MIDDLE ENGLISH PROSE

MIDDLE ENGLISH PROSE

A CRITICAL GUIDE TO MAJOR AUTHORS AND GENRES

Edited by A. S. G. Edwards

Rutgers University Press

New Brunswick, New Jersey

Library of Congress Cataloging in Publication Data
Main entry under title:

Middle English prose.

  Bibliography: p.
  Includes index.
    1. English prose literature—Middle English, 1100–
1500—History and criticism. I. Edwards, A. S. G.
(Anthony Stockwell Garfield), 1942–
√ PR255.M52   1983   828'.108'09   83-2914
ISBN 0–8135–1001–5

Contents

Preface

The purpose of this book is to provide an authoritative guide to a number of important authors and genres of Middle English prose. Although, as the following pages make clear, distinguished work has been undertaken on particular authors or groups of works, no previous study has attempted a comprehensive overview of this highly diversified range of material.

What we have aimed to produce are systematic, critical overviews. Hence each chapter contains a survey of modern scholarship, a statement of desiderata and suggestions for possible avenues of future inquiry, and a bibliography of primary and secondary sources. Each chapter is therefore a succinct, comprehensive reference tool combining evaluative commentary with full, relevant bibliographical materials. It should be particularly noted that the primary bibliographies often include both printed editions and manuscript materials.

The need for such a guide becomes all the more apparent when one reflects, however briefly, on the formidable problems of identification, chronology, and form inherent in any attempt to study almost any prose author or genre of Middle English. We lack a comprehensive index or bibliography of the manuscripts (although one is currently in preparation), and great difficulties can exist in their recovery and identification. The definitions of both "Middle English" and "prose" also pose problems. The chronological boundaries of Middle English cannot be set with any rigidity. And at times the distinction between prose and verse is very blurred.

I would stress that this volume, while comprehensive, is not exhaustive. There are omissions of various kinds in authors and subjects. In some cases works could not be accommodated within the generic categories we established. Other omissions, most notably that of Thomas Malory's *Morte Darthur*, were decided on without much heart searching since there have been in recent years several valuable guides to Malory scholarship, in particular Page West Life's *Sir Thomas Malory and the Morte DArthur: A Survey of Scholarship and Annotated Bibliography* (Charlottesville: University of Virginia Press, 1980) and the collection of essays and bibliography, *Aspects of Malory*, edited by D. S. Brewer and T. Takamiya (Cambridge: D. S. Brewer, 1981). It would have been redundant to include a Malory chapter given such existing guides. We have preferred to devote available space to breaking new ground rather than reworking terrain that has already been well cultivated.

I would like to express my appreciation to all those who have made this volume possible. The various contributors have placed me in their debt by the willingness with which they have undertaken assignments, often of considerable complexity, by the promptness with which they have produced legible drafts, and by their patience with editorial caprice. I am grateful to Herbert F. Mann, former director of Rutgers University Press, who encouraged the planning of this volume, to Leslie Mitchner, managing editor, who has done so much to bring it to completion, and to Barbara Westergaard, whose copyediting has made much straight that was previously askew. For the errors and inconsistencies to which a work of this kind is particularly prone, I am solely responsible.

A. S. G. Edwards

University of Victoria
British Columbia, Canada

Abbreviations

ABR	*American Benedictine Review*
Add.	Additional
AFP	*Archivum Fratrum Praedicatorum*
AHDLMA	*Archives d'histoire doctrinale et littéraire du moyen âge*
AnM	*Annuale médiévale*
Archiv	*Archiv für das Studium der Neueren Sprachen und Literaturen*
BBA	*Bonner Beiträge zur Anglistik*
BGDSL	*Beiträge zur Geschichte der Deutschen Sprache und Literatur*
BHM	*Bulletin of the History of Medicine*
BJRL	*Bulletin of the John Rylands Library*
BL	British Library
BN	Bibliothèque nationale
BNYPL	*Bulletin of the New York Public Library*
ChauR	*Chaucer Review*
DA	*Dissertation Abstracts*
DAI	*Dissertation Abstracts International*
Diss.	Dissertation
DownR	*Downside Review*
EA	*Etudes anglaises*
E&S	*Essays and Studies*
EETS	Early English Text Society. Oxford University Press
EETS, es	Early English Text Society, extra series
EETS, os	Early English Text Society, original series
EGS	*English and Germanic Studies*
EHR	*English Historical Review*
EIC	*Essays in Criticism*
ELN	*English Language Notes*
ES	*English Studies*
EStn	*Englische Studien*
FCEMN	*Fourteenth Century English Mystics Newsletter*
GJ	*Gutenberg Jahrbuch*
HJA&S	*Hitotsubashi Journal of Arts and Sciences*

IMEV	*Index of Middle English Verse.* Edited (1943) by C. Brown and R. H. Robbins. New York: Index Society.
IMEVSupp	*Supplement to the Index of Middle English Verse.* Edited (1965) by R. H. Robbins and J. L. Cutler. Lexington: University of Kentucky Press.
JEGP	*Journal of English and Germanic Philology*
JHM	*Journal of the History of Medicine*
JMRS	*Journal of Medieval and Renaissance Studies*
JRESL	*Jahrbuch für Romanische und Englische Sprache und Literatur*
JWCI	*Journal of the Warburg and Courtauld Institutes*
LeedsSE	*Leeds Studies in English*
LSE	Lund Studies in English
MA	*Le moyen âge*
M&H	*Medievalia et Humanistica*
MAE	*Medium Aevum*
ME	Middle English
MET	Middle English Texts (Heidelberg)
MLN	*Modern Language Notes*
MLQ	*Modern Language Quarterly*
MLR	*Modern Language Review*
MP	*Modern Philology*
MS	*Mediaeval Studies*
N&Q	*Notes & Queries*
Neophil	*Neophilologus*
NM	*Neuphilologische Mitteilungen*
ns	new series
PBA	*Proceedings of the British Academy*
PBSA	*Papers of the Bibliographical Society of America*
PL	*Patrologia Latina*, ed. J. P. Migne
PQ	*Philological Quarterly*
RES	*Review of English Studies*
RPh	*Romance Philology*
RR	*Romanic Review*
RTAM	*Recherches de théologie ancienne et médiévale*
RUO	*University of Ottawa Quarterly/Revue de l'Université d'Ottawa*
SAC	*Studies in the Age of Chaucer*
SB	*Studies in Bibliography*
SN	*Studia Neophilologica*
SP	*Studies in Philology*
STC	*A Short-Title Catalogue of Books Printed in England, Scotland and Ireland, and of English Books Printed Abroad, 1475–1640.*

Compiled (1926) by A. W. Pollard and G. R. Redgrave. London: The Bibliographical Society. Rev. ed. (1976–) by K. Pantzer et al.

TCBS   *Transactions of the Cambridge Bibliographical Society*

TLS   *Times Literary Supplement*

TPS   *Transactions of the Philological Society*

TRHS   *Transactions of the Royal Historical Society*

TSE   *Tulane Studies in English*

UNCSGLL   *University of North Carolina Studies in the Germanic Languages and Literatures*

Wing   *Short-Title Catalogue of Books Printed in England, Scotland, Ireland, Wales and British America, and of English Books Printed in Other Countries, 1641–1700.* Compiled (1945–1951) by Donald Wing. New York: Index Society.

YES   *Yearbook of English Studies*

YSE   *Yale Studies in English*

YWES   *Year's Work in English Studies*

CHAPTER I

Ancrene Wisse, the Katherine Group, and the Wohunge Group

Roger Dahood

This chapter deals with several related early Middle English works associated with the West Midlands. The longest and best known is *Ancrene Wisse* (*AW*), a rule of living written for anchoresses, female religious of more or less solitary life. The Katherine Group (KG) consists of five works in alliterative prose, of which one is a treatise in praise of virginity, *Hali Meiðhad* (*HM*); another is an allegorical homily of body and soul, *Sawles Warde* (*SW*); and three are saints' lives, *Saint Katherine* (*SK*), *Saint Juliana* (*SJ*), and *Saint Margaret* (*SM*). The *Wohunge* or *Wooing* Group (WG) consists of *Þe Wohunge of Ure Lauerd*, *On wel swuðe god Ureisun of God Almihti* (the Lambeth version of which Morris printed under the title *On Ureisun of Ure Louerde*), *Þe Oreisun of Seinte Marie* (the Nero version of which Morris printed under the title *On Lofsong of Ure Lefdi*), and *On Lofsong of Ure Louerde*. The texts of the *WG* are written in alliterative prose and are found almost exclusively in manuscripts also containing texts of *AW* or KG.

ANCRENE WISSE

AW was originally written at the request of three consanguineous sisters for their own use, but the manuscripts testify that it was soon adapted for use by a larger community and eventually for use by men. The textual history, as far as it can be reconstructed from the extant manuscripts, suggests that *AW* enjoyed a great reputation within the religious community of western England from the thirteenth through the sixteenth century. Modern readers have valued it chiefly

Research for this essay was supported in part by a grant from the Humanities Grants Committee of the College of Liberal Arts, University of Arizona.

for its literary qualities. Atkins considers *AW* the "greatest prose work of the time" and "one of the most interesting of the whole Middle English period" (1907, p. 255). Chambers singles it out for its "literary excellence" (1932, pp. xciv–c), elsewhere calling it "the greatest book of its class in either Anglo-Norman or English" (1925, p. 4).

AW consists of an introduction or prologue, followed by eight separate parts. In the introduction the author distinguishes two rules, an outer rule governing external behavior, and a more important inner rule governing matters of the heart. The outer rule is flexible and may be adapted to suit individual needs, capabilities, and circumstances. It serves as a handmaiden to the inflexible inner or "lady" rule. The work is structured so that Parts I and VIII, treating the outer rule, frame Parts II–VII, treating the inner rule. The text reveals its author to have been a learned scholar, a painstaking artist, and an accomplished rhetorician.

The Title

The title *Ancrene Wisse* appears in a colophon of MS Corpus Christi College Cambridge 402 (fol. 144). The precise meaning of the otherwise unrecorded noun *wisse* (from the verb *wissin* "to direct, guide") is not established. *Wisse* is usually translated "guide," but Dobson has made a strong case for "rule" (1976, pp. 51–53).

Although modern scholars often refer to the treatise as *Ancrene Riwle* (or *Ancren Riwle*), only *Ancrene Wisse* has ancient authority. *Ancren Riwle* is the title under which Morton, its first editor, attempting to render Latin *Regula Anachoritarum* or *Regula Inclusarum* into Middle English, published *AW* in 1853. Although in the language of the treatise the genitive plural of *ancre* is *ancrene*, scholars with few exceptions (e.g., Jespersen 1905, who used the grammatically correct form *Ancrene Riwle*, p. 92) followed Morton until Magoun (1937) urged general adoption of *AW*. Since Magoun's note appeared, usage has been divided mainly between *AW* and *Ancrene Riwle*, although the form *Ancren Riwle* persists (e.g., Blake, *HM*, 1972 ed., p. 35). Some scholars reserve the title *AW* for the Corpus text and *Ancrene Riwle* for the rest, but the distinction is not universally observed. One may find any of the three titles used to refer to any manuscript or version of the work.

The Manuscripts

AW survives in seventeen known medieval manuscript codices or fragments, nine in English, four in French, and four in Latin (D'Evelyn 1970, p. 650); an eighteenth, postmedieval manuscript includes some prayers from *AW*. Dobson's partial collation of the manuscripts (1962), indicates that the relationships are complex (esp. p. 137 for the stemma codicum). Although Dobson's method has been faulted and some of his conclusions rejected (reviewed by Stanley, pp. 130–131), his is the only systematic treatment available. The dates given below for the manuscripts are those assigned by D'Evelyn, unless otherwise noted.

Dobson's collation of the primary hands shows the Corpus MS (ca. 1230) to stand apart from the other medieval copies. It is in Dobson's view "a close copy of the author's own final and definitive revision of his work" (1962, p. 163; again, 1966, p. 195). MS Laud 201 (early 17th c.) includes several prayers from *AW*, Part I, copied from Corpus, fols. 6b28–8a1, by the antiquary William Lisle (d. 1637), who deliberately introduced archaisms into his copy (Napier 1909 ed.).

Next in importance is the group comprising MS Cotton Cleopatra C. vi (ca. 1225–1230; Dobson 1972 ed., p. x) and the closely related French text of MS Cotton Vitellius F. vii (early 14th c.), which preserve an earlier version of the text than Corpus. In recent years the Cleopatra MS has received much attention. Although its main text is often marred by careless copying, the numerous inter-lineations and marginal additions by an informed corrector or reviser, "scribe B," are of especial interest. Some of B's additions, in the dialect of the Corpus text and from all indications authorial, appear only in Cleopatra. Other of his additions appear in Corpus. Dobson concludes that B's revisions are "earlier drafts of additions incorporated in the text of which MS. Corpus . . . is a fair copy" (1972 ed., p. ix). He concludes further that B's revisions were composed in the Cleopatra margins, and that B is none other than the author of *AW* (1962, pp. 161–162; 1966, pp. 201–202; 1972 ed., pp. xi, xciii). Dobson's conclusions have great appeal (reviews of 1972 ed. by Frankis, Cottle, and Görlach), but none is beyond doubt. Dobson argues for B's authorship mainly on the grounds that the pronoun *ic* occurs three times among the additions; that some of the additions are "directly occasioned by" blunders in the main text; that the additions show "precision, skill, intelligence, and understanding"; and that B did not work by systematic comparison of the copy against an original, but "as a modern author commonly does in reading his proofs, reading them through for sense" (1972 ed., p. xcvi). The first-person additions, however, could have been copied from another manuscript, and the others could be the work of an intelligent reader with access to a good exemplar. The difficulty with Dobson's fourth point is that not all unsystematic correctors are authors.

Dobson, furthermore, noting the exact fit of two lengthy marginal additions into the available space, concludes that the additions were "first drafted for their places on the Cleopatra page," that is, by the author (1972 ed., p. cxxv). But although text written to fit a limited space suggests a painstaking copyist, it does not imply original composition. Neat copying might well be the work of a scribe other than the author. It is perhaps enough to acknowledge B's additions as the work of a scribe who clearly understood the text, who wrote in the language of the Corpus MS, and who possibly but by no means necessarily was the author.

Another important group of *AW* manuscripts is designated "Nero type," because of affinities to the text of MS Cotton Nero A. xiv (ca. 1225–1250). As Morton's copy text, MS Nero became the basis of most earlier *AW* scholarship. Dobson characterizes Nero as "an innovating manuscript . . . written by a fussy and interfering scribe, constantly archaizing the accidence, attempting to improve the syntax, word-order, and sentence construction (almost invariably with unhappy results), and padding out the phrasing" (1962, p. 133). Nero remains an important text nevertheless, providing in Part I expanded readings of prayers that, if they appear at all in other manuscripts, appear as mere tags. Furthermore, Nero alone preserves the evidence that *AW* was originally composed for three young gentlewomen, "sisters of one father and of one mother," who had abandoned the world to become anchoresses (Day 1952 ed., p. 85:12, 23–26). Closely related to Nero, but having much in common with Corpus, is the Vernon MS (MS Bodleian Eng. poet. a. 1.; late 14th c.). Descriptions of Vernon and its manner of compilation are provided by Serjeantson (1937), Sajavaara (1967a, 1967b), Doyle (1974), and Lewis (1981). Bodleian MS Eng. th.c.70, the Lanhydrock Fragment (ca. 1300–1350), also called Napier's or Lord Robartes's Fragment, consists of a single leaf written in English on both sides. The text is from Part III (corresponding to Morton 1853 ed., pp. 138:25–142:24). Dobson has collated the fragment with all manuscripts and finds that despite readings peculiar to itself, Lanhydrock is of the Nero-Vernon type and is significantly closer to Vernon than to Nero (Dobson, review of Mack and Zettersten 1963 ed.). In several cases, moreover, Lanhydrock agrees in substance and in word order with Corpus against Nero.

Fundamentally similar to Nero is a third, large grouping of manuscripts, designated "Titus type" (Mack 1963 ed., pp. xv–xvii). MS Cotton Titus D. xviii (ca. 1230–1240) is a carelessly copied text, rewritten for use by men as well as women. A noteworthy feature of Titus is its unsystematic substitution of masculine for original feminine pronouns. Of the Titus type are the manuscripts of the second French version of the *AW*, called the "Compilation." The Compilation consists of five originally independent tracts combined into a single "manual emphasizing especially preparation for confession" (Trethewey 1958 ed., pp. x–xi). Of these five, the first two and the last are derived entirely or chiefly from *AW*. The Compilation survives in Trinity College Cambridge MS 883 (R. 14. 7; late 13th–early 14th c.), BN MS Fr. 6276 (attributed by Ker to the early 14th c., according to Trethewey 1958 ed., p. xiv), and partially in MS Bodley 90 (attributed by Ker to the late 13th–early 14th c., according to Trethewey 1958 ed., p. xv).

The Latin version, which survives in four incomplete manuscripts, tends to omit and to compress (Dobson 1962, p. 134). It reflects the revised text of Corpus (D'Evelyn 1949, p. 1174) and in some respects is close to Titus (Dobson 1962, pp. 135–136). Merton College Oxford MS c. 1. 5 (Merton 44; 1300–1350) breaks off after the first nine lines of Part VIII. Magdalen College Oxford MS Latin 67 (ca. 1400) omits Part VIII altogether. MS Cotton Vitellius E. vii (early 14th c.) survives only in charred fragments. MS Royal 7 C. x. (beginning of the 16th c.) ends at the same point as the Merton text and also has lost a large section of Part IV. Closely related to the Latin version is the English text of Parts II and III preserved in British Library MS Royal 8 C. i (15th c.).

Also related to Titus, but not derived from it, is Magdalene College Cambridge MS Pepys 2498 (attributed by Ker to the middle of the second half of the 14th c., according to Zettersten 1976 ed., p. xix, n. 1). The text of Pepys, extensively rewritten (Dobson 1966, p. 194), is addressed to both men and women. Colledge (1939b) and Cottle (review of Zettersten 1976 ed.) associate Pepys with the Lollards.

Dobson has found that both the main text of the Cleopatra MS and scribe B's additions have exerted some influence on the texts of the Nero and Titus types (1962, pp. 139–144; 1972 ed., p. xi) and also on Gonville and Caius College Cambridge MS 234/120 (ca. 1250–1300), which consists of rearranged extracts generalized for a wider audience than the original three sisters (Dobson 1962, p. 132).

Editions and Translations

Until well into the present century Morton's not wholly reliable edition of Nero (1853) was the only complete text of *AW* available in print. Påhlsson's annotated text of Pepys (1918) made available a text far removed from the authorial version. Of fundamental importance to *AW* scholarship, therefore, has been the Early English Text Society's publication of the extant manuscript texts. Each of the English texts is edited separately, as is the French of Vitellius F. vii. The French of the Compilation is edited from MS Trinity with variants from MSS BN 6276 and Bodley 90. The Latin text is from MSS Merton and (for most of Part VIII) Vitellius E. vii with variants from MSS Magdalen (Oxford) and Royal. The series, now completed except for the Vernon MS, is intended to meet highly specialized needs. None of the volumes includes a glossary or explanatory notes. The critical apparatuses, which vary in complexity, are predominantly textual. Paleographical features of all editions except the Latin and the Vitellius French have been treated under the supervision of or in consultation with N. R. Ker. All volumes in the series bracket Morton's pagination in the margins.

Critics have noted numerous shortcomings of the series. Because each manuscript presents special problems of its own, and because the project has involved

numerous editors working over several decades, inconsistencies in emphasis and
presentation have arisen (as noted in, e.g., R. M. Wilson's review of Baugh
1956 ed.). The editions have also been faulted for being little more than transcriptions (Edwards, review of Zettersten 1976 ed.). Furthermore, the transcriptions often are not exact. For example, although editors reproduce manuscript
punctuation and capitalization, they expand abbreviations silently. Such practices
work at cross-purposes. Irregularities of the scribal hands, moreover, often de-
feat editorial efforts to reproduce manuscript word division (as, e.g., Colledge
notes in his review of Day 1952 ed.). In many ways photographic facsimiles
would have been more helpful than attempts at diplomatic transcription (as, e.g.,
d'Ardenne argues in her review of Wilson 1954 ed.).

The series nonetheless provides scholars with a valuable tool. Having all the
texts available in a similar format greatly facilitates comparison of variant readings. Furthermore, if the editions are used with the manuscripts or at least with
photographic copies, the series can be very useful. In the case of heavily corrected
or badly damaged manuscripts, where letters can be discerned only with much
effort or in special light, the edited texts are indispensable. Letters faintly visible
in a manuscript do not always show up in a facsimile. In the case of Lanhydrock,
for example, although the photographs are far more legible than the manuscript
overall, some of the text, especially on the verso, is invisible in the photograph,
and for that portion we must depend on the transcription (Zettersten 1963 ed.,
pp. 166–171). What Dobson has said of the Cleopatra MS applies in some degree to all: "What is necessary is that a single editor should spend the time necessary to solve the problems of the manuscript . . . and find a means of presenting
his results so that others may benefit from his pains; the job should be done thoroughly once, not superficially by each individual user of a facsimile" (1972 ed.,
p. xiii).

Several volumes in the series merit special attention. Tolkien's edition of Corpus (1962), with a paleographical introduction by N. R. Ker, furnishes a generally reliable text. Zettersten and Käsmann supply corrections in their reviews.
Dobson's highly regarded edition of Cleopatra (1972) is a mine of paleographical
and linguistic information. Comparison with the manuscript reveals Dobson's
transcription of the Introduction and Part I to be extremely accurate. Of the few
transcriptional errors the most conspicuous is a misreading of MS *unefne* as
uilefne (fol. 4r, n. i, and p. cxxxix). Herbert's edition of Vitellius F. vii (1944) is
extremely helpful, especially toward the beginning and end of the manuscript,
where shine-through resulting from fire damage has made the surviving text impossible to read except under ultraviolet light.

Day's edition of Nero (1952), based on a transcription by Herbert, is a great
improvement over Morton (reviewed by Samuels, who lists several of Day's transcriptional errors, p. 2, n. 10). Colledge's review is critical of the handling of

word division and punctuation, and contains useful reminders of the dangers inherent in "diplomatic" editions. Comparison of a portion of the edited text with the manuscript shows, furthermore, that the editor is silent in at least two places where the text has been altered by a corrector. Day prints without comment MS *cleane schir inwit* (p. 2:14; fol. 1v8−9), but the *ne* of *cleane*, protruding abnormally into the right margin, and *schir*, protruding abnormally into the left, are written in a different hand (*schir* over an erasure), and the initial *i* of *inwit* has at least been retouched. Again, the first three letters of *hwu-che*, printed without comment, are written in a different hand over an erasure (p. 3:17; MS 2r15). Despite obvious peculiarities in the letter forms of the rewritten text, perhaps the result of writing over erasures, both revisions appear to be the work of the scribe of fols. 120v−end, who may also be responsible for the marginalia discussed in Day's introduction (pp. xvi−xvii).

In the case of the Titus and Lanhydrock editions (1963) a caveat is in order. The appearance in a single volume of the independently edited texts could, since neither editor addresses the issue of manuscript affiliation, lead casual readers to suppose that Lanhydrock is of the Titus type, whereas it is closer to Vernon and Nero, exhibiting none of Titus's vacillation between masculine and feminine pronouns. Zettersten's transcription of Lanhydrock is an advance over Napier's (1898), for Zettersten is able to read more of the text than Napier could. The new transcription, furthermore, is accompanied by a photographic facsimile. Zettersten unfortunately perpetuates Napier's erroneous transcription of MS *nye* as *uye* (fol. 1v13).

D'Evelyn's edition of the Latin text (1944) must be used with care. In comparing only the first two pages of Part VIII against MS Vitellius E. vii, I have found that editorial reconstruction of the text is not always signaled. The first *ri* of D'Evelyn's . . . *rioribus*, for example, cannot be seen in the manuscript because it is partly covered by opaque tape holding the fragment in place (p. 164:12; MS fol. 45b, col. 1). A stroke over what is probably *i* is visible, but the *r* and stem of the *i* cannot be confirmed. Again, the edited text reads *volueritis* (p. 164:20), but the final three letters (*tis*) are editorially reconstructed from vestiges. Most of each letter has crumbled away.

In view of the esteem in which *AW* is held it is somewhat surprising that a full reading text is available only in Morton's now outdated edition of Nero (1853) or in Påhlsson's text of Pepys (1918). Modern annotated editions provide only extracts. Shepherd's edition of Corpus, Parts VI and VII (1959), contains the best introduction to the many problems associated with *AW*. His transcription is reliable, his endnotes and glossary full and informative, and his discussion of literary aspects of the treatise especially perceptive (pp. xl−lxxiii). His introductory section on language (pp. xiv−xxi), however, has been criticized as insufficient, confused, and inaccurate (reviews by Käsmann and Russell-Smith), and his account

of date and authorship should be supplemented by the more recent studies of
Dobson (1966, 1976).

The Ackerman and Dahood edition of Cleopatra, Introduction and Part I
(1984), includes a brief history of monasticism, an account of the monastic day,
and detailed notes identifying the anchoresses' devotions as set forth in Part I.
Briefer selections from *AW* are included in numerous classroom anthologies.
Hall's notes (1920 ed.), superseded in many respects, provide a still useful account of the older scholarship. The notes of Mossé (1952 ed.), Dickins and Wilson (1956 ed.), and Bennett and Smithers (1968 ed.) provide especially useful
information on language and background.

Only two complete Modern English translations are available, both often de-
parting from the sense of the Middle English. They are Morton's translation of
Nero (1853 ed.), later published separately as *The Nun's Rule* (1905), and the
widely used Salu translation of Corpus (1955). The Ackerman and Dahood edition (1984) provides a facing-page translation of the Introduction and Part I.
Meunier's translation into French (1928) is based on Morton.

Date and Author

The question of date and the associated questions of authorship and original audience have provoked some of the most interesting work yet done on *AW*. Tolkien
(1929) was too hasty in dismissing the latter two questions as sentimental, and in
claiming that the last in particular "is not likely to have any importance to scholarship" (p. 116). A firm identification of the author or the original audience
would almost certainly lead to a greater knowledge of the background of *AW* and,
one might hope, a better understanding of *AW* itself.

Earlier attributions of authorship have been rejected. According to a prefatory
note in the Latin MS Magdalen 67, Simon of Ghent, bishop of Salisbury, wrote
AW for his sisters, anchoresses at Tarrant in Dorset. Simon, who died in 1315,
may have been responsible for the Latin, but the English manuscripts long antedate him. On general linguistic grounds Morton assigned the treatise to the early
thirteenth century and speculated that Richard Poor, bishop of Salisbury, 1217–
1228, was the author (1853, p. xv), but no specific link between Poor and *AW* is
known. Hall suggested Saint Gilbert of Sempringham (1089–1189) as the author, but likewise without direct evidence (1920 ed., 2:375–376). Also unconvincing are McNabb's and Kirchberger's arguments for Dominican authorship
(Dobson 1976, p. 14 and n.2).

Believing the three sisters of the Nero version to be three sister-anchoresses
independently documented as having lived at Kilburn Priory, near London, in
the 1130s, Allen (1918b, 1935a) assigned *AW* to the early twelfth century. The
many references in *AW* to works and religious practices dating from the late

twelfth century, however, tell against the earlier date. Shepherd provides a lucid critique of Allen's hypothesis (1959 ed., pp. xxi–xxiii).

More recent authorities consider *AW* a product of the earlier thirteenth century. Even so, the evidence is indirect and somewhat ambiguous. White's attempt (1945) to establish a post-1200 date on the basis of the three-nail crucifix (Corpus, fol. 106a2–3) fails because the three-nail style was known in Europe as early as the mid-twelfth century (Wilson's review of Dobson 1975; Shepherd 1959 ed., p. 27, n. 13).

From the treatment of the sins Bloomfield finds it "hard to date *AW* much before 1225" (1952, p. 148). In *AW*'s use of meditations wrongly attributed to Saint Anselm, Talbot sees evidence for a thirteenth-century date (1951, p. 170). Sitwell (1955) believes that *AW* was composed "just before" 1221, the year the Dominicans, who are alluded to only in the revised texts of Corpus and Vitellius F. vii, came to England. In support of this dating he notes that manuals of confession, whose influence he sees in *AW*, appear in the early years of the thirteenth century. He observes, furthermore, that the Fourth Lateran Council, which convened in 1215, gave a great impetus to the production of these manuals, especially ca. 1217–1222 (pp. xix–xx), and in a recent note Dolan (1974) suggests that the instructions for confession in *AW* show the council's influence.

Shepherd, on the other hand, argues that *AW* cannot have been written either before the last decade of the twelfth century or after 1215, partly because of *AW*'s treatment of love tourneys (1959 ed., p. 54, n. 8f.), but especially because in his view *AW* shows less concern with institutional religion than can be expected in a document composed in the years immediately following the Lateran Council. Shepherd concludes that *AW* "was written about the year 1200, and on the whole probably after, rather than before 1200" (1959 ed., pp. xxi–xxiv).

Dobson (1966) disputes Shepherd's dating, arguing rather that *AW* was written between 1215 and 1222. He successfully challenges the evidence of the love tourney (p. 182). He furthermore suggests that *AW* was indeed influenced by the Lateran Council, citing as evidence on this point, however, only Sitwell's remarks on the increased production of confessional manuals after 1215. He notes, moreover, Sitwell's observations, first, that the anchoresses' devotions are remarkably modern, of the sort one would ordinarily attribute to fifteenth-century works (Sitwell 1955, p. xxii), and second, that *AW* provides the earliest examples both of salutations used in connection with the elevation of the Host and of an elaborate form of the devotion to the Five Joys of Mary (Sitwell 1955, pp. 194, 196). Dobson also cites Talbot's remarks (1956) first, that the Hours of the Holy Ghost date from the end of the twelfth or the beginning of the thirteenth century; second, that no writer would have referred to the elevated Host as "Godes licome" until the question of when transubstantiation occurs in the Mass was settled (1207 at the earliest); and third, that in England writings specifying the mo-

ment of transubstantiation began to appear in the years immediately after 1215
(Dobson 1966, p. 187). In addition, Dobson adduces evidence of monastic
bloodletting and dietary rules (1966, pp. 188–190). He points out that in the
eleventh century bloodletting had been allowed only when necessary but by 1214
at Peterborough had developed into a part of the annual routine as in *AW*. Dobson argues, moreover, that since in other respects the author of *AW* stresses the
relative unimportance of external observances, his exceptional concern for strict
dietary rules is easier to understand if the work was written after the Lateran
Council.

Dobson shows that a post-Lateran date of composition is possible. His evidence, however, does not preclude an earlier date. Although Sitwell observes that
the Lateran Council generated the increased production of confessional manuals,
he avoids concluding that the systematic treatment of confession in *AW* is necessarily post-Lateran (1955, p. xix). Further, Sitwell does not suggest that the correspondences between *AW* and fifteenth-century books of hours can be used in
dating *AW*, and Dobson does not show that they can be. Again, the fact that certain of the devotions in *AW* are the earliest examples of their kinds does not establish a date for *AW*, since the date of composition of the devotions is not known.
Talbot's evidence (1956) seems likewise inconclusive for a post-Lateran date. It
allows a date of composition at least as early as 1207 and possibly earlier, since the
1207 limit depends entirely on Talbot's judgment that the author would not have
written as he did about transubstantiation before then. The evidence from monastic practice in bloodletting and diet also is of uncertain value. Knowles (1963, pp.
456–462) indicates that bloodletting may have been routine before 1214 at some
monastic houses, and that in dietary matters monastic practice was not uniform
throughout England, some houses being stricter than others in adhering to the
ancient rules.

Another consideration is Shepherd's objection that *AW* could not have been
written much after 1200 because "it shows so little acquaintance with the most
recent Parisian theological teaching, and especially with that of Stephen Langton"
(reported in Dobson 1976, p. 315). It is with twelfth-century Paris that the author seems to have most in common (Shepherd 1959 ed., pp. xxviii–xxix). Furthermore, all of the undisputed sources of *AW* antedate 1200. Dobson's recent
attempt (1975) to identify an early thirteenth-century source in the *Moralia super
Evangelia*, well received by some (e.g., review by Wilson), has been vigorously
rejected by others (reviews by Wittig and by Rouse and Wenzel). In their review
Rouse and Wenzel not only reject the parallels as unconvincing, but also argue on
codicological grounds that the *Moralia* was composed too late to have been a
source of *AW*.

The question of date, then, remains open. Although Allen's early dating can be
safely rejected, the best available evidence allows only the broad conclusion that

AW was composed during the later twelfth or early thirteenth century and before 1221, if the fact that friars are mentioned only in the revised text means that the original antedates the arrival of the Dominicans.

The problem of authorship, on the other hand, may be closer to a solution. At least Dobson (1976), who has aroused admiration mingled with varying degrees of caution and skepticism, offers hope (reviews by Arngart, Kristensson, Pearsall, Wenzel). Building upon Brewer's suggestion (1956) that the author was an Augustinian canon, Dobson argues that *AW* was composed in Herefordshire at Wigmore, an Augustinian abbey of the Victorine congregation. He connects the original three anchoresses with Limebrook Priory, near Wigmore, and speculates that the author was their brother, Brian of Lingen, a secular canon of Wigmore, who reveals his name in a cryptogram (1976, pp. 312–368). The evidence for Brian's authorship is inconclusive and without further substantiation is unlikely to win universal acceptance, but the Augustinian backgrounds are now more clearly visible.

Original Language

The early cataloguers, Thomas Smith (1696, pp. 50–51, XIV.1; 97, VII. 6; 103, VII. 1), Humfrey Wanley (1705, pp. 228, 248), and Joseph Planta (1802, p. 581), supposed Latin to have been the original language of *AW*. Bramlette (1893) and later Mühe (1908) attempted to demonstrate the priority of Latin. Macaulay (1914), however, was able to show the unlikelihood of a Latin original, and D'Evelyn (1949) has since strengthened his case.

Morton (1853), followed by Madden (1854), Wülcker (1874b), and others in the nineteenth century, favored English, but did not make conclusive arguments. In this century, since Napier (1909 ed.) refuted Heuser's suggestion (1907 ed.) of an Old English original, the debate has been chiefly between Middle English and French. Macaulay (1914) and recently Lee (1974) have argued for French, but a growing body of evidence points to Middle English. Although the arguments of Dymes (1924) and of Chambers (1925) have not withstood scrutiny, Samuels (1953) and Käsmann (1957) have produced strong evidence for English. Samuels points to many places in the text where for the sake of alliteration the Middle English includes words not required by the sense; nonetheless, the French, which does not alliterate, corresponds word for word with the English. Second, he points to several proverbs in the French that are apparently translated literally from Middle English. Third, he finds word play in the English that is impossible in French. Fourth, he shows that the French lacks originality and repeatedly exhibits a gracelessness most easily explained as the result of translation. Fifth, he finds readings in the French that can be explained only as mistranslations of the English.

After systematically reviewing and rejecting the evidence of Dymes and Chambers, Käsmann (1957) brings forward new evidence of mistranslation in the French. Also, he finds evidence that the French text includes superfluous glosses of French vocabulary, a circumstance best explained by the assumption that a French translator, following an English original in which unfamiliar French borrowings were glossed, slavishly translated both the borrowings and the glosses.

The Language of the Middle English Texts

The early English manuscripts of *AW* have been subjected to intensive grammatical and dialectal study. The earlier scholarship is of limited interest today both because of the greater sophistication of more recent linguistic work and because until this century the importance of the Corpus manuscript was not recognized. Even until well into this century most scholars concentrated on the Nero text, available in Morton's edition (1853); thus Bögholm (1937), Brock (1865), Dahlstedt (1903), Dieth (1919), Funke (1921), Ostermann (1905), Püttmann (1908), Redepenning (1906), Serjeantson (1927), and Wülcker (1874a, 1874b). Kölbing's warning (1876) against excessive reliance on Morton and Nero is a notable exception. By the early years of the twentieth century, however, scholars were beginning to look beyond Nero. Mühe (1901) produced a detailed study of the language of Titus. Shortly thereafter, Williams (1905), comparing fourteen phonological and morphological features of Nero and Cleopatra, observed that the language of Cleopatra is very similar to the language of the KG. Then Macaulay (1914) published his collation demonstrating the superiority of the Corpus text.

A turning point for *AW* studies came with the publication of Tolkien's discovery (1929) that in several respects the language of Corpus (designated A) is identical with the language of MS Bodley 34 (designated B; attributed by Ker to probably the first quarter of the 13th c., *Facsimile*, 1960, p. x), containing several works of the KG. This language he termed AB, attributing the linguistic uniformity of the two manuscripts to obedience to some school or authority. Although it now seems clear that Tolkien somewhat overstated the similarity of language in Corpus and Bodley 34 (McIntosh 1947–1948; Wilson 1959; Clark 1966; Jack 1975; De Caluwé-Dor 1977), the existence of the AB language may be taken as established. Several other of Tolkien's conclusions, however, have met with resistance. From the consistency of language and spelling Tolkien had inferred that the Corpus and Bodley scribes "used naturally the same language as that of their originals" (1929, p. 107). He had recognized but deemed unlikely the possibility that the originals had been written in some other dialect and then translated into AB (pp. 109–112). D'Ardenne, however, disagrees. In her view, "AB as a whole is a language of conscious cultivation, whose users would be likely to translate, and capable of doing it thoroughly" (*SJ*, 1936 ed., pp. xxxiv–xxxv). Hulbert likewise thought that Tolkien overemphasized the difficulties of translation, particularly from a dialect not very different from AB (1946, p. 412). Recently Benskin and Laing have argued for the likelihood of translation (1981, pp. 92–93).

Bliss (1952–1953) reasonably objects that the evidence on the question of scribal translation between dialects is inconclusive, the judgments of his predecessors subjective. He nevertheless speculates that the AB scribes probably would not have been capable of consistent translation from a dialect markedly different from AB. Unlike Tolkien, however, he can conceive of the AB scribes' modernizing of an original written in their own dialect as long as fifty years before their time (pp. 2–6). Bliss's important contribution to the study of the AB language was his demonstration that the Corpus and Bodley scribes fairly consistently observe an orthographical distinction between *oþer* (adj., "other") and *oðer* (conj., "either, or"). Because the distinction is arbitrary, that is, not explainable on phonetic grounds, it is a sure indication that AB was a literary standard, a written language with conventionalized spelling. Jack (1976) provides the most detailed account of the *oþer* / *oðer* convention, arguing persuasively that the many exceptional instances in which the adjective is spelled *oðer* are evidence of an additional, competing convention that Bliss had failed to recognize. In a brief note Stevens (1961) points out that the case for AB is reinforced by the distinctive formulae used exclusively in the titles of Corpus and Bodley 34.

Tolkien's work paved the way for d'Ardenne's edition of *SJ* (1936) with its indispensable account of the AB language. D'Ardenne characterizes AB as a West Midlands dialect related to the Old English of the Vespasian Psalter but does not attempt more precise localization (pp. 178–179). Her discussions of the AB orthography, accidence, and phonology are essential to an understanding of the language of Corpus, although her treatment of the phonology is selective and has been criticized in some of its details (e.g., Dobson, *AW*, 1972 ed., p. lxxxi, n. 3). Moreover, since *AW* and *SJ* have much vocabulary in common, d'Ardenne's comprehensive glossary and etymological appendix are also valuable sources of information about *AW*. Logan's full account of *SK* (1973) is another useful repository of AB forms, although some of Logan's conclusions have been sharply criticized (review by Diensberg). Additional discussions of the AB language appear in the notes to relevant selections of the anthologies mentioned above.

More specialized studies deal with limited aspects of the language. On dialectal evidence from the Vernon index, written later than the rest of the manuscript, Serjeantson assigned Vernon to the area of South Shropshire and South Staffordshire (1937, p. 227), but Sajavaara assigns it to northern Worcestershire (1967b, p. 438). Käsmann (1961) provides information about native and borrowed ecclesiastical vocabulary in *AW*, KG, and *WG*. Zettersten (1965, with important reviews by Bäckman and Jacobsson) treats mainly the vowels in words of Germanic origin in the Corpus, Nero, and Gonville and Caius MSS, and to a lesser extent other linguistic features and other manuscripts. Zettersten (1964) is a companion study dealing with sixteen of the more difficult words, and Zettersten (1969) lists all the French loans in the Corpus, Nero, and Gonville and Caius MSS. Also useful is Diensberg (1975), concerned mainly with verb forms in the Corpus, Cleopatra, and Nero MSS, but also setting out the phonology of the main hands of the three manuscripts.

Articles dealing with individual words or cruces in the text include Baldwin (1976), Dahood (1978), Diensberg (1978a, 1978b, the latter arguing that numerous forms in *AW*, hitherto thought to be West Saxon loans, are native to AB), Dobson (1974), Dolan (1979), Jack (1977), Kenyon (1914), Onions (1928), Salu (1952–1953), Smithers (1949–1950; 1965, but see Dobson 1976, pp. 142–143), Turville-Petre (1969), and Zettersten (1969, pp. 232–234). Smithers (1948–1949), Russell-Smith (1957), and Bennett (1958) deal with the interpretation of *nore* in *AW*.

Redepenning's (1906) and Dieth's (1919) studies, based on Morton, provide useful syntactical information, especially for Nero. Ladd (1961) and Jack (1979) dispute the view, expressed, for example, by d'Ardenne (*SJ*, 1936 ed., p. 222), that the language of Nero is more archaic than that of Corpus. Kivimaa (1966) gives compact accounts of the relative and conjunctive uses of *þe and þet* in *AW* (Nero, Titus), KG, *On Ureisun of Ure Louerde*, and *Wohunge*. Kubouchi's systematic analysis of word order in Parts VI and VII (1975) demonstrates a preponderance of subject-verb word order.

Sources and Influence

In addition to the studies of Talbot (1951, 1956) and Dobson (1966, 1975, 1976), mentioned above in connection with dating, other source studies have appeared. Allen (1934a) called attention to what she termed a "probable" echo of Geoffrey of Monmouth, but the echo is dim. Smyth (1911, pp. 85–100) lists biblical quotations and paraphrases given in English in the Nero text. Owst (1933) discusses specific passages of *AW* in connection with the works of medieval sermon writers and homilists. Clark (1954), Ives (1934), Prins (1948), and Whiting (1935) have treated individual proverbs in *AW*. Brewer (1953) identifies Saint Bernard's *Sermones in Cantica* as a probable source of the backbiters passage. Colledge (1939a), Kaske (1960), Miller (1962), Shepherd (1956), and

Woolf (1962) provide background for understanding individual passages. Woolf (review of Shepherd 1959 ed.) presents an illuminating discussion of love between friends and between body and soul, and of penitential pain and scourging in *AW*. Raw (1974) identifies many of the devotions specified in Part I. She finds that a number of them occur in Old English manuscripts. Ackerman's (1978) analysis of the liturgical day includes discussion, partly drawing on Talbot (1956), Raw (1974), and others, of devotional material in Part I. Barratt (1980) finds Carthusian sources for *AW* in Guigo's *Consuetudines* and Adam of Dryburgh's *Liber de Exercitio Cellae*. Bishop (1979) reports finding outside of *AW* (Corpus, fol. 108b25) another early Middle English reference to Greek fire. Maybury (1977) surveys the exegetical tradition drawn upon in Part III of *AW* for the pelican, owl, and sparrow.

Allen (1918a) touched on the relationship between *AW* and the mystic tradition (pp. 189–193). She then published three articles (1923, 1924, 1929a) identifying purported borrowings from *AW* in other medieval works. Her evidence, however, was not consistently strong, and in one instance (1924) she retracted an earlier identification. A brief summary of her findings may be found in Chambers (1932, p. xcix). Allen's successful identification (1940) of *AW* as a source of the *Tretyse of Loue* has been confirmed in detail by Fisher (*Tretyse*, 1951 ed., pp. xiii–xxii; also Fisher 1949, 1959). Colledge (1939b) finds evidence in the Pepys text that *AW* was used by Lollards. The matter has recently been addressed again by Cottle (review of Zettersten 1976 ed.). Crawford (1930) finds in the Vernon MS text of the *Life of Adam and Eve* a reminiscence of *AW*.

Stylistic and Literary Analyses

In an often-cited study Bethurum, comparing *AW* to the works of the KG, describes its movement as "simple and direct" (1935, p. 554), and recently Rygiel (1976) has analyzed some of the reasons for the impression of simplicity. Although in general *AW* is easier to read than KG, with its more obviously self-conscious prose, *AW* is highly complex in both structure and style. Humbert's respected study (1944) surveys *AW*'s varied and complex iterative patterns. Extremely useful on many aspects of style is Shepherd's discussion (1959 ed., pp. lix–lxxiii). Less successful is Grayson (1974; reviewed by Wenzel), who takes as her point of departure Shepherd's observation that anticipation, accumulation, and recapitulation in the development of themes lend a "curious spiral quality" to the work (Shepherd 1959 ed., p. lxii). For all its complexity, however, the prose is almost always lucid. In his convincing explication of an enumerative sequence in *AW* (Corpus, fol. 106a22), Waldron (1969) stresses the author's concern for clarity.

Koskenniemi studies the various effects of synonymous pairings in the Nero and Corpus texts of *AW* (1968, pp. 68−74) and in *SM* (pp. 61−67). Clark (1968, pp. 370−375) demonstrates how the author uses alliteration for emphasis and also comments on his personal, informal tone. Clark (1978) examines one aspect of the informality, the use of colloquialisms in dialogue. Clark (1977) traces the author's use of grammatical rhyme ultimately to Augustine. Doyle calls attention to the methodical distinction and exemplification, the partial dramatization of the vices, the acute awareness of physical suffering in sentient beings, the antipathy for horrible evil, and the appreciation for details of domestic life as features contributing to the power and effectiveness of *AW* (1954, pp. 70−76). In Georgianna's view, the author of *AW* focuses upon the mundane because the anchoress' relationship with God is defined in terms of the everyday. She observes that the decision to become a solitary does not accomplish so radical a break with the world as the enclosure rite might suggest (1981, p. 5). Kliman argues that "the genial and humane author is not a misogynist but a sexist and an anti-feminist" (1977, p. 43). Rygiel (1980) finds in Part VII a tripartite structure, consisting of divine action, human response, and judgment of that response. Rygiel (1982) subjects Corpus fol. 98b9−21 to close reading with particular attention to the interrelationship and patterning of various stylistic devices.

KATHERINE GROUP AND *WOHUNGE* GROUP

A convenient introduction to the KG may be found in Baugh (1967, pp. 123−126). Of especial interest are the Early English Text Society's photographic facsimile of Bodley 34 (1960) and d'Ardenne's separately published transcription (*HM*, 1977 ed.; the reviews of Millet, Diensberg, and Rynell report numerous errors in the transcription). Apart from matters discussed above in connection with *AW* (in the sections on language and style), scholarly concern with KG has tended to focus on authorship, form, and sources. Works of the KG and *WG* survive in Titus (which preserves not only *AW* but *HM*, *SK*, *SW*, and the unique text of *Wohunge*), Bodley 34, and Royal 17 A. xxvii (early 13th c.). An incomplete version of *On wel swuðe god Ureisun of God Almihti* survives in the Lambeth MS (early 13th c.). Some believe the KG to be the work of a single author, others the work of several. In her edition of *SJ* (1936, pp. xl−xlvii) d'Ardenne reviews the debate and the evidence. She concludes that *AW*, KG, and perhaps *WG* are products of a single center and an indeterminate number of authors. The question of form, whether the KG texts are prose or poetry, has long been settled in favor of rhythmic prose. Modern editors survey the earlier scholarship and set forth the evidence for the prevailing view (*SJ*, d'Ardenne 1936 ed., pp. xxviii–xxix; *SW*, Wilson 1938 ed., pp. xl–xliii).

Except for *HM*, the works of KG are adapted from Latin sources. The sources of *SJ*, *SK*, and *SM* are discussed in the editions of d'Ardenne (1936), d'Ardenne and Dobson (1981), and Mack (1934) respectively. Dobson (1976, pp. 164–165, 429–430) argues that the *Moralia super Evangelia* is the source of a passage in *HM*, but the *Moralia* is probably too late (Rouse and Wenzel, review of Dobson 1975). Dobson (1976, pp. 146–153) and, in more detail, Becker (1980) provide a clearer picture than hitherto available of the relationship between *SW* and its Latin source, *De Custodia Interioris Hominis*, an independent treatise incorporated in the *De Anima*, formerly ascribed to Hugh of Saint Victor.

Articles on specific readings include Furuskog (1946) and the response by d'Ardenne and Tolkien (1947b). The latter includes a spirited account of the editorial task and a sharp critique of Furuskog's work. The authors nevertheless accept several of Furuskog's readings (pp. 70–71), all but one of which later appear among the corrigenda or footnotes in the reprint of d'Ardenne (*SJ*, 1961 ed.). The omission occurs at d'Ardenne 326 (43r20), *þi feader wisdom wisse me þi wum* under erasure after *criste*. Tolkien and d'Ardenne further say that at 729 (51r23) the manuscript reads *oder* not as in her edition *oðer*. In the facsimile the ascender of the letter in question appears crossed, although not in the way characteristic of the scribe's *ð*. D'Ardenne omits the revised reading *oder* from her corrigenda, her silence suggesting a preference for her original *oðer*. Still, a comment on the unusual shape of the letter would be helpful. D'Ardenne and Tolkien (1947b) argue for a MS reading *rw?len* (usually read *iþþlen*) at MS Bodley 72v1, but their reading is rejected by Bennett and Smithers (*SW*, 1968 ed., p. 419:24n). D'Ardenne (1974) points out that Einenkel's *bratewil* (*SK*, 1884 ed.) is a misreading of MS *beatewil*, a form Dobson discusses further (*SK*, d'Ardenne and Dobson 1981 ed., pp. 257–258). Hotchner (1942) finds the source of later Latin *dux vitae* in Old English *lifes lattiow*, a phrase occurring also in *SJ* (as *liues lattow*, 291).

The *WG*, roughly contemporary with *AW* and KG, consists entirely of short works in rhythmic prose. Later English mystical writers, and in particular the author of the *Talkyng of the Loue of God*, draw heavily upon *WG*. Like *AW* and KG the group exhibits features of the AB language. *WG* receives an extensive discussion in Thompson's introduction (1958 ed.), but it has otherwise aroused little scholarly interest. According to Thompson the works of *WG* "derive particularly from the tradition of the mystical marriage of the Heavenly Bridegroom with Holy Church or the human soul" (1958 ed., p. xv), but only one of the texts has been traced to a direct source: *Þe Oreisun of Seinte Marie* is freely translated from Marbod of Rennes's *Oratio ad Sanctam Mariam*, which Thompson prints in an appendix. Thompson has been criticized for giving insufficient attention to the tradition of devotional literature behind the *WG* (review by Salter) and for inadequate treatment of the language (review by Smithers).

FUTURE STUDY

All the works of KG and *WG* are available in modern scholarly editions. The most urgent needs for the future concern *AW*. A critical edition or at least a complete collation in an easily comprehensible form would be welcome, even if it should produce no startling departures from the stemma that Dobson set forth in 1962. Especially needed is a reading text of the whole treatise, annotated on the scale of Shepherd's edition of Parts VI and VII (1959). Selections cannot take the place of a proper edition, and in translations much of what is admirable in *AW*— the skillful alliteration, the prose rhythms, the sometimes dazzling word play— is inevitably obscured or lost. Until a fully annotated text is available, *AW* will remain the province of specialists, an acknowledged but largely inaccessible masterpiece.

In the past the most successful work on *AW* has been linguistic, and much work on the language remains to be done. Tolkien's identification of the AB language and d'Ardenne's edition of *SJ* (1936) have set the course of *AW* language study for the foreseeable future. Subsequent work to date has been in the nature of refinements of or supplements to these contributions. We probably cannot expect from future linguistic studies revelations as dramatic as the identification of the AB language, yet developments in graphemic and dialectal study may eventually increase our knowledge of the center or centers at which AB flourished. Again, careful attention to vocabulary and meanings may considerably enhance our appreciation of the author's art. In his opening section, for example, where he explains the need for a rule, the author plays upon the various meanings of the related words *rectus, regula, richte,* and *riwle* with startling effect. I suspect in *AW* the presence of other passages with comparable but as yet unrecognized word play.

Work also remains to be done on the sources of *AW*. Too often in the past investigators have been willing to accept vague parallels as evidence of borrowing or derivation, where much stronger evidence is required. Dobson, however, has succeeded in directing attention to the largely neglected compilations of the late twelfth and early thirteenth centuries. Further attention also to the devotions in Part I of *AW* could eventually lead to the identification of service books close in form and content to the exemplar from which the sister anchoresses copied their service (Corpus, fol. 6a2). Identification of such sources might provide further clues to the date and circumstances of *AW*'s composition.

BIBLIOGRAPHY

Primary works are listed alphabetically as follows: *Ancrene Wisse*, Katherine Group, *Tretyse of Loue*, *Wohunge* Group. Within the entries, titles of primary works are abbreviated except when abbreviation would be misleading. The following abbreviations are used: *AW* (*Ancrene Wisse*), *AR* (*Ancren* or *Ancrene Riwle*), *HM* (*Hali Meiðhad*), *SJ* (*Saint Juliana*), *SK* (*Saint Katherine*), *SM* (*Saint Margaret*), and *SW* (*Sawles Warde*). For each work or group of works listings include, as appropriate, manuscripts alphabetically by city, facsimiles, printed editions, and translations. Printed editions and translations appear in order of publication. When not otherwise evident, base manuscripts and related information are given within square brackets. Secondary works appear alphabetically by author. For convenient reference, reviews are entered under the works reviewed.

PRIMARY WORKS

ANCRENE WISSE

MANUSCRIPTS

English

Cambridge. Corpus Christi College 402, fols. 1–117v
Cambridge. Gonville and Caius College 234/120, pp. 1–185
Cambridge. Magdalene College Pepys 2498, pp. 371–449
London. BL Cotton Cleopatra C. vi, fols. 4–199
London. BL Cotton Nero A. xiv, fols. 1–120v
London. BL Cotton Titus D. xviii, fols. 14–105
London. BL Royal 8 C. i, fols. 122v–143v
Oxford. Bodleian Library Eng. th. c. 70 (Lanhydrock Fragment)
Oxford. Bodleian Library Eng. poet. a. 1 (Vernon MS), fols. 371v–391v
Oxford. Bodleian Library Laud 201, fols. 264–265

French

Cambridge. Trinity College 883 (R. 14. 7), fols. 1–154v
London. BL Cotton Vitellius F. vii, fols. 2–70
Oxford. Bodleian Library Bodley 90, fols. 1–77
Paris. BN Fr. 6276, fols. 3–127a/36

Latin

London. BL Cotton Vitellius E. vii, in fragments
London. BL Royal 7 C. x, fols. 69v–124v
Oxford. Magdalen College Latin 67, fols. 1–95
Oxford. Merton College c. 1. 5 (Merton 44) fols. 90–165v

PRINTED EDITIONS

English Text

Morton, James, ed. (1853) *The AR: A Treatise on the Rules and Duties of Monastic Life.*
Camden Society, os 57. Repr. (1968) New York: Johnson Reprint Corporation. [Nero]
Napier, Arthur S., ed. (1898) "A Fragment of the *AR.*" *JEGP*, 2, 199–202.
[Lanhydrock]
Paues, A. C., ed. (1902) "A XIVth Century Version of the *AR.*" *EStn*, 30, 344–346.
[Pepys, fols. 224–228b, corresponding to Morton 1853, pp. 412, 424, 426; Zet-
tersten 1976, pp. 182–184 (Part VIII: On Servants)]
Heuser, W., ed. (1907) "Die AR—Ein aus angelsächsischen Zeit überliefertes Denk-
mal." *Anglia*, 30, 103–122. [Laud]
Napier, Arthur S., ed. (1909) "The *AR.*" *MLR*, 4, 433–436. [Laud]
Påhlsson, Joel, ed. (1918) *The Recluse: A Fourteenth-Century Version of the AR.* Lunds
Universitets Arsskrift, N.F. Avd. 1, Bd. 6, Nr. 1. Lund: Gleerup. Repr. of 1911 ed.
with notes. [Pepys]
Hall, Joseph, ed. (1920) *Selections from Early Middle English: 1130–1250.* 2 vols. Oxford: Oxford University Press. Text, I: 54–75; notes, II: 354–407. [Corpus, fols.
56–58 and Caius, pp. 126–134 parallel (Seven Deadly Sins); Corpus, fols. 112v–
117v and Nero, fols. 116–120v parallel with variants from Cleopatra, Titus (Part
VIII: Outer Rule)]
Day, Mabel, ed. (1952) *The English Text of the AR: Cotton Nero A. xiv, on the basis of a
transcript by J. A. Herbert.* EETS, os 225. Reviews: M. L. Samuels (1953) *MAE*,
22, 1–2, esp. n. 10; Eric Colledge (1953) *RES*, ns 4, 278–279.

Mossé, Fernand, ed. (1952) *A Handbook of Middle English.* Translated by James A. Walker. Baltimore: Johns Hopkins Press. Text, pp. 138–148; notes, pp. 343–346. [Corpus fols. 13v–14 (Temptation of Eve), 22–22v (Flatterers), 105–106v (Love of Christ), 112–113 (Renunciation of Goods of This World) with corresponding text from Vitellius French and Merton, Vitellius Latin]

Wilson, R. M., ed. (1954) *The English Text of the AR: Edited from Gonville and Caius College MS. 234/120,* with an introduction by N. R. Ker. EETS, os 229. Review: S. R. T. O. d'Ardenne (1958) *RES,* ns 9, 56–58.

Baugh, Albert C., ed. (1956) *The English Text of the AR: Edited from British Museum MS. Royal 8 C. i.* EETS, os 232. Reviews: R. M. Wilson (1957) *MLR,* 52, 625–626; S. I. Tucker (1958) *RES,* ns 9, 116.

Dickins, Bruce, and Wilson, R. M., eds. (1956) *Early Middle English Texts.* 2d rev. of 1951 ed. London: Bowes and Bowes. Text, pp. 89–94; notes, pp. 206–210. [Nero fols. 20v–21v (Flatterers and Backbiters), Corpus fols. 78v–80 (Dog of Hell)]

Shepherd, Geoffrey, ed. (1959) *AW: Parts Six and Seven.* Repr. Manchester: Manchester University Press, 1972. [Corpus] Reviews: Rosemary Woolf (1961) *EIC,* 11, 210–214; Hans Käsmann (1962) *Anglia,* 80, 327–329; Joy Russell-Smith (1962) *RES,* ns 13, 65–68.

Tolkien, J. R. R., ed. (1962) *The English Text of the AR: AW: Edited from MS. Corpus Christi College Cambridge 402,* with an introduction by N. R. Ker. EETS, os 249. Reviews: Hans Käsmann (1963) *Anglia,* 81, 472–474; Arne Zettersten (1966), *ES,* 47, 290–292.

Mack, Frances M., ed. (1963) *The English Text of the AR: Edited from Cotton MS. Titus D. xviii. Together with the Lanhydrock Fragment, Bodleian MS. Eng. th.c.70,* edited by Arne Zettersten. EETS, os 252. Reviews: Basil Cottle (1964) *JEGP,* 63, 761–762; E. J. Dobson (1967) *MAE,* 36, 187–191.

Zettersten, Arne, ed. (1963). See preceding.

Bennett, J. A. W., and Smithers, G. V., eds. (1968) *Early Middle English Verse and Prose,* with a glossary by Norman Davis. 2d ed. Repr. with corrections Oxford: Oxford University Press, 1974. Text, pp. 223–245; notes, pp. 398–416. [Corpus, fols. 65–70 (Holy Thoughts), 77–79v (Remedies of Sin), 104–108v (Love of Christ)]

Dobson, E. J., ed. (1972) *The English Text of the AR: Edited from B.M. Cotton MS. Cleopatra C. vi.* EETS, os 267. Reviews: Basil Cottle (1974) *JEGP,* 73, 239–240; M. L. Samuels (1974), *MAE,* 43, 78–80; P. J. Frankis (1975) *RES,* ns 26, 196–198; Manfred Görlach (1975) *Anglia,* 93, 222–225.

Zettersten, Arne, ed. (1976) *The English Text of the AR: Edited from Magdalene College, Cambridge MS. Pepys 2498.* EETS, os 274. Reviews: Basil Cottle (1977) *JEGP,* 76, 541–542; A. S. G. Edwards (1979) *ES,* 60, 82–83.

Ackerman, Robert W., and Dahood, Roger, eds. (1984) *AR: Introduction and Part I.* Medieval and Renaissance Texts and Studies. Center for Medieval and Early Renaissance Studies: Binghamton, New York. [Cleopatra]

French Text

Herbert, J. A., ed. (1944) *The French Text of the AR: Edited from British Museum MS. Cotton Vitellius F. vii.* EETS, os 219.

Trethewey, W. H., ed. (1958) *The French Text of the AR: Edited from Trinity College Cambridge MS. R. 14. 7, with Variants from Bibliothèque Nationale MS. F Fr. 6276 and MS. Bodley 90.* EETS, os 240. Review: Joy Russell-Smith (1960) *RES*, ns 11, 421–423.

Latin Text

D'Evelyn, Charlotte, ed. (1944) *The Latin Text of the AR: Edited from Merton College MS. 44 and British Museum MS. Cotton Vitellius E. vii.* EETS, os 216. [includes variants from British Museum MS Royal 7 C. x and Magdalen College Oxford Latin MS 67]

TRANSLATIONS

Morton, James, ed. (1853) s.v. Printed Editions, above.

——, trans. (1905) *The Nun's Rule.* London: A. Moring. Repr. of the translation in Morton, ed. (1853), s.v. Printed Editions, above.

Meunier, G., trans. (1928) *La regle des recluses, dite aussi Le livre de la vie solitaire.* Tours: A. Mame. [Nero into modern French]

Salu, Mary B., trans. (1955) *The AR.* London: Burns and Oates. [Corpus]

Ackerman, Robert, and Dahood, Roger, eds. (1984) s.v. Printed Editions, above.

KATHERINE GROUP

MANUSCRIPTS

London. BL Cotton Titus D. xviii: *HM*, fols. 112v–127; *SK*, fols. 133v–147v; *SW*, fols. 105v–112v.

London. BL Royal 17 A. xxvii: *SJ*, fols. 56–70; *SK*, fols. 11–37; *SM*, fols. 37–56; *SW*, ff. 1–10v.

Oxford. Bodleian Library Bodley 34: *HM*, fols. 52v–71v; *SJ*, fols. 36v–52; *SK*, fols. 1–18; *SM*, fols. 18–36v; *SW*, fols. 72–80v.

FACSIMILE

Facsimile of MS. Bodley 34: SK, SM, SJ, HM, SW (1960), with an introduction by N. R. Ker. EETS, os 247.

Hali Meiðhad

Cockayne, Oswald, ed. (1866) *Hali Meidenhad: An Alliterative Homily of the Thirteenth Century.* EETS, os 18. [Titus]

Furnivall, Frederick J., ed. (1922) Reedition and reissue of preceding. [Titus, Bodley parallel]

Colborn, A. F., ed. (1940) *HM: Edited from MS. Bodley 34 and MS. Cotton Titus D. xviii.* Copenhagen: Einar Munksgaard. [Parallel] Reviews: Dorothy Everett (1941) *RES*, 17, 117–121; S. R. T. O. d'Ardenne (1942) *ES*, 24, 58–62.

Blake, Norman F., ed. (1972) *Holy Virginity.* In *Middle English Religious Prose*, pp. 35–60. London: Edward Arnold. [Bodley, with partly modernized spelling]

d'Ardenne, S. R. T. O., ed. (1977) *The KG. Edited from MS. Bodley 34.* Bibliothèque de la Faculté de Philosophie et Lettres de l'Université de Liège. Fascicule 215. Paris. Reviews: Bella Millet (1979) *RES*, ns 30, 333–334; Bernhard Diensberg (1981) *Anglia*, 99, 226–229; Alarik Rynell (1981) *SN*, 53, 385–387.

Millet, Bella, ed. (1982) *HM.* EETS, os 284. [Bodley, Titus]

Saint Juliana

Cockayne, Oswald, ed. (1872) *Þe Liflade of SJ.* EETS, os 51; repr. 1957. [Royal, Bodley, parallel]

Hall, Joseph, ed. (1920) See s.v. *AW*, Printed Editions, above. Text, I: 138–149; notes, II: 543–553. [Royal, fols. 56–61v; Bodley, fols. 36v–43; parallel]

d'Ardenne, S. R. T. O., ed. (1936) *Þe Liflade ant te Passiun of Seinte Iuliene.* Repr. with corrigenda as EETS, os 248 (1961). [Royal, Bodley parallel with Latin text of MS Bodley 285] Reviews: E. V. Gordon (1937) *MAE*, 6, 131–143; Eilert Ekwall (1939) *ES*, 21, 125–129.

———, ed. (1961) See preceding.

———, ed. (1977) See s.v. *HM*, above.

Saint Katherine

Morton, James, ed. (1841) *The Legend of SK of Alexandria.* London: Abbotsford Club. [Titus with variants from Royal]

Hardwick, Charles, ed. (1849) *A Semi-Saxon Legend of St. Catharine of Alexandria*, appended to his *An Historical Inquiry Touching St. Catharine of Alexandria.* Cambridge: Cambridge Antiquarian Society. [Titus]

Einenkel, Eugen, ed. (1884) *The Life of SK*. EETS, os 80. [Royal (emended), with the
   Latin text of BL MS Cotton Caligula A. viii parallel and variants from Titus and
   Bodley]
Gibbs, Henry H., ed. (1884) *The Life and Martyrdom of SK of Alexandria*. London: Rox-
   burghe Club. Includes repr. of preceding in Appendix.
Hall, Joseph, ed. (1920) See s.v. *AW*, Printed Editions, above. Text, I: 128–131; notes,
   II: 524–531. [Royal, fols. 11–14]
d'Ardenne, S. R. T. O., ed. (1977) See s.v. *HM*, above.
d'Ardenne, S. R. T. O., and Dobson, E. J., eds. (1981) *Seinte Katerine*. EETS, supp.
   ser. 7. [Bodley (emended), Royal, Titus parallel; Latin vulgate *Passio*]

Saint Margaret

Cockayne, Oswald, ed. (1866) *Seinte Marherete: The Meiden ant Martyr*. EETS, os 13.
   [Royal with variants from Bodley]
Mack, Frances M., ed. (1934) *Seinte Marherete: Þe Meiden ant Martyr*. EETS os 193.
   [Royal, Bodley parallel] Reviews: Dorothy Everett (1935) *RES*, 11, 337–341; R. M.
   Wilson (1936) *MLR*, 31, 74–75; E. V. Gordon (1937) *MAE*, 6, 131–143.
Dickins, Bruce, and Wilson, R. M., eds. (1956) See s.v. *AW*, Printed Editions, above.
   Text, pp. 95–98; notes, pp. 210–213. [Bodley, fols. 24–25v (The Dragon)]
d'Ardenne, S. R. T. O., ed. (1977) See s.v. *HM*, above.

Sawles Warde

Morris, Richard, ed. (1868) *Old English Homilies and Homiletic Treatises*, pp. 244–267.
   EETS, os 34. Repr. with os 29 in one vol. (1969) New York: Greenwood Press;
   (1973) New York: Kraus. [Bodley with variants and missing portions supplied from
   Royal]
Wagner, Wilhelm, ed. (1907) See next.
———, ed. (1908) *SW: Kritische Textausgabe auf Grund aller Handschriften mit Einlei-
   tung, Anmerkungen und Glossar*. Bonn: P. Hanstein. Text alone appeared as dissertation
   in 1907. [Royal with variants from Titus and Bodley]
Hall, Joseph, ed. (1920) See s.v. Printed Editions, above. Text, I: 117–128; notes,
   II: 492–524. [Bodley supplemented by Royal]
Wilson, R. M., ed. (1938) *SW: An Early Middle English Homily*. Leeds School of English
   Language Texts and Monographs no. 3. [Titus, Royal, Bodley, *Ayenbyte of Inwyt*, *De
   Anima*; parallel] Review: Dorothy Everett (1940) *RES*, 16, 72–76.
Mossé, Fernand, ed. (1952) See s.v. *AW*, Printed Editions, above. Text, pp. 148–151;
   notes, pp. 343–347. [Bodley fols. 79v–80v supplemented by Royal with correspond-
   ing texts of *Ayenbite of Inwyt* and *De Anima* (Happiness of the Elect)]

Bennett, J. A. W., and Smithers, G. V., eds. (1968) See s.v. *AW*, Printed Editions, above. Text, pp. 246–261; notes, pp. 417–426. [Bodley with variants from Royal, Titus]

d'Ardenne, S. R. T. O., ed. (1977) See s.v. *HM*, above.

TRANSLATIONS

Hali Meidhad

Cockayne, Oswald, ed. (1866) See s.v. Printed Editions, above.

Furnivall, Frederick J., ed. (1922) See s.v. Printed Editions, above.

Saint Juliana

Cockayne, Oswald, and Brock, Edmund, trans. (1872). In Cockayne, ed. (1872) s.v. Printed Editions, above.

Saint Katherine

Morton, James, ed. (1841) See s.v. Printed Editions, above.

Einenkel, Eugen, ed. (1884) See s.v. Printed Editions, above. Repr. of Morton, ed. (1841) translation.

Gibbs, Henry H., ed. (1884) See s.v. Printed Editions, above. Repr. of Morton, ed. (1841) translation.

Saint Margaret

Cockayne, Oswald, ed. (1866) See s.v. Printed Editions, above.

Sawles Warde

Morris, Richard, ed. (1868) See s.v. Printed Editions, above.

d'Ardenne, S. R. T. O., trans. (1979) "La Garde de l'Ame." *MA*, 85, 297–315. [Modern French]

TRETYSE OF LOUE

PRINTED EDITIONS

de Worde, Wynkyn, ed. (1493) London: Wynkyn de Worde. STC 24234.
Fisher, John H., ed. (1951) *The Tretyse of Loue.* EETS, os 223.

WOHUNGE GROUP

MANUSCRIPTS

London. BL Cotton Nero A. xiv, fols. 123v–126v *On wel swuðe god Ureisun of God Almihti*; 126v–128 *Þe Oreisun of Seinte Marie* [untitled in Nero]; 128–131 *On Lofsong of Ure Louerde* [untitled in manuscript].
London. BL Cotton Titus D. xviii, fols. 127–133 *Þe Wohunge of Ure Lauerd.*
London. BL Royal 17 A. xxvii, fols. 70–70v *Þe Oreisun of Seinte Marie.*
London. Lambeth Palace MS 487, fols. 65v–67 *On wel swuðe god Ureisun of God Almihti* [incomplete, untitled in Lambeth].

PRINTED EDITIONS

Morris, Richard, ed. (1868) See s.v. KG, Printed Editions, *SW*, above. *On wel swuðe god Ureisun of God Almihti*, pp. 182–190 [Lambeth], 200–203 [Nero]; *On Lofsong of Ure Louerde*, pp. 208–217; *Þe Oreisun of Seinte Marie*, pp. 204–207 [Nero], 305 [Royal]; *Wohunge*, pp. 268–287.
Sampson, George, ed. (1924) *Cambridge Book of Prose and Verse.* Cambridge: Cambridge University Press. *Þe Oreisun of Seinte Marie*, pp. 196–198. [Nero repr. from preceding entry]
Thompson, W. Meredith, ed. (1958) *Þe Wohunge of Ure Lauerd. Edited from British Museum MS. Cotton Titus D. xviii, together with On Ureisun of Ure Louerde, On Wel Swuðe God Ureisun of God Almihti, On Lofsong of Ure Louerde, On Lofsong of Ure Lefdi, Þe Oreisun of Seinte Marie from the manuscripts in which they occur.* EETS, os 241. Reviews: Elizabeth Salter (1962) *RES*, ns 13, 166–168; G. V. Smithers (1962) *MAE*, 31, 216–218.
Blake, Norman F., ed. (1972) *The Wooing of Our Lord [Wohunge].* In Blake, ed. (1972), pp. 61–72, s.v. KG, Printed Editions, *HM*, above.

TRANSLATIONS

Morris, Richard, ed. (1868) See s.v. KG, Printed Editions, *SW*, above.
Sampson, George, ed. (1924) See s.v. Printed Editions, above.

SECONDARY WORKS

Ackerman, Robert W. (1978) "The Liturgical Day in *AR*." *Speculum*, 53, 734–744.

Allen, Hope E. (1918a) "The Mystical Lyrics of the *Manuel des Pechiez*." *RR* 9, 154–193, esp. 189–193.

———— (1918b) "The Origin of the *AR*." *PMLA* 33, 474–546.

———— (1919) "A New Latin Manuscript of the 'AR.'" *MLR*, 14, 209–210.

———— (1921) "The 'AR' and Kilburn Priory." *MLR*, 16, 316–322.

———— (1922) "Another Latin MS. of the 'AR.'" *MLR*, 17, 403.

———— (1923) "Some Fourteenth Century Borrowings from 'AR.'" *MLR*, 18, 1–8.

———— (1924) "On 'Some Fourteenth Century Borrowings from AR.'" *MLR* 19, 95.

———— (1929a) "Further Borrowings from 'AR.'" *MLR*, 24, 1–15.

———— (1929b) "On the Author of the *AR*." *PMLA*, 44, 635–680.

———— (1933) "The Localization of Bodl. MS. 34." *MLR* 28, 485–487.

———— (1934a) "The 'AR' and Geoffrey of Monmouth." *MLR*, 29, 173.

———— (1934b) "Eleanor Cobham." Letter to *TLS* (March 22), 214.

———— (1935a) "The Three Daughters of Deorman." *PMLA*, 50, 899–902.

———— (1935b) "The Tortington Chartulary." Letter to *TLS* (Feb. 14), 92.

———— (1936a) "The AR." Letter to *TLS* (Oct. 24), 863.

———— (1936b) "Manuscripts of the AR." Letter to *TLS* (Feb. 8), 116.

———— (1940) "Wynkyn de Worde and a Second French Compilation from the 'AR' with a Description of the First." In *Essays and Studies in Honor of Carleton Brown*, pp. 182–219. New York: New York University Press.

Atkins, J. W. H. (1907) "Chapter XI: Early Transition English." In *Cambridge History of English Literature*, vol. 1, edited by Adolphus W. Ward and A. R. Waller, pp. 241–269. New York: G. P. Putnam's Sons.

Baldwin, Mary (1976) "Some Difficult Words in *AR*." *MS*, 38, 268–290.

Barratt, Alexandra (1980) "Anchoritic Aspects of *AW*." *MAE*, 49, 32–56.

Baugh, A. C., ed. (1967) *A Literary History of England*. Vol. I: *The Middle Ages*. 2d ed. *AW*, pp. 127–134; KG, pp. 123–126. New York: Appleton-Century-Crofts.

Becker, Wolfgang (1980) "The Source Text of *SW*." *Manuscripta*, 24, 44–48.

Bennett, J. A. W. (1958) "Lefunge o swefne o nore." *RES*, ns 9, 280–281.

Benskin, Michael, and Laing, Margaret (1981) "Translations and *Mischsprachen* in Middle English Manuscripts." In *So Meny People Longages and Tonges: Philological Essays in Scots and Mediaeval English Presented to Angus McIntosh*, edited by Michael Benskin and M. L. Samuels, pp. 55–106. Edinburgh: privately printed.

Bethurum, Dorothy (1935) "The Connection of the Katherine Group with Old English Prose." *JEGP*, 34, 553–564.

Bishop, Ian (1979) "'Greek Fire' in *AW* and Contemporary Texts." *N&Q*, 224, 198–199.

Bliss, A. J. (1952–1953) "A Note on Language AB." *EGS*, 5, 1–6.

Bloomfield, Morton W. (1952) *The Seven Deadly Sins*. East Lansing: Michigan State College Press.

Bögholm, N. (1937) "Vocabulary and Style of the Middle English *AR*." *ES*, 19, 113–116.

Bramlette, Edgar E. (1893) "The Original Language of the *AR*." *Anglia*, 15, 478–498.

Brewer, Derek S. (1953) "Postscriptum." *MAE*, 22, 123.

———— (1956) "Two Notes on the Augustinian and Possibly West Midland Origin of the *AR*." *N&Q*, 201, 232–235.

Brock, Edmund (1865) "The Grammatical Forms of Southern English (Ab. A.D. 1220–30) Occurring in the *AR*." *TPS*, 150–167.

Chambers, R. W. (1925) "Recent Research upon the *AR*." *RES*, 1, 4–23.

———— (1932) *On the Continuity of English Prose from Alfred to More and His School*. From the introduction to *Nicholas Harpsfield's Life of Sir Thomas More*, edited by Elsie V. Hitchcock, pp. xlv–clxxiv. EETS, os 186. Repr. separately as EETS 191A (1957).

Clark, Cecily (1954) "A Mediaeval Proverb." *ES*, 35, 11–15.

———— (1966) "*AW* and *KG*: A Lexical Divergence." *Neophil*, 50, 117–124.

———— (1968) "Early Middle English Prose: Three Essays in Stylistics." *EIC*, 18, 361–382, esp. 363–375.

———— (1977) "As Seint Austin Seith. . . ." *MAE*, 46, 212–218.

———— (1978) "'Wið Scharpe Sneateres': Some Aspects of Colloquialism in *AW*." *NM*, 79, 341–353.

Colledge, Eric (1939a) "'The Hours of the Planets': An Obscure Passage in 'The Recluse.'" *MLN*, 54, 442–445.

———— (1939b) "*The Recluse*: A Lollard Interpolated Version of the *AR*." *RES*, 15, 1–15, 129–145.

Coulton, G. G. (1922) "The Authorship of 'AR.'" *MLR*, 17, 66–69.

Crawford, S. J. (1930) "The Influence of the 'AR' in the Late Fourteenth Century." *MLR*, 25, 191–192.

Dahlstedt, August (1903) *The Word Order of the AR*. Sundsvall: R. Sahlin.

Dahood, Roger (1978) "A Lexical Puzzle in *AW*." *N&Q*, 223, 1–2, 541.

d'Ardenne, S. R. T. O. (1974) "*Bratewil (Katerine 1690)." *ES* 55, 282–283.

d'Ardenne, S. R. T. O., and Tolkien, J. R. R. (1947a) "'iþþlen' in *SW*." *ES* 28, 168–170.

———— (1947b) "MS. Bodley 34: A Re-collation of a Collation." *SN*, 20, 65–72.

De Caluwé-Dor, Juliette (1977) "Divergence lexicale entre le KG et l'*AR*: valeur statistique des premières attestations de mots d'origine française en anglais." *EA*, 30, 463–472.

D'Evelyn, Charlotte (1949) "Notes on Some Interrelations between the Latin and English Texts of the *AR*." *PMLA*, 64, 1164–1179.

———— (1970) "Bibliography." In *A Manual of the Writings in Middle English, 1050–1500*, vol. 2, edited by J. Burke Severs, pp. 597–598 (*SJ*), 599–600 (*SK*), 606–607 (*SM*), 650–654 (*AW*). New Haven: Connecticut Academy of Arts and Sciences.

Diensberg, Bernhard (1975) "Morphologische Untersuchungen zur AR: Die Verbalflexion nach den MSS Corpus Christi College Cambridge 402, B.M. Cotton Cleopatra C.

vi, B.M. Cotton Nero A. xiv." Diss., Rheinische Friedrich-Wilhelms-Universität. Review: Klaus Bitterling (1978) *Anglia*, 96, 470–471.

——— (1978a) "*AW/R* surquide, caue, creauant/creaunt, trusse, bereget, und babanliche." *Archiv*, 215, 79–82.

——— (1978b) "Westsächsische Lehnwörter im merzischen AB-Dialekt?" *Anglia*, 96, 447–450.

Dieth, Eugen (1919) "Flexivisches und Syntaktisches über das Pronomen in der AR: Ein Beitrag zur mittelenglischen Syntax." Diss., University of Zurich.

Dobson, E. J. (1962) "The Affiliations of the Manuscripts of *AW*." In *English and Medieval Studies Presented to J. R. R. Tolkien on the Occasion of His Seventieth Birthday*, edited by Norman Davis and C. L. Wrenn, pp. 128–163. London: Allen and Unwin. Review: E. G. Stanley (1964) *Archiv*, 201, 130–132.

——— (1966) "The Date and Composition of *AW*." *PBA*, 52, 181–208.

——— (1974) "Two Notes on Early Middle English Texts." *N&Q*, 219, 124–126.

——— (1975) *Moralities on the Gospels: A New Source of AW*. Oxford: Oxford University Press. Reviews: Richard H. Rouse and Siegfried Wenzel (1977) *Speculum*, 52, 648–652; Edward Wilson (1977) *RES*, ns 28, 65–66; Joseph Wittig (1980) *Anglia*, 98, 185–190.

——— (1976) *The Origins of AW*. Oxford: Oxford University Press. Reviews: Derek Pearsall (1977), *RES*, ns. 28, 316–318; O. Arngart (1978), *ES*, 59, 154–155; Siegfried Wenzel (1978) *Speculum*, 53, 354–356; Gillis Kristensson (1981) *SN*, 53, 371–376.

Dolan, T. P. (1974) "The Date of *AW*: A Corroborative Note." *N&Q*, 219, 322–323.

——— (1979) "'Riote' in *AW*." *ELN*, 16, 198–200.

Doyle, A. I. (1954) "A Survey of English Prose in the Middle Ages." In *The Age of Chaucer*, edited by Boris Ford, pp. 68–82. The Pelican Guide to English Literature 1. Baltimore: Penguin.

——— (1974) "The Shaping of the Vernon and Simeon Manuscripts." In *Chaucer and Middle English Studies in Honour of Rossell Hope Robbins*, edited by Beryl Rowland, pp. 328–341. London: Allen and Unwin.

Dymes, Dorothy M. E. (1924) "The Original Language of the *AR*." *E&S*, 9, 31–49.

Fisher, John H. (1949) "Continental Associations for the *AR*." *PMLA*, 64, 1180–1189.

——— (1959) "The French Versions of the *AR*." *University of North Carolina Studies in the Germanic Languages and Literatures*, 26, 65–74.

Funke, O. (1921) "Zur Wortgeschichte der französischen Elemente in Englischen." *EStn*, 55, 1–25.

Furuskog, Ragnar (1946) "A Collation of the *KG* (MS. Bodley 34)." *SN*, 19, 119–166.

Georgianna, Linda (1981) *The Solitary Self: Individuality in the AW*. Cambridge, Mass.: Harvard University Press.

Grayson, Janet (1974) *Structure and Imagery in AW*. Hanover, N.H.: University Press of New England. Review: Siegfried Wenzel (1976) *MAE*, 45, 219–221.

Hotchner, Cecilia A. (1942) "A Note on 'Dux Vitae' and 'Lifes Lattiow.'" *PMLA*, 57, 572–575.

Hulbert, James R. (1946) "A Thirteenth-Century English Literary Standard." *JEGP*, 45, 411–414.

Humbert, Agnes M. (1944) *Verbal Repetition in the AR*. Washington: Catholic University of America Press. Reviews: Gladys D. Willcock (1945) *YWES*, 26, 71; Beatrice White (1946) *RES* 22, 230.

Ives, D. V. (1934) "The Proverbs in the 'AR.'" *MLR*, 29, 257–266.

Jack, George B. (1975) "Relative Pronouns in Language AB." *ES*, 56, 100–107.

────── (1976) "*Oper in the 'AB Language.*'" *Anglia*, 94, 431–435.

────── (1977) "*Luste* in *AW*." *NM*, 78, 24–26.

────── (1979) "Archaizing in the Nero Version of *AW*." *NM*, 80, 325–326.

Jespersen, Otto (1905) *Growth and Structure of the English Language*. Leipzig: G. Teubner.

Kaske, R. E. (1960) "Eve's 'Leaps' in the *AR*." *MAE*, 29, 22–24.

Käsmann, Hans (1957) "Zur Frage der ursprünglichen Fassung der *AR*." *Anglia*, 75, 134–156.

────── (1961) *Studien zum kirchlichen Wortschatz des Mittelenglischen 1100–1350: Ein Beitrag zum Problem der Sprachmischung*. Tübingen: Max Niemeyer.

Kenyon, John S. (1914) "Syntactical Note." *MLN*, 29, 127–128.

Kirchberger, Clare (1954) "Some Notes on the *AR*." *Dominican Studies*, 7, 215–238.

Kivimaa, Kirsti (1966) *Þe and Þat as Clause Connectives in Early Middle English with Especial Consideration of the Emergence of the Pleonastic Þat*. Societas Scientiarum Fennica, Commentationes Humanarum Litterarum 39, no. 1. Review: Tauno Mustanoja (1967) *NM*, 68, 327–329.

Kliman, Bernice W. (1977) "Women in Early English Literature: 'Beowulf' to the 'AW.'" *Nottingham Mediaeval Studies*, 21, 32–49.

Knowles, David (1963) *The Monastic Order in England*. 2d ed. Cambridge: Cambridge University Press.

Kölbing, Eugen (1876) "Zu der AR." *JRESL*, 15, nf 3, 179–197.

Koskenniemi, Inna (1968) *Repetitive Word Pairs in Old and Early Middle English Prose: Expressions of the Type "Whole and Sound" and "Answered and Said" and Other Parallel Constructions*. Turun Yliopiston Julkaisuja. Annales Universitatis Turkuensis. Sarja-Series B OSA, Tom. 107. Turku.

Kubouchi, Tadao (1975) "Word-Order in the *AW*." *HJA&S*, 16, 11–28.

Ladd, C. A. (1961) "A Note on the Language of the *AR*." *N&Q*, 206, 288–290.

Lee, Berta G. (1974) *Linguistic Evidence for the Priority of the French Text of the AW: Based on the Corpus Christi College Cambridge 402 and the British Museum Cotton Vitellius F vii Versions of the AW*. Janua Linguarum. Series Practica 242. The Hague: Mouton.

Lewis, Robert E. (1981) "The Relationship of the Vernon and Simeon Texts of the *Pricke of Conscience*." In *So Meny People Longages and Tonges: Philological Essays in Scots and Mediaeval English Presented to Angus McIntosh*, edited by Michael Benskin and M. L. Samuels, pp. 251–264. Edinburgh: privately printed.

Logan, H. M. (1973) *The Dialect of the Life of SK: A Linguistic Study of the Phonology and Inflections*. Janua Linguarum. Series Practica 130. The Hague: Mouton. Review: Bernhard Diensberg (1980) *Anglia*, 98, 125–130.

Macaulay, G. C. (1914) "The 'AR.'" *MLR*, 9, 63–78, 145–160, 324–331, 463–474.

McIntosh, Angus (1947–1948) "The Relative Pronouns *Þe* and *Þat* in Early Middle English." *EGS*, 1, 73–87.

McNabb, Vincent (1916) "The Authorship of the *AR*." *MLR*, 11, 1–8.

—— (1920) "Further Light on the 'AR.'" *MLR*, 15, 406–409.

—— (1926) "Further Research upon the *AR*." *RES*, 2, 82–85; with a response by R. W. Chambers (including a letter from Herbert Thurston), 85–89; and a reply to that letter by McNabb, 197–198, with another reply from Chambers and another from Thurston, 199–201.

—— (1934) "The Authorship of the *AR*." *AFP*, 4, 49–74.

Madden, Frederic (1854) "The AR." *N&Q*, 9, 5–6.

Magoun, Francis P., Jr. (1937) "*AW* vs. *AR*." *ELH*, 4, 112–113.

Maybury, James F. (1977) "On the Structure and Significance of Part III of the *AR*, with Some Comment on Sources." *ABR*, 28, 95–101.

Miller, B. D. H. (1962) "She Who Hath Drunk Any Potion . . ." *MAE*, 31, 188–193.

Mühe, Th. (1901) *Über den im MS. Cotton Titus D. xviii enthaltenen Text der AR*. Göttingen: diss., E. A. Huth.

—— (1908) "Über die AR." *Anglia*, 31, 399–404.

Onions, C. T. (1928) "Middle English (i) Wite God, Wite Crist, (ii) God It Wite." *RES*, 4, 334–337.

Ostermann, Hermann (1905) "Lautlehre des germanischen Wortschatzes in der von Morton herausgegebenen Handschrift der AR." *BBA*, 19, 1–91.

Owst, G. R. (1933) *Literature and Pulpit in Medieval England: A Neglected Chapter in the History of English Letters and of the English People*. Cambridge: Cambridge University Press.

Planta, J. (1802) *A Catalogue of the Manuscripts in the Cottonian Library Deposited in the British Museum*. London: L. Hansard, printer.

Prins, A. A. (1948) "On Two Proverbs in the *AR*." *ES*, 29, 146–150.

Püttmann, Adolf (1908) "Die Syntax der sogenannten Progressiven Form im Alt- und Frühmittelenglischen." *Anglia*, 31, 405–452.

Raw, Barbara (1974) "The Prayers and Devotions in the *AW*." In *Chaucer and Middle English Studies in Honour of Rossell Hope Robbins*, edited by Beryl Rowland, pp. 260–271. London: Allen and Unwin.

Redepenning, Hermann (1906) "Syntaktische Kapitel aus der *AR*." Diss., Universität Rostock.

Russell-Smith, Joy (1957) "Ridiculosae Sternutationes (*o nore* in *AW*)." *RES*, ns 8, 266–269.

Rygiel, Dennis (1976) "The Allegory of Christ the Lover-Knight in *AW*: An Experiment in Stylistic Analysis." *SP*, 73, 343–364.

—— (1980) "Structure and Style in Part Seven of *AW*." *NM*, 81, 47–56.

—— (1982) "A Holistic Approach to the Style of *AW*." *ChauR*, 16, 270–281.

Sajavaara, Kari (1967a) *The Middle English Translations of Robert Grosseteste's Chateau d'Amour*. Mémoires de la Société Néophilologique de Helsinki 32. Helsinki: Société Néophilologique.

———— (1967b) "The Relationship of the Vernon and Simeon Manuscripts." *NM*, 68, 428–439.

Salu, Mary (1952–1953) "Some Obscure Words in *AW* (MS. C.C.C.C. 402)." *EGS*, 5, 100–102.

Samuels, M. L. (1953) "*AR* Studies." *MAE*, 22, 1–9.

Serjeantson, Mary S. (1927) "The Dialects of the West Midlands in Middle English." *RES*, 3, 54–67, 186–203, 319–331.

———— (1937) "The Index of the Vernon Manuscript." *MLR*, 32, 222–261.

———— (1938) "The Dialect of the Corpus Manuscript of the *AR*." *London Mediaeval Studies*, 1, 225–248.

Shepherd, Geoffrey (1956) "'All the Wealth of Croesus . . .': A Topic in the 'AR.'" *MLR*, 51, 161–167.

Sitwell, Gerard (1955) Introduction and appendix in *The AR*, translated by Mary B. Salu, pp. vii–xxii, 193–196. London: Burns and Oates.

Smith, Thomas (1696) *Catalogus Librorum Manuscriptorum Bibliothecae Cottonianae*. Oxford: Oxford University Press.

Smithers, G. V. (1948–1949) "Four Cruces in Middle English Texts." *EGS*, 2, 59–67.

———— (1949–1950) "Ten Cruces in Middle English Texts." *EGS*, 3, 65–81, esp. 72–73.

———— (1965) "Two Typological Terms in the *AR*." *MAE*, 34, 126–128.

Smyth, Mary W. (1911) *Biblical Quotations in Middle English Literature before 1350*. *YSE* 41. New Haven: Yale University Press.

Stevens, William J. (1961) "The Titles of 'MSS AB.'" *MLN*, 76, 443–444.

Talbot, C. H. (1951) "The 'De institutis inclusarum' of Ailred of Rievaulx." *Analecta Sacri Ordinis Cisterciensis*, 7, 167–217.

———— (1956) "Some Notes on the Dating of the *AR*." *Neophil*, 40, 38–50.

Thurston, Herbert (1926). See s.v. McNabb (1926).

Tolkien, J. R. R. (1929) "*AW* and *HM*." *E&S*, 14, 104–126.

Turville-Petre, Joan (1969) "Two Etymological Notes: AW *eskibah*, *hond þet ilke*." *SN*, 41, 156–161.

Waldron, R. A. (1969) "Enumeration in *AW*." *N&Q*, 214, 86–87.

Wanley, Humfrey (1705) *Antiquae Literaturae Septentrionalis, liber alter*. In George Hickes, *Linguarum Veterum Septentrionalium Thesaurus*. Oxford. Repr. (1970) New York and Hildesheim: Georg Olms.

White, Beatrice (1945) "Whale-Hunting, The Barnacle Goose, and the Date of the 'AR': Three Notes on Old and Middle English." *MLR*, 40, 205–207.

Whiting, B. J. (1935) "Proverbs in the 'AR' and the 'Recluse.'" *MLR*, 30, 502–505.

Williams, Irene F. (1905) "The Language of the Cleopatra MS. of the AR." *Anglia*, 28, 300–304.

Wilson, R. M. (1959) "On the Continuity of English Prose." In *Mélanges de linguistique et de philologie: Fernand Mossé in memoriam*, pp. 486–494, esp. pp. 492–494. Paris: Didier.

Woolf, Rosemary (1962) "The Theme of Christ the Lover-Knight in Medieval English Literature." *RES*, ns 13, 1–16.

Wülcker, Richard (1874a) "Über die Sprache der AR und die der Homilie: Hali Meidenhad." *BGDSL*, 1, 209–239.

———— (1874b) "Übersicht der neuangelsächsischen Sprachdenkmaler." *BGDSL*, 1, 57–88, esp. 71–75.

Zettersten, Arne (1964) *Middle English Word Studies*. Lund Universitets Arsskrift, N.F. Avd. 1, Bd. 56, Nr. 1. Lund: Gleerup.

———— (1965) *Studies in the Dialect and Vocabulary of the AR*. LSE 34. Reviews: Sven Bäckman (1968) *ES* 49, 453–462; Ulf Jacobsson (1966) *SN*, 38, 181–194.

———— (1969) "French Loan-words in the *AR* and Their Frequency." In *Mélanges de philologie offerts à Alf Lombard à l'occasion de son soixante-cinquième anniversaire par ses collègues et ses amis*, pp. 227–250. Etudes Romanes de Lund 18.

CHAPTER 2

Richard Rolle and Related Works

John A. Alford

Richard Rolle, hermit of Hampole, is the chief religious and literary figure in early fourteenth-century England. If not "one of the greatest English writers" (Horstman 1896, 2:xxxv), he was certainly one of the most versatile and prolific, turning out poems, translations, biblical commentaries, and original prose writings, in both English and Latin, so that for a century and a half he was "probably the most widely read in England of all English writers" (Chambers 1932, p. ci). Here, of course, we are concerned only with his English prose writings, although occasional reference will be made to his poetry and Latin writings as well.

BIOGRAPHY

We have more information about Rolle (ca. 1300–1349) than about any of the other fourteenth-century English mystics, more perhaps than about any previous writer in the language. Yet because of the nature of the sources—primarily the *Officium de Sancto Ricardo Heremita* (drawn up by the nuns of Hampole ca. 1383 in hope of his canonization) and the autobiographical statements in his own writings—we must be extremely cautious. The *Officium* is colored by a holy desire to present Rolle as a model of saintliness (Noetinger 1926), and his own statements perhaps by a not-so-holy desire for self-exculpation. Moreover, his attempt to pattern his life after the lives of certain biblical personages—to speak and act and feel as they did—qualifies considerably the meaning of his autobiographical remarks (Alford 1976).

The *Officium* is extant in four MSS, all defective: Bodleian e Musaeo 193, BL Cotton Tiberius A. xv, Lincoln Cath. 209 (printed by Perry 1866), and Uppsala University C. 621 (fragment, printed by Lindkvist 1917). A collated version of the first three MSS appears in the *York Breviary*, Surtees Society 75 (1882), Appendix II (reprinted by Woolley 1919). There are translations in Allen (1927, pp. 55–61) and Comper (both 1914 and 1928).

The basic study of Rolle's life is by Allen (1927, pp. 430–526), although it must be used with care (see Arnould 1957, notes to pp. vii, viii, xxxi, xlix, lii). Comper's biography (1928) is generally satisfactory, although her attempt to construct Rolle's educational background (chaps. 1–3) is less useful than Liegey's (1954). Hodgson (1926) adds little to either Allen or Comper. There are many short accounts of the hermit's life, too numerous to be listed here. Most noteworthy are those by Allen (1931), Noetinger (1926), Whiting (1948), Arnould (1960), and Marzac (1968). Sargent (1981) looks at contemporary criticism of Rolle (by Walter Hilton and the author of *The Cloud of Unknowing*) and the defense by Thomas Basset.

Following are the main details of Rolle's life: born about 1300 at Thornton, near Pickering, in Yorkshire; at nineteen sent to Oxford where his mind (the *Office* says) "was more on theological than secular knowledge"; dropped out and either went to Paris, where he was able to study theology in earnest, or returned directly home, where he began the life of a hermit; took up solitary residence in the house of a family friend, Sir John Dalton; left shortly after his initiation into mystical joy ("the opening of the heavenly door"), the first of several changes of cell for which he was much criticized by his "*detractores*"; began to attract a following through his teaching and Latin writings; turned to English in his later years, apparently for the sake of his female disciples, in particular Margaret Kirkby and an unnamed nun of Yedingham; died at Hampole in 1349.

Among the questions raised about Rolle's life, two in particular have received much attention. First, was he in trouble at one time with local church authorities? On the basis of the phrase *heremita contra episcopum* in the *Melos*, Horstman thought so (1896, 2:xxii), and Allen even tried to identify the bishop involved (1927, pp. 480–488). The theory is rejected by Arnould (1957, Appendix I). Second, did he study theology at Paris? In 1926 Noetinger called attention to the fact that "Richardus de Hampole" is listed as a student at the Sorbonne in several seventeenth-century MSS (Bibliothèque de l'Arsenal), compiled "ex veteribus manuscriptis ac instrumentis publicis." Allen was inclined to accept the evidence (1927, pp. 490–500). Arnould, however, tries to show that the seventeenth-century compilers misinterpreted their sources and thus created a myth (1957, Appendix II). Marzac disagrees and offers new evidence from a Prague MS that "la tradition du passage de Richard Rolle à Paris était donc déjà bien établie dans la première moitié du XVe siècle" (1968, p. 25). Riehle is the latest to reaffirm the tradition (1981, p. 171n).

THE CANON

Two scholars have been most instrumental in establishing the canon of Rolle's English prose writings: Carl Horstman and Hope Emily Allen. In 1895–1896 Horstman brought out his collection of northern texts, *Yorkshire Writers: Richard Rolle . . . and His Followers*, and announced that "henceforth the question will rest on the works here given" (2:xl). The criteria for selection were two: dialect and inclusion in a MS containing other works indisputably by Rolle. In 1927 Allen published her monumental *Writings Ascribed to Richard Rolle*. Having sifted through the texts in Horstman's volumes, as well as hundreds of MSS, she reduced the number of genuine English prose writings to the following:

I. Major Writings   *The English Psalter*
                           Commentaries connected with the Psalter
                           Ego Dormio
                           The Commandment
                           The Form of Living
                           Meditations on the Passion
II. Short Pieces   *The Bee*
                           Desyre and Delit
                           Gastly Gladnesse
                           Seven Gifts of the Holy Ghost
                           On the Ten Commandments

Allen's criteria were mainly four: dialect, attribution to Rolle by at least one MS, style, and certain characteristic themes (e.g., the triad of *calor, dulcor, canor*). Allen was confident that she had established the definitive body of works and said so—"almost no uncertainties enter it" (1927, p. 3). Although most scholars have agreed with her assessment, the issue is by no means settled. Geraldine Hodgson was convinced that several other works printed by Horstman belonged to Rolle, and she habitually spoke of Allen's list as if it were an act of thievery. In the case of *Our Daily Work*, Riehle agrees with her (1981, p. 170), although the research by both Arntz (1981) and Keiser (1981) seems to vindicate Allen's judgment. Morgan (1953) would reduce the canon still further by excluding the *Meditations*; Madigan's study of this work, however, would seem to vindicate Allen once again (1978, Appendix C). Riehle has announced his plans (*FCEMN* 5:3, 1979, p. 4) to reassess the whole question of Rolle's canon.

CRITICISM

This section is divided into general criticism, criticism of particular works, and criticism of related works, that is, Rolle's "school."

General Criticism

In 1956 R. M. Wilson observed, "Much has been written on the Middle English mystics, but almost invariably from a religious point of view, and as writers of English prose they have been little considered except in very general terms" (p. 87). This is no longer true, if indeed it was true even thirty years ago. In the case of Rolle, at least, the two approaches—religious and literary—have a continuous tradition all the way back to the nineteenth century. Often they have merged.

Exclusively religious approaches to Rolle, it must be said, have been too concerned of late with grading his mysticism. Found wanting on that basis, Rolle has been thought not worth discussing on any other. Knowles set the theme in 1961: "As a mystic Rolle has little or nothing to teach" (p. 54), and this has become more or less the received opinion among scholars whose interest is primarily religious (e.g., Sitwell, Colledge, Pepler, Thornton). Having accepted this point of view, the best that Phyllis Hodgson can find to say about Rolle is that "nevertheless . . . he prepared the way for his greater successors, Walter Hilton and the author of *The Cloud of Unknowing*" (1967, p. 21). But in what way Rolle's successors were "greater" remains to be seen. Was their experience more profound, their writing more accomplished, their influence more important? Actually the prejudice against Rolle seems to be rooted in a distrust of affective mysticism in general. As Merton points out, Knowles "clings to a single standard in judging mystics: it is the Dionysian standard of 'unknowing.' Therefore, he cannot accept as genuine a mystic of light like Rolle" (1961, p. 148). Recent studies (Benz 1969; Riehle 1981) that connect Rolle's thought more closely with that of continental mystics may do much to restore his reputation.

In general the most illuminating studies of Rolle's work combine an active sympathy for the religious end and a respect for the literary means used to further it. After all, Rolle's importance does not lie simply in the fact that he enjoyed this or that degree of mystical experience—innumerable souls have felt themselves similarly blessed—but that he chose to *write* about it and, having written, attracted a larger audience than any previous writer in the language. What were the reasons for his extraordinary appeal? Criticism has focused on two in particular: a unique set of characteristic themes and a distinctive prose style.

Among Rolle's characteristic themes, one of the most prominent is his devotion to the Holy Name of Jesus, a hallmark of his writings. The theme appears for the first time in his comment on Cant. 1.2 in the *Tractatus super Cantica Canticorum*. This section, called the *Oleum Effusum* (after the beginning words) or *Encomium Nominis Jhesu*, became extremely popular and circulated as a separate piece in both Latin and English. Included in the comment is an account of Rolle's discovery of the power of the Holy Name in warding off a certain temptress: "Tharefore I turnede me to Gode and with my mynde I said 'A Jhesu how precyous es thi blude!' makand þe crosse with my fyngere in my breste, and als faste scho wexe wayke and sodanly all was awaye; and I thankked Gode þat delyvered me, and sothely fra þat tym furthe I forced me for to luf Jhesu, and ay þe mare I profette in þe luf of Jhesu þe swetter I fand it, and to þis daye it went noghte fra my mynde" (Perry 1866, p. 6). Allen saw in this incident a shift in devotion from the Virgin to the Son (1927, p. 92), but this interpretation is rejected both by Liegey (1956), who points to Rolle's continued devotion to Mary, and by Wilmart, who says, "C'est une question qui, du point de vue catholique, ne se pose pas" (1940, p. 134n). Though partly indicated by the above account, Knowles's description of the Holy Name as "a kind of talisman" for Rolle is hardly adequate; its deeper meaning in his works is explored more fully by Froomberg (1948) and Madigan (1978). Wilmart (1944) gives the historical background of the devotion, especially Bernard's contribution, and reproduces the complete text of Rolle's comment from MS Douai 396.

Unlike the devotion to the Holy Name, which was a European phenomenon, Rolle's identification of the effects of spiritual love as *calor*, *dulcor*, and *canor* seems to have been original. Liegey (1954, 1957) finds possible sources for each but concludes that the triad as such is peculiar to Rolle. Schnell quotes from the *Incendium Amoris* and *Emendatio Vitae* all the passages in which the terms appear (1932, pp. 114–145). Renaudin discusses the motif in two articles, the first (1938) devoted, in part, to *calor* and *dulcor*, the second (1940) to *canor*. In both he stresses that the terms refer to an experience "à la fois spirituelle et sensorielle" (1938, p. 163). The idea of *canor* is probably the most interesting both because it is most distinctively Rolle's and because it is the highest expression of divine love visited upon the soul—"le chant n'est envoyé qu'à celle qui est parvenue à la perfection de l'amour" (1940, p. 68). Several studies examine the poetic implications of mystical *canor*. Olmes is concerned mainly with the metaphorical aspects of the idea (1933, pp. 16–28, 40–42). Liegey points out that Rolle has one style for exposition and another for describing the personal effects of divine love, the latter style marked by increased alliteration and rhythmic regularity: "These are unmistakable signs to the reader that Rolle is now no longer glossing, nor explaining, nor arguing, nor preaching, but singing!" (1954, p. 57). Schulte (1951) elaborates on the musical element in Rolle's thought. Womack (1961) develops the thesis (cf. Knowles 1927; Wilmart 1944) that Rolle was a spiritual troubadour, "standing in sharp contrast to the secular troubadour of the Middle

Ages, whose influence . . . he was consciously attempting to combat"—a view expressly denied by Riehle (1981, p. 54).

Another important triad—it appears in the *Emendatio* and in all the English epistles—is that of the three grades of love, insuperable, inseparable, and singular. There is less doubt about where Rolle got this pattern. Allen points to the same terminology in Richard of Saint Victor's *De IV Gradibus Violentae Charitatis—insuperabilis, inseparabilis, singularis, insatiabilis* (1927, p. 201). Why Rolle reduced the number to three is uncertain. Allen gives several possible reasons (p. 202). But Colledge interprets the reduction as another piece of evidence that Rolle's "knowledge of mysticism, and his capacity for communicating his knowledge, are limited" (1961, p. 58). Somewhat kinder, Jennings nevertheless agrees that the fourth grade of love was not part of Rolle's experience: "Happily he would have stressed that *insuperabilis est qui alii affectui non cedit*; *inseparabilis, qui a memoria nunquam recedit*; *singularis, qui socium non recipit* and just as happily omitted *insatiabilis, cum ei satisfieri non possit*—the truth of which I suspect he doubted himself" (1975, pp. 198–199).

Hahn's study of the sources of Rolle's thought (1900) is largely invalidated by the inclusion of such noncanonical material as *The Prick of Conscience*; the relevant information is extracted by Allen and presented in the notes to her *English Writings* (1931). There is also a chapter on Rolle's sources in Comper (1928).

Rolle's prose style has received nearly as much attention as his thought. Early impetus was provided by Horstman, who called Rolle "the true father of English literature" (1896, 2:xxxv) and by Chambers, who said, "Rolle's date, his style, and his popularity give him a supreme place in the history of English prose" (1932, p. ci). Partly in reaction to such extravagant claims, more recent critics (Morgan 1952a; Wilson 1956; Harris 1970; Relihan 1978) have emphasized the existence of a fully developed prose tradition in the late thirteenth century and have suggested that Rolle consciously drew upon it in his vernacular writings. Not only the vernacular but also the Latin tradition must be taken into account as an influence on Rolle's English prose style. Liegey (1957) points out that Rolle's alliterative tendency may be fed by two streams—one native, going back to Anglo-Saxon practice, and the other Latin and much older still. Alford (1973) seeks to demonstrate that Rolle borrowed from the Latin Bible much of his imagery, language, and even syntax. Rolle's own Latin works probably influenced his English in some way, as Matthews (1962) and others note (e.g., the *Form* derives in part from his *Emendatio*, and the *English Psalter* from his Latin one). To what extent is yet unclear.

As for analyses of Rolle's style itself, numerous studies may be added to the above. Unfortunately two of the chief studies of his syntax depend on works no longer attributed to the hermit. Of the eighteen works used by Henningsen (1911), fewer than half can be considered authentic. Schneider (1906) bases his conclusions in part on such noncanonical writings as *Our Daily Work*. His central thesis, that Rolle's prose exhibits "a style anticipatory of the highly developed Euphuism of Lyly and his school," is criticized at length by Olmes (1933, pp. 85–100). The latter author's own discussion of Rolle's prose style, both English and Latin, is still useful, particularly as an anthology of examples arranged by category. Although Liegey's dissertation (1954) deals primarily with the *Melos*, it shows again and again how Rolle's habits of composition in Latin carried over into his English writings. The use of punctuation in Rolle MSS as a guide to "the text's aural character" is noted by Morgan (1952b) and elaborated in great detail by Smedick (1979).

Several studies mentioned already are concerned with Rolle's imagery (e.g., Benz 1969; Liegey 1954; Olmes 1933; Riehle 1981; Schneider 1906). Taking his imagery to be "a way out of the linguistic impasse of communicating something . . . that was essentially incommunicable and indescribable," Wakelin (1979, p. 197) concentrates on metaphors connected with the theme of mystical love. It may be safely said, however, that Riehle's study now supersedes all others. It is the only one that attempts a comprehensive survey of all Rolle's works and the only one that attempts to explain his imagery in the context of both English and continental mysticism.

Criticism of Particular Works

The earliest of Rolle's works in English (begun ca. 1340) is his *English Psalter*. It survives in over thirty-five MSS. Paues (1902) located many of these and distinguished between two versions: one "pure" and the other interpolated with Lollard material. Her efforts were elaborated in a series of articles by Everett (1922, 1923), whose work in turn served as the foundation for Allen's discussion (1927, pp. 169–192). The only published edition is that of Bramley (1884). It is far from satisfactory. As Allen notes, he "uses only twelve manuscripts . . . and makes no attempt to trace the sources" (1927, p. 170). The need for a new edition has been met in part by several recent dissertations. In 1966 Collins edited forty-four psalms from MS Huntington 148 (though the basis of her selection of particular psalms is unclear), and since 1976 a number of doctoral students at Fordham University have edited various portions of MS University College, Oxford 64. At the present rate, however, the latter project will require ten separate dissertations for completion; and as a practical matter scholars will continue to rely on Bramley.

The *English Psalter* may be described as consisting of three discrete parts: (1) the Latin text, each verse followed by (2) Rolle's English translation, and then by (3) a brief commentary in English. The Latin text was derived primarily from Jerome's Gallican Psalter (Everett, as quoted in Allen 1931, p. 121); and the commentary, from the *catena* of Peter Lombard (Middendorf 1888). How Rolle modified his borrowings from the latter is shown by Allen in her monograph on *The Prick of Conscience* (1910, pp. 148–151). Geraldine Hodgson cites other possible borrowings from Augustine's *Ennarationes* (1926, pp. 151–188). Although parallels exist between the two, Rolle's *English Psalter* is not a translation of his *Latin Psalter* but rather an independent work. According to the verse prologue of a fifteenth-century copy, it was composed for his friend "dame Merget kyrkby" (see below).

The *English Psalter* enjoyed immense popularity. This, Deanesley points out, along with the fact "that Rolle's Psalter was recognized as the only biblical translation which could be used by the orthodox explains the quickness of the Lollards to insert their own teaching among the glosses" (120, p. 231). Muir (1934, 1935) has studied the relation between the Rolle and Wycliffite psalters and their influence on the Authorized Version of 1611. The relation between Rolle's *English Psalter* and the earlier metrical version (the so-called Surtees Psalter, ed. Horstman 1896, 2:130–273) is another problem. For a long time it was supposed that he was the author of both. However, Everett (1922) showed that similarities between the two were better explained by hypothesizing "a partially modernized form of the O. E. glosses" (p. 350) as a common source. The verse rendition of the seven penitential psalms ascribed to Rolle in MS Bodleian Digby 18 (ed. Adler and Kaluza 1887) is also no longer considered to be his.

Following Rolle's Psalter in some MSS are brief commentaries on the six canticles of the Old Testament and on the *Magnificat, Te Deum, Benedictus, Nunc Dimittis*, "Song of the Three Children," and Athanasian Creed. Everett (1922) gives a full account of the MSS, which tend to fall into two groups: those containing only the first seven pieces (ed. Bramley 1884) and those containing all twelve. Because the first six pieces are included also in Rolle's *Latin Psalter*, Everett accepts them as genuine (as does Allen), but about the *Magnificat*, which is not included, she is less sure. Allen, however, confidently attributes it to Rolle (1927, pp. 192ff.). Both reject the other commentaries as the work of a Lollard; and even the genuine pieces where attached to these "have an unmistakable flavour of Lollardry" (Everett 1922, p. 225). The whole twelve, in the interpolated version, will be found in Arnold (1871) and Heseltine (1930, modernized).

The earliest of Rolle's English epistles is thought to be his *Ego Dormio* (13 MSS), written about 1343 for "a certain nun of Yedingham" (MS Dd. 5. 64). In it Rolle exhorts his "dere syster in Criste" to seek above all else the love of God. Toward this end he proposes devotion to the Holy Name and, interestingly enough, meditation on two lyrics written expressly for the purpose. The three grades of love appear here for the first time, though without their labels ("insuperable," etc.), a fact "seeming to indicate that these had not yet been borrowed from Richard of St. Victor" (Allen 1931, p. 60).

Chronologically, Rolle's next English work is *The Commandment* (14 MSS). According to MS Dd. 5. 64, it was written for a nun of Hampole, though probably not Margaret Kirkby, "since it gives so much of the material presented in the *Form*, which was explicitly dedicated to her" (Allen 1931, p. 73). Like the *Ego Dormio*, the epistle exhorts the reader chiefly to love, but its instructions are now more clearly defined: that is, the three degrees of love are specifically labeled, and praise of the Holy Name is more elaborate. Wilson describes the writing as more accomplished and more "individual" than in the earlier work (1956, p. 95). The unique introductory passage in the Gurney MS (now Bradfer-Lawrence MS 10), which Allen rejected as "dragging and insipid" (1927, p. 253), has been identified by Amassian (1979) as a translation of part of the *Emendatio*. Amassian's commentary on the work (1967) is the most extensive.

The last of Rolle's English compositions, the *Form of Living*, seems to have been regarded by the Middle Ages as his best. It survives in well over forty MSS. It was translated into Latin, the first part turned into verse (ed. Horstman 1896, 2: 283–292), and other favorite sections circulated as part of such compilations as *The Pore Caitif* and the *Speculum Spiritualium*. The *Form* is addressed in numerous MSS to "Margaret," apparently a beginning anchoress. Allen argues convincingly (1927, pp. 265–268) that she is the same person to whom the *English Psalter* was addressed, namely Margaret Kirkby, nun of Hampole, who episcopal registers show became a recluse on December 12, 1348. The work must have been written, therefore, in the last months of Rolle's life.

By far the longest of his English epistles, the *Form* is the only one to be divided into chapters. In the copy printed by Horstman (1895) and Allen (1931)—MS Dd. 5. 64—the scribe inserted Rolle's *Seven Gifts* as Chapter 11, apparently in order to bring the total number to twelve, the same as in the *Emendatio*, to which the *Form* closely corresponds. The work exhibits all the hallmarks of Rolle's authorship: a distinctive alliterative style, devotion to the Holy Name, the three degrees of love, the sensuous concomitants of his mysticism (heat, sweetness, song), and pervasive reminiscences from his other writings, the *Emendatio* in particular.

As the finest of Rolle's English works, the *Form* has received the most critical attention. Only a few recent studies can be mentioned here. In an article comparing the *Form* and its verse adaptation, Blake (1974a) observes, "What was a guide to meditation has been transformed into a general guide to a Christian life suitable for the average reader" (p. 301); and on this basis he tentatively concludes that prose was seen as a "specialized medium more suitable for contemplative and similar works," while "poetry was still regarded as the most suitable medium for the instruction of the laity and the lesser clergy" (p. 308). Both Jolliffe (1974) and Brady (1980) deal with other ways in which the *Form* was adapted. Jolliffe lists in detail the borrowings in a treatise titled *Of Actyfe lyfe & con-*

templatyfe declaracion (from MS Add. 37049); and Brady (following Allen's suggestion) shows in parallel columns all the borrowings from the *Form* made by the compiler of *The Pore Caitiff*. Rygiel (1978) provides a structural analysis of the *Form*, first of the whole and then of the individual chapters. Finally, using the punctuation marks in MSS of the *Form*, Smedick (1979) shows how the scribes "help to bring out the author's style and give us some assistance in hearing as well as seeing its characteristic features" (p. 461).

Rolle's *Meditations on the Passion* cannot be dated with any precision, although Allen says that "they are likely to belong to his later years, along with the rest of his English writings" (1931, p. 18). There are two versions. Text I, the shorter version, survives in one MS, Cambridge University Ll. i. 8 (ed. Ullmann 1884; ed. Horstman 1895; ed. Allen 1931). Text II survives in four MSS, Cambridge University Add. 3042 (ed. Horstman 1895), Bodleian e Musaeo 232 (ed. Allen 1927), Uppsala University C. 494 (ed. Lindkvist 1917), and BL Cotton Titus C. 19 (ed. Madigan 1978). The shorter version seems to have been the model for the longer one.

As noted above, there is some question about Rolle's authorship of the *Meditations*. They are unlike any of his other works in both style and content. Moreover, they do not survive in a single MS in a northern dialect. Nevertheless, all but the Uppsala MS ascribe the *Meditations* to him, and Allen is inclined to explain their unique character as a function of their unique purpose: they are essentially penitential works that "seek at every point to move the reader to tears, and the joys of the mystic are hardly hinted at" (1927, p. 283). In 1953 Morgan cast new doubt on the matter by showing the works to be the products of cumulative authorship reaching back to the thirteenth century. Madigan (1978) reaffirms the ascription to Rolle. Hers is the basic critical study, which provides not only a detailed analysis of the *Meditations* but also a comprehensive introduction to Rolle's life and works. (For a negative review of Madigan's work, see Edwards 1980).

Criticism of the remaining short pieces is negligible.

Criticism of Related Works

It has long been common to speak of Rolle's "school," but the concept has never been adequately defined. What are the essential characteristics of such a school, and what are the works that may be said to constitute it? Certainly the existence of a large body of *spuriana* is no evidence in itself of any great following. Scribes routinely affixed Rolle's name to works whose true authors owed nothing to the mystic and in some cases were actually opposed to his practice. They did so mainly to ensure the wider circulation of these works. If we confine the designation of "school" to those writings that actually imitate or further Rolle's modes of

thought and expression, we shall find the number to be much smaller than generally assumed.

To put the matter in perspective, we must go back to Horstman's pioneer work
(1895–1896). The writings printed therein had to meet two criteria—northern
dialect and inclusion in a MS containing at least one work certainly by Rolle.
Horstman published the whole collection as *Yorkshire Writers: Richard Rolle . . .
and His Followers*, even though he recognized the inappropriateness of the title in
many cases. Nevertheless, the designation stuck. When Wells came to compile
his *Manual of the Writings in Middle English* (1916), he adopted the classification
nearly wholesale. He set up a category called "Rolle and His Followers" after
Horstman, and of the sixty-odd pieces listed therein all but a few were taken
directly from Horstman. It is now clear that a majority of these do not fit under
such a heading. For example, several of the works belong to Hilton. Others are
probably earlier than Rolle. Still others are translations from the Latin and show
none of Rolle's stylistic mannerisms; *The Remedy against the Troubles of Temptations*, for example, has been identified as a translation of William Flete's *De Remediis contra Temptaciones* (see Jolliffe 1974, p. 121). There is not room here to
justify the removal of each individual piece from the category of "Rolle's followers." The best that can be done is to present a selection of works that may
reasonably qualify for inclusion. These may be divided into three kinds: (1) English translations of Rolle's Latin works, (2) English translations of works by
other writers that show his influence in some way, and (3) original English
works. (A complete study of Rolle's influence would include a fourth category as
well, translations of his English works into Latin; for an example [*Ego Dormio*],
see Amassian and Lynch 1981.)

English translations of Rolle's Latin works.   The most frequently translated of
Rolle's Latin works was his *Emendatio Vitae*. There are seven ME translations,
all apparently independent, in sixteen MSS. Amassian (1979) describes each of
these versions in detail. Best known to modern readers is Richard Misyn's translation, edited by Harvey (1896). Modernized versions appear in Heseltine
(1935), Comper (1914), and elsewhere. Schnell's study (1932) of Misyn provides biographical information and an analysis of his translation techniques. Still
another translation is represented by Hulme's edition (1918) of Worcester Cathedral MS F. 172. Finally, translations no longer extant may be indicated by the
existence of various fragments. For example, the fragment attached to *The Commandment* in one MS (noted above) does not derive from any of the seven known
versions and "may stand alone as a solitary witness to a lost tradition of the *EV*"
(Amassian 1979, p. 71). Other fragments or extracts appear in compilations like
the *Disce Mori* (Allen 1927, p. 399) and *The Pore Caitif* (see Brady 1981).

The more mystical and much longer *Incendium Amoris* is represented by only one medieval translation, that of Misyn (ed. Harvey 1896), and by several extracts (noted by Allen 1927, p. 224).

The relatively large number of translations of Rolle's comment on *Oleum Effusum* may be explained, in part, by its place in private devotions. One of these translations is found both in Harley 1022 (Horstman 1895, 1:186–191) and in the Thornton MS (Horstman, ibid., and Perry 1866, pp. 1–6; modern versions in Heseltine 1930, pp. 81–85, and Hodgson 1923, pp. 47–53). The Thornton MS breaks it into two separate pieces, however, and titles the last 200 words "Narracio: A tale þat Rycherde hermet [made]." Other translations of the *Oleum* appear in BL Stowe 38 as part of *The Pore Caitif* and in Trinity College Dublin 155. The short piece known as "The Name of Jesus" (Horstman 1895, 1:106; modern version in Hodgson 1923, pp. 54–55) derives in general from the *Oleum* and from the *Form*, Chapter 9.

Finally, we may note a few translations from Rolle's early work the *Judica Me Deus* (ca. 1320–1322), described by Allen as "really a collection of four loosely connected tracts" (1927, p. 93). One of the tales therein, taken from Caesarius of Heisterbach, is rendered into English in *De In-perfecta Contricione* (Perry 1866, pp. 6–7; Horstman 1895, 1:192–193; modern versions in Hodgson 1910, pp. 190–191, and 1923, p. 62). Quite possibly, Allen theorizes (1927, p. 403), an expanded version of the *Judica*, now lost, was the source also of the other tale that makes up *De In-perfecta Contricione* and of the exemplum *De Vita Cuiusdam Puelle* (Horstman 1895, 1:194; modern version in Hodgson 1923, p. 78).

English translations of works by other authors.   Not many examples can be cited with confidence in this category. Probably the most important (24 MSS) is *The Abbey of the Holy Ghost* (Perry 1867; Horstman 1895, 1:321-337; Blake 1972, pp. 88–102), which Allen says "must have emanated from [Rolle's] school" (1927, p. 337). His influence is most apparent in the addition of mystical material not found in the French original (see Allen 1927, pp. 341–342). Consacro, who has done the most recent study of *The Abbey* (1976), has also promised a new edition. The ME translation of Richard of Saint Victor's *Benjamin Minor* (Horstman 1895, 1:162–172) is another work that adds material reminiscent of Rolle's mysticism, in particular the devotion to the name of Jesus. Similarly, the popularity of the ME *Prayer to the Name of Jesus*, a translation from Saint Anselm's *Meditatio*, may have owed something to Rolle's influence (see Allen 1927, pp. 314–317). Except for these few pieces, however, there is little evidence of Rolle's peculiar style or thought in any of the numerous translations associated with his name. Perhaps the most we can say for the time being is that he helped to create a wider audience for such writings.

Original English works.   In this class of writings the most extensive to show Rolle's influence is the work or collection of works known as Þe *Holy Boke Gratia Dei*. It comprises several pieces treated by Horstman as individual compositions.

These are the tracts on "Grace" (Horstman 1895, 1:132–136, 1:305–310; modernized in Hodgson 1910, pp. 169–182), "Our Daily Work" (Horstman 1895, 1:136–156, 1:310–321; modernized in Hodgson 1910, pp. 83–165, and 1929, pp. 26–95), and "Prayer" (Horstman 1895, 1:300–305). These pieces, combined with *The Meditations on the Passion*, and *Of Three Arrows of Doomsday* (Horstman 1895, 1:112–121; modernized in Hodgson 1923, pp. 161–172), "make a continuous whole in the Ingilby MS [now Huntington 148], and probably this was the original arrangement" (Allen 1927, p. 286). Arntz's edition of the work, based on the Huntington MS, appeared in 1981. She sides with Allen against Hodgson on the question of Rolle's authorship. Keiser (1981) does the same and offers evidence that both the MSS and their content point to a Carthusian origin. Also worth noting here, since it imitates the above fragment of the same name, is the short treatise *Of Three Arrows of Doomsday* (Horstman 1896, 2:446–448), extant in at least eight MSS.

Next in importance is *Contemplations of the Dread and Love of God* (Horstman 1896, 2:72–105), titled *Fervor Amoris* in Jolliffe's *Check-List*, which records seventeen MSS (1974, pp. 97–98). Rolle's influence is unmistakable. After citing as his authority "ful holy men of ryght late tyme," the writer goes on to describe the three degrees of love as found both in the *Form* and in *Ego Dormio*.

The three degrees of love also appear by name (insuperable, inseparable, and singular), along with the frequent use of "sweet Jesus," in the *Lambeth Devotion* (Lambeth Palace MS 546). Allen prints the entire piece and says, "It would seem that this little devotion may be by Rolle, but is perhaps more likely to be due to an imitator" (1927, p. 344).

Of the 3,000 words of rhythmical alliterative prose known as *On Prayer* (Horstman 1895, 1:295–300; modernized in Hodgson 1923, pp. 48–160), Allen says, "This interesting work shows Rolle's influence in style and doctrine, and might even be a work by him, though positive evidence (internal or external) is lacking" (1927, p. 81n). Four MSS are known to exist (Jolliffe 1974, p. 129).

Finally, we may note *An Epistle on Salvation by Love of the Name of Jesus* (Horstman 1895, 1:293–295; Perry 1866, pp. 42–45; modernized in Hodgson 1923, pp. 56–61). This little work explains why the Holy Name is so effectual to salvation ("Now þe name of Ihesu es noghte elles bot þis gastely hele") by means of a logic dear to Rolle (see Froomberg 1948). Allen's comment, "It is a rationalization of the devotion to the Holy Name probably directed against the fanatical followers of Rolle" (1927, p. 352), does not, of course, rule out authorship by one of his less fanatical followers.

I have now mentioned most, if not all, of the English prose writings that may be attributed at the present time to Rolle's followers. Although the list is much smaller than that implied by Horstman's work, it still bears impressive testimony to Rolle's influence. Moreover, it should be remembered that his "school" includes not only the prose writings cited here but also a number of lyric poems, discussion of which is beyond the scope of this chapter (see Comper 1928; S. Wilson 1959; Woolf 1968; Knowlton 1973; and Gibinska 1976). It also includes many individuals who wrote in Latin, such as Thomas Basset, hermit, author of *The Defense against the Detractors of Richard* (ed. Allen 1927, pp. 527–537 [incomplete], and Sargent 1981), the Carthusian monk Richard Methley (Allen 1927, pp. 416ff.), and William Stopes, the learned doctor to whom the *Emendatio* may have been dedicated (Allen 1927, pp. 518–520). Whether it should include other individuals sometimes grouped among Rolle's followers, such as John Mirk, William Nassyngton, John Gaytryge, Walter Hilton and Margery Kempe, is uncertain. Finally, we must not forget those nonwriters who promoted and disseminated Rolle's works: the inhabitants of Syon Monastery, of Sheen, Mount Grace, and other Carthusian houses, and of course Rolle's most faithful disciples, the nuns of Hampole.

SUGGESTIONS FOR
FURTHER RESEARCH

The foregoing survey has suggested the need for additional work in the following areas:

The Canon

There seems to be increasing doubt about the criteria used by Allen for establishing the Rolle canon. To the early objections of Hodgson must now be added those of Madigan, Riehle, and others. Riehle, as noted above, has announced his plans to reassess the whole matter.

Editions and Translations

Rolle's *English Psalter* badly needs reediting, the efforts taken in this direction at Fordham University notwithstanding. In 1978, Newton reported on plans for "a popular translation and Middle English critical edition of Rolle's *English Psalter*, scheduled for completion in 1979" (*FCEMN* 4:4, 1978, p. 24). Like the *Psalter*, Rolle's other commentaries in English have not been edited since Bramley (1884). *The Form of Living* has not been edited since Allen (1931). Many of the Latin writings exist only in manuscript. Modern translations are few: we have only those of Heseltine (1935), Wolters (1972), and del Mastro (1981) of the *Incendium*, Theiner's (1968) of the *Contra Amatores Mundi*, and del Mastro's

(1981) of the *Emendatio Vitae* (other translations of the *EV* are all modernizations of Misyn's work). Ironically, the only translation of the *Melos* is in French (Vandenbroucke 1971), although an English translation by Sara deFord is underway (see *FCEMN* 7:4, 1981, p. 156).

Rolle's Thought

Although many studies have been made of various themes in Rolle's works (e.g., *jubilus*, *canor*, love, the Holy Name), there is no comprehensive approach to his thought as a whole. The need is evident. For example, how appropriate is the common attempt to explain Rolle's mysticism by reference to the classical threefold way (purgative, illuminative, unitive)? Jennings (1975) has shown that this scheme cannot be made to fit either of his well-known triads. Whether it plays any part in his thinking at all remains to be seen. But even if we assume that it does—or should—how valid is criticism based primarily on his English writings? Is it true that Rolle "is best represented by such a short English treatise as . . . *Ego Dormio*" (Colledge 1961, p. 57) or that appraisal on this basis is justified "because his English writings all belong to the later period when he was more surely rooted in the illuminative way" (Pepler 1958, p. 165)? Little wonder that by using works addressed chiefly to beginners in the contemplative life, Rolle's critics have been able to present him as little more than a proficient himself. As Riehle (1981) demonstrates repeatedly, however, Rolle's most striking and difficult ideas lie in his Latin works, especially in his *Melos*, which despite the edition by Arnould (1957) continues to be ignored. Scholars who are not able or not willing to read through this formidable body of material probably should leave evaluations of Rolle's mysticism to those who are.

Prose Style

Although considerable attention has been given Rolle's English style, certain aspects of it have hardly been touched. There is no published study of his translation techniques as revealed either in his Psalter or in the biblical and patristic quotations that occur in his other English writings. Of particular interest are his syntax (e.g., lack of the verb in such renderings as "My God my helper" for *Deus meus adiutor meus*, Ps. 17.2) and his use of "translation words" (e.g., "ingo" for *introibo*, "genges" for *gentes*, "uptaker" for *susceptor*). Except for the note by Gilmour (1956), very little has been done with Rolle's possible contributions to the English vocabulary.

Sources

As noted already, Hahn's study (1900) is invalid inasmuch as it depends largely on the noncanonical *Prick of Conscience*. Yet nothing comparable has been undertaken. References continue to be made to "influences" such as Augustine, Gregory, Bernard, Bonaventure, and others, but usually without much specific evidence. Richard of Saint Victor is probably the most important source in Rolle's later (i.e., English) writings, as even a cursory examination will show, and yet little has been done beyond the preliminary observations by Allen (1927, pp. 201 and passim). Until Rolle's debt to the tradition has been established more precisely, it is hardly possible to appreciate his place within it.

Influences

The matter of Rolle's school requires a full investigation. What are the texts that reveal the influence of his style and thought? What are the criteria for determining that influence? What were the lines of transmission? The investigation should not be based on the works printed by Horstman. He confined his search to the libraries of London, Oxford, and Cambridge. Hulme (1918), for one, has already noted possible Rolleana elsewhere, in Worcester Cathedral F. 172. Perhaps separate studies might be made of Rolle's influence as transmitted by popular compilations. Brady (1980) has made a start with her analysis of *The Pore Caitif*, but many other compendia remain to be examined. Particularly likely to bear fruit is the direction pointed by Sargent (1976) in his study of Carthusian materials.

BIBLIOGRAPHY

The following is a select bibliography of primary and secondary materials. Not included are many nineteenth-century studies, notices of work in progress, and the more popular or "inspirational" treatments of Rolle's mysticism. Additional items will be found in the bibliography on Rolle compiled by Valerie Lagorio and Ritamary Bradley in *The Fourteenth-Century English Mystics* (1981, pp. 53–80). The order of presentation below is alphabetical by author, except in the first section, where editions and modernizations of Rolle's English writings are listed chronologically. Full bibliographical information for repeated items is given for the first citation only.

THE ENGLISH PROSE WRITINGS
OF RICHARD ROLLE

THE ENGLISH PSALTER

MANUSCRIPTS

Allen, Hope Emily, ed. (1927) *Writings Ascribed to Richard Rolle, Hermit of Hampole, and Materials for His Biography*, pp. 171–176. MLA Monograph ser. 3. New York: D. C. Heath. Repr. (1966) New York: Kraus.

EDITION

Bramley, H. R., ed. (1884) *The Psalter or Psalms of David and Certain Canticles*. Oxford: Clarendon Press.

SELECTIONS

Allen, Hope Emily, ed. (1931) *English Writings of Richard Rolle, Hermit of Hampole*. Oxford: Clarendon Press, Repr. 1963. Repr. (1971) St. Clair Shores, Mich.: Scholarly Press.

Collins, Marjorie (1966) "Psalms from the English *Psalter Commentary* of Richard Rolle." Ph.D. diss., University of Michigan.

Cavallerano, Jerry D. (1976) "Richard Rolle's *English Psalter*, Psalms 31–45." Ph.D. diss., Fordham University.

Newton, Sandra (1976) "An Edition of Richard Rolle's *English Psalter*, the Prologue through Psalm 15." Ph.D. diss., Fordham University.

Callanan, Marion E. (1977) "An Edition of Richard Rolle's *English Psalter* with Notes and Commentary (Psalms 46–60)." Ph.D. diss., Fordham University.

Carney, Ellen (1980) "Richard Rolle's *English Psalter*, Psalms 91–105: An Edition with an Introductory Essay on Rolle's Style." Ph.D. diss., Fordham University.

Rodriguez, Zane Jose (1980) "Richard Rolle's English Commentary on the Psalter, Psalms 61 to 75: Text and Glossary, with an Introductory Essay on Rolle and the Tradition of Psalm Commentary." Ph.D. diss., Fordham University.

COMMENTARIES CONNECTED WITH THE *PSALTER*

MANUSCRIPTS

Everett, Dorothy (1922) "The Middle English Prose *Psalter* of Richard Rolle of Hampole." *MLR*, 17, 217–227.

EDITIONS

Arnold, Thomas (1869–1871) *Select English Works of John Wyclif*, 3:3–82. 3 vols. Oxford: Clarendon Press.

Bramley (1884), pp. 494–526.

Heseltine, G. C. (1930) *Selected Works of Richard Rolle, Hermit*, pp. 153–237. London: Longmans, Green and Co.

EGO DORMIO

MANUSCRIPTS

Allen (1927), pp. 247–249.

Amassian, Margaret G., and Lynch, Dennis (1981) "The *Ego Dormio* of Richard Rolle in Gonville and Caius MS. 140/80." *MS*, 43, 218–249.

EDITIONS

Horstman, Carl, ed. (1895–1896) *Yorkshire Writers: Richard Rolle of Hampole, An English Father of the Church, and His Followers*, 1:50–61, 415–416. 2 vols. London: Swan Sonnenschein and Co.

Hodgson, Geraldine (1923) *Some Minor Works of Richard Rolle*, pp. 63–78 (modernized). London: John M. Watkins.

Heseltine (1930), pp. 89–100 (modernized).

Allen (1931), pp. 60–72.

Colledge, Eric (1961) *The Mediaeval Mystics of England*, pp. 143–154 (modernized). New York: Scribner.

Amassian and Lynch (1981), pp. 230–248 (transcription only of MS Cambridge University Library Dd. 5. 64).

THE COMMANDMENT

MANUSCRIPTS

Allen (1927), pp. 251–253.

Amassian, Margaret (1979) "The Rolle Material in Bradfer-Lawrence MS 10 and Its Relationships to Other Rolle Manuscripts." *Manuscripta*, 23, 67–78.

EDITIONS

Horstman (1896), 2:61–71.

Hodgson (1923), pp. 80–91 (modernized).

Heseltine (1930), pp. 3–11 (modernized).

Allen (1931), pp. 73–81.

Amassian, Margaret (1967) "An Edition of Richard Rolle's *The Commandment*." Ph.D. diss., Fordham University.

THE FORM OF LIVING

MANUSCRIPTS

Allen (1927), pp. 257–262.

Smedick, Lois (1979) "Parallelism and Pointing in Rolle's Rhythmical Style." *MS*, 41, 404–467 (esp. p. 411).

EDITIONS

Horstman (1895), 1:3–49, 412–415, 416–420.

Hodgson, Geraldine (1910) *The Form of Perfect Living and Other Prose Treatises of Richard Rolle of Hampole*, pp. 1–79 (modernized). London: Thomas Baker.

Heseltine (1930), pp. 15–51 (modernized).

Allen (1931), pp. 85–119.

MEDITATIONS ON THE PASSION

MANUSCRIPTS

Allen (1927), pp. 278–279.

Madigan, Mary F., ed. (1978) *The Passio Domini Theme in the Works of Richard Rolle: His Personal Contribution in Its Religious, Cultural, and Literary Context*. Elizabethan and Renaissance Studies 79. Salzburg: Institut für Englische Sprache und Literatur, Universität Salzburg.

EDITIONS

Ullmann, J., ed. (1884) "Studien zu Richard Rolle de Hampole." *EStn*, 7, 415–472 (short version), with later emendations by J. Zupitza (1889), *EStn*, 12, 463–469.

Horstman (1895), 1:83–91 (short version), and 92–103 (long version).

Lindkvist, Harald, ed. (1917) "Richard Rolle's *Meditatio de Passione Domini*." *Skrifter utgifna af Kungl. Humanistika Vetenskaps—Samfundet i Uppsala*, 19, 1–78 (long version).

Heseltine (1930), pp. 55–72 (modernized).

Allen (1931), pp. 19–36 (both long and short versions).

Madigan (1978), pp. 236–277 (long version).

THE BEE

Manuscripts

Allen (1927), p. 269.

Editions

Perry, George (1866) *English Prose Treatises of Richard Rolle of Hampole*, pp. 8–9.
    EETS, os 20. Repr. (1973) New York: Kraus.
Horstman (1895), 1:193.
Heseltine (1930), pp. 103–104 (modernized).
Allen (1931), pp. 54–56.

DESYRE AND DELIT

Manuscripts

Allen (1927), pp. 271–272.

Editions

Perry (1866), p. 13.
Horstman (1895), 1:197.
Allen (1927), p. 271.
Heseltine (1930), pp. 104–105 (modernized).
Allen (1931), pp. 57–58.

GHASTLY GLADNESSE

Manuscripts

Allen (1927), pp. 272–273.

Editions

Horstman (1895), 1:80.
Allen (1927), p. 273.
Heseltine (1930), p. 106 (modernized).
Allen (1931), pp. 51–52.

THE SEVEN GIFTS OF THE HOLY GHOST

MANUSCRIPTS

Allen (1927), p. 274.

EDITIONS

Perry (1866), p. 12.
Horstman (1895), 1:136, 196.
Hodgson (1923), pp. 92–93 (modernized).

ON THE TEN COMMANDMENTS

MANUSCRIPTS

Allen (1927), p. 276.

EDITIONS

Perry (1866), pp. 9–11.
Horstman (1895), 1:195.
Heseltine (1930), pp. 75–78 (modernized).

OTHER PRIMARY WORKS

Adler, Max, and Kaluza, M. (1887) "Über die Richard Rolle de Hampole: Zugeschrieben Paraphrase der sieben Busspsalmen." *EStn*, 10, 215–255.

Arnould, E. J. F., ed. (1957) *The Melos Amoris of Richard Rolle of Hampole*. Oxford: Basil Blackwell.

Arntz, Mary Luke (1981) *Richard Rolle and þe Holy Boke Gratia Dei: An Edition with Commentary*. Elizabethan and Renaissance Studies 92. Salzburg: Institut für Anglistik und Amerikanistik, Universität Salzburg.

Blake, N. F., ed. (1972) *Middle English Religious Prose*. London: Edward Arnold.

Comper, Frances (1914) *The Fire of Love or Melody of Love and The Mending of Life or Rule of Living*. London: Methuen.

Daly, John Philip (1961) "An Edition of the *Judica Me Deus* of Richard Rolle." Ph.D. diss., University of North Carolina.

Deanesley, Margaret, ed. (1915) *The Incendium Amoris of Richard Rolle of Hampole*. Manchester: University Press. Repr. (1974) Folcroft, Pa.: Folcroft Library Edition.

Harvey, Ralph, ed. (1896) *The Fire of Love and the Mending of Life or The Rule of Living of Richard Rolle.* EETS, os 106. Repr. (1973) New York: Kraus.

Heseltine, George C., trans. (1935) *The Fire of Love.* London: Burns, Oates and Washbourne.

Hodgson, Geraldine (1929) *Rolle and "Our Daily Work."* London: Faith Press.

Hulme, William Henry (1918) "Richard Rolle of Hampole's *Mending of Life,* from the Fifteenth Century Worcester Cathedral Manuscript F. 172." *Western Reserve University Bulletins* ns 21. Cleveland: Western Reserve University Press.

Marzac, Nicole, ed. (1968) *Richard Rolle de Hampole (1300–1349): Vie et oeuvres suivies du tractatus Super Apocalypsim.* Paris: Librarie Philosophique J. Vrin.

Mastro, M. L. del, trans. (1981) *The Fire of Love and the Mending of Life.* Garden City, N.Y.: Image Books.

Murray, Elizabeth M. (1958) "Richard Rolle's *Commentary on the Canticles.* Edited from MS Trinity College, Dublin, 153." Ph.D. diss., Fordham University.

Perry, George (1867) *Religious Pieces in Prose and Verse.* EETS, os 26.

Porter, Mary Louise (1929) "Rolle's *Latin Commentary on the Psalms.*" Ph.D. diss., Cornell University.

Theiner, Paul, ed. and trans. (1968) *The Contra Amatores Mundi of Richard Rolle of Hampole.* University of California Publications, English Studies 33. Berkeley and Los Angeles: University of California Press.

Vandenbroucke, François, ed. (1971) *Le chant d'amour (Melos Amoris).* Translated by Les Moniales de Wisques from the Latin text of E. J. F. Arnould's edition. 2 vols. in 1. Paris: Les Editions du Cerf.

Wolters, Clifton, trans. (1972) *The Fire of Love.* Harmondsworth: Penguin.

Woolley, Reginald, ed. (1919) *The Officium and the Miracula of Richard Rolle of Hampole.* London: SPCK.

SECONDARY WORKS

Alford, John A. (1973) "Biblical *Imitatio* in the Writings of Richard Rolle." *ELH,* 40, 1–23.

———— (1976) "The Biblical Identity of Richard Rolle." *FCEMN,* 2:4, 21–25.

Allen, Hope Emily (1910) *The Authorship of the Prick of Conscience,* pp. 115–170. Radcliffe College Monographs 15. Boston: Ginn and Co.

———— (1917) "The *Speculum Vitae*: Addendum." *PMLA,* 32, 133–162.

———— (1927) *Writings Ascribed to Richard Rolle.*

Amassian, Margaret (1979) "The Rolle Material in Bradfer-Lawrence MS 10."

Arnould, E. J. F. (1960) "Richard Rolle of Hampole." *Month,* ns 23, 13–25.

Benz, Ernst (1969) *Die Vision: Erfahrungsformen und Bilderwelt.* Stuttgart: E. Klett.

Blake, N. F. (1974a) "*The Form of Living* in Prose and Poetry." *Archiv,* 211, 300–308.

—— (1974b) "Varieties of Middle English Prose." *Chaucer and Middle English Studies in*

Honour of Rossell Hope Robbins, edited by Beryl Rowland. London: Allen and Unwin.

Brady, Mary Teresa (1980) "Rolle's 'Form of Living' and 'The Pore Caitif.'" *Traditio*, 36, 426–435.

——— (1981) "Þe Seynt and His Boke: Rolle's *Emendatio Vitae* and *The Pore Caitif*." *FCEMN*, 7:1, 20–31.

Chambers, R. W. (1932) "On the Continuity of English Prose from Alfred to More and His School." Introduction to *Harpsfield's Life of More*, edited by E. V. Hitchcock and R. W. Chambers. EETS, os 186, repr. separately (1957) as vol. 191a.

Comper, Frances M. (1928) *The Life of Richard Rolle, Together with an Edition of His English Lyrics*. London and Toronto: J. M. Dent and Sons; repr. (1969) New York: Barnes and Noble.

Consacro, Peter (1976) "The Author of *The Abbey of the Holy Ghost:* A Popularizer of the Mixed Life." *FCEMN* 2:4, 15–20.

Deanesley, Margaret (1920) *The Lollard Bible and Other Medieval Biblical Versions*. Cambridge: University Press, repr. 1966.

Eaton, Mary Eleanor (1954) "The Use of Scripture by the English Mystics." Ph.D. diss., Stanford University.

Edwards, Anthony S. G. (1980) Review of Mary Felicitas Madigan's *The Passio Domini Theme in the Works of Richard Rolle*. *English Studies in Canada*, 6, 493–500.

Elwin, Verier (1930) *Richard Rolle, A Christian Sannyāsē*. Madras: Christian Literature Society for India.

Everett, Dorothy (1922, 1923) "The Middle English Prose *Psalter* of Richard Rolle of Hampole." *MLR*, 17, 217–227, 337–350; and 18, 381–393.

Froomberg, Hilary (1948) "'The Virtue of Our Lord's Passion' by Richard Rolle of Hampole." *Life of the Spirit*, 3, 221–225.

Gibinska, Marta (1976) "Some Observations on the Themes and Techniques of the Medieval English Religious Love Lyrics." *ES*, 57, 103–114.

Gillespie, Vincent F. (1982) "Mystic's Foot: Rolle and Affectivity." In *The Medieval Mystical Tradition in England: Papers Read at Dartington Hall, July 1982*, edited by Marion Glasscoe, pp. 199–230. Exeter: University of Exeter.

Gilmour, J. (1956) "Notes on the Vocabulary of Richard Rolle." *N&Q*, 201, 94–95.

Hahn, A. (1900) *Quellenuntersuchungen zu Richard Rolles englischen Schriften*. Halle: Vereinigten Friedricks-Universität Halle-Wittenberg.

Harris, Mary E. (1970) "The Word in the Wilderness: Style in English Anchoritic Prose." Ph.D. diss., University of California at Berkeley.

Henningsen, G. H. (1911) *Über die Wortstellung in den Prosaschriften Richard Rolles von Hampole*. Erlangen: Junge und Sohn.

Hodgson, Geraldine (1926) *The Sanity of Mysticism: A Study of Richard Rolle*. London: Faith Press; repr. (1977) Folcroft, Pa.: Folcroft Library Editions.

Hodgson, Phyllis (1967) *Three Fourteenth-Century English Mystics*. London: Published for the British Council and the National Book League by Longmans.

Homier, Donald F. (1975) "The Function of Rhetoric in Suggesting Stages of Contemplation in the Vernacular Writings of the Fourteenth-Century English Mystics." Ph.D. diss., Northern Illinois University.

Jennings, Margaret (1975) "Richard Rolle and the Three Degrees of Love." *DownR*, 93, 193–200.

Jolliffe, P. S. (1974) *A Check-List of Middle English Prose Writings of Spiritual Guidance.* Toronto: Pontifical Institute of Mediaeval Studies.

———— (1975) "Two Middle English Tracts on the Contemplative Life." *MS*, 37, 85–121.

Keiser, George R. (1981) "Þe Holy Boke Gratia Dei." *Viator*, 12, 289–317.

King, Donald Paul (1970) "The Threefold Way: English Contemplatives in the Fourteenth Century." Ph.D. diss., Indiana University.

Knowles, David (1927) *The English Mystics.* London: Burns, Oates and Washbourne.

———— (1961) *The English Mystical Tradition.* New York: Harper.

Knowlton, Mary Arthur (1973) *The Influence of Richard Rolle and of Julian of Norwich on the Middle English Lyrics.* The Hague: Mouton.

Lagorio, Valerie Marie, and Bradley, Ritamary (1981) *The Fourteenth-Century English Mystics. A Comprehensive Annotated Bibliography.* New York: Garland.

Lehmann, Max (1936) *Untersuchungen zur mystischen Terminologie Richard Rolles.* Jena: Gustav Neuenhahn.

Liegey, Gabriel (1954) "The Rhetorical Aspects of Richard Rolle's *Melos Contemplativorum.* Ph.D. diss., Columbia University.

———— (1956) "The 'Canticum Amoris' of Richard Rolle." *Traditio*, 12, 369–391.

———— (1957) "Richard Rolle's Carmen Prosaicum, an Edition and Commentary." *MS*, 19, 15–36.

Matthews, William, ed. (1962) *Later Middle English Prose.* London: Peter Owen.

Merton, Thomas (1961) *Mystics and Zen Masters.* New York: Farrar, Strauss and Giroux.

Middendorf, Heinrich (1888) *Studien zu Richard Rolle von Hampole unter besonderer Berücksichtigung seiner Psalmenkommentar.* Magdeburg: Friese und Fuhrman.

Morgan, Margery (1952a) "*A Talking of the Love of God* and the Continuity of Stylistic Tradition in Middle English Prose Meditations." *RES*, ns 3, 97–116.

———— (1952b) "A Treatise in Cadence." *MLR*, 47, 156–184.

———— (1953) "Versions of the Meditations on the Passion Ascribed to Richard Rolle." *MAE*, 22, 93–103.

Muir, Lawrence (1934) "A Comparison of the Rolle and Wycliffite Psalms with Those of the Authorized Version, together with a History of the Early *English Psalter.*" Ph.D. diss., Cornell University.

———— (1935) "Influence of the Rolle and Wycliffite Psalters upon the Psalter of the Authorized Version." *MLR*, 30, 302–310.

———— (1970) "Translations and Paraphrases of the Bible, and Commentaries." *A Manual of the Writings in Middle English 1050–1500,*" vol. 2, edited by J. Burke Severs, pp. 381–409, 534–552. Hamden: Connecticut Academy of Arts and Sciences.

Niederstenbruch, Alex (1939) "Die geistige Haltung Richard Rolles." *Archiv*, 175, 50–64.

Noetinger, Maurice (1926) "The Biography of Richard Rolle." *Month*, 147, 22–30.

Olmes, Antonie (1933) *Sprache und Stil der englischen Mystik des Mittelalters, unter besonderer Berücksichtigung des Richard Rolle von Hampole*, pp. 1–100. Studien zur englischen Philologie 76. Halle: Niemeyer. Repr. (1973) Wiesbaden: Dr. Martin Sändig.

Paues, Anna (1902) *A Fourteenth Century English Biblical Version*. Cambridge: Cambridge University Press.

Pepler, Conrad (1948) "Love of the Word." *Life of the Spirit*, 2, 540–546.

――― (1958) *The English Religious Heritage*. Saint Louis: Herder.

Relihan, Robert (1978) "Richard Rolle and the Tradition of Thirteenth Century Devotional Literature." *FCEMN*, 4:4, 10–16.

Renaudin, Paul (1938) "Le dénuement et l'amour dans la vie de Richard Rolle." *La vie spirituelle*, 61, 143–162.

――― (1940) "Richard Rolle poète de l'Amour divin." *La vie spirituelle*, 62, 65–80.

――― (1954) *Mystiques anglais*. Paris: Editions Montaigne.

Riehle, Wolfgang (1981) *The Middle English Mystics*. Translated by Bernard Standring. London: Routledge and Kegan Paul.

Rygiel, Dennis (1978) "Structures and Style in Rolle's *The Form of Living*." *FCEMN*, 4:1, 6–15.

Sargent, Michael (1976) "The Transmission by the English Carthusians of Late Medieval Spiritual Writings." *Journal of Ecclesiastical History*, 27, 225–240.

――― (1981) "Contemporary Criticism of Richard Rolle." *Kartäusermystik und -Mystiker*, 1: 160–205. *Analecta Cartusiana* 55 (Proceedings of the Third International Congress on Carthusian History and Spirituality). Salzburg: Institut für Anglistik und Amerikanistik, Universität Salzburg.

Schneider, John P. (1906) *The Prose Style of Richard Rolle of Hampole, with Special Reference to Its Euphuistic Tendencies*. Baltimore: J.H. Furst.

Schnell, Eugen (1932) *Die Traktate des Richard Rolle von Hampole "Incendium Amoris" und "Emendatio Vitae" und deren Übersetzung durch Richard Misyn*. Borna-Leipzig: Universitätsverlag von R. Naske.

Schulte, Franz (1951) "Das musikalische Element in der Mystik Richard Rolles von Hampole." Diss., Bonn University.

Sitwell, Gerard (1961) *Spiritual Writers of the Middle Ages*. New York: Hawthorn Books.

Smedick, Lois (1979) "Parallelism and Pointing in Rolle's Rhythmical Style," *MS*, 41, 404–467.

Thornton, Martin (1963) *English Spirituality*. London: SPCK.

Tuma, George (1977) *The Fourteenth-Century English Mystics: A Comparative Analysis*. Elizabethan and Renaissance Studies 61 and 62. Salzburg: Institut für Anglistik und Amerikanistik, Universität Salzburg.

Wakelin, M. F. (1979) "Richard Rolle and the Language of Mystical Experience in the Fourteenth Century." *DownR*, 97, 192–203.

Wells, John Edwin (1916) *A Manual of the Writings in Middle English 1050–1400*. New Haven: Connecticut Academy of Arts and Sciences. 9 supps., 1919–1952.

Whiting, Charles E. (1948) "Richard Rolle of Hampole." *Yorkshire Archaeological Society Journal*, 37, 5–23.

Wilmart, André (1940) "Le Cantique d'amour de Richard Rolle." *Revue d'ascetique et de mystique*, 21, 131–148.

――― (1944) *Le "Jubilus" dit de Saint Bernard*. Rome: Edizioni di Storia e Letteratura.

Wilson, R. M. (1956) "Three Middle English Mystics." *E&S*, ns 9, 87–112.

———— (1959) "On the Continuity of English Prose." In *Mélanges de linguistique et de philologie: Fernand Mossé in memoriam*, pp. 486–494. Paris: Didier.

Wilson, Sarah (1959) "The Longleat Version of 'Love Is Life'." *RES*, ns 10, 337–346.

Womack, Sam, Jr. (1961) "The *Jubilus* Theme in the Later Writings of Richard Rolle." Ph.D. diss., Duke University.

Woolf, Rosemary (1968) *The English Religious Lyric in the Middle Ages*. Oxford: Clarendon Press.

Workman, Samuel K. (1940) *Fifteenth Century Translation as an Influence on English Prose*. Princeton: Princeton University Press. Repr. (1972) New York: Octagon Books.

Wormald, Francis (1935) "*De Passione Secundum Ricardum* (Possibly a New Work by Richard Rolle)." *Laudate*, 13, 37–48.

Wright, Gilbert G. (1963) "The Definition of Love in Richard Rolle of Hampole." Ph.D. diss., University of Wisconsin.

CHAPTER 3

The Cloud of Unknowing and Walter Hilton's *Scale of Perfection*

Alastair Minnis

The Cloud of Unknowing and Walter Hilton's *Scale of Perfection* are living classics of religious literature.[1] As such, they have received much attention, while scholarly study has lagged behind—a point dramatically illustrated by the fact that, while five modernized versions of the *Scale* have appeared in this century, no edition of the original Middle English text has yet been published. (There are, however, three unpublished partial editions, by Birts 1952, Wykes 1957, and Hussey 1962.) This lack will soon be remedied by the forthcoming edition by S. S. Hussey and A. J. Bliss for the Early English Text Society. Other gaps are in the process of being filled with extensive analyses of the sources, theological doctrines, audiences, dissemination, and literary and linguistic qualities of the *Scale* and the *Cloud*. Doubtless these works shall continue to provide spiritual instruction and inspiration for committed Christians and contemplatives of several religions, but they are also being claimed by specialists in source study, literary criticism, the history of ideas, linguistic theory and practice, and literary theory both medieval and modern. All this testifies to their perennial appeal and challenge.

At the time of writing only two of the Middle English works convincingly attributed to Hilton, the *Eight Chapters on Perfection* and *Of Angels' Song*, are available in critical editions, by F. Kuriyagawa (1958; repr. 1971) and T. Takamiya (1977) respectively. Three short tracts of dubious authenticity, on the *Benedictus*, *Qui Habitat*, and *Bonum Est*, have been edited by Wallner (1954 and 1957). For Hilton's *Epistle on the Mixed Life* one must turn to the transcriptions of two manuscripts in Horstman's *Yorkshire Writers* (1895), or to the modernized version provided by Dorothy Jones in her *Minor Works of Walter Hilton* (1929). Jones's volume also includes modernized texts of *Eight Chapters on Perfection*, *Qui Habitat*, and *Bonum Est*. Clare Kirchberger has printed (1952) a modernized version of a work of doubtful authenticity, *The Goad of Love*, a translation of James of Milan's *Stimulus Amoris*. The Middle English text of this work is available only in an unpublished thesis by Harold J. Kane (1968). An edition of Hilton's Latin works is being prepared by Joy Russell-Smith.

The *Cloud* group of writings has been better served, having been edited in its entirety by P. Hodgson for the Early English Text Society in two volumes (1958a, 1958b). *The Cloud of Unknowing* was probably the earliest work by our anonymous author; *The Book of Privy Counselling* was probably the latest, since in it he refers to the *Cloud*, *The Epistle of Prayer*, and his translations of the *De Mystica Theologia* of Pseudo-Dionysius and the *Benjamin Minor* of Richard of Saint Victor (154/13–18). In addition, Hodgson included a work of doubtful authenticity, the *Epistle of Discretion in Stirrings*, which in her opinion "bears an unmistakable resemblance" to the others (1958a, p. lxxix).

About Hilton's life little is known. It is now generally accepted that he incepted in canon law, probably at Cambridge, spent some time as a hermit, and eventually became an Augustinian canon of the priory of Thurgarton in Nottinghamshire, where he died on March 23, 1396. Even less is known about the *Cloud* author. All that is clear is that he lived in the northeast Midlands, that he knew some of Richard Rolle's works, and that his masterpiece, *The Cloud of Unknowing*, was known to Hilton by the time he wrote the second book of the *Scale*. Various scholars have suggested that he was a secular priest (Noetinger 1924; McCann 1924b), a cloistered monk (Underhill 1912), a Carthusian (Grenehalgh [see Sargent 1979]; B. White 1949; Lees 1981; Walsh 1981), not a Carthusian (Underhill 1912; Jones 1929), a hermit (Hodgson in her first [1944] ed. of the *Cloud*), a recluse (Gardner 1947), and a Dominican (Knowles 1961). The Carthusian and Dominican theories merit special attention in view of the light they throw on the peculiar blend of theological opinion in the *Cloud*. Lees and Walsh postulate the influence of the great Carthusian theologian Hugh of Balma (prior of the Charterhouse of Meyriat in Bresse, 1298–1340), a suggestion to which I shall return. Knowles (1961) and Walsh (1981) have argued that the doctrine of grace found therein was distinctively Thomist, an opinion that has been supported by J. P. H. Clark (1980), who adds that the discussion of the divine names included in *The Book of Privy Counselling* echoes a passage in Saint Thomas's *Summa Theologiae*. But of course, the influence of Aquinas extended far beyond the confines of the Dominican Order—a point of special importance to Walsh, who claims that there is a "wealth of internal evidence for the hypothesis that the author of the *Cloud* . . . was a Carthusian" (1981, p. 9). In particular, Saint Thomas's doctrine of grace was considerably developed and altered by others. More work is urgently needed on fourteenth-century (rather than thirteenth-century) debate on Dionysian themes, in order to make clear just how distinctive the relevant views of Aquinas would have appeared to the *Cloud* author, and whether there is anything in the English treatise that parallels some exclusively Dominican elaboration of the thought of the "common doctor."

The belief that Hilton wrote the *Cloud* seems to have originated with a famous scribe-editor of the late fifteenth century, the Carthusian James Grenehalgh of Sheen Charterhouse. Since modern scholars like McCann (1924b), Jones (1929), Gardner (1947), and Riehle (1977) consider that this is at least possible, the question remains an open one. On the other hand, Hodgson (1955), Knowles (1961), Gatto (1975), Clark (1977), and Lees (1981) have argued impressively against the identification. Knowles quotes with approval Gardner's earlier statement (1933, p. 147) that "'the two authors appear . . . to present strongly marked and different personalities, which no amount of common background or shared phraseology can disguise. Style, manner, vocabulary and imagery can be borrowed, but personality is inalienable'" (1961, p. 69, n. 3). This impressionistic judgment has received powerful support in Clark's recent series of articles in the *Downside Review*, which, by illuminating the sources of the *Cloud* and the *Scale*, have demonstrated that these works represent different traditions of mystical theology, and therefore are almost certainly not by the same author. "The two writers share in part a common theological background," he concludes, "and draw on many of the same figures of speech, but at decisive points their paths diverge, and they use similar language in the interest of diverse theologies" (Clark 1977, p. 109). The following sections of this chapter describe several of these points of divergence, with the purpose of indicating some of the salient doctrinal features of the *Cloud* and the *Scale*.

When the *Cloud* author asserted the superiority of the will over the reason, and the power of love or affection over the power of the understanding, he was tacitly taking sides in a long-running debate on the nature of theology. Several schoolmen, notably Richard Fishacre, Robert Kilwardby, and Giles of Rome, argued that theology is essentially affective, while others, including Albert the Great, Thomas Aquinas, and Henry of Ghent, sought to emphasize (in different ways and to different extents) the rational and intellectual nature of the science of theology (see Minnis 1979, and Chap. 4 of Minnis 1983). Pseudo-Dionysius was cited often in this controversy; conversely, the terms of reference of the debate coloured medieval approaches to the Dionysian corpus. For example, in his commentary on *De Mystica Theologia* (1255) Albert the Great asserted the superiority of the intellect (*intellectus*), by means of which the soul is united with God (see

Völker 1958, pp. 241–245). Writing earlier, Thomas Gallus had assigned this supreme role to the affection or disposition (*affectus*), the loving power of the will (see especially Walsh 1957; for bibliography see Völker 1958, pp. 223–231).

That part of Gallus's work that concerns us here, the exposition of *De Mystica Theologia*, took three forms: a brief commentary or gloss, known as the *Glossa* (1232), an explanatory paraphrase entitled the *Extractio* (1238), and a full commentary entitled the *Explanatio* (1241). Herein one can see Gallus building on Victorine ideas of contemplation—in particular, the thought of Richard of Saint Victor (d. 1173), who is acknowledged as a major source in the *Explanatio*—yet gradually moving towards a considerable modification of Richard's position in emphasizing the *principalis affectio* as the mental power through which the mystic union is effected. By *principalis affectio* (or *apex affectus*) is meant the purest and most sublime activity of the affection, the will's capacity to love rising to its utmost limits with the aid of divine grace, leaving far behind all corporeal involvement and earthly emotion. It is coterminous with the *synderisis scintilla*, the spark of conscience or discernment which leaps up to God like a spark shooting from a fire. Gallus substituted *principalis affectio* for Richard's *intelligentia* (i.e., the superior function of the intellect) as the medium of unitive experience—he did not identify the former with the latter, as Von Ivánka thought (Von Ivánka 1969). We should realise, however, that for Gallus the principal affection was a cognitive power; more precisely, it was the supreme cognitive power possessed by man, whereby the soul obtained knowledge-in-love.

Robert Grosseteste sided with Gallus in affording the *affectus* an elevated status in the mystical union: he believed that the highest knowledge possible in this life is acquired in and through love (see Grosseteste's commentary on *De Mystica Theologia*, ed. Gamba 1942). But it must be emphasized that Grosseteste's Dionysian scholarship was far too erudite for many medieval readers, while the more facile and succinct expositions of Thomas Gallus enjoyed a wide audience. It was Gallus who influenced those masterpieces of affective piety, Hugh of Balma's *De Theologia Mystica* or *Viae Sion Lugent* and Saint Bonaventure's *Itinerarium Mentis in Deum*. He seems to have influenced *The Cloud of Unknowing* also, either directly, or indirectly through intermediate writings that reiterated his teaching. Two facts, the indubitable influence of Gallus on *Deonise Hid Diuinite* and the congruence of the thought in this work and in the *Cloud*, strengthen the case for direct influence, especially in view of the prominent and distinctive position that Gallus occupies among medieval interpreters of Pseudo-Dionysius.

In the prologue to *Deonise Hid Diuinite* the *Cloud* author states that he has "moche folowed þe sentence of þe Abbot of Seinte Victore," "a worþi expositour of þis same book" (2.10–12). This "worþi expositour" was identified by McCann (1924b) as Thomas Gallus, who was abbot of Saint Andrew's at Vercelli from its foundation in 1219 until his death in 1246, a canon regular of the Congregation of Saint Victor. McCann (1924b) and Hodgson (1958a and 1958b) have demonstrated beyond any reasonable doubt that, in translating John the Saracene's version of *De Mystica Theologia*, the *Cloud* author certainly used Gallus's *Extractio*, and probably his *Glossa* and *Explanatio*, on that text. Moreover, both these scholars postulate the influence of Gallus on the *Cloud* as well, a theory recently supported by Clark (1980). *Deonise Hid Diuinite* owes much of its characteristic flavour to the way in which Gallus had "medievalized" *De Mystica Theologia*; the *Cloud* owes much of its characteristic flavour to Gallus's version of Victorine spirituality.

In *The Cloud of Unknowing*, the *Cloud* author's emphasis on love or affection places him firmly beside Gallus. Their terminology is slightly different in some particulars: the *Cloud* author speaks of "loue" where Gallus spoke of *principalis affectio*; in the English treatise the words "affeccion" and "wille" designate the mental faculty that Gallus usually designated as *affectio* or *affectus*. These English terms represent small and natural developments of Gallus's theory of affection— one may point to the same process in *Viae Sion Lugent*, where Hugh of Balma substituted words like *affectio amoris*, *ardor amoris*, and *amor ardentissimus* for Gallus's *principalis affectio* and *apex affectus* (see Völker 1958, pp. 231–235). But there are no essential differences of doctrine: the *Cloud* author shares Gallus's belief in the primacy of love in the soul's ascent to God.

"Þe Abbot of Seinte Victore" believed that the soul is united with God by the principal affection. Similarly, the *Cloud* author states that the spiritual disciples of God may be "onid vnto God in parfite charite" insofar as this is possible in this life (85.7–8). For the *Cloud* author as for Gallus, love is the highest cognitive power, far superior to the powers of reason and intellect. God is incomprehensible to every created intellect (i.e., to the understanding of men and indeed of angels) but not to love (18.17–21). This echoes Gallus's doctrine of ascent "by the principal affection to union with God, which is . . . incomprehensibly located beyond all knowledge both human and angelic" (*Glossa*, in *PL* 122, 272A. Here the work is attributed erroneously to John Scotus Erigena).

According to the *Cloud* author, there are two main mental powers, two types of "principal worching miȝt," the knowing faculty and the loving faculty. God is incomprehensible to the "knowable miȝt" but comprehensible to the "louyng miȝt" (18.22–19.6). This contrast between the *intellectus* and the *affectus* is reiterated constantly throughout the *Cloud*. For the *Cloud* author it is as rigid a distinction as it was for Thomas Gallus, and here both writers are opposed to Richard of Saint Victor, who postulated a progressive movement up the mental hierarchy, an ordered transition from one type of contemplation to another. The *Cloud* author is not prepared to accommodate human reason and intellection in the higher reaches of mystical experience: God "may wel be loued, bot not þouȝt. By loue may he be getyn & holden; bot bi þouȝt neiþer" (26.3–5). In a manner strongly reminiscent of the way in which Gallus expounded Dionysius's advice to his friend Timothy, the *Cloud* author counsels his spiritual friend to reject all the normal processes of human thought, which depend on visible and substantial things. He who would be one with God must suppress all knowledge and feeling about anything less than God (see especially 81.21–83.5).

This emphasis on personal purification and preparation for grace squares with that ethical bias that is a distinctive feature of Gallus's medievalization of *De Mystica Theologia*. For example, Gallus interpreted the Dionysian account of Moses' ascent of Mount Sinai in terms of the process whereby the contemplative separates himself from various material opinions and earthly affections in order to ascend to God (*PL* 122, 274C). One concomitant of this doctrine, in both the *Glossa* and the *Explanatio*, is discrimination between the gentile philosopher who believed that the intellect was supreme and the Christian mystic who recognises the superiority of the principal affection (*Glossa*, in *PL* 122, 269B, 272D–273A; *Explanatio*, in London, British Museum, MS Royal 8. 6. IV, fols. 42v–43r). This may lie behind the *Cloud* author's repeated attacks on learned men who suffer from intellectual pride: these latter-day philosophers refuse to recognise the superiority of love.

The point of the intelligence does not penetrate the divine incomprehensibility, Gallus argues; the eye of intellectual cognition cannot reach so high, whence mystical knowledge is said to be by ignorance. By the power of the principal affection the soul is united with God in that most excellent state which neither the reason reaches by investigation nor the intellect contemplates by vision; by the full affection of the mind we long to be in the superlucent darkness of the "cloud of ignorance" (*caligo ignorantiae*), that is, in a state that is "superintellectual" since the intellect does not see or know it in any way. The parallels with the *Cloud* author's depiction of the cloud of unknowing are striking. When the soul begins to ascend to God it finds "a derknes, & as it were a cloude of vnknowyng, þou wost neuer what, sauyng þat þou felist in þi wille a nakid entent vnto God. Þis derknes & þis cloude is, how-so-euer þou dost, bitwix þee & þi God, & letteþ þee þat þou maist not see him cleerly by liȝt of vnderstonding in þi reson, ne fele him in swetnes of loue in þin affeccion" (16.20–17.5). But the eye of intellectual understanding is of limited avail. In this life knowledge cannot reach up to God but love can (33.11), and so it is necessary to "fele in þin affeccion goostly" a "blynde steryng of loue vnto God for him-self" (34.8–11). One must beat away at the cloud of unknowing "wiþ a scharpe darte of longing loue" (38.12–13), recognising that we can encounter Him only in the darkness of this wonderful cloud: "þer was neuer ȝit pure creature in þis liif, ne neuer ȝit schal be, so hiȝe rauischid in contemplacion & loue of þe Godheed, þat þer ne is euermore a hiȝe & a wonderful cloude of vnknowyng bitwix him & his God" (47.17–20). While the "cleer siȝt" of God is not possible to us in this life, by grace God can give men the "felyng" of Him (34.17–19). Hence, one should cease from intellectual activity and lift up one's love to that cloud, hoping that God will send out a beam of spiritual light to pierce it, thereby revealing some of His secrets. "Þan schalt þou fele þine affeccion enflaumid wiþ þe fiire of his loue, fer more þen I kan telle þee" (62.17–18).

Traces of Gallus's theory of affection may be found even in passages in which the *Cloud* author is following closely Richard of Saint Victor. One example must suffice. As Hodgson has pointed out, Chapters 71–73 of the *Cloud* are based on Richard's *Benjamin Major* iv.22–v.1. From this portion of Richard's text the English writer drew his account of Moses' ascent of Mount Sinai—and perhaps also the central image of his work, the cloud of unknowing, for here Richard described the darkness of unknowing as the cloud of ignorance (*nubes ignorantiae*). But there is one interesting change which may be attributed to the influence of Gallus's replacement of *intelligentia* with *principalis affectio*. The *Cloud* author allegorizes the Ark of the Covenant as love: just as the Ark contained all the jewels and relics of the temple, "riȝt so in þis lityl loue put ben contenid alle þe vertewes of mans soule" (126.21–4). There is nothing to parallel this in *Benjamin Major* iv.22–v.1, but in i.2 Richard had allegorized the Ark as intelligence: "We know that every precious thing—gold and silver, and precious stones—is usually placed in an ark. Therefore, if we consider the treasures of wisdom and knowledge, we shall quickly discover what the storehouse of such treasures is. What ark will be suitable for this activity, except the human intelligence?" (*PL* 196, 65C; Zinn 1979, p. 153). For *intelligentia* the *Cloud* author has substituted "loue," in agreement with the thought of Gallus. This is one of several instances that have convinced me that the English writer read Richard of Saint Victor in the light of the opinions and emphases of "þe Abbot of Seinte Victore."

We are now in a position to question one of the opinions of a great medievalist to whom we are all highly indebted. In *The English Mystical Tradition* David Knowles voices his scepticism concerning the specific influence of Gallus on the *Cloud*: "It is not evident that the abbot of Vercelli inspired what are the peculiar characteristics of the *Cloud* and its companions: the insistence on the blind, 'naked' act of loving attention; the clear distinction between natural and supernatural knowledge, and the incommunicability and the imperceptibility to the natural powers of the light of contemplation. Likewise, there is no hint in Thomas Gallus of the abundant and shrewd practical advice of the *Cloud*. In other words, while the influence of Gallus is very real, it is not the specifying influence" (1961, p. 75). In fact, the peculiar characteristics of the *Cloud* group here listed are substantially the same as distinctive doctrines of Thomas Gallus identified by recent scholarship. In particular, Gallus definitely emphasized the blindness of the affective ascent and firmly distinguished between natural and supernatural types of knowledge. The *Glossa* and the *Explanatio* make much of the Areopagite's exhortation of his beloved "other self" Timothy to leave behind both sensible perceptions and intellectual operations, all sensible and intelligible things, and as far as is humanly possible to be raised up unknowingly to union with God, who is above every substance and all ordinary knowledge. Gallus relished the paradox that the divine light described by Dionysius is the secretly supershining darkness of spoken silence: this is incomprehensibility, he explains, said to be "darkness" on account of the excess of light, to be "spoken" because of the eternal Word which speaks from eternity, to be "secretly supershining" because of the most secret effusion of the divine light, and to be "of silence" because the generation of such a Word is not perceived by the intellectual hearing and therefore cannot be recounted by word of mouth (*PL* 122, 271B; cf. *Explanatio*, MS Royal 8. 6. IV, fols. 43v–44r). In short, the light of contemplation is incommunicable and imperceptible to the natural powers of sense and reason. With regard to the absence of "shrewd practical advice" in Gallus, it should be recognised that considerable differences of genre and audience are involved: Gallus was expounding the intention of his author through *explication de texte*, while the *Cloud* author was offering advice to a budding contemplative. But it is perfectly possible to argue that the *Cloud* author was amplifying and clarifying for his "friend in God" the advice that Dionysius, viewed through the filter of Augustinian ethics, was supposed to have provided for his beloved friend Timothy.

It remains to consider briefly the possibility that the peculiar characteristics of *The Cloud of Unknowing* represent the influence of Gallus not directly but through an intermediate source. The intermediary can hardly have been Thomas Aquinas (as Knowles implies) since he believed that both the *intellectus* and the *affectus* were crucially involved in the ultimate mystical experience. Walsh (1981) has postulated the influence of two Carthusian writers, Hugh of Balma and Guigues du Pont (who died in 1297). However, most if not all of the parallels offered in the footnotes to his new edition of the *Cloud* seem to be reducible to one or another of the following categories: ideas and images of fairly wide currency, with roots in the Fathers and the Victorines; notions expressed with sufficient clarity and amplitude by Gallus himself; logical extensions of Gallus's thought which (one may imagine) the *Cloud* author was perfectly capable of, given his interests and tastes. Working independently, Rosemary A. Lees (1981) singled out Hugh of Balma as the most likely candidate. Her main argument turns on the belief that Hugh went beyond Gallus by disassociating knowledge-in-love from other types of knowledge; in this respect, she concludes, the *Cloud* author followed Hugh rather than Gallus. But Gallus's demarcation of the respective roles of the *intellectus* and the *affectus* provides a quite sufficient precedent for all the major contrasts between "understondyng" and "loue" in the *Cloud*. It may be argued, moreover, that the *Cloud* author shared Gallus's opinions concerning the function of intellect in the lower stages of contemplation and the function of superintellect in the highest possible stage. Finally, the most distinctive feature of Hugh's *Viae Sion Lugent*, its division of the contemplative way into the purgative, illuminative, and unitive stages, is unparalleled in our work, although it does seem to have influenced two fifteenth-century tracts on the contemplative life which contain borrowings from the *Cloud* (see Jolliffe 1975). The insoluble problem faced by Walsh and Lees is that there is nothing in the *Cloud* that can be identified as exclusively Hugonian; the many parallels they cite from *Viae Sion Lugent* should therefore be regarded as analogues rather than sources. Perhaps it is worth making the additional point that those who wish to claim the *Cloud* author for the Carthusian Order need not feel bound to champion the influence on his masterpiece of the great Carthusian doctor: after all, Gallus's Dionysian scholarship was popular among Carthusians, as the mystical theology of Hugh of Balma and Guigues du Pont bears witness.

In the absence of clear evidence to the contrary, the claim for the direct influence of Gallus should be upheld. Sources must not be multiplied beyond necessity, especially when we know, on his own admission in *Deonise Hid Diuinite*, that the *Cloud* author was familiar with Gallus's interpretation of *De Mystica Theologia*. Writing in the *Downside Review* in 1934, Knowles toyed with the idea that "there is a source of the *Cloud*, if only a great and inspiring teacher, whose name we shall never know" (p. 81, n. 1). It is tempting to name that specifying influence as Thomas Gallus. Of course, Gallus did not provide every doctrine and detail in the *Cloud*—one must remember, for example, its Thomistic theory of grace—but it is arguable that his teaching determined the tenor and tone of the work as a whole.

The doctrine of the *Cloud* is essentially private and privileged; it can hardly be expressed and it is appropriate only to a select group of contemplatives. By contrast, while Book I of the *Scale* is addressed to a "Dear Sister in Christ" (apparently an enclosed nun), in its entirety the work guides the reader through the entire process of meditation and contemplation, ranging from an explanation of the kinds of meditative achievement possible in the active life to a description of the supreme achievement of the perfect contemplative who enjoys union with God. As Russell-Smith says, "Hilton was exceptional among writers of his time in giving close attention to the problems of the contemplative life lived in an active state, and . . . different features of the second treatise in the *Scale* illustrate concern with the spiritual progress of all Christians, no matter what their state of life" (1965, p. 196). Those beginners in the spiritual life about whom the *Cloud* author was so scathing would have found in the *Scale* an abundance of doctrine designed to instruct and encourage them. It is little wonder, therefore, that Hilton's work soon became popular among people other than contemplatives. On the other hand, the intended audience of the *Cloud* was small and select, and its actual circulation was narrow. It seems to have been favoured by the Carthusian Order; in 1491 a Latin translation was made by Richard Methley, of the Charterhouse of Mount Grace in Yorkshire.

This difference in appeal is substantiated by the postmedieval dissemination of the two works. In the sixteenth century the *Cloud* slipped into obscurity, to be rediscovered by Augustine Baker (1575–1641), under whose influence it had a brief vogue in English religious houses in exile on the Continent. Then it passed into complete oblivion until Underhill's edition in 1912. The *Scale* fared much better: it was the first English mystical work to be printed, by Wynkyn de Worde in 1494. This edition was followed by one by Julian Notary in 1507 and two by de Worde, in 1525 and 1533. The moderation and comprehensiveness of the *Scale* may account for its acceptance by pious Tudor layfolk as a guide to godliness. Naturally, Hilton's *Epistle on the Mixed Life* had a considerable appeal to that same audience. It was included in de Worde's first edition of the *Scale*, printed on its own by Notary in 1507, and published together with other tracts by Pynson in 1516. (The most comprehensive study of the medieval and early Renaissance dissemination of the *Cloud*, the *Scale*, and many other religious texts remains A. Ian Doyle's unpublished thesis of 1953.)

Hilton's concern with lesser mortals is manifest throughout his writings both in Middle English and in Latin. The addressee of the first book of the *Scale* apparently was unable to read the Latin Bible (i.15), which may explain why Hilton outlines the different ways in which the learned and the unlearned can begin the process of spiritual ascent (i.4–6). The *Epistle on the Mixed Life* assures the devout layman that he too can, in some measure, enjoy the mixed life of activity and contemplation, which is not confined to prelates. In the Latin treatise *De Tolerandis Imaginibus* Saint Gregory's contention that material images and religious objets d'art are the books of the unlearned is reiterated forcefully (see Owst 1961, pp. 137–139). Hilton was tolerant also of images of another kind, the *imagines* or *phantasmata* formed by the imagination. The *Cloud* author believed that the "bodely and fleschely conseintes of hem þat han corious & ymaginatyve wittys ben cause of moche error" (94.22–24), and therefore imaginative thinking must be ruthlessly suppressed: "bot þou bere him doun, he wile bere þee doun" (33.11–20). By contrast, for Hilton such thinking was the basis of a commendable spiritual condition, a state of grace which is the highest that many good Christians attain.

There are, Hilton argues, two ways of knowing God: "On is had principally in ymaginacioun, & litel in vndirstondynge. Þis knowynge is in chosen soules bigynnande & profitande in grace, þat knowen God & lufen Him al manly not gostly, with manly affecciouns & with bodily liknes . . . Anoþer knowynge is principally feled in vndirstandynge, whan it is conforted & illumined bi þe Holy Gost, & litel in ymaginacioun" (ii.31:136/4–13). Echoing ideas from Richard of Saint Victor's *Benjamin Minor* and the first two chapters of Dionysius's *De Caelesti Hierarchia*, Hilton states that it is very difficult for an untutored soul that is weighed down by the body truly to know itself, or an angel, or God (ii.30:124/6–13). It imagines a "bodily schappe," intending in that way to acquire knowledge of itself, and so of God and other spiritual things. But this is impossible, because "alle gostly þinges ere seen & knowen by vndirstandynge of þe soule, not bi ymaginacioun." No matter how much fervour of devotion and fire of love the soul may feel, as long as its conception of God is largely or wholly dependent on imagination rather than intellection, it has not yet attained perfect love or contemplation (125/9–14). However, although much less elevated than the intellectual contemplation of Christ's divinity, imaginative meditation on the humanity of Christ is definitely good and inspired by grace. This is made absolutely clear in Hilton's classification of the three stages of love in the *Scale* (ii.30:125/15–126/6). All these stages are good, but they become progressively better. The first is in faith alone without any knowledge of God given in the imagination or in the intellect by grace; in the second the soul knows God not only by faith but also in the humanity of Jesus through the imagination, while in the third the soul's contemplation extends to the divinity that is united to the humanity (insofar as that is possible in this life). Naturally, few people are able to attain such intellectual contemplation, and therefore God, because of His love of all humanity, made provision for lesser mortals: "Nerþeles vnto swilk soules þat can not þinken of þe Godhed gostly, þat þei schuld not erren in here deuocioun, bot þat þei schuld be conforted & strengþed þurgh sum maner inward beholdynge of Iesu, for to forsake synne & þe luf of þe werld; þerfore oure Lorde Iesu tempreþ His vnseable liȝt of His Godhed, & cloþiþ it vndir bodily liknes of His manhed, & schewiþ it to þe inner eiȝe of a soule & fediþ it with þe luf of His precious flesche gostly" (ii.30:128/5–12).

For Hilton, the human nature of Christ was the major shadow by which the divine light is mediated to men, and imaginative meditation on "þe schadwe of His manhede" was a major step towards eventual vision of the divinity behind the humanity. Those who are not far advanced in their spiritual course can love Jesus only "as it were al manly and fleschly after þe condiciouns & þe liknes of man. And vpon þat rewarde þei schapen al here wirkynge, in here þouȝtes & in here affecciouns" (ii.30:126/9–12). They reverence Him as man, and adore Him and love Him principally through their imaginations.

Hilton's attitude to imagination meant that he could not share the purist doctrine of affection found in the *Cloud*. The *Cloud* author was interested only in the highest reaches of the affective power, when it leaves behind every stimulating image to enter the cloud of unknowing where the hidden God is to be found. Hilton emphasizes that affection is involved in all three degrees of contemplation, and the higher the degree the more purified is the *affectus* (see ii.30 and 35 in toto). In the second or penultimate degree the imagination is dominant, stimulating the soul to human affection ("manly affeccioun"), so-called in contradistinction with the refined and therefore spiritual type of affection present in the third and highest degree (ii.30:131/5−6). Hilton affirms that beginners and those who are not spiritually gifted by nature should foster human and natural love through the imagination, until greater grace be given them. Since such people can think of Jesus only as a man living under earthly conditions, and all their affections are shaped by this limitation, they worship and love Him principally in His human aspect. But of course, the soul should desire to have a spiritual love and understanding of Christ's divine nature as well as His human nature. The divine goodness can transform one's natural aspiration to God into spiritual affection ("gostly affeccioun," ii.35:153/17−18, 157/19). In the manner of Richard of Saint Victor, Hilton conceives of a transition rather than an enormous leap from "manly affeccioun" and "gracious ymaginacioun" to the "gostly affeccioun" and illumined intellect with which the soul, as far as it may in this life, contemplates the Godhead united to manhood in Christ.

And herein lies the major difference of doctrine that separates the *Scale* and the *Cloud*. Hilton's belief that both the *affectus* and the *intellectus* are involved in the ultimate contemplative experience places him along with Richard of Saint Victor and Thomas Aquinas rather than with those thinkers, including Thomas Gallus, Hugh of Balma, and the *Cloud* author, who identified the *affectus* as the faculty by which the soul is united with God. In the first book of the *Scale* Hilton argues that the third and highest degree of contemplation consists of both knowledge and love, in knowing God and the perfect love of Him; by divine grace the intellect is illumined to see Truth itself, which is God, and spiritual matters, while the will is inflamed with a soft, sweet, burning love (i.8). This synthesis is elaborated in the second book, where it is stated that both love and light are found in a pure soul (ii.46:225/7−8). For truly humble souls, the true Sun (i.e., the Lord Jesus) will "illumine here resoun in knowynge of soþfastnes & kyndelen here affeccioun in brennynge of luf, & than schal þei boþ brennen & schynen. Þei schul þurw vertue of þis heuenly sunne bren in perfit luf, & shynen in knowyng of God & gostly þinges" (ii.26:101/19−102/2). However, it would seem that the intellect plays the dominant role. The view of Gallus and the *Cloud* author that the principal affection is a cognitive power, and the highest one possessed by the human soul, is not shared by Hilton, who believes rather that the supreme cognitive faculty is the intellect, which is, considered in relation to the other faculties, superior to the will or *affectus*. In the mental ascent through the degrees of perfection the intellect leads the way, since affection follows intellection: "lufe comiþ oute of knowynge & not knowynge oute of luf" (ii.34:146/16). The soul cannot love what it does not know; the more it knows, the more it loves.

It remains to consider Hilton's imagery of light (and darkness) in rather more detail, in order to make the point that often he and the *Cloud* author use similar images to mean very different things. In the second book of the *Scale* mention is made of a "liȝtsom derknes" or "liȝty mirknes," a "gode niȝt," and a "riche noȝt" (ii.24:88/9, 90/17; ii.25:93/9; ii.27:103/2, 109/16). Is this terminology attributable to the influence of the *Cloud*, which Hilton may have read after completing Book I of the *Scale*? It is quite possible that he may have derived from the *Cloud* a smattering of the language of negative theology, but a smattering is all it is. The references to darkness found in Book II of the *Scale* have nothing to do with the transcendence of intellect, as Clark (1977) has pointed out; it is as if Hilton focused on Chapters 68 and 69 of the *Cloud*, to the exclusion of its earlier references to darkness as a lack of knowing. Hilton's seeker after truth enters a glowing darkness which shuts out the false light and love of the world and ushers in the dawn of the true day (ii.24:88/9−11). This darkness is painful to those who are not yet enlightened and cleansed, but eventually it becomes restful, when the soul is hidden for a time from the painful feeling of all vain thoughts, and "only is restid in desire & longynge to Iesu with a gostly biholdyng" (93/2−5).

In the first book of the *Scale* Hilton had described the darkness of sin (i.52); here in the second book he is employing imagery of night and darkness to describe, in terms strongly reminiscent of Chapters 68 and 69 of the *Cloud*, the process of adjustment from a state of sin to a state of grace. Yet in both Hilton's books the central concept is the same, namely, the Augustinian imperative of restoring in man, through the removal of sin, the divine likeness which is one's true self. For Hilton the lightsome darkness is a means to an end: having passed through the cleansing, and to that extent welcome, darkness, the soul may proceed to higher things. The *intellectus* and *affectus* are raised to their highest possible states as "þe innere iȝe of þe soule" is opened to see Christ as He is in His divinity, "in vndirstandynge þat is counfortid & liȝtned bi þe gifte of þe Holy Gost, with a wondirful reuerence & a priue brennande lufe, & with gostly saueour & heuenly delite, more clerly & more fully þen it may be wryten or seide" (ii.32:137/3−4, 15−19). By contrast, the *Cloud* author believed that "þe souereyn-schinyng derknes" was reached in the penultimate stage of the mystic quest. The higher part of contemplation, as we know it in this life, is wholly caught up in darkness: the soul must wait in this darkness as long as is necessary, striking at the thick cloud of unknowing with the sharp dart of love, until God may, perhaps, send out a shaft of spiritual light to reveal some of his secrets (*Cloud*, 32.5−8; 26.8−12; 62.14−17). The divergence of doctrine could hardly be more radical.

Comparison of the *Cloud* author and Walter Hilton is difficult because their intended audiences and aims in writing were not the same. The *Cloud* is concerned almost exclusively with the highest level of contemplation possible in this life, whereas the *Scale* describes the full range of meditative and contemplative experience, providing both milk for spiritual children and solid food for perfect souls. But it is clear that, in their views on the respective roles of affection and intellection, our writers differ fundamentally. The *Cloud* author shared Gallus's belief in the primacy of the *affectus* in the soul's journey to God, whereas Hilton postulated a synthesis of intellection and affection at every step of the mystic way, including the ultimate stage in which God, who is both Light and Love, illuminates the *intellectus* and inflames the *affectus* to the very limits of their capacities. Hilton was interested in reason and intellect, in the normal operations of human thinking, including imaginative thinking, whereas for the *Cloud* author, who advocated the transcendence of ordinary thought processes, imagining and fantasies were dangerous hinderances to the soul's affective ascent. In view of these quite different theological positions, it is difficult to see how some modern scholars can still be attracted by the theory that Hilton wrote *The Cloud of Unknowing*.

NOTE

1. All references to the works of the *Cloud* author are to the page and line numberings in the editions by Phyllis Hodgson (1958a, 1958b). For Book II of the *Scale* I used S. S. Hussey's unpublished edition. Since this is not easily available, I have provided book and chapter numbers in addition to Hussey's page and line enumeration. For Book I, I used the modernized versions of the *Scale* by Sitwell (1953) and Sherley-Price (1957). I am grateful to Professor John Burrow for his comments on an earlier draft of this chapter, and to Dr. Hussey for allowing me to quote from his unpublished thesis.

BIBLIOGRAPHY

MANUSCRIPTS AND EARLY PRINTED EDITIONS

THE CLOUD OF UNKNOWING

For MSS of the English text and the two Latin translations see Hodgson (1958a), pp. ix–xxvii. For early printed editions see p. lxxxvii.

OTHER WORKS BY THE *CLOUD* AUTHOR

For MSS see Hodgson (1958a), pp. ix–xxv, and Hodgson (1958b), pp. ix–xxiii.

HILTON'S *SCALE OF PERFECTION*

MANUSCRIPTS

The following list is based on T. Takamiya (1975) "The Luttrell Wynne MS of Walter Hilton," *Reports of the Keio Institute of Cultural and Linguistic Studies*, 7, 171–191.

BL, London, Add. 11748	Books I and II
All Souls' College, Oxford 25	Books I and II
Bodleian Library, Oxford, Bodley 100	Books I and II
Bodleian Library, Oxford, Bodley 592	Books I and II
Bibliothèque royale, Brussels, 2544–2545	Books I and II
Cambridge University Library, Add. 6686 (Ashburnham-Young)	Book I
Corpus Christi College, Cambridge, R. 5 (268)	Books I and II
Duke of Devonshire, Chatsworth	Books I and II
Cambridge University Library, Dd. v. 55	Book I
Cambridge University Library, Ee. iv. 30	Books I and II
Edinburgh, Edinburgh Fragments	Book I
Cambridge University Library, Ff. v. 40	Book I
BL, Harley 6579	Books I and II
BL, Harley 330	Book I
BL, Harley 1022	Book I
BL, Harley 1035	Book I
BL, Harley 2387	Books I and II
BL, Harley 2397	Book II
BL, Harley 6573	Books I and II
Huntington Library, San Marino, HM 112	Book I
Huntington Library, San Marino, HM 266	Books I and II
Saint John's College, Cambridge, G. 35 (202)	Book I
Lambeth Palace, London, Lambeth 472	Books I and II
Bodleian Library, Oxford, Laud Misc. 602	Books I and II
BL, Lansdowne 362	Book I
Marquis of Bath, Longleat House, Somerset, Longleat 298	Book I
Takamiya, Tokyo (Luttrell Wynne)	Books I and II
Magdalene College, Cambridge, F. 4. 17	Book II
National Library of Scotland, Edinburgh, 6126 (Borthwick)	Book I
Inner Temple Library, London, Petyt 524	Books I and II
Columbia University Library, New York, Plimpton 257	Books I and II
Bodleian Library, Oxford, Rawlinson C. 285	Books I and II

Boedleian Library, Oxford, Rawlinson C. 894	Book I, extract
Liverpool University Library, Rylands F. 4. 10	
(Harmsworth)	Book I
BL, Add. 22283 (Simeon)	Book I
University of Pennsylvania Library, Philadelphia, Eng. 8	
(Stonor)	Books I and II
Stonyhurst College, Whalley, Lancashire, A. vi. 24	Book I
Trinity College, Cambridge, B. 15. 18 (354)	Books I and II
Trinity College, Cambridge, O. 7. 47 (1375)	Book I
Trinity College, Dublin, A. 5. 7 (122)	Book II, extracts
Trinity College, Dublin, C. 5. 20 (352)	Books I and II, extracts
Lincoln Cathedral Chapter Library, A. 5. 2 (91) (Thornton)	Book I, extract
University College, Oxford, 28	Book I
Bodleian Library, Oxford, Eng. poet. a. 1 (Vernon)	Book I
Pierpoint Morgan Library, New York, Aldenham copy of	
Wynkyn de Worde's edition (1494)	
Westminster Cathedral	Books I and II, extracts
Worcester Cathedral Chapter Library, F. 172	Book I
Westminster School, Winchester	Books I and II

For MSS of the Latin translation by Thomas Fishlake, *Liber de Nobilitate Anime* (ca. 1400), see Hussey (1973) and Colledge (1979).

EARLY PRINTED EDITIONS

Wynkyn de Worde, 1494 (STC 14042)
Julian Notary, 1507 (STC 14043)
de Worde, 1525 (STC 14044)
de Worde, 1533 (STC 14045)
Baker, A., and Cressy, S., eds., London: T. R., 1659
Dalgairns, J. B., ed., London: J. Philp, 1870; repr. (1901) London: Art and Book Co.

MODERN EDITIONS, STUDIES, BACKGROUND

For full bibliography see V. M. Lagorio and R. Bradley, eds. (1981) *The Fourteenth-Century Mystics: A Comprehensive Annotated Bibliography*, New York: Garland. Subsequent bibliography can be found in *The Fourteenth-Century English Mystics Newsletter*, ed. Lagorio and Bradley from the Department of English, the University of Iowa. The following bibliography is selective.

Beale, W. H. (1975) "Walter Hilton and the Concept of 'Medled Lyf.'" *ABR*, 26, 381–394.

Birts, R., ed. (1952) "*The Scale of Perfection* by Walter Hilton Canon at the Augustinian Priory at Thurgarton, Book i, Chapters 38–52." B. Litt. thesis, University of Oxford.

Blake, N. F. (1974) "Varieties of Middle English Religious Prose." In *Chaucer and Middle English Studies in Honour of Rossell Hope Robbins*, edited by Beryl Rowland, pp. 348–356. London: Allen and Unwin.

Brinton, H. H., ed. (1948) *The Cloud of Unknowing*. New York and London: Harper.

Burrow, J. A. (1977) "Fantasy and Language in *The Cloud of Unknowing*." *EIC*, 27, 283–298.

Clark, J. P. H. (1977) "The 'Lightsome Darkness'—Aspects of Walter Hilton's Theological Background." *DownR*, 95, 95–109.

———— (1978a) "*The Cloud of Unknowing*, Walter Hilton and St. John of the Cross: A Comparison." *DownR*, 96, 281–298.

———— (1978b) "Walter Hilton and 'Liberty of Spirit.'" *DownR*, 96, 61–78.

———— (1979a) "Action and Contemplation in Walter Hilton." *DownR*, 97, 258–274.

———— (1979b) "Image and Likeness in Walter Hilton." *DownR*, 97, 204–220.

———— (1979c) "Intention in Walter Hilton." *DownR*, 97, 69–80.

———— (1980) "Sources and Theology in *The Cloud of Unknowing*." *DownR*, 98, 83–109.

———— (1982a) "Augustine, Anselm and Walter Hilton." In *The Medieval Mystical Tradition in England*, edited by Marion Glasscoe, pp. 102–106. Exeter: University of Exeter.

———— (1982b) "Walter Hilton and the Psalm Commentary *Qui Habitat*." *DownR*, 100, 235–262.

Colledge, E. (1956) "Recent Work on Walter Hilton." *Blackfriars*, 37, 265–270.

———— (1961) "The English Mystics and Their Critics." *Life of the Spirit*, 15, 554–559.

———— (1962) *The Mediaeval Mystics of England*. New York: Charles Scribner's Sons.

———— (1979) "*De Nobilitate anime* and *De Ornatu spiritualium nupciarum*." *Quaerendo*, 9, 149–159.

Deanesly, M. (1920) "Vernacular Books in England in the Fourteenth and Fifteenth Centuries." *MLR*, 15, 349–358.

Doyle, A. Ian (1953) "A Survey of the Origins and Circulation of Theological Writings in English in the Fourteenth, Fifteenth and Sixteenth Centuries, with Special Reference to the Part of the Clergy Therein." Ph.D. diss., University of Cambridge.

Ellis, R. (1980) "A Literary Approach to the Middle English Mystics." In *The Medieval Mystical Tradition in England*, edited by Marion Glasscoe, pp. 99–119. Exeter: University of Exeter.

———— (1982) "The Choices of the Translator in the Late Middle English Period." In *The Medieval Mystical Tradition in England*, edited by Marion Glasscoe, pp. 18–46. Exeter: University of Exeter.

Gamba, U., ed. (1942) *Il commento di Roberti Grossatesta al "De Mystica Theologia" del Pseudo-Dionigi Areopagita*. Orbis Romanus 14. Milan: Società Editrice "Vita e Pensiero."

Gardner, E., ed. (1910) Hilton's *Of Angels' Song*. In *The Cell of Self Knowledge*, pp. 61–73. London: Chatto and Windus.

Gardner, Helen L. (1933) "Walter Hilton and the Authorship of *The Cloud of Unknowing.*" *RES*, 9, 129–147.

—— (1936) "The Text of *The Scale of Perfection.*" *MAE*, 5, 11–30.

—— (1937) "Walter Hilton and the Mystical Tradition in England." *E&S*, 22, 103–127.

—— (1947) Review of the *Cloud*, ed. Hodgson. *MAE*, 16, 36–42.

Gatto, L. C. (1975) "The Walter Hilton–*Cloud of Unknowing* Authorship Controversy Reconsidered." *Studies in Medieval Culture*, 5, 181–189.

Glasscoe, Marion, ed. (1980) *The Medieval Mystical Tradition in England: Papers read at the Exeter Symposium, July 1980.* Exeter: University of Exeter.

——, ed. (1982) *The Medieval Mystical Tradition in England: Papers read at Dartington Hall, July 1982.* Exeter: University of Exeter.

Hodgson, P. (1955) "Walter Hilton and *The Cloud of Unknowing*: A Problem of Authorship Reconsidered." *MLR*, 50, 395–406.

——, ed. (1958a) *"The Cloud of Unknowing" and "The Book of Privy Counselling."* EETS, os 218.

——, ed. (1958b) *"Deonise Hid Diuinite" and Other Treatises on Contemplative Prayer Related to "The Cloud of Unknowing."* EETS, os 231.

——, ed. (1982) *"The Cloud of Unknowing" and Related Treatises.* Analecta Cartusiana 3. Salzburg: Universität Salzburg.

Horstman, Carl, ed. (1895) Hilton's *Of Angels' Song* and *The Epistle on the Mixed Life* in *Yorkshire Writers: Richard Rolle of Hampole . . . and His Followers*, 1:173–182, 264–292. London: Swan Sonnenschein and Co.

Hudson, A. (1968) "A Chapter from Walter Hilton in Two Middle English Compilations." *Neophil*, 52, 416–421.

Hughes, A. C. (1962) *Walter Hilton's Direction to Contemplatives.* Rome: Typis Pontificae Universitatis Gregoriana.

Hussey, S. S., ed. (1962) "An Edition, from the Manuscripts, of Book ii of Walter Hilton's *Scale of Perfection.*" Ph.D. diss., University of London.

—— (1964) "The Text of *The Scale of Perfection*, Book ii." *NM*, 65, 75–92.

—— (1973) "Latin and English in *The Scale of Perfection.*" *MS*, 35, 456–476.

—— (1980) "Walter Hilton: Traditionalist?" In *The Medieval Mystical Tradition in England*, edited by Marion Glasscoe, pp. 1–16. Exeter: University of Exeter.

Jolliffe, P. S. (1975) "Two Middle English Tracts on the Contemplative Life." *MS*, 37, 85–121.

Jones, Dorothy, ed. (1929) *Minor Works of Walter Hilton.* London: Burns, Oates and Washbourne.

Kane, Harold J. (1968) "A Critical Edition of the *Prickynge of Love.*" Ph.D. diss., University of Pennsylvania.

Kennedy, D. G. (1979) "The Incarnational Element in Hilton's Spirituality." Ph.D. diss., McGill University.

Kieckhefer, R. (1978) "Mysticism and Social Consciousness in the Fourteenth Century." *RUO*, 48, 179–186.

Kirchberger, Clare, ed. (1952) *The Goad of Love.* London: Faber and Faber.

Knowles, David (1934) "The Excellence of the *Cloud.*" *DownR*, 52, 71–92.

———— (1961) *The English Mystical Tradition*. London: Burns and Oates.

Kuriyagawa, F. (1971) "The Inner Temple MS of Walter Hilton's *Eight Chapters of Perfection*." *Studies in English Literature* (Tokyo), English number, March 1971. Repr. (1980) by Takamiya.

Lagorio, Valerie (1980) "New Avenues of Research in the English Mystics." In *The Medieval Mystical Tradition in England*, edited by Marion Glasscoe, pp. 234–249. Exeter: University of Exeter.

Lees, Rosemary A. (1981) "The Negative Language of the Dionysian School of Mystical Theology: An Approach to *The Cloud of Unknowing*." D. Phil. diss., University of York.

McCann, Justin (1924a) "The Cloud of Unknowing." *Ampleforth Journal*, 29, 192–197.

————, ed. (1924b) *The Cloud of Unknowing etc.* London: Burns, Oates and Co.

Mastro, M. L. del, ed. (1979) *The Staircase of Perfection*. Garden City, N.Y.: Doubleday and Co.

Medcalf, S. (1980) "Medieval Psychology and Medieval Mystics." In *The Medieval Mystical Tradition in England*, edited by Marion Glasscoe, pp. 120–155. Exeter: University of Exeter.

Milosh, J. E. (1966) *"The Scale of Perfection" and the English Mystical Tradition*. Madison: University of Wisconsin Press.

Minnis, A. J. (1979) "Literary Theory in Discussions of *Formae Tractandi* by Medieval Theologians." *New Literary History*, 11, 133–145.

———— (1982) "The Sources of *The Cloud of Unknowing*: A Reconsideration." In *The Medieval Mystical Tradition in England*, edited by Marion Glasscoe, pp. 63–75. Exeter: University of Exeter.

———— (1983) *Medieval Theory of Authorship: Scholastic Literary Attitudes in the Later Middle Ages*. London: Scolar Press.

Nieva, C. S. (1971) *This Transcending God: The Teaching of the Author of "The Cloud of Unknowing."* London: Mitre Press.

———— (1978) *"The Cloud of Unknowing* and St. John of the Cross." *Mount Carmel*, 26, 79–98.

Noetinger, M. (1923) "The Modern Editions of Walter Hilton's *Scala Perfectionis*." *DownR*, 41, 149–157.

———— (1924) "The Authorship of *The Cloud of Unknowing*." *Blackfriars*, 4, 1457–1464.

————, trans. (1925) *Le nuage de l'inconnaissance*. Paris: Maison A. Muse.

Noetinger, M., and Bouvet, E. trans. (1923) *L'echelle de la perfection*. Tours: A. Mame et Fils.

Oblate of Solesmes, ed. (1927) *The Scale of Perfection*. London: Burns, Oates and Washbourne.

O'Connell, P. F. (1981) "The Person and Work of Christ in *The Cloud of Unknowing*." *Contemplative Review*, 14, 1–9, 15–21.

Owst, G. R. (1967) *Literature and Pulpit in Medieval England*. 2d ed. Oxford: B. Blackwell.

Pepler, Conrad (1958) *The English Religious Heritage*. Saint Louis: Herder.

Perry, G. G., ed. (1921) *Of Angels' Song* and *The Epistle on the Mixed Life* in *English Prose Treatises of Richard Rolle*. EETS, os 20. Repr. (1974) New York: Kraus.

Petry, R. C. (1952) "Social Responsibility and the Late Medieval Mystics." *Church History*, 21, 3–19.

————, ed. (1957) *Late Medieval Mysticism*. The Library of Christian Classics 13. London: SCM Press.

Riehle, W. (1977) "The Problem of Walter Hilton's Possible Authorship of *The Cloud of Unknowing* and its Related Tracts." *NM*, 78, 31–45.

————, trans. (1980) *Die Wolke des Nichtwissens*. Einsiedeln: Johannes Verlag.

———— (1981) *The Middle English Mystics*. London: Routledge and Kegan Paul.

Robbins, R. H. (1957) Review of *Deonise Hid Diuinite*, ed. Hodgson. *Speculum*, 32, 406–410.

Rogers, Daniel J. (1982) "Psychotechnical Approaches to the Teaching of the *Cloud*-Author and to the *Showings* of Julian of Norwich." In *The Medieval Mystical Tradition in England*, edited by Marion Glasscoe, pp. 143–160. Exeter: University of Exeter.

Russell-Smith, Joy M. (1960) Review of *Deonise Hid Diuinite*, ed. Hodgson. *ES*, 41, 261–267.

———— (1954) "Walter Hilton and a Tract in Defence of the Veneration of Images." *Dominican Studies*, 7, 180–214.

———— (1965) "Walter Hilton." In *Pre-Reformation English Spirituality*, edited by James Walsh, pp. 182–197. London: Burns and Oates.

Sargent, Michael G. (1976) "The Transmission by the English Carthusians of some Late Medieval Spiritual Writings." *Journal of Ecclesiastical History*, 27, 225–240.

———— (1977) "A New Manuscript of The Chastising of God's Children with an Ascription to Walter Hilton." *MAE*, 46, 49–65.

———— (1979) "James Grenehalgh as Textual Critic." Ph.D. diss., University of Toronto.

———— (1982) "The Organization of *The Scale of Perfection*." In *The Medieval Mystical Tradition in England*, edited by Marion Glasscoe, pp. 231–261. Exeter: University of Exeter.

Schmidt, A. V. C. (1980) "Langland and the Mystical Tradition." In *The Medieval Mystical Tradition in England*, edited by Marion Glasscoe, pp. 17–38. Exeter: University of Exeter.

Sherley-Price, L., ed. (1957) *The Ladder of Perfection*. Harmondsworth: Penguin Books.

Sitwell, G. (1949, 1950) "Contemplation in *The Scale of Perfection*." *DownR*, 67, 276–290; 68, 21–34, 271–289.

————, ed. (1953) *The Scale of Perfection*. London: Burns and Oates.

Steele, Francis J. (1979) "Definitions and Depictions of the Active Life in Middle English Religious Literature in the Thirteenth, Fourteenth and Fifteenth Centuries, including Special Reference to *Piers Plowman*." D. Phil. diss., University of Oxford.

Takamiya, T. (1977) "Walter Hilton's *Of Angels' Song* edited from the British Museum MS Additional 27592." *Studies in English Literature* (Tokyo), English Number, March 1977. Repr. in Takamiya (1980).

———— (1980) *Two Minor Works of Walter Hilton: Eight Chapters of Perfection and Of Angels' Song*. Tokyo: Privately printed by T. Takamiya. Repr. of Kuriyagawa (1971) and Takamiya (1977).

Trethowan, I., ed. (1975) *The Scale of Perfection*. Saint Meinrad, Ind.: Abbey Press.

Tuma, G. W. (1977) *The Fourteenth-Century English Mystics: A Comparative Analysis.* Elizabethan and Renaissance Studies 61 and 62. Salzburg: Institut für Anglistik und Amerikanistik, Universität Salzburg.

Underhill, E., ed. (1912) *The Cloud of Unknowing.* London: John M. Watkins, repr. 1934.

———, ed. (1923) *The Scale of Perfection.* London: John M. Watkins, repr. 1948.

Völker, W. (1958) *Kontemplation und Ekstasie bei Pseudo-Dionysius Areopagita.* Wiesbaden: Franz Steiner.

Von Ivánka, E. (1969) "Zur Überwindung des neuplatonischen Intellektualismus in der Deutung der Mystik: *Intelligentia* oder *Principalis Affectio.*" In *Platonismus in der Philosophie des Mittelalters.* Wege der Forschung 197. Darmstadt: Wissenschaftliche Buchgesellschaft.

Wakelin, M. F. (1980) "English Mysticism and the English Homiletic Tradition." In *The Medieval Mystical Tradition in England,* edited by Marion Glasscoe, pp. 39–54. Exeter: University of Exeter.

Wallner, B., ed. (1954) *An Exposition of "Qui Habitat" and "Bonum Est" in English.* LSE 23. Lund: Gleerup.

———, ed. (1957) *A Commentary on the "Benedictus."* Lund: Gleerup.

Walsh, James (1957) "*Sapientia Christianorum*: The Doctrine of Thomas Gallus, Abbot of Vercelli, on Contemplation." D. Theol. diss., Pontifica Universita Gregoriana, Rome.

——— (1963) "The Cloud of Unknowing." *Month,* December, 325–336.

——— (1965a) "The Cloud of Unknowing." In *Pre-Reformation English Spirituality,* edited by James Walsh, pp. 170–181. London: Burns and Oates.

———, ed. (1965b) *Pre-Reformation English Spirituality.* London: Burns and Oates.

———, ed. (1981) *The Cloud of Unknowing.* Classics of Western Spirituality. Ramsey, N.J.: Paulist Press.

Watson, Katharine (1982) "*The Cloud of Unknowing* and Vedanta." In *The Medieval Mystical Tradition in England,* edited by Marion Glasscoe, pp. 76–101. Exeter: University of Exeter.

White, B. (1949) Review of the *Cloud,* ed. Hodgson. *MLR,* 44, 99–103.

White, H. V. (1962) Review of Knowles (1961) and Colledge (1962). *Speculum,* 37, 447–448.

Wilson, R. M. (1956) "Three Middle English Mystics." *E&S,* ns 9, 87–112.

Wolters, C., ed. (1978) *The Cloud of Unknowing and Other Works.* Harmondsworth: Penguin Books.

———, ed. (1980) *A Study of Wisdom: Three Tracts by the Author of "The Cloud of Unknowing."* Fairacres Publication 75. Oxford: SLG Press.

Wykes, B. E. (1957) "An Edition of Book i of The Scale of Perfection by Walter Hilton." Ph.D. diss., University of Michigan.

Zinn, G. A., trans. (1979) *Richard of St. Victor.* Classics of Western Spirituality. Ramsey, N.J.: Paulist Press.

CHAPTER 4

Nicholas Love

Barbara Nolan

"Explicit compendium Nichol . . . Love . . . Montis . . . monachi."[1] Such
brief traces as this link the fifteenth-century Carthusian prior, Nicholas Love, to
the *Mirrour of the Blessed Lyf of Jesu Christ* and appended treatise on the Sacrament. Love's *Mirrour* is first described in a certificate of approval issued by
Archbishop Thomas Arundel of Canterbury in 1410. In this notice, the author is
not mentioned by name. Arundel describes him as the "compiler" and "translator" and commends his work to the faithful for their "edification" and the "con-
futation" of "heretics and Lollards." A further notice to readers suggests a modest
freedom on the translator's part, promising that passages original with the compiler will be indicated by the letter "N" in the margin. But in spite of modest
additions, about which the annotator may not be entirely trustworthy, the *Mirrour* is best characterized as an abridged translation of the pseudo-Bonaventuran
Meditationes Vitae Christi, now generally attributed to a fourteenth-century Franciscan, John of Caulibus.

Love's hiddenness in relation to the *Mirrour* and the treatise is in keeping with
the nature of his work. The prose is designed to call attention to itself only insofar
as it serves to arouse certain kinds of piety in the ordinary reader, lay as well as
religious. Like the prose style of the best English devotional writing preceding
it, Love's literary style follows upon his sense of a simple audience's needs. His
prose also owes a considerable debt to his Latin sources and to later medieval
religious tradition which encouraged meditation on Christ's life as if it were present to the devout reader. Above all, the Carthusian translator adapts to his use the
"plain and open" style of the great English devotional writers of the fourteenth
century, many of whom had written for "lewed" rather than learned readers.

Although Love's output is slight, his claim to inclusion in a history of English
prose is considerable. His literary style, based in part on Latin models, in part on
English precedent, and always adjusted to his intended audience, is at once elegant, limpid, precise, and direct. In addition, his work represents an important
development in the history of devotional prose. Addressed to an audience wider
than that of its Latin source, the *Mirrour* responded to a growing need for lay

spiritual reading. As the history of the manuscripts and editions attests, Love's
work of translation enjoyed a long and wide popularity, and therefore influence,
in all parts of England. It was, according to Margaret Deanesly, "probably more
popular than any other single book in the Fifteenth Century" (1920b, p. 353).
Elizabeth Salter, who has written the only published monograph on Love, has
mapped major directions for the study of the *Mirrour*, and this chapter refers
often to her work. But much remains to be done. We still lack a critical edition of
the text, a project considerably more complex than early editors had thought. Despite Salter's excellent work, we do not yet have a rigorous, exacting analysis of
Love's prose in relation either to his English predecessors or to his Latin models.
It would be valuable to know just how his English style intersects with and ad-
justs the rules and patterns of Latin rhetorical tradition. Finally, we need a thorough comparative study of the *Mirrour* in relation to its source and analogues in
order to appreciate Love's participation in the history of later medieval spirituality in general, and Carthusian spirituality in particular.

The few facts we know of Love's life have been conveniently collected by Salter
(1974). He was appointed rector, and then prior, of the new Charterhouse of
Mount Grace in Yorkshire in the years 1409–1410. In 1421 he resigned as prior
and in 1424 he died. No information allows us to ascertain his place of birth. On
the basis of manuscript evidence, Salter conjectures that the language of the original *Mirrour* was a variety of northeast Midland English (1974, pp. 23–24). For
the rest we must depend on inference from the status of Mount Grace in the earlier fifteenth century and from the *Mirrour* and the treatise themselves. Love
must have been among the early priors of Mount Grace, founded in 1398, and he
may have been responsible, at least in part, for its role as a center of literary
activity. That Mount Grace had a substantial library is suggested by its gift of a
number of books to the charterhouse at Sheen when it was founded in 1415
(Salter 1974, pp. 31–32).[2] Of Love's own reading, at least among the Latin
writers quoted or mentioned in his text, we cannot be certain. Salter claimed for
him a firm grounding in the writings of Augustine, Gregory, Bernard, and
Thomas Aquinas. But, as we shall see below, until we have a critical edition of his
source, the pseudo-Bonaventuran *Meditationes Vitae Christi*, as well as his own
work, we cannot begin to assess his material additions to the Latin text.

    However we can be reasonably confident that his references to Anglo-Latin
and English devotional texts reflect his own contributions. In the *Mirrour*, in his
treatment of the Annunciation, he alludes to what is probably the *Ancrene Riwle*
(Love 1908, p. 36; Salter 1974, p. 33). At two places, he refers to unnamed

treatises—one on temptation, another on the Pater Noster (Love 1908, pp. 99 and 112). These, he says, are written "not only in latyn but also in englisshe." Clearly Love recognizes his own translation as belonging to the tradition of such treatises. Furthermore, his references imply that he expects his readers to recognize his allusions and to perceive the continuity between his work and others like it. Love's treatise on the Sacrament, which follows the *Mirrour* in most manuscripts, relies on an English translation of Heinrich Suso's *Horologium Sapientiae* which the translator has adapted for his purposes (Salter 1974, p. 33; see also Salter 1957b). In the treatise, he mentions Aelred of Rievaulx's Life of Edward the Confessor as well as the Life of Saint Hugh of Lincoln, prior of the first English Carthusian house (Love 1908, pp. 308 and 311).

One of the most important direct references to Love's reading appears in his instruction in the *Mirrour* concerning silence: "who so wole more pleynely be enformed and tauʒt in Englisshe tonge lete hym loke the tretys that the worthy clerke and holy lyuere maister Walter hyltoun the chanoun of thurgarten wrote in englische" (Love 1908, p. 165).

This reference to Hilton's *Epistle on Mixed Life* reflects a general Carthusian enthusiasm for the fourteenth-century English mystics (Blake 1972, pp. 450–451; Sargent 1976, pp. 231–239). It is clear from manuscript evidence that the best English works were copied assiduously by monks not only in England but also on the Continent. A special affinity between Love's work and Hilton's is further suggested by the appearance of the *Mirrour* together with texts by the earlier mystic in at least two manuscripts. Norman Blake surmises that this sort of juxtaposition may reflect the interests of the audience for whom such manuscripts were compiled; it also implies a fully developed "tradition" in devotional prose of which scribes, writers, and readers were fully aware (Blake 1972).

Of equal interest for a knowledge of Love's spiritual reading as well as his inner life is his description, in the treatise on the Sacrament, of his own affective response to the Eucharist. Here, in terms that echo both Hilton and Rolle, he describes the soul on fire with love, in union with Christ. Yet this rare, deeply personal revelation, serves, as we would expect, an exemplary didactic function. Like Augustine's more famous confession, it operates rhetorically to encourage faith by the testimony of sacramental grace experienced.

In addition, this autobiographical fragment, like the treatise as a whole, seems to have been designed to refute the Lollards. References to the Lollards appear in both the *Mirrour* and the treatise, and they reflect Love's (and the English Church's) immediate political concern with antisacramental reformers who threatened ecclesiastical institutions. While it would be a mistake to overemphasize Love's polemical interests, it is important to recognize the warmth with which he defended the Eucharist. Indeed, it seems likely that the treatise on the Sacrament is appended to the *Mirrour* precisely to define the kind of *sacramental* piety required for a proper meditation on Christ's life. (For discussions of the treatise see Salter 1957a and 1974, pp. 47–49 and Appendix I; see also Schleich 1930.)

A rich manuscript tradition attests the popularity of the *Mirrour* throughout the whole of England, among lay as well as religious readers. The list of extant manuscripts compiled by Salter with the aid of A. I. Doyle includes forty-seven complete copies. The fullest descriptions of the manuscripts are to be found in Doyle's unpublished Ph.D. thesis for Cambridge University (1953) and in Salter's monograph (1974). In this regard, Doyle served as an essential source for Salter; he also provides the basis for the summary given by James Hogg in his recent study (1980).

According to Doyle, the copies of the *Mirrour* are remarkably uniform: "Most copies are on skin, of small quarto or folio size, by practised scribes, with ample colour and illumination of initials, rubrics, headlines, etc., and the Latin notes . . . , contents-table, prologue, side notes, appended treatise varying little in relative disposition" (1953, 1 : 143).

Doyle attributes this uniformity to a "standardised metropolitan manufacture," probably carried on either in Canterbury or in London (1953, 1 : 143; quoted by Hogg 1980, p. 22). Ownership of the manuscripts indicates their wide diffusion both in and out of monasteries. The Charterhouse of Sheen, the Augustinian priory of Newark, Sibilla, abbess of Barking Abbey, Joan, countess of Kent, Edmund, earl of Kent, perhaps even Margery Kempe, owned copies of the *Mirrour* during the course of the fifteenth century (Salter 1974, pp. 12–14).

Two early MSS of northern provenance are of particular interest. At the bottom of one, Cambridge University Library Add. 6578, is written, "Iste liber est de domo Assumpcionis beatae Marie in Monte gracie." At the bottom of the same page, a warning is given, perhaps directed to scribes unfamiliar with northern forms. The note asks that readers recognize northern "gude" for "gode" and "hir" for "heere" in the plural. On the basis of these notes, Salter suggests that this MS may have been the fair copy of Love's original, given out to southern scribes after Archbishop Arundel had approved the text for publication (Salter 1974, p. 11). Another early northern MS, Cambridge University Library Add. 6686, contains the ascription of the *Mirrour* to Love quoted at the beginning of this chapter.

A recent note by Jason Reakes (1980) calls attention to two complex manuscripts—Takamiya MS 20 and the Foyle MS. Both of these MSS include an anonymous fourteenth-century English translation of the Passion section of the

Meditationes Vitae Christi. Reakes believes that these interpolations, in acephalous form, were early and common. And they led, in at least one important instance, to the contamination of Love's text. In Brasenose College MS e. 9 (now in the Bodleian), the base text for the most widely used modern edition of the *Mirrour*, two passages from the anonymous Passion—part of the incipit for Chapter 2 and the concluding paragraph—appear as if they were part of the *Mirrour*. Occurring between the "Die Jovis" and "Die Veneris" sections, they have been taken over unnoticed into Powell's edition (Reakes 1980, pp. 191–202).

A further caution concerning Brasenose College MS e. 9, and all other manuscripts, has been issued by Patrick F. O'Connell (1980). In his study of the *Mirrour* in relation to the *Meditationes*, O'Connell questions the reliability of the annotations in the margins of Love's text. These comments and headings, mainly in Latin, were evidently added very early, perhaps at the time Arundel's certificate of approval was given. The annotator not only seems to have provided incorrect information in identifying those parts of the text original with Love; he may also have made his own additions. O'Connell observes in particular those points at which Love, according to the annotator, transposed materials in his source. In O'Connell's opinion, the translator was simply following a Latin text different from the one available to the annotator. He also suggests tentatively that the last paragraph of the *Mirrour*, which departs in tone and intensity from what precedes it, was written not by Love but by the annotator (1980, p. 34).

O'Connell's hypothesis is that Love's Latin source differed substantially from the text of the *Meditationes* contained in the only modern edition of that work. Although O'Connell has been unable to locate the exact manuscript or version Love used, he presents evidence of sufficient substance to warrant further research.

Above all, the studies by Reakes and O'Connell make it clear that the choice of manuscripts for use in a critical edition of the *Mirrour* and the treatise is more complex than had been thought by earlier editors. Not until further close study of the manuscripts in relation to each other and to their sources has been undertaken can we hope for a sound, reliable text that correctly reflects Love's work.

The earliest printed editions of the *Mirrour* appeared in the last two decades of the fifteenth century. Caxton produced two editions, one in 1486, a second in 1490. Pynson published a first edition in 1494 and a second in 1506; and Wynken de Worde brought out an edition in 1494, with three more in the first decades of the sixteenth century. A slightly revised and modernized version of the *Mirrour* was published at Douai in 1620. And in 1739, a certain E. K. made a modernized translation. From that time until the early twentieth century, no new

edition appeared. Then, in 1908, Lawrence Powell edited the *Mirrour*. This edition is based on Brasenose College MS e. 9, made about 1430. At the time
Powell selected his text, he knew of only twenty-three manuscripts, and he selected the Brasenose MS as "perfect, containing portions intentionally omitted in
other manuscripts" (Powell 1908, p. iii). He collated this manuscript with two
others, the Sherrard MS, then in the possession of Lord Aldenham, and Bodleian
MS e. Musaeo 35. Although Salter, in her monograph, praises the quality of
Powell's edition, she objects to his choice of a manuscript that displays south-
western elements unlikely to have been present in Love's original. To her objection may now be added Reakes's discovery of contamination noted above. Salter
prefers two early northern manuscripts as the basis for a critical edition—Cambridge University Library Add. MSS 6578 and 6686—and she suggests that the
former may even have been the "fair copy made at Mount Grace from Love's
original" (Salter 1974, p. 11). Whether or not this is the case, she argues for the
use of a manuscript of northern provenance as representing the dialect of the region of Mount Grace, and probably of Love.[3]

In 1926, a modernized version of the *Mirrour* was published by a monk of
Parkminster, whom Hogg has identified as Dom Sebastian MacCabe (Salter
1974, p. iii). We are promised a critical edition of the *Mirrour* by Hogg, but
this is not scheduled to appear before 1990. Clearly the task will be a challenging
one, and it will benefit from further studies along the lines established by Reakes
and O'Connell.

Two of the most important literary problems regarding Love's *Mirrour* concern originality in content and prose style. To some extent, these are related, particularly if one wishes to assess the stylistic quality of passages original with Love
as against those that involve direct translation. But the question of style can also
be studied independently, for the *Mirrour* as a whole participates importantly in
the history and development of English devotional prose.

Treatment of the first question, that of material originality, must now take into
account O'Connell's hypothesis noted above. Scholars have universally accepted
the fifteenth-century annotator's judgments concerning Love's additions and modifications. Salter accordingly notes twenty-seven examples of his "originality."
But O'Connell has argued persuasively that twelve of these examples are in fact
paralleled in an independent nineteenth-century translation of the *Meditationes*.
If both Love and the nineteenth-century translator worked from versions of the
source similar to each other but different from that used by the fifteenth-century
annotator, then we cannot rely on the annotator's glossing. Nor can we count on
Peltier's edition of the *Meditationes*. Only with a sound critical edition of the

Latin text, one that records extant variant versions, can we accept or reject O'Connell's findings and determine Love's additions to his source.

On the other hand, there is no question as to the distinctive power and effectiveness of the English author's prose style. So successful was his translation in the fifteenth and sixteenth centuries that Sir Thomas More mentions it as one of three "englysshe bookes as moste may norysshe and encrease deuocyon" (quoted by O'Connell 1980, p. 3). Salter has made a substantial beginning in the analysis of Love's style, both in comparison with his Latin original and in relation to earlier devotional prose. In a valuable chapter on English prose translation, she traces the long history of religious writing from the Old English period to the fifteenth century. In this survey she outlines Love's special place in the history of vernacular devotional prose. Throughout the chapter, Salter argues for a certain degree of continuity in the formation of a native devotional prose style from the high Middle Ages to the fifteenth century. It is a continuity based on the common use of Latin models and rhetorical habits, on the demands of a specialized audience, and on the prevailing religious temper of the times. "The process of translation," she concludes, "especially when carried on in circumstances of religious need, had readily definable influences upon the development of one line of literary prose and . . . those influences worked characteristically towards clarity, moderation and sparing embellishment" (Salter 1974, p. 218). But she also takes pains to insist that the continuity is not a simple one. Here she calls attention to one of the most interesting and challenging questions in relation to Love's *Mirrour*.

The problem of "continuity" in the history of Middle English religious prose is an important one, and it has not yet been satisfactorily treated. R. W. Chambers was the first to argue for an unbroken development from Old to Middle English prose, and then to Thomas More, by looking especially at religious and contemplative texts (1932). But as Salter, Blake, and others have suggested, his principles for establishing this continuity are neither fully defined nor adequate (see N. Davis 1961; Salter 1956a, 1974, p. 215; Wilson 1959). Chambers had described the development as taking place mainly in the West Midlands and then moving northward. Salter, on the other hand, argues, though not systematically, for an eastern as well as a western tradition in Middle English prose, one that includes not only the western *Ancrene Riwle*, but also the thirteenth-century eastern *Virtues and Vices* and the *Mirrour* (Salter 1974, p. 215).

Two very useful articles, widely different in aims and interest, suggest frameworks for a full reconsideration of later medieval English devotional prose, including the continuities observed by Salter. The first, published in 1952 by Margery M. Morgan, deals specifically with a fourteenth-century devotional text, *A Talking of the Love of God*. Morgan describes an English "tradition" which shaped certain kinds of religious writing at least from the early thirteenth century on. Writers in this tradition had a very clearly defined, narrow subject matter on which they meditated deeply and continuously, making their own the devotional idiom of their predecessors. Most of these writers depended not only on each other but on common Latin models. Yet, although their language and their concepts are very largely traditional, most of the texts remain individual, marked by the writer's particular "faith, love and aspiration" (Morgan 1952, p. 97).

Morgan's essay offers an exemplary demonstration of her thesis. By comparing *A Talking* with a few devotional writings current in the early thirteenth century, including the *Wooing of Our Lord* and the *Orison of Our Lord*, she shows dependence as well as originality in the treatment of borrowed materials. Her conclusion—that all three writers "had in mind certain Latin sources and already existing English versions of them"—seems irrefutable (Morgan 1952, p. 99). Though her sample is a very small one, it establishes important directions, I think, for a much larger study of intertextuality in Middle English devotional writing, including Love's *Mirrour*. Such a study would necessarily include medieval Latin as well as English texts; and it would involve discussion not only of themes, imagery, and meditative structures, but also of rhetorical techniques adapted from Latin into English and then transformed to become part of the native literary idiom. Habits of devotional thought and styles of expression, developed among highly gifted writers from century to century, were remarkably homogeneous, and they had a very powerful effect on the formation of English literary prose. If these habits, and the processes by which they evolved, were well defined, we would be in a better position to discuss the style of individual writers like Love and to describe their specific contributions to the history of English prose.

A second framework within which to consider a "tradition" of Middle English religious prose has been proposed by Blake. He looks to homogeneity of audience rather than style, defining audience as the "social milieu in which a work was written and the way in which it was disseminated" (1972, p. 440). He distinguishes between a specialized audience for religious works, one with easily defined interests and expectations, and a general audience for other kinds of works. The devotional pieces form a homogeneous whole, according to Blake, while works outside the "tradition" are "essentially ad hoc affairs," often translations done at the behest of a particular patron (1972, p. 452). Works written within the tradition can be characterized, among other things, by their dependence on Latin rhetorical practices, a dependence that resulted in certain stylistic habits and patterns; by contrast, works for the general audience are "very diverse in style and there will often seem to be little unity between one work and the next" (1972, p. 453).

Blake's argument is general, and it repeats from a different angle what Morgan and Salter had already observed. But it does emphasize an important element in the production of medieval devotional treatises like Love's. The writers, who were also part of the readership for works like their own, were clearly aware of a limited audience whose tastes and expectations they knew well. In this circumstance, a conservative literary style, frequent borrowing and allusion from text to text, and straightforward translation from Latin into a familiar, relatively simple English idiom would naturally play an important part. Indeed, the existence of just this small, select readership must be regarded as a sine qua non for the development of literary prose in later medieval England.

Salter's analysis of Love's style in Chapters 7 and 8 of her monograph, which offers the only sustained study of this kind in print, does not provide the kind of full comparative analysis I have suggested above. It does, however, establish a very useful beginning for further work. In her comparison of Love's prose with his Latin original, she shows both his dependence on his Latin model for certain kinds of rhetorical effect and his preference for clearer, looser, simpler sentence constructions than his original. In her study of vocabulary, she discovers a strong preference for native English diction: though the "Latin-French element is . . . considerable . . . it never rises above one-seventh of the total word content" (1974, pp. 264–273).

Chapter 8 addresses the question of Love's material as well as his stylistic originality in the "Die Veneris" or Passion section of the *Mirrour*. On the basis of O'Connell's findings, it may be necessary to revise certain of Salter's conclusions, particularly with regard to Love's putative transposition of materials and his additions. Nevertheless, it is clear that the translator, taking into account the needs of his audience, did in fact strive to provide his readers with "the mylke of ly3te doctrine" rather than the "sadde mete of grete clergie" in determining content as well as style. To this end he clearly omitted matter that was digressive or overly fraught with exemplary quotation.

Love also added explanatory glosses to frame the matter of his original. One passage of extraordinary beauty at the beginning of the "Die Veneris" section deserves special attention. Here Love almost certainly speaks in his own voice as he describes the young, fair Christ about to be hanged on the cross. I quote it to exemplify the great clarity, simplicity, and power of a style still in need of adequate description:

> Wherfore thou schalt ymagyne and ynwardely thinke of hym in his passioun as of a faire 3onge man of the age of xxxiii 3ere/ that were the faireste/ the wiseste/ and the moste ri3twysse in his leuinge; and moost goodly and innocent that euere was or my3t be in this world so falsely accused so enviously pursewed/ so wrongfully demede/ and so despitously slayne/ as the process of this passioun afterward telleth/ and all for thy loue. Also vnderstonde/ as clerkes seyne and resoun techith/ that in his bodily kynde of man he was of the clennest complexioun that euere was man or my3te be; wherfore hauynge this in mynde he was the more tendre in the body/ and

so foloweth that the peyne in the body were the more sore and bittre and the harder to suffre. (Love 1908, pp. 216–217)

With a doubling of verbs, a careful choice of adjectives, mainly English in origin, and parallel construction, Love achieves a precise, concretely imagined figure of the Christ who is the subject of the meditation or "process" before him. How much this elegantly simple style owes to the devotional tradition, and how much to Love's genius, remains for scholars of Middle English prose to determine.

Love's prose style may also be profitably studied beside another fifteenth-century translation of the *Meditationes Vitae Christi*. The anonymous *Speculum Devotorum*, recently edited by Hogg (1973–1974), was written by a fellow Carthusian who knew of Love's *Mirrour* and may have used it. The two texts differ substantially in style, and a comparative study would certainly help to illuminate the distinctive stylistic habits of both writers. Along the same lines, one might usefully consider both the *Mirrour* and the *Speculum* in relation to the nine known Middle English translations of parts of the *Meditationes*. The study of prose style is not easy either synchronically or diachronically, and it is made the more complex by the fact of translation. Nevertheless, in Love's case, it is a project worthy of pursuit both for its own sake and for the history of English literary prose.

For students of intellectual and spiritual history, a subject of considerable interest is the *Mirrour*'s participation in the genre of devotional lives of Christ. From the later fourteenth century on, these works, including the *Fruyt of the Redemption*, the *Speculum Devotorum*, and Walter Kennedy's *Passioun of Christ*, exhibit an exemplary realism, designed to elicit meditation by the power of the literal word or event. All of them reflect that attitude toward Christ's humanity that had developed through the later Middle Ages under the successive influences of Saint Anselm, Saint Bernard, and the Franciscans. Though Salter gives an excellent outline of this history, close comparative study would yield valuable information about religious expression, iconographic patterns, and meditative practices in the later Middle Ages.

In a related area, substantial attention has already been given to the influence of Love's *Mirrour* on fifteenth-century play cycles which emphasize the literal events of Christ's life in order to provoke meditation. Emile Mâle (1922), Salter (1974), V. A. Kolve (1966), K. S. Block (1922), and Rosemary Woolf (1972) have all observed connections. Most recently the subject has been treated in a dissertation by Marian Davis. She argues that a reviser of the N-Town Cycle, or

Ludus Coventriae, used Love's *Mirrour* in an effort to "unify and enrich" the cycle (M. Davis 1979). Both the *Mirrour* and the plays insist on the importance of contemplating Christ's life as if its events were present to the audience; it is therefore not surprising to find the reviser adapting elements from Love's translation to provide the drama with a systematic meditative structure.

Finally, in terms of Carthusian history, one might well compare Carthusian translations of the *Meditationes Vitae Christi*, including the *Vita Jesu Christi* of Ludolphus of Saxony, Love's *Mirrour*, and the anonymous fifteenth-century *Speculum Devotorum*. These texts vary considerably in their methods of reading their source and glossing or augmenting it. In their divergent developments from the original we may discern distinctive formulations of the meditative process and responses to audience need. Ludolphus's text, produced in the fourteenth century in Latin, is by far the most scholarly of the three and uses traditional methods of exegesis. The events of the Life are glossed closely, often word by word, with citations from the Fathers. The anonymous *Speculum* by a monk of the English Charterhouse of Sheen occupies a middle ground. This translator is scrupulous in his reading of Christ's history, using several sources, but chiefly Peter Comestor and Nicholas of Lyra, to supplement pseudo-Bonaventura. His principal interests, however, are not so much those of the traditional scriptural scholar as those of the meticulous historian and psychologist. He seeks out the circumstantial implications of the text, explaining why, for example, Jesus' traitors were carrying lanterns, what Jesus used to wipe the blood-sweat from his face in the garden of Gethsemane. By contrast, Love's interests are dramatic and meditative. Neither a glossator in the traditional sense, nor a historian, he stresses the immediate imaginative moments in Christ's life for the sake of those that "ben of symple vnderstondynge."

If Love's single work of translation does not qualify him as a "major" writer, the quality of his prose admits him without question to rank among the major English stylists. As heir to the native devotional tradition of the thirteenth and fourteenth centuries, he could draw upon a rich storehouse of diction as well as a complex variety of rhetorical patterns naturalized from Latin. Close comparative analysis of Love's style, study of his audience, and examination of his place in spiritual history all await scholarly attention. These projects, however, should be based upon a sound critical edition of the *Mirrour*.

NOTES

1. Cambridge University Library MS Add. 6686. A. I. Doyle discovered these words on the final page of the MS with the use of ultraviolet light.
2. For a full discussion of the library at Mount Grace, see Hogg (1980, pp. 14–17); for book lists,

see Thompson (1930, pp. 313–334). David Knowles (1955, p. 343) gives a useful summary of Carthusian literary taste.

3. Richard Batteiger (1971) has edited a portion of the *Mirrour* using Cambridge University Library MS Add. 6578.

BIBLIOGRAPHY

PRIMARY WORKS

For a full list of manuscript versions of Love's work see Salter (1981); for details of printed editions see STC 3260–3269 and also

Love, Nicholas (1908) *The Myrrour of the Blessed Lyf of Jesu Christ.* Edited by Lawrence Powell. Oxford: Clarendon Press.

———— (1926) *The Mirror of the Blessed Life of Jesus Christ. Edited by a Monk of Parkminster.* New York: Benziger Bros.

SECONDARY WORKS

Baier, Walter (1977) "Untersuchungen zu den Passionbetrachtungen in der *Vita Christi* des Ludolf von Sachsen." *Analecta Cartusiana*, 44, 325–338.

Batteiger, Richard P. (1971) "Love's *Mirrour* and the Aesthetics of Devotion." *DAI*, 32, 378A–379A.

Bennett, H. S. (1947) *Chaucer and the Fifteenth Century.* Oxford History of English Literature. Oxford: Clarendon Press.

Blake, Norman (1972) "Middle English Prose and Its Audience." *Anglia*, 90, 437–455.

Block, K. S., ed. (1922) *Ludus Coventriae.* EETS, es. 120.

Chambers, R. W. (1932) *On the Continuity of English Prose.* London: Oxford University Press. (A separately published text of the introduction to EETS, os 186.)

Davis, Marian (1979) "Nicholas Love and the N-Town Cycle." *DAI*, 40, 1454A.

Davis, Norman (1961) "Styles in English Prose of the Late Middle and Early Modern Period." In *Langue et littérature*, pp. 165–184. Bibliotheque de la Faculté de Philosophie de l'Université de Liège 161. Paris: [no publisher given].

Deanesly, Margaret (1920a) *The Lollard Bible and Other Medieval Versions.* Cambridge: Cambridge University Press.

———— (1920b) "Vernacular Books in England." *MLR*, 15, 349–358.

Doyle, A. E. (1953) "A Survey of the Origins and Circulation of Theological Writings in English in the Fourteenth, Fifteenth and Sixteenth Centuries." 2 vols. Ph.D. diss., Cambridge University.

Gruys, Albert (1976) *Bibliographie generale: Auteurs cartusiens. Cartusiana*, vol. 1. Paris: CNRS.

———— (1978) *Supplement. Cartusiana*, vol. 3. Paris: CNRS.

Hogg, James, ed. (1973–1974) *Speculum Devotorum*. Analecta Cartusiana, 12–13. Salzburg.

———— (1980) "Mount Grace Charterhouse and Late Medieval Spirituality." *Collectanea Cartusiensia*, 3, 1–43.

Knowles, David D. (1955) *The Religious Orders in England*, vol 2. Cambridge: Cambridge University Press.

Kolve, V. A. (1966) *The Play Called Corpus Christi*. Stanford: Stanford University Press.

Mâle, Emile (1922) *L'art réligieux de la fin du moyen âge en France*. Paris: A. Colin.

Morgan, Margery M. (1952) "*A Talking of the Love of God* and the Continuity of Stylistic Tradition in Middle English Prose Meditations." *RES*, ns 10, 97–116.

O'Connell, Patrick F. (1980) "Love's *Mirror* and the Meditationes Vitae Christi." *Analecta Cartusiana*, 82, 3–44.

Peltier, A. C., ed. (1864–1871) *Opera Omnia Sancti Bonaventurae*. Vol. 12: *Meditationes Vitae Christi* (1868). Paris: Ludovicus Vives.

Reakes, Jason (1980) "A Middle English Prose Translation of the Meditaciones de Passione Christi and Its Links with Manuscripts of Love's *Myrrour*." *N&Q*, 27, 199–202.

Salter, Elizabeth (1956a) "Continuity in Middle English Devotional Prose." *JEGP*, 55, 417–422.

———— (1956b) "Punctuation in an Early Manuscript of Love's *Mirror*." *RES*, ns 7, 11–18.

———— (1957a) "Continuity and Change in Middle English Versions of the *Meditationes Vitae Christi*." *MAE*, 26, 25–31.

———— (1957b) "Two Middle English Versions of a Prayer to the Sacrament." *Archiv*, 194, 113–121.

———— (1964) "Ludolphus of Saxony and His English Translators." *MAE*, 33, 26–35.

———— (1974) *Nicholas Love's Myrrour of the Blessed Lyf of Jesu Christ*. Analecta Cartusiana 10. Salzburg: Institut für englische Sprache und Literatur, Universität Salzburg.

———— (1981) "The Manuscripts of Nicholas Love's *Myrrour of the Blessed Lyf of Jesu Christ* and Related Texts." In *Middle English Prose: Essays on Bibliographical Problems*, edited by A. S. G. Edwards and Derek Pearsall, pp. 115–127. New York: Garland.

Sargent, Michael G. (1976) "The Transmission by the English Carthusians of Some Late Medieval Spiritual Writings." *Journal of Ecclesiastical History*, 27, 225–240.

Schleich, G. (1930) "Über die Enstehungszeit und den Verfasser der mittelenglischen Bearbeitung von Susos Horologium." *Archiv*, 162, 26–34.

Thompson, E. Margaret (1930) *The Carthusian Order in England*. New York and Toronto: Macmillan Co.

Wilson, R. M. (1959) "On the Continuity of English Prose." *Mélanges de linguistique et de philologie: Fernand Mossé in memoriam*, pp. 486–494. Paris: Didier.

Woolf, Rosemary (1972) *The English Mystery Plays*. London: Routledge and Kegan Paul.

Workman, Samuel K. (1940) *Fifteenth Century Translation as an Influence on English Prose*. Princeton: Princeton University Press.

CHAPTER 5

Julian of Norwich

Christina von Nolcken

Julian of Norwich, our "first English woman of letters,"[1] must be today the most familiar and beloved of the fourteenth- and fifteenth-century English mystics. Her work is known in several languages,[2] she features in modern novels, she inspired Florence Nightingale, her name is invoked in the dedication of an organ composition, and her message of hope helps conclude Huxley's *Eyeless in Gaza* and Eliot's "Little Gidding."[3] The site of her anchorhold is visited by members of many denominations, and the six-hundredth anniversary of her "reuelacion of loue" was marked by a festival and a flurry of publication.[4]

In her life, however, she seems to have been relatively unknown: certainly her writings—two versions of a single text—were little circulated. While there are many extant manuscripts of the *Cloud of Unknowing*, Hilton's *Scale of Perfection*, and Rolle's *Form of Living*, the short version of Julian's text is preserved in a single mid-fifteenth-century anthology, and, apart from brief extracts in a collection of ca. 1500, there are only seventeenth- and eighteenth-century witnesses for her Long Text. Julian's comparative obscurity was doubtless partly because she was a woman: "Botte for I am a womann, schulde I therfore leve that I schulde nouʒt telle ʒowe the goodenes of god, syne that I sawe in that same tyme that is his wille, that it be knawenn?" (222/46–48),[5] but it may also be because her work is not reductively didactic or directed at a historically located audience.[6]

Paradoxically, these must also be the reasons why her work has been so valued since her death. Her visions and thought are obviously conditioned by the concerns of her age, but her text finally transcends history. Thanks to recognition of its lasting spiritual value by Augustine Baker and the seventeenth-century English Benedictines on the Continent we know the Long Text.[7] Today this is generally recognized as a "spiritual masterpiece" (Underhill 1932, p. 807), "one of the most valuable documents of ascetical experience in the whole range of mystical literature" (Coleman 1938, p. 132). That the achievement is a woman's gives it particular interest.

Both versions of Julian's text are concerned with her extraordinary experience on May 13, 1373 (285/2–4). Before that she had desired three gifts of God: further acquaintance with Christ's Passion; an illness when she was thirty that might seem mortal even to herself; and the wounds of contrition, compassion, and longing for God. In 1373, when she was thirty and one-half years old, she had such an illness. After she had suffered for about a week and been near death for two days and three nights, the curate came to attend her end. She fastened her eyes upon the cross which he held before her, and from early morning during some hours (631/37–40) she had fifteen "schewings,"[8] mainly focused on the Second Person of the Trinity. While they lasted her only pain was in sympathy with Christ's sufferings at the Passion, but her own then returned, and "as a fule" (266/18; cf. 634/28) she doubted the validity of what she had seen. She was then subjected that night in her sleep to diabolic attack, something she had expected and indeed hoped for. When she awoke she was at last able to accept all in "reste and pees" (267/39; cf. 638/25). A culminating showing of Christ reigning in the soul confirmed her faith, and she then demonstrated to herself the effectiveness of what she had learned by resisting further diabolic attack.

Although her Short Text is extant only in a scribally edited mid-fifteenth-century manuscript, scholars accept that on the whole it represents an account set down soon after this experience. In it Julian declares her intention to ponder the meaning of what she had been shown (247/1). The next version, some six times longer, apparently incorporates the results of twenty years of meditation (520/86, 732/14). The Long Text provides extended and detailed explications of her visions in a commentary that has obviously evolved by stages. During this time Julian seems to have had no further showing, but she did receive further insights—"dyuerse tymes our lord gafe me more syght" (327/35)—as to the meaning of what she had already seen. This notably enabled her to include and discuss at length the example of the lord and the servant (Chap. 51). Even with the Long Text, by any standards a work of genius, she did not consider her task completed: "This boke is begonne by goddys gyfte and his grace, but it is nott yett performyd, as to my syght" (731/2–3).

Julian reveals a good deal, thus, about her spiritual biography, one that Riehle suggests corresponds closely with patterns developed on the Continent by late medieval female mystics (1981, pp. 27–28).[9] We know little about her actual biography. Relevant information has been most completely assembled by Colledge and Walsh (1978a), and it is unlikely that much will be added to this. A scribal preface to the Short Text states that Julian was still alive in 1413, a recluse at Norwich. A will of 1415 supports the early tradition that she was enclosed at the parish church of Saint Julian at Conisford, Norwich. It seems that she adopted its patron's name. We do not know her own, or when she became a recluse, or whether she was ever a nun. At some time between 1402 and 1415 Margery Kempe visited her to discuss revelations (Meech and Allen 1940, pp. 42–43). A bequest in 1416 "a Julian recluz a Norwich" may indicate that she was then still alive, but the reference may be to someone else.

We unfortunately know nothing about Julian's education or who might have influenced her. She describes herself as "leued" (222/41), "a symple creature vnlettyrde" (285/2). Some, like Glasscoe (1976), understand from this that Julian was illiterate and dictated her texts. She need not have been uneducated, for like Margery Kempe she could have had ecclesiastics read aloud to her and instruct her. Others, for example Colledge and Walsh, have dismissed such words as "modest self-disparagement" (1978a, p. 222) and regard Julian as literate, indeed learned, in both Latin and English. That her account of mystical experience is in the vernacular, however, might support scholars like Reynolds (1958, pp. xvi–xxi) and Riehle (1981, p. 29) who argue that she was literate only in English but that she might have known the contents of Latin works from spiritual directors.

Given the great interest and merit of Julian's texts, their comparative brevity, and the paucity of textual evidence for them, it is surprising that editions in Middle English have appeared only recently. Early attempts, notably by Reynolds in the 1940s and 1950s, did not get beyond dissertation form. Finally, in 1976 Glasscoe made available a text based on BL Sloane MS 2499, and in 1978 Beer edited the Short Text. Nineteen seventy-eight also saw publication by Colledge and Walsh of what will surely remain the definitive texts, with full editorial apparatus, of both versions.[10] Yet Julian's work has been well-known for more than a century. Since 1877 there has been a succession of modernized printings of her Long Text, as there has of the Short Text since the rediscovery of its manuscript in 1909.

The history of scholarly discussion of Julian's writings reflects this textual history. Modernizations were directed at readers primarily interested in theological and devotional issues, and most secondary studies had a corresponding emphasis. Much was written on Julian's orthodoxy, and her thoughts on such subjects as prayer, sin and evil, and the motherhood of God. The nature of her experience was discussed, notably by Thouless (1924), who described himself as "a Christian modern psychologist" (p. 5), and by Molinari (1958), who analyzed the modes of the visions and concluded that Julian's sickness was not a form of nervous hysteria. Scholars unfamiliar with Middle English ignored except most superficially the texture of her writings. With a few exceptions, scholars with primarily linguistic or literary interests have turned their attention to Julian only very recently.

In only one area have such scholars been able to build on previous discussion. It has obviously always been of vital relevance to all kinds of analysis to identify the teachings, writings, or artifacts that might have influenced Julian. Some she indicates herself. The story of Saint Cecilia, which she heard recounted by a cleric, seems to have stimulated her initial desire for three wounds (204/46– 206/53, a detail suppressed in the Long Text). She confirms, too, that she must have been influenced by iconography: "I leevyd sadlye alle the peynes of Cryste as halye kyrke schewys and techys, and also the payntyngys of crucyfexes that er made be the grace of god aftere the techynge of haly kyrke to the lyknes of Crystes passyonn, als farfurthe as man ys witte may reche" (202/15–18, also suppressed in the Long Text). In her visions, indeed, "a Gothic crucifix has come to life" (Graef 1959, p. 264), and hers are probably the most compelling and harrowing descriptions of incidents of the Passion in Middle English. Other examples of these kinds of influence are easily traceable: Windeatt (1977, p. 13) points out that her image of the soul as a child springing from the hideous body follows a traditional iconographic idea; Colledge and Walsh trace pervasive influence from the largely Franciscan spirituality of the vernacular lyrics and also suggest that her account of diabolic visitation was influenced by the *Speculum Christiani* (1978a, p. 635).[11]

When trying to give expression to her experience Julian may consciously have drawn on formulations from a wide range of written material, although she never incorporates such formulations wholesale into her text. Commentators have increasingly wished to argue that she was well-read, but as she seldom refers directly to an authority and as she only rarely quotes, and then briefly and inaccurately, discussion has been inconclusive. In places Julian's writings seem to be a tissue of allusion; possibly she was here remembering material rather than consulting it. If she had learned sources, she had entirely assimilated them. In 1952 Reynolds suggested Julian's wide familiarity with the Bible, with such vernacular works as the *Ancrene Riwle*, and (probably in translation) with such works as Richard of Saint Victor's *Benjamin Minor*, Pseudo-Dionysus's *Mystical Theology*, and the writings of Flemish and German mystics. Indeed, some time ago Allen considered the possibility that Flemish and German mysticism was influential in Norfolk (Meech and Allen 1940, p. liv), although Riehle has questioned whether Julian herself was influenced (1981, p. 27). Gradually other works have been proposed that Julian might have known, and the list reaches considerable length in Colledge and Walsh (1978a). Here is claimed for Julian "an exceptionally good grounding in Latin, in Scripture and in the liberal arts" enabling her to have read "widely in Latin and vernacular spiritual classics" (p. 44).

In other areas scholars with literary or linguistic interests have not been able to build on previous discussion. Especially concerning Julian's style early comments now seem imprecise and impressionistic: according to many it was "quaint," it had "le trait un peu grêle de certains sculpteurs médiocres" (Goyau 1913, p. 850). Praise reflected the value a commentator placed on what Julian had to say: her style resembled "a moorland stream" (Coleman 1938, p. 150), her words were "fragrant as ointment poured out" (Knowles 1927, p. 147), with beauty "as of the song of birds on a Spring evening" (Hubbard 1928–1929, p. 140). More incisive literary discussion began in 1956 when Wilson considered Julian's use of such devices of the Latin rhetoricians as she might have learned from other vernacular writers. This discussion was furthered by Reynolds (1958), and Colledge and Walsh (1978a) go so far as to argue that Julian was directly familiar with the writings of the rhetoricians. Other analyses to date consist mainly of Stone's (1970), which associates stylistic features with authorial personality, and Riehle's (1981), which considers the metaphorical language of the medieval English mystics generally.

Discussion of the structure and organization of Julian's texts has followed a similar course. Julian herself considered that her experience was meaningfully ordered: she notes, for example, the significant echo of our Lord's first words to her in his last words (269/29–32, 646/60–63). Such comments, as well as her own verbal echoes and careful cross-references between sections, suggest that she wished to reproduce this order in her own presentation. Even Chapters 73–86 of the Long Text, which read at first like an afterthought, become structurally significant when one realizes the extent to which they sum up years of meditation: "And fro the tyme þat it was shewde, I desyerde oftyn tymes to wytt in what was oure lords menyng. And xv yere after and mor, I was answeryd in gostly vnderstondyng, seyeng thus: What, woldest thou wytt thy lordes menyng in this thyng? Wytt it wele, loue was his menyng. Who shewyth it the? Loue. (What shewid he the? Love.) Wherfore shewyth he it the? For loue" (732/13–733/18). Scholars long overlooked this order, however, and tended to dismiss Julian's writings as "unsystematic" (Webster 1972–1973, p. 230; Sayer 1973, p. 30). Others who saw them as carefully organized—with a "highly artistic structure" (Walsh 1967, p. 49)—supported their claims only incidentally or through paraphrase. Only recently has a more literary approach made possible more incisive analysis. Notably, Windeatt has used the structure of contemporary dream poems to provide "some contemporary literary correlative which can help locate what is most individual in Julian's text, highlighting the way in which autobiographical conditions have been transmuted into literary effects, and so helping toward some critical understanding of what the mystic achieves as an artist" (1980, p. 57).

Literary consideration of what was involved in Julian's revision of her text has also yielded fresh insights. Here too discussion for long did not move beyond confirming Harford's proposal (1911, p. 8) that the Short Text came first and was not a digest of the Long. Again it was Windeatt who effectively pointed a new direction (1977) by analyzing the greater meditative assurance of the Long Text and Julian's increased understanding of its universal relevance as reflected in its larger number of abstract terms and its more complex, varied sentence structure. Schmidt's discussion (1980) of the imaginative rehandling of data that must have taken place between the versions also demonstrated forcibly that Julian's texts are accessible to this kind of literary analysis.

The availability of editions in Middle English, therefore, has encouraged new kinds of analysis of Julian's texts. Literary critics, interested not so much in the nature of Julian's initial inspiration as in subsequent stages of interpretation and expression, will probably pursue the directions outlined above. For many, of course, the main interest of Julian's writings will remain theological and devotional—as, indeed, she would have wished: "For the shewyng I am nott good, but if I loue god the better; and in as much as 3e loue god the better, it is more to 3ow than to me" (321/2–3).[12] But these readers too will be unable to ignore the historical, linguistic, and literary perspectives that are increasingly being established for Julian and her texts.

Colledge and Walsh have done much to locate Julian within English contemplative tradition. Insofar as this tradition is "intimately connected with the beginnings of vernacular literature" (Underhill 1932, p. 805), a place should also be sought for her within the history of English prose; this has been hardly discussed since Chambers (1932). As Julian's work was little circulated, it is unlikely that it will prove to have exerted any appreciable direct influence on later writers.[13] Julian's relationships with her predecessors and immediate contemporaries, however, invite further discussion. When considering her stylistic models, for example, scholars may finally wish to disagree with Colledge and Walsh's contention that she worked with increasing assurance within Latin rhetorical tradition. They may instead stress the influence of more commonplace forms, such as sermons. As D. S. H., a Benedictine of Stanbrook, pointed out, "vernacular eloquence was not necessarily a literary product. Such devices as alliteration, rhetorical repetition, and the numerical classification of which Julian appears so inordinately fond, were familiar pulpit expedients" (1959, p. 707).

The lack of established procedures for analyzing and discussing Middle English prose will delay consideration of Julian's stylistic relationship with her immediate contemporaries. Scholars who regard style as choice or difference constituted by systematic departures from a set of norms will consider that the first desideratum of Middle English stylistic studies is a description of the norms available to the speaker or writer. Doubtless there will eventually be attempts to provide such a description, as well as discussion of how to define and describe individual deviations. For the time being, however, the approach of those who start stylistic analysis at the level of the individual author seems more feasible.

Even discussions with this relatively narrow focus have been few, and Julian's prose demands further consideration. Most insistently, we need to know whether her work was written or dictated. We still do not have convincing criteria for distinguishing a dictated style. Features that Julian's prose shares with that of the illiterate Margery Kempe—such as the frequent use of tautologically paired words and constructions relying on repetition—appear also in much other prose of the period. That Julian revised her work provides a further complication. Stylistic differences between versions perhaps reflect partly the difference between dictated and written composition; Julian may have become literate during the years separating her texts.

We need, indeed, more discussion generally of the stylistic relationship between the Short and the Long texts. Julian evidently worked over an extended period at both interpreting and expressing (whether with or without an amanuensis) the meaning of her showings. Hers was the problem of all mystics who try to communicate the essentially incommunicable: "The nomber of the words passyth my wyttes and my vnderstandyng and alle my myghtes, for they were in þe hyghest, as to my syght, for ther in is comprehendyd I can nott telle what; but the joy that I saw in the shewyng of them passyth alle that hart can thynk or soule may desyre" (403/11−15). To follow how a vigorous means of expression evolves in Julian's texts becomes particularly compelling when we remember how little precedent there was for writing on such matters in English. We see, for example, the coordinating and basically repetitive style of the period increasingly turned to rhetorical advantage. Through the use of repetition and balance in sentence parts Julian conveys her insights at an emotional as well as an intellectual level. The tendency is clear, indeed often marked, in the Short Text, in passages such as 243/30−34, 252/3−7 which define God, for example, or in Julian's apostrophe to sin (271/26−36, suppressed in the later version). The possibility of scribal conflation means, however, that we cannot be sure whether the Short Text always represents Julian's earliest style. Certainly this "rhetoric of accumulation"[14] is even more prominent in the Long Text, again in passages of heightened emotive force such as definitions of God (as at 431/17−19, 493/30−31, 590/13−19, 601/4−602/10) or Julian's well-known statement on the Trinity: "For the trinitie is god, god is the trinitie. The trinitie is our maker, the trinitie is our keper, the trinitie is our everlasting louer, the trinitie is our endlesse ioy and our bleisse, by our lord Jesu Christ, and in our lord Jesu Christ" (295/11−14).

Reynolds (1958, pp. xxiii−xxxi) touches upon Julian's stylistic range, another topic that demands further consideration. Julian describes three modes of revelation, largely corresponding with those traditional since Augustine: "be bodylye

syght, and be worde formede in myne vndyrstandynge, and be gastelye syght"
(224/2–3; cf. 272/58–59, 323/29–30, etc.); the extent to which she modifies
her style to convey each mode needs investigating. Hers seems essentially to have
been a visual imagination, and the concrete, adjectival style of much of her work
appropriately represents this. It vividly conveys what she sees physically, conditioned as this often is by contemporary art: "And after this I saw beholdyng the
body plentuous bledyng in semyng of the scoregyng, as thus. The feyer skynne
was broken full depe in to the tendyr flessch, with sharpe smytynges all a bout the
sweete body. The hote blode ranne out so plentuously that ther was neyther seen
skynne ne wounde, but as it were all blode" (342/3–7). Julian uses this concrete
style also to convey more spiritual insights, for it appears in her analogies (e.g.,
212/8–10, 605/43–607/57), in her metaphors (e.g., 299/4–6, 566/22–
567/29), in "allegorical writing of the highest quality."[15] But Julian can also
control long passages of expository prose, as in the chapters surrounding the
fourteenth revelation in the Long Text. It is probable that Julian's style will finally impress as much for its variety and flexibility as for its vividness and force-
ful patterning.

Analysis reveals the great care with which Julian's work, especially the Long
Text, was composed. Her art reflects the strength of her commitment to communicate her experience. That this art often seems artless reflects her own sincerity
and humility. The profundity of what she says has been much discussed. That she
developed a medium that almost always matches the message has been less frequently remarked. It is to defining more and more precisely the nature of this
achievement that future literary discussion must apply itself.

NOTES

1. The phrase, frequently quoted, is Underhill's (1932, p. 807).
2. Sawyer (1978) lists translations in French, German, and Italian.
3. For such appearances in modern works, see P. F. Chambers (1955, p. 60).
4. Examples are Sayer (1973), and Allchin and the Sisters of the Love of God (1973).
5. All references to Julian's texts are to page and line in Colledge and Walsh (1978a).
6. She frequently refers to this as comprising "alle myne evynn cristene" (219/1–2; cf. 319/33),
   "swylke menn and womenn that for goddes love hates synne and dysposes thamm to do goddes
   wille" (274/6–8), "thame that schalle be safe" (222/52). Once she restricts it to each man and
   woman who "desyres to lyeve contemplatyfelye" (215/42).
7. For a full survey of "people who were interested in the Middle English mystics, who referred to
   them, who quoted them or who took the trouble to possess, or to copy, their works" from the
   seventeenth to the twentieth century, see Birrell (1976).
8. The term is Julian's; it has gained general currency through its use by Reynolds (1958) and by
   Colledge and Walsh (1978a and 1978b).

9. Although references here are to the 1981 translation, Riehle's book appeared in German in 1977.
10. Colledge and Walsh's edition fittingly grew from Reynolds's pioneer work, although her texts were not finally used.
11. Julian also notes where her imagination was not stimulated as one might expect—she does not see angels, for example (710/22–23), or hell or purgatory (427/2–5). At one point she asked to have revealed to her the future of a certain person she loved, but this was not granted (252/14–16, 432/3–6). Some female mystics—Mechtild of Hackeborn, for example—did not hesitate to claim this last kind of information.
12. Colledge and Walsh's modernization and much of the introduction to their edition have such an emphasis; for recent articles demonstrating such continuing interest, see, for example, Børresen (1978), Ryder (1978), and Clark (1981). Roland Maisonneuve's forthcoming "Visionary Universe of Julian of Norwich" will make an important further contribution, as will C. Brant Pelphrey's forthcoming "Love Was His Meaning: The Theology and Mysticism of Julian of Norwich."
13. Knowlton (1973) has discussed Julian's "very slight" influence on later lyric tradition.
14. The phrase is Salter's (1974, p. 270). Much of what she says about Love's style could apply to Julian.
15. Walsh (1961, p. 31) evaluates thus the parable of the lord and the servant.

BIBLIOGRAPHY

Manuscripts and editions of Julian's texts are listed in full; modernizations are listed selectively and are arranged chronologically. Only those secondary studies referred to in the text are included. For fuller bibliography, see Molinari (1958, pp. 199–209), Sawyer (1978, pp. 53–123), and Colledge and Walsh (1978a, pp. 761–773).

PRIMARY WORKS

SHORT TEXT

MANUSCRIPT

BL Add. 37790, fols. 97–115

PRINTED EDITIONS

Beer, Frances, ed. (1978) *Julian of Norwich's Revelations of Divine Love: The Shorter Version ed. from BL Add. MS. 37790.* MET 8. Heidelberg: Carl Winter.
Colledge, Edmund, and Walsh, James, eds. (1978a) *A Book of Showings to the Anchoress Julian of Norwich*, pp. 201–278. 2 vols. Toronto: Pontifical Institute of Mediaeval Studies.

Modernized Versions

Harford, Dundas, ed. (1911) *Comfortable Words for Christ's Lovers, Being the Visions and Voices Vouchsafed to Lady Julian, Recluse at Norwich in 1373.* London: H. R. Allenson.
———— (1912, 1925) *The Shewings of Lady Julian, Recluse at Norwich, 1373.* London: H. R. Allenson; Chicago: W. P. Blessing Co. Repr. of preceding.
Reynolds, Anna M., ed. (1958) *A Shewing of God's Love: The Shorter Version of "Sixteen Revelations of Divine Love" by Julian of Norwich.* London: Longmans, Green and Co.
Colledge, Edmund, and Walsh, James, eds. (1978b) *Julian of Norwich: "Showings,"* pp. 125–170. New York. Paulist Press.

LONG TEXT

Manuscripts

Paris, BN Fonds anglais 40
BL Sloane 2499
BL Sloane 3705

Manuscript Selections

Westminster Cathedral Treasury 4, fols. 72v–112v
The Upholland Anthology (Saint Joseph's College Library, Upholland, Lancashire), fol. 113ff.

Printed Editions

Cressy, R. F. S., ed. (1670) *XVI Revelations of Divine Love, Shewed to a Devout Servant of our Lord, called Mother Juliana, an Anchorete of Norwich: Who lived in the Dayes of King Edward the Third.*
———— (1843) *Sixteen Revelations of Divine Love, Made to a devout Servant of our Lord, called Mother Juliana, an Anchorete of Norwich: Who lived in the days of King Edward the Third.* London: S. Clarke; Leicester: J. S. Crossley. Repr. of preceding with a preface by G. H. Parker.
———— (1902) *XVI Revelations of Divine Love shewed to Mother Juliana of Norwich 1373.* London: Kegan Paul, Trench, Trubner and Co. Repr. of preceding with preface by George Tyrrell. 2d ed. 1920.
Glasscoe, Marion, ed. (1976) *Julian of Norwich, A Revelation of Love.* Exeter: University of Exeter.
Colledge and Walsh, eds. (1978a), pp. 281–734.

MODERNIZED VERSIONS

Collins, Henry, ed. (1877) *Revelations of Divine Love, Shewed to a devout Anchoress, by name Mother Julian of Norwich*. London: Thomas Richardson and Sons.

Warrack, Grace, ed. (1901) *Revelations of Divine Love, Recorded by Julian, Anchoress at Norwich, Anno Domini 1373*. London: Methuen and Co. (By 1952 this had been reprinted fourteen times.)

Hudleston, Roger, ed. (1927) *Revelations of Divine Love, Shewed to a devout Ankress, by name Julian of Norwich*. London: Burns and Oates, 2d ed. 1952.

Walsh, James, ed. (1961) *The Revelations of Divine Love of Julian of Norwich*. London: Burns and Oates. Repr. (1973) Wheathampstead: Anthony Clarke Books.

Wolters, Clifton, ed. (1966) *Julian of Norwich: "Revelations of Divine Love."* Harmondsworth: Penguin Books.

Colledge and Walsh, eds. (1978b), pp. 175–343.

SECONDARY WORKS

Allchin, Arthur M., and the Sisters of the Love of God (1973) *Julian of Norwich: Four Studies to Commemorate the Sixth Centenary of the "Revelations of Divine Love."* Fairacres, Oxford: S. L. G. Press.

Birrell, T. A. (1976) "English Catholic Mystics in Non-Catholic Circles." *DownR*, 94, 60–81, 99–117, 213–231.

Børresen, Kari E. (1978) "Christ Notre Mère, la théologie de Julienne de Norwich." *Cusanus-Gesellschaft*, 13, 320–329.

Chambers, P. Franklin (1955) *Juliana of Norwich: An Introductory Appreciation and an Interpretative Anthology*. London: Victor Gollancz.

Chambers, R. W. (1932) "The Continuity of English Prose from Alfred to More and His School." In Harpsfield's *Life of More*, edited by Elsie V. Hitchcock, pp. xlv–clxxiv. EETS, os 186.

Clark, J. P. H. (1981) "*Fiducia* in Julian of Norwich." *DownR*, 99, 97–108, 214–229.

Coleman, T. W. (1938) *English Mystics of the Fourteenth Century*. London: Epworth Press. Repr. (1971) Westport, Conn.: Greenwood Press.

Glasscoe, Marion, ed. (1980) *The Medieval Mystical Tradition in England: Papers Read at the Exeter Symposium, July 1980*. Exeter: University of Exeter.

Goyau, Lucie F.-F. (1913) "Visions mystiques dans l'Angleterre du moyen âge." *Revue des deux mondes*, 16, 830–856.

Graef, Hilda (1959) *The Light and the Rainbow: A Study in Christian Spirituality from Its Roots in the Old Testament and Its Development through the New Testament and the Fathers to Recent Times*. London: Longmans, Green and Co.

H., D. S., a Benedictine of Stanbrook (1959) "English Spiritual Writers: Dame Julian of Norwich." *Clergy Review*, 44, 705–720.

Hubbard, Irene (1928–1929) "Julian of Norwich." *Modern Churchman*, 18, 139–141.

Knowles, David (1927) *The English Mystics*. London: Burns, Oates and Washbourne.

Knowlton, Mary A. (1973) *The Influence of Richard Rolle and of Julian of Norwich on the Middle English Lyrics*. The Hague: Mouton.

Meech, Sanford B., and Allen, Hope E., eds. (1940) *The Book of Margery Kempe*. EETS, os 212.

Molinari, Paulo (1958) *Julian of Norwich: The Teaching of a 14th Century English Mystic*. London: Longmans, Green and Co.

Reynolds, Anna M. (1952) "Some Literary Influences in the *Revelations* of Julian of Norwich." *LeedsSE*, 7 and 8, 18–28.

Riehle, Wolfgang (1977) *Studien zur englischen Mystik des Mittelalters unter besonderer Berücksichtigung ihrer Metaphorik*. Heidelberg: Carl Winter.

——— (1981) *The Middle English Mystics*. Translated by Bernard Standring. London: Routledge and Kegan Paul. (Translation of preceding)

Ryder, Andrew (1978) "A Note on Julian's Visions." *DownR*, 96, 299–304.

Salter, Elizabeth (1974) *Nicholas Love's "Myrrour of the Blessed Lyf of Jesu Christ."* Analecta Cartusiana 10. Salzburg: Institut für Englische Sprache und Literatur, Universität Salzburg.

Sawyer, Michael E. (1978) *A Bibliographical Index of 5 English Mystics: Richard Rolle, Julian of Norwich, the Author of the Cloud of Unknowing, Walter Hilton, Margery Kempe*. Bibliographia Tripotamopolitana 10. Pittsburgh: Pittsburgh Theological Seminary.

Sayer, Frank D. (1973) *Julian and Her Norwich: Commemorative Essays and a Handbook to the Exhibition "Revelations of Divine Love."* Norwich: Julian of Norwich 1973 Celebration Committee.

Schmidt, A. V. C. (1980) "Langland and the Mystical Tradition." In *The Medieval Mystical Tradition in England*, edited by Marion Glasscoe, pp. 17–38. Exeter: University of Exeter.

Stone, Robert K. (1970) *Middle English Prose Style: Margery Kempe and Julian of Norwich*. The Hague: Mouton.

Thouless, Robert H. (1924) *The Lady Julian, A Psychological Study*. London: Macmillan Co.

Underhill, Evelyn (1932) "Medieval Mysticism." In *The Cambridge Medieval History*, vol. 7, edited by J. R. Tanner, et al., pp. 777–812. Cambridge: Cambridge University Press.

Walsh, James (1967) "Julian of Norwich." In *New Catholic Encyclopedia*, 8:48–49. New York: McGraw-Hill.

Webster, Alan (1972–1973) "Julian of Norwich." *Expository Times*, 84, 228–230.

Wilson, R. M. (1956) "Three Middle English Mystics." *E&S*, ns 9, 87–112.

Windeatt, B. A. (1977) "Julian of Norwich and Her Audience." *RES*, ns 28, 1–17.

——— (1980) "The Art of Mystical Loving: Julian of Norwich." In *The Medieval Mystical Tradition in England*, edited by Marion Glasscoe, pp. 55–71. Exeter: University of Exeter.

CHAPTER 6

Margery Kempe

John C. Hirsh

Few Middle English works have been announced as publicly or greeted as warmly as was the work now universally known as *The Book of Margery Kempe*. A few short extracts were published in the early sixteenth century, but the work as a whole was first made known by Hope Emily Allen in a letter to the London *Times* of December 27, 1934, and when the first (modernized) edition was published twenty-one months later, the *Times* of September 30, 1936, greeted the event with a fourth leader and an article of some length—"Margery Kempe's Own Story"—which together focused on what the *Times* called the "romance" of its discovery, "more unexpected and more important than the discovery of the 'Morte d'Arthur' at Winchester" (p. 13). Materially assisted by such thunder the work became the subject of a large number of often rather uncritical book reviews, and several popular, but by no means unthoughtful, articles. Since the Early English Text Society edition was not published until 1940, early interest centered upon the 1936 edition, which had excised, and placed in an appendix, certain religious matters that its editor deemed uninteresting to the modern reader. This practice did not suppress any part of the work, but it did create the impression, in the popular press, that the work's interest was as social, not as religious, history, a misapprehension that has endured. Under such influences, early scholarship concerned itself less with the formal problems of the text, than with the historical ones, particularly with those that were already under discussion when the work appeared, the psychology of mysticism and social history, both areas in which the *Book*'s contribution is in fact rather specialized. Among these early readers, Evelyn Underhill, writing in the *Spectator* of October 16, 1936, found the book "almost equally important to students of medieval manners, and disconcerting to students of medieval mysticism." For Underhill, Margery's energy, emotionalism, and "hysterical" tendencies (the word recurs often) simply "poured themselves into a religious mould"; there is "very little in Margery's *Book* which can properly be defined as mystical" (p. 642). This same somewhat startled denial of Margery's religiousness emerges in D. L. Douie's review in *History* (1937–1938), which compared Margery to the "women preachers of the Methodist revival" but suspects "a somewhat unbalanced temperament which may have been nurtured too exclusively on the mystical writings of the period" (p. 71). Writing in the *Dublin Review* (1937), Justin McCann found not only "a supreme and amazing egotism, but also that more unattractive quality of 'possessive amorousness,' which would seem to be the special failing of hysterical devotion" (p. 113).

This early sensitivity to, and reaction against, the more psychological aspects of Margery's *Book* seem to have been conditioned by a series of articles examining mysticism psychologically which Herbert Thurston had published in the *Month*.[1] Thurston reviewed the *Book* twice, rejecting the idea that Margery was "no more than a neurotic and self-deluded visionary," and finding instead a "combination of pronounced hysteria with a genuine love of God." Two articles in the American press confirmed this bias in Margery's favor: Sigrid Undset, in an article reprinted in the *Atlantic Monthly*, noted how Margery "fought bravely against her sins and frailties" (1939, p. 233), and Helen C. White's *Commonweal* article of December 3, 1943, accepted Allen's argument (which had appeared in the 1940 EETS edition) that Margery's *Book* shows "a real core of genuine mysticism. The classic stages of mystical awakening and growth are clearly to be discerned, and . . . in its main lines her experience is definitely in accord with that of the great mystics" (p. 164).

In subsequent years this more orthodox view gained ascendency, urged along, rather than argued, by such admiring but uncritical accounts as those of T. W. Coleman (1937) and Catherine Cholmeley (1947), which set out to refute the earlier "hysteria" analyses, but in the course of doing so dismissed, rather than explored, the problems associated with Margery's religious experiences. A somewhat more critical defense is E. I. Watkins's "In Defense of Margery Kempe" (1941), one of the first to modify Allen's view of Margery's mysticism, a task of no little difficulty.

This early reception of the *Book*, then, conditioned as it was by prevailing attitudes toward psychology, mysticism, and medieval social history, was more enthusiastic than critical, even where it leveled strictures against Margery herself. "The circumstances of its discovery perhaps led to some exaggeration of its interest," R. M. Wilson (1956, p. 104) frankly remarked, before turning to a consideration of its prose style, and as late as 1961 David Knowles, influenced no doubt by the first generation of reviewers, declared, "If the *Book* of Margery Kempe has little in it of deep spiritual wisdom, and nothing of true mystical experience, it is a document of the highest value for the religious historian of the age . . . Margery Kempe can only improperly and accidentally be classed among the English mystics, and . . . little of spiritual instruction is to be found in her Book" (148–49). Although Edmund Colledge (1961b) did not take exception to these judgments in his interesting review of Knowles's book, he did in a subsequent article printed in the *Month* (1962), which still stressed, equivocally, the limitations of Margery's spirituality, and found her, with regret and affection, a child of her own Gothic times. But perhaps the best single study of Margery's spirituality is that of an anonymous Benedictine of Stanbrook which appeared in the *Downside Review* (1938), and treated the effect of the Eucharist on her life and thinking. Recently Wolfgang Riehle (1981) has usefully treated certain key words and expressions in contemporary mystical texts, and has turned again to the study of continental parallels, an important concern, one that Colledge, and before him Allen, had shared.

Apart from these more properly religious studies, the historical setting of the *Book* has also had its share of latter-day scrutiny. H. S. Bennett's *Six Medieval Men and Women* (1955) emphasizes certain of the articles—for example, of clothing—that occur in the text, and examines the social implications of some of the action. Louise Collis's historical novel *The Apprentice Saint* (1964), though it should be approached with caution, raises some interesting points, like the conjecture that the illness of Margery's son may have been psychosomatic. A more recent study by Anthony Goodman (1978) treats the way in which Margery's social standing conditioned her behavior, and suggests certain psychological matters that may have tempered her extraordinary personality, an element other critics have treated only in passing. Although he sets aside the important problem of authorship, Goodman's study is of real interest.

Turning from these historical and religious considerations to more particular problems, it should be said that the issue of authorship remains of central importance. The common assumption, endorsed by the EETS edition, was that Margery was the author, and that her scribes acted as her amanuenses, though George R. Coffman (1942) expressed some doubts, as did Knowles (1961), who echoed Bennett's view (1955) that the first scribe was indeed her son. I have argued further (1975) that the second scribe was closely involved in the composition of the work, and that the authorship was essentially collaborative, a view that should condition any historical study. Since the *Book* is not based upon a translation, its language has particular interest, and has been studied by Shibath (1958), Reszkiewicz (1962), and Stone (1970), though Stone's study, carried out without a control, was examined critically by R. M. Wilson (1973) and P. J. C. Field (1973). The *Book* contains many markedly colloquial passages. These have been the subject of much passing comment and a sensitive survey by Wilson (1956), though in comparison with, for example, the Paston letters, the *Book* is less colloquial than some remarks would imply—perhaps because of the second scribe's Latinate training. One other related area concerns the manuscript itself, which was acquired by the British Library from Sotheby's sale of June 24, 1980 (lot 58, see Ker 1964, p. 132). The glosses and annotations in the manuscript require further study. For example, Meech did not record certain rubrications which he called "a-signs" and "n-signs" (these are now recorded in Appendix A, below), which were used by the rubricator to call attention to certain passages and to organize the text for the reader. Taken together they supply a running commentary, albeit a limited one, on the *Book*, by a contemporary hand.[2] Further studies on the scribe are needed, like M. C. Seymour's (to me not convincing) study (1968), which has the advantage of showing how little is known about the scribe who wrote the manuscript.

There is no shortage of desiderata for this work. The style needs further examination, perhaps in the light of authorial considerations. Margery's interest in saints has been often remarked—perhaps most perceptively by Colledge (1961a), who points out her connections with the Low Countries—but we still lack a detailed study of her connection with Saint Bridget, whose life she in many ways sought to imitate. To be most useful, such a hagiographical study should embrace too a study of the devotional context of Margery's religiousness, and in this area at least a good start has been made in Martin Thornton's *Margery Kempe: An Example in the English Pastoral Tradition* (1960). If Thornton does not address the devotional practices current in Margery's time, and by which she was clearly influenced, he does urge the pastoral, not the mystical, quality of her *Book*, and views it as a part of a specially English tradition which achieved a synthesis of affective and speculative practices, influenced by a humane theological optimism. Still, it is difficult to escape the impression that Margery's devotions were linked to her personality and her psychology, as well as to the practices of her time. She shows a tendency to attach herself to—perhaps even to batten on—her male spiritual confessors, and though this dependency was doubtless edifying, her attachment to her confessor-priests played a marked role in her spiritual life, and the relationship should qualify the degree of independence with which, in spite of her travels, she is to be credited. From the same perspective, the fact that priests read to her should not be taken as absolute proof that she herself could not read. A hagiographical examination of the *Book*, then, should concern itself with which saints' lives, particularly which English ones, were likely to have influenced Margery and her scribe, and how far their influence may reasonably be thought to extend. Important as it is, such a study is not without danger, for it seems to me that although hagiographical elements influence the structure of the *Book*, they do not determine it, and the saintly aspirations that Margery undoubtedly entertained did not prevent her from injecting her own extraordinary narrative into the pattern the scribe set down. The choice of, and delineation of, certain incidents may themselves have been influenced by hagiographical considerations. It is doubtful, in this matter, that Margery and her scribe were working at cross-purposes.

So much has been said of Margery's mysticism that it may seem unnecessary to raise the matter again, but there is good reason to do so. The current view of

Margery's mysticism is very much conditioned by Allen's contributions to the 1940 EETS edition of the *Book*, though the second volume of the edition, which was to include much of the documentation for this view, never appeared. During the twenty years Allen was engaged with the second volume her interpretation of late medieval English piety was enlarging (see Appendix B). By the time of her death in 1960 she had turned toward one aspect of what she understood to be the native religious tradition, which she had come to call English contemplative piety. This piety she believed to have been founded in the earlier mystical tradition, but to have come under various influences that had changed its complexion—it was in part for this reason, for example, that at the time of her death she was engaged in a study of Saint Bridget of Sweden and the Bridgettine Order, material she hoped to present in the second volume. Increasingly interested in what she came to regard as the highly ecstatic nature of this piety, Allen was convinced that continuity from earlier periods was only one aspect, and that the cross-currents of late medieval English tradition were more complex than she had earlier believed. Her understanding of mysticism had always been somewhat latitudinarian, and these later refinements and reinterpretations would have been of great interest, had she brought them to conclusion.

Part of the problem in evaluating Margery's mysticism lies in the extremity of scholarly attitudes the publication of her *Book* called up. If she was not, in that decidedly quaint (and somewhat sexist) word, "hysterical," then she must be a great mystic—and perhaps a genius to boot. Or perhaps she was all three. In such a heady atmosphere it became increasingly difficult to estimate Margery's own religious affections, and the personal attachment felt by some of her students—who saw themselves rather as her champions—did nothing to clarify matters. Nor did the personal repulsion which, in other students, she equally evoked. That there are in her book stages of growth and a kind of religious awareness, whether born of literary tradition, imitation and artifice, or personal devout experience, few would deny, but the mixture of these elements, and their historical, literary, and religious contexts, await exploration. But the easy and current bracketing of Margery with Richard Rolle, Julian of Norwich, Walter Hilton, and the *Cloud* author, should be resisted. So should her utter separation from them.

Margery's own intellectual and emotional limitations should not blind the reader to the very great value of her remarkable *Book*. For more than any other document preserved from late medieval England, it gives evidence of the effects and motivations that lie behind the lay practice of certain devotions, of the attitudes of several persons, both clerical and lay, toward the more ecstatic of these practices, and of some of the psychological properties these practices contained. In doing so it reminds us that the study of medieval religious values has to do primarily with what meaning these practices had for those who were involved with them. Without such sympathy, the study of popular devout attitudes such as those Margery manifests becomes too readily the documentation of superstition. These are perhaps more specialized concerns than the broad social significance that, on its first publication, the work was thought to contain, but for the study of late medieval religious attitudes *The Book of Margery Kempe* has few rivals.

NOTES

1. Published well before the discovery and identification of Margery's *Book*, which they do not of course mention, Thurston's articles (1922–1923, 1923) are important for understanding the work's reception.

2, For a study of the MS gloss references to Richard Methley and Prior John Norton see Hogg (1977, esp. n. 2, pp. 91–94).

APPENDIX A:
MS RUBRICATIONS IN THE *BOOK*

Meech did not record in the EETS edition one marginal sign for *nota* where it appeared as *n*, though where it appeared as *no* he did; nor did he record the structural sign he calls the a-sign (p. 3, nn. 2 and 3). These are recorded below, keyed to the passages they identify; where either sign is simply added to a passage already recorded in Meech's apparatus it is not reported. The method here differs slightly from Meech's, which reports the end of the line at which the mark appears, not which passage it indicates, in those passages marked *no*[*ta*] which he did report. Page and line reference to the EETS edition are followed by the first word of the marked passage (a 1 indicates the first and a 2 the second appearance of that word in the line). Where the rubrication is in the outer margin the passage is marked (o); all others are in the inner.

N-sign: *nota*

3/8 Than (o); 5/26 Whan (o); 8/25 And; 10/6 And; 11/15 Alas (o); 11/34 And; 14/32 And; 17/6 And (o); 20/20 A; 21/25 Sodeynly (o); 25/11 Than (o); 28/2 Eyþyr (o); 34/26 An- (o); 41/10 Thys; 44/3 And (o); 46/19 The (o); 49/4 For (o); 50/29 A (o); 52/20 þu (o); 54/20 Also; 57/6 þe 1 (o); 63/12 wher-for (o); 67/21 Owyr (o); 69/19 & 2 (o); 73/7 Dow- (o); 75/24 Dowtyr (o); 78/18 be-cause; 83/31 & 1 (o); 90/14 Ryght (o); 106/27 & (o); 112/2 & (o); 113/17 And (o); 114/4 And (o); 120/5 beyng (o); 130/32 Hauyth (o); 134/16 The (o); 142/6 And; 146/2 but (o); 148/15 We; 154/13 Also (o); 156/9 Dowtyr (o); 158/13 he (o); 158/21 A (o); 160/10 wherfor (o); 161/2 þerfor (o); 162/21 And (o); 162/35 þe (o) *twice*; 173/27 An-oþer; 175/2 and (o); 176/20 For (o); 178/30 and (o); 180/30 and (o); 185/6 Than (o); 185/33 Sum-tyme (o); 199/25 And (o); 201/33 þat (o); 204/8 þat (o); 204/24 Forþermor (o); 206/19 for (o); 208/16 An-oþer (o); 209/5 owr (o); 209/15 An-oþer (o); 210/5 For; 216/31 & (o); 229/21 & 2 (o); 230/9 Owr (o); 235/37 Qui (o); 246/3 A (o); 249/13 As (o); 251/15 I (o); 251/32 Lord (o); 253/10 for 1 (o).

a-sign: paragraphus

3/25 Sum; 6/21 And (o); 7/19 And; 12/4 I (o); 13/17 Sche; 16/32 Dowtyr; 17/13 Thys; 17/25 And; 20/3 sumtyme (o); 21/5 & 2; 29/19 whan; 29/32 Sche; 38/12 I; 41/30 he (o); 42/24 þe; 42/36 And (o); 47/34 & (o); 48/16 Owyr; 49/34 Owyr (o); 51/10 for; 53/29 Also; 54/7 A (o); 54/15 An-oþer (o); 54/20 Also (o); 54/38 Sche; 69/38 þe; 70/21 and (o); 73/3 I (o); 76/16 Go (o); 76/30 Than; 77/34 as; 89/16 & (o); 89/36 And; 90/25 & 1 (o); 93/5 Whan (o); 95/28 whech (o); 97/8 And (o); 97/18 Good (o); 97/32 þan (o); 98/26 I; 104/26 And; 110/19 Al-mythy (o); 111/9 þan; 115/30 whom; 117/19 but (o); 119/1 And (o); 119/27 On (o); 121/9 And (o); 130/37 Alas; 131/24 On (o); 138/6 and; 139/30 & (o); 142/21 I 2; 146/8 þan; 153/10 þe (o); 154/27 sche 1; 155/4 and (o); 156/30 Than; 158/26 For; 159/24 & (o); 163/10 Than (o); 164/25 Lord (o); 167/11 And (o); 169/6 And (o); 171/13 sche; 172/23 3yf; 173/20 So (o); 175/14 A (o); 176/9 Alasse (o); 182/9 for (o); 185/30 Dowtyr; 186/6 Dowtyr (o); 188/9 And (o); 190/26 And (o); 192/24 Alas (o); 197/5 þes (o); 198/29 Hir (o); 199/4 and (o); 202/22 The; 204/10 desyryng; 207/4 Dowtyr; 207/11 For (o); 209/36 whech (o); 211/24 And (o); 215/20 Owr (o); 215/31 A (o); 217/10 for; 218/2 And (o); 220/4 Sum-tyme (o); 227/12 Owr; 230/15 Wauyr (o); 235/1 sche (o); 245/16 sche (o); 248/20 þe (o); 250/34 I (o); 251/19 er 2.

APPENDIX B:
THE HOPE EMILY ALLEN PAPERS
AT BRYN MAWR COLLEGE

Although facsimiles of the medieval manuscripts Allen held at the time of her death are now in the Van Pelt Library of the University of Pennsylvania, her professional papers are in the Miriam Coffin Canaday Library of Bryn Mawr College, Bryn Mawr, Pennsylvania. They are contained in seven Hollinger boxes (10.5 feet), and are presently stored as received, following Allen's death in 1960. Although the boxes observe certain large distinctions—"Women Mystics," "Continental Mystics," "The Book of Margery Kempe II," "Richard Rolle," "The Ancrene Riwle," for example—the contents of each box is heterogeneous, comprising professional correspondence, unpublished drafts (rarely complete) of articles and books, early drafts of published pieces, galley and page proofs, offprints from colleagues and friends, and collections of occasional notes by Allen. Although a rich archive for the biographer or the intellectual historian, the actual use for the student of medieval religion is somewhat limited. The unpublished pieces are by no means ready for the press, though there are passages of great interest scattered throughout. The holdings for the projected second volume of *The Book of Margery Kempe* are disappointing: Allen's work was still at a relatively early stage at the time of her death. Certain appendices were apparently going to advance arguments that would not have moved general agreement, and their examination must await a study of Allen's work. Taken as a whole, the papers will only very rarely answer a specific question, but they contain a wealth of reference and allusion, and can offer more than one insight into medieval religion.

BIBLIOGRAPHY

PRIMARY WORKS

BL Add. MS 61823

PRINTED EDITIONS

de Worde, Wynkyn [1501] *A shorte treatyse of contemplacyon . . . taken out of the boke of Margerie kempe of lynn.* STC 14924.

Pepwell, Henry (1521) *A veray deuoute treatyse (named Benyamyn) . . .* , sigs. D6v–E3v. Repr. of preceding. STC 20972.

Gardner, Edmund G., ed. (1910) *The Cell of Self-Knowledge: Seven Early English Mystical Treatises Printed by Henry Pepwell in 1521,* pp. 49–59. The New Medieval Library. London: Chatto & Windus. Repr. of preceding.

Butler-Bowdon, W., ed. (1936) *The Book of Margery Kempe, 1436,* with an introduction by R. W. Chambers. London: Jonathan Cape. Modernized. Repr. (1944) New York: Devin-Adair Co. (Subsequent reprintings delete date from title.) Repr. (1954) The World's Classics. London and Toronto: Oxford University Press.

Meech, Sanford Brown, ed. (1940) *The Book of Margery Kempe.* The text from the unique MS owned by Colonel W. Butler-Bowdon, vol. 1, with notes and appendices by Hope Emily Allen. EETS, os 212. Corrections by Hope Emily Allen in a letter to the *TLS,* March 22, 1941, p. 139.

REVIEWS

The following list includes the more important reviews of W. Butler-Bowden's modernized version (1936) and the Early English Text Society edition (1940), here marked EETS. These reviews helped to shape early opinion of the newly discovered *Book of Margery Kempe.* Newspaper reviews of the 1936 edition (including one by G. G. Coulton October 11 in the *Observer* and one by Graham Greene October 13 in the *Morning Post*) are surveyed by George Burns (1938) "Margery Kempe Reviewed," *Month,* 171, 238–244.

Bacon, Leonard (1944) *Saturday Review of Literature,* Nov. 4, p. 12.

Brooks, B. G. (1942) *Nineteenth-Century and After,* 132 (July), 30–32, EETS.

Coffman, George (1942) *Speculum*, 17, 138–42, EETS.

Douie, D. L. (1937–1938) *History*, 22, 70–72.

Keenan, Charles (1944) *America*, 72, 33–34.

McCann, Justin (1937) *Dublin Review*, 200, 103–116.

Thurston, Herbert (1936) *Month*, 168, 446–456; *Tablet* Oct. 24, pp. 570–571.

TLS Oct. 10, 1936, p. 805.

TLS March 8, 1941, pp. 111 and 120, EETS.

Underhill, Evelyn (1936) *Spectator*, 157, Oct. 16, p. 642.

SECONDARY WORKS

Atkinson, Clarissa W. (forthcoming) *Mystic and Pilgrim: The Book and the World of Margery Kempe*. Ithaca: Cornell University Press.

A Benedictine of Stanbrook (1938) "Margery Kempe and the Holy Eucharist." *DownR*, 56, 468–482.

Bennett, H. S. (1955) *Six Medieval Men and Women*, pp. 124–150. Cambridge: Cambridge University Press.

Cholmeley, Catherine (1947) *Margery Kempe, Genius and Mystic*. London: Longmans, Green and Co.

Coleman, Thomas W. (1937) "Margery Kempe: Medieval Mystic, Evangelist, and Pilgrim." *London Quarterly and Holborn Review*, 162, 498–502. Expanded in (1938) *English Mystics of the Fourteenth Century*, pp. 153–176. London: Epworth Press.

Colledge, Edmund [formerly Eric] (1961a) *The Medieval Mystics of England*. New York: Scribners.

——— (1961b) Review of David Knowles, *The English Mystical Tradition*. *Life of the Spirit*, 15, 554–550.

——— (1962) "Margery Kempe." *Month*, ns 28 (July), 16–29. Repr. (1965) in *Pre-Reformation English Spirituality*, edited by James Walsh, pp. 210–223. New York: Fordham University Press.

Collis, Louise (1964) *The Apprentice Saint*. London: Michael Joseph. Repr. (1964) as *Memoirs of a Medieval Woman, the Life and Times of Margery Kempe*. New York: Crowell. Repr. (1983) under American title. New York: Harper Books.

Crawford, Joseph (1973) "Independent Woman in a Medieval World." *Spiritual Life*, 20, 199–203.

Delaney, Sheila (1978) "Sexual Economics, Chaucer's Wife of Bath, and *The Book of Margery Kempe*." *Minnesota Review*, 5, 104–115.

Dickman, Susan (1980) "Margery Kempe and the English Devotional Tradition." In *The Medieval Mystical Tradition in England: Papers Read at the Exeter Symposium, July 1980*, edited by Marion Glasscoe, pp. 156–172. Exeter: University of Exeter.

Dinnis, Enid (1940) "Margery Kempe of Lynne." *Thought*, 15, 84–96.

Field, P. J. C. (1973) Review of Robert K. Stone, *Middle English Prose Style. Speculum*, 48, 182–185.

Goodman, Anthony (1978) "The Piety of John Brunham's Daughter, of Lynn." In *Medieval Women, Dedicated and Presented to Professor Rosalind M. T. Hill*, edited by Derek Baker, pp. 347–358. Studies in Church History, Subsidia I. Oxford: Published for the Ecclesiastical History Society by Basil Blackwell.

Hirsh, John C. (1975) "Author and Scribe in *The Book of Margery Kempe*." *MAE*, 44, 145–150.

Hogg, James (1977) "Richard Methley: 'To Hew Heremyte, A Pystyl of Solytary Life Nowadayes.'" *Analecta Cartusiana*, 31, 91–119.

Ker, N. R. (1964) *Medieval Libraries of Great Britain*, p. 132. London: Royal Historical Society.

Knowles, David (1927) *English Mystics*. London: Burns and Oates.

—— (1961) *The English Mystical Tradition*. London: Burns and Oates. Rev. ed. of preceding.

Lagorio, Valerie Marie, and Bradley, Ritamary, eds. (1981). *The Fourteenth-Century English Mystics, A Comprehensive Annotated Bibliography*, pp. 127–132. New York: Garland. Includes some Ph.D. theses not listed here.

Maisonneuve, R. (1982) "Margery Kempe and the Eastern and Western Tradition of the 'Perfect Fool.'" In *The Medieval Mystical Tradition in England: Papers Read at Dartington Hall, July 1982*, edited by Marion Glasscoe, pp. 1–17. Exeter: University of Exeter.

Medcalf, Stephen (1981) *The Later Middle Ages; The Context of English Literature*, pp. 110–121, 160 ff. London: Methuen & Co. Includes a recent psychoanalytic analysis by Dr. Anthony Ryle.

O'Connell, Sir John R. (1937) "Mistress Margery Kempe of Lynn." *DownR*, 55, 174–182.

Pearson, Samuel C., Jr. (1981) "Margery Kempe: Her *Book*, Her Faith, Her World." *ABR*, 32, 365–377.

Reszkiewicz, Alfred (1962) *The Main Sentence Elements in "The Book of Margery Kempe," A Study in Major Syntax*. Komitet Neofilologiczny Polskiej Akademii Nauk. Warsaw.

Riehle, Wolfgang (1981) *The Middle English Mystics*. Translated by Bernard Standring. London. Routledge and Kegan Paul.

Sawyer, Michael E., comp. (1978) *A Bibliographical Index of Five Middle English Mystics*. Bibliographia Tripotamopolitana 10. Pittsburgh: Pittsburgh Theological Seminary, Clifford E. Barbour Library. Includes some M.A. and Ph.D. theses not listed here.

Seymour, M. C. (1968) "A Fifteenth-century East Anglian Scribe." *MAE*, 37, 166–173.

Shibath, Shōzō (1958) "Notes on the Vocabulary of *The Book of Margery Kempe*." In *Studies in English Grammar and Linguistics, A Miscellany in Honor of Professor Takanobu Otsuka*, pp. 209–220. Tokyo: Kenkusha.

Stone, Robert K. (1970) *Middle English Prose Style, Margery Kempe and Julian of Norwich*. Studies in English Literature 36. The Hague and Paris: Mouton.

Thornton, Martin (1960) *Margery Kempe: An Example in the English Pastoral Tradition*. London: SPCK. Argument summarized in Thornton (1963) *English Spirituality, An*

Outline of Ascetical Theology According to the English Pastoral Tradition, pp. 222–229. London: SPCK.

Thurston, Herbert (1922–1923) "Some Physical Phenomena of Mysticism." *Month*, 140, 331–344; 141, 97–109, 227–240, 334–344; and 142, 23–33.

———— (1923) "Pithiatism, Otherwise Called Hysteria." *Month*, 142, 97–108.

———— (1955) *Surprising Mystics*. Edited by J. C. Crehan, pp. 27–37. London: Burns and Oates. A reprint of his review in the *Month*, cited above.

Undset, Sigrid (1939) "Margery Kempe of Lynn." *Atlantic Monthly*, 164, 232–240. Repr. (1938) from *Men, Women and Places*, pp. 81–106. London: Cassell & Co.

Watkin, Edward I. (1941) "In Defense of Margery Kempe." *DownR*, 40, 243–263. Repr. in Watkin (1953) *Poets and Mystics*, pp. 104–135, London: Sheed and Ward; and (1979) *On Julian of Norwich and In Defence of Margery Kempe*, edited by Marion Glasscoe, pp. 35–65, Exeter: University of Exeter.

Webb, Geoffrey (1961) "The Person and the Place—II: At Old St. Julian's." *Life of the Spirit*, 15, 549–554.

Weissman, Hope Phyllis (1982) "Margery Kempe in Jerusalem: *Hysterica Compassio* in the Late Middle Ages." In *Acts of Interpretation, The Text in Its Contexts 700–1600: Essays on Medieval and Renaissance Literature in Honor of E. Talbot Donaldson*, edited by Mary J. Carruthers and Elizabeth D. Kirk, pp. 201–217. Norman, Okla.: Pilgrim Books.

White, Helen C. (1943) "Margery Kempe of Lynn." *Commonweal*, 39, 164–166.

Wilson, R. M. (1956) "Three Middle English Mystics." *E&S*, ns 9, 87–112.

———— (1973) Review of Robert K. Stone, *Middle English Prose Style*. *MAE*, 42, 183–184.

CHAPTER 7

Mandeville

Ralph Hanna III

According to his own account, Sir John Mandeville, knight of Saint Albans, left England in 1322 to travel overseas. During his thirty-four-year absence, he penetrated far into Asia and reached the legendary lands of Cathay and Prester John. And in his old age, for the "solaas" of a reading public eager for knowledge of the marvels of the East, he set down his memoirs. Writing in French for the benefit of the unlearned (although he recognized the primacy of Latin for such works), Sir John set down, insofar as his fallible memory allowed, the highlights of his adventures—a fascinating discussion of oriental potentates and the strange customs of little known races, of topography and natural wonders. This work, *Mandeville's Travels*, if the number of surviving manuscripts gives any accurate indication, was the most popular piece of nonreligious Middle English prose, especially in the first half of the fifteenth century.

But any effort to deal with *Mandeville's Travels* must explore a paradox. For although the biography provided by the work, which I have summarized above, is now taken to be nonhistorical, a purely literary fiction, the deserved popularity of the work reflects "Mandeville" alone. The most consistent appeal of the work, an appeal responsible for its ceaseless republication, translation, and use well into the eighteenth century, is that of a definable personality. Over and above the obvious marvels that the text relates, *Travels* attracts by the creation of a narrative personality—"Mandeville"—a personality constantly vivifying and informing the marvelous Asian world described.

The skeptical insistence that this character has no real-life counterpart, no being outside the work, has stimulated the most substantial research on *Travels*. And although some late hangovers of belief in a historical Sir John Mandeville occur in distinguished places (see Bennett 1954; Letts 1949), the issue was substantially settled before this century. "In the decade 1880–1890 four scholars working independently, Warner in England, Vogels and Bovenschen in Germany, and Lorenzen in Denmark, laid the foundations for all later investigations of *Mandeville's Travels*" (Seymour and Waldron 1963, p. 406). Most devastating to the biographical readings of the work were the researches of Bovenschen

and Warner, for they demonstrated, beyond any doubt, that "Mandeville" had
traveled no further than the shelf of his library and that the full substance of the
marvels he narrates so appealingly had come to him ready-made in the works of
others (Bovenschen 1888; Warner 1889, pp. xv–xxix; usefully summarized in
Seymour 1967, pp. xiv, 276–278). Sir John did not even have to research his
chosen topic in any particularly scholarly way, for he could make use of compendia and collections of travel literature, perhaps most notably Jean le Long's
French translations of oriental materials and Vincent of Beauvais's *Speculum*.

The myth of Sir John Mandeville, knight of Saint Albans, also received major
shocks from the results of detailed manuscript studies. Here the early work of
Johann Vogels (1891) with the English manuscripts set a model for other scholars
to emulate. But the situation has only become clarified in work of the last thirty
years, since study of the French texts has lagged considerably behind that of texts
in other languages (see the appeal in Mossé 1955).

The current state of the art (which has largely developed in response to shortcomings of Bennett 1954, nonetheless a major study) effectively explodes any serious belief in the English genesis of *Travels*—and with it the last vestiges of a
historical Sir John. It is now apparent that the original version of *Mandeville's
Travels* was written in French and on the Continent. The earliest dated manuscript in any language, BN nouv. acq. fr. 4515, already showing a text well advanced in corruption, was copied in 1371 (ed. Letts 1953, 2:226–413) and
gives a "continental version" of the text. And comparison with a recension largely
copied in England, the "insular version" (ed. Warner 1889, from Lo5 and Lo7),
indicates the textual anteriority of the continental texts. These are also anterior in
time: the earliest dated insular texts, BN fr. 5635 and BN fr. 2810, were copied
in 1402 and 1403, respectively (de Poerck 1956).[1]

Such researches allow some fairly specific conclusions about the genesis of
Travels. The work followed very closely the appearance of le Long's accounts (ca.
1350), as if inspired by (and aware of ways of improving upon) them. *Travels*
was composed on the Continent, probably in 1356 or 1357: the main evidence
for such dating is the bit of feigned autobiography near the very end of the work
in all versions (see Seymour 1967, my citation text, p. 229/14–27).[2] Continental composition is implied by the sources used, works not known to have had
English circulation in 1357 (see Seymour 1967, p. 277, an argument that requires fuller evidence).

From this continental French version was derived the insular text. Although,
as noted above, the earliest dated insular MSS were copied shortly after 1400,
this recension, the most important to the English Mandeville, must be somewhat
older. It provided the basis for four Latin translations; a copy of one of these,
Leiden University MS Vulcan 96, is dated 1390 and represents a scribally advanced version both of the insular version source and of the Latin text (Seymour

1964c, p. 48). All things considered, the insular recension must have developed by the late 1370s; directly or otherwise, it was to become the source of all English versions of *Travels*.

This view of the work's genesis effectively scuttles a variety of earlier views, but it also leaves unanswered some pressing questions. The creation of "Mandeville" represents a literary hoax of impressive proportions; but even granting that the author sought primarily to create a particular narrative personality, some of the specific details attached to this persona become troubling. Were we able to believe "Mandeville"'s claim that "now I am comen hom mawgree myself to reste for gowtes artetykes" (p. 229/20–21) and to believe the work a composition of convalescence, some of "Mandeville"'s created biography would make sense. But given a work of continental French composition, one must wonder anew why the chosen narrator should be an Englishman. Or, why should he be given a particular (and recorded) English name? Or, why should he be associated with Saint Albans? Such questions, easy enough to answer if one can believe in a historical Sir John Mandeville, become issues for scholarly investigation once the biographical fiction of the work is exploded.

In Middle English, six separate recensions of *Travels* survive, two in verse (*IMEV* 248.5 and 3117.6). But only one of these, the so-called defective version, has any real claims to be the English *Mandeville*. It is the oldest English version: a number of copies date from shortly after 1400 (Seymour 1966b), and some are bequeathed in wills of the late 1390s (Wilson 1970, pp. 146, 147, 150; Seymour 1966b, p. 174), implying that the work was translated from the insular version by the late 1380s. The defective version also, directly or otherwise, provided source material for three of the five other English recensions (only the Bodley and metrical versions are completely independent).[3] Further, it alone, so far as one can tell, achieved any very wide dissemination: about thirty complete manuscripts, in addition to a number of smaller fragments and abridgments, survive. And this text alone exercised influence on Renaissance readers, providing copy for the first printed version—and all subsequent editions to 1725. The defective version in fact is the common version of the Middle English *Mandeville*.

Yet today this text has become the least known of all the recensions. In part this state of affairs reflects the accidents of publication: Seymour's long-projected EETS edition based on Queen's College 383 has not yet (1983) appeared, and, while all other Middle English versions have appeared in modern critical editions, one must rely on Pynson's 1496 print for a sense of the common version. But, in addition, prevalent scholarly confusion about what a Mandeville text should be has denied the common version that central status it should hold in Middle English studies.

A taste of this confusion can be gained from one scholar's passing statement, confirming the history of twentieth-century editions, that the version of Egerton

1982 represents a "preferred text" (Moseley 1974b, p. 5, n. 1). Offered without explanation, this view apparently reflects a desire to have a complete text corresponding to the full French versions. Such a text the common version does not provide, for it is truly defective in one regard. The French source manuscript for the common version, now lost, apparently lacked a full quire of text so that the unwitting English translator omitted most of Chapters 6–8 and created a textual non sequitur that perturbed all subsequent scribes (see Seymour 1963, p. 364, for quotation of this "Egypt gap," and cf. pp. 25/6–8 and 45/31–33 in the fuller Cotton text).

But this defect should in no wise detract from the use and study of the common version, for lack of absolute fidelity to the full French *Mandeville* scarcely argues against this text. If some absolute reproduction of the original is desired, no English text will do: all are descended from the insular French, which itself lacks authorial materials (see de Poerck 1956, pp. 138–139). But, if fidelity is an issue, the common version more faithfully and carefully reproduces the French than do its competitors: the usually cited Cotton version has generally been viewed as a translation replete with misunderstandings of the source (see, e.g., Hamelius 1923, pp. 16–19 and his notes; Seymour 1967, pp. xix, 259–271). And the Egerton text, insofar as it is independent of the common version, is far removed from any authority, being based upon an English translation of a Latin translation of the insular version. Further, both Egerton and Cotton redactions are, to a large extent, based upon the common version anyway, and a major impetus in their production was filling the gap in the text, an act not beyond the perspicacity of an intelligent, if devious, scribe[4] (see Seymour's account of the Egerton conflation 1961b, esp. pp. 165–166). And, of course, neither version exercised any discernible evidence in either the Middle Ages or the Renaissance. In short, no compelling reason, other than unavailability of the Pynson print, compels one to ignore this centerpiece of the Middle English *Mandeville* tradition.

As the preceding paragraphs should indicate, the unraveling of the textual tradition has proved an intricate and demanding enterprise, and in such a situation studies of a critical nature have lagged somewhat behind. Most treatments have surveyed *Travels* helpfully, but within the broader context of general medieval literary history, and specifically literary studies are yet in their infancy. Perhaps most developed has been scholarly discussion of the work's influence, an obvious topic given its popularity.

Mandeville's Travels exercised passing influence upon a number of later fourteenth-century poets. Chaucer, the *Gawain*-poet, and the authors of the alliterative *Morte* and *Mum and the Sothsegger* all knew some version of *Travels* (Bennett 1953a and 1954, pp. 219–225; Brown 1904; Gollancz 1921, pp. xxv–xxviii, 91–92, 96–98; and, for the only notice of *Mum*, Seymour 1973, p. xvin). In most cases, the scanty evidence does not allow conclusions about the form in which the poets read *Travels*, but some fragmentary evidence suggests the *Gawain*-poet, at least, may have known an English version (Anderson 1977, pp. 6–7, n. 10 and the references there cited, unfortunately without reference to the common version). A good many further allusions have been suggested. But in many of these Mandeville's information reflects literary traditions that are extremely widespread, and the references could have been derived from other sources. One might contrast the sobriety of Lowes (1905), for whom Mandeville explicates, but is not a source for, a Chaucer reference with the ebullience of Lange (1938a and 1938b) or Schofield (1904, pp. 189–190).

Considerable digging remains to be done in this area, for a large number of fifteenth-century Mandeville references certainly remain unnoticed. To date, scholars most usually have noted the production during this period of rearranged and truncated texts (Horner 1980; Moseley 1974b; Seymour 1961c and 1966a). But at least one intriguing reference to *Travels* has come to light, the invocation of Sir John Mandeville to authenticate a book and a relic at Christ Church, Canterbury (Seymour 1974a). More extensive searches among manuscript materials should produce further such oddments. And completely untouched are such unexplored areas as sermons and later books of travel. Did wonders from *Travels* provide exemplary materials for sermons in the same way that information from Bartholomaeus or Higden did? Did the existence of *Travels* influence later travel literature composed in England? Such questions must remain unanswered pending further manuscript research.

Other discussions have explored the connection of *Travels* with larger literary themes. Most notably, scholars have concentrated upon the importance of the work as a vehicle for disseminating conventional ideas about the location and topography of the Earthly Paradise and its environs (Lascelles 1936; Patch 1950). And a modest amount of work addresses Mandeville's use of Prester John materials, although within a European, rather than English, context (Slessarev 1959).

The absence of a definitive text has seriously handicapped any more specific literary study. The most basic philological tasks have yet to be performed upon the English versions. One study has attempted to treat lexicon, but it provides little more than a listing of Cotton version vocabulary (see Osgood 1907). No scholar has yet undertaken even such basic studies as Mandeville's propensity to neologisms or to gallicisms, habits typifying well-known fourteenth-century translators. Stylistic and syntactic studies similarly remain in their infancy, the only such effort being that of van der Meer (1929).

Nor in spite of the obvious attractiveness and monumental popularity of *Travels* has the work inspired much critical commentary. Bennett (1954, pp. 15–86) should have broken ground here with her attractive, but very general,

appreciation of the work's literary merits. But her suggestions have not stimulated any great response. The three main exceptions to this generalization all concentrate upon the persona that animates the work (Bloomfield 1952; Howard
1971 and 1980; Zacher 1976). All insist upon the tolerance expressed by the
speaking voice, upon "Mandeville"'s reliance on a view of natural reason that
animates the world and mankind, and upon the processes involved in creating a
personal world out of books.

Although these studies perform a useful introductory function, they scarcely
exhaust those literary topics that deserve critical concern. A first issue is that of
literary form: when one talks of *Mandeville's Travels*, what kind of work is one
considering? What is its genre? Or is *Travels* a work sui generis? This issue emerges, somewhat covertly, in the editions: when editors divide *Travels* into two portions, the Jerusalem itinerary (Chaps. 1–15) and the Asiatic wanderings (as do
Hamelius 1919; Letts 1953), they imply a separation in kind as well as in geo-
graphical locus. For the opening section plainly belongs within a well-established
literary type, that of guidebooks for pilgrims, be they in Rome or Palestine. But
what changes are wrought in such an established genre by its juncture with what
the editorial division suggests is a literary anomaly?

Two very tentative and somewhat strained answers have been put forward.
These account for the book's apparently broken-backed structure by assuming a
fully satiric intent. Hamelius's notion (1923, pp. 14ff.) that *Travels* is intended
as an antipapal satire is surely misguided. But there is considerably more to be
said for Butturff's suggestion (1972) that the structure of the book establishes the
framework for an antipodean satire in which Europe is implicitly compared, to
its detriment, with other lands. But excepting a very few obvious passages of
complaint, *Travels* seems remarkably even tempered to be written toward such an
end; more cogent than either proposal remains the suggestion that the book reproduces the actions of an open and inquiring mind (Howard 1971, 1980;
Zacher 1976). But such a conclusion, although it speaks directly to the issue of
narrative manner, advances one no further in generic considerations.

A second formal consideration, in part suggested above, concerns the literary
shape of the work. To what extent does *Travels* have what critics take to be literary structure at all? In an obvious way *Travels* shares with many medieval works
an utterly linear narrative, and the island-to-island itineraries which comprise
much of the book surely accentuate this feature. Here a considerable amount of
work remains. To what extent does *Travels* rely upon repeated motifs (gardens or
great emperors, for example) or deliberate juxtapositions of related details or
what might be taken as imagery to give shape to "Mandeville"'s peregrinations?
Or to take another avenue of approach: given that "Mandeville" selected and
edited his texts in an eclectic manner, can his shifting between different accounts,
his additions and suppressions within these accounts, and the junctures he creates

between them reveal any structural intent? The raw materials for such an investigation have long been available through source studies, but some researcher has to lay these findings next to the text to achieve results.

A second large issue, particularly important in the context of this volume, concerns what one might call "the Englishness of the common version." Most critical comments on *Travels* have operated at a level of literary generality that would suit all full texts in any language. These comments thus address a universally European fad, rather than particular features of one or all English versions. One obvious way to focus study upon the specifically English accounts would be to investigate the uniquely English interpolations and their intent (see Moseley 1970b). But for the most part, such a discussion must begin with stylistic features: is it possible that any part of the common version's appeal was based on its manner, rather than its subject matter? Does the author, so far as constant comparison of his source and the translation allows, show facility as an English prose stylist? Or is he merely, as the scholar who knows him best claims (Seymour 1967, p. xix), "workmanlike"? But even if the translator of the common version was only a competent toiler guided by the language of the insular text before him, might one not wish to investigate further what literary virtues might be expressed in a direct or unadorned prose style? And more broadly, do these virtues and forms of plainness reflect concerns similar or alien to those of the original? And do they concur with or differ from the concerns of contemporary translators who seek directness?

Finally, the issue of style returns to the most fundamental appeal of the work—the sense of a personality that informs the narrative. As I've suggested above, the few past discussions of this literary character have not achieved any very clear agreement about his interests or function. In part, this situation reflects an impressionistic mode of approach that has animated much of the criticism. But perhaps by beginning at the very fact that "Mandeville" was produced by a full-scale literary hoax, critics might adopt a more rigorous approach to the work. If one is aware that the work is a feigned first-person narrative, it becomes possible to view *Travels* much as one might a Canterbury tale. In this context, one should be interested in "Mandeville"'s intentions, as they achieve literary expression. Do certain kinds of information interest the speaker more than other kinds? What does he explicitly state to be his designs upon the reader? And how do these stated goals accord with the actual narrative performance?

Most strikingly ignored in past discussions, I would think, has been the narrator's humor. This trait expresses itself, not simply through a skepticism and insistence upon empirical verifiability which flickers throughout a work founded on the miraculous and imaginary, but in a certain deliberate disingenuousness. As an especially flagrant example, one might consider "Mandeville"'s parting apology for not having told more of what he saw, for being selective: the traveler finally

demurs so that those who follow him overseas will still find new marvels to write
of "for men seyn alleweys that newe thinges and newe tydynges ben plesant to
here" (p. 228/21–22). The variety of ironic viewpoints this comment retrospectively casts over *Travels* should remind English readers, at least, of the master fictive ironist Chaucer.

Concluding with Chaucer suggests the fundamental goal of all these desired
studies. For the translator of the common version was also a Ricardian and of the
Ricardians, the one outstanding contributor of a prose piece written for "solaas."
It can scarcely be accidental that the English *Mandeville* industry produced in
this period a major French recension, four separate Latin ones, and at least the
two earliest English versions. In the broadest view, studies of the common version must contribute to our understanding of the literary milieu that produced the
greatest efflorescence of medieval English literature.

NOTES

1. A recension of the continental version, typified by additions concerning Ogier le danois, is sometimes treated as a third form of the text. It was probably created in the 1380s in Liège, perhaps
   by Jean d'Outremeuse.
2. For the problem of which year was intended, see de Poerck (1956, pp. 157–158). Steiner
   (1934) relies upon internal evidence of dubious value and Thomas (1957) upon a Latin interpolation peculiar to insular version texts.
3. The defective version must date from after 1377 since in an original interpolation it describes
   "Mandeville"'s visit to the pope in Rome. The Cotton version was probably composed ca. 1400
   (the MS dates from s. xvi/4, perhaps as early as 1410), and the lost translation from the Latin
   Royal version must be contemporary. The Egerton version must have been composed in the first
   quarter of the fifteenth century since the MS dates from ca. 1425; the Bodley and metrical versions are probably contemporary, although the latter might be slightly more recent (both its MSS
   copied s. xv med.). The stanzaic version (MS s. xvii/4 is the latest of all the forms of the text.
4. I think here of the copyist of Huntington HM 114, who to the horror of modern editors, routinely collated the texts he copied. He apparently discovered the Egypt omission by consultation
   or memory of the French. But rather than fill the gap by a new translation, he simply added, after
   transcribing *Travels*, a unique extract from *The Three Kings of Cologne* which treats one of the
   main Egyptian wonders, the garden of balm (see chap. 7, pp. 35/28–37/17). See Seymour
   (1966b, pp. 188–189, and 1974b).

BIBLIOGRAPHY

PRIMARY SOURCES

The English Prose Versions of *Mandeville's Travels* (*MT*)

Full lists of MSS occur in Bennett (1954, pp. 287–294) and, thoroughly supplanting Bennett, Seymour (1966b, with abbreviated versions in Seymour 1967, pp. 272–278 and 1973, pp. 193–197). Given the expansiveness and availability of these listings, only omissions and corrections are here noted. I list the texts in the probable chronological order of composition.

The common version, thirty-five copies (including one untraced MS) listed by Seymour. His no. 22 is now Cambridge, Fitzwilliam Museum, Bradfer Lawrence Dep BL 7 (see *TCBS* 6, ii [1973], 88); his no. 32, although still unlocated, can be traced further: it was bought at the Sneyd sale by Sir Thomas Brooke, at the Brooke sale (Sotheby, May 31, 1921, lot 921) by Sir Leicester Harmsworth, and resold among Harmsworth's MSS (Sotheby, October 16, 1945, lot 2023). To Seymour's list, add Bodleian Library, MS Lat. misc. 85, fols. 84–91 (a single quire with chaps. 13–14 only, identified by R. H. Robbins [1968] *E&S*, ns 21, 17 and n. 88); MS Digby 88, fol. 28 (notes; see Horner 1980); MS Rawlinson D 652 (a full text overlooked by all past researchers). There is no modern critical edition, although one based on MS no. 5 has been projected by Seymour for twenty years. The most reliable guide to the Middle English text remains Pynson (1496, STC 17246), available in STC microfilm. This text, in successive copies, was republished at least twenty times before 1725 (STC 17247–17254, Wing M 412–417); see Bennett (1954, pp. 346–359) for the fullest list of printed versions.

The Cotton version, unique to BL MS Cotton Titus C. xvi (fol. 60v in facsimile at C. E. Wright [1960] *English Vernacular Hands*, plate 17, Oxford: Clarendon Press). Many times printed: J. Woodman et al. (1725) London, the *editio princeps* (and first edited Mandeville text); A. W. Pollard (1900) repr. (1964) New York: Dover (partly modernized); P. Hamelius (1919–1923) EETS 153–154; and Seymour (1967) Oxford: Clarendon Press.

The Egerton version, unique to BL MS Egerton 1982. Printed by George F. Warner (1889) *The Buke of John Maundeuill*, Roxburghe Club (London: Nichols); and Malcolm Letts (1953) *Mandeville's Travels: Texts and Translations*, Hakluyt Society 2d ser. 101 (modernized), 1:1–223.

The Bodley version, in Bodleian Library, MS e Musaeo 116 and MS Rawlinson D 99. Printed by Letts (1953) Hakluyt Society 2d ser. 102 (modernized), 2:416–481, from Rawlinson; and Seymour (1963), EETS 253, from e Musaeo with collations from Rawlinson.

The English translation from the Latin Royal version does not survive intact but can be partially reconstructed from the agreements of Warner (1889), Letts (1953), and Seymour (1963).

SECONDARY DISCUSSIONS

Anderson, J. J. (1977) *Cleanness*. Manchester: Manchester University Press.

Bennett, Josephine Waters (1953a) "Chaucer and *MT*." *MLN*, 68, 531–534.

———— (1953b) "The Woodcut Illustrations in the English Editions of *MT*." *PBSA*, 47, 59–69.

———— (1954) *The Rediscovery of Sir John Mandeville*. MLA Monographs Series 19. New York: MLA.

Bloomfield, Morton W. (1952) "Chaucer's Sense of History." *JEGP*, 51, 301–313.

Bovenschen, Albert (1888) "Untersuchungen über Johann von Mandeville und die Quellen seiner Reisebeschreibung." *Zeitschrift der Geschichte für Erdkunde zu Berlin*, 23, 177–306.

Brown, Carleton (1904) "Note on the Dependence of *Cleanness* on the *Book of Mandeville*." *PMLA*, 19, 150–153.

Butturff, Douglas R. (1972) "Satire in *MT*." *AnM*, 13, 155–164.

Cawley, A. C. (1957) "A Ripon Fragment of '*MT*.'" *ES*, 38, 262–265.

———— (1972) "'*MT*': A Possible New Source." *N&Q*, 217, 47–48.

Day, Mabel, and Steele, R. (1934) *Mum and the Sothsegger*. EETS 199.

de Backer, Louis (1877) *L'Extreme-Orient au moyen âge*. Paris: E. Leroux.

de Poerck, Guy (1956) "La tradition manuscrite des 'Voyages' de Jean de Mandeville: à propos d'un livre récent." *Romanica Gandensia*, 4, 125–158.

Doyle, Mary, and Seymour, M. C. (1967) "The Irish Epitome of *MT*." *Eigse*, 12, 29–36.

Gollancz, Sir Israel (1921) *Cleanness*. Rev. by D. S. Brewer. Cambridge: Brewer, repr. 1974.

Horner, Patrick J. (1980) "*MT*: A New Manuscript Extract." *Manuscripta*, 24, 171–175.

Howard, Donald R. (1971) "The World of *MT*." *YES*, 1, 1–17.

———— (1980) *Writers and Pilgrims: Medieval Pilgrimage Narratives and Their Posterity*. Berkeley: University of California Press.

Lange, Hugo (1938a) "Chaucer und *MT*." *Archiv*, 174, 179–181.

———— (1938b) "Die Paradiesvorstellung in *MT*." *EStn*, 72, 312–314.

Lascelles, Mary (1936) "Alexander and the Earthly Paradise in Medieval English Writings." *MAE*, 5, 31–47, 79–104, 173–188.

Letts, Malcolm (1949) *Sir John Mandeville: The Man and His Book*. London: Batsworth.

Lidman, Mark J. (1974–1975) "*The Travels of Sir John Mandeville*: A Checklist." *Thoth*, 15:i, 13–18.

Lowes, John Livingston (1905) "The Dry Sea and the Carrenare." *MP*, 3, 1–46.

Moseley, C. W. R. D. (1970a) "The Lost Play of Mandeville." *Library*, 5th ser. 25, 46–49.

———— (1970b) "Sir John Mandeville's Visit to the Pope: The Implications of an Interpolation." *Neophil*, 54, 77–80.

———— (1974a) "Chaucer, Sir John Mandeville, and the Alliterative Revival: A Hypothesis concerning Relationships." *MP*, 72, 182–184.

—— (1974b) "The Metamorphoses of Sir John Mandeville." *YES*, 4, 5–25.

Mossé, Fernand (1955) "Du nouveau sur le Chevalier Jean Mandeville" (review article). *EA*, 8, 321–325.

Osgood, Charles G., Jr. (1907) Review of Robert Herndon Fife, Jr., *Der Wortschatz der englischen Mandeville nach der Version der Cotton Handschrift. American Journal of Philology*, 28, 90–94.

Patch, Howard Rollin (1950) *The Other World According to Descriptions in Medieval Literature*. Cambridge, Mass.: Harvard University Press.

Schepens, Luc (1964) "Quelques observations sur la tradition manuscrite de *Voyage* de Mandeville." *Scriptorium*, 18, 49–54.

Schofield, William Henry (1904) "The Nature and Fabric of *The Pearl*." *PMLA*, 19, 154–216.

Seymour, M. C. (1961a) "A Medieval Redactor at Work." *N&Q*, 206, 169–171.

—— (1961b) "The Origin of the Egerton Version of *MT*." *MAE*, 30, 159–169.

—— (1961c) "Secundum Johannem Maundvyle." *English Studies in Africa*, 4, 148–158.

—— (1963) "The Irish Version of *MT*." *N&Q*, 208, 364–366.

—— (1964a) "The Early English Editions of *MT*." *Library*, 5th ser. 19, 202–207.

—— (1964b) "Mandeville and Marco Polo: A Stanzaic Fragment." *Journal of the Australasian Universities Language and Literature Association*, 21, 39–52.

—— (1964c) "The Scribal Tradition of *MT*: The Insular Version." *Scriptorium*, 18, 34–48.

—— (1966a) "The English Epitome of '*MT*.'" *Anglia*, 84, 27–58.

—— (1966b) "The English Manuscripts of *MT*." *Transactions of the Edinburgh Bibliographical Society*, 4, 169–210.

—— (1968) "A Fifteenth-Century East Anglican Scribe." *MAE*, 37, 166–173.

—— (1973) *The Metrical Version of MT*. EETS 269.

—— (1974a) "A Letter from 'Sir John Mandeville.'" *N&Q*, 219, 326–328.

—— (1974b) "The Scribe of Huntington Library MS. HM 114." *MAE*, 43, 139–143.

—— (1977) "Medieval America and 'Sir John Mandeville.'" In *An English Miscellany Presented to W. S. Mackie*, edited by Brian S. Lee, pp. 46–53. Cape Town: Oxford University Press.

Seymour, M. C. and Waldron, R. A. (1963) "The Danish Version of *MT*." *N&Q*, 208, 406–408.

Slessarev, Vsevolod (1959) *Prester John: The Letter and the Legend*. Minneapolis: University of Minnesota Press.

Steiner, Arpad (1934) "The Date of Composition of *MT*." *Speculum*, 9, 44–47.

Taylor, E. G. R. (1953) "The Cosmographical Ideas of Mandeville's Day." In Letts (1953) *MT*, 1 : li–lix. Hakluyt Society, 2d ser. 102.

Thomas, J. D. (1957) "The Date of *MT*." *MLN*, 72, 165–169.

van der Meer, Hindrikus Johannes (1929) *Main Facts concerning the Syntax of MT*. Utrecht: Kemink.

Vogels, Johann (1891) "Handschriftliche Untersuchungen über die englische Version

Mandeville's" [*sic*]. *Jahresbericht über das Realgymnasium zu Crefeld, Schuljahr 1890–91*, 1. Crefeld: Kühler.

Wilson, R. M. (1970) *The Lost Literature of Medieval England*. 2d ed. London: Methuen.

Zacher, Christian K. (1976) "The Pilgrim as Curious Traveler: *MT*." In *Curiosity and Pilgrimage: The Literature of Discovery in Fourteenth-Century England*, pp. 130–157. Baltimore: Johns Hopkins University Press.

CHAPTER 8

John Trevisa

Anthony S. G. Edwards

Scholarly lack of interest in John Trevisa is simultaneously perplexing and understandable. It is perplexing in that Trevisa is clearly an important figure in the history of Middle English prose. The sheer volume of his work commands attention, running as it does to well over a million words. His major works, the translations of the *Polychronicon* and *De Proprietatibus Rerum*, helped to sustain and broaden the influence of these works during the fifteenth and sixteenth centuries. And his contributions to the development of the English language (though never adequately examined) appear considerable.

But, on the other hand, Trevisa is almost exclusively a translator. Also, much of his oeuvre does not fall directly under the purview of the literary scholar, consisting as it does of renderings of scientific, historical, or didactic works. Nor is there very much in the quality of the translations themselves to quicken literary sensibilities. And much of his corpus remains relatively inaccessible. Even in such thesis-hungry times these factors have constituted sufficiently effective deterrents. But there is much important work to be done.

Curiously enough, while his works have been neglected the life of Trevisa has been the subject of several useful studies. The available details of his life have been assembled by Perry (1925, Fowler (1960, 1962, 1971), and Emden (1959). The following paragraphs summarize the information they present.

Trevisa was born ca. 1342, probably in Cornwall and possibly at Trevessa. It is quite likely that from his youth he enjoyed the patronage of the Berkeley family. He entered Exeter College, Oxford in 1361 or 1362; subsequently he became a fellow of this college. He appears to have vacated this fellowship in 1369 to become a fellow of Queen's College. On June 8, 1370, he was ordained priest, after proceeding rapidly through the lesser orders in the same year.

Details of his subsequent ecclesiastical career are scant. Prior to the translation of the *Polychronicon* (ca. 1385–1387) he appears to have spent some time abroad, visiting Germany and Savoy. (He speaks with approval of the baths in those places: "I have assayed and bathed therein.") But the purpose of his trip is unknown. He became nonresident canon and prebendary of Westbury on Trym, Gloucestershire ca. 1389. It is likely that it was in the following year he became vicar of Berkeley in Cornwall. He was also given leave to travel abroad in 1390 by permission of the king with his letters of general attorney. His purpose is once again unknown.

Before his travels and ecclesiastical preferments Trevisa found himself involved in controversy at Oxford. In 1379 he was expelled from Queen's College together with the provost and other fellows. It was alleged that they refused "to account for certain moneys of the college that came into their hands . . . and have taken away charters, books, jewels and muniments, besides goods belonging to the college" (quoted in Fowler 1960, p. 92). How this matter was resolved, or indeed what it actually signifies is unknown (the best discussion is Fowler 1960), but Trevisa was apparently permitted to resume his fellowship and is recorded as residing in the college between 1383 and 1386. He also rented rooms in the college between 1394 and 1396, when he was no longer a fellow. No details of his final years survive, but he was certainly dead by May 1402.

Neither the chronology nor the canon of Trevisa's works is altogether clear. But some facts can be established.

The earliest work that can be ascribed to Trevisa with certainty is his translation of the *Polychronicon* of Ranulph Higden. Trevisa himself tells us that this was completed on April 18, 1387. And it is clear from internal evidence that he was working on Book I in 1385. To have completed his translation in little more than two years was a remarkable effort of sustained translation. (At a conservative count it runs to over three-quarters of a million words.) The *Polychronicon* is a universal history divided into seven books, dealing with a vast range of biblical and classical history and continuing to the death of Edward III. Trevisa made a number of additions to his source and added a brief continuation taking events down to the treaty of Bretigny. The whole work is prefaced by two brief, apparently original works by Trevisa: the *Dialogue between a Lord and a Clerk on Translation*, and his *Epistle . . . unto Lord Thomas of Barkley upon the translation of Polychronicon. . . .*

The only other work by Trevisa that can be precisely dated is his translation of Bartholomaeus Anglicus's widely popular and influential fourteenth-century encyclopedia, *De Proprietatibus Rerum*, which, he tells us, was completed on February 6, 1398. This was another massive piece of translation, running to over half a million words. Trevisa appears to have made relatively few additions to his source.

None of Trevisa's other certain translations compares in scale with these two, and none can be dated with certainty. His other large translation is of the *De Regimine Principum* of Aegidius Romanus, a work of about two hundred thousand words. It may postdate the translation of *De Proprietatibus Rerum*, but this is not certain. His other translations, of the apocryphal *Gospel of Nichodemus*, Richard Fitzralph's sermon *Defensio Curatorum*, and William Ockham's dialogue on temporal power, *Dialogus inter Militem et Clericum*, are all quite brief. One is tempted to date them between Trevisa's two major translations for no better (or worse) reason than that conjecture abhors a vacuum.

As I have already observed, Trevisa has not been the subject of much scholarly scrutiny. One crucial reason for such neglect is the lack of satisfactory modern editions of his corpus, an obvious necessary preliminary to further study. There are, for example, no published editions of the *Gospel of Nichodemus* or the *De Regimine Principum*. For the *Polychronicon* we must still rely on the Rolls Series edition prepared in the late nineteenth century. This is based on the Saint John's Cambridge manuscript, with partial collation of three others (of the fourteen now known to exist) and Caxton's printed edition. There is very little annotation. It cannot be used with much confidence that it provides a secure basis for conclusions.

Of greater value is Perry's edition of the *Dialogus inter Militem et Clericum* and the *Defensio Curatorum* (1925). These were each based on a collation of five of the six extant manuscripts. (The only one he was unable to examine was what is now the Huntington copy.) The texts appear to be presented with considerable accuracy. There is, however, no commentary and only a perfunctory glossary. In spite of these limitations Perry's edition remains the nearest approach we have to authoritative texts of any of Trevisa's works.

I say this notwithstanding the appearance in 1975 of a collaborative text of the *De Proprietatibus Rerum* under the title *On the Properties of Things* under the general editorship of M. C. Seymour. It is difficult to arrive at a just assessment of this edition without the promised third volume of notes and commentary. The edition is based on a collation of virtually all the known manuscripts and draws on the talents and experience of seventeen editors in several countries. Simply to overcome the enormous logistical problems posed by such an undertaking and to have created a publishable edition is a notable achievement, one that reflects Seymour's courage and single-mindedness. But large questions remain unanswered, particularly about the principles upon which the text was constructed.

One distinctive feature of the edition is the large number of conjectural emendations it makes. These often involve the rejection of defensible readings in the English manuscripts in favor of readings based on the authority of a number of Latin manuscripts of the *De Proprietatibus Rerum*. Since neither Trevisa's Latin exemplar nor his own final draft of his translation appears to be extant, extensive emendation on such principles could be adjudged an unsound undertaking. (I discuss the question of Trevisa's reliability as a translator later.) The matter is complicated by the necessarily selective apparatus accompanying the edition, which is at times inaccurate or contradictory, so that it is not always easy for a reader to be clear about the bases for specific editorial decisions. The projected third volume will no doubt serve to clarify such problems. As it is, the edition is a helpful contribution to medieval studies in that it makes available an important text. The question of the degree to which the form in which it does so can be justly termed Trevisa's remains an open one.

The editorial neglect must be the major impediment to other research on Trevisa. The *Polychronicon* translation has received most attention. The most significant study has been Fristedt's (1973); it has important implications for any study of Trevisa's translations. Fristedt takes as his point of departure the relationship between BL Add. 24194 and the Saint John's, Cambridge manuscripts. The former has a lengthy lacuna (Book VI, chaps. XIV–XXVI) which in the latter is filled by a translation completely different from that occurring in any of the other surviving manuscripts. Fristedt argues (a) that the Saint John's version is nonetheless by Trevisa; (b) that it is an early, literal one; and (c) that it has striking parallels in style and technique with the Early Version of the Wycliffe Bible. These conclusions, if valid, have bearing on questions of major importance to Trevisa studies—his methods as translator and his possible involvement in the translation of the Wycliffe Bible—and their implications are discussed below. The significance of Fristedt's work cannot be overstressed.

Other studies of the *Polychronicon* are of more limited value. The most useful are two studies by A. C. Cawley in 1937 and 1948. The first deals with the relationships between the manuscripts and Caxton's edition. The usefulness of the account is circumscribed by the fact that Cawley was aware of only seven of the fourteen extant manuscripts. But his categorizations provide the beginnings of a classification. His study of the punctuation of the *Polychronicon* (1948) is of much less value since it is based on an examination of only two chapters from Book I.

Other studies deal with more general concerns. John Taylor (1966), although primarily concerned with Higden's Latin original has much useful material that obviously helps to illuminate our understanding of Trevisa's translation. Later studies by Dwyer (1967) and Edwards (1973, 1980) have focused on the influence of the *Polychronicon*. Dwyer suggests possible influence on Chaucer and Lydgate. Edwards identifies an early sixteenth-century version (1973) and attempts to assess the influence and audience of the work down to the seventeenth century (1980). Whiting (1954) and Housman (1947) have notes on particular passages Trevisa added to his translation.

Work on the translation of *De Proprietatibus Rerum* has been meager. Se Boyar's article (1920) still remains the most helpful general account. As with the *Polychronicon* the most useful work has been textual or bibliographical. Most notable has been Mitchner's identification (1951) of the Plimpton manuscript as the copy text for de Worde's 1495 edition. Bitterling (1977b) has printed a manuscript fragment not used by Seymour in his edition. Seymour himself has printed Middle English abstracts of Trevisa's translations of Books VII and XVII (1969, 1973).

Several studies attempt to explore the influence of the work. Steadman (1959) has suggested possible influence on Chaucer's *Nun's Priest's Tale*, Bitterling (1977a) on the *Peterborough Lapidary*, and Dwyer (1979) on Lydgate's *Fall of Princes*. Seymour (1974) in a useful study notes a number of instances of interest in the *De Proprietatibus Rerum* between the fourteenth and sixteenth centuries. Finally, Parrish (1969) examined some of the transformations and accretions the work received in East's enlarged 1582 edition "Batman upon Bartholomew."

Trevisa's shorter works have been virtually ignored. Power's identification (1978) of a new manuscript of the *Gospel of Nichodemus* is the only study of note.

There is one further area of research that is of particular concern to students of Trevisa. This is the question of Trevisa's possible involvement in a translation of the Bible into English, possibly the Early Version of the Wycliffe Bible. There is a tradition that Trevisa did make such a translation. The question has been most recently reexamined by Fowler (1960) and by Fristedt (1973). Both connect Trevisa in different ways to the Wycliffe Bible. And Fristedt feels able to conclude that "Trevisa's close acquaintance with the making of the Wycliffe Bible in all its stages has herewith been disclosed and in consequence he must also have been active in their production" (1973, p. 40).

The validity of this claim is open to some question. But it is useful in that it helps to define several crucial areas in which future Trevisa research is very necessary. These are discussed in the next section.

The first major area for future inquiry must be the question of the Trevisa canon. The fundamental problem of attribution lies in Trevisa's possible involvement in the translation of the Wycliffe Bible. There are some compelling objections to Fristedt's conclusion quoted above. The earliest identification of Trevisa as a Bible translator was made by Caxton in 1482 in his prologue to his edition of Trevisa's translation of the *Polychronicon*. He states there that Trevisa "atte re-

quest of thomas lord barkley translated [the *Polychronicon*], the byble and bar-
tylmewe de proprietatibus rerum out of latyn into english." It should be noted
that Caxton does not identify Trevisa as translator of the *Wycliffe* Bible. In fact,
no specific attribution of it to him seems to have been made before the seventeenth
century. Nor is there any evidence to suggest that either Trevisa or his patron,
Lord Berkeley, had any Wycliffite sympathies.

But Fowler, in his 1960 study, feels able to pronounce with confidence on his
involvement. He places great weight on the fact that Trevisa was at Queen's College during the 1360s and 1370s at a time when his contemporaries included
both Nicholas Hereford, one of the known compilers of the Early Version of the
Wycliffe Bible, and John Wycliffe himself. The presence of three such figures all
concerned in various ways with vernacular translation, at the same time within
the same college, is to say the least, a striking coincidence. And one may wonder,
in passing, how Trevisa may have occupied himself between his arrival at Oxford
ca. 1361–1362 and the beginning of his first dated translation ca. 1385. Even if
it were possible to demonstrate that all his shorter works were composed before
1385 they would scarcely provide a sufficient volume of literary activity to explain credibly the speed with which he translated the *Polychronicon*. We also know
that Trevisa was an advocate of translating the Bible into English; he argues for it
in his *Dialogue between a Lord and a Clerk on Translation* which precedes the *Polychronicon*: "the gospel, and prophecy, and the right faith of holy church must be
told [to Englishmen] . . . in English, and that is not done but by English translation . . . then English translation is good and needful" (Pollard 1903, pp.
206–207). Finally, there are Fristedt's arguments of alleged stylistic correspondences between passages in the Saint John's manuscript of the *Polychronicon* and
the Early Version.

Clearly, the whole problem stands in need of further clarification. Several lines
of inquiry suggest themselves. It is possible that more extensive publication of
Wycliffite writings in both Latin and English may offer new clues about the authorship and methods of preparation of the Bible translations. Also, more study
of theory and practice of translation as it applies to both the Wycliffe Bible and
Trevisa's known works would help to provide firmer criteria for attribution. In
the light of our present knowledge, Trevisa's involvement in Bible translation,
while circumstantially possible, is not yet conclusively established.

The Wycliffe Bible is not the only unresolved problem in the Trevisa canon.
Digby 233 in the Bodleian Library contains in addition to the unique, unedited
copy of Trevisa's translation of Aegidius Romanus's *De Regimine Principum* a
translation of Vegetius's *De Re Militari* sometimes ascribed to Trevisa. (The
work also appears in a number of other manuscripts as noted by Shrader 1979.)
H. N. MacCracken (1913) has argued on internal evidence that it is by Trevisa.

Perry (1925) takes an equivocal position, while Fowler (1962) cites unpublished research ascribing it to John Walton. Two major difficulties exist in any attempt to assign this work to Trevisa: (a) the colophon to the text in Digby 233 states that "þe turnynge of þis book into englisch was wreton & endud in . . . a þousand foure hundred & eiȝte"—six years after Trevisa's death; (b) the colophon to the Digby manuscript which also appears in other copies conceals the identity of the translator by a cryptogram. A variety of solutions have been offered to this cryptogram; the name "Trevisa" is not a convincing one. Such problems must carry considerable weight, even if they do not constitute absolutely insuperable objections to Trevisa's authorship. But until a full edition has been prepared and carefully compared with reliable editions of Trevisa's known works the question cannot be regarded as finally settled.

In general, it seems desirable to establish much clearer canonical criteria for Trevisa's works. Apart from the work of Perry (1937) and Fristedt (1973), both of whom employed very limited bodies of material, no studies exist that attempt to establish linguistic or grammatical characteristics for Trevisa that could be applied to works of disputed authorship. Yet until such criteria are established, we face the prospect of extreme and implausible attributions of the order of Fowler's (1961) attempt to graft *Piers Plowman* onto the Trevisa canon.

As the previous paragraphs suggest, a pressing issue intimately involved with problems of the Trevisa canon is the question of his principles and practice as translator. Trevisa himself has left only a relatively brief statement of principles as a preface to the *Polychronicon*, and none in any of his other writings. The *Polychronicon* statement is not a great deal of help. In it Trevisa insists on literalness and clarity as synonymous terms at the same time as he demonstrates their difference. What does Trevisa mean by his claim that in his translation "the meaning shall stand and not be changed"? Is he a faithful translator? Seymour (1975) argues that "Trevisa was an intelligent and competent Latinist who generally . . . followed the Latin text before him without question, though occasionally interpolating his own comment" (p. xv). This conclusion seems often at odds with Seymour's actual procedures; he makes a large number of conjectural emendations to the text because of its apparent failure to follow accurately the postulated norm of the Latin.

There is further evidence that raises questions about Trevisa's degree of proficiency as a translator. The editors of the *Polychronicon* observe that "Trevisa appears to have been puzzled with the Latinity of Higden . . . It must be owned that [he] has occasionally fallen into the most ludicrous errors . . . it is impossible not to perceive that Higden's scholarship is very far superior to that of his translator" (Babington and Lumby 1865, 1:lix–lx). It is hard to know how much weight to attach to these views since they are based on examination of so few manuscripts of Trevisa's translation. But there is some support for them in the researches of H. K. Kim (1963) who, in an unpublished edition of Trevisa's *Gospel of Nichodemus* has found over twenty passages in a relatively short text (no more than thirteen thousand words) where Trevisa seems to have either mistranslated or included nonsense of his own devising. But such doubts about Trevisa's accuracy have been recently challenged by Lawler in an important study (1983) which concludes that he is "surprisingly fluent and competent . . . by his own criteria, accurate, intelligible, and idiomatic." The question warrants further examination. Apart from Lawler's work, the only study of Trevisa as translator is Perry's very general one (1937).

A necessary preliminary to any conclusions about Trevisa's accuracy as a translator would seem to be some attempt to identify more precisely the source texts for his translations. There are obvious problems here, particularly in the cases of the *Polychronicon* and the *De Proprietatibus Rerum* of which numerous copies survive in the original Latin. Taylor's important work (1966) on the different versions of the *Polychronicon* should provide considerable assistance to any effort to determine which manuscript Trevisa used. As it is, we know that he had access to a text containing both Higden's acrostic spelling of his name and a passage on the diameter of the earth, neither of which appears in the earliest version (unfortunately also the least copied). We also know that during the 1370s Trevisa removed a copy of the *Polychronicon* from Queen's College, a copy for which a *secundo folio* reading exists (see further Fowler 1960). An attempt to identify, if not the text itself, at least the type of text to which Trevisa had access, is an obvious starting point for a study of his translational accuracy.

Similar studies could be undertaken for other works. We lack even a preliminary classification of the manuscripts of the *De Proprietatibus Rerum*. Possibly the completion of Seymour's edition will go some way toward remedying this lack. Kim (1965) has identified with some precision the type of Latin text Trevisa used in his *Gospel of Nichodemus*. It may also be possible to identify the sort of Latin exemplar employed in the Aegidius Romanus translation.

More precise identification of Trevisa's source texts must be studied in conjunction with the larger question of his methods of translation. Fristedt's (1973) hypothesis of two stages of translation in the *Polychronicon*, an initial literal one and then a more polished one, merits further study to see whether it provides a general principle for Trevisa's translational technique. There are some indications that it may. Perry (1925) detects a similar process in the surviving texts of the *Dialogus inter Militem et Clericum*. It may also be evidenced in the manuscripts of the *De Proprietatibus Rerum*. Two of those that appear earliest, Harley 4789 and Bodleian e Musaeo 16, evidence a higher degree of fidelity to the postulated Latin norm and also have a greater frequency of clearly incorrect readings.

The relationship is never clearly set out between these manuscripts and the remaining ones, including the base manuscript BL Add. 27944, but their readings are given considerable weight. It remains to be seen how this way of proceeding can be justified if it can be demonstrated that this text was also an evolving one.

In this, as in most other respects, conclusions will have to wait upon the preparation of reliable critical editions of Trevisa's work. It is only with such editions to hand that we will be able to attempt satisfactory definitions of the distinctive features of Trevisa's translational technique. Did he revise his works? How recurrent is the oft-noted use of doublets? To what degree is he a neologizer? To what extent did he depart from his source texts? In what ways does he add to them?

Finally, it would be helpful to have a clearer sense of the influence of Trevisa's translations, particularly the *Polychronicon* and the *De Proprietatibus Rerum*. Some beginnings have been made by Taylor (1966), Seymour (1974), and Edwards (1980 and forthcoming). But a fuller, more systematic study is needed of the ways in which these translations were used during the later Middle Ages and Renaissance. We already know that the *Polychronicon* was plundered by a variety of later writers and was being reworked as late as the end of the seventeenth century. And the literary influence of the *De Proprietatibus* seems to have been pervasive and constant between the time of Lydgate and that of Burton and Milton. A detailed study is merited. It is only in the eighteenth century that Trevisa sank into obscurity and was seen as of interest only to eccentric antiquarians of the kind satirized by Dr. Johnson as Hirsutus who "when he was serious, he expatiated on the narratives of Johan de Trevisa."[1] Trevisa, one of the most versatile and prolific of translators into Middle English, deserves a better fate than such ridicule.

NOTE

1. *The Rambler*, ed. W. J. Bate and A. B. Strauss (New Haven: Yale University Press, 1969), 3 : 170; the quotation is from no. 177 for November 26, 1751.

BIBLIOGRAPHY

PRIMARY WORKS

Primary works are listed in conjectured chronological order.

DIALOGUE BETWEEN A LORD AND A CLERK ON TRANSLATION

MANUSCRIPTS

BL Cotton Tiberius D. vii, fols. 1–2v
BL Harley 1900, fols. 42–43v
BL Stowe 65, fols. 217–218
Glasgow University MS Hunterian 367, fol. 1
Huntington Library HM 28561, fols. 41–42v

PRINTED EDITION

Pollard, A. W., ed. (1903) *Fifteenth Century Prose and Verse*, pp. 203–208 (modernized). London: Archibald Constable & Co. See under *Polychronicon* for early printed editions.

EPISTLE . . . UNTO LORD THOMAS OF BARKLEY
UPON THE TRANSLATION OF POLYCHRONICON . . .

MANUSCRIPTS

BL Cotton Tiberius D. vii, fol. 2v
BL Harley 1900, fol. 43v
BL Stowe 65, fol. 218
Princeton University Library, Taylor MS, fol. 8v
Huntington HM 28561, fol. 42

PRINTED EDITION

Pollard, A. W., ed. (1903), pp. 209–210. See under *Polychronicon* for early printed editions.

POLYCHRONICON

MANUSCRIPTS

BL Cotton Tiberius D. vii, fols. 6v–296
BL Harley 1900, fols. 44–310v
BL Stowe 65, fols. 1–201
BL Add. 24194, fols. 21–262
Saint John's College, Cambridge MS 204, fols. 34–280
Corpus Christi College, Cambridge MS 354, fols. 1–206
Chetham's Library, Manchester, MS 11379, fols. 37v–178v
Aberdeen University MS 21, fols. 12–171v
Glasgow University MS Hunterian 367, fols. 2ff.
Liverpool Public Library MS, fols. 1–220
Princeton University Library, Garrett 151, fols. 1–212v
Princeton University Library, Taylor MS, fols. 9–225
Huntington Library HM 28561, fols. 24–319
olim Boies Penrose, sold at Sotheby's (London), December 8, 1981

MANUSCRIPT SELECTIONS

BL Lansdowne 210, fols. 67v–73 (printed in part in Edwards 1973)
Bodleian Rawlinson C. 86, fols. 31v–49v
Trinity College, Oxford, MS 29
Asloan MS, fols. 77–86
Huntington HM 144, fols. 54v–64v

PRINTED EDITIONS

Caxton, 1482 (STC 13438)
de Worde, 1495 (STC 13439)
Treveris, 1527 (STC 13440)
Babington, C., and Lumby, J. R., eds. (1865–1886) 9 vols. Rolls Series.
See also *Discripcion of Englande*, Caxton 1480 (STC 13440a) and de Worde 1498 (STC
    13440b), both of which are selections from *Polychronicon*.

DEFENSIO CURATORUM

MANUSCRIPTS

BL Harley 1900, fols. 6–21
BL Stowe 65, fols. 205v–217
BL Add. 24194, fols. 8–21
Saint John's College, Cambridge MS 204, fols. 5–18v

Chetham's Library, Manchester MS 11379, fols. 5v–18v
Huntington Library HM 28561, fols. 5v–20v

PRINTED EDITION

Perry, A. J. (1925) *Dialogus inter Militem et Clericum* [&c], pp. 39–93. EETS, os 167.

DIALOGUS INTER MILITEM ET CLERICUM

MANUSCRIPTS

BL Harley 1900, fols. 1–5v
BL Stowe 65, fols. 202–205v
BL Add. 24194, fols. 4–8
Saint John's College, Cambridge MS 204, fols. 1–5
Chetham's Library, Manchester MS 11379, fols. 1–5v
Huntington Library HM 28561, fols. 1–5v

PRINTED EDITIONS

Berthelet [n.d.] (STC 12511) and [1540?] (STC 12511a)
Perry, A. J. (1925), pp. 1–38.

GOSPEL OF NICHODEMUS

MANUSCRIPTS

BL Add. 16165, fols. 94v–114
Salisbury Cathedral MS 39, fols. 129v–147
Winchester College MS 33, fols. 74–93
Kim, H. D., ed. (1963) "*The Gospel of Nichodemus*, translated by John Trevisa." Ph.D.
diss., University of Washington.

DE PROPRIETATIBUS RERUM

MANUSCRIPTS

BL Harley 614, fols. 1–242
BL Harley 4789, fols. 1–286
BL Add. 27944, fols. 2–330
BL Add. 45680, fols. 48–49 (fragments)
Bodleian e Musaeo 16, fols. 1–310

Cambridge University Library Ii. v. 41, fols. 2–343
Bristol City Library MS 9, fols. 1–137
Columbia University, Plimpton 263, fols. 1–379
Pierpont Morgan Library M 875, fols. 1–337

MANUSCRIPT SELECTIONS

BL Sloane 983, fols. 81–102v (printed Seymour 1969 and 1973)

PRINTED EDITIONS

de Worde, 1495 (STC 1536)
Berthelet, 1535 (STC 1537)
East, 1582 (STC 1538)
Seymour, M. C., et al. (1975) *On the Properties of Things.* 2 vols. Oxford: Clarendon Press.

DE REGIMINE PRINCIPUM

MANUSCRIPT

Bodleian Digby 233, fols. 1–182v

SECONDARY WORKS

Babington, C., and Lumby, J. R. (1865–1886) See *Polychronicon*, Printed Editions.
Bitterling, Klaus B. (1977a) "Notes on the Text of the Peterborough Lapidary." *N&Q*, 222, 303–306.
———— (1977b) "Zwei bisher unbeachtete Fragmente der Mittelenglischen Übersetzungen von Bartholomaeus Anglicus, *De Rerum Proprietatibus*." *NM*, 78, 47–56.
Cawley, A. C. (1937) "Puncutation in the Early Versions of Trevisa." *London Medieval Studies*, 1:1, 116–133.
———— (1948) "Relationships of the Trevisa Manuscripts and Caxton's *Polychronicon*." *London Medieval Studies*, 1:3, 463–482.
Dwyer, Richard A. (1967) "Some Readers of John Trevisa." *N&Q*, 212, 291–292.
———— (1979) "Arthur's Stellification in Lydgate's *Fall of Princes*." *PQ*, 57, 155–171.
Edwards, Anthony S. G. (1973) "A Sixteenth Century Version of Trevisa's *Polychronicon*." *ELN*, 11, 34–38.
———— (1978) "Notes on the *Polychronicon*." *N&Q*, 223, 2–3.
———— (1980) "The Influence and Audience of the *Polychronicon*: Some Observations." *Proceedings of the Leeds Philosophical and Literary Society*, Literary and Historical Section, 17, pt. 6, 113–119.

———— (forthcoming) "Bartholomaeus Anglicus and Medieval English Literature."
Archiv.

Emden, A. B. (1959) Biographical Register of the University of Oxford to A.D. 1500, 3,
1903–1904. Oxford: Clarendon Press.

Fowler, David C. (1960) "John Trevisa and the English Bible." MP, 58, 81–98.

———— (1961) Piers the Plowman, pp. 185–205. Seattle: University of Washington
Press.

———— (1962) "New Light on John Trevisa." Traditio, 18, 289–317.

———— (1971) "More about John Trevisa." MLQ, 32, 243–264.

Fristedt, Sven L. (1973) The Wycliffe Bible: Part III, pp. 8–58. Stockholm: Almqvist &
Wiksell.

Housman, J. E. (1947) "Higden, Trevisa, Caxton and the Beginnings of Arthurian
Criticism." RES, 23, 209–217.

Kim, H. C. (1963) See Gospel of Nichodemus, Manuscripts.

Lawler, Traugott (1983) "On the Properties of John Trevisa's Major Translations." Viator, 14, 267–268.

MacCracken, Henry N. (1913) "Vegetius in English." In Anniversary Papers . . . [for
G. L.] Kittredge, pp. 389–403. Boston: Ginn & Co.

Mitchner, R. W. (1951) "Wynkyn de Worde's Use of the Plimpton Manuscript of De
Proprietatibus Rerum." Library, 5th ser. 6, 7–18.

Parrish, Verna M. (1969) "Batman's Additions from Elyot and Boorde to His English
Edition of Bartholomaeus Anglicus." In Studies in Language, Literature and Culture of
the Middle Ages and Later, edited by E. B. Atwood and A. A. Hill, pp. 337–346.
Austin: University of Texas Press.

Perry, Aaron J. (1925) see Defensio Curatorum and Dialogus, Printed Editions.

———— (1937) "Trevisa as Translator." In Manitoba Essays, pp. 277–289. Toronto:
Macmillan.

Pollard, A. W. (1903) See Dialogue and Epistle, Printed Editions.

Power, Kathleen H. (1978) "A Newly Identified Prose Version of the Trevisa Version of
the Gospel of Nichodemus." N&Q, 223, 5–7.

Se Boyar, G. E. (1920) "Bartholomaeus Anglicus and His Encyclopedia." JEGP, 19,
168–189.

Seymour, Michael C. (1969) "A Middle English Abstract of Bartholomaeus, De Proprietatibus Rerum." Anglia, 87, 1–25.

———— (1973) "More about a Middle English Abstract of Bartholomaeus, De Proprietatibus Rerum." Anglia, 91, 18–34.

———— (1974) "Some Medieval English Owners of De Proprietatibus Rerum." Bodleian
Library Record, 9, 156–165.

Seymour, M. C. et al. (1975) See De Proprietatibus, Printed Editions.

Shrader, C. R. (1979) "A Handlist of Extant Manuscripts Containing the De Re Militari
of Flavius Vegetius Renatus." Scriptorium, 33, 280–305.

Steadman, John M. (1959) "Chauntecleer and Medieval Natural History." Isis, 50,
236–244.

Taylor, John (1966) The Universal Chronicle of Ranulf Higden. Oxford: Clarendon Press.

Whiting, Bartlett Jere (1954) "Miller's Head Revisited." MLN, 69, 309–310.

CHAPTER 9

Minor Devotional Writings

Michael G. Sargent

The purpose of this chapter is to describe those works of religious devotion that cannot be attributed to such major writers as Rolle, Hilton, the author of *The Cloud of Unknowing*, Julian of Norwich, Nicholas Love, or Margery Kempe. Indeed, they are "minor" primarily in this sense, for some of the works described here are among the longest, and some among the most popular, of prose writings in Middle English. They are also "minor works" in the sense that they are derivative: virtually all of them are either direct translations of works originally written in other languages, or compilations made up from such works and earlier English writings. "Devotional" is here taken inclusively to refer to the entire range of piety from simple, affective prayer to works describing, or inciting to, contemplative union, and overlaps to an extent with material covered in other chapters of this survey. Several works of general religious instruction in particular, treated separately by Alexandra Barratt (see Chapter 18), include sections at least that must be described as devotional. I attempt, however, to avoid duplication of treatment here of works more adequately, or more properly, treated elsewhere.

Some of the difficulty in defining the limits of devotional literature, and the rationale for an inclusive approach, can be seen in Valerie Lagorio's essay "Problems in Middle English Mystical Prose" (Edwards and Pearsall 1981, pp. 129–148). A problem at least equal to that of lack of definition of this material, however, is that of lack of access to it. The only adequate reference guide to the manuscripts is Peter Jolliffe's *Check-List* (1974a: hereafter *Check-List*), which lists 349 separate works—or versions of works distinct enough to merit separate entry—that fall roughly into the areas of devotional writing and religious instruction. Jolliffe provides complete manuscript and print bibliography for the listed items, arranged into fifteen overlapping categories of instructional writings, plus cross-reference indices by incipit, manuscript, and author and title, if known. One should be aware, however, of the limits that Jolliffe imposed upon his work: not only are all major works excluded, sermons and Wycliffite tracts, but so are lists and expositions of the articles of the Creed, the Lord's Prayer, the

Commandments, the seven deadly sins, and so forth, intended rather for impersonal instruction than for personal guidance, as well as prayers and tracts for use in affective prayer, religious rules and writings that first occur in printed form (*Check-List*, pp. 25–32). Within these limitations, however, the *Check-List* is an extremely useful research tool. The recent *Incipits of Latin Works on the Virtues and Vices* (Bloomfield, Guyot, Howard, and Kabealo 1979), more fully described by Barratt, provides an indispensable key to the literature underlying the instructional treatises, useful as well for the exploration of the more strictly devotional material. The chapter "Secondary Works" in Valerie Lagorio and Ritamary Bradley's bibliography of the fourteenth-century English mystics (1981, pp. 133–162) lists the material already in print and forthcoming editions of which the editors were aware. The same two editors have also undertaken the revision of the section "Rolle and His Followers" in Wells's *Manual of the Writings in Middle English 1050–1400* (1926). It should be added that a good deal of information on minor devotional writings in Middle English was published by Hope Emily Allen, particularly in *Writings Ascribed to Richard Rolle* (1927), a work that is probably still the best starting point for research in the area. A final reference tool, Peter Revell's *Fifteenth Century English Prayers and Meditations* (1975), must be used with extreme caution. As a finder's list, it is an adequate guide to one of the categories of material excluded by Jolliffe; but the accuracy of Revell's descriptions and attributions depends entirely upon the accuracy of the British Library catalogues of manuscripts and incunabula from which he drew his information, much of which is unfortunately both dated and incorrect. A proper reference work treating manuscript and printed Middle English prayers and meditations has yet to be written.

Another problem of access to minor devotional writings is, of course, the lack of critical editions of many of them. Of the 349 devotional and instructional items listed by Jolliffe, for example, only 40 have been edited critically. Another 28 have been printed, but not in critical editions (including works of which partial critical editions have been produced, or those of which a single-manuscript edition has been produced—usually by Horstman—but of which several more manuscripts are now known), while 9 critical editions have been produced in doctoral dissertations, but never actually published. It should be kept in mind, however, that many of the unedited works listed by Jolliffe, and many of the prayers and meditations not listed, are short pieces occurring in few manuscripts: of the 272 unedited pieces in Jolliffe's *Check-List*, 202 are shorter than five manuscript folios, and 195 occur only in one manuscript; 150 are both. Only 45 pieces occurring in a single manuscript are more than five folios in length, and 52 shorter pieces occur in more than one manuscript; only 25 pieces more than five folios in length occur in more than one manuscript. Yet despite the fact that many of the unedited devotional writings are not long or common enough to be individually significant, the sheer number of such short confessions, prayers, exhortations, and meditations makes them important to any literary history of the period; and it is to be hoped that one of the results of the process of indexing all surviving Middle English prose will be some sort of reference guide to these most truly minor of the minor devotional writings.

The more prominent of the minor works may, with a few late-fifteenth- and early-sixteenth-century exceptions, be divided into two classes: the straightforward translations of works written in other languages and imported into England in Latin or French, and the compilations. These minor devotional writings are not unique in their derivative character: Nicholas Love is known only for his translation of the *Meditationes Vitae Christi*; Hilton's *Eight Chapters* is a professed translation of a no-longer-extant Latin original, and the Middle English *Stimulus Amoris*, the *Prickynge of Love*, is one of the best-known works attributed to him; and among the lesser works of the *Cloud* corpus are two translations and one compilation. Another translation, the *Ladder of Foure Ronges* (*Check-List* M.1), which occurs in one of the manuscripts of the *Cloud* corpus and twice elsewhere, is similar enough in intent to merit its inclusion in Phyllis Hodgson's edition of *Deonise Hid Diuinite* and other tracts (1955, pp. 100–117; see also Hodgson 1949), but not attribution to the author of the *Cloud*. The *Ladder* is a version of the *Scala Claustralium*, a work written for novices on the monastic occupations of reading, meditation, prayer, and contemplation by Guigo II, ninth prior of the Grande Chartreuse (d. 1188), edited in Latin and French and recently reissued in English by Edmund Colledge and James Walsh (1970, 1978). Colledge and Walsh pointed out that the *Ladder* derives from a version of the Latin text the shape of which has been completely rearranged, apparently "to make the treatise less schematic and less obviously didactic, and thus more suitable for devotional reading. . . . The English translator carries this process even further" (Colledge and Walsh 1978, pp. 39–40). The *Ladder of Foure Ronges*, perhaps corrected against its Latin original, also provided some of the material, and possibly even the intent and organization, of *Þe Holy Boke Gratia Dei*, a compilation discussed below.

Another twelfth-century letter of religious instruction later translated into Middle English was the *De Institutione Inclusarum* of the Cistercian abbot Aelred of Rievaulx, probably written in 1163–1164 (ed. Dumont 1961; Hoste and Talbot 1971). Barratt has pointed out that this anachoritic rule, which borrows some of its defense and description of the solitary life from the *Consuetudines* of the Carthusian Order (1977), was later in turn drawn upon by the author of the *Ancrene Wisse* (1980). Further, there exist two separate translations of the *De Institutione Inclusarum* into Middle English, each of which exists in a single manuscript (*Check-List* H.25): one version is found in the Vernon manuscript; and the other in a manuscript copied by Stephen Doddesham, originally of Witham

Charterhouse, but later transferred to Sheen near Richmond, where he died in
1481–1482 (see Barratt 1977, p. 536). The two translations have recently been
edited together by Ayto and Barratt (projected for 1984).

The treatise *De Exterioris et Interioris Hominis Compositione*, a long work for
religious by the Franciscan David of Augsburg (d. 1272), describing the reformation of the fallen soul to the image of God and the extirpation of the image of
sin in three books addressed to spiritual beginners, proficients, and perfect, was
also twice translated into Middle English (*Check-List* H.2a). Both translations,
according to Jolliffe's description (1974b), call themselves *Formula Noviciorum*
after the first book of the Latin original, but declare themselves ignorant of the
name of the author. In fact, although David of Augsburg's authorship of the last
two books has been generally accepted, the Quaracchi editors (1899) noted that
the first book, which occasionally occurs separately, is often, probably falsely, attributed to others. The first of the two Middle English versions of the entire
treatise addresses itself, interestingly, not only to religious who have no Latin,
but also to all—even secular men and women—who desire to serve God. The
second Middle English version exists only in a copy made by Thomas Prestins, a
brother in the Bridgettine convent of Syon in the early sixteenth century, and is
addressed specifically to the Syon nuns. Another manuscript contains an abstract
from the first book of the *De Compositione* (*Check-List* H.2b); a translation of a
single chapter of the first book also exists in two manuscripts (*Check-List* I.4); one
of these also contains a translation of a section of the second book (*Check-List*
D.5), another version of which occurs at the conclusion of the compilation *The
Cleansing of Man's Soul*. None of these versions of the *De Compositione* has yet
been edited.

Several translations exist also of works of the continental women mystics. *The
Booke of Gostlye Grace* translates the *Liber Specialis Gratie* of Mechtild of Hackeborn, a nun in the celebrated Benedictine convent of Helfta (d. 1298). Both the
original Latin text, a record of mystical visions and experiences ("special graces")
in seven books, and a short version in five books, as well as collections of shorter
extracts, circulated throughout Europe; the most accessible edition dates from the
late nineteenth century, and is not entirely satisfactory (Mechtild 1877). Theresa
A. Halligan, who edited the Middle English version (1979), listed twenty-one
extracts, paraphrases, texts, and references in English and Latin found in manuscripts of English provenance. *The Booke of Gostlye Grace*, which survives in two
manuscripts, derives from the shorter, five-book version of the Latin text. Pointing out the connections of English manuscripts of the *Liber Specialis Gratie*,
and the possible connection of MS Bodley 220 of *The Booke of Gostlye Grace*,
with members of the Carthusian and Bridgettine orders, N. F. Blake suggested
(1973) that the Latin text was transmitted to England by the Carthusians, and
translated for the nuns of Syon. Halligan, who admitted that this hypothesis was

"not unreasonable," considered it, however, as no more than a possibility (1974, 1979, p. 53); her edition is in fact based on the northern, less probably Carthusian BL MS Egerton 2006. The anonymous fifteenth-century Carthusian compiler of the *Speculum Devotorum* drew heavily upon the *Liber Specialis Gratie*; and at least four other, unedited Middle English extracts survive (*Check-List* I.31).

The *Dialogo* of Catherine of Siena was also translated into English, specifically for the Bridgettine nuns, as *The Orchard of Syon* (Denise 1958; Hodgson 1964; ed. Hodgson and Liegey 1966). The *Dialogo* was, according to the well-known story, dictated by Catherine in her native Tuscan while rapt in ecstasy; it was completed in 1378, two years before her death. The Middle English translation was made from a contemporary Latin version. Two of the three surviving manuscripts of the *Orchard* date from the early fifteenth century, and seem to have been intended for the first generation of nuns in Syon, founded in 1415, although a connection with the Benedictine convent of Barking has also been suggested (Hodgson 1964). The version of the *Orchard* printed by Wynkyn de Worde in 1519 at the expense of Richard Sutton, steward of Syon, a de luxe edition of some typographical significance, also contains a translation of the introductory prologue to the *Dialogo* by Raymund of Capua, Catherine's confessor for the last four years of her life. The problem of the organization of the *Dialogo*, its division by later redactors into chapters and books, has been discussed and perhaps finally settled by Giuliana Cavallini, in the critical edition of the Italian text (1968); but the division into seven parts, each of five chapters and thirty-five "alleys" in which the nuns might walk, is one of the interesting features of the Middle English version. The Pierpont Morgan manuscript, on the other hand, is divided according to the more usual 170-chapter system, and may represent either an intermediate step in the creation of the format of the *Orchard*, or a reimposition of that of the original.

William Flete, an English Augustinian friar who gave up academic life and moved to the celebrated monastery of his order at Lecceto in Italy in 1359, was a particularly important spiritual adviser to Catherine of Siena during the years from 1362 until 1374, when Raymund of Capua became her confessor. Although Flete's refusal to come to Rome in 1379 in support of Urban VI caused an estrangement between them, Catherine forgave him and reaffirmed her confidence in him before her death the following year. Before Flete left England, however, he wrote an influential tract *De Remediis contra Temptaciones*, of which some thirty-seven manuscripts survive: twenty representing four different recensions of the original Latin, and seventeen of three separate Middle English versions (*Check-List* K.8). The growth of this text has been described in detail by Benedict Hackett (1961; see Hackett, Colledge, and Chadwick 1964); but only the expanded third English version has been published (ed. Colledge and Chadwick

1968; see Horstman 1896, pp. 106–123). The *De Remediis* was also used in several fifteenth-century compilations, including the *Speculum Spiritualium*, the *Fervor Amoris*, and *The Chastising of God's Children*, and even (although perhaps only indirectly known) in Thomas More's *Dialogue of Comfort against Tribulation*. Several other tracts on trial and temptation exist: Jolliffe lists fifteen items, of which two have been edited, the "Sayings of the Six Masters" and the *Dialogue between Reason and Adversity*, based on Petrarch's *De Remediis utriusque Fortunae* (Fisher 1951; Diekstra 1968; *Check-List* J.2, J.9); two of the five versions of the pseudo-Peter of Blois *De Duodecim Utilitatibus Tribulationis* and one other short piece were printed by Horstman (1896, pp. 391–406, 45–60; 1895, p. 106; *Check-List* J.3b, c, J.12); and nine tracts remain unedited. Three of these, and a number of other pieces, are to be edited by Barratt in *The Book of Tribulation* (MS Bodley 423).

Like the books of Mechtild of Hackeborn and Catherine of Siena, the *Revelationes* of Birgitta of Sweden circulated in several forms in late medieval Europe, and surviving extracts are even more common than full translations into English. According to Roger Ellis, who has summarized the critical literature on the original Latin in a recent introductory article on the Middle English versions (1982b; see also Colledge 1956), the first identifiable collection of the *Revelationes* made by Alphonse of Pecha probably contained seven books, the last of which he himself seems definitely to have compiled. An eighth book was added to this before the beginning of the canonization process, within four years of Birgitta's death in 1373, as, later, was a further collection of revelations unavailable in Rome, known as the *Revelationes Extravagantes*. Another collection of revelations, the "tractatus de summis pontificibus," seems also to have been in circulation, although its exact contents are unknown. Further, several compilations of extracts also existed, such as the *Onus Mundi*, which was translated into Middle High German. Most of the manuscripts of the original Latin text of the *Revelationes* circulating in England in the later Middle Ages belonged to a particular subgroup of the seven-book Alphonsine version; and it is this version that was twice translated into Middle English. Besides these two complete translations, two sets of extracts exist, one edited by W. P. Cumming (1929), which make use of material from a different Latin version. *The Myroure of oure Ladye* (ed. Blunt 1873), the Middle English translation of the Bridgettine Office, uses material in its preface from a distinctive version of the *Revelationes Extravagantes*. Four other sets of Middle English extracts from the *Revelationes* also exist: one, a translation of *Revelationes* VI.lxv, survives in five manuscripts (*Check-List* H.13); two translations, of II.xvi and VII.v, survive in two manuscripts each (*Check-List* I.13a and D.10); and one, of VI.xciv, survives in a single copy. Two paraphrases also exist of *Revelationes* II.xvi (*Check-List* I.13b,c); as well as an acknowledged citation of IV.xxxviii in the *Fervor Amoris* which also appears in condensed form in the *Pore Caitif*, and several other unacknowledged borrowings. Besides these more-or-less straightforward versions of the *Revelationes*, Ellis has also traced extracts from, and references to, Birgitta in a number of other named and unnamed Middle English compilations. The majority of this material remains unpublished.

The *Mirror of Simple Souls* is a translation, extant in three manuscripts of the fifteenth century, of *Le Mirouer des simples ames* of Margaret Porete. Because of the work's repeated circulation, its author, as Romana Guarnieri first pointed out (1946; see also 1965), was burned in Paris as a relapsed heretic in 1310. Among the positions for which it was condemned—positions later attributed to Beghards generally—were that "the annihilated soul takes leave of the virtues, nor is any longer in their service," that "such a soul does not, and need not, care for the consolations and gifts of God [including, apparently, the sacraments], for she is intent on God alone, and they would impede her," and that "the soul annihilated in the love of the Creator may without reprehension or remorse of conscience grant to nature whatever it wants and desires" (Colledge and Guarnieri 1968, pp. 359, 364; but see Lerner 1974). The original Old French work exists in only one manuscript, from which it was edited by Guarnieri (1961, 1965); besides the Middle English, an Italian and two Latin translations are known. Marilyn Doiron, the editor of *The Mirror of Simple Souls* (1968), ascribes this version to the mid- to late fourteenth century, although all extant manuscripts are at least half a century more recent. The Middle English translator takes some care to explain the orthodoxy of fifteen passages in the original where "the sense might be mistaken [or taken amiss]," setting off his interpolations with his first and last initials "M.N.," a device used by Nicholas Love in his *Mirror*. Clare Kirchberger, noting the Carthusian provenance of all three extant manuscripts (1927, p. xxxv), suggested that the translator might be Michael of Northburgh, bishop of London and a founder of the London Charterhouse (d. 1361). This identification, however, seems to have nothing in its favor but the coincidence of initials. The Middle English *Mirror of Simple Souls* was, together with *The Cloud of Unknowing*, translated into Latin and further annotated by Richard Methley of Mount Grace Charterhouse. Methley's translation survives in a single manuscript, Pembroke College, Cambridge, 221, by William Darker of Sheen; a marginal annotation before the *Mirror*, referring to the Clementine decretal "Ad nostrum qui" demonstrates at least one late medieval reader's concern for the heterodoxy of its teaching. Doiron, however, has defended the orthodoxy of the original, as interpreted by its Middle English translator (1964). An edition and study of Methley's translations, completed several years ago by James Walsh and Edmund Colledge, are still at press for the *Archivo italiano per la storia della pietà*.

One of the three manuscripts of the "M.N." translation of *The Mirror of Sim-*

ple Souls, BL Add. 37790 (the Amherst manuscript) comprises an interesting collection of fourteenth- and fifteenth-century mystical literature in English, including Richard Misyn's translations of Rolle's *Emendatio Vitae* and *Incendium Amoris*, the *Ego Dormio* and extracts from *The Form of Living*, the unique Short Text of the *Revelations* of Julian of Norwich and Middle English versions of writings of Jan van Ruusbroec and Henry Suso, a letter attributed to Saint Bernard, extracts from the *Revelationes* of Birgitta of Sweden, and a short compilation using material from Rolle, Hilton, the *Cloud* corpus, and Hugh of Balma. Among the more interesting of these pieces is *The Treatise of Perfection of the Sons of God*, the unique copy of the Middle English version of Willem Jordaens's Latin translation, *De Perfectione Filiorum Dei, vel de Calculo Candido*, of Ruusbroec's mystical treatise *Vanden blinckenden Steen* (Colledge 1952; ed. Bazire and Colledge 1957). The Middle English translation was undertaken, according to its author, to help him in understanding this intellectually subtle work: the Netherlands original had, in fact, been written for an anchorite, to serve as a memorandum of Ruusbroec's "conversations concerning mystical theology, and it is indeed not a work for beginners" (Bazire and Colledge 1957, p. 85). Colledge suggested that the *Treatise* was intended for, and circulated among, an audience similar to that the *Cloud* author found for his translation of the *Mystica Theologia*, *Deonise Hid Diuinite*; although this audience could never have been large, it is still obvious from scribal errors that the unique extant copy of *The Treatise of Perfection of the Sons of God* stands at some remove from the original.

The Amherst manuscript also contains a unique copy of one of two Middle English (four pre-Reformation) translations of the *Varia et Brevia Documenta Pie Seu Religiose Vivendi*, a short piece commonly, if spuriously, attributed to Bernard of Clairvaux (*Check-List* H.14). Colledge has published the text of the Amherst translation, called the "Golden Epistle," together with a description of the other English versions (1975). Another text occasionally, if dubiously, attributed to Ruusbroec circulating in late medieval England lists five points concerning the Eucharist. Ian Doyle, who published a discussion and edition of the Latin and English versions of this piece deriving from England (1964), pointed out that versions are found not only in Netherlands, attributed to Ruusbroec or Albert the Great, but in German and Netherlands copies of a sermon attributed to Johannes Tauler, and in Latin attributed to Guyard of Laon. Six manuscripts of the Latin text of the "Five Points" survive, two of which are of English provenance. Of the two Middle English versions, one survives in a single manuscript which seems to reflect the interests of a member of the secular clergy; the second translation exists in five manuscripts which fall into two groups. The first group consists of Douce MS 322 and its congeners Harley 1706 and Trinity College, Cambridge, R. 3. 21; all are of the second half of the fifteenth century, and are connected with the Benedictine and Dominican convents of Barking and Dartford, and with their

London patrons (Doyle 1958, 1959). The second group consists of two early sixteenth-century manuscripts in the production of which William Darker of Sheen took some part, and like others of Darker's books, they were probably both made for the Bridgettine nuns at Syon. Both Middle English versions of the "Five Points" attribute the original Latin text to Albert the Great: John Bale mistakenly attributes the work of translation to Adam of Dryburgh.

The *Imitation of Christ*, the only work of the *devotio moderna* to have had any influence in late medieval England, seems to have circulated there, in both Latin and English, primarily among what Roger Lovatt has termed "a small, conservative, intellectual and spiritual elite" (1968, p. 114), consisting primarily of members of the Carthusian and Bridgettine orders, and the circle that grouped itself around Lady Margaret Beaufort at the end of the fifteenth century. The first of the three translations into English before the dissolution of the monasteries was made from the expanded version of the three-book *Musica Ecclesiastica* form of the original, which seems to have been imported into England by Carthusian agency. The earliest surviving English manuscript of this form of the Latin text was copied by John Dygoun, recluse at Sheen; and two of the four surviving copies of the first Middle English translation were produced there: Trinity College, Dublin, MS 678 was copied by Stephen Doddesham; and Glasgow, Hunterian Library 136 was copied by William Darker for Elizabeth Gibbs, abbess of Syon. J. K. Ingram edited this translation from the other two surviving manuscripts, whose provenance is unknown, in 1893. Ingram also discussed the efforts of William Atkynson, a fellow of Pembroke College who produced the second translation of the *Imitation* in cooperation with the Lady Margaret, to broaden its appeal (1893, pp. xxiv–xxvii). This translation was printed by Richard Pynson and Wynkyn de Worde in 1502 and 1504, and reissued four times by de Worde by 1530. A third translation of the *Imitatio*, by Richard Whytford, the self-styled "wretch" of Syon, was published by Robert Wyer, probably in 1531, and forms the basis of virtually every English version up to the present century (see Hogg 1982).

It should also be mentioned that Middle English translations exist of the short pseudo-Augustinian *Speculum Peccatoris* (*Check-List* F.8), surviving in twenty-two manuscripts, from one of which it was published by Horstman (1896, pp. 436–440), of the *Doctrina Cordis*, the *Doctrine of the Heart* attributed to Gerard of Liège (but see Hendrix 1982), edited by Mary Patrick Candon (1963), and of a number of more strictly didactic treatises as well.

One of the most interesting developments in later medieval English devotional literature was the creation of devotional compilations drawn from the works of the English mystics or from Latin translations of continental writers. Despite the name, these Middle English compilations probably did not derive from the Latin *compilatio*, a collection of *sententiae* of the Fathers and Doctors of the

Church on particular points of theology, philosophy, or law, but rather from the devotional *florilegia*, collections of psalms and prayers, of which Saint Anselm's book of meditations sent to Countess Matilda of Tuscany seems to have been an example, and the later collections of meditations, both his and others, which circulated under his name a natural successor (see Southern 1963, pp. 34–47; Wilmart 1923, 1932, 1940). These collections tended to be personal, and to reflect the concerns of the compiler or the person for whom the compilation was made. An entire spectrum of such collections exists from the period with which we are concerned, ranging from those in which the personality of the collector is predominant and nondevotional materials may also occur, to those made on a single topic, such as tribulation or the *ars moriendi*. We are probably justified in seeing such productions as the *Book of Tribulation* as incipient compilations; as in another way we may view such duplicated collocations of material as occur in the devotional sections of the Vernon and Simeon manuscripts, or in Douce 322 and its congeners. In some cases, however, the compilation transcended its limitation as a collection of snippets from other works and took on an identity and literary form of its own. At times this identity was hard won: the *Pore Caitif* and *Þe Holy Boke Gratia Dei*, for example, occur in more than one form. But other works of this genre exist upon which the author-compiler has succeeded in imposing a lasting identity; and some of these are among the most popular and aesthetically pleasing of the minor devotional writings.

Although the devotional compilation seems to have become most prominent in the vernacular in the fourteenth and fifteenth centuries, its earliest forms were in Latin. We have seen how the revelations of Mechtild of Hackeborn and Birgitta of Sweden circulated as often in shorter compilations as in full form; and the same is true in England of Richard Rolle. One such piece is the "Oleum Effusum" compilation, in which a section of Rolle's *Commentary on the First Verses of the Song of Songs* is joined to a paragraph from a letter of Anselm of Canterbury, Chapters 12 and 15 of Rolle's *Incendium Amoris*, and the first paragraph of Chapter 8; this compilation usually accompanies the short version of the *Incendium*, in which the more personal sections included in the compilation do not occur. Another Latin compilation drawn from Rolle is that entitled *De Excellentia Contemplationis*, possibly deriving from the English Carthusians or Bridgettines (Sargent 1976, p. 231); the *Speculum Spiritualium*, a massive compilation of similar provenance, apparently designed by its compiler to serve as a one-volume library of contemplative literature, also draws heavily upon Rolle and Hilton, as does the third section, the "Exhortacio" of the *Cibus Anime*, the primarily didactic tract from which the *Speculum Christiani* was drawn (ed. Holmstedt 1929; but see Gillespie 1980, 1981, 1982). The short Latin compilation "Quandoque Tribularis," found in association with the *Speculum Spiritualium* and Rolle's *Emendatio Vitae*, is composed of three pieces of the fourth book of the *Ancrene*

Wisse warning the contemplative to "watch and pray that you fall not into temptation," describing the withdrawal of devotion as similar to a game of hide-and-seek between mother and child, and listing a series of comforts in times of tribulation. It occurs independently in Latin, in a version that betrays its English origin (see Allen 1923, pp. 2–3), and is retranslated into English in three larger compilations and the third Middle English version of Flete's *De Remediis contra Temptationes*.

The "Quandoque Tribularis" compilation supplies the title and parts of the first two chapters of *The Chastising of God's Children*, and perhaps the idea for the whole (see Allen 1923, pp. 1–3). The *Chastising*, edited by Joyce Bazire and Eric Colledge (1957), is composed of twenty-seven chapters, each ending with the exhortation to "watch and pray," and dealing generally with the problem of withdrawal of devotion and the temptations that follow upon it. The first chapter also draws upon Suso's *Horologium Sapientiae* for its description of the game of love, and upon Geert Groote's Latin translation, *De Ornatu Spiritualis Desponsationis*, of Jan van Ruusbroec's Middle Netherlands treatise *Die Gheestelijke Brulocht* (Bazire and Colledge 1957, pp. 41–49; De Soer 1959). This Latin translation of Ruusbroec is in fact the primary source for the first third of the *Chastising*, most of the remainder of which is derived from Cassian, Isidore, Gregory, the pseudo-Bonaventuran *Stimulus Amoris*, Flete's *De Remediis*, and Alphonse of Pecha's *Epistola Solitarii ad Reges*. Sections of the *Chastising* amounting to between one-third and one-half of its total volume are used in the didactic compilation *Disce Mori* (*Check-List* A.6), along with material drawn from Rolle, Hilton, and other sources (see Bazire and Colledge 1957, pp. 25–27; Hudson 1968); the manual *Ignorancia Sacerdotum* (*Check-List* A.2), described by Phyllis Hodgson as "a discourse on the Lambeth Constitutions" (1948) is in fact composed almost entirely of sections drawn from the *Disce Mori*, which make up nearly two-thirds of its volume. Jesus College, Oxford, MS 99, according to the editors of the *Chastising* the better of the two manuscripts of the *Disce Mori*, was copied in the latter half of the fifteenth century, and belonged to Dorothe Slyghe, a nun in Syon. The *Ignorancia Sacerdotum*, of which only one copy survives, seems to derive from a manuscript more closely related to the Jesus College text. The manuscript of the *Chastising* to which these two compilations are most closely related is that in Bodley MS 505, procured by Edmund Storoure of London Charterhouse, and containing *The Mirror of Simple Souls* as well. These and other manuscript relations suggest that all three works circulated most commonly among members of the Carthusian and Bridgettine orders; and the known Carthusian interest in Ruusbroec would indicate that it was by their agency that a copy of *Die Gheestelijke Brulocht* was available in England to the compiler of *The Chastising of God's Children* (Bazire and Colledge 1957, pp. 35–41; Sargent 1976, p. 227, 1977).

Reference is also made to the *Chastising* in a penitential compilation, *The Cleansing of Man's Soul* (*Check-List* E.14). This work is divided into three sections, on contrition, confession, and satisfaction, each of which contains seven chapters. The compilation incorporates material from the *Tractatus de Interiori Domo*, erroneously attributed to Bernard of Clairvaux, the thirty-fifth of Bernard's *Sermones de Diversis* and some form of the *Summa Casuum Poenitentiae*; the closing section is similar to the translation of David of Augsburg's *De Compositione* II, 1, 7–10 (*Check-List* D.5). There are four extant manuscripts of the *Cleansing*, two extracts and a related short tract on confession of which two copies survive (*Check-List* C.5). One of the complete manuscripts, Bodley 923, belonged to Sibille de Felton, abbess of Barking in 1394 (d. 1419); the *Cleansing* was edited from this manuscript by Charles L. Regan (1963). Another such compilation is the *Pore Caitif* (*Check-List* B), a large and popular didactic treatise, the majority of which consists of tracts on the Creed, the Lord's Prayer, the commandments, and virginity. Its middle section, however, consists of ten tracts bearing the subtitle "some short sentences exciting men to heavenly desire." Two of these devotional tracts derive from the "Oleum Effusum" compilation, and one from the "Quandoque Tribularis"; three further tracts derive from Rolle's *Emendatio Vitae*; one of these, and two others, depend as well on *The Form of Living* (see Allen 1923, pp. 3–4; Brady 1954a, 1980; Sargent 1979). The *Pore Caitif* was edited by Mary Theresa Brady (1954b); both the edition of the *Cleansing* and that of the *Caitif*, however, were produced for doctoral dissertations, and neither has been published.

An English version of the "Quandoque Tribularis" also occurs in the compilation known as *Þe Holy Boke Gratia Dei* (*Check-List* I.29). This work seems to have taken its inspiration, as well as some of its material, from the introductory discussion of the role of grace in the contemplative life in the *Ladder of Foure Ronges*; although it is possible that the compiler had access as well to the Latin original. This use of the material marks the final stage in the alteration of a schematic treatise on the monastic exercises of reading, meditation, prayer, and contemplation to a work of popular devotion (see Keiser 1981). Mary Luke Arntz, the recent editor of *Þe Holy Boke Gratia Dei*, has pointed out that the work "has been known, for the most part, only in the segments: 'Grace,' 'Prayer,' 'Our Daily Work,' and 'A Meditation on the Passion and of Three Arrows on Doomsday'" (1981, p. vi), attributed by Horstman to Rolle and printed from two of its three manuscripts (1895, pp. 112–121, 132–156, 300–321). The continuity of the entire work can be demonstrated only from the abbreviated version extant in San Marino, California, Huntington MS 148 (the Ingilby manuscript). The *Holy Boke*, which Arntz diagrams to show the progression of its argument (1981, pp. lxviii–lxx), incorporates two sections of the *Milicia Christi*, related to the *Treatise of Ghostly Battle* (see Wells 1926, p. 372), a considerable portion of a treatise on the Lord's Prayer and material from the *Abbey of the Holy Ghost*, *Sawles Warde*, the Middle English *Mirror* of Edmund of Abingdon, and various other patristic and medieval sources (Arntz 1981, pp. xliv–lxiv).

The *Treatise of Ghostly Battle*, a version of which occurs in the *Pore Caitif* as "The Horse and Armour of Heaven," and the *Milicia Christi* are a pair of allegorical tracts describing in detail the "whole armour of God" of the sixth chapter of the Pauline Epistle to the Ephesians. Both were edited by V. Murray, for a doctoral dissertation (1970); the former was printed by Horstman (1896, pp. 420–436). Another tract of the *Pore Caitif*, "The Charter of Christ," is an allegorization of the suffering body of Christ and the instruments of his torture and death as the elements of a legal charter. The "Charters," more common in verse than in prose, were printed by M. C. Spalding (1914). Two other allegorical tracts, *The Abbey of the Holy Ghost* (*Check-List* H.16) and *The Charter of the Abbey of the Holy Ghost* (*Check-List* H.9), are similar in intent and method. An edition of the *Abbey* is projected by Peter Consacro, and of the *Charter of the Abbey* by Elizabeth Fanning; both were printed by Horstman (1895, pp. 321–362). All of these allegorical tracts combine didactic and devotional aims; but the inclusion of what might otherwise be considered primarily a didactic allegory in a devotional compilation must alter the way in which it is perceived.

A Talking of the Love of God is a compilation found only in the Vernon and Simeon manuscripts, and drawn, as M. Konrath first fully demonstrated (1918; but see also Peebles 1911; Allen 1918), from two of the pieces of the twelfth-century devotional "Wooing Group." The demonstration has been restated in detail by C. M. Westra, the editor of the *Talking* (1950), who pointed out that the introductory section derives in part from the introduction to the collection of meditations sent by Anselm of Canterbury to Countess Matilda; the first section of the *Talking* is an expanded translation of the *Wel swuðe god Ureisun of God Almihti*; the second section, which opens with a prayer to Mary similar to that with which the *Ureisun* ends (which is inserted into the third section of the *Talking*), seems to derive from a similar source, now lost; the third section of the *Talking* is based on *Þe Wohunge of ure Lauerd*: it begins as a fairly close translation, but becomes more free as it proceeds. The conclusion of the *Talking* seems to be the creation of the author-compiler, although the thought and expression of the *Wohunge* still underlie the later work. The *Talking* is particularly interesting in that it is a late-fourteenth-century version of a set of late-twelfth- or early-thirteenth-century meditations written in the mode, and probably under the influence, of those written a century earlier by Anselm and his contemporaries. We can see in this the continuity of a type of heavily cadenced prose (if, the author of the *Talking* says in his introduction, it is correctly punctuated), employing alliteration, rhyme, and rhetorical parallelism, which must certainly be judged as one of the sources of Rolle's meditational prose style (see Morgan 1952a, 1952b; Smedick 1975, 1979).

The *Fervor Amoris* (*Check-List* H.15), also known as the *Contemplations of the Dread and Love of God*, is among the more important devotional compilations still in need of critical editing. It deals in several short chapters each of four degrees of love: ordained, clean, steadfast, and perfect. We know that parts of this treatise circulated separately (see *Check-List* K.2, M.15), that parts derive from the *Dialogo* of Catherine of Siena, the *De Remediis* of William Flete, and the *Revelationes* of Birgitta of Sweden, and that the closing section is a version of the nuptial prayer of the Roman rite. The work was printed by Horstman (1896, pp. 72–105) from a 1506 printing by Wynkyn de Worde; some of the sources and the relations among the sixteen surviving manuscripts were described in an article by Curt Bühler (1954) and a note by Jeanne Krochalis (1977). But the only recent edition, that produced for a doctoral dissertation by Anthony William Annunziata (1966), is a diplomatic transcript of the idiosyncratic, abridged text in Pierpont Morgan MS 861. The *Speculum Devotorum*, an early-fifteenth-century compilation drawing upon some of the same sources, and composed for a religious woman by a Carthusian of Sheen, exists in two manuscripts, which James Hogg (1973–1974) is in the process of editing. The author of this treatise states that when he last spoke to the "ghostly sister" to whom it is addressed, he promised her a meditation on the passion; but that he was dissuaded from producing such a piece by the availability of the pseudo-Bonaventuran *Meditationes Vitae Christi*, especially as translated into English by his Carthusian confrere Nicholas Love. In fact, however, he produced a somewhat more ambitious devotional compilation than he seems originally to have planned, drawing heavily upon the revelations of both Mechtild of Hackeborn and Birgitta of Sweden, among other sources.

Another pair of short devotional compilations are the *Via ad Contemplationem* (*Check-List* H.31), found only in the Amherst manuscript, and the slightly longer, related tract *Of Active Life and Contemplative Declaration* (*Check-List* H.11) in BL Add. MS 37049, another English Carthusian production. Both are composed of extracts from *The Cloud of Unknowing* and the related epistles of *Discrecioun of Stirings* and of *Preier*, and Hilton's *Scale of Perfection* arranged according to the description of the purgative, illuminative, and unitive way of contemplation in the treatise *Viae Syon Lugent* (also known as *De Triplici Via* or *De Mystica Theologia*) by Hugh of Balma, prior of the Charterhouse of Meyriat 1289–1304. The tract *Of Active Life* incorporates somewhat more material from the *Scale* and the *Viae Syon Lugent* as well as Rolle's *Form of Living* in meeting a slightly different aim from that of the cognate tract, which deals simply with contemplation. Both were published by Jolliffe (1975).

One last and particularly interesting compilation is the *Seven Points of True Love and Everlasting Wisdom*, the abridged Middle English version of Henry Suso's *Horologium Sapientiae*. As Roger Lovatt pointed out in a recent study (1982), the author-compiler of the *Seven Points* has reorganized his material in such a way as to leave out the more affective and personal passages, and produce a work of pious devotion more appropriate to the use of the English noblewoman for whom he wrote. We can see in the popularity of the *Seven Points* from before the end of the fourteenth century the degree of penetration of continental devotional literature in England; but we can also see that this penetration was achieved by adaptation and alteration of the literature for a different audience. It should also be pointed out that if the conjecture is correct that the Macro play of *Wisdom*, which derives its opening from the *Seven Points*, was first performed in the Inns of Court (see Eccles 1969, p. xxxv), we have even further evidence of the extent to which members of the urban middle class in England came during the fifteenth century to see contemplative literature as in some way appropriate to themselves. The *Seven Points* was printed by Horstman from one of the ten manuscripts in which it survives, in whole or part (1888); the origin, author, and intention of the Middle English abridgment of the *Horologium* were discussed in two series of articles by G. Schleich (1927, 1929, 1930) and Wiltrud Wichgraf (1929, 1930, 1936). Most of this argument was summarized by Pius Künzle, editor of the *Horologium Sapientiae* (1977). Schleich suggested, on the basis of an early manuscript from Beauvale Charterhouse, that the *Seven Points* was a Carthusian product; but this conjecture remains unprovable. Lovatt, in fact, demonstrated the early and widespread popularity of the *Horologium* in both English and Latin. Elizabeth Armstrong produced a critical edition of the "Lerne to Dye" chapter, the most popular in the compilation, for a doctoral dissertation (1966); she and Christina von Nolcken are at work on a critical edition of the whole.

Besides the translations and compilations described above, there were a few original minor devotional works in English, dating particularly from the end of the fifteenth and the beginning of the sixteenth centuries. I should mention, for example, the *Pystyl of Solytary Lyfe Nowadayes* addressed to Hugh, hermit, by the Mount Grace Carthusian Richard Methley, extant in a single copy and edited by James Hogg (1977). Hogg has also recently described some of the works of the Bridgettines of Syon, and particularly Richard Whytford (see Hogg 1982), although these may in fact be considered early modern authors, rather than late medieval.

One important, original devotional work of the mid-fifteenth century is the pair of treatises, separated in time, according to their author, by several years, known as *The Tree & XII Frutes of the Holy Goost*. Employing the modes of allegory and subdivision common in the compilations, these two pieces first compare the religious vocation of the woman to whom they are addressed to a garden in which she is planted and must be pruned and tended to flourish—a conceit perhaps drawn from Catherine of Siena; and second, describe the twelve fruits of virtue, each with four qualities, which she shall produce. It is interesting to note that in two of the three surviving manuscripts, the *Tree & XII Frutes* is preceded by the *Doctrine of the Heart*; the third manuscript is acephalous. All three manuscripts, as well as the printing of the two constituent treatises by Robert Coplande in 1534–1535, were used by J. J. Vaissier for the critical edition of the *Tree & XII Frutes* (1960).

From this survey of the Middle English minor devotional writings, we can see several directions in which profitable work may yet be done. First, it should be noted that only some three dozen of the more important minor works have been described here: there is as yet no adequate survey of the unedited lesser devotional pieces. Further research, particularly in conjunction with the Index of Middle English Prose project, should be able to provide reference guides which will be the first step toward edition and study of this material. The format such editions might take should also be considered: it may be possible to produce an anthology similar to that of Anne Hudson for Wycliffite writings (1978), illustrating the range of devotional themes, styles, and images. On the other hand, it would also be interesting to see editions of some of the major devotional miscellanies, such as Barratt's *Book of Tribulation*—particularly considering the possible relation between these miscellanies and the compilations. Nor have all of the compilations and translations been edited; several of the major pieces described here are still available only in manuscript; and several that have been printed still need critical editing. Further, this criticism must be both textual and literary: we need both complete examination and analysis of the manuscript evidence, and study of the sources and forms of this literature. It has, after all, not been very long since it was considered an adequate introduction to any Middle English religious prose compilation—whether didactic or devotional, confessional, affective, or contemplative—to describe it as an analogue to Chaucer's *Parson's Tale* and derive its shape and intent from mendicant preaching manuals or the Lambeth Constitutions.

The question of the role in Middle English devotional literature of translations of, and compilations from, continental writings in Latin or the other vernacular languages is also worth examination, as is that of the mutual interpenetration of late medieval vernacular devotional literature as a whole. A related issue is that of the difference in the perception of the intent of a work when it is translated or used in a compilation for an audience other than that for whom it was composed. Lovatt demonstrated the extent to which this change of perception occurred in the case of Suso's *Horologium Sapientiae* (1982); but again a general study of the phenomenon would be interesting. Ellis has also pointed out the possibilities, primarily grammatical and rhetorical, that were open to the translator (1982a). This subject, again, would reward study: it might be particularly interesting in the case of the *Imitation of Christ*, for example, which was translated into English thrice in one century, to examine the lexical differences among the three versions. Finally, it is important to study the organizational techniques used in the Middle English compilations. If Chaucer's poetry can be likened to a Gothic cathedral, then these works can be compared to a van Eyck polyptych, in which symmetrically arranged discrete sections can be viewed either separately, as related groups, or as part of a larger whole. And it should be kept in mind that while chronicles, sermon collections, and biographies have an external order imposed upon them, it was primarily in devotional literature that writers of English first faced the technical problems of the composition of book-length prose treatises.

BIBLIOGRAPHY

Because of the number of works described in this chapter, it has not seemed advisable to produce separate bibliographies of primary and secondary literature. Rather, all editions and criticism are listed together alphabetically, where possible under the name of the modern editor or critic. This section is preceded by a reference list in which information is given under the author or title of the original work: the titles of Middle English versions are cross-referred, wherever necessary and practical, to the original.

REFERENCE LIST

OF ACTIVE LIFE AND CONTEMPLATIVE DECLARATION

See Hugh of Balma

AELRED OF RIEVAULX. *DE INSTITUTIONE INCLUSARUM*

EDITIONS

Dumont (1961)
Hoste and Talbot (1971)
Ayto and Barratt (forthcoming) ME
See also Barratt (1977, 1980)

ALBERT THE GREAT (ATTRIBUTED TO). "FIVE POINTS" ON THE EUCHARIST.

EDITION

Doyle (1964) Latin and ME
See also Doyle (1958, 1959)

BERNARD OF CLAIRVAUX. *VARIA ET BREVIA DOCUMENTA* ("GOLDEN EPISTLE")

EDITIONS

Bernard of Clairvaux
Colledge (1975) ME

BIRGITTA OF SWEDEN. *REVELATIONES*

EDITIONS

Birgitta of Sweden
Cumming (1929) ME
See also Colledge (1956); Ellis (1982a, 1982b, 1982c)

THE BOOKE OF GOSTLYE GRACE

See Mechtild of Hackeborn

CATHERINE OF SIENA. *DIALOGO*

EDITIONS

Cavallini (1968)
Hodgson and Liegey (1966) ME
See also Denise (1958); Hodgson (1964)

THE CHASTISING OF GOD'S CHILDREN

See Ruusbroec, Jan van. *Die Gheestelijke Brulocht*

THE CLEANSING OF MAN'S SOUL

EDITION

Regan (1963)

CONTEMPLATIONS OF THE DREAD AND LOVE OF GOD

See *Fervor Amoris*

DAVID OF AUGSBURG. *DE EXTERIORIS ET INTERIORIS HOMINIS COMPOSITIONE*

EDITION

David of Augsburg
See also Jolliffe (1974b)

DE DOCTRINA CORDIS (ATTRIBUTED TO GERARD OF LIÈGE)

EDITION

Candon (1963) ME
See also Hendrix (1982)

DISCE MORI

See Bazire and Colledge (1957); Hudson (1968)

FERVOR AMORIS

EDITION

Annunziata (1966)
See also Bühler (1954); Krochalis (1977)

FLETE, WILLIAM. *DE REMEDIIS CONTRA TEMPTATIONES*

EDITIONS

Horstman (1896, pp. 106–123) ME
Colledge and Chadwick (1968) ME
See also Hackett (1961); Hackett, Colledge, and Chadwick (1964)

FORMULA NOVICIORUM

See David of Augsburg

GUIGO II. *SCALA CLAUSTRALIUM*

EDITIONS

Colledge and Walsh (1970, 1978)
Hodgson (1955) ME
See also Hodgson (1949)

ÞE HOLY BOKE GRATIA DEI

EDITIONS

Arntz (1981)
See also Keiser (1981)

HUGH OF BALMA. *VIAE SYON LUGENT (DE TRIPLICI VIA, DE MYSTICA THEOLOGIA)*

EDITIONS

Hugh of Balma
Jolliffe (1975) ME

IGNORANCIA SACERDOTUM

See Hodgson (1948); Bazire and Colledge (1957); Hudson (1968)

LADDER OF FOURE RONGES

See Guigo II

MARGARET PORETE. *MIROUER DES SIMPLES AMES*

Editions

Guarnieri (1961, 1965)
Doiron (1968) ME
See also Guarnieri (1946); Doiron (1964); Colledge and Guarnieri (1968); Lerner (1974)

MECHTILD OF HACKEBORN. *LIBER SPECIALIS GRATIAE*

Editions

Mechtild of Hackeborn
Halligan (1979) ME
See also Blake (1973); Halligan (1974)

MIRROR OF SIMPLE SOULS

See Margaret Porete

ORCHERD OF SYON

See Catherine of Siena

(PSEUDO) PETER OF BLOIS. *DE DUODECIM UTILITATIBUS TRIBULATIONIS*

Editions

Auer (1952)
Horstman (1896, pp. 45–60, 391–406) ME
See also Hendrix (1982)

PETRARCHA, FRANCESCO. *DE REMEDIIS UTRIUSQUE FORTUNAE*

EDITIONS

Schottländer (1975)
Diekstra (1968) ME

PORE CAITIF

EDITION

Brady (1954b)
See also Allen (1923); Brady (1954a, 1957, 1980); Sargent (1979)

RUUSBROEC, JAN VAN. *DIE GHEESTELIJKE BRULOCHT*

EDITIONS

Reypens and Schurmans (1944–1948, vol. 1)
Bazire and Colledge (1957) ME
See also De Soer (1959); Sargent (1977, 1983)

RUUSBROEC, JAN VAN. *VANDEN BLINCKENDEN STEEN*

EDITIONS

Reypens and Schurmans (1944–1948, vol. 3)
Muller (1921) Latin
Bazire and Colledge (1957) ME
See also Colledge (1952); Sargent (1983)

RUUSBROEC, JAN VAN. (ATTRIBUTED TO). "FIVE POINTS" ON THE EUCHARIST

See Albert the Great

SEVEN POINTS OF TRUE LOVE AND EVERLASTING WISDOM

See Suso, Henry

SUSO, HENRY. *HOROLOGIUM SAPIENTIAE*

EDITIONS

Künzle (1977)
Horstman (1888) ME
Armstrong (1966) ME
See also Schleich (1927, 1929, 1930); Wichgraff (1929, 1930, 1936); Lovatt (1982)

A TALKING OF THE LOVE OF GOD

EDITION

Westra (1950)
See also Peebles (1911); Allen (1918); Morgan (1952a, 1952b); Smedick (1975, 1979)

THOMAS À KEMPIS. *IMITATIO CHRISTI*

EDITIONS

Pohl (1902–1922, vol. 2)
Ingram (1893) ME
See also Lovatt (1968); Hogg (1982)

THE TREATISE OF PERFECTION OF THE SONS OF GOD

See Ruusbroec, Jan van. *Vanden blinckenden Steen*

VIA AD CONTEMPLATIONEM

See Hugh of Balma

EDITIONS AND STUDIES

Allen, Hope Emily (1918) "Mystical Writings of the *Manuel des Péchiez*." *RR*, 9,
154–193.
――― (1923) "Some Fourteenth Century Borrowings from 'Ancren Riwle.'" *MLR*, 18,
1–8.

—————— (1924) "On 'Some Fourteenth Century Borrowings from *Ancren Riwle*.'" *MLR*, 19, 95.

—————— (1927) *Writings Ascribed to Richard Rolle, Hermit of Hampole, and Materials for His Biography*. MLA Monograph ser. 3. New York: D.C. Heath.

—————— (1929) "Further Borrowings from 'Ancren Riwle.'" *MLR*, 24, 1–15.

Annunziata, Anthony William, ed. (1966) "*Contemplations of the Dread and Love of God*, Morgan MS 861." Ph.D. diss., New York University.

Armstrong, Elizabeth Psakis, ed. (1966) "Heinrich Suso in England: An Edition of the *Ars Moriendi* from *The Seven Points of True Love*." Ph.D. diss., Indiana University.

Arntz, Mark Luke, ed. (1981) *Richard Rolle and Þe Holy Boke Gratia Dei: An Edition with Commentary*. Elizabethan and Renaissance Studies 92. Salzburg: Institut für Anglistik und Amerikanistik.

Auer, Albert, ed. (1952) *Leidenstheologie im Spätmittelalter*. Kirchengeschichtliche Quellen und Studien 2. Saint Ottilien, Austria: Eos Verlag.

Ayto, J., and Barratt, Alexandra, eds. (forthcoming) *Two Middle English Translations of Aelred of Rievaulx's "De Institutione Inclusarum."* EETS, os 287.

Barratt, Alexandra (1977) "The 'De Institutione Inclusarum' of Aelred of Rievaulx and the Carthusian Order." *Journal of Theological Studies*, 28, 528–536.

—————— (1980) "Anachoritic Aspects of *Ancrene Wisse*." *MAE*, 49, 32–56.

Bazire, Joyce, and Colledge, Eric, eds. (1957) *The Chastising of God's Children and The Treatise of Perfection of the Sons of God*. Oxford: Blackwell.

Bernard of Clairvaux. *Varia et Brevia Documenta* ("Golden Epistle"). PL 184, cols. 1173–1174.

Birgitta of Sweden. *Revelationes*. Book I, edited by C. G. Undhagen (1978). Book V, edited by B. Bergh (1971). Book VII edited by B. Bergh (1967). *Revelationes Extravagantes*, edited by L. Hollman (1956). Samlingar utg. av Svenska Fornskriftsällskapet ser. 2, vols. 1, 5, 7, 8. Uppsala: Almqvist and Wiksell.

Blake, Norman F. (1973) "Revelations of St. Matilda." *N&Q*, 218, 323–325.

Bloomfield, Morton W.; Guyot, B-G.; Howard, D. R.; and Kabealo, T. B. (1979) *Incipits of Latin Works on the Virtues and Vices*. Cambridge, Mass.: Medieval Academy of America.

Blunt, J. H., ed. (1873) *The Myroure of oure Ladye*. EETS, es 19.

Brady, Mary Teresa (1954a) "*The Pore Caitif*: An Introductory Study." *Traditio*, 10, 529–548.

——————, ed. (1954b) "*The Pore Caitif*: Edited from MS Harley 2336 with Introduction and Notes." Ph.D. diss., Fordham University.

—————— (1957) "The Apostles and the Creed in Manuscripts of *The Pore Caitif*." *Speculum*, 32, 323–325.

—————— (1980) "Rolle's 'Form of Living' and 'The Pore Caitif.'" *Traditio*, 36, 426–435.

Bühler, Curt F. (1954) "The Middle English Texts of Morgan MS 861." *PMLA*, 69, 686–692.

Candon, Mary Patrick (1963) "An Edition of the 15th-Century Middle English Translation of Gerard of Liège's *De Doctrina Cordis*." Ph.D. diss., Fordham University.

Cavallini, Giuliana, ed. (1968) *Il Dialogo della divina providenza*. Rome: Edizioni Cateriniane.

Colledge, Edmund, ed. (1975) "Fifteenth- and Sixteenth-Century English Versions of 'The Golden Epistle of St. Bernard.'" *MS*, 37, 122–129.

Colledge, Edmund, and Chadwick, Noel (1968) *"Remedies Against Temptations*: The Third English Version of William Flete." *Archivo italiano per la storia della pietà*, 5, 199–240.

Colledge, Edmund, and Guarnieri, Romana (1968) "The Glosses by 'M. N.' and Richard Methley to 'The Mirror of Simple Souls.'" *Archivo italiano per la storia della pietà*, 5, 357–382.

Colledge, Edmund, and Walsh, James, eds. (1970) *Guigues II le Chartreux: Lettre sur la vie contemplative (L'échelle des moines), Douze méditations*. Sources Chrétiennes 163. Paris: Editions du Cerf.

———, eds. (1978) *Guigo II. A Letter on the Contemplative Life and Twelve Meditations*. New York: Doubleday. (This is the original version of Colledge and Walsh 1970, of which the French introduction is simply a restructured translation.)

Colledge, Eric (1952) *"The Treatise of Perfection of the Sons of God*, a Fifteenth-Century English Ruysbroek Translation." *ES*, 33, 49–66.

——— (1956) *"Epistola Solitarii ad Reges:* Alphonse of Pecha as Organizer of Birgittine and Urbanist Propaganda." *MS*, 18, 19–49.

Cumming, W. P., ed. (1928) *The Revelations of St. Birgitta*. EETS, os 178.

David of Augsburg (1899) *De Exterioris et Interioris Hominis Compositione, Secundum Triplicem Statum Incipientium, Proficientium et Perfectorum*. Quaracchi: Collegium S. Bonaventurae.

Denise, Mary (1958) *"The Orchard of Syon*: An Introduction." *Traditio*, 14, 269–293.

De Soer, Bernard (1959) "The Relationship of the Latin Versions of Ruysbroeck's 'Die Geestelike Brulocht' to 'The Chastising of God's Children.'" *MS*, 21, 129–146.

Diekstra, F. N. M., ed. (1968) *A Dialogue between Reason and Adversity*. Assen: Van Gorcum.

Doiron, Marilyn (1964) "The Middle English Translation of *Le mirouer des simples ames*." In *Dr. L. Reypens Album*, edited by Albert Ampe, pp. 131–152. Studien en Tekstuitgaven van *Ons Geestelijk Erf* 16. Antwerp: Ruusbroec-Genootschap.

———, ed. (1968) "'The Mirror of Simple Souls' a Middle English Translation." *Archivo italiano per la storia della pietà*, 5, 241–356.

Doyle, A. I. (1958) "Books Connected with the Vere Family and Barking Abbey." *Transactions of the Essex Archaeological Society*, 25, 222–243.

——— (1959) "An Unrecognized Piece of *Piers the Ploughman's Creed* and Other Work by Its Scribe." *Speculum*, 34, 428–436.

———, ed. (1964) "A Text Attributed to Ruusbroec Circulating in England." In *Dr. L. Reypens Album*, edited by Albert Ampe, pp. 153–171. Studien en Tekstuitgaven van *Ons Geestelijk Erf* 16. Antwerp: Ruusbroec-Genootschap.

Dumont, Charles, ed. (1961) *Aelred de Rievaulx: La vie de recluse, la prière pastorale*. Sources Chrétiennes 76. Paris: Editions du Cerf.

Eccles, Mark (1969) *The Macro Plays*. EETS, os 262.

Edwards, A. S. G., and Pearsall, Derek, eds. (1981) *Middle English Prose: Essays on Bibliographical Problems*. New York: Garland.

Ellis, Roger (1982a) "The Choices of the Translator in the Late Middle English Period."

In *The Medieval Mystical Tradition in England*, edited by Marian Glasscoe, pp. 18–46. Exeter: University of Exeter.

——— (1982b) "Flores ad Fabricandam . . . Coronam: An Investigation into the Uses of the Revelations of St. Bridget of Sweden in Fifteenth-Century England." *MAE*, 51, 163–186.

——— (1982c) "A Note on the Spirituality of St. Bridget of Sweden." In *Spiritualität Heute und Gestern*, edited by James Hogg. Analecta Cartusiana 35, 1:157–166. Salzburg.

Fisher, J. H. (1951) *The Tretyse of Loue*. EETS, os 223.

Gillespie, Vincent (1980) "*Doctrina* and *Predicacio*: The Design and Function of Some Pastoral Manuals." *Leeds SE*, ns 11, 36–50.

——— (1981) "The Literary Form of the Middle English Pastoral Manual, with Particular Reference to the *Speculum Christiani* and Some Related Texts." Diss., Oxford University.

——— (1982) "The *Cibus Anime*, Book 3: A Guide for Contemplatives?" In *Spiritualität Heute und Gestern*, edited by James Hogg. Analecta Cartusiana 35. Salzburg.

Glasscoe, Marion (1982) *The Medieval Mystical Tradition in England: Papers Read at Dartington Hall, July 1982*. Exeter: University of Exeter.

Guarnieri, Romana (1946) "Lo '*Specchio delle anime semplici*' e Margherita Poirette." *L'osservatore romano*, June 16, p. 3.

———, ed. (1961) *Le Mirouer des Simples Ames anienties et qui Seulement Demourent en Voulior et Desir d'Amour*. Rome: privately printed; repr. in Guarnieri (1965, pp. 513–635).

———, ed. (1965) "Il movimento del libero spirito." *Archivo italiano per la storia della pietà*, 4, 351–708.

Hackett, Benedict (1961) "William Flete and the *De Remediis Contra Temptaciones*." In *Medieval Studies Presented to Aubrey Gwynn, S.J.*, edited by J. A. Watt, J. B. Morrall, and F. X. Martin, pp. 330–348. Dublin: Three Candles.

Hackett, Benedict; Colledge, Eric; and Chadwick, Noel (1964) "William Flete's *De Remediis Contra Temptaciones* in Its Latin and English Recensions: The Growth of a Text." *MS*, 26, 210–230.

Halligan, Theresa A. (1974) "The Revelations of St. Matilda in English: 'The Booke of Gostlye Grace.'" *N&Q*, 219, 443–446.

———, ed. (1979) *The Booke of Gostlye Grace of Mechtild of Hackeborn*. Toronto: Pontifical Institute of Mediaeval Studies.

Hendrix, Guido (1982) "Kleine Queste naar de Auteur van *De Duodecim Utilitatibus Tribulationum*." *Ons Geestelijk Erf*, 56, 109–124.

Hodgson, Phyllis (1948) "*Ignorancia Sacerdotum*: A Fifteenth-Century Discourse on the Lambeth Constitutions." *RES*, 24, 1–11.

——— (1949) "*A Ladder of Foure Ronges by the Whiche Men Mowe Wele Clyme to Heaven*: A Study of the Prose Style of a Middle English Translation." *MLR*, 44, 465–475.

———, ed. (1955) *Deonise Hid Diuinite and Other Treatises on Contemplative Prayer Related to "The Cloud of Unknowing."* EETS, os 231.

——— (1964) "*The Orcherd of Syon* and the English Mystical Tradition." *PBA*, 50, 229–249.

Hodgson, Phyllis, and Liegey, Gabriel, eds. (1966) *The Orcherd of Syon.* EETS, os 258.

Hogg, James (1973–1974) *The Speculum Devotorum of an Anonymous Carthusian of Sheen,* vols. 2, 3. Analecta Cartusiana 12, 13. Salzburg.

——— (1977) "Richard Methley: To Hew Heremyte a Pystyl of Solytary Lyfe Nowadayes." *Miscellanea Cartusiensia* 1:91–119. Analecta Cartusiana 31. Salzburg.

——— (1982) "The Brigittine Contribution to Late Medieval English Spirituality." In *Spiritualität Heute und Gestern,* edited by James Hogg. Analecta Cartusiana 35. Salzburg.

——— (1983) "English Charterhouses and the *Devotio Moderna.*" In *Historia et Spiritualitas Cartusienses: Colloquii Quarti Internationalis Acta,* edited by Jan de Grauwe. Ghent: Jan de Grauwe.

Holmstedt, G., ed. (1929) *Speculum Christiani.* EETS, os 182.

Horstman, Carl, ed. (1888) "Orologium Sapientiae, or The Seven Poyntes of Trewe Wisdom, aus MS Douce 114." *Anglia,* 10, 323–389.

———, ed. (1895, 1896) *Yorkshire Writers: Richard Rolle of Hampole . . . and His Followers.* 2 vols. London: Swan Sonnenschein and Co.

Hoste, A., and Talbot, C. H., eds. (1971) *Aelredi Rievallensis Opera Omnia.* 1 *Opera Ascetica.* Corpus Christianorum, Continuatio Medievalis 1. Turnholt: Brepols.

Hudson, Anne (1968) "A Chapter from Walter Hilton in Two Middle English Compilations." *Neophil,* 52, 416–421.

——— (1978) *Selections from English Wycliffite Writings.* Cambridge: Cambridge University Press.

Hugh of Balma (1866) *Viae Syon Lugent* (*De Triplici Via,* or *De Mystica Theologia*). In *S.R.E. Cardinalis Bonaventurae . . . Opera Omnia,* edited by A. C. Peltier, 8: pp. 1–53. Paris: Vives.

Ingram, J. K., ed. (1893) *Thomas à Kempis's De Imitatione Christi.* EETS, es 63.

Jolliffe, P. S. (1974a) *A Check-List of Middle English Prose Writings of Spiritual Guidance.* Toronto: Pontifical Institute of Mediaeval Studies.

——— (1974b) "Middle English Translations of *De Exterioris et Interioris Hominis Compositione.*" *MS,* 36, 259–277.

———, ed. (1975) "Two Middle English Tracts on the Contemplative Life." *MS,* 37, 85–121.

Keiser, George R. (1981) "Þe Holy Boke Gratia Dei." *Viator,* 12, 289–317.

Kirchberger, Clare (1927) *The Mirror of Simple Souls.* London: Burns, Oates and Washbourne.

Konrath, M. (1918) "Eine übersehene Fassung der *Ureisun of Oure Louerde,* bez. *Ureisun of God Almihti,* und der *Wohunge of Ure Lauerd.*" *Anglia,* 42, 85–98.

Krochalis, Jeanne (1977) "*Contemplations of the Dread and Love of God*: Two Newly Identified Pennsylvania Manuscripts." *University of Pennsylvania Library Chronicle,* 42, 3–22.

Künzle, Pius, ed. (1977) *Heinrich Seuses Horologium Sapientiae: Erste kritische Ausgabe unter Benützung der Vorarbeiten von Dominikus Planzer, O.P.* Spicilegium Friburgense 23. Freiburg in der Schweiz.

Lagorio, Valerie (1981) "Problems in Middle English Mystical Prose." In *Middle En-*

glish Prose, edited by A. S. G. Edwards and Derek Pearsall, pp. 129–148. New York: Garland.

Lagorio, Valerie Marie, and Bradley, Ritamary (1981) *The Fourteenth-Century English Mystics: A Comprehensive Annotated Bibliography*. New York: Garland.

Lerner, Robert (1974) "A Note on the University Career of Jacques Fournier, O. Cist., Later Pope Benedict XII." *Analecta Cisterciensia*, 30, 66–69.

Lovatt, Roger (1968) "The *Imitation of Christ* in Late Medieval England." *TRHS*, 18, 97–121.

——— (1982) "Henry Suso and the Medieval Mystical Tradition in England." In *The Medieval Mystical Tradition in England*, edited by Marion Glasscoe, pp. 47–62. Exeter: University of Exeter.

Mechtild of Hackeborn (1875–1877) In *Revelationes Gertrudianae ac Mechtildianae*, vol. 2. Paris.

Morgan, Margery (1952a) "*A Talking of the Love of God* and the Continuity of Stylistic Tradition in Middle English Prose Meditations." *RES*, ns 3, 97–116.

——— (1952b) "A Treatise in Cadence." *MLR*, 47, 156–164.

Muller, D. P., ed. (1921) *Jan van Ruysbroek: Van den blinckenden Steen met W. Jordaens latijnsche Vertaling*. Louvain.

Murray, V., ed. (1970) "An Edition of *A Tretyse of Gostlye Batayle* and *Milicia Christi*." Diss. Oxford University.

Peebles, Rose Jeffries (1911) *The Legend of Longinus*. Bryn Mawr Monographs 9. Baltimore: J. H. Furst.

Pohl, Michael Josephus, ed. (1902–1922) *Opera Omnia Thomae Hemerken à Kempis*, vol. 2. Freiburg im Breisgau: Herder.

Regan, Charles L., ed. (1963) "*The Cleansing of Man's Soul*, Edited from MS Bodley 923 with Introduction, Notes and Glossary." Ph.D. diss., Harvard University.

Revell, Peter (1975) *Fifteenth Century English Prayers and Meditations: A Descriptive List of Manuscripts in the British Library*. New York: Garland.

Reypens, L., and Schurmans, M., eds. (1944–1948) *Jan van Ruusbroec: Werken*. 4 vols. Tielt: Lannoo.

Sargent, Michael G. (1976) "The Transmission by the English Carthusians of Some Late Medieval Spiritual Writings." *Journal of Ecclesiastical History*, 27, 225–240.

——— (1977) "A New Manuscript of *The Chastising of God's Children* with an Ascription to Walter Hilton." *MAE*, 46, 49–65.

——— (1979) "A Source of the *Poor Caitiff* Tract 'Of Man's Will.'" *MS*, 41, 535–539.

——— (1983) "Ruusbroec in England: *The Chastising of God's Children* and Related Works." In *Historia et Spiritualitas Cartusienses: Colloquii Quarti Internationalis Acta*, edited by Jan de Grauwe. Ghent: Jan de Grauwe.

Schleich, G. (1927) "Zur Textgestaltung der mittelenglischen Bearbeitung von Susos Orologium Sapientiae." *Archiv*, ns 52, 36–50, 178–192.

——— (1929) "Auf den Spuren Susos in England." *Archiv*, ns 56, 184–194.

——— (1930) "Über die Entstehungszeit und den Verfasser der mittelenglischen Bearbeitung von Susos Horologium." *Archiv*, ns 57, 26–34.

Schottländer, Rudolf, ed. (1975) *Francesco Petrarcha: De Remediis utriusque Fortunae*. Humanistische Bibliothek. Munich: Wilhelm Fink.

Smedick, Lois K. (1975) "Cursus in Middle English: *A Talkyng of þe Loue of God* Reconsidered." *MS*, 37, 387–406.

———— (1979) "Parallelism and Pointing in Rolle's Rhythmical Style." *MS*, 41, 404–467.

Southern, R. W. (1963) *Saint Anselm and His Biographer: A Study of Monastic Life and Thought.* Cambridge: Cambridge University Press.

Spalding, M .C. (1914) *The Middle English Charters of Christ.* Bryn Mawr College Monographs 15. Bryn Mawr, Pa.: Bryn Mawr College.

Vaissier, J. J., ed. (1960) *A deuout treatyse called the tree & xii. frutes of the holy goost.* Groningen: J. B. Wolters.

Wells, John Edwin (1926) *A Manual of the Writings in Middle English 1050–1400.* New Haven: Connecticut Academy of Arts and Sciences. "Rolle and His Followers" pp. 444–464, plus supplements. The revision of the *Manual* is proceeding under the editorship of J. Burke Severs and Albert E. Hartung. The revision of the Rolle section has been undertaken by Valerie Lagorio and Ritamary Bradley.

Westra, Cecelia Maria, ed. (1950) *A Talkyng of þe Loue of God.* 's Grauenhage: Nijhoff.

Wichgraf, Wiltrud (1929) "Susos Horologium Sapientiae in England nach Handschriften des 15. Jahrhunderts." *Anglia*, 41, 123–133, 269–287, 345–373.

———— (1930) "Susos Horologium Sapientiae in England: Nachlese." *Anglia*, 42, 351–352.

———— (1936) "Heinrich Susos Horologium Sapientiae in England." *Archiv*, ns 169, 176–181.

Wilmart, André (1923) Introduction in A. Castel, *Méditations et Prières de S. Anselme*, pp. xxv–xxvi. Paris, Bruges.

———— (1932) *Auteurs spirituels et textes dévots du moyen âge latin.* Paris: Bloud et Gay; reissued Paris: Etudes Augustiniennes, 1971.

———— (1940) *Precum Libelli Quattuor Aevi Karolini.* Rome: Ephemerides liturgicae.

CHAPTER 10

Sermon Literature

Thomas J. Heffernan

Discussion of the Middle English sermon must begin with a caveat: with few exceptions the authentic *ad populum* sermon of medieval England was intended to teach the faithful the truths of scripture and the faith viva voce (Owst 1926b, pp. 222–229). What are the implications of this for the modern student? If we accept the premise that the sermon was meant chiefly for oral presentation, we must then address ourselves to the nature of those texts that survive, sparsely from the late twelfth through the mid-fourteenth centuries but in some abundance from the late fourteenth century on. Are these texts representative of the matter as it was preached? Middle English sermons exhibit considerable variety in both form and theme. Ross's edition of the prose sermons in MS Royal 18. B XXIII (1940) illustrates the application of rhetorical techniques borrowed from the *artes praedicandi*; these thematic sermons were designed with an upper-class lay congregation in mind. The Corpus Christi sermons edited by Horstmann (1889), on the other hand, which are of approximately the same date as the thematic sermons edited by Ross, are written in octosyllabic rhymed couplets. Addressed to a lay congregation, they are devoid of biblical exegesis and are, at times, virulently anti-Semitic. Sermon length can vary widely: a verse sermon for the *Festum omnium sanctorum* in MS Ashmolean 61 (Horstmann 1887a) is 600 lines of octosyllabic rhymed couplets, while "A lutel soth Sermun" (Morris 1872, pp. 186–188) is a mere 100 irregularly rhymed short lines. Sermon length varies even in single collections: the sermon for Quadragesima Sunday in the original recension of the *Northern Homily Cycle* is approximately 1,288 lines of rhymed octosyllabic verse while the average length of sermons in that collection is slightly in excess of 300 lines. Although the majority of Middle English sermons—especially those in prose—take their theme from scripture, there are examples of sermons that use popular songs as the theme, such as "Atte wrastlinge mi lemman i ches" (Förster 1918). Mendicant sermons in the vernacular, as "At a Sarmoun þer I seet" suggests, often selected themes from the traditional repertoire of fasting, penance, the avoidance of sin, and the terrors of doomsday (Furnivall 1901b, pp. 476–478). Of course the doomsday sermon has a long history in Middle English and was used effectively throughout this period. Förster (1918) has printed an interesting example of a doomsday sermon from the first half of the thirteenth century which takes as its theme the Latin tag "Quam diu fuero." Sermons were written for every occasion. There are sermon collections composed for the entire liturgical year like the *Northern Homily Cycle*: "Expliciunt euangelia dominicalia totius anni in vulgaria lingua exposita" (Bodleian Library, MS Ashmolean 42, fol. 257v). There are also separate collections for the *temporale* or the *sanctorale*; and smaller collections that contain liturgical days of some importance, such as sermons for the Quadragesima Sundays. And of course there are individual sermons on shrift, on the importance of new feasts, on the sacraments, on the saints, and on the teachings of the Church, which can be found in florilegia of Latin, French, and English texts (Reichl 1973). Middle English sermons were written in prose and in verse, and some are Menippean; their themes vary widely—some collections like Mirk's *Festial* illustrate these themes through an abundance of exempla while others like the "Trinity College" homilies (Morris 1873) use virtually no exempla. Such variety in form, in theme, and in both intellectual and literary merit should make us wary of thinking of the English sermons composed between 1150 and 1450 as homogeneous.

The starting place for the study of the sermon must be its *sitz im leben*: what was the function for which this exposition was intended? And what do we mean when we label this sermon but that homily? Once these questions have been answered, the tools of literary criticism may very well reveal much about the merits of a text under consideration.

Literary historians interested in the study of the sermon or homily might begin by discussing what is meant in late medieval England by the terms "sermon" and "homily." They might begin to look at the bishops' registers, ordination lists, synodal legislation, and demographic studies of the clergy, and assess the wealth of other catechetical literature in order to address what might be termed the social archaeology of the sermon. Once the civic roots of the sermon have been plumbed, its ecclesial crown might be assayed—that is the role of preaching, whether on scripture or the faith, in the liturgy. I consider these issues below.

In my opening remark concerning the nature of the sermon, I stressed the obvious, that the sermon was intended to teach—that is the sermon as we find it in England, at least from the first quarter of the thirteenth century through the end of our period, was a response to an episcopal command to educate the laity in the faith and to raise its moral sights.

The use of the single term "sermon" to identify varied aspects of preaching is an oversimplification, and distorts the situation as we find it in the Middle Ages. The medieval preacher had different words to describe related but different ministries. Indeed there is a very real problem which still awaits solution and which I now want to address briefly: what was understood by the use of the terms "sermon" and "homily" in Middle English documents? There has been some confusion about the use of both terms. Part of the confusion concerns the similarity of the function of the sermon and the homily. Both words identify preaching as their central activity, but they differ with respect to the circumstances and the sources of that preaching.

For the Middle Ages *sermo* and *homilia* referred to two distinct ministerial functions. But as late as 1955, de Gaiffier (pp. 127–128), concluded that the terms *sermo* and *homilia* were understood throughout the Middle Ages as synonyms. It is only recently, especially in work on Anglo-Saxon England done by Smetana (1978, p. 78) and Gatch (1977, p. 45), that we can discern the distinctions between what these two words signified in the medieval mind. *Homilia* is a name applied to an edifying discourse based on a text of sacred scripture that is itself traditionally tied to a particular liturgical day or event. *Sermo*, on the other hand, need not be based on a scriptural text nor need it be tied to a particular liturgical function. In brief then, *homilia* is an exegetical commentary on scripture composed for a specific liturgical celebration; *sermo* is an edifying discourse meant to bring the faithful closer to Christian truth with no *prescriptive* theme— scriptural or otherwise—and no obligatory connection to a liturgical event. This distinction is observed in vernacular texts, whether in English or Anglo-Norman, up until the last third of the fourteenth century. The closing decades of the fourteenth century saw an increasing use of the term *sermo* to designate those Middle English texts that in earlier times would have been labeled *homilia*. The increased use of the term *sermo*, and indeed the increased composition of what are clearly sermons from this period, appear to reflect an urgency within the episcopacy to implement the program for ecclesial reform outlined a century and a half earlier by the Fourth Lateran Council.

The English *ad populum* sermon after the last third of the fourteenth century is chiefly concerned with explaining the proper disposition for Christian living in a besotted world. Although such a pastoral attitude may not seem novel in the late Middle Ages, what is interesting in the orthodox sermon is the curious lack of interest in a serious explication of scripture. Indeed, though we still see many sermons beginning with a scriptural pericope, the exegetical commentary is reduced either to a mere footnote in the zeal to apply the scripture to behavior or treated to the most preposterous of allegorizations. The catechetical thesis most prevalent in English preaching during this period is twofold: to continue the Church's efforts at reform and to raise the laity's ecclesial literacy and public morality through the aegis of preaching Church dogma. It is somewhat ironic that in this age of the call for scripture in English, so little serious scriptural pedagogy is presented in the English sermon.

Of the reforms implemented by the English episcopacy in response to the canons of the Fourth Lateran Council, canon twenty-one, which made mandatory the attendance at annual private confession for the laity, apparently had the greatest impact on the pastoral ministry of the Church. Although the primary point of *omnis utriusque Sexus* was intended to provide that this obligatory, annual, and complete confession was to prepare the penitent for reception of the Eucharist during the Easter season, a secondary effect was to elevate the importance of the preacher and his ministry for the establishment of a system of precepts with which to monitor behavior. The effect of the canon was to place the local parish priest in a position of enormous importance: penitents were obliged to confess to him or else seek his permission to seek shrift elsewhere. Such a right to enter into the personal lives of parishioners was bound to give the local parish clergy a kind of moral leverage it had not had before (de jure). The Church, through the implementation of the canon, had granted itself the power to regulate both the spiritual and secular lives of its subjects. The power of the confessional was double-edged: that is, it was both the power to forgive and the power to withhold. And since the issue concerned was the salvation of one's immortal soul, the attainment of forgiveness was of obvious importance on both the spiritual and the secular levels. But such far-reaching powers brought with them a host of problems. Parish priests, often with little formal training in even rudimentary theology and Church dogma, were suddenly invested with daunting powers, which could be used for good and ill. The English episcopacy's response was twofold: it moved to improve the intellectual level of its clergy, and at the same time it began the implementation of a vast program of reform. If sins were to be forgiven, penitents must be clear about the nature of the sin, the degree of sinfulness of their actions, and the consequent punishment for sin. An important effect of this need for greater lay understanding in the faith was to invest the office of the preacher with new and far-reaching responsibilities. Hence the success of canon twenty-one depended on, and at the same time facilitated, the growth in preaching in English from the second decade of the thirteenth century to the end of the Middle English period. The episcopacy in England, with remarkably few exceptions, from Poore (d. 1237) through Arundel (d. 1413)—though Cheney (1973, pp. 185–186) points to the diocesan statutes of Stephen Langton for Canterbury (1213–1214) as calling for a similar ecclesial renewal—was genuinely concerned with and actively involved in ensuring the spiritual and moral well-being of its flocks. Bishop Poore of Salisbury prescribed that the priests of the diocese should have his constitutions frequently before their eyes "*ipsas [constitutiones] frequenter habentes pre oculis* (Cheney 1973, pp. 185–186).

Powicke's work (1928, p. 151), although over half a century old, still contains much insight in this area of episcopal concern for pastoral catechesis. One of the very best one-volume overviews of the efforts of the English episcopacy to implement the Lateran program is still that of Gibbs and Lang (1934). Douie's work (1952) on the great Franciscan John Pecham and his place in clerical reform, pastoral catechesis, and diocesan administration is still standard. For the period immediately preceding the Lateran Council and its impact on this reform spirit see Morey (1937) and Cheney (1956). Morey's volume, which is a careful portrait of Bartholomew of Exeter, shows how the stage was set for the growing importance of the sacrament of penance and a new interest in theological aspects of penance which in turn were seminal in the later discussion of penance by the Fourth Lateran Council.

One need only look at the episcopal constitutions throughout the thirteenth century, where the same concerns continually appear: education of the faithful in the sacraments, in the way to pray, in how to avoid temptation, and in how to make a correct confession. Further, this program for spiritual renewal should be implemented in the language of the people. Walter Cantilupe, bishop of Worcester, in his Constitutions of 1240, spells out the need for this active catechesis through *frequenter praedicent*. And that great polymath cleric of the northeast, Robert Grosseteste, bishop of Lincoln, was quite clear on the duties of the parish priests in his diocese: "Sciat insuper saltem simpliciter septem ecclesiastica sacramenta, et hii qui sunt sacerdotes maxime sciant que exiguntur ad vere confessionis et penitentie sacramentum, formamque baptizandi doceant frequenter laicos in ydiomate communi" (Cheney 1973, p. 189): for texts of the councils and synods see Wilkins (1737) and Powicke and Cheney (1964).

This activity was not simply the ageless continuation of the Church's *magesterium*. The episcopal directives concerning the catechesis of thirteenth- and fourteenth-century England were carefully programmatic. There was a comprehensive plan of action administered by the hierarchy. The renewal of the Church, envisioned by Innocent III and promulgated in the canons of the Fourth Lateran Council, sought the spiritual and moral reforms of both the clergy and the faithful. We see such concern in synod after synod; the Statutes of the Synod of Gerona (1260), for example, urged the priests of the diocese to make clear to their parishioners the canons of the Council in their sermons (Mansi 1900–1927, 23:929). Indeed Innocent's plan of reform had been building for some time as evidenced by his letter to the diocese and archbishop of Metz (July 1199): "Licet autem scientia valde sit necessaria sacerdotibus ad doctrinam, quia juxta verbum propheticum labia sacerdotis custodiunt scientiam et legem exquirunt ex ore ejus; non est tamen simplicibus sacerdotibus etiam a scholasticis detrahendum, cum in eis sacerdotale ministerium debeat honorari" (PL 214:697).

The opening words of canon twenty-seven of the Fourth Lateran Council put the matter of ecclesial reform quite succinctly: *Cum sit artium regimen animarum* (since the government of souls is the art of arts; see Powicke's important discussion, 1953, pp. 445–509). The word *regimen* is ambiguous: of course we are meant to govern our own souls, but it is the clergy, a spiritually and morally literate clergy, who is to provide us with the necessary means for this exercise of responsibility. Owst (1926b, pp. 1–47) and especially D. W. Robertson (1949) have discussed the impact of these episcopal promulgations. It was this episcopal legislation that served as the stimulus for the increase in preaching that took place in late medieval England. It was the bishops and their legislation, managed by effective assistants, like William of Nassington who worked in the *familia* of the archbishop of York, and the impact of that legislation particularly on the secular priesthood and those orders of canons under the effective aegis of the bishop, that brought about so much in the way of pastoral catechesis through the medium of preaching and the use of didactic tracts. Nassington himself has been credited with the composition of several vernacular treatises including the *Northern Homily Cycle*—although the evidence for this latter attribution is very slight. Brentano (1955) has written perceptively about the powers of the members of the episcopal *familia*; his work (1959) on Archbishop Wickwane of York is of considerable importance in illustrating the power of the metropolitan over his suffragan bishops.

The sermons of this period were a response to a call to reform. Did this command prescribe a particular type or pattern of preaching? If so, what are the characteristics of this pattern? Were the models proposed in the *artes praedicandi* appropriate to and used in the *ad populum* sermon? The pedagogic program and liturgy informed the shape of the sermon to the laity. The overwhelming majority of Middle English sermon codices that survive are liturgical—that is they reflect the exigencies of use in a church service. And of this number the sermons for the Sunday gospels represent the largest block. Who were these preachers? Was their effort successful? Did the continual promulgation of episcopal decrees effect the hoped for reforms? It is probably true that the aims of the Lateran Council were doomed to failure for the universal Church but successful in particular instances. Gibbs and Lang (1934, p. 179) sensibly point out that Church law cannot alone lead to spiritual rebirth. The complaints concerning clerical illiteracy heard in the thirteenth century continue to echo in the late fourteenth and the fifteenth centuries. Some of the hierarchy like Pecham were pragmatists—indeed Pecham went so far as to suggest that if the parish priest had difficulty in following the precepts of *Ignorancia Sacerdotum* with respect to preaching or hearing confession he should seek the help of qualified holy men or *viros sanctos*. Although it is not clear from the context who these *viros sanctos* were, it is well to underscore the archbishop's practical concern for his priests' lack of training. More than a century later we hear John Purvey, someone with a very different position, offering similar advice to the uneducated clergy: "If for sothe he [the parish priest] vnderstode no Latyn, go he to oon of his neigtobris that vnderstandith, wiche wole charitabily expone it to hym; and thus edifie he his flock, that is his puple" (Deanesly 1920a, p. 442).

As I indicated at the outset of this discussion, the *ad populum* sermon of England in the period from the early thirteenth through the early fifteenth century is chiefly an oral presentation either liturgically based or extraliturgic. The *terminus post quem* of the early fifteenth century is arbitrary, as we still have in the famous Elizabethan collection *Certaine Sermons or Homilies* a thoroughly medieval outlook (with the exception of their virulent antipapism), a medieval methodology in the structure of the sermon, and a medieval use of the citation of authorities. But to return to the discussion of the oral nature of the sermon and its consequences for scholarly study, since preaching was almost certainly of regular occurrence (i.e., weekly), it had to contain two elements that at first sight seem somewhat at odds: tradition and novelty. The traditional element in preaching is inherent in the mission of the preacher to persuade the listener of the rightness of the Church's view and consequently that truth's ability to rescue the individual soul from perdition. And indeed the liturgy itself was a further reinforcement of the forces of tradition. Hence the themes, the place, and the authorities cited in the majority of the orthodox sermons in English from this period tend to reinforce this traditional element. Novelty, on the other hand, is best seen in the sermon's incorporation of an enormous body of exemplary literature into its purview. Crane (1890), Owst (1961, pp. 149–209), Pfander (1934), and others have commented on this rich body of narrative expropriated by the late medieval preacher from a rich variety of sources.

Eadmer tells us that when Saint Anselm preached he set forth each point with familiar examples "sub vulgaribus et notis exemplis proponens," to ensure that his listeners would retain his instruction (Southern 1962, p. 56). It was Jocelin of Brakelond's story of Samson (Arnold 1890, p. 245), abbot of Bury Saint Edmunds (1185–1211), preaching in his Norfolk dialect ("et Anglice sermocinari solebat populo, sed secundum linguam Norfolchiae ubi natus et nutritus erat") that served as the stimulus for Robert Grosseteste's own vernacular preaching (Stevenson 1899, p. 32). The thirteenth century was conscious of its heritage; it was to become the great age of preaching and pioneer in the use of sermon exempla (de la Marche 1886, p. 299). The use of the exemplum was the single most important development in the success of the *ad populum* sermon of late medieval England. The English episcopacy was soon to recognize the power of the exemplum in pursuit of its goal of implementing the canons of the Lateran Council. Roger Wesenham, bishop of Coventry, underlined the value of the exemplum in his *Instituta* (1245–1254); its power to persuade was not lost on the regular clergy as is apparent in comments made by William of Malmsbury (Stubbs 1889, p. 355).

The sermon exempla were drawn from fables, hagiography, fabliaux, bestiaries, and natural history. Wright (1842, p. vi) and de la Marche (1868, pp. 278–280), pioneers in the study of sermon exempla, illustrate the didactic purpose for which the exempla were used and the sources from which they were drawn. Paris (1913, p. 246) and Ten Brink (1895, 1:264) point to the parable and Aesopian fable in the sermon exempla as one of the favorite devices of the preacher. Meyer (1885, p. 390) and Herbert (1910, 3:1–3, 31–33) counter and suggest that neither the fable nor the parable should be included under the rubric of exempla. Crane was the first (1890, pp. xvii, xviii) to suggest that sermon exempla are unique to the late Middle Ages. Mosher (1911, p. 1) gave us the first analysis of the structure of the exemplum, indicating brevity and the presence of human characters as chief properties. Welter (1927, p. 3) added that the exemplum must also be moral, applicable to human behavior, and narrative in form. Pfander (1934, p. 13) wanted to restrict the term to an illustrative story used only in a sermon designed for teaching or entertainment, while D. W. Robertson (1962, pp. 366–367) has extended its use so far—to "a study with an implication"—that its value as a critical term is diminished.

In England, the mendicants were, shortly after their arrival, the most potent force in vernacular preaching. They rode this crest from the late 1220s until the close of the thirteenth century. Their popularity diminished, however, throughout the fourteenth century. The antimendicant pieces written at the close of the fourteenth century are so numerous as to virtually constitute a genre. The mendicants were also skilled in the university or thematic sermon which grew apace with the scholastic movement. Pelster (1934, pp. 192–204) and Davy (1931, pp. 149–414) illustrate the mendicant contribution to the thematic sermon. Charland's work (1936) on the principal tool for the composition of the thematic sermon, the *artes praedicandi*, and on the principles of sermon composition is still the standard work (see also Caplan 1934 and Murphy 1974, pp. 268–355). However, there seems to have been little influence from the *artes praedicandi* on the vernacular *ad populum* sermon. Spearing correctly suggests (1972, p. 115) that the vernacular sermon only loosely adopted some techniques from the thematic sermon (e.g., repetitive patterning). But as Owst has shown it was in their rapid and virtually complete acceptance by the people that the Franciscans and the Dominicans made their major impact. The reasons he suggests for this great popularity—the Franciscans' and Dominicans' vast repertoire of sermon exempla, their superior education over that of their parochial clergy, and their exposure to life outside the perimeter of the parish—are undoubtedly correct (1926b, p. 81). Wolpers (1964, p. 213) attributed their successes to the clarity and directness of expression of their sermons. Collections of exempla drawn from texts like de Voragine's *Legenda Aurea*, the hagiographic epitomes in Vincent of Beauvais's *Speculum Historiale*, and the legends of Odo of Cheriton, to name only a few, were used exhaustively throughout the thirteenth, fourteenth, and first quarter of the fifteenth centuries by the mendicants and other clergy involved in vernacular preaching. Of course, this exhaustive and often indiscriminate use of exempla led to its demise.

Dante (Petrocchi 1966–1967, 4:485–488) was one of the first to criticize the friars' use of exempla at the expense of preaching the gospel. Such criticism became a commonplace as the century wore on. In England the Wycliffites and their sympathizers, and orthodox monk-scholars like Uthred of Boldon, were severe critics (Matthew 1880, pp. 8, 16; Skeat 1867, p. 19). Wyclif appears to be criticizing this practice in his plea for plain speaking in sermons "plana locuio de pertinentibus" (Hargreaves 1966, pp. 3, 11). Despite the complaints, certain segments of the populace still delighted in such racy anecdotes as the preacher was able to summon—Mirk's *Festial* is ample testimony to this.

A curious characteristic of the extant manuscripts is the virtually complete absence of topical reference. With rare exception the catechetical literature of medieval England, and here I include the penitential treatise, the saint's life (the life of Saint Kenelm in the *South English Legendary* is a notable exception), the catechism, the sermon, and the homily, makes little reference to specific current events. The absence of this element, which one assumes was a necessary part of this oral discourse—delivered by a member of the community, who, in some instances, lived at or even below the economic level of some of his parishioners—is striking. Would it be too much to construe the lack of such topical remarks in the surviving manuscripts as an indication that many of these texts are source materials and not the sermons as preached—a written record meant to be read from and amplified during the reading? This lack of the topical, the absence of references to the living tissue of the community, raises a related problem: how does one assess the place of an individual sermon within the tradition when the corpus is so scant, and when some of those that do survive may have been written more as models than as representatives of the item preached? What part of the extant corpus is representative of the text actually preached—all, half, some none? Obviously this question is more pertinent for those comparatively few texts surviving from the late twelfth through the early fourteenth centuries. Starting in the mid-fourteenth century there is a dramatic increase in the materials that survive; and hence a sermon's merit is discernible through comparison.

Perhaps one way to learn, albeit indirectly, something concerning the "type" of preaching likely to have been heard by the largest congregations would be to find out what particular clerical group was doing most of the preaching at a particular time. Despite the paucity of extant codices for the late twelfth through the early fourteenth centuries, if we can discern who was involved in preaching and the degree of this involvement, we may then be able to draw some cautious conclusions about the nature of this particular preaching. An examination of pertinent ordination lists, poll tax records, episcopal registers, clerical population figures, and other sources of statistics should reveal the strength of particular clerical groups at a specified time in a defined region. Once this information is secured, hypotheses about the likelihood of a particular type of preaching (e.g., Franciscan emphasis on the virtue of voluntary poverty) and its frequency in a particular locale might be framed.

Preaching in England was carried on by a heterogeneous group of clerics who were members of the secular clergy and of religious orders. Richardson's work (1912) on the parish clergy, although somewhat dated, is still useful. H. S. Bennett's (1957, pp. 28–34) work on ordination lists and the requirements for ordination illuminate the educational background of the secular clergy. The hierarchy did attempt to certify that all those proposed for ordination were literate, old enough, and of good character. In his widely disseminated manual for priests, the *Pupilla Oculi*, John de Burgos puts the three major requirements for ordination succinctly: "Tria vero in ordinandis potissime requiruntur: sc. literatura sufficiens, aetas legitima, morum honesta" (H. S. Bennett 1957, p. 31). The parish clergy was being drawn from an increasingly lower strata of society as the fourteenth century wore on, and its numbers dropped precipitously after the first incidence of the plague in 1349. The implications for preaching, depending as it does on a certain standard of literacy, are marked. Would such a situation lend itself to a more extempore preaching ministry? With the consequent reduction in the ability to read, preaching would become more emotional, depend less on the traditional commentary on scripture (which we see in any number of thirteenth-century English sermons), and rely more on a rote presentation of the Lateran program of education of the faithful in the Pater Noster, the Ave, the Decalogue, the Seven Deadly Sins, the rudiments for making a good confession, and so on. It is interesting that there is a dearth of Middle English sermon manuscripts that can be reliably dated just after mid-century; there is a sharp increase at the end of the century. This paucity of surviving manuscripts can be explained by a number of factors, but the exigencies of reduced clerical literacy and the increase of extempore preaching should be considered. What we can learn from the complaints of contemporaries—Brinton, Wimbledon, Bromyard, Wyclif, and Mirk—all tends to confirm this lack of intellectual rigor on the clergy's part. For an informative discussion of local clergy, see Bill's work (1966) on the five classes of clergy in Warwickshire. Edwards (1949) has ruled out a major role for the cathedral clergy in the preaching ministry and in the copying of books. There are some exceptions to this, for example, the long-standing practice of the canons of Lincoln Cathedral in preaching the Sunday sermon to the local laity (see Foster and Major 1931). Indeed Lincolnshire and other selected areas of the Northeast were singularly blessed with respect to medieval preachers. The Austin canons were very active in Lincoln; Sempringham was the home of the only uniquely English regular foundation (and there is evidence that despite their constitutions the Gilbertines were active in the copying of works for the pastoral ministry); and the diocese of Lincoln had a history of reform-minded bishops (e.g., Grosseteste) who were mindful of the importance of preaching in the vernacular for the success of the Lateran program. Bowker (1968) presents a full picture of the secular clergy in the diocese of Lincoln in the late fifteenth century; her valuable bibliography is especially noteworthy for those citations that discuss matters of clerical literacy and the possession of books by the secular clergy. Dickens's work (1952) on the clergy of south Yorkshire is an antidote to the emphasis on clerical illiteracy, and a reminder that we must be careful to avoid generalizations for the country. He finds a disproportionately high incidence of book ownership among this clergy and as a result suggests a higher standard of clerical culture.

Thompson's observations (1938, p. 134) on the presence of monks and particularly canons resident in vicarages must broaden our understanding of who was doing the preaching and the nature of the sermon. Indeed some abbeys had altars in the conventual church reserved for Sunday mass for the lay residents of the area. The varied orders of canons, particularly the Augustinians and closely affiliated groups (e.g., Premonstratensians) appear to have played a crucial role—albeit as yet little documented—in preaching; they continued in this activity into the sixteenth century according to Wolsey's Statutes (Wilkins 1737, 3:683) and influenced parish liturgies under their aegis (J. C. Robertson 1877, p. 310). James (1909) shows the eclectic spirit of the Austin canons of York, whose library before the dissolution consisted of 646 volumes which clearly constituted the nucleus of a first-rate preaching workshop: they had volumes of *sermones dominicales*, *ars praedicandi*, *distinctiones*, Pennafort's *Summa Confessorum*, Peraldus's *Summa de Viciis et Virtutibus*, Pagula's *Oculis Sacerdotis*, the homilies of Gregory and Bede, volumes of *legendae sanctorum*, and *postilliae* on the Old and New Testaments. Dickinson (1951) makes an intelligible whole out of the fragmented and loosely structured beginnings of the Premonstratensians and their early settlements in England. Manuel (1922, p. xxi), Thompson (1938, p. 34), and Colvin (1951, p. 284) all give ample evidence of Premonstratensians holding cures in parish churches, sometimes in perpetuity and at some distance from their abbey. Bishops' registers from the thirteenth century contain statements about the flexibility of the Augustinian rule and their staffing of parishes. Anthony Bec, bishop of Durham (1283–1311), gave permission to the prior and convent of the Austin canons of Guisborough to serve the vicarage of Hart with two canons for the lifetime of the canons "ita quod eidem vicarie per duos honestos et discretos canonicos faciant interim congrue, debite et assidue deserviri et hospitalitatem pauperum in eadem vicaria quatenus poterunt observari" (Fraser 1953, pp. 14–15). Bec also ordered that the office of matins be moved from its usual time of approximately 2:A.M. to early morning so that lay parishioners could attend. And Augustinian breviaries confirm that at matins sermons were preached chiefly on scripture and hagiographic items. Further, Graham (1929, p. 174) has pointed out that sometimes when Austin canons assumed the cure of a parish they also assumed the responsibility for running the local schools (e.g., Waltham, Huntingdon, Bedford). Like their more cloistered brethren, they were not above being absentees and sometimes served dependent parishes through "conducts" (e.g., the Collegiate Church at Ripon) by means of small annual stipends (see Page 1907, 3:369). The Austin canons in England in the later Middle Ages had a considerable part to play in the dissemination of the Lateran program, especially with respect to the *cura animarum*, and as a group are probably responsible for a considerable amount of the vernacular preaching done in this period. This is an area that needs more study.

The mendicants and their part in the Lateran reforms have received considerable attention since the turn of the century. The Franciscans have been served well by Little (1908), Zawart (1928), Moorman (1952 and 1955), Ooms (1961), Fleming (1977), Jones (1974), and Courtenay 1978 (especially his discussion of Franciscan educational practices). On the Dominicans see Hinnebusch (1951), Forte (1958), Emden (1962), and Gleeson (1972). Owst of course gave a prominent place, perhaps too prominent, to the role of the mendicants in vernacular preaching (see Little's review, 1927, pp. 276–277, and more recently Boyle's critique of Owst's method, 1964, pp. 277–230). The standard work on the Austin friars is by Roth (1966). On less important mendicant orders like the Carmelites and the Trinitarians see Rickert (1952) and Jennings (1970, p. 103) respectively. William's work (1960) on the relationships between the mendicants and the seculars is a fully documented, careful survey.

Van Dijk's rhetorical question and answer concerning the importance of the medieval liturgy for those interested in the culture of the Middle Ages are worth quoting: "Was hat das mit mittelalterlicher Liturgie zu tun? Alles!" (1969, p. 86). The student of medieval preaching may not be as obtuse as van Dijk's questioner, but little has been done with respect to the liturgy and the sermon. The liturgy can be of enormous importance to the student of Middle English sermons as I hope to illustrate. The bulk of Middle English sermon codices are liturgical—that is they were composed with a specific ceremonial function in mind. The single most common liturgical setting for these sermons was the commentary on the Sunday gospel pericope. As early as Gratian's *Decretal* (PL 187:209) priests

were expected to have in their possession books that contained homilies for the
Sundays in the church year. Jungmann (1952) on the Roman mass is still standard, but van Dijk and Walker (1960, pp. 52–87) should be consulted, especially for Franciscan practices. Although Gatch (1977) and others have identified
the *prone* as the most auspicious moment in the mass for preaching before the
tenth century, the place of the sermon or homily in late medieval vernacular
preaching is not quite as clear. The great medieval liturgists like Durandus suggest that preaching might have been done after the exposition of the scripture
readings. But the situation in fourteenth-century England varies. The mid-
fourteenth-century *Officium* written to celebrate the presumed imminent canonization of Richard Rolle indicates the preaching should follow the gospel: "Cum
autem in Missa Evangelium esset lectum, petita prius benedictione presbyter,
pulpitum pradicantium adiit, et sermonem . . . fecit ad populum" (Woolley
1919 p. 12). The *Speculum Sacerdotale*, a fifteenth-century English *liber fes-
tivialis*, suggests that the proper time for the exposition of the great deeds of the
saint is after the "redyng of the gospel, and of the offertorie at masse" (Weatherly
1936, p. 2). The Sarum Pontifical for 1315–1329 in the Office for the Consecration of Nuns points to the time after the offertory: "Hic si placet, fiat sermo"
(Simmons and Nolloth 1879, p. 318). When the preaching was done has a bearing on the matter and length of the sermon and should be explored in those sermons that are unambiguously liturgical. But let me return to the importance of
the liturgy as an aid in discerning the provenance and authorship of Middle English sermons. The medieval liturgy can be a bewildering labyrinth of complex
ceremonial practices. Vogel (1965, pp. 5–6) has written a very useful guide
through the maze. In English secular cathedrals there are certain differences in
the liturgical rubrics used in sermon codices that can assist our identification of
these manuscripts (see Frere 1940, p. 159 on York and Canterbury) since Middle English sermons are seldom explicit about such matters. But let me offer one
example: the two most important liturgical uses in late medieval England before
the middle of the fourteenth century were those followed at Sarum and York. The
two sees had different gospel readings for the fifth Sunday after the Epiphany.
York and all its dependencies read the gospel of Luke 4:14–22 for this Sunday
(Henderson 1874, p. 10). Sarum and its dependencies, on the other hand, read
Matthew 13:24–30 (Procter and Wordsworth 1882, 3:ccclxviii). This difference in gospel pericopes was very carefully observed until the time (post
1350s) that the Sarum liturgy began to usurp that of York even in the North;
after this time one must use additional cruces in determining the provenance of
the gospels on the basis of the pericopes. A Middle English sermon then for the
fifth Sunday after the Epiphany that reads Matthew 13:24–30, if it can be
clearly dated from before the second quarter of the fourteenth century, even if
written in a northeast dialect, is not a secular product since it does not follow the

York use. Of course, to determine the provenance one would want to examine a number of cruces, and one would need a knowledge of the gospel readings for this Sunday of the relevant mendicant groups, canons and regulars, if pertinent. Using such a system, I have been able to determine that the *Northern Homily Cycle* is neither a secular nor a mendicant product, as has been argued, but very likely the product of an order of canons, with the Austin canons and the Gilbertines the likeliest candidates. Beissel (1907), Klauser (1935), and Frere (1930) have done significant work in this area, but a complete benchmark of gospel pericopal rubrics of various groups requires investigation of individual missals, breviaries, lectionaries, and sermon codices that can be attributed to a particular group with certainty. Van Dijk's unprinted work on the Bodleian liturgical manuscripts is quite good but must be used with care. Ker (1954, Appendix) has shown that the missal was the book found most often in the possession of the parish church and hence used by the cure. Nevanlinna (1972, 1:26) has worked on the relationship between the York Missal and British Library MSS Harley 4196 and Cotton Tiberius E. VII. The dismemberment of service books for use in the bindings of early printed books from the 1540s (see Woolley 1927, p. xv and Ker 1954, p. ix) has hampered an exact understanding of the variety of service books in England. Bale (Graham 1901, p. 203) reports the astonishment of the Dutch at the arrival in Dutch ports of English ships laden with manuscripts which were sold for next to nothing. The two most important liturgical books for assigning provenance and authorship of Middle English sermons are the missal and the breviary. Baumstark's (1929) work on the Roman Missal is very good. Hohler (1975) has justifiably referred to Legg's (1897) third volume of his Westminster Missal as a "priceless" work of scholarship. A more general discussion of liturgical books used in England can be found in Wordsworth and Littlehales (1910), Maskell (1846, 2:cxcvi), Swete (1914), and Frere (1940). Bäumer (1905) is a solid introduction to the Missal. Batiffol (1893) presents the history of the Roman breviary most intelligibly. The best thing done on the breviary with respect to things English (albeit monastic) is Tolhurst's discussion of Hyde Abbey, Winchester (1942, 6:143–237). The individual uses and their liturgical practices are now easily accessible in Pfaff (1982). King's four volumes (1955, 1957a, 1957b, 1959) are very helpful introductions.

Although most of the earliest of the modern editions of Middle English sermons are a printing of the text of a single manuscript, these Victorian editions—some the work of enthusiastic amateurs—are often notable for the accuracy of their transcriptions. Small's edition (1862) of the Royal College of Physicians manuscript of the *Northern Homily Cycle* is a good example of a typical mid- to late Victorian edition. Small, like many another nineteenth-century editor, was content to place the text at the reader's disposal and make some brief remarks concerning its historical import—more lengthy comments they saved for their discussion of the language. Indeed their inordinate concern with things philologic sometimes caused them to blunder. Belfour's edition of *Twelfth Century Homilies* (1909), despite his title, contains nothing but pre-Conquest items which have been larded with twelfth-century spellings as well as some changes in syntax and vocabulary (see Pope 1967, 1:5). Morris's first collection of homilies (1867–1868) which he printed chiefly for their "philological value" are chiefly Old English *de tempore* sermons transliterated into later lexical forms (Pope 1967, 1:147). Morris's edition of the Kentish Sermons (1872) contains no critical introduction with the exception of his remarks on their language. These are important sermons as they reflect the immediate impact of the popularity of the preaching of Maurice de Sully, bishop of Paris, in early thirteenth-century England. Bennett and Smither's (1974, pp. 213–222, 390–398) more recent edition is good, but since that volume was intended as a reader for Oxford students, the discussions are limited and usually slanted to matters linguistic and pedagogic. Perry's remark (1867, p. v) concerning his edition of "Dan Jon Gaytryge's Sermon" as a "good and idiomatic specimen of a mediaeval sermon . . . preached in obedience to the command of 'oure ffadire þe byshcope'" is mistaken. This text is clearly within the tradition of the pious treatise—a presentation of the essentials of the Lateran program for ecclesial reform, which program the vicar was to make sure his parishioners knew. There is no compelling internal evidence that it was preached. Similar sentiments in a prose text with a strong oral flavor can be found in such clerical nonpreaching volumes as the late-fourteenth-century *Speculum Christiani*; I do not find convincing the arguments that sections of this composition (especially Tabula V) were used in vernacular preaching. Weatherly's edition (1936) of the *Speculum Sacerdotale* is the first modern edition of a complete Middle English collection of *sermones de tempore et de sanctis*. Since the *Speculum Sacerdotale* survives only in BL Add. MS 36791, Weatherly was not faced with the problem of editing numerous manuscripts of a single work, a problem that the editor of Middle English sermon manuscripts must usually face. Weatherly's introduction is sensible and balanced; he is cautious in his observation on how these particular sermons were used (p. xxxix). Although Weatherly was correct in noting their similarity to the sermons in Mirk's *Festial*, he was never able to conclude anything definite concerning their provenance or authorship—questions that need answers. Although the dominical sermons in the collection seem to have an appropriate length for preaching within a formally organized liturgical setting (the sermon for Quinquagesima Sunday is atypical), contain a number of instances when a congregation is being addressed (though I find no instances when males and females are specifically addressed as in a typical salutation e.g., "lordinges and leuedis," or "cristene man and cristene womman"), and present the traditional matter of the Middle English sermon of this period, they do not contain references to the Sunday gospel. This latter situation may suggest that they were preached at a service sometime other than that of the mass. There is evidence of lay congregations in attendance at liturgical services other than Sunday mass. For example, a Corpus Christi sermon from the late fourteenth century (Horstmann 1889) indicates the presence of the laity at matins and evensong, "And at þe matins who wald be, / A hundred daies haue suld he; / And at þe first euin-sang byfore / A hundreth daies by þe sex score." These lay congregations were preached and read to in the vernacular. The "prologue" to the text of the *South English Legendary* in MS Laud. Misc. 108 (Horstmann 1887a, pp. 177–178, 11.1–26) suggests the liturgical practice of reading from a saint's life in church on his anniversary; this may be a reference to the local *Proprium Sanctorum*, "Al þis bok is i-maked of holi dawes; and of holie mannes liues / þat soffreden for ore louerdes loue: pinene manie and riue, / þat ne spareden for none eiȝe: godes weorkes to wurche; / Of ȝwas liues ȝwane heore feste fallez: men redez in holi churche." However, the last line is slightly ambiguous as the nature of the liturgical service is not clearly indicated; for example, *men redez in holi churche* could equally refer to the *lectiones* in the nocturns or the custom of reading from a vita following the gospel in place of the more familiar catechetical sermon. And of course communities of nuns, who often had lay women within the cloister, used the vernacular extensively in their liturgical worship. The Bridgettine Sisters at Syon Abbey, Isleworth, Middlesex had the entirety of their martyrology rendered into English by one Richard Whytford who tells us "Trustynge therfore in your charite / that ye wyll ascrybe applye / & take all thynge vnto ye best / we haue sent forth this martiloge / which we dyd translate out of latyn in to englysshe for the edificacyon of certayn religyus persones vnlerned / that dayly dyd the same martiloge in latyn / not vnderstandynge what they redde" (Procter and Dewick 1893, p. 1). Lay congregations varied considerably as extant sermons appear to have been composed for either the literate landed or the lewid, but seldom for a congregation containing both groups. The *Sermo in Die Epiphanie* (Morris 1872, p. 28) is clearly written for an intelligent congregation of propertied individuals. Of course the bulk of Middle English sermons were composed for less literate congregations. A Corpus Christi sermon in MS Harley 4196 opens with what had become by the late fourteenth century a well-established prologue, "Laude men herto take hede- / ffor vnto clerkes it es no mede, / In þaire bukes may þai se / þe gudenes of goddes preuete." Similar sentiments are contained in the prologue to a copy of the *Northern Homily Cycle* (Bodleian Library, MS Ashmolean 42, fol. 1v) "Forthi will I of my pouerte, / Schewe some thinge I haue in herte, / On ynglihsse tonge þat all maye, / Understand what I will saue, / For lewid men hase mare mistere, /

Goddes worde for to here, / þan clerkes þat þare merour lokes, / þat seese how þai sall lieu in bokes."

Grisdale (1939) has edited three early-fifteenth-century English sermons from Worcester Chapter Library. Hugo Legat, monk of Saint Albans (1380?–1430?) wrote the first of these three—his text is a discussion of the passion of Christ. The other two sermons are anonymous. All three are composed in the thematic style and show certain influences from the *artes praedicandi*. Grisdale has provided a simple presentation of their form with an accompanying explanation of the thematic method. The sermons are for the fourth and fifth Sundays in Lent, and take as their themes the Epistles for those days, namely the Epistle to Galatians 4.31 and Hebrews 9.14–15 respectively. All three sermons quote a considerable amount of scripture from both the Old and New Testaments. The scriptural quotations, which are often lengthy, are quoted first in Latin and then immediately translated into English, which does at times dislocate the movement of the authors' argument. All three sermons use a considerable amount of alliterative phrasing, and Legat employs verse, for example quoting from Virgil's *Eclogues*. The three sermons are all the products of learned authors, and there is little doubt that they were meant for other than a literate congregation. A likely setting for the delivery for such sermons—keeping in mind Legat's authorship—would have been a monastic cathedral; the length, complexity, and tone of these sermons point to a chiefly clerical congregation, although there may have been some laity present.

Ross's edition (1940) of the fifty-one sermons in BL MS Royal 18. B. XXIII bears, in its execution, some resemblance to that of Weatherly's—both Ross's and Weatherly's editions were the fruits of their doctoral studies conducted under the guidance of Karl Young. The sermons printed by Ross illustrate some application of the techniques of the thematic sermon to Middle English *ad populum* sermons. It is interesting to speculate on the marked absence of exempla accompanying these sermons; had the criticism of the Wycliffites and others against the overuse of the exempla begun to tell in educated orthodox circles? The question of their authorship and provenance remains unanswered. The task here is more difficult than it was for Weatherly, as these fifty-one sermons clearly have multiple authorship. Ross made some valuable observations about the composition of the congregation, suggesting the different levels of the laity who might be in attendance.

Although Latin and French figured in Middle English sermons in a variety of ways throughout the period—as glossed scriptural quotations, as argument to authority, as snatches of verses, as an indication of the preacher's erudition—their use has, of itself, never precluded the idea that the particular sermon in question might have been preached. The fifteenth-century "sermo obiti" for Thomas Beauchamp, earl of Warwick (ed. Horner 1978), if actually preached, would have required an entirely bilingual Latin-English congregation. But such an extraordinary pastiche—the label macaronic is not appropriate—of Latin and English surely suggests that this text was not preached but was rather composed as a sui generis specimen used to teach the method of the thematic form; it does not seem unreasonable to suggest that such a text also served some pedagogic function—perhaps as a primer for reading Latin.

Nevanlinna's edition of the final recension of the *Northern Homily Cycle* in Harley MS 4196 (1972) is a sound piece of editing. Her final volume of the projected three-volume edition is scheduled for publication in 1983. Nevanlinna's edition raises a question that editors of Middle English sermons have to address. Do multiple manuscript variants of a single sermon require the kind of collation and annotation one might expend on a text like Chaucer's *Troilus and Criseyde*? I am presently engaged in editing the original version of the *Northern Homily Cycle* which is extant in twenty manuscripts. The complete text runs to over 20,000 lines—simple arithmetic indicates that a completely collated edition of this collection requires the collation of something under a half a million lines. There is of course no substitute for gaining an intimacy with your text short of this sort of work, but the costs must be weighed in advance against the particular document in question. The advantage of having the edition of the original version of this collection and the final recension—they are separated from one another by almost a century—are manifold: their differences will allow us to discern the likes and dislikes of the populace and clergy, changes in the structure of the sermon, and changes in the program of ecclesial reform.

Pantin (1955, p. 235) wrote that "what we badly need is a systematic catalogue or repertory of medieval English preachers and their sermons." Although there has been important work done on individual preachers (Roberts 1968) we still lack the comprehensive catalogue envisioned by Pantin. For vernacular sermons and their authors such a catalogue will have to await the completion of the index of Middle English prose. Wakelin's (1967) and Fletcher's work on the manuscripts of Mirk's *Festial* (1980, pp. 514–522)—although they represent the sort of work that scholars should be about—are descriptions and listings of the sermons of one of the most notable and identifiable English preachers of the later Middle Ages. The great corpus of Middle English sermons is anonymous and lacks such distinctiveness. Before any genuine classification can get under way we shall have to have a repertory of the sort Pantin had in mind.

The student of medieval preaching can gain much valuable information from a review of the work being done in the area of clerical demography. For example, the relative lack of surviving preaching codices from the thirteenth century may suggest something about the clerical group most active in pastoral ministry at this time. If we consider that the population of England from the eleventh through the fourteenth centuries increased steadily from approximately 1.1 million at the time of Domesday to 2.2 million by 1377, and that the clerical population in 1377 constituted 1.6 percent of the entire population (3 percent of the male population), and then conservatively estimate that the number of those clerics permitted to preach was approximately half this total or .08 percent of the entire population in the years immediately before the first onset of the plague, we arrive at a figure of approximately 15,500 clerics who had at least the potential to preach in the generation before the plague. Although the regular clergy achieved its greatest numbers in the period 1275–1300, it maintained an equilibrium until the late 1340s. The secular clergy's membership was highest in the generation following the plague. The regular clergy, with small exception, was engaged in little pastoral preaching during this period. Hence one would want to examine the practices of the seculars, the Austin canons (an important and neglected arm of the Church's preaching ministry), and the mendicant orders in a given region. For example, there seems to have been something of an active tradition of *ad populum* preaching and copying of catechetical literature in the northeast of England, often with a Yorkshire provenance, from the end of the thirteenth century through the fourteenth century. If we examine the clerical population of Yorkshire during the period before the first onset of the plague we notice a manageable clergy (particularly the secular clergy) to laity ratio. In the diocese of York, between 1342 and 1345, the average annual number of clergy ordained to each of the orders of subdeacon, deacon, and priest was approximately 150 seculars and 70 regulars. In addition about 300 seculars and 45 regulars were ordained acolyte each year. Robinson (1969) has estimated the ordained secular population of Yorkshire at this time, ca. 1300–1348, at approximately 3,750. The ranks of the secular clergy varied enormously, from the beneficed scholar-civil servant in the employment of the metropolitan (e.g., William of Nassington) to the unbeneficed cure, almost certainly illiterate (without Latin) drawn from the peasant community he served. We do know that the ratio of beneficed to unbeneficed clergy in Yorkshire was approximately 1.4. Using Russell's (1944) estimate of Yorkshire's total population, based on the poll tax returns of 1377 and making a conservative estimate of a decrease in population from the four incidents of plagues between 1348 and 1377, we can estimate the preplague population of Yorkshire at about 285,000. If we then compare Robinson's estimate of secular clergy at 3,750 to this figure for the total population, we get a secular clergy to laity ratio of 1.76. This is a somewhat greater ratio than Russell's figure for the country as a whole, but his figures are based on the population of 1377, and the ratio of 1.76 is a preplague estimate. If we add to this estimate the population of the mendicants and the Austin canons active in Yorkshire, we have a clergy to laity ratio of 1.63. If we then remove the nonresident beneficed clergy the ratio goes up to 1.84. The ratio is not a large one; it may help place in perspective the tasks of the parish priest, since the average size of the congregation was in the vicinity of eighty souls.

What these ratios do illustrate is that the bulk of the Church's pastoral ministry was performed by the unbeneficed resident clergy. Unfortunately it is not possible to assess the number of unbeneficed clergy with accuracy. The bishops' registers are comparatively silent concerning this body of clergy obliged to perform the important duty of *cura animae*. Although there are the obvious exceptions to this homely picture of the ill-trained, impoverished resident, exceptions like the zealous William Pagula, it does appear that the bulk of the Church's work was done by this group. The silence of the bishops' registers does speak, however, and eloquently: their unspoken message is that the assumption of the responsibility for the *regimen animarum*, which was of such moment to the Fourth Lateran Council and the reform bishops of England, was work, difficult work. But that work was the essence of the unbeneficed clergy's clerical vocation. During the first half of the fourteenth century the clerical group most influential with the majority of the faithful in Yorkshire was the resident unbeneficed clergy. This group delivered its sermons extempore in English (hence the comparative lack of codices); since they were resident they probably employed topical allusion in their preaching; since they were secular they followed the episcopal commands concerning what they were to teach, and they preached the prescribed liturgical gospels for the Sundays in the church year.

BIBLIOGRAPHY

The bibliography does not list items in manuscript or Ph.D. dissertations. Only Middle English versions of major primary sources are included.

MAJOR PRIMARY SOURCES

Belfour, Algernon O., ed. (1909) *Twelfth Century Homilies in MS. Bodley 343*. EETS, os 137.

Blake, Norman F., ed. (1972) *Middle English Religious Prose*. Evanston, Ill.: Northwestern University Press.

————, ed. (1975) *Quattuor Sermones Printed by William Caxton*. MET 2. Heidelberg: Carl Winter.

Brandeis, Arthur, ed. (1900) *Jacob's Well*. EETS, os 115.

Erb, Peter C., ed. (1971) "Vernacular Material for Preaching in MS Cambridge University Library Ii.III.8." *MS*, 33, 63–84.

Erbe, Theodor, ed. (1905) *Mirk's Festial*. EETS, es 96.

Förster, Max, ed. (1918) "Kleinere Mittelenglische Texte." *Anglia*, 42, 145–224.

Grisdale, D. M., ed. (1939) *Three Middle English Sermons from the Worcester Chapter Manuscript F.10*. Leeds School of English Language. Texts and Monographs 5.

Heuser, W., ed. (1904) "With an O and an I." *Anglia*, 27, 290–300.

Holmstedt, Gustaf, ed. (1933) *Speculum Christiani*. EETS, os 182.

Horner, Patrick, ed. (1978) "A Sermon on the Anniversary of the Death of Thomas Beauchamp Earl of Warwick." *Traditio*, 34, 381–401.

Horstmann, Carl, ed. (1877) "Die evangeliengeschichten der homiliensammlung des MS Vernon." *Archiv*, 57, 241–316.

———, ed. (1878) *Sammlung Altenglischer Legenden*. Heilbronn: Gebr. Henninger.

———, ed. (1881) *Altenglische Legenden: Neue Folge*. Heilbronn: Gebr. Henninger.

———, ed. (1887b) "Nachträge zu den Legenden." *Archiv*, 79, 411–470.

———, ed. (1888) "Proprium Sanctorum: Zusatz-Homilien des Ms. Vernon CCXV zur nördlichen Sammlung der Dominicalia evangelia." *Archiv*, 81, 83–114, 299–321.

———, ed. (1889) "Sermo in Festo Corporis Christi." *Archiv*, 82, 167–197.

Knight, Ione K., ed. (1967) *Wimbledon's Sermon "Redde rationem villicationis tue": A Middle English Sermon of the Fourteenth Century*. Pittsburgh: Duquesne University Press.

Matthew, F. D., ed. (1880) *The English Works of Wyclif*. EETS, os 74.

Morris, Richard, ed. (1867–1868) *Old English Homilies and Homiletic Treatises of the Twelfth and Thirteenth Centuries*. 3 vols. EETS, os 29, 34, 53.

———, ed. (1872) *An Old English Miscellany*. EETS, os 49.

Munro, J. J., ed. (1910) *John Capgrave's Lives of St. Augustine and St. Gilbert of Sempringham and a Sermon*. EETS, os 140.

Nevanlinna, Saara, ed. (1972) *The Northern Homily Cycle*. Mémoires de la Société Néophilologique de Helsinki. 2 vols.

Owen, Nancy H., ed. (1966) "Thomas Wimbledon's Sermon: 'Redde racionem villicationis tue.'" *MS*, 28, 176–197.

Perry, George G., ed. (1867) *Religious Pieces in Prose and Verse*. EETS, os 26.

Ross, Woodburn O., ed. (1940) *Middle English Sermons*. EETS, os 209.

Small, John, ed. (1862) *English Metrical Homilies*. Edinburgh: William Patterson.

Steckman, L. L. (1936) "A Late Fifteenth Century Revision of Mirk's Festial." *SP*, 34, 36–48.

Weatherly, Edward H., ed. (1936) *Speculum Sacerdotale*. EETS, os 200.

OTHER PRIMARY SOURCES
(Sermons and Aids to Sermon Composition)

Banks, Mary M., ed. (1904–1905) *An Alphabet of Tales*. 2 vols. EETS, os 126, 127.

Boyle, Leonard E. (1973) "The Date of the *Summa Praedicantium* of John Bromyard." *Speculum*, 48, 533–537.

Broomfield, F., ed. (1968) *Thomas de Cobham: Summa Confessorum.* Analecta Mediaevalia Namurcensia 25. Louvain: Editions Navwelaerfs.

Caplan, Harry, ed. (1934–1936) *Medieval Artes Praedicandi: A Handlist.* Cornell Studies in Classical Philology 24, 25. Ithaca: Cornell University Press.

Caplan, Harry, and King, Henry, eds. (1949) "Latin Tractates on Preaching: A Booklist." *Harvard Theological Review,* 42, no. 3.

Charland, T. M., ed. (1936) *Artes Praedicandi, Contribution à l'histoire de la rhétorique au moyen âge.* Publications de l'Institut d'études médiévales d'Ottawa 7.

Crane, T. F., ed. (1890) *The Exempla or Illustrative Stories from the Sermones Vulgares of Jacques de Vitry.* London Folklore Society 26. London: D. Nutt.

———, ed. (1917) "Medieval Sermon-Books and Stories and Their Study since 1883." *Proceedings of the American Philosophical Society,* 56, no. 5.

Davy, Marie M., ed. (1931) *Les sermons universitaires parisiens de 1230–31: Contribution à l'histoire de la prédication médiévale.* Paris: J. Vrin.

Deanesly, Margaret (1922) *Gospel-Harmony of John de Caulibus.* British Society of Franciscan Studies 10. Manchester: Manchester University Press.

Devlin, Mary A., ed. (1954) *The Sermons of Thomas Brinton, Bishop of Rochester* (1373–1389). 2 vols. Camden Society ser. 3, 85, 86.

Fletcher, A. J. (1980) "Unnoticed Sermons from John Mirk's *Festial.*" *Speculum,* 55, 514–522.

Forte, S. L., ed. (1958) "A Cambridge Dominican Collector of Exempla in the Thirteenth Century." *AFP,* 28, 115–148.

Furnivall, Frederick J., ed. (1901a) *The Minor Poems of the Vernon MS.* EETS, os 117.

———, ed. (1901b, 1903) *Robert of Brunne's Handlyng Synne.* 2 vols. EETS, os 119, 123.

Gregg, J. Y., ed. (1977) "The Exempla of *Jacob's Well*: A Study in the Transmission of Medieval Sermon Stories." *Traditio,* 33, 359–380.

Gwynn, Aubrey O., ed. "The Sermon-Diary of Richard Fitzralph, Archbishop of Armagh." *Proceedings of the Royal Irish Academy,* 44, 1–57.

Hackett, B. M., ed. (1964) "William Flet's *De remediis temptacionis* in Its Latin and English Recensions: The Growth of the Text." *MS,* 26, 210–230.

Herbert, J. A., ed. (1910) *Catalogue of Romances in the Department of Manuscripts in the British Museum.* 3 vols. London: Trustees of the British Museum.

Herrtage, Sidney J. H., ed. (1879) *The Early English Versions of the Gesta Romanorum.* EETS, es 33.

Horstmann, Carl, ed., (1887a) *The Early South-English Legendary.* EETS, os 87.

———, ed. (1892) *The Minor Poems of the Vernon MS.* EETS, os 98.

James, Montague R., ed. (1909) "The Catalogue of the Library of Augustinian Friars at York." *Fasciculus Ioanni Willis Clark dicatus.* Cambridge: Cambridge University Press.

Little, Andrew G., ed. (1908) *Liber Exemplorum ad Usum Praedicantium.* Aberdeen: Typis Academicis.

Mansi, G., ed. (1900–1927) *Sacrorum Conciliorum Nova, et Amplissima Collectio.* 53 vols. Paris: H. Welter.

Marche, Albert Lecoy de la, ed. (1886) *La chaire française au moyen âge, spécialement au XIIIe siècle, d'après les manuscrits contemporains.* 2d ed. Paris: Renouard.

Mosher, Joseph A., ed. (1911) *The Exemplum in the Early Religious and Didactic Literature of England*. New York: Columbia University Press.

Murphy, James J., ed. (1974) *Rhetoric in the Middle Ages*. Berkeley: University of California Press.

Nolcken, Christina von, ed. (1979) *The Middle English Translation of the Rosarium Theologie*. MET 10. Heidelberg: Carl Winter.

Oesterley, Hermann, ed. (1872) *Gesta Romanorum*. Berlin: Weidmann.

Pelster, Franz, ed. (1934) "Sermons and Preachers at the University of Oxford in the Years 1290–1293." In *Oxford Theology and Theologians circa A.D. 1282–1302*, edited by A. G. Little and F. Pelster. Oxford: Clarendon Press.

Pfander, Homer G., ed. (1934) "The Medieval Friars and Some Alphabetical Reference-Books for Sermons." *MAE*, 3, 19–29.

Roberts, Phyllis B., ed. (1968) *Stephanus de Lingua-Tonante: Studies in the Sermons of Stephen Langton*. Toronto: Pontifical Institute of Mediaeval Studies.

———, ed. (1980) "Master Stephen Langton Preaches to the People and Clergy: Sermon Texts from Twelfth-Century Paris." *Traditio*, 36, 237–268.

Ross, Woodburn O., ed. (1937) "A Brief Forma predicandi." *MP* 34, 337–344.

Rouse, Richard H., and Rouse, Mary A., eds. (1979) *Preachers, Florilegia and Sermons: Studies on the Manipulus florum of Thomas of Ireland*. Toronto: Pontifical Institute of Mediaeval Studies, Studies and Texts 47.

Roth, D., ed. (1956) *Die mittelalterliche Predigtheorie und das "Manuae Curatorum" des Johann Ulrich Surgant*. Basler beiträge zur Geschichtswissenschaft 58. Basel and Stuttgart: Helbing and Lichtenhahn.

Smith, Lucy T., and Meyer, Paul, eds. (1889) *Les contes moralisés de Nicole Bozon*. Paris: Firmin Didot.

Toal, F. M., ed. (1960) *The Sunday Sermons of the Great Fathers*. 4 vols. London: Longmans, Green.

Welter, J. T., ed. (1914) *Le Speculum Laicorum: Edition d'une collection d'exempla, composée en Angleterre à la fin du XIIIe siècle*. Thesaurus exemplorum fasc. 5. Paris: A. Picard.

———, ed. (1927) *L'exemplum dans la littérature religieuse et didactique du moyen âge*. Paris: E. H. Guitard.

SECONDARY MATERIALS

Arnold, Thomas, ed. (1890) *Memorials of Saint Edmund's Abbey*. London: Eyre and Spottiswoode.

Batiffol, Pierre (1893) *Histoire du bréviaire romain*. Paris: Picard.

Bäumer, Suitbert (1905) *Histoire du bréviaire*. 2 vols. Paris: Letouzey and Ane.

Baumstark, Anton (1929) *Missale Romanum: Seine Entwicklung, ihre wichtigsten Urkunden und Probleme*. Nijmegen: W. van Eupen.

Beissel, Stephan (1907) *Entstehung der Perikopen des Römischen Messbuches: zur Geschichte der Evangeliebücher in der Ersten Hälfte des Mittelalters.* Repr. 1967. Freiburg: Herder Rom.

Bennett, H. S. (1957) "Medieval Ordination Lists in the English Episcopal Registers." In *Studies Presented to Sir Hilary Jenkinson*, edited by J. Conway Davies. London: Oxford University Press.

Bennett, J. A. W., and Smithers, G. V., eds. (1974) *Early Middle English Verse and Prose*. Oxford: Clarendon Press.

Bennett, Ralph F., ed. (1937) *The Early Dominicans. Studies in Thirteenth-Century Dominican History*. Cambridge: Cambridge University Press.

Berlioz, J., and David, J.-M., eds. (1980–1981) *L'exemplum et le mòdele de comportement dans le discours antique et médiéval.* Mélanges de l'Ecole de Rome, Moyen âge—Temps modernes 92. Paris.

Bill, P. A., ed. (1966) "Five Aspects of the Medieval Parochial Clergy of Warwickshire." *University of Birmingham Historical Journal*, 10, 95–116.

Blench, J. W., ed. (1964) *Preaching in England in the Late Fifteenth and Sixteenth Centuries*. Oxford: Blackwell.

Boyle, Leonard E., ed. (1955) "The Oculus Sacerdotis and Some Other Works of William of Pagula." *TRHS* ser. 5, 5, 81–100.

———— (1964) Review of the 2d ed. of G. R. Owst's *Literature and Pulpit in Medieval England. MAE*, 33, 227–230.

———— (1978) "Aspects of Clerical Education in Fourteenth-Century England." In *The Fourteenth Century*, edited by Paul Szarmach and Bernard Levy. Acta 4. Binghampton: State University of New York Press.

Bowker, Margaret, ed. (1968) *The Secular Clergy in the Diocese of Lincoln, 1495–1520.* Cambridge: Cambridge University Press.

Brentano, Robert (1955) "Late Medieval Changes in the Administration of Vacant Suffragan Dioceses: Province of York." *Yorkshire Archaelogical Journal*, 37, 496–502.

———— (1959) *York Metropolitan Jurisdiction and Papal Judges' Delegates (1279–1296).* University of California Publications in History 58. Berkeley: University of California Press.

Brewer, Derek S. (1954) "Observations on a Fifteenth-Century Manuscript." *Anglia*, 72, 390–399.

Brown, Beatrice D., ed. (1927) *The Southern Passion*. EETS, os 169.

Caplan, Harry (1929) "The Four Senses of Scriptural Interpretation and the Medieval Theory of Preaching." *Speculum*, 4, 282–290.

———— (1933) "Classical Rhetoric and Medieval Theory of Preaching." *Classical Philology*, 28, 73–96.

Caplan, Harry, and King, Henry (1955) *Pulpit Eloquence*. Baton Rouge, La.: Speech Association of America.

Cheney, Christopher R. (1956) *From Becket to Langton: English Church Government 1170–1213*. Manchester: Manchester University Press.

———— (1973) "Some Aspects of Diocesan Legislation in England during the Thirteenth Century." In *Medieval Texts and Studies*, edited by C. R. Cheney. London: Oxford University Press.

———— (1976) *Pope Innocent III and England*. Stuttgart: Hiersemann.

Cigman, Gloria, ed. (1978–1979) "Middle English Sermons in Manuscripts: Ubi sunt." *Medieval Sermon Studies Newsletter*, 3, 5–7.

Colvin, H. M. (1951) *The White Canons in England*. Oxford: Clarendon Press.

Courtenay, William J. (1978) *Adam Wodeham: An Introduction to His Life and Writings*. Leiden: Brill.

Cruel, Rudolf (1966) *Geschichte der deutschen Predigt im Mittelalter*. Hildesheim: G. Olms.

Deanesly, Margaret (1920a) *The Lollard Bible*. Cambridge: Cambridge University Press.

——— (1920b) "Vernacular Books in England in the Fourteenth and Fifteenth Centuries." *MLR*, 15, 349–358.

D'Evelyn, Charlotte, and Mill, Anne J., eds. (1956–1959) *The South English Legendary*. 3 vols. EETS, os 235, 236, 244.

Devlin, Mary (1939) "Bishop Brunton and His Sermons." *Speculum*, 14, 324–344.

Dickens, A. G. (1952) "Aspects of Intellectual Transition amongst the English Parish Clergy of the Reformation Period: A Regional Example." *Archiv für Reformationsgeschichte*, 43, 51–70.

Dickinson, John C. (1951) "English Regular Canons and the Continent in the Twelfth Century." *TRHS*, 5th ser. 1, 71–89.

Dijk, S. J. P. van. (1960) "The Authentic Missal of the Papal Chapel." *Scriptorium*, 14, 257–314.

——— (1963) *Sources of the Modern Roman Liturgy*. Leiden: Brill.

——— (1969) "Ursprung und Inhalt der franziskanischen Liturgie des 13. Jahrhunderts." *Franziskanische Studien*, 51, 86–116, 192–217.

Dijk, S. J. P. van, and Walker, Joan H. (1960) *The Origins of the Modern Roman Liturgy*. London: Darton, Longmans & Todd.

Dobson, Eric J. (1975) *Moralities on the Gospels*. Oxford: Clarendon Press.

Dolan, T. P. (1979) "The Source of the Early Middle English Sermon 'Alse Longe As I Live In Þis Werld.'" *N&Q*, 224, 100–101.

Douie, Decima L. (1952) *Archbishop Pecham*. London: Oxford University Press.

Edwards, Kathleen (1949) *The English Secular Cathedrals in the Middle Ages*. Manchester: Manchester University Press.

Emden, Alfred B. (1962) "Dominican Confessors and Preachers Licensed by Medieval English Bishops." *AFP*, 32, 180–210.

——— (1967) *A Survey of Dominicans in England, Based on the Ordination Lists in Episcopal Registers (1268 to 1538)*. Rome: S. Sabina.

Fisher, John H., ed. (1977) *The Complete Poetry and Prose of Geoffrey Chaucer*. New York: Holt, Rinehart and Winston.

Fleming, John V. (1977) *An Introduction to the Franciscan Literature of the Middle Ages*. Chicago: Franciscan Herald Press.

Fletcher, Alan J. (1978) "'I Sing of a Maiden': A Fifteenth-Century Sermon Reminiscence." *N&Q*, 223, 107–108.

Fletcher, Alan, J., and Powell, Susan (1978) "The Origins of a Fifteenth-Century Sermon Collection: MSS. Harley 2247 and Royal 18 B XXV." *Leeds SE*, ns 10, 74–96.

Forshall, Josiah, and Madden, Frederic, eds. (1850) *The Holy Bible Containing the Old and New Testaments with the Apocryphal Books*. 4 vols. London: Oxford University Press.

Foster, Brian, ed. (1976) *The Anglo-Norman Alexander*. 2 vols. Anglo-Norman Text
    Society.
Foster, C. W., and Major, K. (1931) *The Registrum Antiquissimum of the Cathedral Church
    of Lincoln*. 10 vols. Lincoln Record Society.
Foster, Frances A., ed. (1913, 1916) *The Northern Passion*. 2 vols. EETS, os 145, 147.
———, ed. (1926) *A Stanzaic Life of Christ*. EETS, os 166.
Fraser, C. M. (1953) *Records of Anthony Bec, Bishop and Patriarch 1283–1311*. Surtees
    Society 162. Durham: Andrews.
Frere, Walter, H. (1898, 1901) *The Use of Sarum*. 2 vols. Cambridge: Cambridge Uni-
    versity Press.
——— (1930) *Studies in Early Roman Liturgy: The Roman Gospel-Lectionary*. Alcuin
    Club Collections 30. London: Oxford University Press.
——— (1940) *A Collection of His Papers on Liturgical and Historical Subjects*. Alcuin
    Club Collections 35. London: Oxford University Press.
Gaiffier, B. de. (1955) "L'Homiliaire-Legendier de Valere." *Analecta Bollandiana*, 73,
    119–139.
Gatch, Milton McC. (1977) *Preaching and Theology in Anglo-Saxon England: Aelfric and
    Wulfstan*. Toronto: University of Toronto Press.
Gerould, Gordon H. (1902) *The North-English Homily Collection*. Lancaster, Pa.:
    New Era.
——— (1907) "The North-English Homily Collection." *MLN*, 22, 95–96.
Ghellinck, J. de (1914) "Medieval Theology in Verse." *Irish Theological Quarterly*, 9,
    336–354.
Gibbs, Marion, and Lang, Jane (1934) *Bishops and Reform 1215–1272*. London: Oxford
    University Press.
Gleeson, Philip (1972) "Dominican Liturgical Manuscripts from before 1254." *AFP*,
    42, 81–135.
Goates, Margery, ed. (1922) *The Pepysian Gospel Harmony*. EETS, os 157.
Godefroy, Frédéric (1937–1938) *Dictionnaire de l'ancienne langue française*. 10 vols.
    Paris: Libraririe des sciences et des Arts.
Graham, Rose (1901) *St. Gilbert of Sempringham and the Gilbertines*. London: Elliot
    Stock.
——— (1929) *English Ecclesiastical Studies*. London: SPCK.
Grant, Judith, ed. (1978) *La Passiun de Seint Edmund*. Anglo-Norman Text Society.
Haines, R. M. (1975) "Church, Society and Politics in the Early Fifteenth Century as
    Viewed from an English Pulpit." *Studies in Church History*, 12, 143–157.
Hargreaves, H. (1966) "Wyclif's Prose." *E&S*, ns 19, 1–17.
Harjunpaa, T. (1965) *Preaching in England during the Later Middle Ages*. Acta Academiae
    Aboensis, ser. A. 29.
Heffernan, Thomas J. (1981a) "Four Middle English Religious Lyrics from the Thir-
    teenth Century." *MS*, 43, 131–150.
——— (1981b) "On the Importance of "Schrifte": A Middle English Poem on Pen-
    ance." *NM*, 82, 362–367.
——— (1982) "Unpublished Middle English Verses on the 'Three Sorrowful Things.'"
    NM, 83, 31–33.

Henderson, W. G., ed. (1874) *Missale ad usum insignis Ecclesiae Eboracensis*. 2 vols. Surtees Society 59, 60. Durham: Andrews.

Hinnebusch, William A. (1951) *The Early English Friars Preachers*. Rome: S. Sabinae.

Hohler, C. (1975) "Some Service Books of the Later Saxon Church." In *Tenth-Century Studies*, edited by David Parsons. London: Phillmore.

Holthausen, F., ed. (1878) *Vices and Virtues*. EETS, os 89.

Jeffrey, David L. (1975) *The Early English Lyric and Franciscan Spirituality*. Lincoln: University of Nebraska Press.

Jennings, Bernard, ed. (1970) *A History of Harrogate and Knaresborough*. Huddersfield: Advertiser Press.

Jones, W. R. (1974) "Franciscan Education and Monastic Libraries: Some Documents." *Traditio*, 30, 435–445.

Jungmann, Josef A. (1952) *Missarum Sollemnia: Eine Genetische Erklärung der Römischen Messe*. Vienna: Herder.

Ker, Neil R. (1954) *Fragments of Medieval Manuscripts Used as Pastedowns in Oxford Bindings with a Survey of Oxford Bindings c. 1515–1620*. Oxford Bibliographical Society Publications, ns 5.

King, Archdale A. (1955) *Liturgies of the Religious Orders*. London: Longmans, Green and Company.

——— (1957a) *Liturgies of the Primatial Sees*. London: Longmans, Green and Company.

——— (1957b) *The Liturgy of the Roman Church*. London: Longmans, Green and Company.

——— (1959) *Liturgies of the Past*. London: Longmans, Green and Company.

Kittendorf, D. E. (1977) "Cleanness and the Fourteenth Century *Artes Praedicandi*." *Michigan Academician*, 11, 319–330.

Klauser, Theodor (1935) *"Das romische" Capitulare Evangeliorum*. Liturgiegeschichtliche Quellen und Forschungen 28. Münster.

Kristensson, Gillis, ed. (1974) *John Mirk's Instructions for Parish Priests*. LSE 49. Lund: Gleerup.

Lawton, D. A. (1979) "Gaytryge's Sermons, *Dictamen*, and Middle English Alliterative Verse." *MP*, 76, 329–343.

Legg, John W., ed. (1891–1897) *Missale ad usum Ecclesie Westmonasteriensis*. 3 vols. Henry Bradshaw Society 1, 5, 12. London. Harrison and Sons.

———, ed. (1916) *The Sarum Missal*. Oxford: Clarendon Press.

Legge, Mary D. (1950) *Anglo-Norman in the Cloisters*. Edinburgh: Edinburgh University Press.

Little, Andrew G. (1917) *Studies in English Franciscan History*. Manchester: Manchester University Press.

——— (1927) Review of G. R. Owst's *Preaching in Medieval England*. *EHR*, 42, 276–277.

Long, Mary McD. (1955) "Undetected Verse in Mirk's Festial." *MLN*, 70, 13–15.

Manuel, D. G. (1922) *Dryburgh Abbey*. Edinburgh: Blackwood.

Marche, Albert lecoy de la. (1868) *La chaire française au moyen âge*. Paris: Didier.

Maskell, William (1846) *Monumenta ritualia ecclesiae Anglicanae*. 2 vols. Oxford: W. Pickering.

Mason, E. (1976) "The Role of the English Parishioner, 1100–1500." *Journal of Ecclesiastical History*, 27, 17–29.

Meyer, P. (1885) "Une ancienne version française des fables d'eude de Cherrington." *Romania*, 14, 381–397.

————— (1886) "Manuscrits français de Cambridge." *Romania*, 15, 236–357.

Michaud, M. (1961) *Les livres liturgiques: des Sacramentaires au Missel. L'église dans sa liturgie et ses rites xme partie*. Paris: Fayard.

Michaud-Quantin, Pierre (1962) *Soomes de casuistiques et manuels de confession au moyen-âge (Xll^e–XVl^e siècles)*. Analecta Mediaevalia Namurcensia 13. Louvain: Editions Nauwelaerts.

Moorman, John R. H. (1944) "The Medieval Parsonage and Its Occupants." *BJRL*, 28, 137–153.

————— (1952) *The Grey Friars in Cambridge, 1225–1538*. Cambridge: Cambridge University Press.

————— (1953) *A History of the Church in England*. London: A. & C. Black.

————— (1955) *Church Life in England in the Thirteenth Century*. Cambridge: Cambridge University Press.

Morey, Adrian (1937) *Bartholomew of Exeter, Bishop and Canonist*. Cambridge: Cambridge University Press.

Morris, Richard, ed. (1866) *Dan Michel's "Ayenbite of Inwyt."* EETS, os 23.

—————, ed. (1874–1893) *Cursor Mundi*. EETS, os 62.

Neale, John M. (1856) *Mediaeval Preachers and Mediaeval Preaching*. London: J. C. Mozley.

Ooms, H., ed. (1961) *Bibliographia de bibliographia franciscana*. Brussels: Commission belge de bibliographie.

Owst, Gerald R. (1926a) "The People's Sunday Amusements in the Preaching of Medieval England." *Holborn Review*, 68, 32–45.

————— (1926b) *Preaching in Medieval England*. Cambridge: Cambridge University Press.

————— (1952) *The Destructorium viciorum of Alexander Carpenter*. London: SPCK.

————— (1957) "Sortilegium in English Homiletic Literature of the Fourteenth Century." In *Studies Presented to Sir Hilary Jenkinson*, edited by J. C. Davies, pp. 272–303. London: Oxford University Press.

————— (1961) *Literature and Pulpit in Medieval England*. 2d ed. Oxford: Blackwell.

Page, William (1907) *The Victoria History of the Counties of England: Gloucestershire*. 3 vols. London: Constable & Company.

Pantin, William A. (1955) *The English Church in the Fourteenth Century*. Cambridge: Cambridge University Press.

Paris, Gaston (1913) *La litterature française au moyen âge*. Paris: Hachette.

Paul, J. (1977) "La religion populaire au moyen âge." *Revue d'histoire de l'église de France*, 63, 79–86.

Petrocchi, Giorgio, ed. (1966–1967) *La Commedia secondo l'antica vulgata*. Milan: Mondadori.

Pfaff, Richard W., ed. (1982) *Medieval Latin Liturgy: A Select Bibliography*. Toronto: University of Toronto Press.

Pfander, Homer G. (1936) "Some Medieval Manuals of Religious Instruction in England and Observations on Chaucer's Parson's Tale." *JEGP*, 35, 243–258.

―――― (1937) *The Popular Sermon of the Medieval Friar in England.* New York: New York University Press.

Pope, John C., ed. (1967) *Homilies of Aelfric.* 2 vols. EETS, os 259, 260.

Powicke, Frederick M. (1928) *Stephen Langton.* Oxford: Clarendon Press.

―――― (1953) *The Thirteenth Century 1216–1307.* Oxford: Clarendon Press.

Powicke, Frederick M., and Cheney, C. R., eds. (1964) *Councils and Synods with Other Documents Relating to the English Church.* 2 vols. Oxford: Clarendon Press.

Procter, Francis, and Dewick, E. S., eds. (1893) *The Martiloge in Englysshe after the Use of the Chirche of Salisbury and as it is Redde in Syon, with Addicyons.* Henry Bradshaw Society 3. London: Harrison and Sons.

Procter, Francis, and Wordsworth, C., eds. (1882) *Breviarium ad usum insignis ecclesiae Sarum.* 3 vols. Cambridge: Cambridge University Press.

Reichl, Karl (1973) *Religiöse Dichtung in englischen Hochmittelalter.* Munich: Fink.

Richardson, H. G. (1912) "The Parish Clergy of the Thirteenth and Fourteenth Centuries." *TRHS*, 3rd ser. 6, 89–128.

Rickert, Margaret (1952) *The Reconstructed Carmelite Missal.* Chicago: University of Chicago Press.

Rickey, Mary Ellen, and Stroup, Thomas B. (1968) *Certaine Sermons or Homilies.* Gainesville, Fla.: Scholars Facsimiles and Reprints.

Robertson, D. W., Jr. (1947) "The Cultural Tradition of 'Handlyng Synne.'" *Speculum*, 22, 162–185.

―――― (1949) "Frequency of Preaching in Thirteenth Century England." *Speculum*, 24, 376–388.

―――― (1962) *A Preface to Chaucer.* Princeton: Princeton University Press.

Robertson, J. C., ed. (1877) *Materials for the History of Thomas Becket.* London: Longman.

Robinson, D. (1969) *Beneficed Clergy in Cleveland and the East Riding 1306–1340.* Borthwick Papers 37. York: St. Anthony's Press.

Robson, C. A. (1952) *Maurice of Sully and the Medieval Vernacular Homily.* Oxford: Blackwell.

Roth, Francis X. (1966) *The English Austin Friars.* New York: Augustinian Historical Institute.

Russell, D. W., ed. (1976) *La Vie de Saint Laurent.* Anglo-Norman Text Society.

Russell, Josiah C. (1944) "Clerical Population of Medieval England." *Traditio*, 2, 177–212.

―――― (1948) *British Medieval Population.* Albuquerque: University of New Mexico Press.

Schneyer, Johann B. (1969) *Geschichte der katholischen Predigt.* Freiburg: Seelsorge.

―――― (1969–1975) *Repertorium der lateinischen Sermones des Mittelalters.* 6 vols. Beiträge zur Geschichte der philosophie und theologie des Mittelalters, Texte und Untersuchungen 43. Münster: Aschendorff.

Simmons, Thomas, and Nolloth, H. E., ed. (1879) *The Lay Folks Mass-Book.* EETS, os 71.

Skeat, Walter W., ed. (1867) *Pierce the Ploughmans Creed.* EETS, os 30.

Smalley, Beryl (1964) *The Study of the Bible in the Middle Ages.* 2d ed. Notre Dame, Ind.: University of Notre Dame Press.

Smetana, Cyril L. (1978) "Paul the Deacon's Patristic Anthology." In *The Old English Homily and Its Backgrounds,* edited by Paul E. Szarmach and Bernard F. Huppé. Albany: State University of New York Press.

Smith, Lucy T. (1892) "English Popular Preaching in the Fourteenth Century." *EHR,* 7, 25–36.

Smyth, Charles H. E. (1940) *The Art of Preaching.* London: SPCK.

Southern, Richard W., ed. and trans. (1962) *The Life of St. Anselm Archbishop of Canterbury by Eadmer.* London: Thomas Nelson.

Spearing, A. C. (1972) "The Art of Preaching and 'Piers Plowman.'" In *Criticism and Medieval Poetry,* pp. 107–134. London: E. Arnold.

Spencer, Helen (1977) "A Fifteenth-Century Translation of a Late Twelfth-Century Sermon Collection." *RES,* ns 28, 257–267.

Stevenson, Francis S., ed. (1899) *Robert Grosseteste; Bishop of Lincoln.* London: Macmillan.

Strayer, J. R. (1940) "The Laicization of French and English Society in the Fourteenth Century." *Speculum,* 15, 76–86.

Stubbs, William, ed. (1887, 1889) *Willelmi Malmesbiriensis Monachi De gestis Regum Anglorum Libri Quinque.* 2 vols. London: Eyre and Spottiswoode.

Swete, Henry B. (1914) *Church Services and Service-Books before the Reformation.* London: SPCK.

Ten Brink, B. (1895) *History of English Literature.* Translated by H. M. Kennedy. London: George Bell.

Thompson, A. H. (1938) *The Premonstratensian Abbey of Welbeck.* London: Faber and Faber.

Thorpe, Benjamin (1844) *The Homilies of the Anglo-Saxon Church.* 2 vols. London: Aelfric Society.

Tolhurst, John B. L., ed. (1932–1942) *The Monastic Breviary of Hyde Abbey, Winchester.* 6 vols. Henry Bradshaw Society 69–71, 76, 78, 80. London: Harrison and Sons.

Tubach, F. C. (1962) "Exempla in the Decline." *Traditio,* 18, 407–417.

Vogel, C. (1965) *Introduction aux sources de l'histoire du culte chretien au moyen âge.* Spoleto: Biblioteca degli studi medievali.

Wakelin, M .F. (1967) "The Manuscripts of John Mirk's *Festial.*" Leeds SE, ns 1, 93–118.

Walsh, Katherine (1981) *A Fourteenth-Century Scholar and Primate: Richard FitzRalph in Oxford, Avignon and Armagh.* Oxford: Clarendon Press.

Wells, John E., ed. (1916–1941) *A Manual of the Writings in Middle English.* New Haven: Connecticut Academy of Arts and Sciences.

Wenzel, Siegfried (1974) "Unrecorded Middle-English Verses." *Anglia,* 92, 55–78.

———— (1976a) "Chaucer and the Language of Contemporary Preaching." *SP,* 73, 138–161.

———— (1976b) "Vices, Virtues, and Popular Preaching." In *Medieval and Renaissance*

Studies. Proceedings of the Southeastern Institute of Medieval and Renaissance Studies; Summer 1974, edited by D. B. J. Randall. Durham, N.C.: Duke University Press.

———— (1978) *Verses in Sermons. "Fasciculus Morum" and its Middle English Poems*. Cambridge, Mass.: Medieval Academy of America.

———— (1979) "The Joyous Art of Preaching; Or the Preacher and the Fabliau." *Anglia*, 97, 304–325.

Wilkins, D., ed. (1737) *Concilia Magnae Britanniae et Hiberniae*, vol. 1. London.

Williams, Arnold (1960) "Relations between the Mendicant Friars and the Regular Clergy in the Later-Fourteenth Century." *AnM* 1, 22–95.

Wilson, E. (1973) *A Descriptive Index of the English Lyrics in John of Grimestone's Preaching Book*. Medium Aevum Monographs. Oxford. Basil Blackwell.

Wolpers, Theodor (1964) *Die Englische Heiligenlegende des Mittelalters*. Tübingen: Niemeyer.

Woolley, Reginald M., ed. (1919) *The Officium and Miracula of Richard Rolle of Hampole*. London: SPCK.

———— (1927) *Catalogue of the Manuscripts of Lincoln Cathedral Chapter Library*. London: Oxford University Press.

Wordsworth, C., and Littlehales, H. (1910) *The Old Service-Books of the English Church*. London: Methuen.

Wright, T., ed. (1842) *A Selection of Latin Stories*. London: Percy Society.

Zawart, A. (1928) *The History of Franciscan Preaching and of Franciscan Preachers*. New York: J.F. Wagner.

CHAPTER 11

Historical Prose

Lister M. Matheson

With the cessation in the mid-twelfth century of continuations to the Anglo-Saxon Chronicle, the writing of historical prose in English lapsed until the late fourteenth century, although verse chronicles such as those of Layamon, Robert of Gloucester, and Robert Mannyng of Brunne and the *Short English Metrical Chronicle* continued to be written. Prose chroniclers preferred Latin and Anglo-Norman, and the process of reestablishing English as a medium for historical prose began with translations from those languages, primarily John Trevisa's translation of Higden's *Polychronicon* (which is dealt with in Chapter 8) and the English translation of the *Brut*. Accordingly, the majority of works discussed in this chapter belong to the fifteenth century, but in this century English became the predominant medium for historical writings and governmental records, and the amount of extant material is extremely large.

For present purposes historical prose has been mainly limited to writings on history or extracts from the official records. Though often of great incidental historical value, private correspondence, such as the Paston, Stonor, Cely, and Shillingford letters, has been excluded as not primarily historical in intent. So too have governmental proceedings recorded in the *Rolls of Parliament* (which are sorely in need of a major new, accurate edition) and the *Proceedings of the Privy Council*. The Public Record Office and local record offices still contain vast amounts of unpublished material—indentures, agreements, depositions, deeds, inventories, petitions, and other documents.

For a general survey of historical writing in the fifteenth century in England, in English and in other languages, scholars continue to depend upon the valuable work of Kingsford (1913). Kingsford, however, writes from a historian's point of view and is primarily concerned with the more contemporary portions of the works he discusses. Thus he does not discuss sections that deal with legendary material, which, although now considered unhistorical, were considered historical by the medieval reader. A revision of Kingsford (1913), updated in the light of the scholarship of the past half-century, would be welcome.

The English *Brut* is a legendary and, in its later section and continuations, a historical chronicle of England. The basic text to the year 1333 was translated from the Long Version of the Anglo-Norman *Brut*, which is based on Geoffrey of Monmouth's *Historia Regum Britanniae* to which continuations were added. It was translated into English about 1400, and the English text received in its turn a number of continuations by a process of accretion over the next sixty years. The translator of the basic text and the compilers and authors of the continuations are anonymous, although dialectal evidence suggests that the original translation may have been made in Herefordshire. A second translation of the basic Anglo-Norman text survives in BL Harley 4690 and College of Arms Arundel 58, and Brie (1905) ascribes this translation to "John Maundevyle" on the basis of a sixteenth-century note found in BL Harley 2279, a text of the first translation. The note appears to be a copy of verses originally found at the end of the second translation, dating its completion in 1435 and naming the translator as "Sire Iohn the Maundeuyle that hath ben person but a whyle In Brunham Thorp." Brie (1905) records contemporary references to a John Maundevyle who was rector of Burnham Thorpe in Norfolk from 1427 to 1441. He was born ca. 1380 and lived most of his life in obscure parishes in Norfolk, Lincolnshire, and apparently Worcestershire.

The *Brut* has received little scholarly attention since the beginning of the century. It was, however, the most popular secular work of the Middle Ages in England, an honor sometimes attributed erroneously to the *Polychronicon*. Matheson (1979) lists over 160 manuscripts of the Middle English translation and its derivative texts, a number of manuscripts of a Middle English work exceeded only by that of the manuscripts of the two Wycliffite translations of the Bible. Under the title *The Chronicles of England* the *Brut* was the first chronicle printed in England, and passed through thirteen editions between 1480 and 1528. There are also at least 50 extant manuscripts of the Anglo-Norman text and at least 15 extant Latin manuscripts. The influence of the *Brut* on how Englishmen in the fifteenth and sixteenth centuries viewed their native history was enormous. Matheson (1979) mentions a number of medieval owners, and Ker (1964) assigns the ownership of several manuscripts to religious houses. Fifteenth-century chroniclers were often highly indebted to the *Brut*, and later chroniclers such as Waurin, Hall, Stow, and Holinshed also used it.

For studies of the relationships of the manuscripts of the *Brut*, modern scholars are dependent on Brie (1905) and Kingsford (1913), which superseded the studies of the English and Anglo-Norman texts in Madden (1856) and Meyer (1878). Brie (1905) is an abstract of his intended introduction to his EETS edition of the Middle English *Brut*, but the final volume never appeared, and the abstract remains the single attempt at a definitive study published to date.

Brie lists 167 manuscripts in Anglo-Norman, English, and Latin, 147 of which he examined personally. He attempts to classify the manuscripts and to identify the sources of the continuations to the basic text. Although founded on Meyer (1878), the modified classification of the Anglo-Norman manuscripts is based on considerably more texts than the earlier scholar knew of, and it has never been seriously criticized or altered in toto.[1] Uncritical scholarly references to Brie's treatment of the English *Brut* are frequently found, but a number of adverse criticisms can be made (many of which can be applied equally to his treatment of the Anglo-Norman texts). A number of mistakes are made in the descriptions of manuscripts made by Brie's correspondents, as with the Hunterian manuscripts, and where Brie had to rely on inaccurate printed descriptions, as with Peterhouse 190 (Warkworth's *Chronicle*). A more serious criticism can be made of Brie's method of classifying manuscripts simply by the type of continuations found to constitute the text. Textual differences between manuscripts that possess basically similar continuations are seldom taken into account, and although stylistic alterations and abbreviations are occasionally mentioned, on only one occasion are they used as primary factors in distinguishing a group of manuscripts within the Common Version. It is typical that Brie says of the manuscripts of this group that they are "für die Textkritik völlig unbrauchbar" (1905, p. 65). It must be borne in mind when reading Brie's descriptions that phrases like "enthält den gewöhnlichen fortgesetzten Text" (p. 74), "Prolog und Text stimmen genau zum Vorigen" (p. 83), and "der Text stimmt von Anfang bis zu Ende in jeder Beziehung mit dem vorigen überein" (p. 87), do not refer to exact verbal likeness, but to a similarity of content. The lack of detailed textual analyses or comparisons occasionally prevents Brie from differentiating between groups and leads to oversimplification in determining relationships. "Good" manuscripts are those that possess the same contents and do not diverge stylistically from the norm, unless they contain historically interesting details not found elsewhere. Thus the inclusion of the intrusive Cadwallader episode (taken from Geoffrey of Monmouth) is not used as a criterion for classification, but is simply the mark of a "bad" text. Brie fails to mention the intrusive passage containing Queen Isabella's letter to the citizens of London, which can also be used as a criterion in classification. Although he recognizes the existence of an Extended Version (which adds an exordium and minor literary details) and an Abbreviated Version (which Brie thought erroneously to be a simple abbreviation of the Extended Version), he discounts both versions as worthless (approximately 38 manuscripts). However, he must admit that he cannot decide whether some manuscripts belong to the Common Version or to the Extended Version because they lack a couple of folios at the beginning. In fact, Brie classifies several manuscripts wrongly as Common Version texts that should belong to the Extended Version.

Brie's choice of texts for his EETS edition of 1906 and 1908 is largely based on his classification according to continuation outlined in his earlier work. Only one complete text is presented, from Bodleian Rawlinson B. 171 (though the second part of this manuscript, written in a later hand, is not printed), and since this manuscript represents the earliest stage in the development of the English text, it includes neither the Cadwallader episode nor Queen Isabella's letter. In all, twenty-six manuscripts are used by Brie; sixteen provide sections of continuous text, and eleven are used for purposes of collation (Lambeth 6 appears in both functions). The edition is generally accurate and gives a good selection of texts and continuations, but the following points should be noted. BL Add. 24859 (lettered "T" by Brie), used to collate the texts 1333–1377 and 1377–1419, is not a text of the Common Version as Brie thought, but belongs to an Extended Version group (Group B in my classification; see below). Appendix C (Brie 1908, pp. 392–393), from Bodleian Rawlinson B. 173, is not unique to this manuscript; it is also found in the group of texts to which Hunterian 74 belongs. The latter part of BL Harley 3730, used to collate BL Add. 10099 for the text from 1419 to 1461, is copied from the "Liber Ultimus" of Caxton's 1482 edition of the *Polychronicon*, which was based in this part on the printer's 1480 edition of the *Brut*. It should also be noted that the lacunae noted by Brie in this latter work, also used for collation with BL Add. 10099, represent leaves missing only in the particular BL volume that he used, and that gaps are not found in other copies of the same edition.

Kingsford (1913), in his chapter on the *Brut*, is primarily concerned with the historical value of the continuations that take 1377 as their starting point, and he points out the close relationships between these and the London chronicles. From such comparisons, and on the evidence of internal historical details, Kingsford attempts to date approximately the composition of the continuations, and there seems little reason to doubt his conclusions in this respect. His comments on the relationships of the texts are more open to argument, since they are principally (but not exclusively) based on that selection of texts printed by Brie. The assertion (p. 119) that "the version of 1430 is not, even for the early part of the reign of Henry V derived from the other version" (i.e., the one ending in 1419, the conclusion of many manuscripts) is contradicted by the evidence of texts inadequately examined by Brie and unexamined by Kingsford that include textual characteristics of both versions. Of the peculiar versions of the *Brut* contained in BL Harley 53 and Lambeth 84 and in *Davies's Chronicle*, and of their relationships to the Latin *Brut* and to the main *Brut* tradition, Kingsford remarks that "the overlapping and interlacing of these Chronicles [i.e., in their contents] make the history of their development a difficult problem" (p. 128). Further investigation of the Latin texts is required, but my classification makes unlikely Kingsford's suggestion that there were "earlier recensions of the English Brut than that great one which ended in 1419 at the fall of Rouen . . . one perhaps ending in November 1415 or in October 1416, and others more certainly in July 1417 and November 1417" (p. 133).

My forthcoming classification of the English manuscripts is intended to clear up many of the problems and misconceptions concerning the development of the text. Broadly speaking, the manuscripts fall into four main categories within which many smaller groups can be distinguished: the Common Version, which originally took the narrative to 1333, but to which numerous additions were made, eventually bringing one group to the year 1461; the Extended Version, with an added exordium and details taken from the *Short English Metrical Chronicle*; the Abbreviated Version, which is a shortened cross between the Common and Extended Versions; and an amorphous grouping called "Peculiar Texts and Versions," consisting of a number of texts linked to the Latin *Brut*s (which were translated from the English) and of individual reworkings of English texts. I have included a number of extremely short works based on the *Brut* that are little more than lists of kings with the lengths of their reigns, such as are found in Cambridge University Library Ff. 1.6, Bodleian Digby 196, and Folger Shakespeare Library V. a. 198, which are often of value in dating the manuscripts in which they occur.

The only study of the literary value of the *Brut* to date is found in Starke (1935). A valid distinction is made between what Kingsford (1913) called "the more set and artistic continuations" (p. 115) and the continuations taken verbatim from London chronicles, since the latter are based on the mayoral years while the former transform the same material into continuous narrative in which the chapter is the basic formal unit. A second important distinction is that the former continuations are not open-ended like civic chronicles, for they end at important historical junctures. Starke remarks on the use to which poetical material is put in various descriptions of wars and battles, and further remarks on the dramatic quality imparted by the use of direct speech in many scenes, even those that are relatively unimportant. On linguistic points relating to style Starke says little, although he mentions a number of valid points concerning "die Schwächen einer frühen Prosa" (1935, p. 134).

Brie's edition has been discussed above. Davies (1856) presents the text from 1377 to 1461 of what is now Bodleian Lyell 34, and Gairdner (1880) edits the extremely abbreviated text of Lambeth 306. Kingsford (1913) prints extracts from a manuscript group ending in 1430 from BL Cotton Galba E. viii. Further extracts from manuscripts are edited by Böddeker (1874; the Arthurian section from BL Harley 24, compared with short extracts from Wace, Robert of Gloucester, and from another *Brut* in BL Harley 53), von Scherling (1937; the Lear story from what is now University of Virginia 38–173), and Powell (1937; part of the Vortiger story from Jesus College, Oxford 5). Unpublished dissertations that include edited texts are by Reese (1947; University of Virginia 38–173), Matheson (1977; Hunterian 74 and 443), and Engel (1981; the continuation from 1377 to 1419 from University of Sydney Nicholson 13).

Studies that make more than simple historical reference to the *Brut* are rare. Fletcher (1906) mentions the main differences from other recorded Arthurian legends shown by the Anglo-Norman texts, for an account of which he depends on Meyer (1878). He calls the English translation "a fine example of sturdy English" (1906, p. 220). Taylor (1966, pp. 13–16) includes an outline description of the development of the *Brut* based on Brie (1905), but unfortunately Taylor here and in his earlier article (1957) appears to confuse the Anglo-Norman and the English texts. Cottle (1969), although he uses less than sixty pages of Brie's edition, gives a number of interesting cross-references between the *Brut*'s account of events between 1350 and 1400 and allusions and mentions made by contemporary literary authors.

The paucity of studies dealing with the *Brut* has prevented many modern scholars from fully realizing its central position in fifteenth-century historical writing and its great influence on the shaping of English national consciousness in the fifteenth and sixteenth centuries. Such a large corpus of manuscripts and early printed editions of one work offers many potential areas for future linguistic, semantic, dialectal, paleographical, and scribal researches. Both for its own sake and as an aid in studying the English translations, work is required on the Anglo-Norman texts. A new list and classification of the Anglo-Norman manuscripts updating those of Meyer (1878), Brie (1905), and Vising (1923) are needed as a preliminary toward an edition of the Anglo-Norman *Brut*.

In addition to the translation of the *Brut* the fifteenth century saw several other translations of historical works into English. Trevisa's translation of Higden's *Polychronicon* in the late fourteenth century is dealt with in Chapter 8; a second, anonymous, translation of Higden's work is found in BL Harley 2261 and is printed in Babington and Lumby (1865–1882).[2] This translation of the Latin text ends in 1344, and a continuation in the same hand takes the narrative to 1401. Whether the original translator was also the author (or translator) of the continuation is uncertain. A possibly significant error in the chapter numeration occurs in the first chapter of the continuation (which is numbered 40, although the last chapter of the preceding text is numbered 43), which may mark a change of exemplar. Babington, followed by Kinkade (1934) and Taylor (1966, pp. 139–142), dates the translation between 1432 and 1450 on the basis of the appearance of Lydgate's verses on the kings of England, ending with Henry VI, at the end of the manuscript. However, these popular verses may have been added by the scribe of the single known copy of the text, which appears to have been written about 1475. An alternative tentative date for the translation is the first quarter of the fifteenth century, since the continuation ends in 1401 and it is unlikely that the compiler would have written much later without making use of later historical material. The slavish translation technique, using Latinate constructions and vocabulary, also suggests the earlier date.

The *Expugnatio Hibernica* of Giraldus Cambrensis provides the ultimate basis for an English work entitled *The English Conquest of Ireland*. Furnivall (1896) prints parallel texts from Trinity College, Dublin 592 (of which Trinity College, Dublin 593 may be a sixteenth-century transcript) and Bodleian Rawlinson B. 490. Heuser (1904) edits short extracts from Lambeth 598 and 623 and the single leaf in Bodleian Laud 526 as examples of the Anglo-Irish dialect. The text found in the last is much altered, and appears to be complete as it stands. Although no study of the manuscript relationships has yet been made, it seems unlikely that it represents a separate translation. In Lambeth 598 a later hand, possibly that of Sir George Carew, ascribes the work to a Thomas Bray; the text of this manuscript has been fully edited by Brewer and Bullen (1871), following in their edition the text of the sixteenth-century *Book of Howth*, which also contains a version of the *Conquest of Ireland*. Brewer and Bullen suggest strongly that the basis for the English texts was not Giraldus Cambrensis himself, but a Latin chronicle ultimately based on him.

John Shirley (ca. 1366–1456) translated an account of the murder in 1437 of James I of Scotland as *The Dethe of the Kynge of Scotis*, "translated oute of Latyne into oure moders Englisshe tong" as he says in the colophon to BL Add. 5467. This manuscript contains two further translations by Shirley, and is described in Gärtner (1904) and Manzalaoui (1977). It belongs to the second half of the fifteenth century, and neither of the two hands is Shirley's. The text has been edited thrice from this manuscript: by Pinkerton (1797), in *Miscellanea Scotica* (1818), and by Stevenson (1837). A second manuscript, BL Add. 38690, is noted in Balfour-Melville (1936), which appears to have been overlooked by Shirley scholars. The relationship between the two manuscripts has not yet been examined. However, BL Add. 38690 is probably the earlier, and was probably written about 1440. This is the date of the three preceding items in the manuscript (which was originally a roll), for they are paralleled in official records. Two subsequent items, also abstracted from official records, refer to events occurring in 1460, but these are written in a different hand. The colophon attributing the translation to Shirley is absent. Whereas the text of BL Add. 5467 is incomplete near the beginning owing to a missing leaf, the text of BL Add. 38690 is complete. The lacuna in the former manuscript was filled in 1904 by George Neilson from a seventeenth-century copy of the work in Advocates' Library 17. I. 22, which also lacks the colophon. A new edition and study of this "fulle lamentable cronycle" are needed.

John Shirley was a noted bibliophile, translator, and recorder of works by Chaucer and Lydgate. The best biographical account is Doyle (1961), which supplements and corrects accounts in Gärtner (1904), Hammond (1908, pp. 515–517, 1927, pp. 191–194), and Brusendorff (1925).

College of Arms Arundel 22 contains an unpublished work that was described erroneously by W. H. Black in the *Catalogue of Arundel Manuscripts* (1829, pp. 31–33) as a translation of Geoffrey of Monmouth's *Historia Regum Britanniae*. Caldwell (1954) corrects this description. The work, which Caldwell calls *History of the Kings of Britain*, is a translation of Geoffrey's Latin from the "Description of Britain" to the wrestling match between Corineus and Gogmagog, and thereafter it is a translation of the Anglo-Norman of Wace's *Le Roman de Brut*. The text is incomplete, and an ending from Geoffrey of Monmouth was supplied in 1588 by the collector and antiquary Joseph Holand, who owned the manuscript. Caldwell gives a full description of the contents of the text, comparing it with the texts of Geoffrey and Wace. The extant manuscript is clearly a later compilation and not the original of the translation. The compiler added the verse *Seege of Troye* as a prologue, and rather inexpertly inserted the Latin text of Geoffrey's *Prophecies of Merlin* into the translation from Wace. On the basis of a misreading of *Guace* "Wace" (corrected by Caldwell), Black (1829), followed by Barnicle (1927), attributed the text to "Maister Gnaor," whom he assumed to be a Welshman. Barnicle's attempt to associate the manuscript with Shrewsbury rests on a mistaken identification of a coat of arms assigned to Achilles in the *Seege of Troye* text with the arms of the earls of Shrewsbury. Achilles' arms are said to be a gold lion on an indented azure field; the Talbot arms were gules, a lion rampant within a bordure engrailed or. Possibly Achilles' arms are significant, but I have been unsuccessful so far in identifying them. Caldwell's suggestion that the text may have been intended to bolster the Mortimer claim to the crown in the fourteenth century depends on the date of the text, which he believes to be "of the fourteenth century, nearer the middle than the beginning or end" (1954, p. 643). Neil Ker, however, calls Arundel 22 "certainly fifteenth century" (private letter to the Middle English Dictionary, October 27, 1949). An edition of the text and a linguistic study of the manuscript, which does appear to have pronounced dialectal features, are sorely needed.

Harvard English 938 contains an apparently unique copy of a translation of the Anglo-Norman *Chronicles* of Nicholas Trevet, to which material from a *Brut* text has been added as a continuation. The text of Trevet's *Chronicles* begins with the Creation and ends at the same point as the Anglo-Norman text of BL Arundel 56. Dean (1962) remarks that "the translation does not seem to have been made from any of the extant Anglo-Norman MSS. It has the shorter ending of the majority of them, but does not agree consistently with any one group. It has brief interpolations of its own, and its style is more literal than literary" (p. 99, n. 10). Only the story of Constance has been published, by the Chaucer Society (Furnivall, Brook, and Clouston 1876), but an edition of the translation is currently being prepared. The *Brut* continuation was probably based on a *Brut* text ending in 1419 with the siege of Rouen, although the manuscript is now incomplete. The material has been abbreviated and adapted to fit more closely with the style of the preceding text. Thus the murder of Edward II is taken out of its chronological place in the *Brut* text and placed before the coronation of Edward III in order to complete the account of the reign of the former king. The reign of each successive king is narrated in one long chapter, and chapter headings, which are usual in the *Brut*, are omitted in order to conform to the earlier Trevet text.

A number of genealogical chronicles in Latin and English have survived that trace the ancestry of Edward IV to biblical and legendary figures. Many of the manuscripts are listed and classified in de la Mare (1971, pp. 80–85), and Allan (1979) places them in their historical context and stresses their propagandist purpose. The manuscripts that primarily concern us fall into four types, which Allan has named the "Long Latin" and "Long English" pedigrees and the "Short Latin" and "Short English" pedigrees. The Long Latin pedigree is based in its introductory section on the *Compendium Historiae in Genealogia Christi* of Peter of Poitiers (of which a fifteenth-century English translation exists in Bodleian Barlow 53). De la Mare lists five manuscripts of the Long English translation, to which should be added College of Arms Arundel 53. The Short Latin and Short English pedigrees are similar in omitting the preface from Peter of Poitiers and in reducing the genealogy of Christ to a simple line of descent. De la Mare lists three English manuscripts, which are apparently not direct translations of the Latin text, and to these should be added College of Arms Arundel 23. Many of these genealogical chronicles were probably the product of a single workshop that specialized in this type of material, for, as de la Mare points out, many are "identical in text, script, layout, decoration, or all four" (1971, p. 82). The precise relationships between the versions mentioned above and other Latin genealogical chronicles, especially that attributed to Roger of Saint Albans, are yet to be determined.[3]

Two further unpublished chronicles illustrate an aspect of historical prose, akin to translation, that has received little previous study. Each is a prose paraphrase of considerable length of an earlier historical poem,[4] to which continuations from the *Brut* have been added to make the narrative more up to date. The first is found in Cambridge University Library Ll. 2. 14, and is a paraphrase of Robert of Gloucester's *Metrical Chronicle*. The manuscript is incomplete at the beginning, and the narrative begins during a speech by Goscelin, bishop of London, to his fellow citizens, fainthearted at the prospect of the Romans abandoning Britain. The original text ends with the banishment of the countess of Leicester in the reign of Henry III, and is followed immediately by the *Brut* continuation, which is written by the same hand but in a lighter ink. The *Brut* text belongs to one of the Peculiar Versions, and ends incompletely with the return of the exiled Bolingbroke during the reign of Richard II. It may be remarked in passing that in two other manuscripts the *Brut* is used as a continuation to Robert of Gloucester's *Chronicle*, in Cambridge University Library Ee. 4. 31 and in College of Arms Arundel 58. The latter contains the C-text of Robert of Gloucester, which contains many prose interpolations that require study (some are printed as footnotes in Hearne's edition of Robert of Gloucester). The introduction to the Robert of Gloucester text in the College of Arms manuscript and the continuation that follows it are taken from the second translation of the *Brut*, attributed to John Maundevyle. All three combinations of Robert of Gloucester and the *Brut* were made independently.

The second work is found in Woburn Abbey 181, which contains a prose chronicle to which a *Brut* continuation and other historical pieces have been appended. The only description of its contents is found in the unpublished notes of Sir Frederic Madden in BL Egerton 2257 (followed by Davies 1856, Brie 1905, and this chapter). The prose chronicle appears to be a paraphrase of Robert Mannyng of Brunne's *Chronicle*, Part 2, which is based on Peter Langtoft's Anglo-Norman *Chronicle*. The basis of the paraphrase may have been a text of Mannyng similar to that found in Lambeth 131, which contains the interpolated Havelok story (printed in Skeat's edition of *Havelok* and in Sisam's revision of Skeat, and studied in Putnam 1900). Madden noted that he intended to insert a transcript of the Havelok story from the Woburn manuscript into his copy of his edition of the romance, and Brie (1905) deduced that this meant that the story differed from that found in Langtoft's *Chronicle*. This is borne out by Madden's transcription in his notes of the beginning of the table of contents in the manuscript, from which it is clear that an extended form of the Havelok story is found in the chronicle, and that the names of the characters agree with those in the Lambeth interpolation. It may be noted in passing that several of the chapter headings noted by Madden agree well with the marginal rubrics printed as sidenotes in Hearne's edition of Mannyng's *Chronicle*, Part 2, from Inner Temple MS Petyt 511, vol. 7. The paraphrase begins with Alfred and ends with Edward I and contains several interpolations dealing with noteworthy events in the history of the Abbey of Saint Albans. The continuation from the *Brut* takes the narrative from Edward II to the siege of Rouen in 1419, and again contains several lengthy interpolations; those occurring under the eighteenth and nineteenth years of Richard II are printed in Davies (1856) from Madden's transcriptions. There follow several "occasional" pieces: the *Deposition of Richard II*, an account of the

parliament at Bury in 1447 and of the death of the duke of Gloucester (printed in
Davies 1856), the acts of the parliament at Winchester in 1449, some verses on
the deposition of Richard II, and some orders of the common council of London
concerning cooks and butlers and fees and customs at the lord mayor's feast. The
compiler of the manuscript names himself as Richard Fox of Saint Albans, and
gives the date of writing as 1448 after the *Deposition of Richard II*. The subsequent items were probably written soon after July 1449. Fox is presumably the
"Ricardus Fox, litteratus" who is mentioned in John of Amundesham's *Annales* as
a proxy for the abbey in an arbitration case in 1434.

Although it is not a pure translation, we may consider here Capgrave's *Chronicle*,⁵ which is derived mainly from Walsingham's *Historia Anglicana*. The
chronicle is found in Cambridge University Library Gg. 4. 12 (the autograph,
probably intended for presentation to Edward IV) and Corpus Christi College,
Cambridge 167 (written ca. 1500), and was edited in the Rolls Series by Hingeston in 1858. This inaccurate edition is totally inadequate and is now replaced by
that of P. J. Lucas (1983). The details of Capgrave's life are given by de Meijer
(1955, supplemented by his 1957 article), and some additional details are presented by Lucas (1973). The unpublished dissertation of Fredeman (1971) gives
background information on fifteenth-century Augustinian life and education.
Briefly, John Capgrave was born in 1393 and raised in Lynn, Norfolk. He entered the Augustinian order there, probably about 1410, and later studied at
London and Cambridge. By 1446 he was presumably prior at Lynn, and hosted
Henry VI's visit to the priory in that year. Capgrave was appointed prior provincial of the Augustinian Order in England' in 1453 and continued in that office
until 1457. He spent his remaining years in study and writing until his death in
1464. Capgrave's *Chronicle* was completed ca. 1462 and is dedicated to Edward
IV. It begins as a universal chronicle, but concentrates on the kings of England
from the year 1216 on, and ends abruptly in 1417 with a reference to the Council
of Constance (1414–1418), which is mistakenly said to have taken place at Basel
(presumably by confusion with the Council of Basel, which was convoked in
1431). Much discussion has centered around the identity of the scribe of this and
of other of Capgrave's works. Lucas (1969) argues that Cambridge University
Library Gg. 4. 12 was written by Capgrave himself, in the more formal of the
two scripts that he used. Lucas also argues that this manuscript was intended as a
presentation copy for Edward IV, and that it was finished hastily and the dedication added in order to dispatch the work as quickly as possible to the new king.
Colledge (1974) disputes Lucas's conclusions and attempts to show from the evidence of errors and corrections that the scribe was a professional, possibly a fellow friar, employed by Capgrave. He believes further that Cambridge University Library Gg. 4. 12 was not a presentation copy since it does not have a
miniature of Capgrave presenting the book to a patron, but has only a decorated

initial and border. On balance, however, Lucas's arguments seem stronger than Colledge's. Valuable detailed studies by Lucas have appeared dealing with the punctuation of Cambridge University Library Gg. 4. 12 (1971) and with the orthography of the manuscript (1973), and the appearance of Lucas's edition (1983) will doubtless encourage further studies of Capgrave's *Chronicle*.

Closely associated with the later continuations of the *Brut* are the civic chronicles of London. Although there existed earlier Latin and Anglo-Norman chronicles of London, there was a virtually complete hiatus of over half a century between the last of these and the first of the English chronicles in the early fifteenth century. Kingsford (1905) suggests that in their texts to the end of the fourteenth century the English chronicles had a common original (possibly in Latin, as Flenley 1911 conjectures); they first show signs of having been written contemporaneously with the events they describe during the reign of Henry IV. A further sign of a common original is that all complete texts begin in 1189. The surviving manuscripts belong to the mid-fifteenth century or later, and it is an indication of the popularity and usefulness of the London chronicles that manuscripts continued to be made until well into the sixteenth century. Printed works in city chronicle form, some containing documents and other material otherwise unknown, continued to appear until the end of the sixteenth century.

The annalistic form of the chronicles, headed by the names of the current mayor and sheriffs and arranged according to the mayoral year (beginning on October 29), was probably derived from early official records. In those instances in which city chronicle material underlies the more literary continuations to the *Brut*, the material was assimilated to the normal chapter style of the *Brut*. In other instances, however, in which city chronicles were simply appended to *Brut* texts to bring them up to date, the material was left in its original annalistic form, and the switch from narrative based on the regnal year to narrative based on the mayoral year was apparently considered unimportant.

Almost all the London chronicles are anonymously written, and only a few have been associated with specific individuals. Trinity College, Dublin 509 is ascribed to Robert Bale, native of London and a notary public and judge of the civil courts in that city, by his namesake John Bale, bishop of Ossory, in his *Scriptorum Illustrium Maioris Brytannie Catalogus* (Basel, 1557). The chronicle ends in 1461, and was presumably written soon after that date. Kingsford (1916) describes three lawsuits in 1457, 1465–1470, and 1473–1475 involving a Robert Bale of London, "scryvener," who may be identified with the chronicler.

The authorship of at least part of BL Egerton 1995 has often been ascribed to William Gregory, skinner, alderman, and mayor of London in 1451, who died in 1466 or 1467. Since the manuscript is written in one hand, and the chronicle ends incompletely in 1470, Gregory could not be the author of the work as it now stands. The evidence for his supposed authorship of an earlier part of the text occurs in the entry for 1451 – 1452, when Gregory was mayor. The entry consists almost entirely of an account of a papal pardon, which is called "the grettyste pardon that euyr come to Inglonde from the conqueste vnto thys tyme of my yere, beyng mayre of London." Kingsford (1913) makes the point that if Gregory were the author of the chronicle, it is strange that he omits all important events in the year of his mayoralty; alternatively, Kingsford makes the plausible suggestion that the two notices for 1451 – 1453 were added by Gregory as personal notes at the end of his copy of the preceding chronicle, and these were subsequently copied down in the copy that received the apparently unified continuation to 1470. J. A. F. Thomson (1972), while believing mistakenly that Kingsford accepted Gregory's authorship of the earlier portion, puts forward a tentative identification of the author of the last section of the chronicle as Thomas Eborall, a prominent London clergyman whose name is linked to Gregory, but the evidence is scanty and circumstantial.

From internal evidence Flenley (1911) suggests that the author of Gough London 10 may have been Miles Adys, goldsmith and chamberlain from 1479 to 1484. It is possible that this manuscript belonged to William Capel, draper, alderman, sheriff in 1489, and twice mayor of London, in 1503 and 1509. Capel died in 1519.

From an exhaustive examination of all aspects of the evidence, Thomas and Thornley (1938) conclude that the author of the later section of Guildhall 3313 (*The Great Chronicle*) was almost certainly Robert Fabyan, draper, alderman, sheriff in 1493 – 1494, who died on February 28, 1513. In establishing this attribution Thomas and Thornley were confirming the opinions of John Foxe the Martyrologist (1516 – 1587) and John Stow (d. 1605), who both owned the manuscript, and of Richard Hakluyt, who used the manuscript. Kingsford (1913) discounted the attribution, but on insufficient and erroneous evidence, since his examination of the manuscript, which was then in the hands of the bookseller Quaritch, was necessarily brief. Fabyan also produced the *New Chronicles of England and France*, published posthumously and anonymously in 1516 by Richard Pynson, but attributed to his authorship in John Rastell's edition of 1533. Pynson's "copy" text was probably the two manuscripts that are now Holkham 671 and BL Cotton Nero C. xi, which together constitute the full text of Fabyan's *New Chronicles*. Thomas and Thornley deduce that they are the original author's manuscript from the evidence of a double ending to Holkham 671. Holkham 671, BL Cotton Nero C. xi, and the later section of Guildhall 3313 are all in the same hand.

The Tudor historians of the sixteenth century, whose work descended from and sometimes relied on the work of the medieval chroniclers, are described in McKisack (1971) and Trimble (1950). We may, however, mention Richard Arnold, haberdasher, whose *Customs of London*, printed at Antwerp in ?1503 and reprinted at Southwark in 1521, contains a much abbreviated London chronicle. The well-known commonplace book of Richard Hill, grocer, contains a city chronicle based on Arnold from 1413 to 1490, but independent from 1490 to its abrupt end in 1536.

The contents of the chronicles reflect the interests and tastes of their authors and owners—aldermen, wealthy merchants, and members of the city guilds and companies. The central position of London in national affairs kept the chronicles from being records of purely municipal affairs; documents of national importance occur, and some parliamentary records in the chronicles present better texts than the corresponding texts in the *Rolls of Parliament*. Documents of international importance also occur, such as copies of treaties or letters from the king, beside notes on the price of wheat, the state of the weather, and the menu of a coronation feast. The manuscripts are often either commonplace books or miscellanies containing items of varied interest. Even Arnold's printed *Customs of London* is a commonplace book, with recipes for ink, gunpowder, beer, and other materials intermixed with letters, ordinances, and miscellaneous historical items.

The London chronicles have been reasonably well served editorially. The old edition of BL Harley 565, collated with BL Cotton Julius B. i, published by Nicolas and Tyrrell in 1827 is still serviceable. Kingsford (1905) publishes the texts of BL Cotton Julius B. ii, Cotton Cleopatra C. iv, and Cotton Vitellius A. xvi (the last two chronicles of Cotton Vitellius A. xvi; a collation of the first chronicle with Gregory's *Chronicle* is given as an appendix). Flenley (1911) prints extracts from the later parts of the Longleat manuscript, Bale's *Chronicle*, and Bodleian Gough London 10 where they differ substantially from the other extant published chronicles. Kingsford (1913) prints extracts from BL Harley 3775 and Harley 540 and from College of Arms Arundel 19; Kingsford (1914) prints a short extract from the London chronicle in Hatfield 281, a historical miscellany. Less good editions of BL Egerton 1995 (Gregory's *Chronicle*) and Lambeth 306 (*Short English Chronicle*) appear in Gairdner (1876 and 1880 respectively). Several of the continuations found in *Brut* manuscripts can be considered as London chronicles. Brie (1906, 1908) prints extracts from Cambridge University Library Hh. 6. 9 (as Appendix D); BL Egerton 650 (as continuation E); Bodleian Rawlinson B. 173 (as Appendix E); Trinity College, Cambridge O. 9. 1, collated with Cambridge University Library Hh. 6. 9 (as continuation F).[6] Guildhall 3313 (*The Great Chronicle*) was excellently edited by Thomas and Thornley (1938), with a full comparison in the notes with other London chronicles. The original edition, limited to 500 copies, is now available in a microprint format. With regard to the later chronicles mentioned above, Richard Hill's commonplace book has been edited by Dyboski (1907); Arnold's *Customs of London* were reprinted by Douce (1811); and Fabyan's *New Chronicles* were reprinted by Ellis (1811).

Starke (1935) discusses the London chronicles from a stylistic viewpoint, and reaches conclusions similar to those mentioned above in his study of the *Brut*. Scholarly study has concentrated on the classification of the manuscripts and early printed texts (apart from using the edited texts as historical sources). In an amplification of his earlier remarks in his edition of 1905, Kingsford (1913) attempts to assign the extant texts to a series of recensions that began almost immediately after the composition of the first English chronicles of London. He believes that "between 1414 and 1430 the London Chronicles were undergoing a constant process of rewriting and continuation" (p. 76), and that major recensions were made in 1430, 1431, 1432, 1440, 1445, 1446 (with continuations to 1452, 1461, 1462, and 1465; no copy to 1446 itself was known), and 1440–1485 (texts belonging to "The Main City Chronicle" tradition). Kingsford bases his assignments mainly on passages common to different texts up to certain dates, and adduces the *Brut*, for which he conjectures a similar development, as confirmation of his method and conclusions. However, as we have seen, the *Brut* texts did not develop in this manner, and Kingsford's methodology of classification is seriously criticized in the introduction to Thomas and Thornley (1938). They note that it was quite possible for a scribe to change from one manuscript exemplar to another for his material, not because the text from which he was copying had ended, but because another text gave him a better narrative. In addition, it should be noted that in assigning a manuscript to a particular version, Kingsford does not mean that the text of the manuscript ends at that point. BL Harley 565 is assigned to the version of 1430, but was written in one hand soon after 1442, in which year the text ends. Thomas and Thornley believe that Kingsford's analysis suffers from oversimplification, and that he assigns too great an importance to similar passages in chronicles that are otherwise widely different.

Thomas and Thornley's analysis of the relationship of the first part of the *Great Chronicle* to the other chronicles bears out this view. The compiler appears to have "had before him in a finished form the main constituents of the other chronicles, and made a greater effort to produce a work which should be comprehensive" (1938, pp. xxxv–xxxvi). Kingsford's opinion that the *Great Chronicle* is the "most ample representation of the English Chronicles of London in their earliest form" (1913, p. 82) is modified by Thomas and Thornley, who conclude that the work "sometimes lacks that fulness and wealth of civic detail, which distinguishes Harley 565, and that accuracy of names and dates, which is a feature of the far more meagre chronicle Julius B II. It is in the inclusion of important

public documents that the Great Chronicle surpasses the other manuscripts; of
these some are preserved by Vitellius F IX and Julius B I, others by Julius B II
and the Longleat MS. The Great Chronicle combines the information of all
four" (1938, p. xxvi). Thomas and Thornley make a detailed comparison of the
similarities and differences in various groupings of the manuscripts for the period before 1399 and for the period 1399–1439, which must form the basis for
any future investigation of the manuscript relationships. Studies of the *Brut*
manuscripts that make use of London chronicle material may also be of value in
such investigations. With regard to the later section of the *Great Chronicle*, written by Fabyan, Thomas and Thornley show that it, Fabyan's other chronicle in
BL Cotton Nero C. xi, and BL Cotton Vitellius A. xvi had a common source to
1503 in the now lost "Main City Chronicle," although again they reject Kingsford's suggestion of various recensions of this lost work.

Political events of the fifteenth century induced a number of contemporary ob-
servers to write short narratives in English; those occasioned by the War of the
Roses are usually written from a Yorkist point of view. Some of these pieces are
clearly semiofficial accounts (reflecting an increasingly perceived need for improved public relations), and presumably were intended for popular circulation,
but in the majority of cases these short narratives are extant in only one or two
known copies. The majority were edited and published in the nineteenth century
and suffer from now inadequate introductions and commentaries.

Warkworth's *Chronicle* covers the first thirteen years of the reign of Edward
IV, from 1461 to 1474, including the abortive attempt of Henry VI to regain his
throne, and the chronicle is particularly important as a historical source for the
years 1470–1471 in its account of the turbulent events in the north of England.
It was edited by Halliwell in 1839 from Peterhouse, Cambridge 190, which has
been considered to be the unique copy.[7] Matheson (1978) notes a second copy in
Hunterian 83, on which he is basing a new study of the chronicle, and the following discussion is a synopsis of information to be found therein.

Hunterian 83 is identified wrongly in the catalogue of Hunterian manuscripts
as a copy of Trevisa's translation of the *Polychronicon*. It is a late medieval compilation of texts, formed by adding quires containing introduction and continuation to an originally discrete *Brut* text. The introduction is taken from the 1483
Saint Albans edition of the *Chronicles of England* (i.e., the *Brut*), and after completing the imperfect *Brut* text the same hand adds a continuation to 1461, which
for the first few chapters follows the normal *Brut* continuation to 1461, but then
changes to the text used by Caxton in his 1482 edition of the *Polychronicon* as part

of what the printer called the "Liber Ultimus." The same hand then continues with Warkworth's *Chronicle*, but unfortunately the folio that would have contained the end of Caxton's "Liber Ultimus" and the beginning of the chronicle is missing.

The catalogue of Peterhouse manuscripts wrongly describes the first part of Peterhouse 190 as a copy of Caxton's printed edition of 1482 of the *Brut*, an error initiated by Halliwell (1839) in his edition of Warkworth's *Chronicle*, and continued by many scholars since, among them Kingsford (1913), James Gairdner in his *D.N.B.* article on Warkworth, Emden (1959, pp. 1992–1993), and Lander (1967). As in the case of the Hunterian manuscript, the Peterhouse manuscript consists of an original *Brut* text (although of a different group), to which a second hand has added a continuation to 1461 similar to that found in the Hunterian manuscript, followed by Warkworth's *Chronicle*.

A third manuscript, BL Harley 3730, is incomplete and does not contain Warkworth's *Chronicle*, but the surviving text is closely similar to those contained in the Hunterian manuscript and in the latter part of the Peterhouse manuscript. The relationship between the three manuscripts is not entirely clear, but the Hunterian text may be the original from which the other manuscripts were copied.

John Warkworth's career is fully described by Gairdner and Emden. He was a native of the diocese of Durham, and acquired an M.A. at Oxford in 1449. In 1473 William Grey, bishop of Ely, who had earlier employed Warkworth as personal chaplain, appointed Warkworth master of Peterhouse, Cambridge. He held this position until his death in October or November 1500. He donated an astrolabe and fifty-five books to the library of Peterhouse, recorded in the old catalogue under the year 1481 (not 1483 as stated by Halliwell 1839, Kingsford 1913, and Lander 1967). Of these books the only English text is a *Liber Cronicorum in Anglicis*, the present Peterhouse 190. The ascription of the authorship of the chronicle continuation of this manuscript to Warkworth rests solely on the introductory phrase referring the scribe to "my copey in whyche is wretyn a remanente lyke to this forseyd werke," by which the Hunterian manuscript may be meant. The continuation to the Peterhouse *Brut* cannot, however, have been written before the publication of Caxton's edition of the *Polychronicon* in 1482. The additions to the Hunterian manuscript cannot have been made before the publication of the Saint Albans edition of the *Chronicles of England* in 1483. Warkworth's *Chronicle* cannot have been added to either manuscript until after Warkworth's gift of Peterhouse 190 to the library. If the Hunterian manuscript was Warkworth's personal copy, then the case for his authorship of the additions found therein is strong.

The *Chronicle of the Rebellion in Lincolnshire, 1470* was edited by Nichols in 1847 from the apparently unique copy in College of Arms Vincent 435. The author is anonymous, but clearly he was in the entourage of Edward IV and wrote his narrative as a semiofficial account, making frequent references to official documents and letters.[8]

Two further semiofficial documents have been preserved by John Stow in his transcripts in BL Harley 543. The first is known as *The Manner and Guiding of the Earl of Warwick at Angiers* from the opening words of its heading; it describes the negotiations between Warwick and Margaret of Anjou after the former's flight from England in 1470, and was published by Ellis in his *Original Letters* (1827). The second piece is the *Historie of the Arrivall of King Edward IV*, edited by Bruce in 1838, which recounts the recovery of the throne by Edward IV in 1471. Three manuscripts of a shorter French text (the Short Arrival) exist, and J. A. F. Thomson (1971) suggested that they represented a translation of "a brief and rather bare English newsletter, now lost" (p. 92), which also formed the basis of the longer *Historie*. However, Green (1981) prints the text of an English version of the Short Arrival found in College of Arms 2M 16 and BL Add. 46354, both texts in mid-sixteenth-century hands. From the evidence of a textual comparison Green presents a tentative but convincing reconstruction of the textual relationships. Between May 26, 1471 (the date of the conclusion of the narrative) and May 28, 1471 (on which date Edward IV sent a copy enclosed with a letter to the duke of Burgundy), the French Short Arrival was composed as a newsletter. Probably before April 25, 1472, the French text was translated into English, and, independently, used as a source for the longer official account, the *Historie of the Arrivall*. The author of the original French text may have been a Yorkist herald or pursuivant with the otherwise unknown heraldic title "Marpisse." The compiler of the *Historie of the Arrivall* calls himself in the preamble "a seruant of the Kyngs, that presently saw in effect a great parte of his exploytes, and the resydewe knewe by true relation of them that were present at every tyme." Kingsford (1913) suggests very tentatively that he may also have been the author of the second *Continuation of the Croyland Chronicle*, who styles himself one of the king's councillors and a doctor of canon law, but the suggestion rests only on some points of resemblance between the *Continuation* and the *Historie of the Arrivall*, the latter of which had presumably circulated among many of the members of the king's entourage.

Although it is not a narrative, the Lancastrian politico-legal *Somnium Vigilantis*, edited by Gilson (1911), deserves mention as one of the oldest political pamphlets in English prose. It was written in late 1459 or early 1460, though the extant text in BL Royal 17. D. xv was copied around 1475. The beginning is lost, and the title (which may, however, be original) is found in a seventeenth-century catalogue. The text is in the form of a legal debate; a first speaker argues clemency for the defeated Yorkist lords, while a second speaker represents the royal position and argues for severe punishment. A third speaker provides a conclusion in French supporting the royal position. The Latinate, but vigorous, style suggested to Gilson and Kingsford (1913) that the author, who was clearly a lawyer, might have been Sir John Fortescue, whose *Declaration upon Certain Writings*, refuting his earlier arguments for the Lancastrians, appears in the same manuscript.

A similar desire for news or accurate information about events is reflected in other shorter items that survive, usually in later copies or collections, for it is of the nature of such items to be ephemeral. Armstrong (1948) describes the methods available for the distribution of news during the Wars of the Roses. Kingsford (1913) discusses a number of news items in his chapter on private and official correspondence.[9] The following are examples of such material; no doubt many more await discovery and publication.

A newsletter written by John Stodeley in 1454 concerning political events, using information gathered by a number of people, is printed in Gairdner's edition of the *Paston Letters* (1904) from BL Egerton 914. It is not part of the Paston correspondence, and is addressed to an unknown lord. Also printed in Gairdner (1904, no. 283) is an English narrative of the first battle of Saint Albans in 1455, giving a Yorkist account of the battle. The document belongs among the Stonor papers, but its presence there seems to be accidental. The Pastons did receive a list of participants and of the slain (Gairdner 1904, no. 284) that was probably a news-bill. Copies of accounts of particular interest were also made from the official records, such as the copy of the articles of impeachment brought against the duke of Suffolk in 1450, found among the Paston papers with the title "Coumpleyntys ayens the Dewke of Suffolk" (Gairdner 1904, no. 101; parallel to the text in the *Rolls of Parliament* 5: 177–179).

Kingsford (1913) says that copies are common of a Yorkist political document entitled "The Claim of the Duke of York, 1460," but records specifically only two copies, in Harley Rolls C. 5 and C. 7. A quotation from the latter in the notes to Halliwell (1839) shows the document to be a synopsis of the intricate legal debate and agreement recorded officially in the *Rolls of Parliament* (5: 375–380), which settled the succession to the crown on Richard, duke of York, after the death of Henry VI. The synopsis was presumably produced for circulation among Richard's adherents. Other manuscripts, apart from copies of Parliament Rolls, in which this material is found include BL Add. 38690 and 48031, BL Cotton Tiberius E. viii, and BL Hargrave 335. No study has been made of the manuscripts, and some are probably verbatim extracts from the *Rolls of Parliament*.

There is evidence for the circulation at an earlier date of pamphlets based on the official records describing the deposition of Richard II in 1399. Versions of the formal parliamentary proceedings in Latin and French and of the speeches in English, found in the *Rolls of Parliament* (3: 416–445), are frequently incorporated into chronicles (see Kingsford 1905 and Duls 1975), but in a number of manuscripts the narrative is found standing alone. I have noted the following, although this list is doubtless incomplete: College of Arms Arundel 29 (a historical miscellany; this version contains three extracts from the *Rolls of Parliament*, of which two are in English); Woburn Abbey 181 (see above); BL Add. 48031 (a miscellany); Lambeth 738 (an English *Brut*); BL Stowe 66 (only two folios, containing four extracts, of which two are in English). The texts represent different versions and selections from the *Rolls of Parliament*; the text found in Lambeth 738 (and possibly in Woburn 181) is entirely in English and parallels the long English version found in the London chronicle in BL Cotton Julius B. ii, printed in Kingsford (1905). The relationship of this version to the account in the *Rolls of Parliament* and the Latin and French narrative in Bodleian 596 is discussed in Kingsford's notes, but an examination of all the versions remains to be made.

To a large extent items published from volumes of historical notes consist of material similar to that described above—newsletters, pamphlets, bills, extracts from official records, and other miscellaneous but current material. Kingsford (1913) prints as the *Collections of a Yorkist Partisan* the prose pieces from BL Cotton Roll II. 23 (with the exeption of Article 1, an extract from the *Rolls of Parliament*), a number of which had previously been printed separately. Parallel documents and copies are noted by Kingsford, including "a Bill, on a ragged sheet of paper, preserved at Magdalen College, Oxford . . . perhaps one of the copies originally circulated" of the "Proclamation of Jack Cade" (1913, p. 359). Kingsford also prints the short *Memoranda* of John Piggot, probably a Londoner, preserved in John Stow's transcript in BL Harley 543, and calendars other material relating to fifteenth-century history in this manuscript and in the further collection by Stow in BL Harley 545. More memoranda by Stow are found in Lambeth 306 (a peculiar version of the *Brut*, followed by a London chronicle), a number of which are copies of fifteenth-century documents. These are printed in Gairdner (1880), together with other historical notes in various hands found in the same manuscript.

The fifteenth century also saw the beginnings of biographies in English prose of secular historical figures, although the number of works that survive, or that can be shown to have existed, is not large.

The only well authenticated prose work by John Lydgate, the *Serpent of Division*, is called in the colophon to one manuscript "the cronycule of Julius Caesar" (the modern title derives from the early printed editions). The work is an account of the civil war between Caesar and Pompey, written in 1422 at the request of

Duke Humphrey of Gloucester. It was edited by MacCracken (1911) and the edition is marred by a number of wrong transcriptions and typographical errors. In a supplementary note in 1913 MacCracken defends his dating of the composition. Like the later biographies of the Wars of the Roses, the *Serpent of Division* was written not only as an account of a historical personage, but also with a political moral in mind, in this case the danger of civil strife attendant upon the accession of the infant king Henry V. Accordingly, MacCracken calls the tract "one of the very earliest political pamphlets in English history" (1911, p. 2). Lydgate's varied sources and his treatment of them are studied in great detail by MacCracken in his introduction. Schlauch (1967) discusses the "heightened style" of the work, which she associates with the propaganda aim, and distinguishes it from the more "straightforward style of chroniclers like Trevisa" (p. 1768). Lydgate's life and an account of the monastic background at the abbey of Saint Edmund's at Bury are related in Pearsall (1970, pp. 22−45).

The English roll chronicle of John Rous was written from a similarly political, though more personal, motive. The details of Rous's life are given in Emden (1959, pp. 1596−1597), Kendrick (1950), and Wright (1956). Briefly, he was a native of Warwickshire, to which he returned after attending Oxford, becoming a chantry priest at Guy's Cliffe, a foundation of the earl of Warwick. Rous was the author of a number of antiquarian works, and those that survive are analysed in Kendrick (1950). He died in 1491. The English roll, now BL Add. 48976, is described by Wagner (1950, pp. 116−120) and Wright, and was published in facsimile in 1859 with an introduction by Courthope and a transcript of the text by Larking. This edition was reprinted in 1980 with a historical introduction by C. D. Ross. It traces the genealogy of the earls of Warwick from mythical times to Richard III, and is illustrated with fine, line-drawn portraits and coats of arms. The drawings are accompanied by biographical narratives drawn from a wide range of sources, such as Giraldus Cambrensis, William of Malmesbury, Marianus Scotus, John Hardyng, Domesday Book, Welsh chronicles, and the author's own knowledge and observations. The work was written before 1485, and its tone is strongly Yorkist; a Latin version in the College of Arms, also originally written before 1485, but revised after that date, reflects in its revision the changed political situation and is Lancastrian in sympathy. As Wright remarks, a detailed comparison of the two rolls would establish their artistic, literary, historical, and heraldic importance.

A second text is closely linked with the English Warwick Roll. *The Pageant of the Birth, Life, and Death of Richard Beauchamp, Earl of Warwick* has twice been reproduced in modern times in facsimile from the unique copy in BL Cotton Julius E. iv. Like the Warwick Roll, it combines text with drawings; forty-eight drawings show the major events in the earl's life, and five drawings illustrate royal events, while prose rubrics identify the event and provide historical context.

The work is usually dated between 1485 and 1492, but Scott (1976) argues for a date between 1483 and 1487. E. M. Thompson (1903) suggested that it was possibly made at the instigation of the earl's daughter, Anne, countess of Warwick, who died in 1493. Scott wonders whether the English and Latin Warwick Rolls "were not products of the same atelier as the *Beauchamp pageants*" (1976, p. 62), and suggests that the motive behind these works might have been the attempts of Anne Beauchamp to recover the Warwick possessions, which were forfeited from her and divided between her daughters and their husbands in 1474. The act of forfeiture was annulled in 1487. Traditionally, the *Pageant* was attributed to John Rous, but Kendrick (1950) notes that the hand is not that of Rous, although he does not indicate where he thought the hand of Rous was indeed found. Of the three hands (at least) of the English Warwick Roll, Wright suggests that the one that makes corrections and additions may be that of Rous, which seems a plausible supposition. Wright also notes that the style of drawing differs entirely in the two works, and Scott identifies the artist as the Caxton Master.

Several Latin biographies of Henry V have survived, but of two English versions only traces remain in later manuscripts and works. The first, made soon after 1455, is known through the use made of it by the "Translator of Livius" in the work called by Kingsford, who edited it in 1911, *The First English Life of Henry V*. This was written in 1513 and now exists in two seventeenth-century copies. It is a compilation made from several sources, the principal one of which was the *Vita Henrici Quinti* of Titus Livy Frulovisi, which was written in 1437 or 1438. The Translator also used a lost work that included information derived from James Butler, fourth earl of Ormonde, who died in 1452. Since this lost work could not have been finished before 1455, as internal evidence shows, the author could not have been Ormonde; Kingsford suggests that the author was in Ormonde's service, and that his work may have taken the form of a biography of Henry V, though it may possibly have been more general in character. Some of Ormonde's stories passed through the Translator's work to Stow and Holinshed, and thus helped form the traditional view of the character of Henry V.

The second lost work was an abridgment in English, also made about 1455, of the *Vita et Gesta Henrici Quinti*. The Latin work was attributed to Thomas of Elmham by Thomas Hearne, but Kingsford (1913) shows that Hearne had no evidence for this attribution, and the Latin work must be considered anonymous. The English version survives only in some fragments copied for John Stow in his manuscript collection in BL Harley 530, which is described in Kingsford (1910).

Thomas Hearne preserves a fragment of a late chronicle of Edward IV, breaking off in 1470, as an appendix to his edition (1719) of the *Cronica* of Thomas Sprott. Hearne made his copy from a manuscript lent to him by a friend, but this manuscript is now untraced. Although the work is that of a purported eyewitness, especially between 1468 and 1482 as the writer says, Kingsford (1913) shows from internal references to other works that it must have been written from memory between 1516 and 1522. The author may have been a member of the household of the duke of Norfolk, presumably a gentleman or clerk since he claims to record utterances of the king that he heard personally, and since he also claims to be reporting events that he witnessed personally, both in England and abroad. Although the overall tone is avowedly partisan, "Hearne's Fragment" has some of the characteristics of critical biography, and is thus of some interest in literary history as a transitional work between the medieval and renaissance approaches to biography.

The field of historical literature written in Middle English prose offers many untouched areas for future study. Historical writings have tended to fall between two stools; the historian is primarily concerned with factual historical data contained in published works, while the textual scholar tends to be more interested in literary texts. New, in some cases full, editions are required of texts last edited in the nineteenth century, and first-time editions are needed of previously unpublished texts. The unpublished works noted above are not, nor are they intended to be, a complete listing of such material. A glance in the catalogue of any major manuscript collection will almost invariably reveal unpublished historical items in English, frequently identified or attributed erroneously. The familiar truism that the fifteenth century is largely devoid of significant historical texts reflects the political historian's point of view. For the student of manuscripts, the English language, and medieval intellectual history, historical prose can provide a large corpus of texts, written in various styles and dialects, that formed the basis of the historical consciousness of Englishmen until the nineteenth century.

NOTES

1. Individual areas have, however, been questioned. In the introduction to her edition of the poem that prefaces a number of the Anglo-Norman texts, Brereton (1937) finds her views on the relationships of the manuscripts with which she is concerned to be "diametrically opposed to those of Brie" (p. xviii). Similarly, Brie's ascription of authorship of part of the Long Version of the Anglo-Norman *Brut* to William Pakington has been successfully refuted by Taylor (1957).

2. Higden's *Polychronicon* also forms the basis of a Lollard chronicle of the papacy in Emmanuel College, Cambridge 85, which is edited and discussed in Talbert (1942). The translated material from Higden is supplemented from Martin of Troppau's *Chronicon Pontificum et Imperatorum* (third recension, containing the story of Popess Joan), to form what Talbert calls "an essentially fanatical account of the 'rablement of the popes'" (p. 164). The author, who was probably a

follower of Wyclif, has selected from and abridged his historical sources for doctrinal reasons, in order "to show that papal claims to supremacy in matters of temporal jurisdiction are unfounded" (p. 164). The work was probably composed ca. 1379, although the extant manuscript belongs to the early fifteenth century. In passing, we may note an unprinted English translation from the third recension of Martin of Troppau's *Chronicon* in Ashmole 791, fols. 60–84v, that begins with the birth of Christ and breaks off incompletely with Pope Lando.

3. Kingsford (1913) confuses the different versions and gives an inaccurate list of texts of the genealogical chronicle of Roger of Saint Albans, of which he believed BL Stowe 73 to be a translation. Nine manuscripts of Roger's work are listed in de la Mare (1971; four of these are described in Ker 1969); Allan (1979) adds John Rylands Library Chronicle Roll 2, Queen's College, Oxford 168 (noted in Kingsford 1913), and Emmanuel College, Cambridge 231.

4. Two semihistorical prose works in the same general genre are found in Bodleian Rawlinson D. 82, fols. 1–10v and 11–24v. These, *The Sege of Thebes* and *The Sege of Troy*, are short abstracts or adaptations of Lydgate's long poems the *Siege of Thebes* and the *Troy Book*. They are described and edited by Brie (1913); Chaucerian influence on the character of Calchas in *The Sege of Troy* is noted in Benson (1971).

5. The title *The Chronicle of England* used by Hingeston is misleading; Lucas (1969 and 1983) uses the title *Abbreuiacion of Cronicles*.

6. University of Chicago 254 possesses a continuation similar to that found in Cambridge University Library Hh. 6. 9 and Trinity College, Cambridge O. 9. 1.

7. In his notes Halliwell presents documents from several manuscripts otherwise unpublished: BL Harley Roll C. 7, College of Arms Arundel 59, Ashmole 1160 (a roll), and BL Cotton Charter XVII. 11.

8. Two such, the "Confession of Sir Robert Welles" (from BL Harley 283) and a royal mandate to the city of Coventry, are printed in the notes to Nichols's edition.

9. He also mentions a number of occasional pieces, mainly descriptions of ceremonial events. A number of pieces preserved by John Stow, in Lambeth 306 and elsewhere, are of this nature.

BIBLIOGRAPHY

Middle English works that are primary sources are listed in the order in which they are discussed in the text. Editions are listed in chronological order after each work; where no edition is noted, the work is unpublished.

PRIMARY SOURCES

PROSE *BRUT*

MANUSCRIPTS

See Matheson (1979) for a list of 166 MSS. The following emendations should be made to that list. Delete: BL Egerton 2257; BL Add. 27879; Princeton University Garrett

142. Add: Woburn Abbey 181; Bodleian Digby 196, fols. 26–27, 156v–158; Cambridge University Library Ff. 1. 6 (Findern Manuscript), fols. 110–113; Yale University, Beinecke Library 323; Pennsylvania State University 3A. The new total is 168 MSS.

PRINTED EDITIONS

See Matheson (1979) for a list of thirteen early editions published between 1480 and 1528.

Davies, John S., ed. (1856) *An English Chronicle of the Reigns of Richard II, Henry IV, Henry V, and Henry VI*. Camden Society 64.

Gairdner, James, ed. (1880) *Three Fifteenth-Century Chronicles*, pp. 1–28. Camden Society, ns 28.

Brie, Friedrich W. D., ed. (1906, 1908) *The Brut or The Chronicles of England*. EETS, os 131, 136.

SHORT EXTRACTS

Böddeker, K. (1874) "Die Geschichte des Königs Arthur." *Archiv*, 52, 10–29.

Powell, E. O. (1937) "From The Brute of the Chronicle of England." *Folklore*, 48, 91–93.

Scherling, Erik von (1937) "History of King Lear in an Early 15th Century Manuscript." *Rotulus*, 4, 1–5.

Kingsford, Charles L. (1913) *English Historical Literature in the Fifteenth Century*, pp. 299–309. Oxford: Clarendon Press. Repr. (1962) New York: Burt Franklin.

UNPUBLISHED EDITIONS

Reese, George H. (1947) "The Alderman Brut: A Diplomatic Transcript, Edited with a Study of the Text." Ph.D. diss., University of Virginia.

Matheson, Lister M. (1977) "The Prose *Brut*: A Parallel Edition of Glasgow Hunterian MSS. T.3.12 and V.5.13." Ph.D. diss., University of Glasgow.

Engel, Margaret H. (1981) "An Edition of MS. Nicholson 13: f. 161r–f. 177v." M.A. diss., University of Sydney.

ANONYMOUS TRANSLATION OF HIGDEN'S *POLYCHRONICON*

MANUSCRIPT

BL Harley 2261

Printed Edition

Babington, Churchill, and Lumby, Joseph R., eds. (1865–1882) *Polychronicon Ranulphi Higden*. Rolls Series. Repr. (1964) Wiesbaden: Kraus, vols. 1–8, lower half of right-hand pages.

THE ENGLISH CONQUEST OF IRELAND

Manuscripts

Trinity College, Dublin 592 (E. 3. 31)
Trinity College, Dublin 593 (F. 4. 4)
Bodleian Rawlinson B. 490
Lambeth 598, fols. 1–31
Lambeth 623 (*Book of Howth*), fols. 6–59v
Bodleian Laud 526, single leaf at end

Printed Editions

Furnivall, Frederick J., ed. (1896) *The English Conquest of Ireland*. EETS, os 107.
Brewer, J. S., and Bullen, William, eds. (1871) *Calendar of the Carew Manuscripts*, 5:36–117, 261–317. Rolls Series.

Short Extracts

Heuser, W., ed. (1904) *Die Kildare-Gedichte*. Bonner Beiträge zur Anglistik 14. Bonn: P. Hanstein's Verlag. Repr. (1965) Darmstadt: Wissenschaftliche Buchgesellschaft, pp. 216–218, 220–222.

JOHN SHIRLEY, *THE DETHE OF THE KYNGE OF SCOTIS*

Manuscripts

BL Add. 5467, fols. 72v–82v
BL Add. 38690, fols. 9–16
National Library of Scotland, Advocates' 17. 1. 22

Printed Editions

Pinkerton, John (1797) *The History of Scotland*. London, vol. 1, app. 13.
Miscellanea Scotica, 2:1–29. (1818) Glasgow.
Stevenson, Joseph, ed. (1837) *The Life and Death of King James the First of Scotland*, pp. 45–67. Maitland Club 42. Edinburgh.

N[eilson], G[eorge] (1904) "Missing Section of 'The Dethe of the Kynge of Scotis,' Recovered." *Scottish Historical Review*, 2, 97–99.

HISTORY OF THE KINGS OF BRITAIN

MANUSCRIPT

College of Arms Arundel 22, fols. 8–80v

TRANSLATION OF NICHOLAS TREVET'S *CHRONICLES*

MANUSCRIPT

Harvard University, Houghton Library, Eng. 938, fols. 9–91

PRINTED EXTRACT

Furnivall, F. J.; Brook, Edmund; and Clouston, W. A., eds. (1876) *Originals and Analogues of Some of Chaucer's Canterbury Tales, Part III*, pp. 223–250. Chaucer Society, 2d ser. 15. London: N. Trübner.

GENEALOGICAL CHRONICLES OF EDWARD IV

"LONG ENGLISH" PEDIGREE

MANUSCRIPTS

Bodleian Lyell 33
Bodleian e Musaeo 42
Corpus Christi College, Cambridge 207
Yale University Library, Marston 242
College of Arms Arundel 53
BL King's 395 (continued to Henry VIII)

"SHORT ENGLISH" PEDIGREE

MANUSCRIPTS

Magdalene College, Cambridge, Pepys 2244
BL Add. 31950
College of Arms Arundel 23

PARAPHRASE OF ROBERT OF GLOUCESTER'S
METRICAL CHRONICLE

MANUSCRIPT

Cambridge University Library Ll. 2. 14, fols. 1–143

PARAPHRASE OF ROBERT MANNYNG OF BRUNNE'S
CHRONICLE, PART 2

MANUSCRIPT

Woburn Abbey 181

JOHN CAPGRAVE, *CHRONICLE*

MANUSCRIPTS

Cambridge University Library Gg. 4. 12
Corpus Christi College, Cambridge 167

PRINTED EDITIONS

Hingeston, Francis C., ed. (1858) *The Chronicle of England*. Rolls Series. Repr. (1972)
    Nendeln, Liechtenstein: Kraus.
Lucas, Peter J., ed. (1983) *John Capgrave's Abbreuiacion of Cronicles*. EETS, os 285.

CHRONICLES OF LONDON

MANUSCRIPTS

BL Cotton Julius B. i, fols. 2–90v
BL Cotton Julius B. ii
BL Cotton Vitellius A. xvi, fols. 2–209
BL Cotton Vitellius F. ix, fols. 1–70v
BL Cotton Cleopatra C. iv, fols. 22–61v
BL Cotton Vespasian A. xxv, fols. 28–37
BL Egerton 650, fols. 111v–114v
BL Egerton 1995, fols. 113–222v (Gregory's *Chronicle*)
BL Harley 540, fols. 7–21, 40–45
BL Harley 541, fols. 215–219
BL Harley 543, fols. 150–160

BL Harley 565
BL Harley 3775, fols. 78–99v
BL Harley Roll C. 8
College of Arms Arundel 19
Guildhall Library 3313
Lambeth 306, fols. 18v–46
Bodleian Gough London 10, fols. 19v–52
Bodleian Rawlinson B. 173, fols. 225–227v
Saint John's College, Oxford 57, fols. 138–222
Balliol College, Oxford 354 (Richard Hill's commonplace book), fols. 232–247
Cambridge University Library Hh. 6. 9
Trinity College, Cambridge O. 9. 1, fols. 197v–226v
Trinity College, Dublin 509, pp. 121–218 (Robert Bale's *Chronicle*)
Longleat MS
Hatfield 281, fols. 32–88
University of Chicago 254, fols. 126v–149v
Eshton Hall MS (untraced; for list of contents see *Third Report of the Royal Commission on Historical Manuscripts*, London, 1872, p. 299)

ROBERT FABYAN, *CHRONICLE*

MANUSCRIPTS

Holkham Hall 671
BL Cotton Nero C. xi

EARLY PRINTED EDITIONS

Place of publication is London unless otherwise noted. For the works of John Stow the STC numbers are taken from the published second volume of the revised STC. Some late printed works in civic chronicle form are listed, although they are not discussed in the text, to show the popularity of the form.

Arnold, Richard. *Customs of London.*

Antwerp: A. van Berghen, ?1503 (STC 782)
Southwark: P. Treveris, 1521 (STC 783)

Fabyan, Robert. *Chronicle.*

R. Pynson, 1516 (STC 10659)
W. Rastell, 1533 (STC 10660)

W. Bonham, 1542 (STC 10661)
J. Reynes, 1542 (STC 10662)
J. Kingston, 1559 (two issues: STC 10663, 10664)

A Short Cronycle

J. Byddell, 1539 (STC 10021)

A Cronicle of Yeres

J. Byddell, 1542 (STC 9986)
T. Petyt, 1543 (STC 9987)
W. Myddylton, 1544 (STC 9988)
W. Powell, 1552 (STC 9989)
J. Judson, ?1558 (STC 9990)

Stow, John. *A Summarie of Englyshe Chronicles*

T. Marshe, 1565 (STC 23319)
———, 1566 (STC 23319.5)
———, 1570 (STC 23322)
———, 1573 (STC 23323.5)
H. Binneman, 1574 (STC 23324)
R. Tottle and H. Binneman, 1575 (STC 23325)
R. Newbery, 1590 (STC 23325.2)

Stow, John. *The Summarie of Englyshe Chronicles . . . nowe abridged.*

T. Marshe, 1566 (STC 23325.4)
———, 1567 (STC 23325.5)
———, 1573 (STC 23325.6)
R. Tottle and H. Binneman, 1579 (STC 23325.7)
R. Newbery and H. Denham, 1584 (STC 23325.8)
———, 1587 (STC 23326)
R. Bradocke, 1598 (STC 23328)
———, 1598 (STC 23328.5)
J. Harison, 1604 (STC 23329)
J. Windet, 1607 (STC 23330)
N. Okes, W. Hall, and T. Haveland, 1611 (STC 23331)
E. Allde and N. Okes, 1618 (STC 23332)

Stow, John. *The Chronicles of England.*

H. Binneman for R. Newbery, 1580 (STC 23333)

MODERN PRINTED EDITIONS

[Douce, Francis, ed.] (1811) *The Customs of London, otherwise called Arnold's Chronicle.* London: F. C. and J. Rivington, T. Payne, [etc.].

Ellis, Henry, ed. (1811) *The New Chronicles of England and France, by Robert Fabyan, named by himself the Concordance of Histories.* London: F. C. and J. Rivington.

[Nicolas, N. H., and Tyrrell, Edward, eds.] (1827) *A Chronicle of London.* London: Longman, Rees, Orme, [etc.]. [Harley 565, Julius B. i]

Gairdner, James, ed. (1876) *The Historical Collections of a Citizen of London*, pp. 57–239. Camden Society, ns 17. [Egerton 1995]

————, ed. (1880) *Three Fifteenth-Century Chronicles*, pp. 31–80. Camden Society, ns 28. [Lambeth 306]

Kingsford, Charles L., ed. (1905) *Chronicles of London.* Oxford: Clarendon Press. [Julius B. ii, Cleopatra C. iv, extracts from Vitellius A. xvi]

Dyboski, Roman, ed. (1907) *Songs, Carols, and Other Miscellaneous Poems, from the Balliol MS. 354*, pp. 142–167. EETS, es 101. [Richard Hill's commonplace book]

Flenley, Ralph, ed. (1911) *Six Town Chronicles of England*, pp. 99–101, 114–166. Oxford: Clarendon Press. [Extracts from Longleat MS, Trinity College, Dublin 509 (Bale's *Chronicle*), Gough London 10]

Kingsford (1913) *English Historical Literature*, pp. 292–298. [Extracts from Harley 3775, Harley 540 (transcript by John Stow), Arundel 19]

———— (1914) "An Historical Collection of the Fifteenth Century." *EHR*, 29, 505–515. [Extract from Hatfield 281]

Thomas, A. H., and Thornley, I. D., eds. (1938) *The Great Chronicle of London.* London and Aylesbury. Repr. (1983) Gloucester: Alan Sutton. [Guildhall 3313]

WARKWORTH'S *CHRONICLE*

MANUSCRIPTS

Peterhouse, Cambridge 190, fols. 214v–225
University of Glasgow Hunterian 83 (T. 3. 21), fols. 141–148v

PRINTED EDITIONS

Halliwell, James O., ed. (1839) *A Chronicle of the First Thirteen Years of King Edward the Fourth, by John Warkworth, D.D.* Camden Society 10.

[Giles, John A., ed.] (1843) *The Chronicles of the White Rose of York*, pp. 97–142. London: Bohn. [Modernized]

CHRONICLE OF THE REBELLION IN LINCOLNSHIRE, 1470

MANUSCRIPT

College of Arms Vincent 435, article 9

PRINTED EDITION

Nichols, John G., ed. (1847) *Chronicle of the Rebellion in Lincolnshire, 1470*. Camden Miscellany 1; Camden Society 39.

THE MANNER AND GUIDING OF THE EARL OF WARWICK AT ANGIERS

MANUSCRIPT

BL Harley 543, fols. 168–169 (transcript by John Stow)

PRINTED EDITIONS

Ellis, Henry, ed. (1827) *Original Letters Illustrative of English History, Second Series*, 1:132–135. London: Harding and Lepard.
Giles (1843) *Chronicles of the White Rose*, pp. 229–238. [Modernized]

HISTORIE OF THE ARRIVALL OF KING EDWARD IV

MANUSCRIPTS

BL Harley 543, fols. 31–49v (transcript by John Stow)
BL Add. 46354, fols. 32v–36
College of Arms 2M 16, fols. 33v–36

PRINTED EDITIONS

Bruce, John, ed. (1838) *The Historie of the Arrivall of King Edward IV*. Camden Society 1.
Giles (1843) *Chronicles of the White Rose*, pp. 31–96. [Modernized]
Green, Richard F. (1981) "The Short Version of *The Arrival of Edward IV*." *Speculum*, 56, 324–326.

SOMNIUM VIGILANTIS

MANUSCRIPT

BL Royal 17. D. xv, fols. 302–310v

PRINTED EDITION

Gilson, Julius P. (1911) "A Defence of the Proscription of the Yorkists in 1459." *EHR*, 26, 512–525.

NEWSLETTER OF JOHN STODELEY

MANUSCRIPT

BL Egerton 914

PRINTED EDITION

Gairdner, James, ed. (1904) *The Paston Letters A.D. 1422–1509*, 2:295–299 (no. 235). London: Chatto & Windus; Exeter: James G. Commin.

FIRST BATTLE OF SAINT ALBANS (1)

MANUSCRIPT

Public Record Office, London, Chancery Miscellanea, 37, File III.4–11

PRINTED EDITIONS

Bayley, John (1824) "An Account of the First Battle of St. Albans from a Contemporary Manuscript." *Archaeologia*, 20, 519–523.
Gairdner (1904) *Paston Letters*, 3:25–29 (no. 283).

FIRST BATTLE OF SAINT ALBANS (2)

MANUSCRIPT

BL Add. 39848

PRINTED EDITION

Gairdner (1904) *Paston Letters*, 3 : 29–30 (no. 284).

COUMPLEYNTYS AYENS THE DEWKE OF SUFFOLK

MANUSCRIPT

Olim John Fenn

PRINTED EDITION

Gairdner (1904) *Paston Letters*, 2 : 120–127 (no. 101).

THE CLAIM OF THE DUKE OF YORK, 1460

MANUSCRIPTS

BL Harley Roll C. 5
BL Harley Roll C. 7
BL Add. 48031

PRINTED EXTRACT

Halliwell (1839) *Chronicle . . . by John Warkworth*, pp. 59–60.

DEPOSITION OF RICHARD II

MANUSCRIPTS

College of Arms Arundel 29, fols. 24v–37v
Woburn Abbey 181
BL Add. 48031
Lambeth 738, fols. 232–243v
BL Stowe 66

PRINTED EDITION

Not printed, but see Kingsford (1905, pp. 19–62) for a parallel text.

COLLECTIONS OF A YORKIST PARTISAN

MANUSCRIPT

BL Cotton Roll II.23

PRINTED EDITION

Kingsford (1913) *English Historical Literature*, pp. 358–368.

JOHN PIGGOT, *MEMORANDA*

MANUSCRIPT

BL Harley 543, fol. 144 (transcript by John Stow)

PRINTED EDITION

Kingsford (1913) *English Historical Literature*, pp. 369–373.

JOHN STOW, *MEMORANDA*

MANUSCRIPT

Lambeth 306, fols. 49–63v

PRINTED EDITION

Gairdner (1880) *Three Fifteenth-Century Chronicles*, pp. 96–147.

JOHN LYDGATE, *SERPENT OF DIVISION*

MANUSCRIPTS

BL Add. 48031 (olim Calthorpe/Yelverton 35), fols. 146v–156v
Fitzwilliam Museum, Cambridge, McClean 182, fols. 1–9v, 11
Magdalene College, Cambridge, Pepys 2006, pp. 191–209
Harvard University, Houghton Library, Eng. 530, fols. 49–57v

PRINTED EDITIONS

London: R. Redman, ca. 1535 (STC 17027.5)
London: O. Rogers, 1559 (STC 17028)
London: E. Allde for J. Perrin, 1590 (STC 17029)
MacCracken, Henry N., ed. (1911) *The Serpent of Division*. London: Oxford University Press.

JOHN ROUS, *WARWICK ROLL*

MANUSCRIPT

BL Add. 48976

PRINTED EDITION

[*The Rows Roll*], transcribed by L. Larking, with preface and introduction by W. Courthope; dated 1845 on title page; published (1859) London: H. G. Bohn; repr. (1980) as John Rous, *The Rous Roll*, introduction by C. D. Ross, Gloucester: A. J. Sutton.

THE PAGEANT OF THE BIRTH, LIFE, AND DEATH OF RICHARD BEAUCHAMP, EARL OF WARWICK

MANUSCRIPT

BL Cotton Julius E. iv, part 6 (bound separately)

PRINTED EDITIONS

Carysfort, William, earl of, ed. (1908) *The Pageants of Richard Beauchamp, Earl of Warwick*. Oxford: Roxburghe Club.
Dillon, Viscount, and St. John Hope, W. H., eds. (1914) *Pageant of the Birth, Life, and Death of Richard Beauchamp, Earl of Warwick, K.G., 1389–1439*. London: Longmans, Green, and Co.

"TRANSLATOR OF LIVIUS," *ENGLISH LIFE OF HENRY V*

MANUSCRIPTS

Bodleian Library Bodley 966, pp. 1–91
BL Harley 35
BL Harley 6216, fol. 23 (brief quotation)

PRINTED EDITION

Kingsford, Charles L., ed. (1911) *The First English Life of Henry V*. Oxford: Clarendon Press.

ABRIDGMENT OF THE *VITA ET GESTA HENRICI QUINTI*

MANUSCRIPT

BL Harley 530, fols. 19–30v (transcript for John Stow)

HEARNE'S FRAGMENT

MANUSCRIPT

unknown

PRINTED EDITIONS

Hearne, Thomas, ed. (1719) *Thomae Sprotti Cronica*, pp. 283–306. Oxford.
Giles (1843) *Chronicles of the White Rose*, pp. 1–30. [Modernized]

SECONDARY SOURCES

Allan, Alison (1979) "Yorkist Propaganda: Pedigree, Prophecy and the 'British History' in the Reign of Edward IV." In *Patronage, Pedigree and Power*, edited by Charles Ross, pp. 171–192. Gloucester: Alan Sutton.
Armstrong, Charles A. J. (1948) "Some Examples of the Distribution and Speed of News in England at the Time of the Wars of the Roses." In *Studies in Medieval History Presented to Frederick Maurice Powicke*, edited by R. W. Hunt, W. A. Pantin, and R. W. Southern, pp. 429–454. Oxford: Clarendon Press; repr. 1969.
Balfour-Melville, E. W. M. (1936) *James I, King of Scots 1406–1437*. London: Methuen.
Barnicle, Mary E., ed. (1927) *The Seege or Batayle of Troye*. pp. xvii–xviii, xxvi–xxviii. EETS, os 172.
Benson, C. David (1971) "Chaucer's Influence on the Prose 'Sege of Troy.'" *N&Q*, 261, 127–130.
[Bentley, Samuel, ed.] (1833) *Excerpta Historica*. London: Richard Bentley.
[Black, W. H.] (1829) *Catalogue of the Arundel MSS. in the Library of the College of Arms*. London: "not published."

Brereton, Georgine E., ed. (1937) *Des Grauntz Geanz*, pp. xviii–xxi. Medium Aevum Monographs 2. Oxford: B. Blackwell.

Brie, Friedrich W. D. (1905) *Geschichte und Quellen der mittelenglischen Prosachronik "The Brut of England" oder "The Chronicles of England."* Marburg: N. G. Elwert'sche Verlagsbuchhandlung.

——— (1913) "Zwei mittelenglische Prosaromane: The Sege of Thebes und The Sege of Troy." *Archiv*, 130, 40–52, 269–285.

Brusendorff, Aage (1925) *The Chaucer Tradition*, pp. 207–285. London: Oxford University Press.

Caldwell, Robert A. (1954) "The 'History of the Kings of Britain' in College of Arms MS. Arundel XXII." *PMLA*, 69, 643–654.

Colledge, Edmund (1974) "The Capgrave 'Autographs.'" *TCBS*, 6, 137–148.

Cottle, Basil (1969) *The Triumph of English 1350–1400*. London: Blandford.

Dean, Ruth J. (1962) "The Manuscripts of Nicholas Trevet's Anglo-Norman *Cronicles*." *M&H*, 14, 95–105.

de la Mare, Albinia (1971) *Catalogue of the Collection of Mediaeval Manuscripts Bequeathed to the Bodleian Library, Oxford, by James P. R. Lyell*. Oxford: Clarendon Press.

Doyle, A. I. (1961) "More Light on John Shirley." *MAE*, 30, 93–101.

Duls, Louisa D. (1975) *Richard II in the Early Chronicles*. Studies in English Literature 79. The Hague and Paris: Mouton.

Emden, A. B. (1959) *Biographical Register of the University of Oxford to A.D. 1500*. Oxford: Clarendon Press.

Fletcher, Robert H. (1906) *The Arthurian Material in the Chronicles Especially Those of Great Britain and France*. Studies and Notes in Philology and Literature 10. Boston: Ginn.

Fredeman, Elta J. (1971) "The Life and English Writings of John Capgrave." *DAI*, 31, 6009-A.

Gärtner, Otto (1904) *John Shirley: Sein Leben und Wirken*. Halle: E. Karras.

Hammond, Eleanor P. (1908) *Chaucer: A Bibliographical Manual*. New York: Macmillan.

———, ed. (1927) *English Verse between Chaucer and Surrey*. Durham, N.C.: Duke University Press.

Hearne, Thomas, ed. (1724) *Robert of Gloucester's Chronicle*. 2 vols. Oxford. Repr. (1810) as Vols. 1 & 2 of *Works*. London: Samuel Bagster.

———, ed. (1725) *Peter Langtoft's "Chronicle," as improved by Robert of Brunne*. 2 vols. Oxford. Repr. (1810) as vols. 3 and 4 of *Works*. London: Samuel Bagster.

Kendrick, T. D. (1950) *British Antiquity*. London: Methuen.

Ker, N. R. (1964) *Medieval Libraries of Great Britain*. 2d ed. London: Royal Historical Society.

——— (1969) *Medieval Manuscripts in British Libraries*. I: *London*. Oxford: Clarendon Press.

Kinkade, Bert L. (1934) "The English Translations of Higden's Polychronicon." Ph.D. diss., University of Illinois.

Kingsford, Charles L. (1910) "The Early Biographies of Henry V." *EHR*, 25, 58–92.

——— (1913) *English Historical Literature in the Fifteenth Century*. Oxford: Clarendon Press. Repr. (1972) New York: Burt Franklin.

———— (1916) "Robert Bale, the London Chronicler." *EHR*, 31, 126–128.

Lander, J. R. (1967) "The Treason and Death of the Duke of Clarence: A Reinterpretation." *Canadian Journal of History*, 2, 1–28. Repr. (1976) in J. R. Lander, *Crown and Nobility 1450–1509*, pp. 242–266. Montreal: McGill's-Queen's University Press.

Lucas, Peter J. (1969) "John Capgrave, O.S.A. (1393–1464), Scribe and 'Publisher.'" *TCBS*, 5, 1–35.

———— (1971) "Sense-Units and the Use of Punctuation-Markers in John Capgrave's *Chronicle*." *Archivum Linguisticum*, ns 2, 1–24.

———— (1973) "Consistency and Correctness in the Orthographic Usage of John Capgrave's *Chronicle*." *SN*, 45, 323–355.

MacCracken, Henry N. (1913) "Lydgate's 'Serpent of Division.'" *MLR*, 8, 103–104.

McKisack, May (1971) *Medieval History in the Tudor Age*. Oxford: Clarendon Press.

Madden, Frederic. Unpublished notes in BL Egerton 2257.

———— (1856) "Prose Chronicles of England Called the Brute." *N&Q*, 2d ser. 1, 1–4.

Manzalaoui, M. A., ed. (1977) *Secretum Secretorum: Nine English Versions*, pp. xxxiii–xxxviii. EETS, os 276.

Matheson, Lister M. (1978) "A New Text of 'Warkworth's' *Chronicle*." *Manuscripta*, 22, 15–16. [Abstract of paper]

———— (1979) "The Middle English Prose *Brut*: A Location List of the Manuscripts and Early Printed Editions." *Analytical & Enumerative Bibliography*, 3, 254–266.

Meijer, Alberic de (1955, 1957) "John Capgrave, O.E.S.A." *Augustiniana*, 5, 400–440; 7, 531–575.

Meyer, Paul (1878) "De quelques chroniques anglo-normandes qui ont porté le nom de *Brut*." *Bulletin de la Société des anciens textes français*, 104–145.

Pearsall, Derek (1970) *John Lydgate*. Charlottesville: University Press of Virginia.

Putnam, Edward W. (1900) "The Lambeth Version of Havelok." *PMLA*, 15, 1–16.

Schlauch, Margaret (1967) "Stylistic Attributes of John Lydgate's Prose." In *To Honor Roman Jakobson*, III, pp. 1757–1768. *Janua Linguarum*, Series Maior 33. The Hague and Paris: Mouton.

Scott, Kathleen L. (1976) *The Caxton Master and His Patrons*, pp. 55–56. Cambridge Bibliographical Society Monograph 8. Cambridge: Cambridge University Library.

Starke, Fritz-Joachim (1935) *Populäre Englische Chroniken des 15. Jahrhunderts*. Neue Deutsche Forschungen 3. Berlin: Junker und Dünnhaupt Verlag.

Talbert, Ernest W. (1942) "A Lollard Chronicle of the Papacy." *JEGP*, 41, 163–193.

Taylor, John (1957) "The French 'Brut' and the Reign of Edward II." *EHR*, 72, 423–437.

———— (1966) *The "Universal Chronicle" of Ranulf Higden*, Oxford: Clarendon Press.

Thompson, Edward Maunde (1903) "The Pageants of Richard Beauchamp, Earl of Warwick, commonly called the Warwick MS." *Burlington Magazine*, 1, 151–164.

Thomson, J. A. F. (1971) "'The Arrival of Edward IV'—the Development of the Text." *Speculum*, 46, 84–93.

———— (1972) "The Continuation of 'Gregory's Chronicle'—A Possible Author?" *British Museum Quarterly*, 36, 92–96.

Trimble, William R. (1950) "Early Tudor Historiography 1485–1548." *Journal of the History of Ideas*, 11, 30–41.

Vising, Johan (1923) *Anglo-Norman Language and Literature*. London: Oxford University Press. Repr. (1970) Westport, Conn.: Greenwood Press.

Wagner, Anthony R. (1950) *A Catalogue of English Mediaeval Rolls of Arms*. Oxford: Oxford University Press.

Wright, C. E. (1956) "The Rous Roll: The English Version." *British Museum Quarterly*, 30, 77–81.

CHAPTER 12

Wycliffite Prose

Anne Hudson

If this chapter had been written one hundred, or perhaps even forty, years ago, it would have had the bolder, simpler title "Wyclif," and been couched throughout in more confident terms. Admittedly, when Loserth in 1925 revised Shirley's *Catalogue of the Extant Works of John Wyclif*, originally published in 1865, he omitted the second half of the bibliography, which had contained the English writings; but it is not clear that Loserth did this because of his serious doubts about the authenticity of the vernacular material rather than because, as one interested in the transmission of Wyclif's Latin writings to Hus, he thought the English works not worth the effort of investigation.[1] Research in the past fifty years has increased scholars' scepticism that any of Wyclif's recorded works were in English, though it is plain that the reformer, to gain the popular sympathy that the chroniclers attest in London in the late 1370s, must have preached from time to time in the vernacular.[2] At the same time, more sophisticated analysis of medieval satire has made it evident that, aside from the question of detailed authorial attribution, the boundaries of "Wycliffite prose" are very hard to define. On the one hand, the Lollards, like Wyclif, used conventions of criticism that had existed for several hundred years before Wyclif himself, conventions that the outspokenly anti-Lollard Gower used equally (particularly in the *Vox Clamantis*).[3] On the other hand, after 1382 and increasingly with the stages of the anti-Lollard legislation in 1401, 1407, and 1414, Lollard writers might avoid the explicit teaching of the quintessence of Wyclif's heresy, especially on the Eucharist and dominion, because of fear. Many of the texts produced by the movement are not, as the uninitiated reader might expect, proseletysing works, but rather allude to a body of ideas shared by reader and writer. More recently it has become clear that in the early period between Wyclif's death in 1384 and about 1400 writing in the vernacular went hand in hand with compilation in Latin, and that to study the one without the other is to blinker and distort our understanding. (See further below; Hudson 1972a and 1975; and von Nolcken 1979.)

The title of this chapter, however, implies a major claim: that Wyclif (or Wycliffe), though not the author of any of the works to be discussed, was the main originator of those writings in that his ideas both inspired them and suggested their composition in the vernacular. My usage hitherto indicates a second disputable claim: that to distinguish between *Wycliffite* and *Lollard* is to introduce a division that contemporaries, whether friends or foes, would not have recognized. Some modern critics have tried to keep the term *Wycliffite* for those disciples who could have known Wyclif directly, most of them Oxford men, while using *Lollard* for the more popular movement, many members of which were removed in time, place, and social status from these academics. This is a division that it is impossible in practice to draw, and one that separates material that in every way belongs together. The term *Lollard*, notoriously obscure in origin and in early use, was applied to the followers of Wyclif first by Henry Crump in 1382 and censured in the convocation at Oxford University; the men he was thinking of were undoubtedly academics, in the year when Wyclif's teaching was first formally condemned. It was declaredly an insult, and the term was regarded as offensive by the Wycliffites for several years. By the end of the century, however, those abused had accepted the name, and the two titles were used, as here, synonymously.[4]

Because of the importance of Wyclif, albeit not as author, a brief biography of him must be given. The date of his birth is obscure, but he seems to have come to Oxford about 1354. The earliest of his Latin writings to have survived, texts on logic, date from about 1361. Some nine years later he began teaching in theology, and continued for much of the following eleven years to teach and write in Oxford; his activities in the political field, the precise extent of which is debatable, may have been influential in gaining subsequent adherents to his views, but the teaching of ideas having political significance was entirely within the academic framework of the university. In 1377 Pope Gregory XI issued a bull condemning nineteen opinions from Wyclif's Latin writings, but it was not until 1380 that any censure was passed in England. In 1381 Wyclif withdrew from Oxford to his living at Lutterworth, and a year later at the Blackfriars' Council in London ten heresies and fourteen errors were condemned. At Lutterworth Wyclif continued writing, still largely in academic form, and revising his earlier works. He died in 1384.

The most distinctive of his heretical views was that on the Eucharist; he denied the contemporary explanations of the sacrament, maintaining that material bread and wine remained after the consecration. Coupled with this and likewise diminishing the status of the priesthood was the view that, since God alone could assess the contrition of the penitent and know the final destination of his soul, the sacerdotal absolution after oral confession was unnecessary, at best confirmatory but at worst blasphemous. The aim of the contemporary church should be the closest adherence to the teaching of Christ as set out in the gospels, and the imitation of the practice of the early church revealed in the Pauline and Petrine epistles and Acts; all beliefs and practices that could not be founded directly on this source were a potential impediment to evangelical purity. Since many of the practices that Wyclif regarded as unfounded there were also acknowledged as corrupt in the contemporary church, the impediment was actual and not merely potential. All forms of "private religion," that is any way of life, monastic, fraternal, or anchoritic, that removed the individual from normal society, came under this condemnation. They, together with prayers for the dead, indulgences, worship of images, pilgrimages, and the sale of any sacraments, should be abolished. To restore the clergy to the state that Christ ordained, all the temporalities of the church should be removed and returned to secular ownership, and no priest should hold secular office nor own more than was necessary for the immediate sustaining of life. The true pope, the vicar of Christ on earth, was the most righteous man alive, an individual known only to God but demonstrably at the time of the Great Schism neither of the contending parties. The primary, indeed the only, duty of a priest was the preaching of God's word as revealed in the Bible. (See Leff 1967, 2:494–558 for a general survey of Wyclif's thought.)

The way in which Wyclif's ideas were disseminated in the century and a half after the heresiarch's adumbration of them is a problem primarily for the historian. Recent work has stressed how important is the evidence of Wycliffite writing, rather than the documentary sources which, almost without exception, derive from authorities hostile to Wyclif and the Lollards.[5] The problem of these writings for the historian is that the majority are undated and unlocalized, many undatable and unlocalizable, and most are anonymous. Two Latin works can be fairly precisely dated. The *Opus Arduum* (see Hudson 1978a), a commentary on the Apocalypse, was written by an imprisoned Lollard between Christmas 1389 and Easter 1390; it uses the biblical text for outspoken criticism of the contemporary church. The *Floretum*, abbreviated under the title of *Rosarium* (see Hudson 1972a and von Nolcken 1979 and 1981), a set of alphabetical *distinctiones* on topics biblical, theological, ecclesiastical, and moral, with extensive specified quotation from Wyclif himself, was compiled between 1384 and 1396. Both are learned, academic productions and plainly envisaged the existence of a similar Wycliffite audience. Authorship of neither can be ascertained. A name that has recurred as a Wycliffite author throughout the past three hundred years is that of John Purvey, the disciple who, Knighton recounted, accompanied Wyclif in his retirement at Lutterworth. However, further investigation has shown that there is no reliable evidence for the attribution of any surviving work to Purvey (Hudson 1981). Other Lollard authors who name themselves are few. There is a sermon preserved in one manuscript (Bodley MS Douce 53) attributed to William Taylor, the Lollard principal of Saint Edmund Hall, Oxford, in the early fifteenth century. More extensive are two works by a single unnamed preacher: the later, which alludes to the other, is found in BL MS Cotton Titus D. v and was written between the death of Henry IV in March 1413 and that of Archbishop Arundel in February 1414. Perhaps the most remarkable text to name its author is the autobiographical account of his own trial before Arundel in August 1407 by William Thorpe, remarkable because it seems so improbable that this account should have gained currency: Thorpe in it maintains his absolute refusal to recant, and yet it seems hard to explain how, had he not done so, he could have come by the material to compose the account, let alone smuggle it out of prison. The text differs from the other trial documents that survive, many of them in Latin rather than in English, in that it gives from the defendant's viewpoint an account of the procedure and a reasoned defence of the opinions.[6]

The fact that the vast majority of Lollard texts are anonymous is for various reasons hardly surprising. At the most obvious level, the need to evade persecution, a need that became ever more pressing as time went on, dictated anonymity as elementary prudence. For the same reason very few Lollard manuscripts contain medieval marks of ownership. From 1384, ownership of heretical books was prime evidence of heresy; after 1407 ownership of books in the vernacular of any kind could rouse suspicion, and possession of vernacular scriptures was forbidden without the prior permission of the diocesan bishop, permission that would only be given for translations that antedated Wyclif.[7] But beyond this there seem to have been more positive reasons for anonymity. Though Wyclif is sometimes mentioned as a noble and much-wronged thinker, there is in English Lollardy no trace of the eminence that led to his nomination as the fifth Evangelist in Hussite Bohemia. On the other hand, Knighton comments at an early date on the way in which Lollards became all alike in their ideas and in their manner of argument and even of speech. This Knighton attributed to the effectiveness of the schools and *conventiculae* in which sympathisers were instructed. It seems fairly clear that many of the texts described below were devised for use in these groups. Certainly a reading of many Lollard texts bears out Knighton's observation, and it seems that it is to this similarity of background that echoes between the texts are to be attributed and not, as early critics thought, to their composition by one or two named heretics.[8]

The best known of the Wycliffite texts, and that to which most modern scholarship has been devoted, is the translation of the Bible. Knighton attributed this work to Wyclif himself, but it seems very unlikely that the heresiarch could have found time for the extent of meticulous work that this translation involved; his time was fully absorbed with the numerous Latin tracts that poured from his pen. The claim that Knighton makes is, however, evidence for a connection in inspiration if not in authorship.[9] At the opposite extreme, Michael Wilks (1975, pp. 160–161) recently argued that the Wycliffites used an already existing version of a complete vernacular Bible and merely revised that. This seems very improbable: there are many tracts defending vernacular scriptures dating from the late fourteenth or early fifteenth century, some but not all by Wycliffite writers, but none claims that there was a full rendering before their own time—a claim that would have been of much value for their argument.[10] It seems plain that the first stage of the translation consisted in a very literal rendering, heavily influenced in vocabulary, syntax, and even to some extent word order by the Vulgate, a rendering known as the Early Version. Lindberg (1959–1969, 1973) has produced a critical edition of the manuscripts that contain the Old Testament part of this version. There is an apparent break at Baruch 3.20: at this point Bodleian MS Douce 369 has a note "Explicit translacionem Nicholay de herford," Cambridge University Library MS Ee. 1. 10 has a related note, and MS Bodley 959 abruptly breaks off. The attribution may not be significant (it is difficult to fit sufficient leisure for the work into Hereford's life), but the break seems to be. It may be, however, that even this most literal stage, best represented by Bodley 959, represents a revision in the direction of idiomatic rendering. Fristedt (1969) edited a fascinating manuscript of the pseudo-Augustine tract *De Salutaribus Documentis*, which he argued showed a much earlier stage in a similar process of translation and one that might underlie the Early Version.[11]

The number of manuscripts of the Early Version is not large. Much more common is the Later Version, a text in which revision has gone a very long way in the direction of idiomatic rendering. This version has since the early eighteenth century been attributed for no good reason to John Purvey. But it is clear that the process of revision was infinitely more complex than the efforts of one man could explain. Hargreaves (1969 and bibliography given there) and Fristedt (1953–1973) have indicated some of the stages in the process that can be traced from peculiarities of individual manuscripts. Much work remains to be done on the many problems of the Bible translation. A start has recently been made on the paleographical description and analysis of the 250-odd manuscripts that contain all or a part of the translation. But until a complete collation of all the manuscripts has been undertaken (an enterprise that could sensibly begin by using one or two of the shortest biblical books), it will remain unclear how uniform the Late Version text is, or the extent to which revision between Early and Late versions is traceable. Another area that awaits investigation is of the various prefaces and prologues that are attached to individual books in some of the manuscripts, and of occasional glosses of more or less extensive kind. The so-called General

Prologue, a tract in fifteen chapters, the last of which purports to give an account of the making and revising of the Wycliffite rendering, survives only in ten manuscripts, many of them incomplete. Lindberg (1978) has recently produced a complete edition of the translation of Jerome's preface, found in thirteen manuscripts. Some of the others were printed by Forshall and Madden (1850), but without indication of the frequency of their appearance or of their existence apart from the Wycliffite Bible as independent units.[12]

As has been said, there are a number of Wycliffite tracts in defence of the vernacular scriptures, forbidden by Arundel's Constitutions in 1407. One of these was edited by Deanesly (1920), and more fully by Bühler (1938), but without the Latin source on which it was based; this, the work of the orthodox Richard Ullerston in 1401 at Oxford, survives complete only in a single manuscript, Vienna 4133 (see Hudson 1975). Similar use of preexisting, orthodox material is seen in some of the tracts in Cambridge University Library MS Ii. 6. 26; these remain to be properly investigated. The importance that the Lollards attached to the Bible is well attested in many works that deal with various issues, and in the name "Bible-men" that Pecock said they commonly used. Possibly of Lollard origin is a translation of Clement of Lanthony's harmony of the gospels, a text that awaits a modern edition.[13]

Closely related to the biblical translation, both because they use a somewhat revised Early Version rendering for the gospel texts and because they show the same preoccupation with the accurate interpretation of the text, are the Glossed Gospels, extensively investigated by Hargreaves (1979 and bibliography given there). It seems that there were three versions of the text, a shorter version, a longer one, and one in which only the dominical gospel lections are used but the longer version was further supplemented. In the case of Mark and John the longer version is only known through this extended rearranged selection. As their name implies, the texts consist of gospel text, divided into short passages of a few verses in each, with a commentary following drawn mainly from patristic sources. A substantial amount of the material derives from compilations such as Aquinas's *Catena Aurea*, but it is clear that the translators had recourse to the original texts from which Aquinas had drawn his extracts. The work could only have been done with access to a well-stocked library, probably in Oxford. In the shorter version Lollard concerns are not much in evidence; the bias is much clearer in some passages in the longer version and in the large additions made to some extracts in the rearranged text (only known in York Minster Library XVI. D. 2). Though it seems clear that the York text represents an augmentation of an already existing commentary, it has not yet been ascertained whether the short or the long version was the original. Hargreaves has promised a selection from the York text, but of the other versions only the briefest extracts have been published (see Hudson 1978b). Work also remains to be done on a number of other gospel commentaries (British Library Egerton 842, Cambridge University Library Ii. 2. 12, and Corpus Christi College Cambridge 32), whose relation, if any, to the Glossed Gospels in particular and to the Lollard movement in general, is completely unknown.[14]

The Wycliffites also revised and extended Rolle's commentary on the Psalter. Uncompleted work done for a thesis has in the main confirmed Everett's analysis (1922, 1923) as an outline of the revisions, but has shown that the detail is much more complicated and that there is a strong probability of the involvement of more than one reviser even within what appears to be one version. The commentaries found in MSS Bodley 288, Bodley 877, Lambeth Palace 34, and its continuation in BL Royal 18 C. xxvi seem particularly worthy of attention. Now that the collaborative edition of Rolle's original commentary approaches completion in thesis form, it is to be hoped that its publication will encourage more study of these revisions, study both of textual relations and of ideological outlook.[15]

Apart from the Wycliffite Bible, the text that gained most circulation was a long series of sermons, in its complete extent numbering 298. Of this series thirty-one manuscripts, complete or fragmentary, survive. This is only about an eighth of the Bible manuscripts, but its significance is much greater. While the Bible translation, save for the few manuscripts that contain the General Prologue and the equally small number that have contentious glosses, is entirely uncontroversial and could only be identified as Lollard by comparison with a manuscript declaring its origin, the sermon cycle shouts its heterodoxy from every page. Ownership would be highly dangerous, and any copies that fell into the hands of episcopal officers would instantly be recognized as heterodox and destroyed. It is far from clear, however, that such danger was apprehended when the cycle was composed and copied. The large majority of the manuscripts are handsome, professional productions, well arranged, carefully rubricated to show the lection for the occasion but not to mark incidental biblical quotation, and carefully corrected down to the most insignificant and trivial detail. Work has been going on for the past ten years on this cycle, and it is only possible to summarise the conclusions here; the details will be set out in full in the forthcoming edition.[16]

The 298 sermons are based upon lections of the Sarum rite, almost all expounding those lections in close detail so that the occasion of each sermon is fixed. As originally written, the sermons were in five sets, on the lections for the Sunday gospels and epistles, for the Commune and a limited Proprium Sanctorum order, and over one hundred for specified weekday occasions. Two liturgically comprehensible, and probably authorised, rearrangements were made: by interca-

lating the Sunday epistle and gospel sermons to produce a single dominical cycle
with two sermons for each Sunday, and second by further adding into this the
appropriate weekday sermons after those for the Sunday. Like the other texts
hitherto described, the sermons plainly have a learned background. Their affiliation with Wyclif is, despite some small near-contemporary indications, not of
authorship but of ideas. Some of the English sermons seem to derive material
from Wyclif's Latin sermons for the same occasions or verbally from elsewhere
in his writings. But almost all of the ideas in the vernacular sermons can be traced
back to Wyclif, and there is little of the further radicalization of his views that
can be seen in later Lollard texts. All the indications are that the sermons date
from about the same time as the *Opus Arduum*, around 1389–1390, and they
share its preoccupations. Being much briefer, however, they often expressed those
preoccupations elliptically; the most important part of the new edition will be the
explanatory notes, without which some sections of the text are highly obscure.
The proportion of exegesis to polemic in the sermons is very variable: a few are
almost entirely exegetical, and often these contain little that could be considered
heterodox; others expound the lection very briefly before continuing to a lengthy
diatribe on some Wycliffite matter, more or less relevant to the text at issue. The
method of biblical exegesis is not entirely what one might expect. Despite the
Wycliffite stress on the "literal" interpretation of scripture, much allegorical
reading, of a traditional kind even if not in all details conventional, is encountered.[17] Attached to the sermon cycle in many manuscripts, and apparently regarded as an appendix to it, are two longer sermons, one on Matthew 23 and the
other on Matthew 24. Both use the invitation of the biblical texts to castigate in
the most outspoken terms the abuses in the contemporary church and particularly
the friars. They are being edited with the cycle.

It has already become plain that the sermons of this cycle, as well as gaining
direct circulation through the numerous manuscripts, were modified and adapted
by men who did not share all the sympathies of the original writer. Most simply,
one manuscript excised a considerable amount of the controversial material, especially on the friars (see Hudson 1971b). Four more complicated derivatives have
been found. They range from one manuscript in which only a few brief passages
and phrases have been adopted, to another set of Sunday sermons, found in three
manuscripts, in which large sections were taken over, including most of the biblical translation and much comment, but with the material rearranged and supplemented. It appears from two of the derivatives that the biblical translation in the
cycle sermons was particularly valued. In the originals the lection is often divided
up into sentences or even phrases by comment from the preacher, though it is
always visually marked by rubrication. Two of the derivative groups took considerable pains to draw this material together to provide a single coherent rendering
at the start of the sermon. It is clear that the revisers must in each case have had

access either to a Vulgate or, less probably, to another vernacular translation since in some cases the original sermon had departed too far from the original text (for instance by turning direct into indirect speech to facilitate its incorporation into the exegesis) for use. But apparently the revisers felt the cycle's rendering was so good that this laborious effort was worthwhile. In many respects these derivative sermons seem to offer to the average preacher more than the originals on which they were based: less complicated theological argument, more direct moral instruction, and a simpler, more explicit language. Almost all the derivative material so far traced comes from the Sunday gospel sermons. This is hardly surprising: this would be the material most needed by the ordinary priest, a fact borne out by the greater number of manuscripts of the original set for these occasions. It is likely that, as further work is done on fifteenth-century sermons, more such borrowing and influence will be found.[18]

A sermon group that appears to be Lollard in sympathy but is not related to the large cycle is found in two manuscripts, BL Add. 41321 and Bodleian Library Rawlinson c. 751, in neither of which is the text complete. An edition of this group is under way. The views of the preacher are not outspokenly Wycliffite, but the stress on the need for preaching and the dangers that attend lay reading of the gospels seems, along with other hints, to associate the speaker with Lollardy: "if þei [the laity] taken it [þe worde of God] hemself, þat is, rede it or comoun þerof togidre, þei shullen be beten wiþ somonyng, cursyng and pursuyng and prisonyng." It has also been shown that some of the sermons used the *Rosarium* for their material and even their structure.[19]

To attempt to survey the remaining Wycliffite material in similar detail is a hopeless task: there is too much of it, and each text has its own problems and peculiarities. In what follows I try to describe some characteristic examples. First there are texts that reflect the Wycliffite attempt to enter the political field, notably the *Twelve Conclusions of the Lollards* and the so-called *Lollard Disendowment Bill* (texts in Hudson 1978b, nos. 3 and 27). The first of these survives now only in copies of Roger Dymmock's refutation, but from this and from contemporary chroniclers it emerges that the *Conclusions* were originally fixed in poster form to the doors of Westminster Hall and Saint Paul's Cathedral during the session of Parliament in 1395 (between January 25 and February 15). They were apparently intended for debate in Parliament, whether or not they were formally presented. They contain all the central Lollard claims, denial of transsubstantiation and of the need for oral confession, of the legitimacy of vows of chastity and of prayers for the dead, of images and pilgrimages; they urge that private religions should be abolished and temporalities (that is, income derived from secular lands or tenements, as opposed to spiritualities, the income derived from benefices, tithes, or similar ecclesiastical sources) removed from the clergy, that clerics should not hold secular office and, less expectedly, that all killing, whether in battle or following legal process, is unjustifiable. It seems clear from a reference within the *Conclusions* that some version of the *Bill* existed from 1395, though it would appear from the chroniclers that this second was not presented until 1410. The proposal of the bill was the removal from specified bishoprics and abbacies (mainly those held by the orders of Benedictines, Cistercians, or Augustinian canons) of all temporalities. It seems plain that the proposal was regarded as a first step towards eventual further disendowment, including the removal of the wealth of the friars. The money accruing to the king from the alienation was to provide for a specified number of earls, knights, and squires, to set up fifteen universities, and to provide in each town an almshouse and proper endowment for the relief of the poor. With the hindsight of the complete loss of political force from the Lollard cause after the Oldcastle rising in 1413, it is hard to take these proposals seriously. But the persistence of legislation against the Wycliffites from 1384 to 1420 and later should make clear that that cause was not so clearly hopeless to contemporaries as it appears to us.

Allusion has already been made to the schools and *conventiculae* in which Lollards were instructed in their beliefs. We can discover quite a lot about these from episcopal registers, and more from the texts designed to be used in them. The courtbook recently edited by Norman Tanner (1977), describing in detail cases from the Norwich diocese in the period 1428–1431, provides interesting information about the way in which preachers travelled from community to community, on the importance of books and pamphlets in spreading beliefs and sustaining discussion, and on the effect of a few dedicated believers in a small village, propagating their opinions within the village and, through relatives and friends, in neighbouring villages. It is worth putting alongside this courtbook the long text, declaredly a sermon, that survives in three early fifteenth-century and one sixteenth-century manuscripts. Two of the earlier manuscripts are in the same hand; all three are of the same pocket format. The preacher concludes his sermon:

> Now siris þe dai is al ydo, and I mai tarie ʒou no lenger, and I haue no tyme to make now a recapitulacioun of my sermoun. Neþeles I purpose to leue it writun among ʒou, and whoso likiþ mai ouerse it. . . . And certis, if I haue seid ony þing amys, and I mai now haue redi knouleche þerof, I shal amende it er I go. And if I haue such knouleche herafter, I shal wiþ beter will come and amende my defautis þan I seie þis at þis tyme. And of anoþir þing I biseche ʒou here þat, if ony aduersarie of myn replie aʒens ony conclusioun þat I haue shewid to ʒou at þis tyme, reportiþ redili hise euydencis, and nameli if he take ony euydence or colour of hooli

scripture, and, if almy3ti God wole vouchesaaf to graunte me grace or leiser to
declare mysilf in þese poyntis þat I haue moued in þis sermoun, I shal þoru3 þe
help of him in whom is al help declare me, so þat he shal holde him answerid.

A number of points emerge from this interesting passage: first that the preacher
was itinerant and that he carried with him copies of his address to hand out to
each congregation; second that he expected the congregation would have the energy and opportunity to ponder over the text entrusted to it; third that he antici-
pated that others or another would follow him, and that the congregation would
have sufficient intelligence and memory to note the arguments produced in opposition and to distinguish the biblical texts used to support those arguments;
fourth, and most obvious, that the preacher intended to revisit his disciples. The
account given in the Norwich courtbook of the activities of William White, a
notorious Lollard preacher about whom Netter had much to say, and of his effect
on devotees such as Marjorie Baxter of Martham, suggests that the implications
deduced from this passage are not far-fetched. The ideas set out in this long sermon are various, but deal primarily with the need for absolute clerical poverty
and the evils of the friars' mendicancy, two of the opinions early objected against
White.[20]

This sermon was declaredly for instructional use. Other texts do not so helpfully proclaim their purpose, but seem likely to have been intended for use in
schools. There are a number of texts that have the form of a series of arguments
with biblical and patristic texts in support of a central Lollard claim. Examples of
these are various tracts on images (for instance in BL MS Add. 24202, fols.
26–28v, Bodleian MS Eng. th. f. 39, fols. 1–8 and 37–38, the latter reappear-
ing in Trinity College Cambridge B. 14. 50, fols. 34–35), and on the Eucharist
(for instance in Trinity College Dublin 245, fols. 145–146v, Cambridge University Library Ff. 6. 31 (3), fols. 27v–37v). Use of such lists of proof texts in
trials, produced in the form of a roll from the pocket or fold of a cloak, is recorded several times.[21] More elaborate texts, using the same method but linking a
number of subjects, include *Sixteen Points on which the Bishops accuse Lollards*
(Hudson 1978b, no. 2), the *Lantern of Li3t*, and *The Apology for Lollard Doctrines*. The first and third of these survive in only a single manuscript each. The
Lanterne is found in two manuscripts and in a print of about 1535 that was based
on a third, similar, manuscript; a fourth was in the possession of John Claydon of
London when he was arrested for heresy in 1415. Here the academic origin of
the text is immediately apparent: long passages of patristic argument are quoted
first in their original Latin, and then translated. This, like the *Apology*, uses a
sophisticated method of debate; both are written in a plain but effective style.[22]

Perhaps the best way to exemplify briefly Wycliffite writings outside the central area is to describe three representative manuscripts. The first is now Norwich

Castle Museum 158. 926 4g. 3 in a hand of the early fifteenth century. The first item is a copy of the *Thirty-Seven Conclusions*; here a number of Lollard claims are examined in academic fashion, with the citation of canon law and patristic authorities to support a radical standpoint. There follow four items of more pastoral concern, a commentary on the *Pater Noster* (as Arnold 1869–1871, 3:98–110), one on the *Ave Maria* (as Matthew 204–208), on the Creed (not as Arnold 1869–1871, 3:114–116), and on the Ten Commandments (not as any of the printed versions). A translation of Daniel 3 follows, and then a series of translated biblical quotations of an edifying kind with a little added comment; the translations do not appear to be from either version of the Wycliffite Bible. The last item declares itself to be a translation of part of the *Compendium Theologicae Veritatis* and concerns the definition of antichrist (part is also found in BL Harley 272, fol. 155v). This is a very typical Wycliffite anthology, combining biblical, polemical, and pastoral concerns, with no clear indication of audience or the use to which the manuscript was to be put.[23] The second example, Trinity College Cambridge B. 14. 50, is fairly clearly an informal, probably personal, notebook. It is in two parts. The first twenty-five folios contain sermon notes, partly in English partly in Latin, referring to the *Rosarium* as a source for amplification, further Latin notes including quotations from Grosseteste, and one of Wyclif's briefest Latin texts. The second part includes four English Wycliffite tracts, the first on the need for biblical translation (printed by Deanesly 1920 and Bühler 1938), then the *Sixteen Points* (Hudson 1978b, no. 2), a brief tract against the worship of images, and finally a dialogue between Jon and Richard against the friars. These English texts are followed by another Latin text of Wyclif, the *De Fide Sacramenti*, a group of quotations from the *Rosarium* including a passage on images attributed to Wyclif, and a quotation from Hildegard of Bingen against the friars. Here we have a more eclectic, but also more academic collection of material. The two parts, despite being in different hands, are united by their quotation of Wyclif and of the *Rosarium*. It would seem that the manuscript is a preacher's assemblage, some, like the sermon notes, intended for his use alone, others, such as the four English tracts, probably to be passed on to others (Hudson 1972a, pp. 77–78 and von Nolcken 1979, pp. 36–37).

The third example, now BL Add. 24202, is the one most likely to attract the modern reader, and yet is the most atypical. The first item is a long tract in twenty-three articles concerning the allegiance of a bishop to the pope, written, to judge by internal references during the pontificate of Urban VI (1378–1389). The last, now defective at beginning and end, is another long treatise against the religious orders in the course of which Wyclif is quoted. Between these two are a pair of treatises against the worship of images, one against dice playing, and one concerning tithes and offerings. Pastoral concerns are reflected by *Of weddid men and wifis* (as Arnold 1869–1871, 3 : 188–201), a brief note on the soul, and two extracts from Gaytrigg's *Lay Folks' Catechism*;[24] a short *Tretise of Pristis* takes up the interest of the first item. Best known is the *Tretise of miraclis pleyinge*, uniquely preserved here, a text that has gained critical notice disproportionate to its medieval dissemination under the title of "The Lollard Text against Miracle Plays," a title it only deserves, if at all, because of its context in the manuscript and not from any unequivocally heterodox views within it. The manuscript is unrepresentative because of the large proportion of unique texts that it contains, and because of the interest it shows in topics such as plays and dicing, not a normal part of Wycliffite concerns. The first and last items, however, show very characteristic views, and the manuscript, since so many items are unique, may stand as an indication of the amount of material that has been lost.

Dating many of these texts, and particularly the shorter ones, is a very difficult task. But there seems little positive evidence to suggest that they derive from later than about 1425. Copying, however, proceeded throughout the fifteenth century, and it is clear from documentary evidence that the reading of vernacular books was a persistent mark of Lollard communities, and was often the means for their detection. Interest in Wycliffite texts did not cease with the coming of continental Lutheran heresy. Old Lollard communities received readily the new reforming ideas, and bishops did not always easily distinguish Lollardy from Lutheranism.[25] Between about 1530 and 1550 a number of Lollard texts were printed by the reformers, first in Antwerp and later in London. In most cases, though not all, indication of the antiquity of the text is given. For two of the texts, *The praier and complaynte of the ploweman* and *Wycklyffes wycket*, no medieval manuscript now survives. The second of these is an intriguing case: the terms in which the Eucharist is discussed in it are not quite those familiar from other Lollard tracts on the subject, but the text was certainly notorious before the arrival of the Lutheran heresy in England. As well as printed versions, there are sixteenth-century manuscripts of Lollard works prior to the production of antiquarian copies. An interesting case is Cambridge University Library Ff. 6.2 which contains copies of *Jack Upland* and of the long sermon described above, as well as the unique copy of one of the Lollard versions of the satirical *Epistola Sathanae* (Hudson 1978b, no. 17). In all of them medieval spelling and idiom are well preserved, though with a few modernizations and some mistakes because of misapprehension of the unfamiliar language.[26]

The preceding sections of this chapter have attempted to indicate the present state of scholarship on Wycliffite prose, the work currently in progress and, in some cases, the texts for which editions are needed. From my own study of this area some more general observations emerge. Older editions of Wycliffite texts were inadequate in a number of ways. Most obviously, there was a tendency to choose a single manuscript arbitrarily and to ignore, or consult only haphazardly, all other versions; this resulted in editions that by modern standards are not sufficiently reliable. But, more seriously, almost all the older editions provided little if any annotation. Many of the texts are written in a highly allusive style that is to a modern reader, even one versed in the Middle English of Chaucer or Langland, almost unintelligible. Any new editions of the texts must provide ample commentaries, explaining the allusions and elucidating the often complex arguments. It would, furthermore, be difficult to exaggerate the extent to which, behind this allusive style, a learned tradition exists. Sometimes, as with the Glossed Gospels or the *Lanterne of Li3t*, erudition is evident from the constant citation of patristic or later writers, with precise reference in the former case, Latin quotation before translation in the latter. Even more striking is the endless string of citations, with detailed references, that makes up the whole of the *Floretum*; a comparable technique, though with intervening argument couched in disputation form, is found in the *Thirty-Seven Conclusions*. But sometimes the learning is more concealed. The sermon cycle, for instance, contains few specific references to authors, none to precise sections of works, but is certainly based on a similar academic tradition. One sermon, for example, seems to show knowledge of Wyclif's sermons, of his *Trialogus* and *De Veritate Sacre Scripture*, as well as of Augustine's *De Doctrina Christiana* and Aristotle's *Prior Analytics* (see Hudson 1978b, no. 21B). Another distinguishes three methods of vision, direct, reflected, and *reflexed*; the first two are obvious enough, the third refers to phenomena such as are revealed by the experiment of placing a coin in a vessel—the coin may be invisible from certain angles, but, if the vessel is filled with water, the coin from the same vantage point comes into view. The language is technical, and the matter seems to derive from a fuller account in one of Wyclif's Latin sermons, though not that for the same occasion as this English instance. More work needs to be done on the extent and nature of the background of learning: for instance, the citation of canon law, despite constant castigation of its practitioners, in texts such as the *Thirty-Seven Conclusions*, would repay investigation. Debt to Wyclif is another area in which further work remains to be done. Despite the simplification, development, in some cases radicalization, in other cases debasement, that Wyclif's ideas underwent in the writings of his vernacular followers, it is striking how frequently ideas, comparisons, or phraseology can be traced back to Wyclif's Latin. For instance, an obscure allusion to speculation on the name of Tobias's dog in one of the English sermons is traceable back to Wyclif's *De Gradibus Cleri* where it is used as a type of useless academic argument.[27]

Another area for investigation concerns the grey area between overtly Wycliffite texts and the more radical but orthodox writings. A good instance is *Dives and Pauper*, where evidence external to the text is directly conflicting. In 1431 the work was cited as evidence of the heresy of its owner in Bury St. Edmund's. But between 1420 and 1440 Abbot Whethamstede of St. Alban's, that pillar of orthodoxy, ordered a copy to be made for his abbey's library. I think it is possible to understand both attitudes. *Dives and Pauper* deals with many issues, such as clerical wealth, images, or pilgrimages, that by the 1420s had become identified as Wycliffite, and it shows considerable sympathy with the desire for reform of the contemporary abuses in the church; on the other hand, while radical concerning practice, it is essentially conservative and orthodox concerning doctrine.[28] If, however, contemporaries were uncertain about a text's orthodoxy, it is hardly surprising that we find it hard to make distinctions in every case. On the one hand, "Wycliffite" or "Lollard" in the fifteenth century were terms like "communist," "red," or "fascist" today, often used as labels of abuse without any very precise semantic content. That a text was described as such is not conclusive proof that we should accept its derivation from such a background. On the other hand, one of the main reasons for the initial success of the Wycliffite movement, and for its persistence despite persecution up to the Reformation, was that it articulated into a coherent scheme many of the criticisms that had long been felt about the contemporary church. Since, despite some gestures in the direction of reform at the time of the Council of Pisa, most of these abuses continued, it is inevitable that Lollard criticism will find echoes in much orthodox writing in the fifteenth century. The road of the modern editor or critic who attempts to make firm distinctions in this area is full of potholes.[29]

A more productive line of enquiry could be the influence of Wycliffite writings on fifteenth-century prose. Perhaps this can be expressed most clearly as a series of questions. Is there any evidence that the upsurge of vernacular didactic prose in the century after Wyclif's death was an attempt to answer the challenge of heresy on its own ground? Two examples immediately spring to mind as positive answers to that question: Nicholas Love's translation of the pseudo-Bonaventuran *Meditationes Vitae Christi*, authorized by Archbishop Arundel in 1410, and Pecock's tracts.[30] But can the same be shown from, for instance, vernacular sermons (as opposed to the macaronic confections of William Paunteley)? Is there any evidence that the methods and progressive modifications of the Wycliffite Bible influenced the technique of translation in the fifteenth century? Or does the literal version that Fristedt (1973) has traced in one *Polychronicon* manuscript suggest that the Wycliffites, like Trevisa, were working within an already existing methodology? Did the Lollard insistence that the vernacular could and should be used for matters of learning, theology, and ecclesiastical affairs arouse a taste for English discussion which the orthodox realised they had to satisfy? How far is it possible to trace Wycliffite influence on the vocabulary, or on the spread of a standard language?[31]

Many of these questions are far-ranging, and it seems likely that until more editorial work has been done to make available more of the mass of prose, orthodox and heretical, from the period, they cannot usefully be investigated. But it is important to stress that in the Wycliffite field, whether in editorial or critical matters, no easy answers or quick results can be found. Work requires considerable familiarity with history and with theology, as well as with literary traditions and editorial skills. Willingness to investigate all sorts of material, unpublished episcopal registers, the lengthy and often obscure works of Wyclif, and the even more rebarbative polemics of his opponents, all in Latin, as well as familiarity with the idiom of the vernacular writings—all of these are needed before any useful findings will emerge. This is an area in which much needs to be done, an area in which the medieval writers were engaged with many of the central issues of their time, but it is not beginners' ground.

NOTES

1. J. Loserth's best-known work is his (1884) *Wyclif und Hus*, Munich and Berlin: R. Oldenburg, in its English translation by M. J. Evans (1884), London: Hodder and Stoughton, but of more lasting use are his articles on limited aspects of Wyclif's writings; these are listed in Talbert and Thomson (1970, pp. 517–519).

2. See Walsingham's *Historia Anglicana*, ed. (1863–1864) H. T. Riley, London: Rolls Series, p. 335.

3. *The Complete Works of John Gower*, ed. (1899–1902) G. C. Macaulay, Oxford: Clarendon Press, *Vox Clamantis, Carmen super Multiplici Viciorum Pestilencia*, pp. 13ff., *Confessio Amantis*, Prol. 346ff., v. 1803ff. For an excellent survey of the traditions of satire that provides numerous parallels to Lollard writings see J. Mann (1973) *Chaucer and Medieval Estates Satire*, Cambridge: Cambridge University Press.

4. Thomas Netter in his *Doctrinale*, written between 1420 and 1430, ed. (1757–1759) B. Blanciotti, Venice: Antonius Bassanesius, calls the followers of Wyclif indifferently *Wycliffistae* and *Lollardi*. For the Crumpe story see *Fasciculi Zizaniorum*, ed. (1858) W. W. Shirley, London: Rolls Series, pp. 311–312.

5. See Hudson (1978b, pp. 258–259). The chief documentary sources are episcopal registers recording details of suspects' beliefs in trials; for the difficulties of this sort of evidence see A. Hudson (1973b) "The Examination of Lollards," *Bulletin of the Institute of Historical Research*, 46, 145–159, esp. pp. 151–152.

6. Thorpe's account survives in a single Middle English manuscript and a print of about 1530; the latter was modernized by Pollard (1903).

7. Arundel's Constitutions of 1407 are printed in D. Wilkins (1737) *Concilia Magnae Britanniae et Hiberniae*, London: R. Gosling, F. Gyles, T. Woodward, and C. Davis, 3:314–319.

8. Henry Knighton, *Chronicon*, ed. (1889–1895) J. R. Lumby, London: Rolls Series, 2:186–187; some aspects of this observation are explored in Hudson (1981a) and (1981b) "A Lollard Sect Vocabulary?," *So Meny People Longages and Tonges: Philological Essays in Scots and Mediaeval English Presented to Angus McIntosh*, ed. M. Benskin and M. L. Samuels, Edinburgh: privately printed, pp. 15–30.

9. Knighton, *Chronicon*, 2:151–152. The tradition that Wyclif was responsible for the Bible translation was continued into the modern period by men such as Robert Crowley (1550) *The Vision of Pierce Plowman* . . . , London: Robert Crowley, sig.*2, and John Bale (1557–1559) *Scriptorum Illustrium Maioris Brytannie . . . Catalogus*, Basel: Ionannis Oporinus, 1:456.

10. Texts in defence of vernacular scriptures are discussed below. The antecedents quoted are commonly those of Rolle, Bede, and Alfred, the last credited with responsibility for Psalter and gospel versions in Old English.

11. For Hereford's life see Emden (1958, 2:913–915) and Hudson (1975, pp. 272–275). A much more literal translation than the Early Version is shown by the version of the *Letter of Alexander to Aristotle*, ed. (1978) V. DiMarco and L. Perelman, Amsterdam: Rodopi, a fact completely unremarked by the editors. For a nearer contemporary version showing some literalism see Chapter 8 and Fristedt (1973).

12. See bibliography under Wycliffite Bible. The translations of Jerome's prefaces to individual books are found in Forshall and Madden (1850) in their appropriate positions; other prefaces are scattered between the introduction (1:v–xxxiv), the biblical position to which they belong, and an appendix (4:681b–695b). For the ten manuscripts containing the General Prologue, to which should be added Scheide, Princeton, MS 12, see Hudson (1978b, p. 173).

13. For one of the Cambridge tracts see Hudson (1978b, no. 20); the tract on fols. 51v–58v of the same manuscript comes from the *Mirror*, a Middle English translation of Robert of Greatham's *Miroir* unlikely to be of Lollard origin. Pecock (1860) used the name in *The Repressor of Over Much Blaming of the Clergy*, London: Rolls Series, 1:36. For the gospel harmony see L. Muir (1970) "Translations and Paraphrases of the Bible, and Commentaries," in *A Manual of the Writings in Middle English 1050–1500*, 2:545, ed. J. B. Severs, Hamden: Connecticut Academy of Arts and Sciences, though the list of manuscripts is not complete.

14. Alastair Minnis has recently indicated that he hopes to investigate these texts further. A brief account of the Corpus Christi College manuscript is to be found in M. J. Powell (1916) *The Pauline Epistles*, EETS, es 116, pp. ix–xvi; the text she edited forms the second part of Corpus Christi College Cambridge 32.

15. The collaborative edition has been done by various doctoral students at Fordham University, to replace the old edition by H. R. Bramley (1884) Oxford: Clarendon Press; for details see Chapter 2.

16. The new edition, under the title *English Wycliffite Sermons*, is by the present author and Pamela Gradon; the first volume (1983, Oxford: Clarendon Press) contains the sermons on the Sunday gospels and epistles with introductory material for the whole cycle.

17. For an example of exegesis in allegorical terms, even if all the details of that allegory are hard to trace to any source, see Arnold (1869–1871), 1:11–14, 17–19; for a more polemical instance see 1:131–134 or 138–141.

18. A brief account of the adaptations mentioned appears in the new edition of the original sermons. The expurgated version of the cycle is in Bodleian MS Don. c. 13, for which see A. Hudson (1971a) "The Expurgation of a Lollard Sermon-Cycle," *Journal of Theological Studies*, ns 22, 451–465. The derivatives, in order of their description in the chapter above, are: (i) MS Bodley 806, of which Helen Spencer is preparing an edition; (ii) a set virtually complete in Trinity College Dublin 241, and partially preserved in St. John's College Cambridge G. 22 and in Cambridge University Library Add. 5338, first part; (iii) Cambridge University Library Add.

5338, second part, and Lambeth Palace 392, both incomplete but overlapping in their contents, being edited by Ruth Evans.

19. The sermons are being edited by Gloria Cigman; see further C. von Nolcken (1981).

20. For preliminary details about the text quoted see Hudson (1978b, no. 18 and notes); I do not mean to imply that the text was written by White, or had anything directly to do with him, but only that his history and the contents of the text are mutually illuminating. I am presently editing this sermon (found in BL MS Egerton 2820 and other manuscripts) as well as the sermon by Taylor, the trial account of William Thorpe, and the tract in BL MS Cotton Titus D. v. For White see Tanner (1977) and *Fasciculi Zizaniorum* (above n. 4), pp. 417–432 and Netter's *Doctrinale* (above n. 4), 3:354, 412, 414, 417, 630, etc.

21. See A. Hudson (1972b) "Some Aspects of Lollard Book Production," *Studies in Church History*, 9, 149–150.

22. For Claydon's text see *The Register of Henry Chichele*, ed. (1938–1947) E. F. Jacob, Oxford: Clarendon Press, 4:132–138 at p. 134.

23. The final text is roughly based on *Compendium* vii:8–9 but with additions. The complicated relations between various Middle English commentaries on the Ten Commandments were not satisfactorily covered in the paper by Kellogg and Talbert (1960); a new and wider analysis is being done by Rachel Pyper.

24. Ed. (1901) T. F. Simmons and H. E. Nolloth, EETS, os 118, text T, lines 269–347, 372–435.

25. See, for instance, the material recorded in Foxe's *Acts and Monuments*, ed. (1837–1841) S. R. Cattley, London: R. B. Seeley and W. Burnside, 4:221–241; also A. G. Dickens (1959) *Lollards and Protestants in the Diocese of York 1509–1558*, London: Oxford University Press, and C. Cross (1976) *Church and People 1450–1660*, Glasgow: Fontana/Collins. For the importance of literacy see Aston (1977).

26. See Aston (1964, 1965) and my forthcoming paper "*No Newe Thyng*: The Printing of Medieval Texts in the Early Reformation Period."

27. Arnold (1889–1871, 1:13). Wyclif, *De Gradibus Cleri Ecclesie* in *Opera Minora*, ed. (1913) J. Loserth, London: Wyclif Society, p. 141/7–9: "et quesitum est a tali discolo quis vocatus est canis Tobie, quia sicut una questio est inutilis sic et alia."

28. The text has been edited by P. H. Barnum (1976, 1980) EETS, os 275 and 280; for the heresy trial see Tanner (1977, pp. 99–102) and for Whethamstede's commission *Annales Monasterium Sancti Albani*, ed. (1870–1871) H. T. Riley, London: Rolls Series, 2:269.

29. The classic case, of course, in which attempts at distinction have foundered is *Piers Plowman*; for a balanced consideration of the issue see P. Gradon (1980) "Langland and the Ideology of Dissent," *PBA*, 66, 179–205.

30. The first was edited by L. F. Powell (1908) London: Clarendon Press, but the authorization is incomplete in the copy Powell used; for it see E. Salter (1974) *Nicholas Love's Myrrour of the Blessed Lyf of Jesu Crist*, pp. 1–2, Analecta Cartusiana 10, Salzburg: Institute für englische Sprache und Literatur, Universität Salzburg.

31. For preliminary discussion of these issues see my (1982) "Lollardy: The English Heresy?," *Studies in Church History*, 18, 261–283.

BIBLIOGRAPHY

The material is divided into the Wycliffite Bible, the Glossed Gospels, revisions of Rolle's Psalter commentary, the sermon cycle, editions of other writings, and critical material. To give a comprehensive bibliography of primary sources is not possible, partly because of the very large number of texts, many unedited, to be covered, but more important, because the limits of the field are still uncharted. The second item listed below is unsatisfactory for both reasons.

Hudson, Anne (1973a) "Contributions to a Bibliography of Wycliffite Writings." *N&Q*, ns 20, 443–453.

Talbert, E. W., and Thomson, S. H. (1970) "Wyclif and His Followers." In *A Manual of the Writings in Middle English 1050–1500*, vol. 2, edited by J. Burke Severs, pp. 354–380, 521–535. Hamden: Connecticut Academy of Arts and Sciences.

THE WYCLIFFITE BIBLE

MANUSCRIPTS

Lindberg, Conrad (1970) "The Manuscripts and Versions of the Wycliffite Bible: A Preliminary Survey." *SN*, 42, 333–347. (This list is currently being corrected and brought up to date.)

PRINTED EDITIONS

Forshall, Josiah, and Madden, Frederick (1850) *The Holy Bible . . . Made from the Latin Vulgate by John Wycliffe and His Followers*. Oxford: Clarendon Press. (Contains both versions from selected manuscripts.)

Lindberg, Conrad (1959–1969) *MS Bodley 959 Genesis-Baruch 3.20 in the Earlier Version of the Wycliffite Bible*. Stockholm: Almqvist and Wiksell. (Early Version from all manuscripts.)

————— (1973) *The Earlier Version of the Wycliffite Bible*. Stockholm: Almqvist and Wiksell. (Baruch 3.20 to end of Old Testament from Christ Church Oxford MS 145)

————— (1978) *The Middle English Bible: Prefatory Epistles of St. Jerome*. Oslo, Bergen, and Troms: Universitetsforlaget.

STUDIES OF THE TRANSLATION

Only the most important studies are listed. The later ones include up-to-date bibliographies. A paleographical study of the manuscripts of the Bible translation is being undertaken by Stephen Halasey.

Fristedt, Sven L. (1953–1973) *The Wycliffe Bible*. Stockholm: Almqvist and Wiksell.

Hargreaves, Henry (1969) "The Wycliffite Versions." In *The Cambridge History of the Bible*, vol. 2, ed. G. W. H. Lampe, pp. 387–415.

Wilks, Michael (1975) "Misleading Manuscripts: Wyclif and the Non-Wycliffite Bible." *Studies in Church History*, 11, 147–161.

THE GLOSSED GOSPELS

MANUSCRIPTS

Matthew: shorter BL Add. 41175; longer BL Add. 28026, with a somewhat reduced
form in Bodleian Laud misc. 235 and Fitzwilliam McClean 133.

Mark: shorter BL Add. 41175.

Luke: shorter Bodley 143 and Bodley 243; longer Cambridge University Library Kk.
2. 9.

John: shorter Bodley 243 and Trinity College Cambridge B. 1. 38.

Rearranged version of longer commentary with additions, for the Sunday gospel lections
only: York Minster XVI. D. 2.

STUDIES

Only the most recent statement on these by the scholar who almost alone has investigated them is included.

Hargreaves, Henry (1979) "Popularising Biblical Scholarship: The Role of the Wycliffite Glossed Gospels." In *The Bible and Medieval Culture*, ed. W. Lourdaux and
D. Verhelst, pp. 171–189. Louvain: University Press.

REVISIONS OF ROLLE'S PSALTER COMMENTARY

The listed item contains the only published material. A fuller analysis, and an edition of
selections from MS Bodley 288, are being prepared by Edmund Weiner.

PUBLISHED MATERIAL

Everett, Dorothy (1922, 1923) "The Middle English Prose Psalter of Richard Rolle of
Hampole." *MLR*, 17, 217–227, 337–350 and 18, 381–393.

SERMON CYCLE

MANUSCRIPTS

Hudson, Anne (1971b) "A Lollard Sermon-Cycle and Its Implications." *MAE*, 40,
142–156. (Contains a provisional account of this cycle.)
——— (1983) *English Wycliffite Sermons*, vol. 1. Oxford: Clarendon Press. (Contains a
full account of the manuscripts.)

PRINTED EDITIONS

Arnold, T. (1869–1871) *Select English Works of Wyclif*, vols. 1–2. Oxford: Clarendon Press. (MS Bodley 788)

Hudson, Anne (1983) *English Wycliffite Sermons*, vol. 1 (Edition from all known manuscripts of sermons on Sunday gospels and epistles; further volumes to be edited by Pamela Gradon and Anne Hudson will complete the edition and provide commentary.)

EDITIONS OF OTHER WRITINGS

COLLECTIONS OF SHORTER WYCLIFFITE TEXTS

Vaughan, R. (1845) *Tracts and Treatises by John de Wycliffe, D.D.* London: Blackburn and Pardon. (Modernized, and to be treated with caution.)

Arnold, T. (1869–1871) *Select English Works of Wyclif*, vol. 3 Oxford: Clarendon Press.

Matthew, F. D. (1880) *The English Works of Wyclif Hitherto Unprinted.* EETS, os 74. 2d rev. ed. 1902.

Wynn, H. E. (1929) *Wyclif Select English Writings.* Oxford: Clarendon Press.

Hudson, Anne (1978b) *Selections from English Wycliffite Writings.* Cambridge: University Press.

INDIVIDUAL TEXTS

Bühler, Curt F. (1938) "A Lollard Tract: On Translating the Bible into English." *MAE*, 7, 167–183.

Forshall, Josiah (1851) *Remonstrance against Romish Corruptions.* London: Spottiswoode and Shaw. (More usually known as the *Thirty-Seven Conclusions.*)

Genet, Jean-Philippe (1977) *"Tractatus de Regibus"* in *"Four English Political Tracts of the Later Middle Ages."* Camden Society 4th ser. 18.

Halliwell, J. O. (1841–1843) "A Sermon against Miracle-Plays." In *Reliquiae Antiquae*, 2:42–57. London: William Pickering.

Heyworth, Peter L. (1968) *Jack Upland, Friar Daw's Reply and Upland's Rejoinder.* London: Oxford University Press.

Pollard, A. W. (1903) "The Examination of Master William Thorpe." In *Fifteenth Century Prose and Verse*, pp. 101–167. London: Constable. (Modernized version of the [1530?] print.)

Scattergood, V. J. (1975) "The Two Ways." In *The Works of Sir John Clanvowe*, pp. 57–80. Cambridge: D. S. Brewer.

Swinburn, L. M. (1917) *The Lanterne of Lizt.* EETS, os 151.

Talbert, E. W. (1942) "A Lollard Chronicle of the Papacy." *JEGP*, 41, 163–193.

Todd, J. H. (1842) *An Apology for Lollard Doctrines.* Camden Society 1st ser. 20.

Von Nolcken, Christina (1979) *The Middle English Translation of the Rosarium Theologie.* MET 10. Heidelberg: Carl Winter.

CRITICAL MATERIAL ON WYCLIF,
THE WYCLIFFITE MOVEMENT, AND ITS TEXTS

Aston, Margaret (1960) "Lollardy and Sedition, 1381–1431." *Past and Present*, 17, 1–44.

———— (1964) "Lollardy and the Reformation: Survival or Revival?" *History*, 49, 149–170.

———— (1965) "John Wycliffe's Reformation Reputation." *Past and Present*, 30, 23–51.

———— (1977) "Lollardy and Literacy." *History*, 62, 347–371.

———— (1980) "Lollard Women Priests?" *Journal of Ecclesiastical History*, 31, 441–461.

Deanesly, Margaret (1920) *The Lollard Bible*. Cambridge: University Press.

Emden, A. B. (1957–1959) *A Biographical Register of the University of Oxford to A. D. 1500*. Oxford: Clarendon Press.

Hudson, Anne (1972a) "A Lollard Compilation and the Dissemination of Wycliffite Thought." *Journal of Theological Studies*, ns. 23, 65–81.

———— (1975) "The Debate on Bible Translation, Oxford 1401." *EHR*, 90, 1–18.

———— (1978a) "A Neglected Wycliffite Text." *Journal of Ecclesiastical History*, 29, 257–279.

———— (1981) "John Purvey: A Reconsideration of the Evidence for His Life and Writings." *Viator*, 12, 355–380.

Kellogg, A. L., and Talbert, E. W. (1960) "The Wycliffite *Pater Noster* and *Ten Commandments*, with Special Reference to English MSS 85 and 90 in the John Rylands Library." *BJRL*, 42, 345–377.

Lambert, M. D. (1977) *Medieval Heresy: Popular Movements from Bogomil to Hus*, pp. 217–271. London: Arnold.

Leff, G. (1967) *Heresy in the Later Middle Ages*, 2:494–605. Manchester: University Press.

McFarlane, K. B. (1952) *John Wycliffe and the Beginnings of English Nonconformity*. London: English Universities Press.

———— (1972) *Lancastrian Kings and Lollard Knights*. Oxford: Clarendon Press. (A posthumously published collection, the section on Lollardy dating mainly from lectures given in 1966.)

Tanner, Norman (1977) *Heresy Trials in the Diocese of Norwich, 1428–1431*. Camden Society 4th ser. 20.

Thomson, J. A. F. (1965) *The Later Lollards 1414–1520*. Oxford: Clarendon Press.

Von Nolcken, Christina (1981) "Some Alphabetical Compendia and How Preachers Used Them in Fourteenth-Century England." *Viator*, 12, 271–288.

Woolf, Rosemary (1972) *The English Mystery Plays*. London: Routledge and Kegan Paul. (Discusses the *Tretise of miraclis pleyinge* on pp. 84–101.)

Workman, H. B. (1926) *John Wyclif*. Oxford: Clarendon Press.

CHAPTER 13

The Romances

George R. Keiser

The medieval English romances are stories in verse which deal with the adventures of noble men and women and which end happily. . . . Many of the fifteenth-century examples (generally inferior) and all the thirteenth- and fourteenth-century ones are written in verse, prose romances being of negligible importance if we except the works of Malory.
Schmidt and Jacobs 1980, 1 : 1.

The prose romances occur very late in the history of the Middle English romance, and their appearance reflects a change in taste that had developed on the Continent in the fourteenth century and did not reach England until the mid-fifteenth century. Some prose romances were written before 1450, but most were produced between 1460 and 1520, with Caxton's publication of his own translations and Malory's *Morte Darthur* in the 1470s and 1480s being the artistic high-water mark. While the total number of extant prose romances is not great, their bulk is formidable, for many are of very great length. This fact, in conjunction with a lack of compelling artistry in all but a few of them, explains why the prose romances have received little critical attention even though many have been available in competent EETS editions for more than fifty years. Perhaps with the burgeoning interest in Middle English romances, in fifteenth-century English culture, and in the development of Middle English prose, we may expect that these long neglected works will soon receive more critical scrutiny. In anticipation of that brighter day for these poor relations among the Middle English romances, this is a good time to look at the canon, the state of scholarship and criticism, and directions for future studies.[1]

In view of how little attention they have received, it is not surprising that there have been no satisfactory attempts to describe the canon of prose romances. The obvious starting place is the chronological list of Middle English romances prepared by Helaine Newstead for the first volume of the revised *Manual of the Writings in Middle English* (Severs 1967, pp. 13–16.) Though very useful, this list is not without its problems. First, it includes works written in the first third of the sixteenth century, well beyond the usual limit of Middle English and of the *Manual* itself. Still, while their language cannot be described as Middle English, inclusion of these works is defensible, for they are so close in character, substance, style, and attitude to pre-1500 works that their exclusion would seem arbitrary. Second, apparently having chosen inclusiveness rather than selectivity as the ideal, Newstead (and, presumably, the other editors of the volume) held to no very rigid definition of *romance* in compiling the list. Thus, several works appear only, it would seem, because they treat the so-called matters of romance. The works in question can best be described as epitomes, which are interesting to consider in relation to the romances, though they cannot themselves be called romances, no matter how elastic a definition of romance we may use. Finally despite the apparent tendency toward inclusiveness, the list in the *Manual*, for reasons that are not apparent, omits several works, some of which are mentioned incidentally in the later parts of the *Manual*.

Adding these missing works, we come up with the list found in the first section of the bibliography at the end of this chapter. Ideally, underlying a list that purports to describe the canon of a genre should be a generally accepted definition of that genre, not simply a critical tradition (and in the present instance an admittedly thin one) of regarding the works as belonging to it. However, in the case of Middle English romance, whether in verse or in prose, we are far from an ideal. The long debate about the nature of the genre, and indeed whether it is a genre at all, seems far from resolution. In the circumstances, any list of prose romances should be inclusive, as this one is, even perhaps to an excess.

Although contributions to this debate seldom take the prose romances into account, two recent studies do so and, thus, deserve some notice here. In a chapter whose title, "The Romance Mode," reflects her idea that "it is doubtful whether the romance can be indeed regarded as a genre at all," Gradon (1971, p. 269) looks at several prose romances. Observing that the aristocratic ideals found in the *chansons de geste* and Old English poetry persist in the romance, Gradon calls attention to the importance of the vendetta in Malory's *Morte Darthur*, the heroic ideal in Caxton's *The Foure Sonnes of Aymon*, and the theme of feudal loyalty in Lord Berners's *Huon of Burdeux*. Elsewhere, commenting on the blending of secular and religious ideals in the romance mode, Gradon makes use of the account of Ponthus's success as constable for the king of Little Britain in the earlier version of *King Ponthus*. Additionally, she makes extensive use of the *Morte Darthur* in discussing the marvellous and the exotic, the treatment of character, and the conventions of love in the romance mode. Though she has only incidental references to other prose romances, many of Gradon's observations, especially those concerning the effect of "bringing together objects of sense perception and objects of apprehension in such a way that the familiar and the unfamiliar merge" (p. 238), seem pertinent to such works as *Melusine*, *Valentine and Orson*, and *Huon of Burdeux*.

In contrast to Gradon's doubt that the romance can be regarded as a genre is the argument by Hume that there was "a definite notion of romance form" (1974, p. 161) among the writers whose works are traditionally described as romances—that is, the authors of the works on Newstead's list. Hume compares the romance to other contemporary forms—the folktale, the saint's life and secular vita, and historical writings—to show both their influences on the romance and the differences that give romance an integrity of its own as a genre. Of special interest to the present study is Hume's attempt to argue that we find in the romances a "spectrum of narrative types generated by varying the relation of the hero to the background," which "does help explain how Middle English romances could have been viewed as a homogeneous form" (p. 169). Hume's Type A consists of works in which the hero (or heroes), on whose activities the narrative remains focused at all times, moves from a peaceful and ordered existence to one in which he must undergo a series of tests and quests in order to restore harmony in his life. As prose works of this type Hume cites *Valentine and Orson*, *King Ponthus*, and Caxton's *Paris and Vienne*. At the other end of her spectrum is the Type C romance, in which the events overshadow the hero, if indeed the work has a single hero. Works of this type are *Melusine*, *The Foure Sonnes of Aymon*, and those recounting the sieges of Troy, Thebes, and Jerusalem. Type B romances, at the midpoint of the spectrum, have individual heroes who move against a specific historical background that is both important for its own sake and necessary to the story. Prose works of this type, according to Hume, include Caxton's *Charles the Grete*, *History of Jason*, *Eneydos*, and *Godefroy of Boloyne*. Placing them along a spectrum, Hume rejects absolute boundaries or distinctions among the three types and can, therefore, accommodate Malory's *Morte Darthur* (taking it as a single work, not a collection of romances) and the Prose *Merlin* by placing them between Types B and C. Aside from its usefulness and inclusiveness, the virtue of Hume's approach to defining the romance as a genre is that it confronts head-on questions that must inevitably arise when one attempts to justify the assignment of those prose works that call themselves histories to the romance genre.

The place of the Middle English prose romances in literary history is a subject that has received scant attention. Pearsall views their development as inevitable, "given the influence of continental models and demands of an increasing reading public" (1976, p. 71). Malory and Caxton, understandably, receive the greatest attention from Pearsall, though he does take some notice of those attempts in prose that preceded their work. The Prose *Alexander*, *The Sege of Thebes*, *The Sege of Troy*, and the two manuscript versions of the *Siege of Jerusalem* he describes as "straightforward redactions of the 'matter of antiquity,' attempts to provide 'compendious' summaries," in which "the impulse to composition is historical and factual rather than literary" (p. 73). Four other early works—*Ipomedon*, the Prose *Merlin*, *Melusine*, and *King Ponthus*—he admires for their success in offering more readable versions of stories formerly done in verse. Finally, he mentions later works, including *The Three Kings' Sons* and the romances printed by Wynkyn de Worde and other early sixteenth-century printers, which carry on the tradition of Caxton, though serving a wider audience than his.

Schlauch (1963) examines the place of the prose romances in social and literary history. Setting them into a historical context, Schlauch asserts that the romances preserve an outmoded chivalric ideal which had lost its social function but which appealed to both the new middle classes and the old feudal nobility because of their mutual opposition to a centralized monarchy. Also enhancing this appeal, Schlauch observes, was the fall of Constantinople in 1453, which revived the crusading spirit. Considering their place in literary history, Schlauch finds that the prose romances in general lack an assured, flexible prose style and complexity of character and motivation—qualities that, in her view, would anticipate the modern novel. Caxton's *Recuyell of the Histories of Troy*, *Kynge Appolyn*, and *King Ponthus* do, however, show some occasional insights into human feelings, according to Schlauch. Three works that she admires for possibly making "some sort of contribution to the shaping of later fiction in a realistic vein" (p. 65) are Caxton's *Blanchardyn and Eglantine*, his *Paris and Vienne*, and Lord Berners's *Arthur of Lyttell Brytayne*. Arguing that these works contain elements of sophisticated social comedy, Schlauch discusses their heroines at some length, attempting to demonstrate the liveliness and complexity of each and to show that in the latter two works, where the ladies and their lovers come from different social classes, the social realism is especially successful.

While there are some dubious literary and historical assumptions underlying this study, it deserves serious attention from any prospective student of the prose romances. Schlauch has a keen critical sense and can make very telling points about style and characterization when she deals with the particular.

The last attempt, as of this writing, at a comprehensive view of the prose romances as a whole is Scanlon (1977). In characterizing the romances, Scanlon calls attention to an ostensible concern with fact that causes a blurring of distinctions between family chronicle and romance, "a greater integrity of parts and a tighter motivation of incident and character, as well as an overall clarification (if reduction) of theme and event," and an "overwhelmingly didactic and utilitarian" purpose resulting from the displacement of courtly love by religious concerns (p. 2). Scanlon qualifies this last point by noting the great use made of the marvellous and sensational. In the history of the prose romance, he argues, Caxton exercised the most profound influence on the direction of its development by importing the chivalric ideal nourished by the court at Burgundy, which is closely related to the revival of the crusading spirit after the fall of Constantinople. Specifically, he singles out Caxton's Charlemagne romances, whose mood he describes as "heroically religious" (p. 8), as having the greatest influence on future work in the genre. That later work, and particularly the romances printed by Wynkyn de Worde, popularizes the romance by tempering chivalric conventions with a sense of egalitarianism, increasing the importance of the religious content, and making greater use of materials with folkloric origins and with significant elements of magic, wonder, and comic realism. Scanlon closes his survey with a brief discussion of the "eclipse" of the romance, which resulted, he believes, at least in part from the new learning and the new religion.

Turning now to studies of individual works, we find that few of them, except for *Arthur of Lyttell Brytayne*, have had any significant amount of attention in recent years. Surprisingly, they have not even attracted the notice of many dissertation writers. *Melusine*, one of the more intriguing romances, has been the subject of only two U.S. dissertations since 1970—those of Nolan (1971) and Rigsby (1980)—both apparently more concerned with the legend underlying it than with the romance itself. *The Three Kings' Sons* has been the subject of a dissertation by Grinberg (1969), which examines the French original as a product of the Burgundian milieu in which it originated, as well as the relations of the English text and the extant French manuscript and printed versions. According to Grinberg (1975), the research into textual relations reveals that none of the extant French versions could have been the source for the English version. The final items to be noted in this survey of dissertations are Mitchell (1969), a critical edition of *Arthur of Lyttell Brytayne*; Neeson (1972), a critical edition of the Prose *Alexander*; and Lombardo (1977), a critical edition of *Helyas*.

The Prose *Alexander*, *Robert the Deuyll*, *Valentine and Orson*, and *Paris and Vienne* have been examined in some detail by V. B. Richmond (1975), whose work has not had an entirely favorable critical reception. Unfortunately, because of the very restricted and not altogether clear focus of the book, much of the criticism is justified. Still, it has some positive virtues, not the least of which is that it calls attention to four long-neglected prose romances and offers some specific evidence of their serious, didactic purposes. Richmond takes up the romances individually, and she traces the exposition of a central theme in each: in the Prose *Alexander* the theme of fortune, in *Robert the Deuyll* penance, in *Valentine and Orson* brotherhood, and in *Paris and Vienne* love. Richmond argues vigorously that a firmly Christian moral vision informs each romance and shapes the thematic development.

For some time now it has been generally accepted that *The Sege of Troy* is a prose summary of John Lydgate's *Troy Book*. Benson (1971) has qualified that idea by showing that in several instances in which the prose work disagrees with Lydgate's account, it agrees with the account given by Chaucer in *Troilus and Criseyde*. The fact that the author of *The Sege* made use of Chaucer, as Benson notes, is probably of more interest for what it reveals about the widespread knowledge of Chaucer than for what it reveals about a prose work of slight artistic value.

Perhaps the most dramatic developments concern prose accounts of the siege of Jerusalem. The lost Aldenham MS, which contains a prose narrative different from that printed by Pynson and de Worde, was traced to the Cleveland Public Library by Hornstein (1971). Upon examination, the Cleveland *Siege* was found to be a translation of Roger d'Argenteuil's *Bible en françois*, according to Moe (1966). Kurvinen (1969) presents an edition of yet another prose version, *The Sege of Jerusaleme*, which is extant in MS Porkington 10 and which summarizes an abbreviated text of the Middle English couplet version of *Titus and Vespasian*.

Huon of Burdeux and *Arthur of Lyttell Brytayne* have been treated in surveys of the life and literary activities of Lord Berners by Taylor (1969) and Blake (1971). The latter advances important arguments about the dates of composition of the two romances. Concerning *Huon*, Blake proposes that the first edition was printed in Berners's lifetime (i.e., before 1533) without a prologue; that a lost second edition was printed for Francis Hastings, second earl of Huntingdon, between 1545 and 1561 with the preface and colophon extant now only in the 1601 edition; "that there was a possible 1570 edition, and that the 1601 edition is the fourth edition" (p. 125). Concerning *Arthur*, Blake proposes that its prologue may be "an amalgam" (p. 125) of Caxton's prologues to *Recuyell of the Histories of Troy* and *Morte Darthur*. From these arguments Blake proceeds to the suggestion that Berners completed both works before leaving England to serve as deputy of Calais in 1520 and, thus, before translating Froissart's *Chronicles*. *Huon* may have been done sometime after 1513 and *Arthur* sometime after 1514—the dates, respectively, of the French printed versions which Blake believes that Berners used as sources.

The publication history of *Arthur* has been the subject of study by Mitchell (1972), who argues against an idea preserved in some literary histories that there was an edition of *Arthur* printed between 1520 and 1540, suggesting that a careless error by the eighteenth-century scholar, Joseph Ames, is the source of the idea. Mitchell has also argued (Michel 1979) that the Redbourne print of *Arthur* may have appeared as late as 1566 and the East print as early as 1567.

Oberempt (1976) responds to Blake and Mitchell. Regarding the idea that an edition of *Arthur* was printed between 1520 and 1540, he raises the possibility that such an edition may be extant in the Martin Bodmer Library.[2] Further, Oberempt adduces evidence to suggest that the source of *Arthur* was a fifteenth-century French print, not the 1514 print proposed by Blake; accepting Blake's idea that *Huon* and *Arthur* were completed before 1520, he suggests that *Arthur* may be the earlier work. To this debate Morgan (1974) contributes the information that the revised STC will date the early print of *Huon* as ca. 1515 and the first extant editions of *Arthur* as 1560?.

Examining the plot of *Arthur*, Morgan admires "its comprehensiveness and its artful construction," but concludes that it "carries no great burden of meaning" (p. 376). The most significant artistic accomplishment of the romance, Morgan shows, is its "precise and delicate delineations of social situations" (p. 384). Oberempt (1974) complements Morgan's work by demonstrating that Berners frequently writes in a more elevated style than he found in his source, thereby diminishing the mimetic effect and enhancing "the courtly ceremony that is half-hidden in the background" of the French source (p. 197). Interestingly, both of these persuasive studies recall Schlauch's observations about *Arthur*.

From this survey we can see that while some important ground has been broken and some important beginnings have been made, much more remains to be done. More than a decade ago Hornstein (1971) wrote an essay describing in detail the state of Middle English romance studies and setting forth desiderata. Most of what she said in that essay about the need for further studies is, alas, still pertinent, especially in regard to the prose romances. Students of these romances are still faced with "the absence of *modern*, well-edited and well-indexed editions of French, German, and Latin medieval texts—works of literature and works of criticism—which are basic to a study of the English romances" (p. 59). Grinberg (1975) and Oberempt (1976) attest to the difficulties of establishing the sources, respectively, of *The Three Kings' Sons* and *Arthur of Lyttell Brytayne* and, therefore, of comparing the English works to their sources in order to determine their originality. The absence of a critical edition of the French Prose *Merlin* means that the student of the English Prose *Merlin* must rely on the classification of the manuscripts of the French work done by Mead (1899) more than eighty years ago.

Also lacking are "*modern*, well-edited and well-indexed editions" of the English prose romances themselves. Apart from Kurvinen (1969), Moe (1977), and the work of dissertation writers, there has been no new edition of a prose romance published in the past half-century. Indeed, some of the romances—including *Kynge Appolyn* and *The Dystruccyon of Iherusalem*—have never been edited. *Robert the Deuyll*, *Virgilius*, *Arthur of Lyttell Brytayne*, *Olyuer of Castylle*, and *Helyas, Knyght of the Swanne* are accessible only in editions prepared for a general audience in the nineteenth century. *The Three Kings' Sons*, the Prose *Alexander*, *Melusine*, *The Sege of Thebes*, *The Sege of Troy*, and *King Arthur* are available in editions that seem to approach an acceptable scholarly standard, but these editions lack critical apparatus that would facilitate further study of the works.

We have at least a general idea of the audience for the romances printed by Caxton and Wynkyn de Worde, but we are still very much in the dark about the audience for the other romances. A possible means to enlightenment is to study the forms in which the romances are preserved, as can be seen in two instances in which we know who owned manuscripts containing prose romances. The unique text of the Prose *Alexander* is preserved in the well-known Lincoln Cathedral MS 91, which was copied by Robert Thornton of East Newton, a member of the minor gentry in northern Yorkshire. From recent investigations into the manuscripts, life, and milieu of Robert Thornton (Brewer and Owen 1977; Keiser 1979, 1983), we have learned that the scribe who found the *Alexander* worthy of preservation for himself and his family was a man of limited education, modest means, considerable piety, with esteem for the written word—a man who in many ways reflects the interests and ambitions of his social milieu. *Ponthus* appears in a manuscript that belonged to some member of the Hopton family, which also had its origins in the Yorkshire gentry. As the Hoptons were more prosperous and, consequently, more active than the Thorntons, we have available more information about them, which has been examined at length by Colin Richmond (1981). What we learn from this information is that, given a necessary adjustment of scale on account of their prosperity, the Hoptons as a whole had interests and ambitions not so very different from those of Robert Thornton.

Other aspects of the romances, such as their didacticism, may provide clues about the nature of the audience for which they were intended and, thus, about the ways in which they reflect the values and beliefs of their age. Looking again at *Ponthus* and *Alexander*, we see that in many respects the spirit that informs these romances is very like that which informs the *Instructions to His Son* written by Peter Idley, a member of the Oxford gentry and a contemporary of the Hoptons and the Thorntons. Aside from the entertainment that *Ponthus* and *Alexander* provided, there can be no doubt that a considerable part of their appeal was the guidance that they offer in both social etiquette and morality. Fortune, that appropriately besetting concern of this age of ambition, is a central theme of *Alexander*, and its lesson, "alway thynke on the laste ende" (Westlake 1913, p. 55), is one that Peter Idley also delivers, "This day alyeve, to-morow in thy grave" (D'Evelyn 1935, p. 91). In *Ponthus* the instruction is no less pointed. The hero is a model of humility and piety, who regularly reminds us that "in the mercy of Gode is all" and that "we oughte mo to love our saules then our bodyes that be mortall, and from day to day drawen to an ende" (Mather 1897, pp. 16, 76). Near the conclusion of the work Ponthus delivers a lecture on proper conduct to his cousin-german Pollides, who is about to become king of England (it is not surprising that Hoccleve's *De regimine principum* precedes *Ponthus* in the Hopton book), and he touches on such subjects as loyalty to one's wife and generosity to the poor, which were dear to the heart of Peter Idley and doubtless to the heart of whichever Hopton commissioned the manuscript.

Melusine, following the tradition of mothers in romance at least from the time of the first Perceval story, twice delivers lectures filled with practical advice, often echoing Peter Idley's instructions, to sons about to depart in search of adventure. Elsewhere in *Melusine* we find frequent use of the language of land law, which reminds us of another preoccupation of the gentry, reflected in Peter Idley's advice that his son learn as much as he can about the law and Agnes Paston's exhortation to her son Edmund that he learn the law in order to defend the family's interests. Indeed, the ease with which the author of *Melusine* uses this language when, for instance, Anthony gives the king of Anssay directions for endowing a priory—"and ye shal endowe & empossesse them with rentes & reuenue conuenable for theire lyuyng & for their successours for euermore" (Donald 1895, p. 210)—indicates a thorough familiarity with it, such as we might find in a clerk accustomed to writing deeds and charters. Certainly, he expects his readers to be familiar with it too and impressed with the air of authority that it imparts.

Clearly, this question of who formed the audience of the prose romances demands further investigation. Comparing the instruction embedded in the romances with that set forth in contemporary courtesy books and books of nurture may help us to appreciate the spirit of the romances and to understand more fully the meaning and delight they would have had for their contemporary audience.

In a similar and more obvious vein, we need to reconsider and explore at greater length the traditional notions about the chivalric ideal as it is portrayed in the prose romances. Students of medieval literature and history have long been under the spell of the great Johan Huizinga, whose influence has been transmitted in such important works as those by Kilgour (1937) and Ferguson (1960). The titles of these books provide a clear indication of the theses they explore— principally, that in the late Middle Ages chivalry had declined from its early days of vigor, that it was merely an outmoded ideal, which had little to do with contemporary life or indeed with warfare. "As chivalric pastimes and symbols came to be removed from the practical realm, the ludic motive became predominant," as one of Huizinga's spiritual grandchildren wrote recently (Bornstein 1975, p. 20).

This traditional view of the decline of chivalry has been subjected to intense scrutiny by several students of later medieval culture in the past decade. The historical studies that have so far come out of this reevaluation stress a continuity of the chivalric ideal from the twelfth century until well into the sixteenth, with a steady adaptation by the English and French nobility to suit changing political conditions and thus to keep it alive and vigorous. Typical of the newly emerging view is this corrective to the notion that the chivalric display of the later Middle Ages was a mere playing with illusion: "The Dukes of Burgundy and René of Anjou were skilled masters of theatre, but their political ambitions were not frivolous. They understood how to make a marriage between ostentatious cultivation of chivalry and the service of their own ends. Chivalry was something that they as secular princes could exploit, not because it was an enjoyable game, but because it was an ideal with largely secular foundations . . . which was still taken seriously by a very important sector of people" (Keen 1977, pp. 16–17). To the evidence, marshaled by Kilgour in particular, of contemporary complaints about the decline of chivalry in the later Middle Ages, these scholars retort that similar complaints are to be found in writings of the twelfth century, that from its beginnings the habit of chivalry was to look to the past for its models, that "the contrast between the degeneracy of modern knighthood and its antique vigor came to be repeated so often as to suggest that it became a *topos*" (Keen 1977, p. 6). (For additional studies in this vein, see Keen 1976 and Vale 1981.)

The relevance of this revised view of late medieval chivalry for students of literature is made clear in Larry Benson's book-length study of Malory. Arguing that "a taste for realism . . . and an admiration for romance chivalry apparently complemented each other," Benson demonstrates that the *Morte Darthur* "reflect[s] the real chivalry of the time, heightened and idealized but based firmly enough on reality that the gentlemen for whom Malory wrote could recognize the contours and many of the actual details of the chivalric life of their own day" (1976, pp. 137, 139). That this idea may hold true in the case of other prose romances is suggested by an analysis of the *pas d'armes* in *King Ponthus*, in which Benson shows that what may seem "the most fantastic episode in the whole romance . . . is in some ways the most realistic" (p. 183). The value of this approach for a wide range of chivalric literature in the late Middle Ages is argued forcefully and persuasively in a volume of essays edited by Benson and John Leyerle (1980). While only one essay in the volume ("Fidelity, Suffering and Humor in *Paris and Vienne*" by W. T. Cotton) treats a prose romance, all the others deserve, for both their substance and their methods, the careful attention of any prospective students of the romance.

The nature and influence of Burgundian chivalry, which, as a result of the current revisionism, are being reevaluated, are topics of great importance for the student of Middle English prose romances. The role of Caxton as an importer of Burgundian literary tastes has been demonstrated by Blake (1969) and Bornstein (1976). In addition, Kipling (1977) has argued that Burgundian tastes and ideals were cultivated by Henry VII more seriously and more thoroughly than by Edward IV, in part owing to the influence of the Woodvilles at his court. Kipling singles out Lord Berners as successor to the Woodville Burgundians in carrying on the Burgundian tradition at the Tudor court.

The humanists' debate over the concept of nobility certainly made its way from Burgundy to England and probably had some effect on the history of the prose romance. Willard (1969) has delineated the sources and terms of the debate, which had its ultimate origins in Italian humanism, and she has demonstrated the interest in it at the court of Burgundy in the mid-fifteenth century. (Vale 1981, pp. 14–32, further develops the latter point.) From Burgundy the debate made its way to England, like many of the romances, at least in part through the offices of William Caxton. The topic was clearly of interest to the English author-translators of the prose romances, in which the question of whether birth or virtue is the source of nobility frequently assumes importance, especially when the central heroes are in disguise or are temporarily dispossessed of their noble positions, as in *Ponthus*, *Melusine*, *Valentine and Orson*, and *The Three Kings' Sons*. In the last work the concept of nobility is of the utmost importance, for not only are the sons in disguise, but each has chosen to test his nobility through virtuous chivalric action despite the objections of parents beset by concern for their son's safety.

Narrative technique is yet another and obvious area for further study of the English prose romances, for which we have two useful, though very different, models. L. D. Benson (1976) has shown that a straightforward narrative structure with self-contained episodes is characteristic of the Middle English romances, whose authors often chose to unravel the *entrelacement* of the French sources and to develop their narratives along a direct line. Benson's detailed discussion of the English narrative style and its influence on Malory points an important direction for studies of other prose romances. Wittig (1977) makes use of continental criticism to examine the construction of a group of English verse romances. While not entirely satisfactory, Wittig's study is a significant attempt to subject these works to a structuralist analysis, and, though she seems to imply the contrary, it would appear that the conventional, episodic structure in the prose romances makes them fit subjects for similar analysis.

In the romances the quality of narrative technique varies greatly. In *Arthur of Lyttell Brytayne*, for example, we find a very adroit handling of the narrative, in the Prose *Alexander* and *The Three Kings' Sons* a very competent performance. In others we find less success; the author of *Melusine* sometimes struggles clumsily to get from one episode to another, while Henry Watson all too frequently (following his source) gives long and apparently unnecessary summaries of preceding action in *Valentine and Orson*. In this area of study, which is virtually untouched, comparison of the romances with their French sources and, in some cases, with earlier English versions in verse is necessary to get a true sense of the narrative skill among the authors and to show how they continued the tradition of their English predecessors.

Finally, we come to the need for studies of the prose style in the romances, an area in which so little work has been done that I am hard pressed to find models.

The pioneering efforts of Workman (1940) on fifteenth-century translations and of Schlauch (1950, 1952) on Chaucerian prose remain important and useful seminal studies, suggesting ways to approach the analysis of later medieval English prose. Elsewhere, as I noted above, Schlauch (1963) offers valuable, if brief, insights into the stylistic accomplishments (or lack of them) in several prose romances. Book-length studies of Malory by Field (1971) and Lambert (1975), each admirable in its own way, suggest approaches that, with some modifications, might be useful in examining the prose romances. Indeed, both Field and Lambert do subject brief portions of some of the prose romances under discussion here to stylistic analysis, though usually in a way that emphasizes their shortcomings as compared to Malory's achievements. The only attempt at an extended stylistic analysis of any of these romances is by Oberempt (1974) who, building upon some important foundations laid by the study of Caxton's prose by Blake (1968), considers the accomplishments of Lord Berners's prose in *Arthur of Lyttell Brytayne*.

The prose style—more accurately perhaps, styles—of the romances is a cultivated taste, whose cultivation requires some considerable patience. (At times one is ready to cry out with Gertrude, "More matter with less art.") Still, there are rewards, however hard-won they may be. Lord Berners, unquestionably the best prose writer among the romancers, provides frequent delights with his elegance and wit. The author of *The Three Kings' Sons* demands admiration for an ability to write with lucidity and directness in an even, firm, idiomatic style which, though without any peaks, rarely falters. The Prose *Alexander*, a remarkably skillful piece of writing, especially in view of its early date, contains some very impressive feats of balance, such as this self-assured passage in which Darius reevaluates his original, derogatory opinion of the hero: "'I see wele,' quoþ he, 'þat he, this Alexander, þat gase thus abowte werrayand, waxeþ gretly in wirchipe, and aywhare whare he comme3 he hase þe victory. I wende he hadd bene a theeffe & a robbour, þat hadde went till cuntre3 þat ere wayke & feble, and durst no3te agayne-stande hym, & robbed þam and spoyled þam. Bot now, I see wele, he es a doghty man of Armes, & a noble werrayour'" (Westlake 1913, p. 36). The author of *Melusine*, despite a tendency to overload his prose with doublets, can at times achieve some very powerful effects in his monologues and dialogues, especially in the scenes leading up to the separation of Melusine and Raymondin. While these speeches do not lend themselves to quotation out of context, an earlier remark by Raymondin, in response to a scolding by the earl of Poitier for marrying a woman of unknown lineage, illustrates the power of the author's prose: "'My lord,' said Raymondyn, 'sith it suffyseth me as therof, ye oughte wel to be playsed, For I take no wyf that shall brawle or stryue with you / but only with me / and I alone shall bere eyther joye or sorowe for it, after that it shall please to god'" (Donald 1895, p. 49). Even such uneven hackwork as Henry Watson's *Valentine and Orson* often impresses with its vigor and charm, as in this passage in which the bear takes the infant Orson to her cave:

> The Beer that had taken one of the chyldren of Bellyssant, deuoured it not, but bare it in to his cauerne that was profounde and obscure. In the whiche was foure younge Beers strong and puyssaunt. The Beer caste the chylde amonge hys whelpes to be eaten, but God that neuer forgeteth his frendes shewed an euydent myracle. For the younge Beeres dydde it no harme, but with theyr roughe pawes strooked it softelye. When the Beer sawe that her lytle whelpes would not deuoure it, she was right amorous of the chylde (so much) that she kepte it and gaue it souke a hole yeare. (Dickson 1937, pp 37–38)

Although their straining for effects sometimes detracts from their accomplishments, one frequently finds oneself looking with admiration and interest at the efforts of these prose writers to master the new medium, adapting it to the needs of their narrative and to the demands of rhetoric and decorum.

NOTES

1. The best and best known of the prose romances, those of Malory and Caxton, are beyond the purview of this chapter and receive only incidental attention here.
2. Katherine F. Pantzer of the Houghton Library has informed me that the Bodmer Library copy was examined by F. S. Ferguson at the Ham House sale at Sotheby's in 1938. As a result of his testimony that it was produced from the same typesetting as the edition set for R. Redbourne by William Copland and now dated 1560?, the revised STC will list the Bodmer copy as "A variant, omitting colophon," published by W. Copland, and also dated 1560?. For arguments concerning the dates of editions of another work, *Robert the Devil*, see Sajavaara (1979).

BIBLIOGRAPHY

The following list of Middle English prose romances, arranged chronologically, is intended to be used in conjunction with the first volume of *Manual of the Writings in Middle English, 1050–1500* (Severs 1967). For works discussed in that volume I have provided the entry number in parentheses following the date. For works in manuscripts not discussed in the *Manual* I have provided manuscript information. For all printed works I have provided STC numbers and publication information as these appear (or will appear) in the revised STC.

PRIMARY SOURCES

KING ARTHUR, 1400–1425

BL MS Harley 24, fols. 38b–51a
BL MS Harley 53, fols. 43b–44b

THE PROSE *ALEXANDER*, 1400–1450 (67)

KING PONTHUS AND THE FAIR SIDONE, 1400–1450 (4)

THE SEGE OF TROY, 1425–1450 (76)

THE SEGE OF THEBES, CA. 1450 (77)

THE PROSE *MERLIN*, CA. 1450 (19)

THE SEGE OF JERUSALEME, 1450–1500

MS Porkington 10, fols. 157b–184a

THE DUBLIN *ALEXANDER EPITOME*, 1450–1500 (70)

IPOMEDON, CA. 1460 (102)

THE CLEVELAND *SIEGE OF JERUSALEM*, CA. 1470 (107)

THE THREE KINGS' SONS, CA. 1500 (108)

MELUSINE, CA. 1500 (109)

W. de Worde, 1510 (STC 14648)

ROBERT THE DEUYLL (93)

W. de Worde, 1500? (STC 21070)
W. de Worde, 1517? (STC 21071)
R. Pynson?, 1510? (STC 21071.5)

HENRY WATSON?, *KYNGE PONTHUS* (4)

W. de Worde, 1509? (STC 20107)
R. Pynson?, ca. 1510 (STC 20107.5, formerly 23435a)
W. de Worde, 1511 (STC 20108)

ROBERT COPLAND, *KYNGE APPOLYN OF THYRE* (95)

W. de Worde, 1510 (STC 708.5)

HENRY WATSON, *VALENTINE AND ORSON* (103)

W. de Worde, ca. 1510 (STC 24571.3)
W. Copland, ca. 1555 (STC 24571.7, formerly 24572a)
W. Copland, ca. 1565 (STC 24572)
T. Purfoot, 1637 (STC 24573)

ROBERT COPLAND, *HELYAS, KNYGHT OF THE SWANNE* (63)

W. de Worde, 1512 (STC 7571)
W. Copland, 1550? (STC 7572)

THE DYSTRUCCYON OF IHERUSALEM BY VASPAZYAN AND TYTUS

R. Pynson, 1513? (STC 14517)
W. de Worde, 1510? (STC 14518)
W. de Worde, 1528 (STC 14519)

WILLIAM OF PALERMO (11)

W. de Worde, ca. 1515 (STC 25707.5)

JOHN BOURCHIER, LORD BERNERS, *HUON OF BURDEUX*, 1500–1515

J. Notary, ca. 1515 (STC 13998.5)
T. Purfoot, 1601 (STC 13999)

DE SANCTO JOSEPH (42)

R. Pynson, 1516 (STC 4602)

HENRY WATSON, *OLYUER OF CASTYLLE*

W. de Worde, 1518 (STC 18808)

VIRGILIUS

Anwarpe, J. Doesborcke, 1518? (STC 24828)
W. Copland, 1562? (STC 24829)

JOSEPH OF ARAMATHY (42)

R. Pynson, 1520 (STC 14807)

JOHN BOURCHIER, LORD BERNERS, *ARTHUR OF LYTTELL BRYTAYNE*, 1500–1520 (44)

W. Copland for R. Redbourne, 1560? (STC 807)
W. Copland, 1560? (STC 807.5)
T. East, 1582 (STC 808)

SECONDARY SOURCES

Ashbee, E. W., ed. (1870) *The Romance of "Kynge Apollyn of Thyre."* London: privately printed.

Benson, C. David (1971) "Chaucer's Influence on the Prose 'Sege of Troy.'" *N&Q*, 261, 127–130.

Benson, Larry D. (1976) *Malory's Morte Darthur.* Cambridge, Mass. and London: Harvard University Press.

Benson, Larry D., and Leyerle, John (1980) *Chivalric Literature*. Kalamazoo: Western Michigan University Press; Toronto: University of Toronto Press.

Blake, N. F. (1968) "Caxton and Courtly Style." *E&S*, ns 21, 29–45.

———— (1969) *Caxton and His World*. London: André Deutsch.

———— (1971) "Lord Berners: A Survey," *M&H*, ns 2, 119–132.

Böddeker, K. (1874) "Die Geschichte des Königs Arthur nach einer Chronik des Britischen Museums." *Archiv*, 52, 1–32.

Bornstein, Diane (1975) *Mirrors of Courtesy*. Hamden, Conn.: Archon Books.

———— (1976) "William Caxton's Chivalric Romances and the Burgundian Renaissance in England." *ES*, 57, 1–10.

Brewer, Derek, and Owen, A. E. B. (1977) Introductions to *The Thornton Manuscript*, rev. ed. London: Scolar Press.

D'Evelyn, Charlotte, ed. (1935) *Peter Idley's Instructions to His Son*. Boston: Modern Language Association of America.

Dickson, Arthur (1937) *Valentine and Orson*. EETS, os 204.

Donald, A. K., ed. (1895) *Melusine*. EETS, es 68.

Ferguson, Arthur B. (1960) *The Indian Summer of English Chivalry*. Durham, N.C.: Duke University Press.

Field, P. J. C. (1971) *Romance and Chronicle*. Bloomington and London: Indiana University Press.

Flynn, Elizabeth A. (1968) "The Marvelous Element in the Middle English Alexander Romances." *DAI*, 29, 1866A.

Gradon, Pamela (1971) *Form and Style in Early English Literature*. London: Methuen.

Graves, R. E., ed. (1898) *The History of Oliver of Castile*. London: Blades, East, and Blades.

Grinberg, Henry (1969) "*The Three Kings' Sons*: Notes and Critical Commentary." *DAI*, 30, 280A–281A.

———— (1975) "*The Three Kings' Sons* and *Les Trois Fils de Rois*: Manuscript and Textual Filiation in an Anglo-Burgundian Romance." *RPh*, 28, 521–529.

Guddat-Figge, Gisela (1976) *Catalogue of Manuscripts Containing Middle English Romances*. Munich: W. Fink.

Hornstein, Lillian H. (1971) "Middle English Romances." In *Recent Middle English Scholarship and Criticism*, edited by J. Burke Severs, pp. 55–95. Pittsburgh: Duquesne University Press.

Hume, Kathryn (1974) "The Formal Nature of Middle English Romance." *PQ*, 53, 158–180.

Keen, Maurice (1976) "Chivalry, Nobility, and the Man-at-Arms." *War, Literature, and Politics in the Late Middle Ages*, edited by C. T. Allmand. Liverpool: Liverpool University Press.

———— (1977) "Huizinga, Kilgour and the Decline of Chivalry." *M&H*, ns 8, 1–20.

Keiser, George R. (1979) "Lincoln Cathedral Library MS. 91: Life and Milieu of the Scribe." *SB*, 32, 158–179.

———— (1983) "More Light on the Life and Milieu of Robert Thornton." *SB*, 36, 111–119.

Kilgour, R. L. (1937) *The Decline of Chivalry as Shown in the French Literature of the Late Middle Ages.* Cambridge, Mass.: Harvard University Press.

Kipling, Gordon (1977) *The Triumph of Honour.* Leiden: Leiden University Press.

Kurvinen, Auvo, ed. (1969) *The Siege of Jerusalem in Prose.* Helsinki: Société Néophilologique.

Lagorio, Valerie M. (1971) "The Evolving Legend of St. Joseph of Glastonbury." *Speculum,* 46, 209–231.

Lambert, Mark (1975) *Style and Vision in Le Morte Darthur.* New Haven and London: Yale University Press.

Lombardo, S. D. (1977) "Wynkyn de Worde and His 1512 Edition of *Helyas, Knyght of the Swanne.*" *DAI,* 37, 5107A.

Mather, F. J. (1897) "King Ponthus and the Faire Sidone," *PMLA,* 12, i–150.

Mead, W. E. (1899) "Outlines of the History of the Legend of Merlin." In *Merlin,* edited by H. B. Wheatley. EETS, es 10.

Michel, G. E. (1979) "The Folio and Quarto Editions of *Arthur of Little Britain.*" *Revue belge de philologie et d' histoire,* 57, 664–666.

Mitchell, G. E. (1969) "A Textual Edition on Modern Principles of *Arthur of Little Britain,* A Romance of the Sixteenth Century Translated by John Bourchier, Lord Berners." *DAI,* 29, 4463A.

———— (1972) "The Sixteenth Century Editions of 'Arthur of Little Britain.'" *Revue belge de philologie et d' histoire,* 50, 793–795.

Moe, Phyllis (1960) "Cleveland Manuscript W q901.92–C468 and the Veronica Legend." *BNYPL,* 70, 459–470.

————, ed. (1977) *The ME Prose Translation of Roger D'Argenteuil's Bible en François.* Heidelberg: Carl Winter.

Morgan, Alice B. (1974) "'Honor & Right' in *Arthur of Little Britain.*" In *The Learned and the Lewed,* edited by L. D. Benson, pp. 371–384. Cambridge, Mass.: Harvard University Press.

Neeson, Marjorie, C. S. J. (1972) "*The Prose Alexander*: A Critical Edition." *DAI,* 32, 4012A.

Nolan, Robert J. (1971) "An Introduction to the English Version of *Mélusine*: A Medieval Prose Romance." *DAI,* 31, 5370A.

Oberempt, Kenneth J. (1974) "Lord Berners' Translation of *Artus de la Petite Bretagne.*" *M&H,* ns 5, 191–199.

———— (1976) "Lord Berners' *Arthur of Lyttell Brytayne*: Its Date of Composition and French Source." *NM,* 77, 241–252.

O'Dell, Sterg (1954) *A Chronological List of Prose Fiction in English Printed in England and Other Countries, 1475–1640.* Cambridge, Mass.: The Technology Press of M.I.T.

Pearsall, Derek (1976) "The English Romance in the Fifteenth Century." *E&S,* ns 29, 53–83.

Richmond, Colin (1981) *John Hopton: A Fifteenth Century Suffolk Gentleman.* Cambridge: Cambridge University Press.

Richmond, Velma B. (1975) *The Popularity of Middle English Romances.* Bowling Green: Bowling Green University Popular Press.

Rigsby, Robert K. (1980) "'In Fourme of a Serpent fro the Nauel Dounward': The Literary Function of the Anima in *Melusine*." *DAI*, 40, 5436A.

Sajavaara, Kari (1962) "The Two English Prose Texts of *Robert the Devil* Printed by Wynkyn de Worde." *NM*, 63, 62–68.

——— (1979) "The Sixteenth-Century Versions of *Robert the Devil*." *NM*, 80, 335–347.

Scanlon, Paul A. (1977) "Pre-Elizabethan Prose Romances in English." *Cahiers elisabéthains*, 12, 1–20.

——— (1978) "A Checklist of Prose Romances in English, 1474–1603." *Library*, 5th ser. 33, 143–152.

Schlauch, Margaret (1950) "Chaucer's Prose Rhythms." *PMLA*, 65, 568–589.

——— (1952) "Chaucer's Colloquial English, Its Structural Traits." *PMLA*, 67, 1103–1116.

——— (1963) *Antecedents of the English Novel, 1400–1600*. Warsaw: PWN–Polish Scientific Publishers; London: Oxford University Press.

Schmidt, A. V. C., and Jacobs, Nicholas (1980) *Medieval English Romances*. London: Hodder and Stoughton.

Severs, J. Burke, ed. (1967) *A Manual of the Writings in Middle English, 1050–1500*, vol. 1. New Haven: Connecticut Academy of Arts and Sciences.

Taylor, Ann R. (1969) "*Grant Translateur*: The Life and Translations of John Bourchier, Second Baron Berners." *DAI*, 30, 343A.

Thoms, William J., ed. (1858) *Early English Prose Romances*. London: Routledge.

Vale, Malcolm (1981) *War and Literature*. Athens: University of Georgia Press.

Westlake, J. S., ed. (1913) *The Prose Life of Alexander*. EETS, os 143.

Willard, C. C. (1969) "The Concept of True Nobility at the Burgundian Court." *Studies in the Renaissance*, 14, 33–48.

Wittig, Susan (1978) *Stylistic and Narrative Structures in the Middle English Romances*. Austin and London: University of Texas Press.

Workman, S. K. (1940) *Fifteenth Century Translation as an Influence on English Prose*. Princeton: Princeton University Press.

CHAPTER 14

Chaucer

Traugott Lawler

The facts of Chaucer's life are well known and easily available. The records on which our knowledge of it is based are collected in Crow and Olson (1966). As *House of Fame* 652–660 attests, Chaucer seems to have worked at his writing throughout his active career of civil service. His diplomatic journeys abroad may have a special bearing on his prose. The skill at languages which presumably both qualified him for the journeys and was sharpened by them has its literary counterpart in his translations. Such works as *Boece* (*Bo*) and *Melibee* (*Mel*), both set in Italy, may have first come to his attention there, and are perhaps to be included among the Italian influences on him. And both have a clear political dimension; *Mel* in particular implies reflection on the contentious people and events he came so regularly into contact with.

The only prose piece definitely dated is the *Treatise on the Astrolabe* (*Astr*), which gives a calculation for a date in 1391, and was presumably in process in that year. Both because of its subject and because it is mentioned in the *Legend of Good Women*, scholars universally agree in assigning *Bo* to the *Troilus* period, that is, 1381–1385, and usually early in it. The dating of *Mel* and the *Parson's Tale* (*ParsT*) is quite uncertain, especially since both contain themes, ideas, and even phrases echoed elsewhere in the *Canterbury Tales* (*CT*). Those who dislike them put them early; in view of the echoes, most now put them in the Canterbury period (1386–1400), but before the poems that echo them; Patterson (1978), who believes *ParsT* echoes the other tales, puts it late in that period. The Retraction is presumably latest of all.

No one reads Chaucer's prose without feeling the absence of the skill and aplomb of the poetry; nevertheless, there have been many attempts both to define its general characteristics, and to distinguish the style of each piece from the others. Krapp (1915, pp. 4–10) offers a representative, though more than usually sympathetic, general treatment. He found *Bo* full of "crudity and awkwardness, even

at times obscurity, of expression," *Mel* and *ParsT* "freely and idiomatically written"; he assigns the difference to "how much easier Chaucer found it to translate
from French than from Latin." *Astr* is also "simple and much more idiomatic"
than *Bo*, and in the originally composed introduction to *Astr* Krapp finds "the
quaint simplicity and humor which constitute the main charm of [Chaucer's]
verse." Krapp noted in *Bo* some alliteration and occasional rhyme. Others have
found less to praise, and distinctions little worth making. Fifty years later, in a
book comparable to Krapp's, Ian Gordon (1966) devotes one paragraph to Chaucer (p. 54), and spends it all on abuse.

The idea of seeking verse effects in the prose was taken up by Baum (1946).
Several scholars had noted that some phrases at the opening of *Mel* could be scan-
ned as blank verse; Baum reports that further experiments show that such "metrical prose" is present everywhere in *Mel*, though less densely than at the start; and
comparison with *Bo* and *ParsT* shows that "nowhere has Chaucer indulged his ear
. . . with metrical insets in his prose as he has in the Melibeus" (p. 41). Baum
draws attention to *House of Fame* 623, in which the eagle says that Chaucer has
composed "in ryme, or elles in cadence," and argues that "cadence" means merely
prose, not rhythmical prose.

These brief suggestions form the background for the two major articles to
date on Chaucer's prose style, both by Margaret Schlauch. In "Chaucer's Prose
Rhythms" (1950), she argued that "cadence" meant the Latin *cursus*, of which,
with certain English modifications, Chaucer made constant use. She found such
cadence dense in *Mel* and *Bo*, moderate in *ParsT* and *Astr*, and almost nonexis-
tent in the Retraction and the introduction to *Astr*. In "The Art of Chaucer's
Prose" (1966), Schlauch again attempts to discover several levels of style, this
time on the basis of syntax, rhetoric, and diction rather than rhythm: "the plain
style of scientific exposition" (p. 143) in *Astr* (and in *The Equatorie of the Planetis*); the "heightened style of homiletic discourse" (p. 148) in *ParsT*; and the
"eloquent style" (p. 153) of *Mel* and *Bo*, achieved again by "heightening," and
chiefly, apparently, by *cursus*. She finds more decorative and emotional effects in
Mel and *Bo*, but emphasizes that Chaucer did not overuse them; his prose is
"laudably moderate" and occasionally the eloquence is "truly moving" (161–162).
Schlauch's studies are ambitious, literate, appreciative, and frequently perceptive; but her larger theses give way to vagueness at crucial points.

Jefferson's earlier analysis (1917) of the style of *Bo* (pp. 25–46), because it is
so thorough and because he alludes regularly to *ParsT* and *Mel*, is in effect an
analysis of Chaucer's prose style itself. He isolates several characteristic traits of
sentence structure, none particularly admirable, and various devices "to secure
dignity of style." He regards *Bo* (and, by implication, the others) as very much
"the translation of a poet."

A recent attempt to survey all of Chaucer's prose is Elliott's chapter "I speke in prose" (1974, pp. 132–180). He treats such matters as syntax, sentence structure, stylistic range, and above all diction in *Astr*, *ParsT*, *Bo*, and *Mel* in turn, occasionally generalizing about the prose as a whole. He is good at singling out moments of strikingly effective expression. His account of *Bo* is notably sympathetic, including a neat analysis of how Chaucer used Jean de Meun; he considers it "invaluable practice-ground" for Chaucer, and offers the convincing example of neologisms in "un-," of which *Bo* is full, and which, as is well known, account for some of the most moving lines in *Troilus*. I find his analysis of the "poetic prose" that appears from time to time in *Bo* sound, and his general reference to "controlled rhythm" or "characteristic English rhythms" wiser than Schlauch's too-specific theory of *cursus*. I have not seen Wilson's dissertation (1956), which draws distinctions among the four works largely on the basis of sentence structure and use of rhetorical devices, and relates Chaucer's prose to fourteenth-century prose at large. Mersand (1937) gives percentages of Romance words in the prose works and notes that "Chaucer's prose is richer in Romance words than his poetry" (p. 112).

A specific analysis in the Schlauch tradition is Bornstein's of *Mel* (1978); she provides a taxonomy of Chaucer's changes from his French original, and argues that they constitute "deliberate cultivation" of the "style clergial, the style of the chancellory of the Middle Ages . . . transferred to vernacular writing" (pp. 240, 237). Her lists and analyses are useful, but she makes little attempt to establish the "style clergial" as a firm and definite category, and can cite only one medieval use of the phrase. Bornstein made no use of Geissman's dissertation (1969), a less sympathetic but also more disinterested and more wide-ranging analysis of Chaucer's translations; Geissman makes much clearer than Bornstein Chaucer's constant attempts to achieve absolute clarity by expressing words understood in the French, by putting nouns for pronouns, in general by "consciously striving for greater definiteness, greater concreteness, greater clarity" (p. 116). Though Bornstein claims that "reliance on the passive voice" (p. 237) is a feature of the clergial style, she ignores that feature in her analysis; Geissman makes the extremely interesting finding that translating active verbs as passives is a characteristic of Chaucer's style, and suggests that it is "in part responsible for the heaviness and indirectness of his prose" (p. 140). Among other comparative stylistic judgments, one may mention Jefferson's finding "more finish" in sentence structure in *Mel* than in either *ParsT* or *Bo* (1917, p. 30), and Palomo's finding more careful high style in *Mel* than in *Bo* (1974). In view of the singular lack of consensus, either in description or evaluation, these general studies have produced, it is perhaps no wonder that many readers have shied away from specific formulations, contenting themselves, like Norton-Smith, with sensing that "the style, cursus, and construction of paragraphs" of *ParsT* are "quite unlike" those of *Mel* (1974, p. 156). We still need an accurate comparative stylistic analysis.

The ultimate basis of *Mel* is Albertano of Brescia's *Liber Consolationis et Consilii* (1246); sometime after 1336, Renaud de Louens produced a fairly free French adaptation entitled *Livre de Mellibee et Prudence*, which Chaucer translated, apparently without reference to the Latin. The translation is close, as Severs's edition of the French (1941) makes clear, and yet not as absolutely faithful "phrase for phrase" as Severs asserts (p. 564): there is a certain freedom of syntax and phraseology, as Bornstein (1978) and Geissman (1969) have shown. Chaucer has also added a few proverbs; thus he does indeed "varie as in [his] speche" and "telle somwhat moore / Of proverbes," as he says in his prologue that he did.

Probably the most common opinion of *Mel* is that it is dull, and part of an elaborate literary joke: Chaucer starts the exquisite *Thopas*, is cut off by the Host who does not understand it, then amuses us by assigning to himself, the only real poet on the pilgrimage, this dreary piece of prose. This opinion knows no time or place. Close to it are arguments derived from the "dramatic theory" of the *CT*. This theory, with its emphasis on the tellers at the expense of the tales, has had a bad effect on the understanding of *Mel*, deflecting attention from what it says. Thus even Ruggiers (1965), who takes *Mel* seriously as the "counsel of reason" (p. 21), sees it ultimately from an ironic point of view, as the product of Chaucer the pilgrim, an artificial self, "an artist concerned with prudence and morality" (p. 22), as against the ironic artist of experience that Chaucer really is. (See, however, Ruggiers 1973 and 1979, where he abandons the ironic reading.) Miskimin (1975) expresses this point of view most extremely, arguing that *Mel* is as parodic as *Thopas*, and like it directs irony at "the impotent poet who is unable to master his art" (p. 118). I shall not bother instancing the "joke" or "irony" or "parody" reading further, but treat instead critics and scholars who have made the sensible assumption that Chaucer would not have either translated *Mel* or put it in the *CT* if he despised it.

Tatlock (1907), expanding on a suggestion of Skeat's, argued that the tale was intended first for the Man of Law, and put forward an eloquent argument for taking it seriously. He pointed out, as had Koeppel (1891), that some material from it is used in the Merchant's Tale. Hotson (1921, p. 430) argued that the tale was "a political tract designed to dissuade John of Gaunt from launching on the invasion of Castile in 1386" (a theory expanded further by Williams 1965, who sees John of Gaunt everywhere in Chaucer's work). In 1940, Lawrence published the first full attempt to take *Mel* seriously on its own terms. He found that the allegory "creaks . . . at the end," since to make amends and submit is "not the way the world, the flesh, and the devil usually treat a sinner" (p. 105), and that the insistence on peace is a much more striking feature of the tale than the allegory; he relates it to the history of the struggle to replace private vengeance with public punishment, and also to contemporary English conditions, though less specifically than Hotson. He argued that with *Mel* and *Thopas* Chaucer "solved very neatly the problem of not seeming to compete himself for the dinner," and "secured that happy mingling of the grave and gay which is so clear a part of his design" (p. 109); *Mel* has also in it the "germ" of the discussion of marriage, a point Lawrence had made long before. Stillwell (1944) filled out Lawrence's historical remarks by relating the tale to various events and conditions of the late 1380s and 1390s.

Robertson (1963, p. 369) argued that the prologue means that the sentence of *Melibee* is the sentence of the *CT*, but made no attempt to analyze the allegory in detail. Those who have have not been convincing. Strohm (1967) argued that the allegorical point is that we should make our peace with God, and trust God, not self-defense, to preserve us; but this fails to account for the emphasis the tale places on acting prudently on one's own behalf. Wimsatt (1970, pp. 104–105) treated it as an "allegory of the intellect," prudence being a function of Melibee's mind, but he fails to take the emphasis on forgiveness into account. Huppé (1964) called it an "allegory of Penance and . . . of the Lord's Prayer: forgive us our sins as we forgive those who have sinned against us" (p. 239); but Huppé does not ask whether one can forgive one's own sins, or forgive the world, the flesh, and the devil. The fact is that, despite intermittent "tropological" or "analogical" applications, *Mel* does not work as a consistent formal allegory. Owen (1973) has treated the allegory with fine penetration, arguing that medieval allegory does not in fact require "a constant and exact relationship between the literal detail and the meaning it points to" (p. 275). Owen's essay is to my mind far superior to anything else that anyone has ever written on *Mel*. He reads the allegory flexibly; he sees its relevance not merely to the theme of forgiveness in the *CT*, but to Chaucer's characteristic amiability, tolerance, and confidence, and to the problems still caused by men's and nations' urge to act violently. He reaches the happy insight that in finding within the evil that seemed at first to be without, the tale focuses on the same deep human issue as *Oedipus* and *Hamlet* do. Owen's insight applies to *Mel* criticism: those who focus on artistic issues, or confine the thematic importance of the tale to relations among Fragment VII tales or the *CT* at large, are similarly opting for externalism; Owen forces us, as Prudence forces Melibee, to look inside, at how the tale works out its complex meanings. The result is a far larger sense of its outward relevance than has ever been granted it.

Christmas (1969) associates *Mel* with the genre of *consolatio* and argues for various kinds of thematic relevance to the other tales of Fragment VII, especially *Sir Thopas*, since both Melibee and Thopas are "vengeful and contemptuous of women." Matthews (1972) relates it to the tales that exploit the "latent comic ingredients" in subjects such as women, maistrie, counsel, pedantry; Chaucer saw "substantial germs of humor" in the story as a struggle for maistrie. Ruggiers

(1973) associates *Mel* with comedy in a different way, by opposing its ideas on fortune and providence to those in the Monk's tragedies; as against his helpless complaints against the "unwar strook" of fortune, Prudence urges "rational self-control and Christian resignation to a Providence that works out its own justice" (p. 97). Ruggiers suggests the possibility that *Mel* like *ParsT* "was intended to exert a pervasive influence throughout the structure" of the *CT*, *Mel* exhibiting "the prudence of this world," *ParsT* "the prudence of the other life" (p. 99n). This notion receives more extended treatment in Ruggiers (1979) and also in Lawler (1980).

Modern study of *ParsT* begins with Koeppel (1891) and Spies (1913), who put aside forever the questions of authorship and interpolation. Koeppel identified all the echoes or parallel passages between the verse tales and *ParsT*; Spies showed it was unified, and by Chaucer. Both thought it early, and thought the two parts ill-joined; Patterson (1978) has shown that the view of *ParsT* as "journeyman work completed early" still largely holds. Since 1913 there has been intermittent work on sources and genre; much critical writing, especially since 1955, on the question whether *ParsT* is serious, and a suitable ending to the *CT*; and, in the last decade, brilliant and important work by two scholars which represents clear steps forward.

For a summary of early work on sources, see Petersen (1901), Dempster (1941), and Robinson (1957). There is a general agreement that the material on the deadly sins bears some relation to the *Summa de Viciis* of Gulielmus Peraldus (before 1261), and the material on penitence to Raymund of Pennaforte's *Summa Poenitentiae* (before 1243). But Pfander (1936) points out that these works were so vast, so widely influential, and in many details so different that the relation is quite distant. A major issue has been whether Chaucer joined the two parts or found them together in his source, and another has been whether the language of the source or sources was Latin or French, or both. Pfander and Petersen both posited an immediate source in a manual yet unidentified, which Petersen thought was in Latin, Pfander in French. Pfander thought "the whole set-up" of *ParsT* "French in tone and manner," and that "it is merely a translation" (1936, p. 257). Robinson points out in his notes a few words and phrases that seem to imply a French original, and Elliott (1974) adds lexical, linguistic, and syntactic evidence. Opinions about the date are all relative. Skeat and Koeppel put it early, Koch and Ten Brink put it late (see Robinson 1957, p. 766).

Recent work has brought us closer to Chaucer's sources. Hazleton (1960) adduced parallels to the *Moralium Dogma Philosophorum* (twelfth century), but Wenzel (1971) showed that that work could only have been a remote source; he himself adduces convincing evidence that the *remedia* or corrective virtues for each of the deadly sins come from a thirteenth-century work on the virtues beginning "Postquam dictum est de morbis ipsius anime." In 1974 Wenzel brought us a step farther by analyzing two late-thirteenth-century abbreviations of Peraldus's *Summa*, one a shortening of the other (the longer begins "Quoniam ut ait sapiens," the shorter "Primo videndum est"), both made in England. He showed that either or both are consistently nearer than Peraldus to Chaucer's treatment of the sins: in the sequence of the sins, in wording, and in certain material that they share with it that is not only not in Peraldus but not in any treatise known to Wenzel, whose knowledge of the literature on the capital sins is unparalleled. Wenzel ends his second article by expressing the hope that "perhaps a lucky find will yet reveal a treatise or a sermon which actually combines material on the sins from *Quoniam* with material on the virtues from *Postquam*, and perhaps even with material on penance from Pennaforte or a similarly derived work; though the suggestion that Chaucer may have combined these ingredients himself still remains a distinct possibility."

The other recent student of *ParsT* who has taken our understanding to a new level is Patterson. Based on a wide-ranging study of penitential materials, and taking advantage of Wenzel's findings, Patterson's 1978 essay is the first in the history of Chaucer criticism to take *ParsT* fully seriously, that is, to regard it as wrought by Chaucer, with clear artistic and moral purpose. He first establishes its genre (not a sermon but a manual for penitents, and of a rare kind that eschews larger matters of faith for a rigorous attention to penance only), and shows that it is cohesive, intellectually ambitious, balanced, and orderly; its order itself expresses its fundamental metaphysic of a sacramentally ordered universe. Patterson's assumption that *ParsT* matters to us and mattered to Chaucer enables him to distinguish between carefully wrought and more careless parts, something no one else ever seems to have thought of doing. The well-known verbal echoes, which Koeppel (1891) thought evidence for an early date, Patterson finds mostly conventional: they prove nothing. From a residue of four distinctive and substantial echoes, he then argues that in every case "the lines of influence are from the tales to the *ParsT* and that the *ParsT* was therefore composed after them" (p. 369). (Actually, this is the conclusion reached in the brief special studies of Sister Mariella 1938 and of Owen 1956.) Nor are the echoes pointed at individual pilgrims. The tale is intentionally general: it is "not irrelevant to what precedes it, but it is no more relevant to that than to anything else" (p. 370). Finally, to apply it retrospectively to the tales is to ignore its devaluation of them and of tale-telling itself: it is "not a fulfillment to the tales but an alternative" (p. 379), and "there seems no reason not to accept the obvious biographical implication that it was [Chaucer's] last work" (p. 380). Implicitly throughout, and explicitly in a footnote on page 340, Patterson accepts Wenzel's suggestion that Chaucer may have combined the separate sources himself. But Patterson does more than accept the possibility of that; he alternately assumes it and tries to prove it. To his assumption, and to the crucial portion of his essay in which he tries to show that the other tales predate *ParsT*, one may object that he never considers the possibility that Chaucer translated someone else's combination of the sources. There is no reason why even the four "distinctive" echoes might not have come to the tales from a work Chaucer was translating. On the other hand, one of Patterson's most telling arguments is that three of the four passages occur where Chaucer is revising material in the source in which he seems to have prior knowledge and interest: marriage, oathmaking, gentilesse. This certainly suggests that Chaucer, not someone else, was doing the revising. One wishes that Patterson had provided the evidence for his statement on page 361 that "a comparison [with the sources] shows that there are substantial alterations in just three areas"—the three just mentioned. This is surprising; how does it square, say, with Wenzel's acknowledgment that *Postquam* on remedies has nothing in common with Chaucer's remedy for pride? But Patterson's essay remains a superior piece of scholarship, perhaps in part because it raises as well as answers questions.

Many writers besides Patterson have treated the genre of *ParsT*. Chapman (1928), Myers (1967, 1972), and Delasanta (1978) relate it to the sermon, and writers on Chaucer habitually call it a sermon; though others who have written on Chaucer's use of sermon material, such as Gallick (1975), Shain (1955), and, by silence, Wenzel (1976) have reservations. Pfander (1936), in an important article, related *ParsT* to manuals of religious instruction, and Pantin (1955) and Robertson (1963) have related it to penitential manuals for laymen. Donaldson called it a priest's manual (1975, p. 1112). Tupper (1914) tried to argue that the seven deadly sins were an organizing principle for the *CT*, but he was silenced by Lowes (1915). Critical writing perhaps takes its modern beginning from Baldwin (1955), whose defense of the seriousness of *ParsT*, and its aptness to the large scheme of the *CT*, has proven seminal. Some representative (and quite different) extensions of Baldwin's insistence on the positive thematic relevance of *ParsT* include Huppé (1964), the fullest detailed explicator of the allegorical approach sketched by Baldwin and given full weight with reference to medieval aesthetics by Robertson (1963); Leyerle (1976), who insists that the Parson "knits up" the themes of sex, food, gold, and death but "does not resolve the complexities" (p. 112); Howard (1976), who argues that *ParsT* provides an essential contrast with the rest, which "makes the work complete" (p. 386); Lawler (1980), who offers the fullest treatment of *ParsT* in a book on the *CT* since Baldwin—he stresses its positive values and by exploring various relations with the tales argues that *ParsT* provides effective closure to the work (an opinion he is by no means the first to have expressed); and Delasanta (1968, 1970, 1978) and Peck (1967), who have laid particular emphasis on the framework of *ParsT*, the Prologue and Retraction. Ruggiers (1979) provides a brief but grave and thoughtful statement of how both *Mel* and *ParsT* convey Chaucer's moral purpose. Finlayson (1971) and Allen (1973), in contrast, strive to see dramatic irony at the Parson's expense. Kaske (1975) argues that the Parson's opinions on human destiny and on marriage are set against those of the Knight and Franklin, respectively, providing a "double perspective" of "experience" on their side and "authority" on his, between which Chaucer does not choose; she interprets changes from *Postquam* in the direction of severity on sex as indicating that Chaucer purposely portrayed the Parson as an extremist in this matter. Others have continued to view *ParsT* as simply an ignorable aberration, for example, Donaldson (1970) and all who in fact ignore it, or to emphasize its difference from the rest of the *CT*, for example, Norton-Smith (1974, pp. 154–159). Jordan (1967) acknowledges the great difference in purpose and subject, but finds a "deep kinship in structural predispositions" (p. 237); he analyzes the structure carefully. His remark that "the presence of the Parson's Tale at the end of the *Canterbury Tales* is more important than the tale itself" (p. 230) perhaps sums up perfectly the opinion of the many who are persuaded by Baldwin's scheme but still unable to pay serious attention to the tale.

The Retraction need not detain us long. It stands as a refutation of the commonly made statement that the introduction to *Astr* is the only piece of original prose we have from Chaucer; short though it is, it deserves stylistic analysis, which as far as I know it has never received. There is hardly a book on the *CT* or on Chaucer in which the author does not express his opinion of the Retraction. Opinions are conveniently reviewed by James Gordon (1961), who concludes his review with the acute remark that "part of the genius of Chaucer was his farsighted intimation of new and greatly enlarged possibilities for the literary artist. What he lacked was a theory to sustain him." Sayce (1971), in the most informative treatment to date, offers convincing evidence that the Retraction is full of the topoi of prologues and epilogues; its language and ideas are quite conventional. This leads her to conclude that "far from being a personal confession of literary sin, it is a conventional structural motif which is used as a vehicle for the expression of opposing aesthetic standpoints" (pp. 245–246). She argues that various phrases are humorously allusive or ironic. Her interpretation of her findings has been contested by Delasanta (1978); and Patterson's finding that *ParsT* is late and carefully wrought leads him to assert at the end of his article that both the tale and the Retraction are "a part of the fitting shape of the Christian life . . . an inevitable and gratifying process of change and fulfillment."

Scholarship on *Bo* has been dominated by the question of Chaucer's sources: what Latin text he used, how far he relied on Jean de Meun's French translation, and where he got his glosses. Though Skeat (1900) and others have pronounced differently, no one who has ever studied the matter has doubted that Chaucer made constant use of Jean de Meun. Liddell (1895) concluded from excerpts that Chaucer used both French and Latin, and offered many citations from the French in the notes to his Globe text. Lowes (1917) confirmed Liddell's opinion further, as did Jefferson (1917). Dedeck-Héry (1937) made this sure conclusion surer by listing Jean's errors that Chaucer repeated; he (Dedeck-Héry 1944) found the fragmentary MS Bodley Rawlinson 641 the closest MS to Chaucer's putative copy text of the French, Besançon 434 and Rennes 2435 the closest complete MSS; and he (Dedeck-Héry 1952) edited Jean's text. It was actually Dedeck-Héry's widow who published this; in an introduction, A. J. Denomy asserts that "the editor deliberately included all variants, however minute, to provide the machinery for one day determining the definite Latin manuscript and French commentary that Chaucer used in his translation" (p. 166).

Meanwhile, Liddell (1897) claimed that Chaucer had drawn his glosses from the commentary ascribed to Aquinas. But Petersen (1903) showed that he used Trivet, not Pseudo-Aquinas; since Trivet incorporated Pseudo-Aquinas into his commentary, 300 of the 370 glosses are common to both—but the other 70 are Trivet's (as for 5 glosses that are in Pseudo-Aquinas and not in Trivet, she supposes that Chaucer's MS of Trivet had marginal glosses in it). She suggests that Chaucer used a MS like Paris BN Latin 18424, which has Boethius, Jean de Meun, and Trivet together. Petersen did not study the French text beyond one meter; Jefferson (1917), studying more French but by no means all, concluded that Chaucer's gloss has two sources, Trivet and the French glosses embedded in Jean's translation; a complete comparison of Chaucer's translation with Jean's "would probably show that the influence of the latter on his glosses was greater than Miss Petersen supposes" (p. 15). Lowes (1917) hints at a similar conclusion.

Still no one had studied the French text completely. When Dedeck-Héry did that in 1937, he confirmed that many of the glosses come from Jean, but also that many do not, and supposed that Chaucer had used a Latin commentary such as Trivet's or William of Conches's. Meanwhile Silk in his 1930 dissertation (Silk 1970), which Dedeck-Héry did not know, had studied the entire matter, and was the first to examine Jean de Meun whole. He concluded that the relation to Jean is varying and complex, but stressed how often Chaucer does not depend on Jean for his glosses. He instead championed the cause of Trivet: Chaucer was "chiefly dependent" on him; it is "unsafe to conclude that Chaucer has borrowed a given gloss from Jean de Meun until it is ascertained that he cannot have borrowed it from Trivet" (p. 32). Chaucer followed a text of Boethius he could only have found in Trivet; indeed Cambridge University Library (CUL) MS Ii. 3. 21, which contains one of the best texts of *Bo*, along with a Latin text that incorporates some Trivet and is regularly accompanied in the margins by the Trivet commentary (plus occasional others), is "a copy of the Latin text from which [Chaucer] worked" (pp. 42–43n).

Kottler (1955, 1971) disputed Silk's conclusions. On the basis of partial collation of forty-five MSS, he showed that what Silk thought were readings unique to the text that accompanies the Trivet commentary were actually available elsewhere, and common rather to what he calls a "vulgate text" of Boethius, established by the fourteenth century. Chaucer's Latin text has a "tendency to accept" the new readings, though it need not have all of them. Since many putative Chaucer readings that Silk thought unique to CUL Ii. 3. 21 in fact are not, Silk's confident conclusion that it was a copy of Chaucer's exemplar cannot be upheld; nevertheless some of those readings *are* unique to it, and it remains the closest MS to Chaucer yet to be studied. What Kottler's work did was to show that the question of Chaucer's exact relation to Jean, to commentaries, and to Boethius's text itself will not be advanced until we can determine what MS, or at least what kind of MS, he used. No further advance has been made since Kottler.

All this work has incidentally made it clear that Chaucer's errors, once a favorite subject of commentators on *Bo* (e.g., Skeat 1900; Liddell 1897; Jefferson 1917) may very well be due largely to the state of the text he used. Brief disdainful estimates of the style of *Bo* also abound. The most cogent, perhaps, are those that compare "the elegant rendering of Boethian dicta in Chaucer's verse with their fumbling expression in the prose translation" (Fisher 1977, p. 815); see also Stewart (1891), Jefferson (1917), Patch (1935), and Elliott (1974), who says sympathetically that the comparison merely illustrates Chaucer's "growing mastery of English expression," and points out further that the prose is not always bad, "nor is the verse invariably a great step forward" (p. 168). Other work on *Bo* can be briefly reviewed. Koch (1922) offers a valuable part-by-part analysis of *Bo*, including all certain, probable, and possible places where Chaucer's poetry shows verbal echoes of the translation (for another list of verbal correspondences, arranged, not by *Bo*, but by the poems, see Skeat 1900, pp. xxvii–xxxvii). Science (1923) showed that Walton used Chaucer so closely he can provide textual evidence for the reading *forlinen* at 3p6.50; his edition (1927) gives more extensive evidence of Walton's borrowings. Cline (1928, 1936) associated Chaucer's and Jean de Meun's ideal of translation with the theory of "open" translation of Latin described in the preface to the second version of the Wycliffite Bible. Burnley (1979) gives a brief but instructive analysis of a cluster of Boethian words associated with philosophical stoicism, and of the words Jean and Chaucer used to translate them.

Articles on *Astr* are rare. There is not even a thorough study of the style except for Nagucka's syntactical analysis (1968), which is occasionally revealing about Middle English but in general too given to the algebra of transformational grammar. The general studies of Chaucer's style treated above give shortest shrift to *Astr*; commonly one praises the introduction for its ease and the rest for its straightforwardness. Pintelon (1940) offers seven pages on style (76–82); among his many interesting points is a clear distinction between a style dominated by nouns in Part I and a more flexible verbal style in Part II; and a sharp focus on the way in which, in his "exaggerated explicitness," Chaucer overuses what Pintelon calls "retrospective words" (*this, this same, this foresaide,* etc.) to such a degree that they "tend to blur out the clear contours of each sentence."

Two useful guides for grasping *Astr* are the running paraphrase and explanation provided by Skeat at the bottom of the page in both his editions (1872, 1900), and Gunther's translation (1929) of MS CUL Dd. 3. 53 and reproduction of all of its sixty-two diagrams. One can supplement these diagrams by xeroxing Skeat's drawings of the different parts and constructing a paper astrolabe. The very good photographs of actual instruments in Gunther (1923) are also useful, as are Brae's (1870) and Skeat's notes. Hogben (1943) gives instructions for making and using an astrolabe; and North (1974) gives excellent diagrams and lucid explanations of how the astrolabe manages to represent the celestial sphere on a plane surface.

The fullest attempt to relate the knowledge of astronomical calculation Chaucer reveals in *Astr* to his poetry is North (1969). He makes incidental use of *Astr* at numerous places in his article, and also discusses the dates used or implied in it, and its missing parts, concluding that Chaucer may still have been working on the text in 1393, but probably never provided any of the three parts promised in the introduction but not extant, and seems to have abandoned astronomy after 1393 or 1394. Bennett's chapter "The Men of Merton" (1974) provides a wealth of useful background for understanding Chaucer's knowledge of astronomy. North's article raises the interesting possibility that Chaucer found astrology plausible for a while but eventually became disillusioned with it—a possibility not entertained by Wood (1970) when he argues that *Astr* proves that Chaucer put no faith whatever in astrology. In general Wood's book is an attempt to place Chaucer's use of astrology in an ironic light, as an unorthodox and inadequate system of belief; he cites *Astr* only rarely. Wood and North dismiss Curry (1960) as completely inadequate on astronomy and astrology. Manzalaoui (1974) offers an excellent general treatment of Chaucer and science.

Elmquist (1941) reminds us that several statements in the introduction suggest that Chaucer had in mind a wider audience than little Lewis his son, and makes the appealing suggestion that *Astr* was "intended from the beginning as a literary translation (similar to the *Boece*), but was cast into the conventional form of a piece of private instruction" (p. 534). It would be nice to know how conventional such a form was. Cross (1955) takes the opposite tack, isolating the stylistic features that carry through Chaucer's elementary pedagogical intentions; it is useful to have these identified, but some question remains whether they are necessarily peculiar to a text for a small child; and Cross does not face the question of how hard some of the material is.

Chaucer's principal source was the second part of Messahala's *Compositio et Operatio Astrolabii*, printed in Skeat (1872) and translated by Gunther (1929), who also prints a facsimile of MS CUL Ii. 3.3. Harvey (1935) showed that while Messahala provided the outline, Chaucer ransacked Sacrobosco's *De Sphaera* for many of his details, and digested both. Veazie (1940) gives a sneering but well-informed account of the contents and history of Sacrobosco's book. Harvey promises further proof that Daniel of Morley's *Liber de Naturis Inferiorum et Superiorum* is also a source, but that proof never appeared. As against Robinson's conjecture that "the exact compilation, based upon Messahala, that Chaucer used" (1957, p. 545) may yet be found, Masi (1975) prefers to assume that the arrangement of conclusions in Part II is Chaucer's own. But as against the ordinary supposition that Chaucer made his adjustments to Messahala's substance on the basis of his own understanding of and experience with the instrument, Masi argues that Chaucer actually knew the collection of astronomical treatises in MS Bodley Selden Supra 78, which was in England in the fourteenth century, and made use of marginal notes in it. Eisner (1976) showed that Chaucer used Nicholas of Lynn's calendar, not in *Astr* where he mentions it, but for several dates in the *CT*; he demonstrates clearly that Chaucer knew this text well, and is generally informative, both here and in his subsequent edition of the Calendar (1980), on Chaucer's knowledge and use of astronomy.

In 1955, Derek Price published an edition of an English treatise he names *The Equatorie of the Planetis*, written in 1392 and surviving in Cambridge Peterhouse College 75; the edition includes a linguistic analysis by R. M. Wilson. The work is an account of how to make and use an instrument for computing geometrically the position of the sun, moon, Mercury, Venus, Mars, Jupiter, and Saturn. Price puts forward cautiously the theory that the MS is an author's holograph of a free adaptation of a Latin work—and that its author is Chaucer. Chaucer's name appears in the MS in the phrase "radix Chaucer" for 1392; that is, the root date for all the calculations in the work is 1392, and this is called "Chaucer's root." Furthermore, *Astr* is quoted; the handwriting is identical to that of the one record in the Public Record Office probably in Chaucer's hand; the language and style are in accord with those of *Astr* and of the best MSS of Chaucer's work in general; and a treatise on the *equatorium* is a more fitting companion piece to *Astr* than the "theoretical" portions promised in the introduction to *Astr*; the dates 1391 and 1392 used in the text fit *Astr* nicely. This theory has been received even more cautiously than it was put forth, but not tested further except briefly by Herdan (1956). Fisher included the *Equatorie* in his edition of the works (1977).

The manuscripts of the *CT* were studied by Manly and Rickert (M-R) (1940). *Mel* is in most *CT* MSS, and in three MSS without anything else of the *CT*, and in two with one other tale: MS Pepys 2006 includes in a collection *Mel* and *ParsT* only of the *CT* (M-R 1:406ff., 2:371ff., 7:200ff.). Manly and Rickert find the manuscript situation of *Mel* unusually complex. They suggest (2:388) that like the number of MSS this is evidence of popularity, and also that Chaucer allowed an early version of the translation to circulate. Hartung's dissertation (1957) takes issue with some of Manly's findings; he concludes, like Manly, but for the reason that of two textual traditions one is closer to the French, that Chaucer made the translation, circulated it, and then later revised it.

ParsT is in fewer MSS, but only because it is at the end, and thus was lost in some MSS and never reached in those that were left incomplete by their scribes. Of those that have it, many have gaps, especially at the end, due to lost leaves. Nevertheless there are ample full witnesses, and Manly and Rickert found the textual evidence "overwhelming" for including *ParsT* among the *CT* (2:454ff., 4:359ff., 8:175ff.). The MSS fall, despite inconsistencies, into two main lines of descent; the interesting textual fact here is that the archetype demonstrably contained errors, errors that "Chaucer would certainly have corrected if he had seen them" (2:455). This led Manly to the theory that some literary executor, not Chaucer, combined the two parts (Manly 1931; M-R 2:455; the further essay promised here never appeared). The Retraction occurs in 29 MSS, but is in "practically all the MSS that have the whole of PsT"; this fact and the persistence of the same textual relations cause Manly and Rickert to conclude that the Retraction "was in the ancestor of all the MSS of PsT," but does not lead them to conclude either that Chaucer wrote it or that he intended *ParsT* and the Retraction for the *CT* (2:471–472).

Bo exists in eleven MSS and two early prints, by Caxton (1477–1478) and Thynne (1532). Its treatment by modern editors has not been as careful as that of Chaucer's poems and the prose of the *CT*. Robinson (1957) lists ten MSS. He did not know of Cambridge Pembroke College 215, nor of a fragment recently discovered at the University of Missouri (see Pace and Voigts 1979); on the other hand, his Phillips 9472 is a ghost. Liddell edited the text for the Globe Chaucer (1898), classifying the known MSS into two groups, and collating them all. Other editors have been content to choose either of the two major MSS, CUL Ii. 1. 38 (C1) or CUL Ii. 3. 21 (C2) as their base and collate it with the other and/or with one or two other witnesses. Skeat (1900) used C2, collating BL Add. 10340 (A1), Caxton, and Thynne. Liddell's base was C1, as was Robinson's; Robinson (1957) collated C2, A1, Caxton, and Thynne. Fisher (1977) used C2 only, but drew readings from C1, A1, and Caxton on the basis of the reports of other editors. It must be admitted that the MSS do not vary greatly.

Pintelon (1940) describes twenty-three MSS of *Astr*, four quite fragmentary and few quite complete, confirming Skeat's division, on the basis of the order of conclusions in Part II, into two classes. (Skeat's two editions are virtually identical: 1900 omits some introductory matter, describes four additional MSS, and presents a normalized text and fewer textual notes; the explanatory notes are little changed.) Skeat identified five virtually complete "first-class" MSS, basing his text on CUL Dd. 3. 53, which contains corrections he thought possibly by Chaucer. Brae (1870) had employed three MSS of the second class. Liddell in the Globe edition further classified Skeat's five, choosing Bodley 619 as closest to the original, and the basis for his text, and collating nine others. Robinson also based his text on Bodley 619, comparing it with Skeat's and Brae's editions and the *editio princeps* of Thynne, and reporting variants also from three MSS now in the United States. Of these, two were unknown to Pintelon, and so would raise his total to twenty-five. Robinson reports Derek Price's opinion that these two "perhaps [represent] a missing link between the two main groups" (1957, p. 921). Pintelon printed a facsimile of the Brussels MS, collating the introduction with the sixteen other MSS known to him that contain it. Fisher, like Skeat, used CUL Dd. 3. 53, collating also Bodley 619 and two others. North (1969) reports on a further MS, Aberdeen University Library 123, but says it is "unlikely to augment our knowledge of Chaucer" (p. 432n). Sigmund Eisner is editing *Astr* for the Variorum Chaucer, and John Reidy for the third edition of Robinson. In a private communication, Professor Eisner informs me that several more MSS have been located, though no printed notice of them has yet appeared.

One hesitates to call for further scholarship on *Mel* and *ParsT*, since the last twenty years have produced such a spate of interpretation, especially of *ParsT*. Nevertheless, we still need, following the lead of Ruggiers (1979), Owen (1973), and Patterson (1978), to think more imaginatively and sympathetically about the role the two prose tales play in the scheme of the *CT*. Perhaps the primary need is for editors and teachers to stop deceiving students into thinking they can know the *CT* without reading the prose tales. *ParsT* has prompted far more and far better critical writing than *Mel*; one would like to see the balanced righted somewhat. Some remarks by Ruggiers (1979) suggest to me that a careful study of the medieval concept of prudence—a more dignified and commodious concept than ours—would be very useful.

Some final identification of the most proximate source of *ParsT* is a great desideratum; but even without that it will perhaps be possible to prove, as Patterson has gone far toward doing, that Chaucer did not translate *ParsT* but wrote it. This would open the way for a study of Chaucer's art of prose composition as opposed to mere style. A similar effort of source study and close analysis may similarly vindicate the originality of *Astr*, though surely *Astr* will never reveal the same range of skill and affectiveness as *ParsT* seems capable of revealing.

As far as I know, no one has ever taken up Hartung's theory (1957) that the textual tradition of *Mel* indicates that there were two versions. There are a few teasing places in *Bo* that just might indicate something similar. It is possible that study of these may bring us closer to an understanding of Chaucer's habits of composition, and shed light on the apparent revision of *Troilus* and the *Legend of Good Women*. Indeed, there is material available for a major general study of revision in medieval texts which would be of value to paleographers and editors as well as to students of literature. It is curious that evidence of revision in medieval texts is almost always assessed ad hoc, rather than in the light of some general theory or overview of revision in a scribal culture.

Clearly the major need in *Bo* scholarship is a new text, and more information on French and Latin MSS and commentaries. These are of course related needs, since most textual problems cannot be solved without reference to French, Latin, and the commentaries. Ralph Hanna III and I are preparing a new edition from all the MSS for the forthcoming third edition of Robinson; we hope to advance knowledge of MS Besançon 434 of Jean de Meun (of which Dedeck-Héry 1952 ed. does *not* list all the variants), and of Chaucer's use of Trivet and other commentaries, but we have relied on the Latin text in CUL Ii. 3. 21. A new edition from all MSS is also being prepared by Jerome Taylor for the Variorum Chaucer; in a talk at the annual meeting of the MLA in 1979, Taylor voiced agreement with Petersen's opinion (1903) that Chaucer had a single MS that contained both Latin and French texts and a commentary. The Chaucer Library (see Kirby 1981) lists editions in progress of a French text (in fact, Besançon 434) by Richard Dwyer and a Latin text by Barnett Kottler. When Edmund Silk died in 1981, he left a typescript of an edition from six representative MSS of Trivet's commentary, which Eleanor Silk is hoping to publish. In short, in a few years we may well know *Bo* and its background much better than we do now. Chaucer's use of Jean de Meun still needs further study. Silk's contention that it varied is perhaps misleading; more likely Chaucer used Jean steadily as a model for syntax and diction, and accepted most of his additions, but at the same time always made sure to translate the Latin accurately. The old notion that Chaucer was a poor Latinist is unlikely to be sustained. But it would be better to get off the question of how exactly he used Jean and move to other areas of potentially greater interest. We need further analysis of the relation of *Bo* to Chaucer's poems; it is conceivable that such analysis may upset the received notion of the date of *Bo*: Lowes suggested in 1917 that Chaucer may well have made at least some of the poetic passages directly from the French. It is conceivable also that a more exact knowledge of what lies behind *Bo*, providing as it does a clear control, may help solve textual and interpretative problems in the poetry by giving us a sounder sense of Chaucer's usage. It is likely also to provide a sounder basis for deciding whether Chaucer used cursus or not—if anyone still thinks he did. And Walton, Usk, and others who demonstrably used *Bo* might yield valuable textual information.

Just as the primary need for *ParsT* and *Mel* is that teachers and students should read them and take them seriously, the primary need for both *Astr* and the *Equatorie* is simply that more Chaucerians read them and understand them. We simply do not do justice to Chaucer's astonishingly capacious mind if we ignore its scientific side. Price's theory of the authorship of the *Equatorie* needs a definitive response; after thirty years, it is high time that the skeptics either challenge it decisively or accept it. The diagrams in the *Astr* MSS have never had careful study, of which two kinds are needed. The first is redrawing, probably of those in CUL Dd. 3. 53, according to the best modern graphic techniques, accompanied by explanations, in order to make them do what they were meant to do, illuminate the text. The second is a comparative study of all the diagrams in all the MSS with the aim of deepening our knowledge of the MSS relationships as well as of the diagrams. Further work on the sources is needed (Masi is editing Messahala for the Chaucer Library, as he and Kirby report). Finally, Skeat's claim that the corrections in CUL Dd. 3. 53 are Chaucer's own needs to be vindicated or disproved; these too have a bearing on the large question of revision. Some or all of these desiderata are, of course, likely to be satisfied or allayed by the two editions now in progress.

BIBLIOGRAPHY

Since there are so many extant manuscripts of Chaucer's works, and information on them is readily available, they are not listed here. The editions by Liddell (1898), Manly-Rickert (1940), Pintelon (1940), Price (1955), and Skeat (1872, 1900) give information on manuscripts; corrections are given in the text of the chapter. For the *Canterbury Tales*, see especially Manly-Rickert (1940) and Mc-Cormick (1933); and for *Melibee*, Hartung (1957). For full bibliography of Chaucer studies, consult the following (all of which devote a special section to manuscripts):

Baird, Lorrayne Y. (1977) *A Bibliography of Chaucer, 1964–1973*. Boston: G. K. Hall.

Crawford, William R. (1967) *Bibliography of Chaucer, 1954–63*. Seattle and London: University of Washington Press.

Griffith, Dudley David (1955) *Bibliography of Chaucer, 1908–53*. Seattle: University of Washington Press.

Hammond, Eleanor Prescott (1908) *Chaucer: A Bibliographical Manual*. New York: Macmillan. Repr. (1933) New York: Peter Smith.

PRIMARY WORKS

Brae, Andrew E., ed. (1870) *The Treatise on the Astrolabe of Geoffrey Chaucer*. London: J. R. Smith.

Bryan, W. F., and Dempster, Germaine, eds. (1941) *Sources and Analogues of Chaucer's Canterbury Tales*. Chicago: University of Chicago Press.

Crow, Martin M., and Olson, Clair C., eds. (1966) *Chaucer Life Records*. Oxford: Clarendon Press.

Dedeck-Héry, V. L., ed. (1952) "Boethius' *De Consolatione* by Jean de Meun." *MS*, 14, 165–275.

Dempster, Germaine (1941) "The Parson's Tale." In Bryan and Dempster (1941), pp. 723–760.

Donaldson, E. Talbot, ed. (1975) *Chaucer's Poetry: An Anthology for the Modern Reader*. 2d ed. New York: Ronald Press.

Eisner, Sigmund, ed. (1980) *The Kalendarium of Nicholas of Lynn*. The Chaucer Library 2. Athens: University of Georgia Press.

Fisher, John Hurt, ed. (1977) *The Complete Poetry and Prose of Geoffrey Chaucer*. New York: Holt, Rinehart and Winston.

Gunther, R. T. (1923) *Early Science in Oxford*, vol. 2. Oxford: Printed for the Subscribers.

――― (1929) *Early Science in Oxford*, vol. 5. Oxford: Printed for the Subscribers.

Liddell, Mark H., ed. (1898) "Boece" and "A Treatise on the Astrolabe." In *The Works of*

Geoffrey Chaucer, edited by A. W. Pollard, H. F. Heath, M. H. Liddell, and W. S. McCormick. London: Macmillan. (The Globe Chaucer)

Manly, John Matthews, and Rickert, Edith, eds. (1940) *The Text of the Canterbury Tales, Studied on the Basis of All Known Manuscripts*. 8 vols. Chicago and London: University of Chicago Press.

Pace, George B., and Voigts, Linda E. (1979) "A 'Boece' Fragment." *SAC*, 1, 143–150.

Petersen, Kate O. (1901) *The Sources of the Parson's Tale*. Boston: Ginn.

Pintelon, P. (1940) *Chaucer's Treatise on the Astrolabe: MS 4862–4869 of the Royal Library in Brussels*. Antwerp: De Sikkel.

Price, Derek J., ed. (1955) *The Equatorie of the Planetis*. Cambridge: Cambridge University Press.

Robinson, F. N., ed. (1957) *The Works of Geoffrey Chaucer*. 2d ed. Boston: Houghton Mifflin.

Science, Mark, ed. (1927) *Boethius: De Consolatione Philosophiae, translated by John Walton*. EETS, os 170.

Severs, J. Burke (1941) "The Tale of Melibeus." In Bryan and Dempster (1941), pp. 560–614.

Silk, Edmund Taite (1970) "Cambridge MS Ii. 3. 21 and the Relation of Chaucer's *Boethius* to Trivet and Jean de Meung." *DAI*, 31, 2355A. (1930 diss.)

Skeat, Walter W., ed. (1872) *A Treatise on the Astrolabe*. EETS, es 16.

———, ed. (1900) *The Complete Works of Geoffrey Chaucer*. 2d ed. 7 vols. Oxford: Oxford University Press.

SECONDARY WORKS

Allen, Judson B. (1973) "The Old Way and the Parson's Way: An Ironic Reading of the Parson's Tale." *JMRS*, 3, 255–271.

Baldwin, Ralph (1955) *The Unity of the Canterbury Tales*. Anglistica 5. Copenhagen: Rosenkilde and Bagger.

Baum, Paull F. (1946) "Chaucer's Metrical Prose." *JEGP*, 45, 38–42.

Bennett, J. A. W. (1974) *Chaucer at Oxford and at Cambridge*. Oxford: Clarendon Press.

Bornstein, Diane (1978) "Chaucer's *Tale of Melibee* as an Example of the *Style Clergial*." *ChauR*, 12, 236–254.

Burnley, J. D. (1979) *Chaucer's Language and the Philosophers' Tradition*. Totowa, N.J.: Rowman and Littlefield.

Chapman, C. O. (1928) "The Parson's Tale: A Mediaeval Sermon." *MLN*, 43, 229–234.

Christmas, Robert A. (1969) "Chaucer's *Tale of Melibee*: Its Tradition and Its Function in Fragment VII of the *Canterbury Tales*." *DA*, 29, 3093A.

Cline, James M. (1928) "A Study in the Prose of Chaucer's Boethius." Ph.D. diss., Princeton University.

——— (1936) "Chaucer and Jean de Meun: De Consolatione Philosophiae." *ELH*, 3, 170–181.

Cross, J. E. (1955) "Teaching Method, 1391: Notes on Chaucer's Astrolabe." *English*, 10, 172–175.

Curry, Walter Clyde (1960) *Chaucer and the Mediaeval Sciences.* 2d ed. London: Allen and Unwin.

Dedeck-Héry, V. L. (1937) "Jean de Meun et Chaucer, traducteurs de la Consolation de Boèce." *PMLA*, 52, 967–991.

—— (1940) "The Manuscripts of the Translation of Boethius' *Consolatio* by Jean de Meung." *Speculum*, 15, 432–443.

—— (1944) "La Boèce de Chaucer et les manuscrits français de la *Consolatio* de J. de Meun." *PMLA*, 59, 18–25.

Delasanta, Rodney (1968) "The Horsemen of the *Canterbury Tales*." *ChauR*, 3, 29–36.

—— (1970) "The Theme of Judgment in the *Canterbury Tales*." *MLQ*, 31, 298–307.

—— (1978) "Penance and Poetry in the *Canterbury Tales*." *PMLA*, 93, 240–247.

Donaldson, E. Talbot (1970) "Medieval Poetry and Medieval Sin." In his *Speaking of Chaucer*, pp. 164–174. London: Athlone Press.

Eisner, Sigmund (1976) "Chaucer's Use of Nicholas of Lynn's Calendar." *E&S*, ns 29, 1–22.

Elliott, Ralph W. V. (1974) *Chaucer's English.* London: André Deutsch.

Elmquist, Karl E. (1941) "An Observation on Chaucer's *Astrolabe*." *MLN*, 56, 530–534.

Finlayson, John (1971) "The Satiric Mode and the Parson's Tale." *ChauR*, 6, 94–116.

Gallick, Susan (1975) "A Look at Chaucer and His Preachers." *Speculum*, 50, 456–476.

Geissman, Erwin (1969) "The Style and Technique of Chaucer's Translations from the French." *DAI*, 30, 320A. (1952 diss.)

Gordon, Ian A. (1966) *The Movement of English Prose.* London: Longmans.

Gordon, James D. (1961) "Chaucer's Retraction: A Review of Opinion." In *Studies in Medieval Literature in Honor of Prof. Albert Croll Baugh*, edited by MacEdward Leach, pp. 81–96. Philadelphia: University of Pennsylvania Press.

Hartung, Albert E. (1957) "A Study of the Textual Affiliations of Chaucer's Melibeus Considered in Its Relation to the French Source." *DA*, 17, 2259–2260.

Harvey, S. W. (1935) "Chaucer's Debt to Sacrobosco." *JEGP*, 34, 34–38.

Hazelton, Richard (1960) "Chaucer's Parson's Tale and the *Moralium Dogma Philosophorum*." *Traditio*, 16, 255–274.

Herdan, G. (1956) "Chaucer's Authorship of *The Equatorie of the Planetis*: The Use of Romance Vocabulary as Evidence." *Language*, 32, 254–259.

Hogben, Lancelot T. (1938) *Science for the Citizen.* New York: Knopf.

Hotson, J. Leslie (1921) "The *Tale of Melibeus* and John of Gaunt." *SP*, 18, 429–452.

Howard, Donald R. (1976) *The Idea of the Canterbury Tales.* Berkeley and Los Angeles: University of California Press.

Huppé, Bernard F. (1964) *A Reading of the Canterbury Tales.* Binghamton: State University of New York Press.

Jefferson, Bernard L. (1917) *Chaucer and the Consolation of Philosophy of Boethius.* Princeton: Princeton University Press.

Jordan, Robert M. (1967) *Chaucer and the Shape of Creation.* Cambridge: Harvard University Press.

Kaske, Carol V. (1975) "Getting around the Parson's Tale: An Alternative to Allegory and Irony." In *Chaucer at Albany*, edited by Rossell Hope Robbins, pp. 147–177. New York: Bert Franklin.

Kirby, Thomas A. (1981) "Chaucer Research, 1980: Report No. 41." *ChauR*, 15, 356–379.

Koch, John (1922) "Chaucers Boethiusübersetzung: ein Beitrag zur Bestimmung der Chronologie seiner Werke." *Anglia*, 46, 1–51.

Koeppel, Emil (1891) "Über das Verhältniss von Chaucers Prosawerken zu seinen Dichtungen, und die Echtheit der Parsons Tale." *Archiv*, 87, 33–54.

Kottler, Barnett (1955) "The Vulgate Tradition of the *Consolatio Philosophiae* in the Fourteenth Century." *MS*, 17, 209–214.

———— (1971) "Chaucer's *Boece* and the Late Medieval Textual Tradition of the *Consolatio Philosophiae*." *DAI*, 31, 6013A–6014A. (1953 diss.)

Krapp, George Philip (1915) *The Rise of English Literary Prose*. New York and London: Oxford University Press.

Lawler, Traugott (1980) *The One and the Many in the Canterbury Tales*. Hamden, Conn.: Archon Books.

Lawrence, William Witherle (1940) "The Tale of Melibeus." In *Essays and Studies in Honor of Carleton Brown*, pp. 100–110. New York: New York University Press. Repr. (1968) as "Chaucer's Tale of Melibeus" in *Chaucer and His Contemporaries: Essays on Medieval Literature and Thought*, edited by Helaine Newstead, pp. 207–217. Greenwich, Conn.: Fawcett.

Leyerle, John (1976) "Thematic Interlace in 'The Canterbury Tales.'" *E&S*, ns 29, 107–121.

Liddell, Mark H. (1895) "Chaucer's Translation of Boece's 'Boke of Comfort.'" *Academy*, 48 (September 21), 227.

———— (1897) "One of Chaucer's Sources." *Nation*, 64 (February 18), 124–125.

Lowes, John Livingston (1915) "Chaucer and the Seven Deadly Sins." *PMLA*, 30, 237–371.

———— (1917) "Chaucer's *Boethius* and Jean de Meun." *RR*, 8, 383–400.

McCormick, Sir William (1933) *The Manuscripts of Chaucer's Canterbury Tales: A Critical Description of Their Contents*. Oxford: Clarendon Press.

Manly, John Matthews (1931) "Tales of the Homeward Journey." *SP*, 28, 613–617.

Manzalaoui, Mahmoud (1974) "Chaucer and Science." In *Geoffrey Chaucer*, edited by D. S. Brewer, pp. 224–261. London: Bell.

Sister Mariella (1938) "The Parson's Tale and the Marriage Group." *MLN*, 53, 251–256.

Masi, Michael (1975) "Chaucer, Messahala, and Bodleian Selden Supra 78." *Manuscripta*, 19, 36–47.

Matthews, Lloyd J. (1972) "The Latent Comic Dimensions of Geoffrey Chaucer's *Tale of Melibee*." *DAI*, 32, 4572A.

Mersand, Joseph (1937) *Chaucer's Romance Vocabulary*. New York: Comet Press.

Miskimin, Alice S. (1975) *The Renaissance Chaucer*. New Haven: Yale University Press.

Myers, Doris E. T. (1967) "The *Artes Praedicandi* and Chaucer's Canterbury Preachers." *DA*, 28, 2215–2216A.

———— (1972) "Justesse rationelle: Le 'Myrie Tale in Prose' de Chaucer." *MA*, 78, 267–286.

Nagucka, Ruta (1968) *The Syntactic Component of Chaucer's Astrolabe.* Zeszyty Naukowe Uniwersytetu Jagiellońskiego 199; Prace Językoznawcze, Zeszyt 23. Cracow: Nakładem Uniwersytetu Jagiellońskiego.

North, J. D. (1969) "Kalenderes Enlumyned Ben They: Some Astronomical Themes in Chaucer," *RES*, ns 20, 129–154; 257–283; 418–444.

———— (1974) "The Astrolabe." *Scientific American*, 230, 96–106.

Norton-Smith, John (1974) *Geoffrey Chaucer.* London and Boston: Routledge and Kegan Paul.

Owen, Charles A., Jr. (1956) "Relationship between the Physician's Tale and the Parson's Tale." *MLN*, 71, 84–87.

———— (1973) "The *Tale of Melibee.*" *ChauR*, 7, 267–280.

Palomo, Dolores (1974) "What Chaucer Really Did to *Le Livre de Melibee.*" *PQ*, 53, 304–320.

Pantin, W. A. (1955) *The English Church in the Fourteenth Century.* Cambridge: Cambridge University Press.

Patch, Howard Rollin (1935) *The Tradition of Boethius: A Study of His Importance in Medieval Culture.* New York: Oxford University Press.

Patterson, Lee W. (1978) "The 'Parson's Tale' and the Quitting of the 'Canterbury Tales.'" *Traditio*, 34, 331–380.

Peck, Russell A. (1967) "Number Symbolism in the Prologue to Chaucer's *Parson's Tale.*" *ES*, 48, 205–215.

Petersen, Kate O. (1903) "Chaucer and Trivet." *PMLA*, 18, 173–193.

Pfander, Homer G. (1936) "Some Medieval Manuals of Religious Instruction in England and Observations on Chaucer's Parson's Tale." *JEGP*, 35, 243–258.

Robertson, D. W., Jr. (1963) *A Preface to Chaucer.* Princeton: Princeton University Press.

Ruggiers, Paul G. (1965) *The Art of the Canterbury Tales.* Madison and Milwaukee: University of Wisconsin Press.

———— (1973) "Notes toward a Theory of Tragedy in Chaucer." *ChauR*, 8, 89–99.

———— (1979) "Serious Chaucer: The *Tale of Melibeus* and the Parson's Tale." In *Chaucerian Problems and Perspectives: Essays Presented to Paul E. Beichner, C.S.C.*, edited by Edward Vasta and Zacharias P. Thundy, pp. 83–94. Notre Dame, Ind. and London: University of Notre Dame Press.

Sayce, Olive (1971) "Chaucer's 'Retractions': The Conclusion of the *Canterbury Tales* and Its Place in Literary Tradition." *MAE*, 40, 230–248.

Schlauch, Margaret (1950) "Chaucer's Prose Rhythms." *PMLA*, 65, 568–589.

———— (1966) "The Art of Chaucer's Prose." In *Chaucer and Chaucerians: Critical Studies in Middle English Literature*, edited by D. S. Brewer, pp. 140–163. London and University, Ala.: University of Alabama Press.

Science, Mark (1923) "A Suggested Correction of the Text of Chaucer's Boethius." *TLS*, March 22, pp. 199–200.

Shain, Charles E. (1955) "Pulpit Rhetoric in Three Canterbury Tales." *MLN*, 70, 235–245.

Spies, Heinrich (1913) "Chaucers religiöse Grundstimmung und die Echtheit der Parson's Tale: eine textkritische Untersuchung." In *Festschrift für Lorenz Morsbach*, edited by F. Holthausen and H. Spies, pp. 626–721. Halle: M. Niemeyer.

Stewart, Hugh Fraser (1891) *Boethius: An Essay*. Edinburgh and London: Blackwood.

Stillwell, Gardiner (1944) "The Political Meaning of Chaucer's *Tale of Melibee*." *Speculum*, 19, 433–444.

Strohm, Paul (1967) "The Allegory of the *Tale of Melibee*." *ChauR*, 2, 32–42.

Tatlock, John S. P. (1907) *The Development and Chronology of Chaucer's Works*. London: Chaucer Society.

Tupper, Frederick (1914) "Chaucer and the Seven Deadly Sins." *PMLA*, 29, 93–128.

Veazie, Walter B. (1940) "Chaucer's Text-Book of Astronomy: Johannes de Sacrobosco." *University of Colorado Studies, Series B, Studies in the Humanities*, 1, 169–182.

Wenzel, Sigfried (1971) "The Source for the 'Remedia' of the Parson's Tale." *Traditio*, 27, 433–453.

—— (1974) "The Source of Chaucer's Seven Deadly Sins." *Traditio*, 30, 351–378.

—— (1976) "Chaucer and the Language of Contemporary Preaching." *SP*, 73, 138–161.

Williams, George G. (1965) *A New View of Chaucer*. Durham, N.C.: Duke University Press.

Wilson, Herman Pledger (1956) "Chaucer as a Prose Writer." *DA*, 16, 2154.

Wimsatt, James I. (1970) *Allegory and Mirror: Tradition and Structure in Middle English Literature*. New York: Pegasus.

Wood, Chauncey (1970) *Chaucer and the Country of the Stars*. Princeton: Princeton University Press.

CHAPTER 15

Medical Prose

Linda Ehrsam Voigts

Medical writing from post-Conquest medieval England survives, for the most part, in fourteenth- and fifteenth-century manuscripts. This considerable body of writing, like other *Fachliteratur*, includes both highly learned and popular, traditional material. The range of texts—or, indeed, any text within the substantial corpus—demands some understanding of medieval medicine, of the larger body of Latin writings and the smaller body of Anglo-Norman medical texts, and of the close connections between prose and verse.

Written medicine is the record of the theory and practice of what was both science and craft, and it must be understood in the context of its use and users. To work with these fourteenth- and fifteenth-century texts necessitates approaching them with as great an understanding as possible of the technology they record. To be sure, there is much we do not know, but a number of basic studies are helpful: Charles H. Talbot's *Medicine in Medieval England* (1967); books on the earlier period by Stanley Rubin (1974) and Edward J. Kealey (1981); Huling Ussery's *Chaucer's Physician* (1971); the studies of D'Arcy Power (1913, 1931) and George Gask (1950); and a series of books and articles by Vern L. Bullough (1959, 1961a, 1961b, 1961c, 1962a, 1962b, 1966, 1978). A valuable guide to particular medical practitioners, university-trained physicians, surgeons, barber surgeons, and empirics is Talbot and E. A. Hammond, *Medical Practitioners in Medieval England* (1965), and the student of medical texts can also gain insight into the users of these works by consulting the documents reproduced in *Memorials of the Craft of Surgery in England* (South 1886) and *The Annals of the Barber-Surgeons of London* (Young 1890).

Not only must Middle English medical texts be understood as the written residue of the theory and practice of a science and craft, they must also be understood in terms of—indeed they cannot be separated from—the Latin tradition. Most Middle English texts are translations of or are derived from Latin medicine, and polyglot manuscripts and polyglot texts in which Middle English is inextricably linked to Latin (and sometimes Anglo-Norman) are commonplace. A number of examples should make this point. A composite manuscript from the fourteenth and fifteenth centuries owned by Irwin J. Pincus of Los Angeles is comprised of Latin (e.g., the *Regimen Sanitatis Salernitanum*), Middle English (e.g., a *"de gradibus"* text giving the degrees of heat, cold, moisture, and aridity of botanical simples), and mixed Latin–Middle English texts (e.g., two receptaria), some with Anglo-Norman glosses. Another example is University of Missouri *Fragmenta Manuscripta* no. 175v (correctly recto) of ca. 1400, in which the text changes from English to Latin to Anglo-Norman in the first three lines. Similarly, Latin phrases cannot be separated from the university-derived Middle English texts that contain them in Gonville and Caius MS 176/97. Further evidence that these examples are not sports is the fact that of the seven manuscripts containing Middle English medical texts in Harvard University libraries (Law Library MSS 4, 10, 61; Houghton Library MS lat. 235; Countway Library of Medicine MSS 7, 18, 19), none is an exclusively English-language codex. All contain Latin texts, and some contain Anglo-Norman material as well.

One of the Countway manuscripts provides a clear illustration of the way in which Latin and English texts can be inextricably linked. A manuscript from the William Norton Bullard Collection, it is MS 19 in the Ballard *Catalogue* (1944; see Harley forthcoming), an attractive vade mecum that A. I. Doyle suspects to be the medical book the scribe William Ebesham copied for John Paston in 1468. In this manuscript, the Middle English treatise on urine is followed by the Latin "Expositione Urinarum in Ordine." The English "John of Burdeux" plague tract is a paraphrase or summary of the Latin "Tractatus contra Morbum Epidemialem" which precedes it. The vernacular version is followed by yet another portion of the Latin version of the tract beginning "Exhortatio bona contra morbum pestilentiam." The penultimate work, a Middle English treatise on the planets, is followed by Latin discussions of astrological signs. Clearly, one cannot deal with the English writings in this codex apart from their companion texts in Latin.

To work with Middle English medical writing is, accordingly, to work with Latin medical writing, and one has access to surviving Latin texts via the author or incipit through Thorndike and Kibre *Incipits* (1963), and to surviving manuscripts in British libraries through Ker (1964, 1969, 1977). It is, of course, important to consider Latin texts for which specific codices may not survive, and here medieval booklists are valuable. Cases in point include medical manuscripts listed in the *Customary* of Canterbury and London monasteries (Thompson 1902, 1904), the fourteenth-century will of Simon de Bredon (Powicke 1931), and the fourteenth-century catalogue of the Augustinian friary at York (James 1909). This and other material will become more fully accessible once the National Institutes of Health computer project directed by Karen Reeds, "Medical and Scientific Books in Medieval Libraries," is complete. That computer-bank of information will also make it possible to call up citations to Middle

English medical manuscripts identified in medieval catalogues in order to search out the provenance of codices that survive and to look for records of those that perished.

Anglo-Norman medical writing is indexed in Vising (1923), particularly nos. 313–320. We are fortunate that the prodigious editing efforts of Paul Meyer (see Vising 1923) provide us with published extracts of most of those texts, including two surgery treatises, a 2,000-line poem dealing with elements of medical theory, and a number of receptaria. These texts are discussed later in some detail. Suffice it to say at this point that the revision of Vising will doubtless provide us with more texts.

Just as one cannot consider Middle English apart from Latin or Anglo-Norman texts, so it is artificial to separate prose from verse in considering Middle English medical writings. Verse is often preferred for the communication of lists, as, for example, enumeration of the thirty-two common bloodletting veins. The appeal of verse as against prose is a mnemonic rather than an aesthetic one. As Robbins makes clear in his essential "Medical Manuscripts in Middle English" (1970a), a great many texts can be found in both prose and verse versions. Texts in verse include prognostications, bloodletting guides that list appropriate veins, and herbal remedies. There are both prose and verse versions of the Latin verse *Macer Floridus de viribus / virtutibus herbarum*, and the "rosemary herbal" was translated from Latin and French into English by a number of translators, sometimes into verse, and sometimes into prose (Harvey 1972). Robbins also cites a number of prose remedybooks with verse introductions and conclusions. In these instances it would be particularly difficult to separate verse from prose.

Verse has, however, received more bibliographical attention than has prose; a high percentage of surviving Middle English medical verse has been identified and catalogued in the *Index of Middle English Verse* and *Supplement*, and someone working with a prose text could find analogous verse treatments of the subject by using those tools. To be sure, other instances of Middle English verse will doubtless turn up; for example, Linne R. Mooney (1981) has discovered additional variant instances of *Index of Middle English Verse* 3848, "Veynes þer be XXX[ti] and two." However, our perception of the contours of the corpus are not likely to change.

For prose, however, we lack any resource comparable to the *Index of Middle English Verse*. We do have the handwritten cards of Dorothea Waley Singer's "Hand-List of Western Scientific Manuscripts in Great Britain and Ireland from before the Sixteenth Century" which may be consulted at the British Library or via microfilm. This pathfinding work, undertaken early in the century, poses problems in use and is not complete. In her 1916 article on the survey, she computes a total of 1,032 manuscripts containing Middle English medical writings from the period 1200–1500. The handwritten handlist should be consulted by those who work with Middle English texts, mindful of the caveats concerning it raised by Rossell Hope Robbins (1970b). Work with this handlist should, however, build upon a careful study of Rossell Hope Robbins's landmark survey of Middle English medicine in more than 350 codices (1970a). The importance of Robbins's handlist can scarcely be overstated. It is the place to begin all work with Middle English medicine, and subsequent analyses, such as Voigts (1982) and this chapter, should be viewed as supplements to it.

To be sure, the Robbins handlist is a preliminary survey, as the author himself emphasized. Robbins has estimated (1981, p. xii) that the codices surveyed in the handlist make up less than one-fourth of the total, and discovery of additional manuscripts—most likely prose—and further work with known ones may bring about a reevaluation of some of his 1970 conclusions. Robbins's emphasis on the dominance of the popular remedybook associated with the empiric healer may need revision. So too may his insistence on the limited number of university-trained physicians, particularly in view of Bullough's conclusions concerning the anomalous status of medicine at Oxford and Cambridge. At the two English universities medicine could be studied as a "minor," and far more students undertook some medical study than incepted as doctors of medicine (Bullough 1961b, 1962a, 1962b, 1966). That fact may be related to the high percentages of clerics among English physicians—but never surgeons—in the fourteenth and fifteenth centuries, a point emphasized in Ussery (1971) and Hammond (1960).

Another of Robbins's convictions that may well need reexamination is that university-trained physicians should be associated only with Latin texts, an observation that may be called into question by Robbins's own citation of manuscripts containing Middle English that were owned by graduate physicians (1970a, p. 408). Furthermore, James (1907) and Rhodes (1956) suggested that Gonville and Caius MS 84/166 belonged to John Argentine, doctor of medicine, cleric, royal physician, and provost of King's College, Cambridge; yet this codex contains—in addition to Latin texts from Galen, Avicenna, and Walter of Agilon—a number of commonplace Middle English texts (recipes, prognostications, herbals) including the second, shorter Middle English version of a theoretical phlebotomy (also found in long Latin and English versions; see the Voigts and McVaugh edition, forthcoming). Two recent Canadian dissertation editions of learned Middle English medical texts provide evidence that vernacular medical writing in fourteenth- and fifteenth-century England was more learned than Robbins has suggested; the sources of these texts must have been, ultimately, the faculty of medicine at a university. Faye Getz (1981) identified and edited a Middle English version of the *Compendium Medicine* or *Laurea Anglica* of Gilbertus Anglicus in Wellcome MS 537, and Richard Grothé (1982) has completed an edition of two texts in Wellcome MS 564: a Middle English redaction of Henry of Mondeville's *Surgery*, and what may be an original English-language surgery.

The long *Articella*-like compendium in Gonville and Caius MS 176/97 with which I am now working may also suggest learned participation in vernacular medicine. This early fifteenth-century academic compilation was Englished for a barber-surgeon and citizen of London, Thomas Plawdon, by an "Austin" who— one can infer from his comments—seems to have been a "clerc," perhaps with university training in theology and medicine.

In short, Robbins's "Medical Manuscripts" (1970a) contains generalizations that will need reevaluating when more information is available, but it is nonetheless an extraordinarily valuable tool that will serve us—with periodic supplements—until an index of Middle English prose is available. That index is perhaps the greatest desideratum in Middle English medical studies, for, until it is available, any edition of a prose medical text will be tentative, and no editor can be certain to have seen all the manuscripts nor hope to know the best. A classic instance of this problem is the *Liber de Diversis Medicinis* edited by Ogden (1969) from the text in Lincoln Cathedral MS A. 5. 2 (Thornton Miscellany). George Keiser (1978, 1980) has found nine additional manuscripts containing the text, some of which resolve textual problems in the Thornton version.

The preceding discussion of the contexts in which Middle English medical prose must be understood and addressed has already raised other problems involved in studying or editing these texts: the artificiality of dealing with them apart from the Latin or Anglo-Norman to which they may be integrally related, and the close connections between verse and prose. Three other, perhaps narrower, issues need to be raised, but sound inferences regarding them may be impossible before the appearance of the index of Middle English prose and a larger body of edited Middle English texts, particularly those deriving from academic medicine. The three include the question of medical writing in texts and manuscripts not primarily medical; the issue of "authors"; and the matter of a taxonomy of Middle English medical writings. Given the expense and effort involved in producing a manuscript book and the universal and common concern for health, it is not surprising that medical material is often to be found in books, and indeed texts, that are primarily nonmedical. Robbins cites scores of instances of single recipes or small groups of recipes in manuscripts, many of which are not primarily medical (1970a, p. 403, n. 28). The three Harvard Law manuscripts cited above, MSS 4, 10, and 61, are indeed legal manuscripts, but each of them contains flyleaf recipes. The problems involved in identifying and indexing ubiquitous flyleaf recipes have proved vexing for the editors of handlists for the index of Middle English prose because the recipes are so frequently encountered.

Flyleaf recipes are, however, comparatively easy to consider apart from the codices in which they are contained; they have almost always been added later. The same cannot be said for medical sections occurring in texts not thought of as primarily medical. There are medical sections in the didactic poem *Sidrak and Bokkus* (Nichols 1968), and similar situations obtain for prose as well. For example, *The Commonplace Book of Robert Reynes of Acle* (Louis 1980) contains not only interspersed charms, but also a short treatise on bloodletting which appears to be made up of rudimentary and commonsensical remarks, but which in fact is a condensed version of major issues addressed in university texts on the subject. Medical material also appears in the *Secreta Secretorum* (see Chapter 16), and there are extensive medical sections in the *De Proprietatibus Rerum* of Bartholomaeus Anglicus translated into Middle English by John Trevisa (see Chapter 8). Indeed, two books of Trevisa's Middle English version, 7 and 17, were transmitted in medieval England as independent medical works with other medical writings as companion texts (Seymour 1969, 1973). Certainly, these medical texts encapsulated in more general works need to be sorted out and studied in connection with other medical writings, but—given the number of tasks to be undertaken with texts that are exclusively medical—that study may not be so pressing as other needs, like the editing of basic texts.

A second issue is the question of whether or not we should speak of the "authors" of medical texts. Here, too, conclusions may be premature. Only with an index of Middle English prose and substantially more editions ·of medical texts can we have enough information to make sound generalizations. A number of factors compound the problem. One is that most medical writing is translated, so we are speaking in most instances of translators rather than authors. Another is that most medical works are anonymous, depending for their *auctoritas* on citations to the antique (e.g., Hippocrates, Galen, Dioscorides), Arabic (e.g., Avicenna, Rhazes), or university authority (e.g., Henry of Mondeville, Bernard of Gordon, William of Saliceto), rather than on the name of the English translator-author. In some instances, we are given initials rather than names for the translator-author, for example, *R.B./B.R.* in the case of the Harvard medical manuscript (Ballard *Catalogue* 19) mentioned above (Harley forthcoming). In others, we are given only forenames as in the instance of the long compendium in Gonville and Caius MS 176/97 where the university-trained compiler-cum-translator identifies himself as "Austin." When names *are* given, the identification is often ambiguous, as in phrases like "þe boke of *x*," so that it is difficult to know if the identification is of a translator-author, a scribe, or an owner.

There are, it must be acknowledged, some names to be reckoned with, and both Robbins (1970a) and Talbot and Hammond (1965) summarize much of the available information on the better-known figures like Henry Daniel, O.P., who may well have practiced medicine and is known from numerous manuscript references to have translated the treatise on urines of Isaac Judaeus, the "rosemary herbal" of Philippa, queen to Edward III, and a work on botanical medicaments. The three also deal with the lesser-known John Freind/Frend and John Harwe named in manuscripts. Robbins (1970a), but not Talbot and Hammond (1965), also identifies manuscripts of John Lelamour's translation of the "Macer" herbal and provides us with other names of translators or physician-users not listed in Talbot and Hammond: T. Kytte, Richard Dod, William of Kylingholme (the same as William Kylinghale in Talbot and Hammond?), John Leke of North-creyke, and Dionysius Cyriton. Talbot (1967) gives us Thomas Multon, O.P., and Friar Randolf/Roland, and Talbot (1967) and Talbot and Hammond (1965) give us the following names not listed by Robbins (1970a): Thomas Morstede, an influential surgeon for Henry V's campaign of 1415 (see also Beck 1974 and Gask 1950) and author in 1446 of the *Boke of Fayre Surgery*; John Stipse (Sloane MS 3866); and William of Kylinghale (Wellcome MS 408; the same as William of Kylinghome named by Robbins 1970a from York Cathedral MS xvi. E. 32?). Another problematic name is that of Roger Marshall (ca. 1417–1477), a some-time royal physician (to Edward IV) who held positions at Cambridge. Robbins (1970a) does not deal with New York Academy of Medicine MS 13 containing four Middle English medical texts and thought to be a Marshall holograph. Talbot and Hammond (1965) identify Marshall as the author of the first text, but Talbot (1967) questions that attribution. Marshall's connection with the other three texts remains unresolved.

Two other figures identified with Middle English medical texts are treated at some length by Robbins (1970a) and by Talbot and Hammond (1965), but their associations with vernacular texts are problematic. One is John Arderne, the fa-mous Newark surgeon, who may have had a role in the translation into Middle English of a number of his texts in Emmanuel College MS 69. The other is John Crophill whose holograph, Harley MS 1735, fols. 28r–52v, has received much attention (Robbins 1970a, p. 411; Talbert 1942; Talbot 1967; Talbot and Ham-mond 1965) because the notebook has been interpreted as including a record of fees and Crophill's *consilia*. However, some conclusions about this manuscript have been called into question by Mustain (1972) on the basis of other Crophill records. Further work with medical writing may clear up some of the problems involved in authorship-owner questions and, indeed, bring to light further translator-authors, but many names will remain unidentified, and most texts will remain anonymous.

The third question that can be approached only in a preliminary way, given the state of studies at this time, is the matter of a taxonomy of medical texts. I have dealt with this issue at some length elsewhere (1982) and shall here simply sum-marize those arguments which are, of course, subject to revision when the whole scope of studies is clearer. Robbins used a system of classification by subject mat-ter, that is to say, by diagnosis, prognosis, or therapeutics. This division is not, however, particularly consonant with the technology of medieval medical practice. Bloodletting, for example, is a procedure that was used for diagnosis, prognostics, and therapy. Medieval commentators like Dino del Garbo were uncertain as to how to classify phlebotomy, but only because it was difficult to know if the procedure was medicine or surgery, not because they perceived the categories of medical writing as diagnosis, prognosis, or therapeutics (del Garbo 1514, fol. 116; see also Siraisi 1981).

Similarly, long compendia—like the one at the end of Gonville and Caius MS 176/97—with continuous chapter numbering are clearly intended to be taken as single medical works; the Gonville and Caius text contains a lengthy section on etiology that would be difficult to categorize by one of Robbins's three labels, a section on uroscopy (prognosis and diagnosis), and one on fevers (all three); only the last section, devoted to compound remedies, falls squarely in a Robbins category. Surgeries too—of which there are many Middle English versions (Lanfranc, Guy de Chauliac, Henry of Mondeville, to name a few)—are more than therapeutic manuals, although they include therapies for wounds, fractures, and dislocations, as well as surgical information. Not altogether therapeutic are the sections in surgeries dealing with anatomy and dietary regimens to preserve existing good health, both difficult to categorize as diagnosis, prognosis, or therapeutics.

There may well be other systems of classification that work better for understanding medieval medicine than the diagnosis, prognosis, therapeutics division. One that works well for sixteenth-century printed texts is that of intended audience (Slack 1979). The problem with that system for manuscript material is that we often have no way of knowing what audience was intended, and, when we do know it, it may surprise us. We would not expect the popular material in Gonville and Caius MS 84/166 to be in a book owned by the university-trained royal physician John Argentine, and it is likewise surprising to learn that the long compendium in Gonville and Caius MS 176/97, with one debate on whether disease is caused by malfunction of the members or of the humors and another on a difference between Galen and Avicenna on the nature of synochal fever was Englished for a barber.

A taxonomy that I have suggested (1982), at least until the vast body of material is under better control, is the classification of remedybooks on one hand—open, adaptable, flexible—and academic texts on the other—that is, texts originating in university medicine, subject to simplification and condensation at times, but less subject to revision than the remedybook. This division may be closer to a medieval understanding of texts, but it derives, essentially, from modern needs, because different editorial principles are required for editing remedybooks and academic texts. Middle English medical writing from before the mid-fourteenth century is of the remedybook sort, and a number of the as yet uncounted remedybooks have been edited (see Robbins 1970a for the following: Dawson, Ogden 1969, Henslow, Heinrich, Müller, and Stephens; add to that Schöffler 1919) and studied (see Robbins 1970a for the following: Bühler, Mayer, and Talbert; add to that Harland 1877). Remedybooks obviously provide remedies, although they sometimes contain prognostic material, such as guides to zodiacal prognostication, and they sometimes contain diagnostic-prognostic material such as uroscopy. The bulk of material in them is treatment for symptoms— minor surgical treatments, nontheoretical phlebotomy and cautery, cupping, diets, charms, prayers, ritual action, and that element that bulks largest— recipes. Recipes may be simple or compound, may call for animal, lapidary, or vegetable ingredients, and may be organized by ailments (often from head to foot), or by plants (in the case of herbal remedies), or randomly. Individual recipes ordinarily have a common format, however much they vary in specifics (Stannard 1982).

And vary they do, as is made clear by Henry Hargreaves's comparison of the sometimes radically different forms of a single recipe found in forty codices (1981b; see also the Grymonprez edition 1981). This sort of variation has been of concern to editors of remedybooks in Old English (Voigts 1979) and in other languages who have argued (Crossgrove 1982), that these variations are not necessarily deteriorations of the text, although that may be the case; in some instances a change in a recipe represents an empirically based "improvement" in the technology that the text represents, and editorial emendation would be ill advised.

The other category of texts to be edited has been more neglected by editors, but in many ways it is more critical at the moment to our understanding of fourteenth- and fifteenth-century medicine. These works are the learned Middle English texts derived from formally educated physicians and surgeons, antique and Arabic authors, and members of the faculties of medicine in medieval universities. Of these texts, surgeries have received editorial attention from Beck (1974), Ogden (1971), Wallner (1964, 1969, 1970, 1976, 1979), von Fleischhacker, and Power (see Robbins 1970a for these last two), but others remain unedited. Editions of surgeries yet needed include the Middle English versions of the surgeries of Roger of Salerno (Sloane MS 240), William of Saliceto (Sloane MS 6, BL Add. MS 10, 440), and a composite text in Hunterian MS 95.

In an intermediate stage between medicine and surgery are two Middle English versions of a theoretical phlebotomy edited by Voigts and McVaugh (forthcoming). Recent effort has been devoted to two editions of gynecological treatises (Rowland 1981 and Hallaert 1982), and the Middle English *Compendium* or *Laurea* of Gilbertus Anglicus has been edited in a dissertation (Getz 1981). Many important texts remain only in manuscript, however. Among these cited by Robbins are a work attributed to Copho (BL Add. 34111), three "Galen" manuscripts (York Cathedral MS xvi. E. 32; BL Egerton MS 2433; Harley MS 78), the *Regimen Sanitatis Salernitanum* (six manuscripts), a theoretical text in Hunterian MS 307, and another in Sloane MS 965. There are also other categories that deserve new or additional work: Middle English "Hippocratic" writings cited by Kibre (1975, see esp. 1977), a Middle English version of Bernard of Gordon's *De Prognosticatione* in a Takamiya manuscript, and the text on the medical degrees of botanical simples in the Pincus manuscript. Additional study of Middle English plague texts is needed to further the contributions of Sudhoff and of Dorothea Waley Singer and Annie Anderson (see Robbins 1970a). I shall continue to work with the quaestiones from the *Isagoge* of Johannitius (Ḥunayn ibn Isḥāq) in Gonville and Caius MS 176/97 and the long compendium at the end of that manuscript. It is highly probable that further instances of learned writing will turn up among the many medical manuscripts in the Sloane Collection that lack adequate description, and some of them will likely deserve editing.

As the first two sections of this chapter reveal, any discussion of Middle English medical texts is perforce a discussion of scholarly desiderata. Nonetheless, there is something to be said for an enumeration. The greatest need for Middle English medical studies is for the completion of the index of Middle English prose. Even before the final indices by incipit and translator-author are available, the existence of handlists of those collections like the Sloane and Wellcome, which are rich in Middle English medical texts, will prove invaluable.

Also greatly to be desired are the completion of partial editions and the publication of editions now in dissertation form. It is good to have Margaret Ogden's (1971) text of the *Cyrurgie of Guy de Chauliac* (from Paris BN MS anglais 25), but we await the introduction, commentary, and glossary in another volume. In the case of Björn Wallner's (1970, 1976, 1979) edition of Guy's *Chirurgia Magna* as found in the New York Academy of Medicine MS 12, we have text and notes for the books on anatomy, wounds, and fractures and dislocations, but still to appear are those on apostemes, ulcers, other ailments, and the antidotary. Likewise the publication of the dissertation editions of Getz (1981), Grothé (1982), and Elaine Miller ("In Hoote Somere," a remedybook found in Trinity College Cambridge MS R. 14. 51, 1978) is to be wished.

A third desideratum, the need for editions of texts that remain yet in manuscript, has been discussed at some length in the second section. There is at this writing less pressing need for more editions of remedybooks than for editions of learned texts: the other surgeries and works attributed to Galen, Hippocrates, Johannitius, Bernard of Gordon, and the like. One possible exception to this suggestion for a moratorium on editions of remedybooks would be an edition of the Middle English translation of the *Thesaurus Pauperum* that compares its fifteenth-century uses with those of the sixteenth century as studied by Slack (1979). Robbins regretted that in 1970 it was necessary to issue a plea for research in scientific vernacular manuscripts of the Middle Ages when that plea was a repetition of the one made by Dorothea Waley Singer in 1919. In little more than a decade since Robbins's plea (1970a), however, a number of editions have appeared (Ogden 1971; Rowland 1981; Grymonprez 1981; Hallaert 1982; and others); others will appear in the near future (for example, Harley, forthcoming; and Voigts and McVaugh, forthcoming); and others, now in dissertation form, await publication. This evidence of editing effort is cause for cautious optimism.

Another desideratum is that the study of—and likewise the editing of—medical prose will become less Insular and draw not only on work in the history of medieval medicine in the larger sense, but also on work with other vernacular traditions as well. Signal work on late thirteenth- and early fourteenth-century university medicine has appeared in the last decade, and those concerned with English medicine ignore it at their peril. For example, Nancy Siraisi's important study on the faculty of medicine at Bologna (1981; see also Siraisi 1982) is significant when we note that Simon de Bredon left a copy of Taddeo Alderotti's Commentary on the *Aphorisms* of Hippocrates to Merton College in 1372 (Powicke 1931) and another copy was to be found in the same year in the library of the Augustinian friars at York (James 1909). Similarly, our awareness of the presence of the Middle English version of Bernard of Gordon's *De Prognosticatione* in a Takamiya manuscript makes Luke Demaitre's study of Bernard's writing (1981) germane to Middle English medicine.

It is essential then to study the Middle English texts in the context of the larger Latin tradition from which they derive, and it is likewise necessary for us to be aware of work with comparable texts in other European vernaculars of the era. I have already mentioned the analysis of editing problems in versions of Macer's herbal that are common to German and English versions (Crossgrove 1982), but one can also find analogues in languages geographically and culturally closer to fourteenth- and fifteenth-century English. Relevant here are writings in Middle Scots like Patric Scot's Medical Book (Hargreaves 1981a) and Henryson's parody "Sum Practysis of Medecyne" (Fox 1972), and two fifteenth-century translations into Irish (by a physician in Ulster and a member of the O'Hickey family in Munster) of Bernard of Gordon's *Practica Dicta Lilium Medicine* (Demaitre 1980).

Particularly relevant to Middle English studies, of course, are editions and studies of Anglo-Norman and French translations of Latin texts in the thirteenth, fourteenth, and fifteenth centuries. The bulk of Anglo-Norman medical texts represents translation efforts in England a century before significant medical translation into English. Most Anglo-Norman medical texts date from the thirteenth century, and, as I have mentioned, excerpts from many of them have been published by Paul Meyer (for references see Vising 1923). Not surprisingly, remedybooks dominate. For Vising 319, "Medical prescriptions," there are eighteen manuscript citations. The prose *Euperiston*, 317, is made up of treatments organized *a capite ad calcem* as is 314, a work misleadingly titled *La novele cirurgerie*. Two brief metrical collections of recipes (316)—some cosmetic—for women also fall into the remedybook category. I am grateful to Ruth Dean for her comments on some of these texts and for informing me that 318, *De Generaus Medecines*, is in fact a homiletic rather than a medical text. Further study of Anglo-Norman recipes is being undertaken by Marthe Faribault at the Université de Montréal.

Only two of the entries in Vising (1923) appear to fall in the category of learned medicine (one must remember, of course, that these texts were translated in England long before any learned medical texts were Englished). These include 313, a medical poem of nearly 2,000 lines that begins with a discussion of the four elements (etiology), and 315, two—apparently independent—prose translations of the surgery of Roger of Parma, usually known as Roger of Salerno. Vising lists no medical treatises for the fourteenth century, but Anglo-Norman continued to be used in manuscripts later than the thirteenth century in glosses (as in the Pincus manuscript), in polyglot manuscripts (e.g., Harvard Houghton MS lat. 235), and in polyglot texts (e.g., University of Missouri *Fragmenta Manuscripta* no. 175). Work with any Middle English medical text demands the investigation of possible Anglo-Norman analogues.

Continental French texts may, of course, also bear on Middle English medical manuscripts. This is not the place to survey the considerable body of French vernacular medical writings, but a few points should be made. As in the case of Anglo-Norman, translation of learned medicine into French began a century before we find the practice in English (Bossuat 1951, 1955, 1961). From the thirteenth century there survives a French version of Gerard of Cremona's Latin text of the surgery of Albucasis (Stone 1968; see also 1953, 1954), and the early fourteenth century saw a remarkable spate of translation, including the surgery of Roger of Salerno, the *Circa Instans*, treatises on urines, fevers, deontology, gynecology, Constantine on melancholy, the *Antidotarium Nicolai*, and, of course, hundreds of recipes (excerpts of these texts are in Meyer 1915). The early fourteenth century also saw the beginning of original medical composition in French in the form of the *Régime du corps* of Aldebrandin of Sienna.

This pattern of translation and composition continued in France in the fourteenth and fifteenth centuries; the fourteenth-century translation of Martin of Saint Gille's commentary on the *Aphorisms* of Hippocrates survives in fact in a manuscript copied by the surgeon to the duke of Bedford (Lafeuille 1954 and 1964). Charles V had eleven medical books in his library, and most were French-language manuscripts. Study of these French translations and compositions is important to the study of Middle English medicine not only because of the possibility that some English texts may be translations from French, but also because the study of the translation processes used for French medical texts is more sophisticated than has been the case for English, and some of the methodology used in studying French translation practices might well prove applicable to English (see Beaujouan 1968; Pallister 1980; and Stone 1953, 1954, and 1968).

A final desideratum for the study of Middle English medical prose is the need for those who work with these texts to place individual works, particularly translations of texts of university origin, in the context of the development of the English language during this period. Medical writings represent the first substantial body of university texts to be Englished (astronomical and alchemical writings are few by comparison). While theology remained essentially Latin and law remained Latin and legal French, considerable medical writing of some intellectual weight was translated from the last third of the fourteenth century. The availability of these texts should enable us to do what French and German scholars have done for some time, that is, study the methods of translation of technical writing and their impact on the language into which the texts are translated. In the case of English texts specific questions relating these translations to other translation methods must be asked. Do the medical writings draw on the translation techniques espoused by Wycliffite translators (see Chapter 12)? Are the translation theory and practices of John Trevisa comparable to those used for academic medical texts (see Chapter 8)?

Furthermore, we must inquire if the body of medical translation confirms or refutes the oft-repeated generalization that Middle English translators and prose writers worked in isolation from one another and were unaware of one another's work (Blake 1977; Matthews 1963; Workman 1940). Are the generalizations based on the numerous translations of the *Secreta Secretorum* and the *De Re Militarii* of Vegetius applicable to academic medical prose where there may be less duplication? This question must be asked in light of the fact that late medieval medical communities in England were not large, that collegiality was enforced by guilds and licensing, and that sources of works being translated may well have been Oxford and Cambridge libraries.

The place of Middle English medical writings in the development of the language is not confined to translation practices or the question of duplication of translation efforts. The language of learned medicine should be studied in relation to the development of Chancery Standard. Furthermore, we must investigate the connections between the translation of this body of highly technical Latin prose and the expansion of the grammatical capabilities of English during the late fourteenth and the fifteenth centuries. By 1500 English had acquired other Latin-modeled tenses beyond its native past and present tenses and had appropriated independent verbs to serve as modal auxiliaries. Furthermore, by the end of the fifteenth century, English was no longer essentially a paratactic language depending on coordinating conjunctions, repetition, parallelism, balance, and contrast; it had adopted many of the hypotactic capacities of Latin, had developed subordinating conjunctions, and had seen the emergence of a variety of subordinating devices that encourage expressions of qualification, causality, and doubt. It would be overweening to credit the body of medical writing with the responsibility for all these changes, but the inescapable fact is that by the end of the period many of these features new to English are to be found in academic medical prose, the first large body of highly technical prose to be translated into English. The study of Middle English medical writing bears, pari passu, on the larger concerns of the linguistic, cultural, and intellectual history of England in the later Middle Ages, and those who work with these texts must make that case.

BIBLIOGRAPHY

This bibliography must be used as a supplement to Robbins, "Medical Manuscripts in Middle English" (1970a). In that article, in addition to the 350 manuscript references, Robbins cited nearly seventy printed sources, most of them editions of Middle English medical texts. The first section of this bibliography lists manuscripts containing Middle English medical texts not cited in Robbins. I am grateful to Devra Kunin and Gail Berlin for information on Boston Public Library MS fMed. 92 and to Kathleen Scott for information on Wellcome MS 290. The second section is made up of editions of Middle English texts published or accepted as dissertations since the Robbins articles or not mentioned in it. Editions are listed by the editor. Secondary works and editions of relevant primary materials in Latin (e.g., *The Annals of the Barber-Surgeons of London*), in Anglo-Norman, and in French are cited in the third section. This list does not duplicate works cited in Robbins (1970a) except for works discussed in this chapter. No edition of an Anglo-Norman text listed in Vising (1923) is duplicated in the third section.

MANUSCRIPTS

Boston, Mass. Boston Public Library MS fMed. 92.
    Contains two medical recipes.
Boston, Mass. Countway Library of Medicine MS 7
    Contains material for zodiacal computation.
Boston, Mass. Countway Library of Medicine MS 18
    Contains ca. 200 recipes, mainly medical, scattered throughout.

Boston, Mass. Countway Library of Medicine MS 19
  Contains treatise on urines; ME translation of John of Bordeaux plague treatise; discussion of the planets (ed. Harley, forthcoming).
Cambridge. Gonville and Caius College MS 176/97
  Contains "Of Phlebotomie," ME translation of long version of text attributed to Henry of Winchester (ed. Voigts and McVaugh, forthcoming); series of short ME texts, some verse, including *quaestiones* based on the *Isagoge*; long compendium translated for "Thomas Plawdon," barber surgeon, by "Austin," contains sections on etiology, the *Isagoge*, urines, fevers, a receptarium.
Cambridge. Peterhouse MS 118
  Contains ME translation of surgery of Henry of Mondeville.
Cambridge, Mass. Harvard University Law MS 4
  Contains five medical recipes.
Cambridge, Mass. Harvard University Law MS 10
  Contains two recipes, one medical.
Cambridge, Mass. Harvard University Law MS 61
  Contains one medical recipe.
Columbia, Mo. University of Missouri *Fragmenta Manuscripta* no. 175
  Contains one leaf from a polyglot remedybook.
Glasgow. Glasgow University MS Hunterian 95
  Contains a surgery, based in part on Henry of Mondeville.
London. Wellcome Institute MS 290 (8 full-page colored drawings)
  Contains Pseudo-Galen, *Anatomy*; *Anathomia Porci*.
Los Angeles. Collection of Irwin J. Pincus, *Regimen* MS
  Contains two polyglot receptaria; a treatise on degrees of heat, cold, moisture, aridity of botanical simples; the "rosemary herbal" translated by Henry Daniel.
New York. New York Academy of Medicine MS 13 (Roger Marshall holograph)
  Contains "Lanterne of fisiciens" based on Guy de Chauliac; list of bloodletting veins; a text dealing with wounds, fractures, and diseases (based on university masters); and an antidotary.
Tokyo. Collection of Toshiyuki Takamiya, Bernard of Gordon MS
  (olim Manchester, Chetham's Library)
  Contains ME translation of Bernard of Gordon, *De Prognosticatione*.
Tokyo. Collection of Toshiyuki Takamiya, Guy de Chauliac MS
  (olim Manchester, Chetham's Library)
  Contains ME translation of the surgery of Guy de Chauliac.

EDITIONS OF MIDDLE ENGLISH MEDICAL TEXTS NOT CITED IN ROBBINS

Bain, D. C. (1940) "A Note on an English Manuscript Receipt Book." *BHM*, 8, 1246–1248. [Osler MS 7591]
Beck, R. Theodore (1974) *The Cutting Edge: Early History of the Surgeons of London.* Lon-

don: Lund Humphries. [Includes partial edition of BL Harley MS 1736, thought by Beck to be *The Boke of Fayre Surgery of Thomas Morstede*]

Getz, Faye Marie (1981) "An Edition of the Middle English Gilbertus Anglicus Found in Wellcome MS. 537." Ph.D. diss., University of Toronto.

Grothé, Richard (1982) "Le ms. Wellcome 564: deux traités de chirurgie en moyen-anglais." Ph.D. diss., Université de Montréal.

Grymonprez, Pol (1981) *"Here Men May Se the Vertues off Herbes": A Middle English Herbal (MS. Bodley 483, fols. 57r–67v)*. Scripta 3. Brussels: Omirel.

Hallaert, M.-R. (1982) *The "sekenesse of wymmen": A Middle English Treatise on Diseases in Women*. Scripta 8. Brussels: Omirel. [New Haven, Yale Medical Library MS 47]

Harley, Marta Powell (forthcoming) "The Middle English Contents of a Fifteenth-Century Physician's Handbook." *Mediaevalia*. [Boston, Countway Library of Medicine MS 19 (Ballard *Catalogue*)]

Harvey, John H. (1972) "Mediaeval Plantsmanship in England: The Culture of Rosemary." *Garden History*, 1, 14–21. [The "rosemary herbal" translated by Henry Daniel from Cambridge, Trinity College MS O. I. 13, fols. 77v–82v]

Louis, Cameron (1980) *The Commonplace Book of Robert Reynes of Acle: An Edition of Tanner MS. 407*. Garland Medieval Texts 1. New York: Garland.

Miller, Elaine M. (1978) "'In Hoote somere': A Fifteenth-Century Medical Manuscript." Ph.D. diss., Princeton University. [Cambridge, Trinity College MS R. 14. 51]

Mooney, Linne R. (1981) "Practical Didactic Works in Middle English: Edition and Analysis of the Class of Short Middle English Works Containing Useful Information." Ph.D. diss., University of Toronto.

Nichols, Robert E., Jr. (1968) "Medical Lore from *Sidrak and Bokkus*: A Miscellany in Middle English Verse." *JHM*, 23, 167–172. [London, BL Lansdowne MS 793]

Ogden, Margaret S. (1969) *The "Liber de Diversis Medicinis."* EETS 207. [Lincoln Cathedral MS A. 5. 2]

————— (1971) *The Cyrurgie of Guy de Chauliac*, vol. 1. EETS 265. [Paris, BN MS ang. 25]

Rowland, Beryl (1981) *Medieval Woman's Guide to Health: The First English Gynecological Handbook*. Kent, Ohio: Kent State University Press. [London, BL Sloane MS 2363]

Schöffler, Herbert (1919) *Beiträge zur mittelenglischen Medizinliteratur*. Sächsische Forschungsinstitut in Leipzig III; Anglistische Abteilung, Heft 1. Halle: Niemeyer. [Includes an edition of the ME *Practica phisicalia* of John of Bordeaux/Burgundy (Oxford, Bodleian Rawlinson MS D. 251)]

Seymour, M. C. (1969) "A Middle English Abstract of Bartholomaeus, *De proprietatibus rerum*." *Anglia*, 87, 1–25. [London, BL Sloane MS 983]

————— (1973) "More of a Middle English Abstract of Bartholomaeus, *De proprietatibus rerum*." *Anglia*, 91, 18–34. [London, BL Sloane MS 983]

Seymour, M. C., et al. (1975) *On the Properties of Things: John Trevisa's Translation of Bartholomaeus Anglicus De Proprietatibus Rerum*. 2 vols. Oxford: Clarendon Press. [See Chapter 8 for a discussion of this edition and the MSS.]

Sheldon, Sue Eastman (1977) "The Eagle: Bird of Magic and Medicine in a Middle

English Translation of the *Kyranides.*" *TSE*, 22, 1–31. [London, BL Add. MS 34111]

Voigts, Linda Ehrsam, and McVaugh, Michael R. (forthcoming) *A Latin Technical Phlebotomy and Its Middle English Translation.* Transactions of the American Philosophical Society. [Cambridge, Gonville and Caius MSS 176/97 and 84/166]

Wallner, Björn (1970) *A Middle English Version of the Introduction to Guy de Chauliac's "Chirurgia Magna."* Lund: Gleerup. [New York Academy of Medicine MS 12]

———— (1976) *The Middle English Translation of Guy de Chauliac's Treatise on Wounds.* Vol. 1: *Text.* Lund: Gleerup.

———— (1979) *The Middle English Translation of Guy de Chauliac's Treatise on Wounds.* Vol. 2: *Notes, Glossary and Latin Appendix.* Stockholm: Almqvist and Wiksell.

Wright, Thomas, and Halliwell, James O. (1845) *Reliquiae Antiquae*, vol. 1. London: John Russell Smith. [ME remedybook materials, pp. 51–55, 70, 194–197, 315 (MSS not identified)]

Zettersten, Arne (1967) *The Virtues of Herbs in the Loscombe Manuscript: A Contribution to Anglo-Irish Language and Literature.* Lund: Gleerup.

STUDIES AND EDITIONS OF RELATED TEXTS

Alford, John (1979) "Medicine in the Middle Ages: The Theory of a Profession." *Centennial Review*, 23, 377–396.

Amundsen, Darrel W. (1978) "Medieval Canon Law on Medical and Surgical Practice by the Clergy." *BHM*, 52, 22–44.

Ballard, James F. (1944) *A Catalogue of the Medieval and Renaissance Manuscripts and Incunabula in the Boston Medical Library.* Boston: privately printed.

Beaujouan, Guy (1968) "Fautes et obscurités dans les traductions médicales du Moyen Age." *Revue de synthèse*, 89, 145–152.

Beaujouan, Guy; Poulle-Drieux, Yvonne; and Dureau-Lapeyssonnie, Jeanne-Marie. (1966) *Médecine humaine et vétérinaire à la fin du moyen âge.* Centre de Recherches d'Histoire et de Philologie 5. Hautes Etudes Médiévales et Modernes 2. Geneva: Droz.

Blake, Norman F. (1977) *The English Language in Medieval Literature.* London: Dent.

Bossuat, Robert (1951, 1955, 1961) *Manuel bibliographique de la littératur française du moyen âge.* Melun: D'Argences. *Supplément (1949–1953).* Paris: D'Argences. *Second supplément (1954–1960).* Paris: D'Argences.

Bullough, Vern L. (1959) "Training of the Nonuniversity-Educated Medical Practitioners in the Later Middle Ages." *JHM*, 14, 447–458.

———— (1961a) "Duke Humphrey and His Medical Collections." *Renaissance News*, 14, 87–91.

———— (1961b) "Medical Study at Mediaeval Oxford." *Speculum*, 36, 600–612.

———— (1961c) "Status and Medieval Medicine." *Journal of Health and Human Behavior*, 2, 204–210.

———— (1962a) "The Mediaeval Medical School at Cambridge." *MS*, 24, 161–168.

———— (1962b) "Population and the Study and Practice of Medieval Medicine." *BHM*, 36, 62–69.

———— (1966) *The Development of Medicine as a Profession*. New York: Hafner.

———— (1978) "Achievement, Professionalization and the University." In *The Universities in the Late Middle Ages*, edited by Jozef Ijsewijn and Jacques Pacquet, pp. 497–510. Leuven: Leuven University Press.

Clay, Rotha Mary (1909) *The Mediaeval Hospitals of England*. Repr. (1966) London: Cass.

Cosman, Madeleine Pelner (1973) "Medieval Malpractice: The Dicta and the Dockets." *Bulletin of the New York Academy of Medicine*, 2d ser. 49, 22–47.

Crossgrove, William C. (1971) "The Forms of Medieval Technical Literature: Some Suggestions for Further Work." *Jahrbuch für Internationale Germanistik*, 3, 13–21.

———— (1982) "Textual Criticism in a Fourteenth Century Scientific Manuscript." In *Studies on Medieval Fachliteratur*, edited by William Eamon, pp. 45–58. Scripta 6. Brussels: Omirel.

Demaitre, Luke F. (1976) "Scholasticism in Compendia of Practical Medicine, 1240–1450." *Manuscripta*, 20, 81–95.

———— (1980) *Doctor Bernard de Gordon: Professor and Practitioner*. Toronto: Pontifical Institute of Mediaeval Studies.

Faribault, Marthe (1982) "La chirurgie par rimes." *Fifteenth-Century Studies*, 5, 47–59. [deals with several Anglo-Norman manuscripts]

Flemming, Percy (1928–1929) "The Medical Aspects of the Mediaeval Monastery in England." *Proceedings of the Royal Society of Medicine*, Section on History of Medicine, 22, 771–782.

Fox, Denton (1972) "Henryson's 'Sum Practysis of Medecyne.'" *SP*, 69, 453–460.

Garbo, Dino del (1514) *Dyni Florentini super Quarta fen Primi Avicene Preclarissima Commentaria*. Venice.

Gask, George E. (1950) *Essays in the History of Medicine*. London: Butterworth. [See especially "The Medical Staff of Edward the Third," pp. 77–93, and "The Medical Services of Henry the Fifth's Campaign of the Somme in 1415," pp. 94–102.]

Gottfried, Robert S. (1978) *Epidemic Disease in Fifteenth-Century England: The Medical Response and Demographic Consequences*. New Brunswick, N.J.: Rutgers University Press.

Hammond, E. A. (1960) "Incomes of Medieval English Doctors." *JHM*, 15, 154–169.

Hargreaves, Henry (1981a) "Patric Scot's Medical Book." In *So Meny People Longages and Tonges: Philological Essays in Scots and Mediaeval English Presented to Angus McIntosh*, edited by Michael Benskin and M. L. Samuels, pp. 309–319. Edinburgh: privately printed.

———— (1981b) "Some Problems in Indexing Middle English Recipes." In *Middle English Prose: Essays on Bibliographical Problems*, edited by A. S. G. Edwards and Derek Pearsall, pp. 91–113. New York: Garland.

Harland, J. (1877) "Some Account of a Curious Astronomical, Astrological and Medical MS. in the Chetham Library, Manchester." *Transactions of the Historical Society of Lancashire and Cheshire*, 29th session, 3d ser. 5, 1–8.

James, Montague R. (1907, 1908, 1914) *A Descriptive Catalogue of the Manuscripts in the Library of Gonville and Caius College*. 2 vols. and supp. Cambridge: Cambridge University Press.

——— (1909) "The Catalogue of the Library of the Augustinian Friars at York." In *Fasciculus Ioanni Willis Clark Dictatus*. Cambridge: Cambridge University Press.

Kealey, Edward J. (1981) *Medieval Medicus: A Social History of Anglo-Norman Medicine*. Baltimore: Johns Hopkins University Press.

Ker, N. R. (1964) *Medieval Libraries of Great Britain: A List of Surviving Books*. 2d ed. London: Royal Historical Society.

——— (1969, 1977) *Medieval Manuscripts in British Libraries*. Vol. 1, London; vol. 2, Abbotsford-Keele. Oxford: Clarendon Press.

——— (1978) "Oxford College Libraries before 1500." In *The Universities in the Late Middle Ages*, edited by Jozef Ijsewijn and Jacques Pacquet, pp. 294–311. Leuven: Leuven University Press.

Keiser, George K. (1978) "'Epwort': A Ghost Word in the *Middle English Dictionary*." *ELN*, 15, 163–164.

——— (1980) "MS. Rawlinson A. 393: Another Findern Manuscript." *TCBS*, 7, 445–448.

Kibre, Pearl (1975, 1977) "Hippocrates Latinus: Repertorium of Hippocratic Writings in the Latin Middle Ages." *Traditio*, 31–. [Vol. 33 (1977) lists ME texts]

——— (1978) "Arts and Medicine in the Universities of the Later Middle Ages." In *The Universities in the Late Middle Ages*, edited by Jozef Ijsewijn and Jacques Pacquet, pp. 213–227. Leuven: Leuven University Press.

Lafeuille, Germaine (1954) *Les amphorismes ypocras de Martin de Saint-Gille*. Geneva: Droz.

——— (1964) *Les commentaires de Martin de Saint-Gille sur les amphorismes ypocras*. Geneva: Droz.

Matthews, William (1963) *Later Medieval English Prose*. New York: Appleton-Century-Crofts.

Meyer, Paul (1915) "Manuscrits médicaux en francais." *Romania*, 44, 161–214.

Minnis, Alastair (1979) "Late-Medieval Discussions of *Compilatio* and the Role of the Compilator." *BGDSL*, 101, 385–421.

Mustain, James K. (1972) "A Rural Medical Practitioner in Fifteenth-Century England." *BHM*, 46, 469–476.

Pallister, Janis L. (1980) "Fifteenth-Century Surgery in France: Contributions to Language and Literature." *Fifteenth-Century Studies*, 3, 147–153.

Parkes, Malcolm B. (1976) "The Influence of the Concepts of *Ordinatio* and *Compilatio* on the Development of the Book." In *Medieval Learning and Literature: Essays Presented to R. W. Hunt*, edited by J. J. G. Alexander and M. T. Gibson, pp. 115–141. Oxford: Clarendon Press.

Power, D'Arcy (1913) "The Lesser Writings of John Arderne." *Seventeenth International Medical Congress*, Section 23, History of Medicine, 107–133.

——— (1931) "English Medicine and Surgery in the Fourteenth Century." In *Selected Writings*. Oxford: Clarendon Press.

Powicke, F. M. (1931) *The Medieval Books of Merton College*. Oxford: Clarendon Press.

Rhodes, Dennis (1956) "Provost Argentine of King's and His Books." *TCBS*, 2, 205–212.

Riddle, John M. (1974) "Theory and Practice in Medieval Medicine." *Viator*, 5, 157–184.

Robbins, Rossell Hope (1970a) "Medical Manuscripts in Middle English." *Speculum*, 45, 393–415.

———— (1970b) "A Note on the Singer Survey of Medical Manuscripts in the British Isles." *ChauR*, 4, 66–70.

———— (1981) Foreword to *Medieval Woman's Guide to Health*, edited by Beryl Rowland. Kent, Ohio: Kent State University Press.

Rubin, Stanley (1974) *Medieval English Medicine*. New York: Barnes and Noble.

Russell, J. C. (1935) "Medical Writers of Thirteenth-Century England." *Annals of Medical History*, ns 7, 327–340.

Siraisi, Nancy G. (1981) *Taddeo Alderotti and His Pupils*. Princeton: Princeton University Press.

———— (1982) "Some Recent Work on Western European Medical Learning, ca. 1200– ca. 1500." *History of Universities*, 2, 225–238.

Slack, Paul (1979) "Mirrors of Health and Treasures of Poor Men: The Uses of the Vernacular Medical Literature of Tudor England." In *Health, Medicine and Mortality in the Sixteenth Century*, edited by Charles Webster, pp. 237–273. Cambridge: Cambridge University Press.

South, John Flint (1886) *Memorials of the Craft of Surgery in England*. Edited by D'Arcy Power. London: Cassell.

Stannard, Jerry (1982) "*Rezeptliteratur* as *Fachliteratur*." In *Studies on Medieval Fachliteratur*, edited by William Eamon, pp. 59–73. Scripta 6. Brussels: Omirel.

Stone, Howard (1953) "Cushioned Loan Words." *Word*, 9, 12–15.

———— (1954) "Learned By-Forms in Middle French Medical Terminology." *Lingua*, 4, 81–88.

———— (1968) "Puzzling Translations in the Thirteenth Century Multiple Equivalents in Early French Medical Terminology." *Romance Notes*, 10, 174–179.

Sudhoff, Karl (1914) *Beiträge zur Geschichte der Chirurgie im Mittelalter*, Erster Teil. Studien zur Geschichte der Medizin 10. Leipzig: Barth.

Talbert, Ernest W. (1942) "The Notebook of a Fifteenth-Century Practicing Physician." *Texas Studies in English*, 21, 5–30.

Talbot, C. H. (1967) *Medicine in Medieval England*. London: Oldbourne.

Talbot, C. H., and Hammond, E. A. (1965) *Medical Practitioners in Medieval England*. London: Wellcome.

Thompson, E. Maunde (1902, 1904) *Customary of Benedictine Monasteries of St. Augustine, Canterbury, and St. Peter, Westminster*. Henry Bradshaw Society 23, 27. London: Henry Bradshaw Society.

Thorndike, Lynn, and Kibre, Pearl (1963) *A Catalogue of Incipits of Mediaeval Scientific Writings in Latin*. Rev. ed. Cambridge, Mass.: Mediaeval Academy of America.

Thornton, John (1966) *Medical Books, Libraries and Collectors*. 2d rev. ed. London: André Deutsch.

Ussery, Huling E. (1971) *Chaucer's Physician: Medicine and Literature in Fourteenth-Century England.* Tulane Studies in English 19. New Orleans: Department of English, Tulane University.

Vising, Johan (1923) *Anglo-Norman Language and Literature.* London: Oxford University Press.

Voigts, Linda Ehrsam (1979) "Anglo-Saxon Plant Remedies and the Anglo-Saxons." *Isis,* 70, 250–268.

———— (1982) "Editing Middle English Medical Texts: Needs and Issues." In *Editing Texts in the History of Science and Medicine,* edited by Trevor H. Levere. New York: Garland.

Wallner, Björn (1964) "Lexical Matter in the ME Translation of Guy de Chauliac." In *English Studies Presented to R. W. Zandvoort,* pp. 150–156. Amsterdam: Swets and Zeitlinger.

———— (1969) "A Note on Some Middle English Medical Terms." *ES,* 50, 499–503.

Workman, Samuel K. (1940) *Fifteenth Century Translation as an Influence on English Prose.* Princeton: Princeton University Press.

Young, Sidney (1890) *The Annals of the Barber-Surgeons of London.* London: Blades, Scot and Blades.

Zettersten, Arne (1970) "A MS. of *Agnus Castus* in the Huntington Library." *N&Q,* ns 18, 130–131.

CHAPTER 16

Utilitarian and Scientific Prose

Laurel Braswell

Unlike the other chapters in this volume, this one must examine an area that is comparatively uncharted. There are fewer published texts and a resultant paucity of secondary matter. The smaller number of texts can be traced to their relative lack of interest for scholars more concerned with the "literary" than the technical aspects of *Fachliteratur*. Another factor may be the incompleteness of bibliographical identification, since many of these texts are still being discovered in manuscript collections, and many are currently being reclassified in view of our ever-expanding view of Middle English prose.

That such works were enormously popular during the fourteenth and fifteenth centuries is attested by their variety and the large number of variant manuscripts. From the thirteenth century on, the scope and range of such informative and practical works are well reflected in Vincent of Beauvais's *Speculum Naturale*, and the compulsion to catalogue and describe the "properties of things" exemplified in Bartholomaeus Anglicus's *De Proprietatibus Rerum*, with Trevisa's translation an illustration of the late medieval compulsion to transmit information to laymen in the vernacular. Indeed, by the fifteenth century such was the urgency that Pecock had to apologize for writing his *Folewer to the Donat* in English rather than Latin, for had he taken the time for the latter, he says, "Y schulde neuer write it, neiþer in lay tunge neiþer in latyn tunge, and þat for greet prece of many oþire maters profryng hem silf daili to be writen and to be delyuerid into knowyng" (ed. Hitchcock 1924, p. 29).

Although it was a period of education in the broadest sense, the works described below reflect an entirely different audience from that defined by Blake (1972) in his article on the textual traditions of religious writers such as Rolle and Hilton and the widely circulated compendia of devotional material. Utilitarian and scientific works suggest a larger cross-section of society, both lay and religious, both courtly and bourgeois, but a group motivated on the one hand by *utilitas* and on the other by *curiositas*.

The following survey can provide only an initial description of scientific and utilitarian prose, as more texts continue to be discovered and others reclassified. They do, however, appear to fall into four major categories: theoretical, practical, prognostical, and occult. Even this statement must immediately be qualified, since distinctions between categories are not always clear. Theoretical works on astronomy and physiognomy, for example, may introduce judiciary notions which are prognostic, while prognostic works such as the lunary often rely upon the calculations of astronomical texts for their interpretation. Distinctions between the theoretical and the practical, too, are not always easy to make; to which, for example, should music or grammar be assigned? For the purposes of this chapter, music and grammar are included under theoretical works on the grounds that they present, basically, theoretical assumptions about the subject and that they, along with arithmetic, geometry, astronomy, rhetoric, and logic, form the seven liberal arts, hence the essentials of theoretical education.

Given the lacunae in scholarship for the following works and the newness of the discovery of many, it seems advisable to give a descriptive survey first, before attempting a critical summary of present and potential areas of investigation.

Central to theoretical works are astronomical and astrological treatises, the distinction between them seldom strictly observed, but the first providing in practice that factual data about the universe that the latter interprets for human action. Among the more important English prose treatises on astronomy is the late fourteenth-century, anonymous, translation of the *Exafrenon*, a Latin treatise attributed to Richard of Wallingford, Abbot of Bury Saint Edmunds, ca. 1320, and based largely upon Robert Grosseteste's work on the spheres, originally through John Sacrobosco's *De Sphaera* (ca. 1250) and Gerard of Cremona's translation (ca. 1175) of Albumasar's version to Ptolemy's *Almagest*. With reference to tables of radices and others, and to various figures, and with some glosses on the original, this work instructs the reader on how to make precise calculations of the positions of the sun and moon, and how to interpret the nature and effects of the various relations between signs and planets.

Other English adaptations of the Ptolemaic-astronomical treatises may be found in MS Digby 88, fols. 16–23v, which begins imperfectly ("sol ys hote and drye but not as mars") and cites Ptolemy specifically on fol. 17; it then proceeds to describe the nature of the planets and provides tables on their houses, triplicities, and aspects. The treatise may be dated early fifteenth century. It represents a characteristic feature of many such works insofar as it is inserted into a manuscript collection of related prognosticary works, including lunaries. The *Boke of Astronomie* is extant in many manuscripts, among them Huntington Library HM 64 and Ashmole 189, with the latter beginning "Here begynnythe the boke of astronomy and phylosophy conceiuyd and made be þe wysest phyloso-phers and astronomyars," and asserting that wise Englishmen have "studied and compiled this book out of Greek into English." It then goes on to enumerate the heavens, the governance of the planets, the complexions of the signs, and their influence upon personality, the last of utmost importance for the *Secreta* tradition.

But here we begin to enter the prognosticary category, for closely related to these essentially astronomical works are others, which are actually adaptations (through Haly's *De Judiciis Astrorum*) of Ptolemy's more astrological work, the *Tetrabiblos*, which describes the effects of astronomical conditions upon the natural world of man. The Middle English prose adaptations have as their sources Firmin of Beauval's *Prognostica* (whose source is Alkindus); Roger Bacon's *Judicia Astronomiae*; John Estwood's *Summa Astrologiae Judicialis*; and Bartholomew of Parma's *Breviloquium*. The English adaptations discuss the complexions of the planets and signs as they are composed of the four elements and qualities, and the series of mutations consequently taking place as a result of the movements of heavenly bodies. In such a way would weather, agriculture, commerce, and other activities be affected, just as human complexions (humors) would be determined at birth by the qualities of natal signs and the position of dominant planets. The two texts that make up BL MS Sloane 213 describe "howe the seuen planetes are frendes and enemyes" and characterize the four elements and complexions. The late fifteenth-century treatise in Bodleian Library MS Ashmole 210 affirms the "sothfast connyng of astrologie" and the effects of the moon upon the complexions of the signs. It appears to be a version of Haly's *De Proprietatibus Lune*, and also provides one of the theoretical bases for the prognostic lunary, discussed later in this chapter. Another group of texts suggests adaptations of Ptolemy's *Tetrabiblos*, but with more interest in aspects of physiognomy, while BL MS Harley 2320 appears to be an adaptation of Bartholomew of Parma's *Breviloquium*, beginning "Destinary of þe hye sotille Bartholomew" (see [*On the Planets and Signs*] and *The Boke of Knowledge*). *The Boke of Knowledge* supports its discussion of human complexion by a table showing ruling planets within the signs. This manuscript was copied in Scotland in 1586 by one Robert Denham, partly from printed books and partly from earlier manuscripts, "thrown out of the chapter chest by the baillies"; it thus preserves at this late date a common, earlier type of astronomical-astrological manuscript collection used for both theoretical and practical knowledge.

Closely related to such material are the many versions and adaptations of the *Secreta Secretorum*, an enormously popular encyclopedic work deriving from the pseudo-Aristotelian *Sirr al-Asrar*, or the *Book of the Secret of Secrets*, compiled in Arabic in the tenth century. Originally considered as a "mirror for princes," it was enlarged with scientific and other matter, the most important being the section on physiognomy. The two Latin versions are by John of Spain (mid-twelfth century) and Philip of Tripole (early thirteenth). Thus far, twelve English translations have been published, three in Middle English prose by Steele (1898) and nine—of which seven are in prose—by Manzalaoui (1977), who gives a full account of the work's complex textual history (pp. ix–xlvii). The compendium of matter surveys most of the subjects included in this chapter. Beginning with the exchange of letters between Aristotle and Alexander, the text discusses the conduct of a king, the health of the body, medicine, physiognomy, justice, matters of state, powers of the planets, and the properties of stones and herbs. Steele's editions represent more or less complete texts, while some of Manzalaoui's are fragments or partial texts. Of these manuscripts, MS Sloane 213 is the earliest, ca. 1400, and MS Honeyman the latest, ca. 1484, an English translation of Johannes de Caritate's version.

From the *Secreta* an expanded physiognomy section, which appears to have bypassed the vulgate recension, was popular as a separate text (see Manzalaoui 1977, p. xvii). The fact is attested by several English prose versions, of which only MS Sloane 213 is edited by Manzalaoui. Most notable is John Metham's *Physnomy*, which he included in his compilation of literary and utilitarian material dedicated to his patrons, Sir Miles and Lady Stapleton of Norfolk, ca. 1448; Metham describes the "dysposycion off man, as be the werkyng of nature" (ed. Craig 1916, p. 119), and then goes on to establish personalities by glance, hair, eyes, brows, feet, and regional origin. With the Sloane fragment edited by Manzalaoui may be compared the text of MS Ashmole 189, which also contains the Hippocrates-Philemon story. The extract included in National Library of Medicine MS 49, fols. 93–93v, acknowledges its source as Albertus Magnus.

Lapidaries, or treatises on stones and their properties, form a large part of theoretical works in English, especially if one includes those sections of the *Secreta* and Trevisa's translation of the *De Proprietatibus Rerum*. Origins of the lapidary go back to the detailed descriptions in Isidore of Seville's *Etymologiae*, to Bede's glosses on the twelve apocalyptic stones, and, more immediately, to Marbode of Rennes's *De Gemmis* (ca. 1070) and Phillipe de Thaon's Anglo-Norman *Lapidaire* (ca. 1120), which works increasingly expanded information on the properties and uses of stones. If one overlooks Trevisa's section on stones and metals (ed. Seymour et al. 1975, pp. 825–881), then the earliest English prose lapidary dates from the early fifteenth-century in a Southeast Midland dialect (MS Douce 291). This work represents an independent translation of a mid-fourteenth-century French lapidary, commissioned by King Philip of France, with the English author adding passages from Marbode. The stones are listed in the usual bipartite structure, that is, the twelve stones named by God to Moses, and the eleven stones mentioned in the Apocalypse, beginning with *sardes*, then describing its protective powers, its association with Adam through its red-earth color, and its identification with the blood of Christ's passion (ed. Evans and Serjeantson 1933, pp. 18–19). The latest and most expanded English prose lapidary, although drawing upon at least four earlier Anglo-Norman sources, owes much of its material to Trevisa and is organized in a strictly alphabetical fashion, from *absittus* to *periot*.

The arts proper are represented, first, by grammatical texts. These are extant in at least thirty-six known manuscripts. Versions include the *Accedence* (an English adaptation of Donatus's *Ars Minor* (ca. 350); the *Comparacio* (on comparison); the *Informacio* (on syntax); and the *Formula* (an expansion of the *Informacio*). Donatus's work is a simple textbook, which indeed later provided the name "donat" as a synonym for "primer," outlining the eight parts of speech. It is usually presented in traditional medieval dialogue form between master and students, and begins by naming nouns, pronouns, verbs, adverbs, participles, conjunctions, prepositions, and interjections; and then proceeds to a discussion of genders, numbers, cases, declensions, moods, and tense; and concludes with the uses of prepositions. Some authors can be identified from manuscript and other evidence, as, for example, John Leylond, a grammarian associated with Queen's College, Oxford, from 1415 to 1418, who appears to be responsible for the *Informacio* treatise in some manuscripts (see Thomson 1979, pp. 9–10).

That only three versions of arithmetical texts plus several fragments and diagrams have been identified seems somewhat surprising, especially in view of the essential importance of arithmetic for the study of astronomy and music. Trevisa remarks, in fact, that if we "take away noumbre and tale, . . . all þinges beþ ylost," and if we take away "compot and acountes" everything is full of "lewednesse and vnconnynge" (Trevisa, ed. Seymour et al. 1975, 2:1354; see also the sections "On Numbers and Arithmetic," 2:1353–1360, and "On Geometry," 2:1367–1372). The *Crafte of Nombrynge*, in a Northeast Midland dialect of the early fifteenth century, derives from a glossed version of Alexander de Villa Dei's *De Algorismo* (ca. 1220), while the *Art of Nombryng* is a translation of John of Sacrobosco's *De Arte Numerandi*. Included in Steele's (1922) edition of these two works are a short, fourteenth-century *Treatise on Computation*, explaining arabic numerals and possibly based upon John of Sacrobosco's *De Algorismo*, and an illustrated treatise on *Accomptynge by Counters*, from the printed edition of Robert Record's *Arithmetic*. Steele assumes the last is the only known English version, but proposes that it is based upon earlier, fifteenth-century translations of treatises on the use of the abacus or counting board (1922, pp. vi–vii, xvii–xviii).

Although the virtues of music are extolled by Bartholomaeus insofar as they reveal the mystical meaning of Holy Writ and "abate the evil spirits in mankind," the technical aspects of that subject are more fully set out in three early fifteenth-century treatises edited by Meech (1935c). The first is attributed to Lionel Power, whose compositions are extant in the Hall manuscript and several others. The second is anonymous, while the third is attributed to one "Chilston," thus far unidentified. It is possible that John Wylde, the scribe of BL MS Lansdowne 763, was the translator. Power's treatise is on counterpoint for "syngers or makers or techers," and deals with the intervals in harmonizing the mean, treble, and quatreble parts with plainsong or the tenth part. The second treatise explains the intervals of the descant, counter, countertenor, and faux bourdon parts, while Chilston's (?) treatise considers musical proportions: harmonical, geometrical, and arithmetical. The first two treatises are illustrated by musical notations. There are, in addition, several late fifteenth-century whole and fragmentary treatises which have only in part been edited.

Practical works include, first, those that could be called "instructions for conduct." By far, the largest category of these are courtesy books and related treatises. Their original models lie most likely in the instructions for conduct portions of the *Secreta Secretorum*. Whereas these are directed toward the nature of kingship, however, courtesy and related works are directed initially toward the nature of chivalry and knighthood, later toward the behavior and service of the aristocracy and upper middle class. Their immediate origins probably lie in Italian works such as Brunetto Latini's *Tesoretto*, ultimately in the *Liber Faceti* attributed to John of Garland.

Some of these texts, both in verse and prose, were published by Caxton, a fact that attests immediately to their popularity and currency. Others include anonymous collections, or a large variety of individual but related texts. Furnivall's *Early English Meals and Manners* (1868) published mainly verse treatises, but three are in prose: the *Boke of Keruynge* (first published by Wynkyn de Worde in 1508); a translation of Bishop Grosseteste's *Household Statutes*, ca. 1450–1460; and the anonymous *For to Serve a Lord* of about the same date; the *Boke of Keruynge* is a prose version of John Russell's verse *Boke of Nurture*, ca. 1465. The *General Rule to Teche Every Man to Serve a Lorde or Mayster*, edited by Chambers (1914), describes the duties of the marshal of a hall (possibly Talaton, Devon) and those for other servants as they arrange tables, order the serving of meals, and manage household accounts. Chambers also includes in this edition a short text on carving (p. 17), which bears some relationship to Russell's *Boke of Nurture*. *The Black Book*, compiled for the household management of Edward VI, is filled with practical information on monetary matters and aspects of service, concerned, as the book states, with graduating its readers from the "scole of urbanitie."

Chivalric manuals, strictly speaking, are represented by Caxton's important *Book of the Ordre of Chyvalry* (1484), which falls outside this chapter. It is related to several earlier prose works, most of them deriving ultimately from Ramon Lull's Catalonian *Libre del ordre de cavaleria*, ca. 1276. This work, through the anonymous French *Livre de l'ordre de chevalerie*, was translated by

Sir Gilbert Hay as the *Buke of the Ordre of Knychthede*; although this Scottish work does not properly belong in a survey of Middle English prose, it must be cited as Caxton's source. More theoretical and idealized than utilitarian, the *Buke* discusses such matters as the responsibilities of a knight and his relation to the Church and the rest of the social hierarchy. Representative of a more philosophical type of chivalric manual is the fifteenth-century translation of Christine de Pisan's *Le livre du corps de policie*.

Combining historical and political theory with practical application is the *Tretis on Armes*, ca. 1400, translated by one "john," possibly from Francis de Foveis's *De Picturis Armorum*. It begins with an account of heraldry from the siege of Troy, then elaborates on the technical terms of the subject.

Some military manuals may also fall more into a theoretical than a utilitarian category of prose. In their first inception, however, they were intended as the latter in their explanation of the more technical aspects of military strategy. Texts based upon Vegetius's *De Re Militari*, ca. 375, circulated widely in Latin and vernacular verse and prose. The first English translation, made for Thomas, Lord Berkely, and ascribed to one "Clifton" in the Douce manuscript, was evidently used in his campaign against the Welsh in the early 1400s. An anonymous prose Scottish translation of this work lies outside the province of this survey.[1]

Many of the works described above can be found copied into collections for wealthy patrons, collections that might appropriately be called "Books of Knighthood"—the title, indeed, of Sir John Paston's *Grete Booke*, ca. 1480, and a work nearly duplicated in its balance of practical, chivalric, and utilitarian matter by the collection in Pierpont Morgan MS 775 (see Arthur 1900–1901).

A related aspect of practical, chivalric material is sports, and the subject provides a large number of prose works. The earliest treatise on hunting popular in England was *L'art de vénerie*, written in Anglo-Norman, ca. 1327, by Twiti, the court huntsman of Edward II (see Danielsson 1977, introduction). It was translated anonymously about 1420 into thirty-five English verses, plus eleven short prose sections, and instructs the reader on the techniques of hunting hare, hart, buck, and boar. A few years earlier, Edward, duke of York and grandson of Edward III, translated the major part of another popular French hunting treatise into English prose, and thus Gaston de Foix's *Livre de chasse* (1387) appeared in English as *The Master of Game*. That it was enormously popular is suggested by its two versions, the longer extant in a number of manuscripts, many beautifully illuminated, and the shorter in at least four. A still later version of Twiti, known as *The Craft of Venery*, ca. 1450, includes some additions and provides the source for the treatise on hunting in Paston's *Grete Booke* (MS Lansdowne 285). Twiti's treatise is also the basis for the verse hunting treatise in Dame Juliana Berner's *Boke of St. Albans*, printed at Saint Albans in 1486 and by Wynkyn de Worde, with some additions, in 1498. This "reprint" also includes hawking and fishing treatises, the latter expressing a preference for this "gentler" sport; the printed version has been traced to the earlier Tuxedo Park manuscript. There are at least three versions of the hawking treatise, with MSS Harley 2340, Sloane 3488, and Egerton 1995 the most closely related textually; these provide, or are themselves based upon, that treatise later appearing in the *Boke of St. Albans.*

While treatises on hunting and hawking generally include the care and treatment of animals and birds, there are several works extant dealing more specifically with the care and selection of horses. The late fifteenth-century Wood manuscript, for example, contains a treatise on equestrian medicine and is attributed to one "Sothebe." This treatise is followed in the same manuscript by *The Book of Marchalsie,* which enumerates the good qualities of a horse and how to recognize them. Some relationship is evident between these works and the verse "Fifteen Properties," found in this and other manuscripts, including the *Boke of St. Albans.* The short scrap "On Knowing a Horse of Good Entail," found in Bodleian Library MS Douce 291, is a prose paraphrase of that poem.

Of all these works, the most practical and utilitarian are recipes. There are at least four major categories of prose recipes: medical, that is, prescriptions; cooking; codicological, that is, book production; and agricultural. Medical recipes more properly belong to Chapter 15, although they, like cooking recipes, are so numerous and widely scattered that it would be impossible to cite them all.

There appear to be at least five major collections of recipes extant for cooking and preparing food, dating from ca. 1380 to the end of the fifteenth century. Many more have been noted on scraps or inserted into other types of manuscripts. Perhaps the best known is the *Forme of Cury,* compiled for Richard II and extant complete in at least two manuscripts and partially in four others. This collection, like the others, was intended for the chefs of a large household and was based upon earlier Latin *De Coquina.* The recipes include fish and meat dishes, each with appropriate sauces, and many desserts such as elaborate custards requiring as many as sixty eggs. Most are rubricated in some way, for example, "For to make . . . ," but are rarely consistently organized; many, in fact, are interspersed with medical prescriptions.

Codicological recipes, based upon earlier *De Arte Illuminandi* and related works, offer detailed recipes and instructions for making parchment, pigments, colored leather for bindings, glue, and a variety of other items related to book production. Often, as in Bodleian Library MS Douce 54, they are interspersed with the original Latin recipe or additional Latin recipes.

Agricultural and other household recipes include those represented in MS Douce 54 on grafting and planting fruit trees, growing herbs, and growing roses. Some offer such intriguing instructions as those on "how to make holly leaves shine as silver," or "how to make a red rose green," or "how to make an apple grow in a glass," or "how to drive fleas out of a chamber" (fols. 18–21).

The recipe for gunpowder appears occasionally in other collections, as in MS Pierpont Morgan 775, fol. 275, but this text is associated with alchemical writing, a topic discussed below under "occult works."

Of practical value, too, are the various guidebooks to travel, mainly intended for pilgrims to the Holy Land and other shrines. The best-known travel literature for this period is, of course, by Margery Kempe and Sir John Mandeville (see Chapters 6 and 7). But almost as important are John Capgrave's travelogue of the Holy City, written ca. 1450, and William Wey's *Itineraries* to Jerusalem (1458, 1462) and to Saint James of Compostella (1456). Capgrave, an Austin friar of Lynn, and Wey, a fellow of Eton College, describe their journeys and offer detailed advice to prospective travelers. An anonymous *Handbook* is extant in one manuscript, which describes traveling conditions and advisable conduct for travelers going from Calais through Venice to the Holy Land, Turkey, and Rhodes, then returning by way of the Straits of Gibraltar. It also includes medical prescriptions for various foreign ailments; its present title, *Informacion for Pylgrymes unto the Holy Londe*, derives from Wynkyn de Worde's 1948 edition. Travel lists, outlining cities, shires, and their main features, may be found often in verse (see Bodleian Library MS Douce 98), but at least one prose version is extant in the late thirteenth-century manuscript, Jesus College (Oxford) 29.

Miscellaneous practical works that might also be mentioned in this chapter include a wide variety of texts and approaches to the medium of instruction. A fifteenth-century *Treatise on Sailing* is extant in three known manuscripts, of which two are directly associated with William Ebesham. A *Treatise on Lacemaking* is directed not entirely toward women, since the manuscript refers to "he" on fol. 53, the man who reads out the complex directions to the knotters, and the remaining contents also include general household matter such as medical recipes, a Latin calendar, and astrological-prognosticary works. Instructions for weights and measures are found in the late fifteenth-century Bodleian Library MS Douce 16, which defines the weights of assize bread in a close translation of Latin statutes on *Panis de Coket*, and is inserted on a blank half-sheet in a later hand than the remainder of the manuscript. A *Treatise on Time* in BL MS Harley 4011, ca. 1445, calculates the times of the world (Before the Law, Under the Law, and Time of Grace), and enumerates the number of seconds, minutes, hours, days, weeks, and months for the year; it then, in monthly sequence, estimates the lengthening and shortening of days by hours and minutes.

Instructions for the construction and use of instruments are well-represented by Chaucer's treatises on the astrolabe and equatory (see Chapter 14). Lesser known are the anonymous instructions for making an obscure type of sundial known as "the little ship of Venice," a geometrico-mechanical computing device, ultimately based upon spherical projection derived from Hellenistic theories mentioned in Ptolemy's *Planisphaerium*. The Middle English prose translation in a late fourteenth-century manuscript, which also contains other translations of astrological and astronomical matter, may be based upon an earlier Latin treatise.

Documents of a prognosticary and prescriptive nature are found in nearly every type of manuscript, from the most sumptuously produced parchment chronicle to the poorest commonplace book. Almost all owe their basic assumptions to the principles of judicial astrology, and in many instances the theoretical treatises on that subject, along with technical tables of radices, lunar mansions, and other calculations are included in the manuscripts. Many more of these documents appear to be extant in verse than in prose, owing to the mnemonic function of verse, but there nevertheless remain a large number of prose examples.

The largest group of such texts includes almanacs and related works, used for daily consultation in all practical matters of daily life. What they all possess in common is an overall organization based upon certain chronologies, whether days, months, zodiacal signs, or astronomical positions, and a series of predictions determined by the astronomical or meteorological conditions present during specified periods of time.

Most widely proliferated among such almanac-type of documents were lunaries, regularly consulted according to the positions of the moon. This could be calculated either by the cycle the moon makes throughout its twenty-eight to thirty *mansions* or days, or by its zodiacal cycle through the twelve signs, basically corresponding to the twelve calendar months but beginning with Aries (March). That the lunary form should be the most popular type of almanac is not surprising in view of the then current notion that the moon had more direct influence upon the earth as a result of its closer position. The outcome of every earthly event could consequently be established according to the position of the moon and the quality or complexion of the day or sign in which it was to be found at any given time.

At least seven lunaries are extant in prose, none of them directly related to any other and each therefore representing a different version. Their sources are the highly popular Latin *lunaria*, and possibly more immediately, Anglo-Norman versions, although the Latin calendar of Friar John Somer (of which an exemplar is found in MS Digby 88) provides a close version to those that assign biblical figures to each day or month, for example, "On the first day of the moon Adam was created and made."

John Metham, although not following the biblical pattern, included a full version of a prose lunary among his texts in the Garrett manuscript, and it is approximately contemporary (ca. 1448) with most of the other extant prose lunaries. It may be of some interest to historians of astrology that Metham expresses considerable skepticism about the validity of many of his prognostications and, qualifying them with such remarks as "the fourth day is good for travelling if the wind will serve," or "the sixth day is propitious for hunting if the weather be prophitable," concludes with the warning that the lunary must be used with "dyscrecion and resun" (Metham, ed. Craig 1916, p. 156).

Some prose lunaries are more specialized than generally prognostic; for example, the Longleat and Selden Supra MSS are concerned chiefly with medical and phlebotomy prognostications. Still others are so specialized as to single out only one area of activity, such as the travel lunary in MS Ashmole 210, which is based upon the zodiacal signs, with the months glossed in the margins. The quality and provenance of prose lunary manuscripts vary but reflect both lay and ecclesiastical use among all classes; marginal notations and horoscopes, added in later hands indicate that many continued to be used until the end of the sixteenth century.

A solar-type of almanac, one based upon the position of the sun within the signs of the zodiac, is the *Boke of Fortune* found in Bodleian Library MS Ashmole 343, mid-fifteenth century. Rather than beginning with the ascendance of Aries, however, its prognostications begin with the calendar year, although its information is similar to that contained in the months of the moon.

The *Critical Days* type of almanac, based ultimately upon Galen's *De Diebus Criticis* and the assumption that the moon's influence is more beneficial during its first two quarters, is primarily a guide to phlebotomy. Its principles were employed for more general prognostics, however; MS Sloane 213, for example, cites the critical days and their consequences if a man or woman be born on them. Related to this type of work is *The Four Houses*, an adaptation of Arnald de Villanova's *Quatuor Domus*, which describes the influence of the planets within their *domus naturales*.

The *Erra Pater*, or *Prophecies of Esdras*, are found usually in verse, but John Metham included a prose version in the Garrett manuscript and several others have been noted. They predict the weather, and fortune and sickness as well, according to the day upon which Christmas or New Year's Day falls. Thus, if Christmas falls upon a Sunday, the "wyntyr folyng schuld be fulle of wyndys," with "great peace in the land," and he that is born that day is "fortunat to the world" (Metham, ed. Craig 1916, p. 146).

Still another type of prognosticary almanac is concerned with the state of the weather, especially the effect of thunder upon human activities. It seems to have been a very early type of popular almanac, as evidenced by the late Old English version found in BL Cotton Vespasian MS D. XIV, fols. 75v and 103; the Middle English versions derive from several Latin sources, including John Estwood's succinct account in the *Summa Astrologiae Judicialis*. While Trevisa, in his translation of *De Proprietatibus Rerum* (Bk. 11), notes that thunder may have considerable effect upon certain agricultural activities, the Middle English prognosticary *Erra Pater* texts relate the day or sign during which thunder occurs to the outcome of various activities on the basis of the astrological complexions.

A distinction between prognosticary works and those considered occult is somewhat difficult to delineate or justify, since such works as the prophecies of *Esdras* clearly involve some occult notions about portends. Yet, whereas the *Esdras* prophecies are ultimately based upon astrological and astronomical principles, works more narrowly defined as "occult" may determine portends by symbolical associations such as those of Hermaneutical alchemy or the *gnosis* principle of alchemical knowledge. Occult texts extant in Middle English prose defined in this way include those on dreams, chiromancy, geomancy, charms, and alchemy.

Dream books, usually entitled the *Dream of Daniel* or *Somniale Danielis* (a title, incidentally, occasionally given to lunaries and other almanac-type works), are extant in at least four prose manuscripts. They diagnose dreams by predicting, in curiously pre-Jungian symbols, the significance of objects and events occurring during a particular dream. To dream of archery, for example, betokens change; water betokens sickness. Some versions similar to MS Lansdowne 388 arrange the objects in alphabetical order (e.g., "archery"-*zonam*, "gyrdyll") for convenient reference.

Chiromancy, or palmestry, is represented in three known manuscripts: John Metham's version in the Garrett and All Souls College manuscripts and an anonymous translation in Bodleian Library MS Digby 88, the last slightly earlier, ca. 1420. Latin treatises on chiromancy, originating from twelfth-century translations from Arabic, were attributed to Adelard of Bath and John of Seville. These circulated widely, and Metham's English treatise, attributed by him to "Aurelian," thus far unidentified, is clearly a version of Adelard's *Linii Naturales*. This work belongs to the second group of *Summae Chiromantiae* described in Craig's introduction (1916, pp. xxvi–xxix). It defines the four principal lines and the general proportions of the hands, nails, and joints. Obviously such notions relate to the pseudo-Aristotelian theories of physiognomy; for example, small fingers denote a person who is "enuyus, proud, hardy, and bold" (ed. Craig 1916, p. 112). Many of the Latin treatises and the English versions in MSS Digby 88 and Digby Roll IV are illustrated by diagrams.

Geomancy appears to be represented in Middle English prose versions by only one manuscript, dating from the early fifteenth century. It may be an adaptation of Martin of Spain's illustrated treatise, a copy of which is to be found in the same manuscript, fols. 76v–80. The English work describes the technique of divination by which handfuls of earth are thrown down at random, or by figures or lines made between random dots. Predictions are then made about the good or bad outcome of events associated with such figures and their governing planets and signs.

Charms in Middle English prose border often upon medical prescriptions (see Chapter 15). Some charms, however, are of wider application. These may be used for magic, or as preventive measures against evil—hence their relationship to prognosticary matter. Those based upon the magical properties of the eagle, for example, derive ultimately from Latin translations of the Greek *Kyranides*, and clearly extend in many instances to more than medical applications. Thus, the right eye of the eagle "gives grace and friendship," while the left eye protects against all harm (ed. Sheldon 1977, p. 24). Having angels in mind while rising from bed, while it thunders, or while eating or drinking, may evoke protection (MS Sloane 2584). Invoking Dismas, the good thief crucified on Christ's right hand (MS Sloane 2389), or the three Magi (same manuscript) will protect against thieves.

The largest number of such works pertain to alchemy, which is also the case for verse texts (Reidy 1975, pp. ix–xxi). The prose texts can be classified into approximately fifteen groups. Among the most important are the fifteenth-century translations of the *Liber de Turba* by "Magister Panton"; Albertus Magnus's *Speculum Lucis*; and Johannes de Rupeseissa's (Jean de Roquetaillade's) *Liber de Consideratione Quintae Essentiae*, or *Liber Lucis*, written ca. 1350. The last work was probably the most popular, and is extant in at least thirty-five Latin manuscripts and five English prose ones. Hermes' *Secreta*, also known as *De Salibus et Corporibus*, is a seven-part treatise, each part corresponding to one of the seven planets, with instructions for turning base metals into silver or gold; MS Ashmole 1451 contains two versions of it within the same manuscript. Garland's *Rosarium* and Hermes' *Dicta* are concerned mainly with the philosopher's stone, as are the two short prose treatises on procedures for making the philosopher's stone ascribed to Chaucer, although the manuscript containing them is early sixteenth century and the verses accompanying them in the same manuscript are related to Ripley's *Compound of Alchemie*. Robert Frunitor, identified as Robert Barkar of Bongeye, Suffolk, is the only other known English prose author; his work is dated 1456. Several manuscripts contain both prose and verse alchemical texts; for example, Bodleian Library Ashmole 1451 includes an English prose translation of Hermes' *Secreta* and an extract of Norton's *Ordinal* (the latter on fols. 2v, 9v–11). Among the large number of alchemical collections of recipes and other types of instructions are recipes on metallic waters (MS Sloane 1091), waters of salt (MS Sloane 776), making a furnace (MS Trinity College Cambridge 916), and oil of transmutation (MS Sloane 1091), and a collection of maxims (MSS Ashmole 759 and Ashmole 1451). Several collections intersperse Latin with English recipes in the manner of cooking and household collections or herbals. While none of these works is original, and indeed this is true even for Norton's alchemical poem in the sense that it makes no innovative use of the usual topoi or more imaginatively describes the symbolic aspects of colors and elements than its sources (and see also Trevisa's translation of the *De Proprietatibus Rerum*, Bks. 16 and 19), the English prose texts do, however, display an unusually extensive knowledge and use of the more technical Latin treatises.

Preliminary surveys of utilitarian and scientific prose were made by Wells in 1916 and Bennett in 1944, with Bennett extending the bibliographical references to include fifteenth-century works. Unfortunately, the Burke Severs's revision to this section of Wells's *Manual* has not yet been completed, while Bennett's modest summary article must now be seen as sketchy and incomplete.

If there is one area of Middle English scientific prose in obvious need of extensive textual criticism and study, it is that of astronomy and astrology. While Chaucer's knowledge and treatment of the original Latin texts have been closely studied by a large number of scholars such as Wedel (1920), their derivatives in other Middle English forms have been neglected. The list of Middle English prose astronomical manuscripts given in the bibliography below probably represents only a selection of extant works. Among these, only the translation of Richard of Wallingford's *Exafrenon* has been published. *The Boke of Astronomie*, with its remarkable combination of astronomical data and Christian imagery, begs for publication in a full critical edition; Ralph Hanna reports that he is currently compiling a complete survey of manuscripts, and I am indebted to him for the present list. The texts, whole and fragmentary, on the signs and complexions need to be studied more fully in view of their relation to the *Secreta Secretorum* and, further, as a background to Renaissance physiopsychological theories. Boll (1903), Sarton (1950), and Thorndike (1929) are useful for early bibliography, but more recent scholars such as Grant (1971, 1974) indicate the extent of desiderata.

The list of known English manuscripts of the *Secreta Secretorum* provided by Workman (1940, pp. 167–169) has now been accounted for in printed texts, whether by Steele (1898) or Manzalaoui (1977). There remain the related and more fragmentary texts to edit and study as part of this encompassing tradition. As we await publication of Manzalaoui's promised second EETS volume, containing notes and bibliography, several studies of the *Secreta* provide at least a beginning, among them Workman's (1940) linguistic analysis of translation techniques.

As for the neglected lapidaries, two articles concerning the Peterborough manuscript by Bitterling (1977, 1979) demonstrate the many errors and obscurities of Evans and Serjeantson's EETS edition (1933) and prepare the way for a revised and nondiplomatic text. The background material has been surveyed but insufficiently studied by Studer and Evans (1924), Basier (1936), Legge (1963), and Meier (1977). It is curious, in view of the many prose lapidary texts, that no Middle English prose bestiaries have come to light in the tradition of the earlier verse *Physiologus*, apart from its reworking in the *De Proprietatibus Rerum* and Trevisa's translation. Yet Latin and French bestiaries appear to have had considerable influence upon medieval vernacular literature, as the bibliographical surveys of White (1954), McCulloch (1962), and Rowland (1973, 1978) suggest. Perhaps a Middle English prose bestiary is yet to be discovered.

Many valuable aids to the further study of the natural sciences are already available. Since the appearance of Sarton's (1948) pioneer survey, several significant historical studies have been published, for example, by Crombie (1959), Grant (1971), and Weisheipl (1971). Grant's source book (1974) includes representative Latin treatises and full bibliographies. Most recently, Jayawardene (1978) has published a comprehensive checklist of pre-1600 scientific manuscripts, and Braswell's (1981) paleographical handbook indicates further manuscript catalogues, first-line indexes, and other aids.

Thomson's detailed catalogue (1979), with its many printed extracts, has provided a valuable starting point for future scholarship on grammatical texts, while Murphy (1974, pp. 32–33) analyzes some of the Latin background. Both the large number of grammatical manuscripts, attesting to the importance of such works for medieval education, and the paucity of editions suggest a real need for textual work as well as background study of pedagogical function, whether in secular schools such as the Exeter City grammar school (identified, for example, with MS Peniarth 356B) or the parish and monastic schools (identified with the lost Syon Abbey manuscript; see Thomson 1979, p. 4). Thomson's recently completed edition of selected Middle English prose grammatical treatises for the Garland Medieval Texts Series will, no doubt, promote further scholarship along these lines. In the related area of the *ars dictaminis*, Voigts (1981) has recently published an article describing a newly discovered *Dictaminal Formulary* of the second half of the fifteenth century, which also contains an English letter with Latin rhetorical labels. Surely one must consider this a type of utilitarian prose, although the lines of demarcation between the *ars dictaminis* and the *ars rhetorica* are not always clear (see Murphy 1974). The grammarian John Leylond should receive more notice, especially concerning his identity and contributions to the traditional Donatian *Informacio*.

For arithmetical texts, Steele's edition (1922) needs accurate collation with the manuscripts. A more complete study of these texts in relation to Latin sources needs to be attempted, especially with regard to the treatises of John Sacrobosco, Thomas of York, Samson of Worcester, Adelard of Bath, and Gerard of Cremona. Apart from Sarton's (1948) survey of Latin arithmetical texts, there has been little study of medieval English arithmetic and the systems of the abacus and counter. Several texts remain to be edited for the first time, such as the treatise on accountancy in MS Sloane 213, and the treatises on numbering in MSS Cambridge University Library LI. IV. 14 (III) and Bodleian Library 790. G. VII. Geometry has been largely ignored, apart from Manzalaoui's obscure reference to "an English treatise" in BL MS Sloane 213 (1977, p. xxvi) and Trevisa's translation of the "*De Geometria*" section of the *De Proprietatibus Rerum*.

In music, Meech's edition (1935c) of three treatises remains the only major contribution to texts in that subject. Much remains to be done; for example, the two Corpus Christi College (Cambridge) and Bodleian Library manuscripts have only been partially edited. Hughes's splendid bibliography (1974) now makes it possible to explore potentially fruitful manuscript collections (see especially his items 56a–74), as well as secondary matter (e.g., items 1749–1815). Carter's *Dictionary* (1968) will greatly facilitate the study of such texts.

Courtesy and related practical texts have proven a popular area for research: see Bornstein's study (1976) and analysis (1977) of the *Livre du corps du policie*. All known texts have been edited, with a modernized version of several texts published by Rickert (1923). Yet clearly Furnivall's edition (1868) is unsatisfactory, and both his and Chambers's (1914) texts should be reedited in view of more recent scholarship, especially with regard to studies in other vernaculars, such as Parson's of Anglo-Norman texts (1929). Myers's account (1959) of the textual traditions of *The Black Book* ought to be investigated: is the Society of Antiquaries manuscript an early copy of an original now lost, as stated? And how does it compare with the sixteenth- and seventeenth-century copies? McFarlane (1973) provides some useful background as a starting point.

In the area of military manuals, the number of unedited prose manuscripts of Vegetius's *De Re Militari* calls for more texts and studies. Bornstein (1975) and Shrader (1979) provide finding lists of manuscripts. The possibility that Trevisa wrote some of the texts is considered in Chapter 8. For some years now, Katherine Gavin has been reported to be editing Lord Berkeley's version for EETS, but the date of its appearance is still unknown. A closer comparison of translation techniques among these versions might yield interesting conclusions along the lines of Workman's linguistic observations (1940) or Bornstein's (1977) analysis of the English *Livre du corps de policie*. Although Jones's (1943) edition of the *Tretis on Armes* provides a valuable text, the authorship, sources, and other aspects of the treatise need further study.

Hunting and other sports have also proven popular topics for research; see, for example, Savage (1933). Tilander's attractive edition of the English Twiti versions (1956), along with that of the French original from BL MS Add. 46919, invites further study, which will now be facilitated by his excellent introduction, bibliography, and full glossary. Tilander's remarks about the obscure manuscript history of the *Craft of Venery* (1956, p. 12) are intriguing and should be investigated. Workman (1940) comments extensively upon the translation techniques of the *Boke of St. Albans* and *The Master of Game*, thereby calling attention to the fact that better textual criticism should replace the inadequate Baillie-Grohman edition (1904) of the latter; the former has been reproduced only in facsimile from the 1486 edition, apart from Wynkyn de Worde's print of 1498, which appends additional matter much in need of source study. The *Boke of St. Albans* and Sir John Paston's *Grete Booke* have received detailed study by Bühler (1941), Jacob (1944), Doyle (1957), and Hands (1967); Doyle examines and confirms the identity of Paston's *Grete Booke* as MS Lansdowne 285. Tilander, in his critical edition of Juliana Berners's verse *Boke of Huntyng* (1964), which is based upon the incunabula version in the *Boke of St. Albans* and Blades's facsimile, studies this text with regard to earlier hunting treatises and compares it with the text found in Bodleian Library MS Rawlinson Poet. 143.[2] Bitterling (1981) has edited a second manuscript version of the treatise on fishing in the *Boke of St. Albans*, a manuscript originally cited as a verse version in *IMEVSupp*, no. 1502.5. Swaen (1943) and Shirley Leggatt (1950) provide useful editions of the treatise on hawking found in three manuscripts, and Hands (1967) adds further context. However, the attribution to Prince Edward, the work's relationship to the *Boke of St. Albans*, and its background in works such as Frederick II's *De Arte Venandi cum Avibus*, Albertus Magnus's *De Falconibus*, and Adelard of Bath's twelfth-century version need to be further explored.

On horsemanship and care of horses, the most popular extant text is the verse "Fifteen Properties," although Hands (1972) describes two still unedited but possibly related, prose treatises on the care and selection of horses, in the Wood manuscript. Until now the prose scrap in Bodleian Library MS Douce 291 has remained unnoticed. While these texts are related to each other and to the hunting manuals, they may also derive in part from Palladius's *Opus Agriculturae*, extant only in verse.[3]

Because of their usual lack of consistent grouping and classification, most recipes have remained without critical editions, apart from Austin's EETS edition (1888) of one of the larger collections. Another fairly large collection, which might easily and usefully be edited, is found in Bodleian Library MS Douce 257. Most recently, interest has tended to focus upon the viable and practical aspects of these recipes, as witnessed by three attractively produced and modernized cookbooks published by Sass (1975; I am grateful to Sass for providing me with a list of her manuscripts), Hieatt and Butler (1976), and Cosman (1976). These may be considered useful to scholars insofar as they contain some introductory and bibliographical matter. It is now possible to compare these cooking recipes more extensively with French and other vernacular parallels by means of the *Index* compiled by Goldberg and Saye (1933). Wilson (1973) offers a useful introduction to the subject of medieval cooking in general, while Serjeantson (1937) studies its vocabulary.

Codicological and household recipes are varied in nature and may be mixed in the same manuscript with unrelated texts. Our knowledge of the extent and nature of Latin sources and what they tell us about medieval book-making practices owes much to Thompson's editions and bibliographical survey (1935), while Braswell (1981) has updated and enlarged the bibliographical resources, both primary and secondary.

Travel texts have received workable editions and have been studied in terms of historical context (see, e.g., Barber 1957). One might single out Amiran's revised and annotated edition of Röhricht's (1890; rev. 1963) chronological bibliography of travel works on the Holy Land, a welcome reference work to supplement Schefer and Cordier's *Recueil de voyages*. Among general studies of English pilgrims are those by Mitchell (1964), Hall (1966), and Zacher (1976), the latter mainly with reference to Chaucer but full of valuable general references. Certainly more could be done along the lines of Lucas's close study (1969) of Capgrave's autograph manuscripts.

Finally, among the miscellaneous practical texts that offer instruction are those for sailing, which have received an edition based upon only one of the three known manuscripts (Gairdner 1889); those for lacemaking, which has been edited by Stanley (1974) and conjecturally explained with regard to some of the technical terms, such as *compon* and *piol*; and those describing weights for assize bread. It would be useful in a larger context to have the last edited with supporting research into the whole problem of medieval English weights and measures.

Among the practical texts offering information on keeping time is Horstmann's unannotated edition (1887), which is disappointing and in need of further study. The edition of the treatise describing the making of a "little ship of Venice"—a form of sundial—by Price (1960) contributes much to our knowledge of such instruments, although the editor fails to explain its more technical aspects and its relationship to Latin sources; some help is provided in this respect by Gunther (1923, 2:40–41).

Among prognosticary texts, the most productive area of scholarship thus far has been for verse texts, with Robbins (1939) outlining those for the *Erra Pater* and the *IMEV* and *IMEVSupp* identifying verse prognosticary texts by incipit. Their prose equivalents have been sadly neglected.

Introductory scholarship on the English prose lunary began in 1916 with Craig's remarks about Metham's text in the Garrett manuscript, but it was Förster (1944) who placed the lunary in its larger Latin and vernacular contexts. Yet Förster did no more than provide the text of MS Ashmole 391 and samples of others. Braswell's (1978) study and forthcoming collective critical edition of all the Middle English lunary texts listed below (MET, Heidelberg) attempt to explain their principles and practical use. Unless additional texts are identified, lunary criticism is at the moment a less viable field for research than that for astronomical-astrological texts which establish the theoretical bases for their prognostications.

Among the related prognosticary texts such as the *Boke of Fortune*, however, only two manuscripts have been edited. *The Four Houses* appears to be of considerable interest in view of its rarity, and the *Erra Pater* prose texts could most profitably be assembled and studied as a collective group. Kurvinen (1957) and Silverstein (1959) suggest rich areas for source studies in weather and thunder books, while Robbins's (1939) survey needs revision and expansion.

Occult works have always attracted much interest, as Briggs (1962) and Thomas (1971) suggest. Once again, however, the number of well-edited texts in Middle English is astonishingly small. Most desirable would be an edition of a prose alchemical text comparable in quality and scope to Reidy's edition (1975) of Norton's *Ordinal*. The Latin backgrounds of dream books, chiromancy, and especially alchemy have been studied by Martin (1977), Powell (1976), Read (1966), and Thorndike (1953 and 1965). A few recent theses, for example Sheldon's (1978), have contributed to our general knowledge of medieval English occult works. It is surprising that McBryde's (1917) survey of some Middle English verse and prose charms fails to specify the manuscripts used; one hopes that future editions will indicate the textual transmissions and backgrounds of this genre more accurately. An obvious invitation to publish comes from the geomancy treatise in MS Ashmole 360. A potential editor might wish to consider whether its source was Martin of Spain or John de Mor, and whether there might be a connection between this text and prognostic picture lunaries, some of which use similar dot patterns.

Apart from its relation to Chaucer (see, e.g., Duncan 1968), alchemy has received the least attention in proportion to its number of extant Middle English prose manuscripts. In view of Singer's comprehensive catalogue of alchemical manuscripts in Latin and the vernacular (Singer, Anderson, and Addis 1931), Wilson's survey of North American manuscripts (1939), and Robbins's addenda to the *IMEV* of certain manuscripts also containing prose (1966), it is surprising that so few prose texts have been edited. In addition, substantial aids to the study of such texts are now available through Bidez's catalogues (1924–1935, 1939–1951) and Biedermann's *Handlexikon* (1973), while hermaneutical symbolism is surveyed and documented by Telle (1980). Plessner (1954) provides a useful introduction to the *Turba Philosophorum*, and Powell (1976) to the historical development of alchemy.

In concluding this necessarily brief survey of utilitarian and scientific prose, it should be emphasized that, seen collectively, the manuscript texts represent an extraordinarily large body of vernacular material for fourteenth- and fifteenth-century England. Such material appears to have belonged to laymen as well as to professionals, and to private as well as to religious libraries. The fact is attested by the known provenances of some of the manuscripts. It is also, to approach the matter from the opposite direction, reflected in those extant wills that mention bequests of books: the lawyer Peter Arderne, for example, bequeathed in 1467 not only Boethius's *Consolation of Philosophy* but also books on hunting and grammar; Witham Charterhouse earlier in the century was given a collection of books that included a *tractatus de armis in anglicis* (Wilson 1970, pp. 144, 154). But which books were these? And were they additional Twiti or Vegetius or Donatus manuscripts to those listed in this chapter? The question raises a most important implication in connection with scholarship in these and other areas of scientific and utilitarian prose: there is so much more to be done.

NOTES

1. Diane Bornstein, ed. (1971) "The Scottish Prose Version of Vegetius' *De re militari*: Introduction and Text," *Studies in Scottish Literature*, 8, 174–183.
2. Gunnar Tilander, ed. (1964) *Juliana Barnes, Boke of Huntyng*. Cynegetica 11, Karlshamm: E.G. Johansson. The text and its relationship to MS Rawlinson Poet. 143 are studied by Kathleen L. Smith (1962–1967) "A Fifteenth-Century Vernacular Manuscript Reconstructed," *Bodleian Library Record*, 734–741.
3. See *Palladius on Husbondrie*, ed. (1872, 1879) Barton Lodge, EETS, os 52, 72, and the extract in *A Glastonbury Miscellany of the Fifteenth Century*, ed. (1968) A. G. Rigg, London: Oxford University Press, pp. 103–116.

BIBLIOGRAPHY

The two major divisions of the bibliography are made according to the distinctions between primary and secondary sources. Primary sources include manuscripts and their editions, when these exist. Secondary sources include studies and reference works.

In the primary section, texts are listed according to their classification within my descriptive discussion. Within the four main divisions of theoretical, practical, prognosticary, and occult works, distinctions are made according to the particular category and more precise nature of each work. I have listed authors when known and placed a question mark after those normally so identified but not verified. Titles in square brackets are conjectural and have usually been supplied by me. The lists of manuscripts is doubtless in many cases still incomplete, for reasons discussed above. Each manuscript or group of manuscripts is followed by reference to a printed edition if such exists; where there is no such reference, the work may be assumed to be still unedited.

PRIMARY SOURCES

THEORETICAL WORKS

The Natural Sciences

Astronomical-Astrological

Translation of Richard of Wallingford's (?) *Exafrenon*

MANUSCRIPTS

Bodleian Library Digby 67, fols. 6–12v
Bodleian Library Digby Roll, 3 (outer surface)
Trinity College (Cambridge) o. 5. 26, fols. 171–181 (as renumbered fols. 163–173)

PRINTED EDITION

North, J. D., ed. (1976) *Richard of Wallingford: An Edition of His Writing with Introductions, English Translation and Commentary.* 3 vols. Oxford: Oxford University Press.

[*On the Planets and Signs*]

MANUSCRIPTS

Bodleian Library Ashmole 391, fols. 5v–16v
Bodleian Library Digby 88, fols. 16–23v, 34–36v (fragment)
Bodleian Library Digby 210, fols. 21v, 81–97
National Library of Medicine 49, fols. 1–18
BL Sloane 1315, fols. 33–36v

The Boke of Astronomie

MANUSCRIPTS

Huntington Library HM 64 (olim Phillipps 6883), fols. 52–61v
BL Add. 12195, fols. 127v–135
BL Egerton 827, fols. 1–23v
BL Egerton 2433, fols. 1–18v

BL Royal 17. A. iii, fols. 76v–80v
BL Royal 17. A. xxxii, fols. 8–20v
BL Sloane 965, fols. 143v–163
BL Sloane 1317, fols. 103v–115
BL Sloane 1609, fols. 11–27
BL Sloane 2453, fols. 1–14
BL Sloane 3553, fols. 1–20
University College (London) Angl. 6, fol. 1
Wellcome Institute 411, fols. 32–37v
Bodleian Library Add. B. 17, fols. 3–18v
Bodleian Library Ashmole 189 (1), fols. 1–63v
Bodleian Library Ashmole 1405, pp. 123–127
Bodleian Library Ashmole 1443, pp. 13–81
Bodleian Library Ashmole 1477 (3), fols. 1v–2
Bodleian Library Rawlinson D 1220, fols. 3–29v
Bodleian Library Selden supra 73 (1), fols. 3–18v
Cambridge University Library Ll. iv. 14, fols. 143–146
Gonville and Caius College (Cambridge) 457, fols. 1–7v
Magdalene College (Cambridge) Pepys 878, pp. 1–37
Trinity College (Cambridge) R. 14. 51, fols. 77v–94v
Yale University 163, fols. 103–112v
Columbia University Plimpton 260
Takamiya 39

PRINTED EDITION

Krochalis, Jeanne, and Peters, Edward, eds. (1975) *The World of Piers Plowman*, pp.
3–17. Philadelphia: University of Pennsylvania Press. (Cambridge University Library Ll. iv. 14)

The Boke of Knowledge

MANUSCRIPT

National Library of Medicine 49, fols. 64–73v

[*On the Planets, Signs, and Complexions*]

Manuscripts

Bodleian Library Ashmole 391, fols. 1–1v (fragment)
Bodleian Library Ashmole 189, fols. 115–126v
Bodleian Library Ashmole 210, fol. 21 (fragment)
Bodleian Library Digby 88, fols. 89–91v (fragment)
BL Sloane 213, fols. 115–118 (fragment)
Longleat Library 176, fols. 42–49
Saint John's College (Cambridge) 237, pp. 1–2 (fragment)

Destinarie

Manuscript

BL Harley 2320, fols. 5–31

Astrological-Physiological

Secreta Secretorum

Manuscripts

BL Royal 18. A. vii, fols. 2–26
Lambeth Palace Library 501, fols. 1–42
Bodleian Library Rawlinson B. 490, fols. 28–72 (the "James Yonge" version of 1422)
Bodleian Library Rawlinson C. 83, fols. 1v–8v (*The Booke of Goode Governance* by Johannes Hispaniensis)
BL Sloane 213, fols. 118v–121
Bodleian Library Ashmole 396, fols. 1–47 (with emendations from MS Bodleian Library Lyell 36)
Honeyman (San Juan, Capistrana, Calif.), fols. 4–109v (*Þe Priuyte of Priuyteis*)
Bodleian Library Ashmole 59, fols. 1–12v ("Marmaduke" version)
BL Add. 5467, fols. 211–224v (by John Shirley)
University College (Oxford) 85, pp. 70–134
Princeton Library Garrett, fols. 57–75v (fragment)

Printed Editions

Steele, R., ed. (1898) *Secreta Secretorum*. EETS, os 74. (first three MSS)
Matthews, William (1962) *Later Medieval English Prose*, pp. 211–212. New York: Appleton-Century-Crofts. (extract from Rawlinson B. 490)

Manzalaoui, M. A., ed. (1977) *Secreta Secretorum: Nine English Versions*. EETS 276. (fourth through tenth MSS)

Lapidaries

[Lapidarie]

MANUSCRIPTS

Bodleian Library Douce 291, fols. 121–135
Bodleian Library Ashmole 1447, fols. 37–38
Bodleian Library Add. A. 106, fols. 44–47v, 126–136
Bodleian Library Eng. misc. e. 558 ("Mostyn")
Peterborough Cathedral 33, fols. 1–16
BL Egerton 827, fols. 39–47v

PRINTED EDITIONS

Evans, J., and Serjeantson, Mary S., eds. (1933) *English Mediaeval Lapidaries*. EETS, os 190. (first four MSS)

Zettersten, Arne, ed. (1968) *A Middle English Lapidary*. Acta Universitas Lundensis 1. Lund: University Press. (the "Mostyn" MS)

Bitterling, Klaus (1977) "Notes on the Text of the 'Peterborough Lapidary.'" *N&Q*, 222, 303–306. (Peterborough Cathedral MS collated with Evans and Serjeantson ed.)

———— (1979) "Further Notes on the Text of the 'Peterborough Lapidary.'" *N&Q*, 224, ns 26, 6–8.

THE ARTS

Grammar

Accedence

MANUSCRIPTS

National Library of Wales Peniarth 356B, fols. 48, 54v–57v, 163, 165–167
Saint John's College (Cambridge) F. 26, fols. 1–12
Trinity College (Cambridge) O. 5. 4, fols. 4v–6v
BL Add. 12195, fol. 66

BL Add. 37075, fols. 1–6v
PRO c. 47/34/13, fols. 22–23
Norwich Record Office Colman 111, fol. 1v
Bodleian Library Digby 26, fols. 5v, 62v–63v
Bodleian Library Douce 103, fols. 53–57
Bodleian Library Rawlinson D. 328, fols. 119–126
Worcester Cathedral Library F. 123, fol. 99v

PRINTED EDITIONS

Meech, S. B., ed. (1935a) "Early Applications of Latin Grammars to English." *PMLA*, 1, 1012–1032. (second and ninth MSS)
————, ed. (1935b) "An Early Treatise in English Concerning Latin Grammar." In *Essays and Studies in English and Comparative Literature*, pp. 81–125. University of Michigan Publications 13. Ann Arbor: Michigan University Press. (third MS)

Comparacio

MANUSCRIPTS

National Library of Wales Peniarth 356B, fols. 9v, 163–164v
Cambridge University Library Add. 2830, fols. 54v–56v
Bodleian Library Rawlinson D. 328, fols. 80–83
Worcester Cathedral Library F. 123, fols. 99v–100

PRINTED EDITION

Meech, S. B., ed. (1934) "John Drury and His English Writings." *Speculum*, 9, 70–83. (second MS)

Informacio

MANUSCRIPTS

National Library of Wales 423D, fols. 11v–17
National Library of Wales Peniarth 356B, fols. 1–9v, 167v–168
Lincoln Cathedral Library 88, fols. 91v–95 (margin)
Bodleian Library Hatton 58, fols. 46–54v
Bodleian Library Rawlinson D. 328, fols. 8–15v, 73v

Formula

MANUSCRIPTS

Corpus Christi College (Cambridge) 233, fols. 164–169v
BL Add. 37075, fols. 30v–37, 41
BL Harley 1002, fols. 1–12
Bodleian Library Rawlinson D. 328, fols. 76–79v, 83v–89

[*Notes on Cases Used, with Place Names*]

MANUSCRIPT

Gonville and Caius College (Cambridge) 417/447, fol. 15v

[*Treatise on Syntax and Parts of Speech*]

MANUSCRIPTS

Trinity College (Cambridge) O. 5. 4, fols. 4, 6v–7v
Trinity College (Dublin) 430, pp. 3–11
Durham Cathedral Library B. IV. 19, fols. 1–1v

PRINTED EDITIONS

Kitchin, G. W., ed. (1907) "A Medieval Latin Grammar." *Durham University Journal*, 17, 194–196. (last item)
Smyly, J. G., ed. (1930) "A Latin Grammar in English." *Hermathena*, 20, 353–359. (first two MSS)

Arithmetic

The Crafte of Nombrynge

MANUSCRIPT

BL Egerton 2622, fols. 136–165

The Art of Nombryng

MANUSCRIPT

Bodleian Library Ashmole 396, fols. 48–56

[Treatise on the Numeration of Algorism]

MANUSCRIPTS

BL Sloane 213, fols. 121–123
BL Egerton 2852, fols. 5–13

PRINTED EDITIONS

Halliwell-Phillips, J. O., ed. (1839) *Rara Mathematica*, p. 72. London: J. W. Parker. (extracts from Sloane 213)
Steele, Robert, ed. (1922) *The Earliest Arithmetics in English*. EETS, os 118. (includes *Crafte of Nombrynge*, Egerton 2622 and *Art of Nombryng*, Ashmole 396)

Of Augrym

MANUSCRIPT

Bodleian Library 790. G. VII, fols. 146–154 (fragment)

[On Numbering]

MANUSCRIPT

Cambridge University Library LI. IV. 14 (III), fols. 121–142

Music

Lionel Power, [*Treatise on Music*]

MANUSCRIPT

BL Lansdowne 763, fols. 104v–107v

[*Treatise on Music*]

MANUSCRIPT

BL Lansdowne 763, fols. 112v–115v

Chilston (?), [*Treatise on Music*]

MANUSCRIPT

BL Lansdowne 763, fols. 116–117v

PRINTED EDITION

Meech, S. B. (1935c) "Three Musical Treatises in English from a Fifteenth-Century Manuscript." *Speculum*, 10, 235–269. (includes all three items from MS Lansdowne 763)

[*Treatise on Music*]

MANUSCRIPTS

Corpus Christi College (Cambridge) 410, II, fols. 13v–15v (fragment)
Bodleian Library 842, fols. 12–16v

PRINTED EDITION

Burney, Charles (1789, repr. 1935) *A General History of Music.* 2d ed., 2:433–435. London: G.T. Foulis. (extracts from both MSS)

PRACTICAL WORKS

RULES FOR CONDUCT

Courtesy Books and Related Works

Boke of Keruynge

MANUSCRIPT

BL Add. 37969, fols. 2–8

PRINTED EDITIONS

de Worde. 1508 (STC 3289).
Chambers, R. W., ed. (1914) *A Fifteenth-Century Courtesy Book*, pp. 11–17. EETS, os 148.
Matthews, W. (1962) *Later Medieval English Prose*, pp. 95–99. (extract)

Translation of Bishop Grosseteste's *Household Statutes*

MANUSCRIPT

BL Sloane 1986, fols. 100–102

PRINTED EDITIONS

Furnivall, F. J., ed. (1868) *Early English Meals and Manners*, 328–331. EETS, os 32.
Rickert, Edith (1908) *The Babees' Book: Medieval Manners for the Young*. New York: Duffield. (modern translation)

For to Serve a Lord

MANUSCRIPT

Bromley

PRINTED EDITION

Furnivall, F. J., ed. (1868) *Early English Meals and Manners*, pp. 366–377.

The Black Book

MANUSCRIPT

Society of Antiquaries 211

PRINTED EDITION

Myers, Alec R., ed. (1959) *The Household of Edward IV: The Black Book and the Ordinance of 1478*. Manchester: University Press.

Translation of Christine de Pisan's *Livre du corps de policie*

MANUSCRIPT

Cambridge University Library Kk. 1. 5, fols. 1−79v

PRINTED EDITIONS

John Skot. 1521 (STC 7270).
Bornstein, Diane, ed. (1977) *The Middle English Translation of Christine de Pisan's "Livre du corps de policie."* MET 7. Heidelberg: Carl Winter.

Chivalric Prescriptions
And Military Manuals

Tretis on Armes

MANUSCRIPTS

BL Add. 34648, fols. 3v−8v
BL Harley 6097, fols. 1−10, 12−49v
Bodleian Library Laud Misc. 733, fols. 1−17v

PRINTED EDITION

Jones, Evan John, ed. (1943) *Medieval Heraldry: Some Fourteenth-Century Heraldic Works*, pp. 213−220. Cardiff: William Lewis. (all three MSS)

Translation of Vegetius's *De Re Militari*

MANUSCRIPTS

For a list of the seventeen manuscripts of the *De Re Militari* in Middle English or Scots, see Shrader (1979), pp. 302–304.

Sports

Translation of Guillaume Twiti's *L'art de vénerie*

MANUSCRIPTS

BL Cotton Vespasian B. XII, fols. 5–9
Phillipps 12086, fols. 37–40 (the "John Porter" MS)
BL Lansdowne 285, fols. 215–216

PRINTED EDITIONS

Wright, Thomas, and Halliwell-Phillipps, J. O., eds. (1845) *Reliquae Antiquae*, 1 : 149–154, London: J.R. Smith. (first MS)
Tilander, Gunnar (1956) *La vénerie de Twiti*, pp. 44–50. Cynegetica 2. Uppsala: Almqvist and Wiksell. (all three MSS)
Danielsson, B., ed. (1977) *William Twiti, "The Art of Hunting," 1327*, pp. 41–51. Cynegetica Anglica 1. Stockholm Studies in English 37. Stockholm: Almkvist and Wiksell.

Edward, duke of York, *The Master of Game*

MANUSCRIPTS

Baillie-Grohman, W. A. and Baillie-Grohman, F., eds. (1904) *The Master of Game*, London: Ballantyne, Hanson, for the Authors, pp. 241–243, list 19 MSS; the following should also be included:
Yale University 101
Yale University 163, fols. 134v–136
Duke of Gloucester, York House 45

Bodleian Library James 11, p. 157 (extracts)
Takamiya MS 19
Takamiya MS 16 (olim Phillipps 10364)

PRINTED EDITION

Baillie-Grohman, W. A., and Baillie-Grohman, F., eds. (1904) *The Master of Game*. (all
    except last three MSS)

Treatyse of Fysshynge wyth an Angle

MANUSCRIPTS

Denison (Tuxedo Park, N.Y.)
BL Sloane 1698, fols. 12–13

PRINTED EDITIONS

de Worde. 1498 (STC 3309). (Denison MS)
Watkins, M. G., ed. (1880) *The Treatyse of Fysshynge wyth an Angle*. London: E. Stock.
    (facsimile of de Worde)
Satchell, Thomas, ed. (1883) *An Older Form of the "Treatyse of Fysshynge wyth an Angle."*
    English Dialect Society 141. London: W. Satchell. (first MS)
Bitterling, Klaus, ed. (1981) "A Middle English Treatise from BL MS. Sloane 1698."
    ES, 62, 110–114. (Sloane MS)

Boke of Hawkyng

MANUSCRIPTS

BL Harley 2340, fols. 50–103
BL Sloane 2721, fols. 1–37
BL Sloane 3488, fols. 1–3
Bodleian Library Rawlinson C. 506, fols. 310–320
Duke of Gloucester, York House 45, p. 158
Bodleian Library Ashmole 1432, fol. 12 (fragment)
Trinity College (Cambridge) O. 9. 38, fol. 21
Bl Lansdowne 285

Printed Editions

The Boke of St. Albans. 1486 (STC 3308). (MS unspecified)

Wright, T., and Halliwell-Phillipps, J. O , eds. (1845) *Reliquae Antiquae,* pp. 293–308. (first MS)

Swaen, A. E., ed. (1943) *"The Booke of Hawkyng after Prince Edward Kynge of Englande* and Its Relation to the *Book of St. Albans." SN,* 16, 5–32. (first MS)

Shirley Leggatt, N. J., ed. (1950) "The *Book of St. Albans* and the Origins of Its Treatise on Hawking." *SN,* 22, 135–145. (third MS)

Hands, Rachel (1975) *English Hawking and Hunting in "The Boke of St. Albans."* Oxford English Monographs. Oxford: Clarendon Press. (facsimile ed. of Lansdowne MS)

Sothebe (?), [*Treatise on Horses*]

Manuscript

Bodleian Library Wood 18, fols. 61–79v

The Boke of Marchalsie

Manuscript

Bodleian Library Wood 18, fols. 84–112

"On Knowing a Horse of Good Entail"

Manuscript

Bodleian Library Douce 291, fol. 136

Recipes

Cookbooks

[*Recipe Collections*]

Manuscripts

BL Harley 279, fols. 1–48v
BL Harley 4016, fols. 1–28

Bodleian Library Ashmole 1439, fols. 36–37v
Bodleian Library Laud 553, fols. 5–6
Bodleian Library Douce 55, fols. 34–76
Bodleian Library Douce 257, fols. 86–99v
BL Sloane 7, fols. 95–105v
BL Sloane 442, fols. 6–25v
BL Harley 1605, fols. 98–118

PRINTED EDITIONS

Furnivall, F. J., ed. (1868) *Early English Meals and Manners*, p. 60. (extract from first MS)
Austin, T., ed. (1888) *Two Fifteenth-Century Cookery Books*. EETS, os 91. (first two MSS)

A Noble Boke of Cookry ffor a Prynce Houssolde or eny other Estately Houssolde

MANUSCRIPT

Holkham (earl of Leicester)

PRINTED EDITION

Napier, Robina, ed. (1882) *A Noble Boke of Cookry*. London: Elliot Stock.

The Forme of Cury

MANUSCRIPTS

BL Add. 5016 (Roll)
BL Cotton Julius D. VIII, fols. 90v–96v
BL Harley 1605, fols. 98–118
Durham Cosin V. III. 11, fols. 61v–72v
Rylands 7, fols. 1–91
Bühler 36 (Roll)

PRINTED EDITIONS

Pegge, Samuel, ed. (1780) *The Forme of Cury*. London: J. Nichols. (first MS)
Sass, Lorna J. (1975) *To the King's Taste: Richard II's Book of Feasts and Recipes Adapted for Modern Cooking*. New York: Metropolitan Museum of Art. (modernized version of all MSS)

Codicological and Household

[*Miscellaneous Collections*]

MANUSCRIPTS

Bodleian Library Douce 54, fols. 10–22v
Bodleian Library Douce 45, fols. 31–49v
BL Sloane 1584, fol. 39
BL Sloane 73, fols. 196–197, 201
BL Sloane 122, fols. 90–106v
BL Sloane 345, fol. 34
BL Sloane 1764, fol. 4
BL Sloane 962, fol. 152
BL Egerton 2852, fol. 4
BL Harley 665, fol. 1
BL Harley 665, fol. 1
BL Harley 2390, fol. 80
BL Harley 218, fol. 71
BL Cotton Julius D. VIII, fol. 88
BL Sloane 1698, fol. 89
BL Add. 14252, fol. 114
Bodleian Library Ashmole 1477, fols. 51–52
Trinity College (Cambridge) R. 14. 45, fols. 77–118
Pierpont Morgan Library 775, fol. 275

TRAVEL

Pilgrimage

John Capgrave, *Ye Solace of Pilgrims*

MANUSCRIPTS

Bodleian Library 423, fols. 355–414v
All Souls College (Oxford) 17 (flyleaves)
Balliol College (Oxford) 190, fols. 118–119

PRINTED EDITION

Mills, C. A., ed. (1911) *Ye Solace of Pilgrims*. London: British and American Archaeological Society.

William Wey, *Itineraries*

MANUSCRIPTS

Bodleian Library 565, fols. 1–105
Bodleian Library Douce 389 (scroll map)

PRINTED EDITIONS

Williams, G., ed. (1857) *The Itineraries of William Wey*. Roxburghe Club. London: J.B. Nichols. (first MS)
Matthews, W. (1962) *Later Medieval English Prose*, pp. 224–228. (extract of first MS)

Informacion for Pylgrymes unto the Holy Londe

MANUSCRIPT

BL Cotton Append. VIII, fols. 108–112

Miscellaneous Travel

[*Shires and Hundreds of England*]

MANUSCRIPT

Jesus College (Oxford) 29, fol. 267

Miscellaneous Instruction

Sailing

[*Directions for Sailing*]

Manuscripts

BL Lansdowne 285
BL Lansdowne 48
Pierpont Morgan Library 775, fols. 131–138v

Printed Edition

Gairdner, James, ed. (1889) *Sailing Directions for the Circumnavigation of England.* Hakluyt Society. London: The Society. (MS Lansdowne 48)

Printed Editions

de Worde. 1498 (STC 14081).
Horstmann, C., ed. (1885) "Ratschläge für eine Orientreise: aus Cotten Append. VIII." *EStn*, 8, 227–284.
Duff, E. G., ed. (1893) *Informacion for Pylgrymes unto the Holy Londe.* London: Lawrence and Bullen. (facsimile ed.)

Lacemaking

[*Instructions for Lacemaking*]

Manuscript

BL Harley 2320, fols. 52–70v

Printed Edition

Stanley, E. G., ed. (1974) "Many Sorts of Laces." In *Chaucer and Middle English Studies in Honour of Rossell Hope Robbins*, edited by Beryl Rowland, pp. 89–103.

Time

[*Treatise on Time*]

MANUSCRIPT

BL Harley 4011, fols. 164–168

PRINTED EDITION

Horstmann, C., ed. (1887) "Ueber Zeitrechnung." *EStn*, 10, 34–41.

Weights

[*Weights for Assize Bread*]

MANUSCRIPT

Bodleian Library Douce 16, fol. 230v

Sundial

[*Treatise on Making a "Little Ship of Venice"*]

MANUSCRIPT

Trinity College (Cambridge) O. 5. 26, fols. 121–122v

PRINTED EDITION

Price, Derek de Solla, ed. (1960) "The Little Ship of Venice—A Middle English Instrument Tract." *JHM*, 15, 402–407.

PROGNOSTICARY WORKS

ALMANACS AND RELATED TEXTS

Lunaries

[*The Days of the Moon*]

MANUSCRIPTS

Bodleian Library Ashmole 391, fols. 3v–5
Princeton University Library Garrett, fols. 79–84 (by John Metham)
Bodleian Library Ashmole 189, fols. 64–67 (fragment)
Longleat Library 176, fols. 39v–41

PRINTED EDITIONS

Craig, Hardin, ed. (1916) *The Works of John Metham*, pp. 148–156. EETS, os 132.
    (Garrett MS)
Förster, Max, ed. (1944) "Vom Fortleben antiker Samellunare im englischen und in an-
    deren Volkssprachen." *Anglia*, 67, 137–143. (first MS, with extract from third MS)

[*The Months of the Moon*]

MANUSCRIPTS

Bodleian Library Ashmole 189, fols. 68–68v
Bodleian Library Ashmole 189, fol. 67v
Bodleian Library Ashmole 210, fol. 23
Bodleian Library Selden supra 90, fols. 16v–21v

Related Works

Boke of Fortune

MANUSCRIPT

Bodleian Library Ashmole 343, fols. 2–22v

[*Critical Days*]

MANUSCRIPTS

BL Harley 1735, fols. 29–36
BL Sloane 213, fol. 112v

[*The Four Houses*]

MANUSCRIPT

Bodleian Library Ashmole 391, fols. 5v–16v

Erra Pater (or *The Prophecies of Esdras*)

MANUSCRIPTS

Princeton University Library Garrett, fols. 78–78v ([*Christmas Day*], by John Metham)
Gonville and Caius College (Cambridge) 457, fol. 58 ([*Christmas Day*])
Saint John's College (Cambridge) 269, fol. 58 ([*Christmas Day*])
BL Harley 671, fol. 25 ([*New Year's Day*])
BL Sloane 218, fol. 111 ([*New Year's Day*])
Huntington Library HM 1336, fol. 35 ([*New Year's Day*])

PRINTED EDITION

Craig, Hardin, ed. (1916) *The Works of John Metham*, pp. 146–147. (Garrett MS)

Dyuers Tokens of Wedder (or *Thunder Books*)

MANUSCRIPTS

Bodleian Library Digby 88, fols. 42v–43v
Pierpont Morgan Library 775, fols. 281v–282v
Huntington Library HM 49, fols. 96–96v
National Library of Wales Porkington 10, fols. 8v–11

PRINTED EDITIONS

Bühler, Curt F., ed. (1941) "Astrological Prognostications in MS. 775 of the Pierpont
    Morgan Library." *MLN*, 56, 351–355. (Morgan MS)

Kurvinen, Auvo, ed. (1957) "Impressions Concerning ðe Weduryng.'" *NM*, 58, 46–69. (Porkington MS)

OCCULT WORKS

Diagnostic and Prophetic

Dream Books

Somnia Danielis

Manuscripts

BL Royal 12. E. XVI, fols. 1–2v
BL Sloane 1609, fols. 29v–32
Trinity College (Cambridge) O. 9. 37, fols. 26–30
BL Lansdowne 388, fol. 372v

Printed Editions

Förster, Max (1910) "Ein mittelenglisches Prosa-Traumbuch des 14. Jahrhunderts." *Archiv*, 127, 48–84. (first three MSS).
Bühler, Curt F., ed. (1962) "Two Middle English Texts of the *Somnia Danielis*." *Anglia*, 80, 264–273. (MS Lansdowne 388)

Chiromancy

John Metham, *The Syens of Palmestre*

Manuscripts

Princeton University Library Garrett, fols. 1–11v
All Souls College (Oxford) 81, fols. 202–212

Printed Edition

Craig, Hardin, ed. (1916) *The Works of John Metham*, pp. 118–145. (second MS)

[*Treatise on Palmestrie*]

MANUSCRIPTS

Bodleian Library Digby 88, fols. 44–46v
Bodleian Library Digby Roll IV

PRINTED EDITION

Price, D. J., ed. (1953) *An Old Palmestry*. Cambridge: W. Heffer and Sons. (second MS)

Geomancy

Translation of Martin of Spain's *De Geomancia* (?)

MANUSCRIPT

Bodleian Library Ashmole 360, fols. 15v–27v

MEDICO-CHEMICAL

Charms and Related Texts

Virtutes Aquila

MANUSCRIPT

BL Add. 34111, fols. 195–196v

PRINTED EDITION

Sheldon, Suzanne, ed. (1977) "The Eagle; Bird of Magic and Medicine in a Middle
English Translation of the *Kyranides*." *TSE*, 22, 1–31.

Alexander Alexius, [*Compendium*]

Manuscripts

BL SLoane 353, fols. 51v–56
BL Sloane 2948, fols. 52–56
BL Sloane 73, fols. 4–7v
All Souls College (Oxford) 81, fols. 133v–145

Printed Edition

Singer, Dorothea Waley, with Anderson, Annie, and Addis, Robina (1931) *Catalogue of Latin and Vernacular Alchemical Manuscripts in Great Britain and Ireland Dating from Before the Sixteenth Century*, 3:772–773. Brussels: UAI. (extracts)

[*Charm Based on the Measurement of Christ's Body*]

Manuscripts

Rotulus Harley 43. A. 14
Glazier 39
Bodleian Library 177
Rotulus Harley T. 11

Printed Editions

Simpson, W. Sparrow, ed. (1892) "On a Magical Roll Preserved in the British Museum." *Journal of the British Archaeological Association*, 48, 50–54. (fourth MS)
Onions, C. T., ed. (1918) "A Devotion to the Cross Written in the South-West of England." *MLR*, 13, 228–230. (third MS)
Bühler, Curt F., ed. (1964) "Prayers and Charms in Certain Middle English Scrolls." *Speculum*, 39, 274–277. (Glazier 39)

[*Charm Based on the Length of Nails with Which Christ Was Fastened to the Cross*]

Manuscript

Rotulus Harley T. 11

Printed Edition

Bühler, Curt F., ed. (1964) "Prayers and Charms in Certain Middle English Scrolls," pp. 274–277.

[*Charm Based on Remembering Angels*]

MANUSCRIPT

BL Sloane 2584, fol. 37

PRINTED EDITION

Gray, Douglas, ed. (1974) "Notes on Some Middle English Charms." In *Chaucer and Middle English Studies*, edited by Beryl Rowland, p. 58.

[*Charms against Thieves*]

MANUSCRIPT

BL Sloane 2389, fol. 26

PRINTED EDITION

Bühler, Curt F., ed. (1962) "Three Middle English Prose Charms from MS. Harley 2389." *N&Q*, 207, 48.

Alchemy and Related Texts

Translation of Magister Panton's *Liber de Turba*

MANUSCRIPTS

BL Sloane 1091, fols. 82–84
Trinity College (Cambridge) 1312, fols. 8–12
Cambridge University Library Kk. VI. 30, fol. 36

Translation of Hermes' *Dicta Philosophorum*

MANUSCRIPT

Bodleian Library Ashmole 759, fols. 136–146v

Translation of *Mercher ad Fledium*

MANUSCRIPT

Corpus Christi College (Oxford) 226, fols. 34–94v

Translation of Hermes' *Secreta*

MANUSCRIPT

Bodleian Library Ashmole 1451, fols. 43–43v, 68–70

Translation of Ebrardus's (?) *Summa Aurea*

MANUSCRIPT

BL Sloane 1118, fols. 34–36

Translation of John of Garland's *Rosarium Parvum*

MANUSCRIPT

BL Sloane 1091, fols. 125–132

Translation of Albertus Magnus's *Semita Recta*

MANUSCRIPTS

Cambridge University Library Ee. I. 13, fols. 141–148v
BL Sloane 2128, fols. 1–13v

Translation of Albertus Magnus's *Mirror of Light*

MANUSCRIPTS

Trinity College (Cambridge) 916, pp. 121–142
Cambridge University Library Kk. VI. 30, fols. 1–35v.
BL Sloane 513, fols. 155–168

Translation of Roger Bacon's *De Leone Viridi*

MANUSCRIPTS

BL Sloane 1091, fols. 102–104v

Translation of Arnaldus de Villa Nova's *Visio Mystica*

MANUSCRIPT

Trinity College (Cambridge) R. 14. 45, fols. 34–40

Translation of Raymund Lull's *Epistola*

MANUSCRIPTS

BL Sloane 1091, fols. 97–101v
Bodleian Library Ashmole 1450, fols. 147–155v, 165–168v

Translation of Jean de Roquetaillade's *Liber de Consideratione Quintae Essentiae*

MANUSCRIPTS

BL Sloane 73, fols. 11–25v
BL Sloane 353, fols. 2–51
BL Sloane 480, fols. 26–161
Bodleian Library Ashmole 1450, fols. 157–160, 168v–176
Bodleian Library E. Mus. 52, fols. 33v–42v

PRINTED EDITIONS

Furnivall, F. J., ed. (1866) *The Book of Quinte Essence or Fifth Being*. EETS, os 16. (MS
    Sloane 353)
Matthews, W. (1962) *Later Medieval English Prose*, pp. 213–215. (extract from MS
    Sloane 353)

Robert Frunitor, *The Wordis of the Philosophers*

MANUSCRIPT

BL Stowe 1070, fols. 26–32

Dialogue

MANUSCRIPTS

BL Harley 2407, fols. 68v–69
BL Sloane 3747, fols. 66–71v

[Recipe Collections and Maxims]

MANUSCRIPTS

BL Sloane 2135, fols. 10v–11
BL Sloane 1091, fol. 133
BL Sloane 513, fols. 39–39v
BL Sloane 1698, fols. 45–52v
BL Sloane 3747, fols. 16–24v
BL Harley 2407, fols. 1–2v
Bodleian Library Ashmole 759, fols. 56–65, 78v, 134–135
Bodleian Library Ashmole 1451, fols. 1–36, 71–79

Geoffrey Chaucer (?), [Treatises on Making the Philosopher's Stone]

MANUSCRIPT

Trinity College (Dublin) D. 28, fols. 96–104v

PRINTED EDITION

Dunleavy, Gareth W., ed. (1965) "The Chaucer Ascription in Trinity College Dublin
    MS. D. 28." *Ambix*, 13, 13–20.

SECONDARY SOURCES

Arthur, Harold, Viscount Dillon (1900–1901) "On a MS. Collection of Ordinances of Chivalry of the Fifteenth Century Belonging to Lord Hastings." *Archaeologia*, 57, 33–34.

Barber, M. J. (1957) "The Englishman Abroad in the Fifteenth Century." *M&H*, 11, 67–77.

Basier, L. (1936) The *"Lapidaire chrétien." Its Influences, Its Sources.* Washington, D.C.: Catholic University of America.

Bennett, H. S. (1944) "Science and Information in English Writings of the Fifteenth Century." *MLR*, 39, 1–8.

Bidez, J. (1924–1935) *Catalogue des manuscrits alchemiques grecs.* 2 vols. Brussels: M. Lemertin.

———— (1939–1951) *Catalogue des manuscrits alchemiques latins.* 3 vols. Brussels: UAI.

Biedermann, Hans (1973) *Handlexikon der magischen Künde von der spätantike bis zum 19. Jahrhundert.* 2d ed. Graz: Akademische Druck- und Verlagsanstalt.

Blake, N. F. (1972) "Middle English Prose and Its Audience." *Anglia*, 90, 437–455.

Boll, Franz (1903) *Sphaera.* Hildesheim: Georg Olms.

Bornstein, Diane (1975) "Military Manuals in Fifteenth-Century England." *MS*, 37, 467–477.

———— (1976) *Mirrors of Courtesy.* Hamden, Conn.: Archon.

———— (1977) "French Influence on Fifteenth-Century English Prose as Exemplified by the Translation of Christine de Pisan's *Livre du corps de policie." MS*, 39, 369–396.

Braswell, Laurel (1978) "Popular Lunar Astrology in the Late Middle Ages." *RUO*, 48, 187–194.

———— (1981) *Western Manuscripts from Classical Antiquity to the Renaissance: A Handbook.* New York: Garland.

Briggs, Katherine Mary (1962) *Pale Hecate's Team.* London: Routledge and Kegan Paul.

Bühler, Curt F. (1941) "Sir John Paston's *Grete Booke*, a Fifteenth-Century Best-Seller." *MLN*, 56, 345–351.

Carter, Henry H. (1961) *A Dictionary of Middle English Music Terms.* Bloomington: Indiana University Press.

Cosman, Madeleine Pelner (1976) *Fabulous Feasts.* New York: George Braziller.

Crombie, Alistair Cameron (1959) *Medieval and Early Modern Science.* 2d ed. Garden City, N.Y.: Doubleday.

Doyle, A. I. (1957) "The Work of a Fifteenth-Century Scribe, William Ebesham." *BJRL*, 39, 298–325.

Duncan, Edgar H. (1968) "Alchemy and Chaucer's Canon's Yeoman's Tale." *Speculum*, 43, 633–656.

Evans, Joan (1922) *Magical Jewels of the Middle Ages and the Renaissance, Particularly in England.* Oxford: Clarendon Press.

Goldberg, Ada, and Saye, Hyman (1933) "An Index to Mediaeval French Medical Receipts of the Middle Ages That Have Been Published." *BHM*, 1, 435–466.

Grant, Edward (1971) *Physical Science in the Middle Ages.* New York: Wiley.

———— (1974) *A Source Book in Medieval Science.* Cambridge, Mass.: Harvard University Press.

Gundel, Wilhelm (1931) *Sternglaube, Sternreligion und Sternorakeln.* 4th ed. Berlin: Teubner.

Gunther, R. W. T. (1925–1945) *Early Science in Oxford.* 14 vols. Oxford: The Author.

Hall, Donald J. (1966) *English Medieval Pilgrimage.* London: Routledge and Kegan Paul.

Hands, Rachel (1967) "Juliana Berners and the *Book of St. Albans.*" *RES*, ns 18, 373–386.

———— (1971) "The Names of All Manner of Hawks, and to Whom They Belong." *N&Q*, ns 18, 85–88.

———— (1972) "Horse-Dealing Lore, or a Fifteenth-Century 'Help to Discourse'?" *MAE*, 41, 230–239.

Hieatt, Constance B., and Butler, Sharon (1976) *Pleyn Delit.* Toronto: University of Toronto Press.

Hitchcock, Elsie, ed. (1924) *Folewer to the Donet.* EETS, os 164.

Hughes, Andrew (1974) *Medieval Music: The Sixth Liberal Art.* Toronto Medieval Bibliographies 4. Toronto: University of Toronto Press.

Jacob, E. F. (1944) *"The Book of St. Albans."* *BJRL*, 28, 99–118.

Jayawardene, S. A. (1978) "Western Scientific Manuscripts before 1680: A Checklist of Published Catalogues." *Annals of Science*, 35, 143–172.

Legge, M. D. (1963) *Anglo-Norman Literature and Its Background.* Oxford: Clarendon Press.

Lucas, P. J. (1969) "John Capgrave, O.S.A. (1393–1464): Scribe and 'Publisher.'" *TCBS*, 5, 1–35.

McBryde, John M. (1917) "Some Middle English Charms." *Sewanee Review*, 25, 297–304.

McCulloch, Florence (1962) *Mediaeval Latin and French Bestiaries.* Rev. ed. Chapel Hill: University of North Carolina Press.

McFarlane, K. B. (1973) *The Nobility of Later Medieval England.* Oxford: Clarendon Press.

Martin, Lawrence Thomas (1977) "The *Somniale Danielis*, An Edition of the Medieval Latin Dream Interpretation Handbook." *DAI*, 38. 4150A.

Meier, Christel (1977) Gemma Spiritualis: Methode und Gebrauch der Edelsteinallegorese von frühen Christentum bis ins 18. Jahrhundert, pt. 1. Münsterische Mittelalterschriften 34/1. Munich: W. Fink.

Mitchell, R. J. (1964) *The Spring Voyage: The Jerusalem Pilgrimage in 1458.* London: John Murphy.

Murphy, James J. (1974) *Rhetoric in the Middle Ages: A History of Rhetorical Theory from Saint Augustine to the Renaissance.* Berkeley: University of California Press.

Parson, Rosamund H. (1929) "Anglo-Norman Books of Courtesy and Nurture." *PMLA*, 44, 313–455.

Plessner, M. (1954) "The Place of the *Turba Philosophorum* in the Development of Alchemy." *Isis*, 45, 331–338.

Powell, Niel (1976) *Alchemy, the Ancient Science.* Garden City, N.Y.: Doubleday.

Read, John (1966) *Prelude to Chemistry. An Outline of Alchemy. Its Literature and Relationships.* 2d ed. Cambridge, Mass.: Harvard University Press.

Reidy, John, ed. (1975) *Thomas Norton. Ordinal of Alchemy.* EETS 272.

Robbins, Rossell Hope (1939) "English Almanacks of the Fifteenth Century." *PQ*, 18, 321–331.

———— (1966) "Alchemical Texts in Middle English Verse: Corrigenda and Addenda." *Ambix*, 13, 62–73.

Röhricht, Reinhold (1890), rev. Amiran, David H. K. (1963) *Bibliotheca Geographica Palaestinae: Chronologisches Verzeichnis der von 333 bis 1878 verfassten Literatur über das Heilige Land mit dem Versuch einer Kartographie.* Jerusalem: Universitas Booksellers.

Rowland, Beryl (1973) *Animals with Human Faces: A Guide to Animal Symbolism.* Knoxville: University of Tennessee Press.

————, ed. (1974) *Chaucer and Middle English Studies in Honour of Rossell Hope Robbins.* London: Allen and Unwin.

———— (1978) *Birds with Human Souls: A Guide to Bird Symbolism.* Knoxville: University of Tennessee Press.

Sarton, George (1948) *Introduction to the History of Science,* 3 vols. in 5 pts. Baltimore: Williams and Williams.

Savage, H. (1933) "Hunting in the Middle Ages." *Speculum,* 8, 30–41.

Serjeantson, M. S. (1937) "The Vocabulary of Cooking in the Fifteenth Century." *E&S*, 23, 25–37.

Seymour, M. C., et al. (1975) *On the Properties of Things: John Trevisa's Translation of Bartholomaeus Anglicus De Proprietatibus Rerum.* 2 vols. Oxford: Clarendon Press.

Sheldon, Suzanne (1978) "Middle English and Latin Charms, Amulets, and Talismans from Vernacular Literature." *DAI* 39. 4233A.

Shrader, C. R. (1979) "A Handlist of Extant Manuscripts Containing the *De Re Militari* of Favius Vegetius Renatus." *Scriptorium,* 33, 280–305.

Shumaker, Wayne (1972) *The Occult Sciences in the Renaissance (A Study in Intellectual Patterns).* Berkeley: University of California Press.

Silverstein, Theodore (1959) "On the Source of an English Thunder-Treatise of the Fifteenth Century." In *A Festschrift for John G. Kunstmann,* pp. 85–98. *UNCSGLL* 26. Chapel Hill: University of North Carolina Press.

Studer, Paul, and Evans, Joan (1924) *Anglo-Norman Lapidaries.* Paris: E. Champion.

Telle, Joachim (1980) *Sol und Luna: Literar- und alchemiegeschichtliche Studien zu einem altdeutschen Bildgedicht.* Hürtgenwald: Guido Pressler.

Thomas, Keith (1971) *Religion and the Decline of Magic: Studies in Popular Beliefs in Sixteenth- and Seventeenth-Century England.* London: Weidenfeld and Nicolson.

Thompson, Daniel V. (1935) "Trial Index to Some Unpublished Sources for the History of Medieval Craftsmanship." *Speculum,* 10, 410–431.

Thomson, David (1979) *A Descriptive Catalogue of Middle English Grammatical Texts.* New York: Garland.

Thorndike, Lynn (1923–1958) *A History of Magic and Experimental Science.* 8 vols. New York: Macmillan.

———— (1965) "Chiromancy in Mediaeval Latin Manuscripts." *Speculum*, 40, 674–706.

Voigts, Linda Ehrsam (1981) "A Letter from a Middle English Dictaminal Formulary in Harvard Law Library MS. 43." *Speculum*, 56, 575–581.

Wedel, Theodore Otto (1920) *The Medieval Attitude toward Astrology*. New Haven: Yale University Press.

Weisheipl, James (1971) *A Development of Physical Theory in the Middle Ages*. Ann Arbor: University of Michigan Press.

Wells, J. E. (1916–1957) *A Manual of the Writings in Middle English 1050–1400*, with Supplements. Hamden: Connecticut Academy of Arts and Sciences.

White, T. H. (1954) *The Bestiary: A Book of Beasts, Being a Translation from a Latin Bestiary of the Twelfth Century*. London: Cape.

Wilson, C. Anne (1973) *Food and Drink in Britain*. London: Constable.

Wilson, R. M. (1970) *The Lost Literature of Medieval England*. 2d ed. London: Methuen.

Wilson, William J. (1939) "Catalogue of Latin and Vernacular Alchemical Manuscripts in the United States and Canada." *Osiris*, 6, entire issue.

Workman, Samuel K. (1940) *Fifteenth Century Translation as an Influence on English Prose*. Princeton: Princeton University Press. Repr. (1972). New York: Octagon Books.

Zacher, Christian K. (1976) *Curiosity and Pilgrimage: The Literature of Discovery in Fourteenth-Century England*. Baltimore: Johns Hopkins University Press.

CHAPTER 17

William Caxton

Norman Blake

William Caxton's name is familiar to most English-speaking people as the man who introduced printing into England, and the celebration in 1976 of the quincentenary of the first book printed in England witnessed a spate of books about him. He therefore differs from most of the writers dealt with in this volume in that scholarship has to contend not so much with ignorance, as with romantic ideas and conflicting interpretations. Through his life and work he impinges on history, economics, literary history and criticism, bibliography, and early printing. As no man can be familiar with all these areas, an expert in one discipline may pick up debatable interpretations from another; and this can breed controversy. For the literary scholar Caxton falls into that gap between Chaucer and the Elizabethans which is often dismissed as a barren age, and so he has been more praised as a printer of Chaucer and Malory than as an author in his own right. In the eighteenth century he was dismissed as a person of no discrimination who published inferior vernacular texts instead of the Latin classics; in the nineteenth a reaction against this view set in, and he was uncritically adulated as a scholar who tried to emulate continental publishers by printing his country's major writers; and in the twentieth century there has been a growing realisation of the different roles he played in his life and of their interaction. Too often, though, scholars have been quick to attack or defend Caxton for a particular characteristic, such as his haste in translation, while the important task of editing and cataloguing his editions remains neglected.

With Caxton it is important to know something about his life for it sheds light upon his literary career. Even so, many details remain obscure. The reasons for this ignorance are partly the paucity of sources, partly the commonness of the name Caxton, and partly the social milieu into which he is likely to have been born. It is widely accepted that he was born in the Weald of Kent which was then a formidable and sizable forest not far from London. This is because in his prologue to the *History of Troy* he wrote that he "was born and lerned myn Englissh in Kente in the Weeld, where I doubte not is spoken as brode and rude Englissh as is in ony place of Englond" (Blake 1973, p. 98). However, it is necessary to bear in mind that when Caxton gives information about himself in his prologues and epilogues, he does so not to inform posterity about his life, but to build up his "blurb." As a publisher he was trying to sell books printed on his presses, and to do that he included prologues and epilogues that would attract potential purchasers. At the end of the Middle Ages writers frequently threw their attainments into the worst possible light as part of the so-called humility formula. This was a means whereby the writer craved the indulgence of the reader for the imperfections of his work that sprang from his own shortcomings. What goes into these formulas is often exaggerated, and so one cannot take their evidence at face value. Thus although it remains probable that Caxton was born in Kent, it is not necessary to assume that his birthplace was in the Weald, which was introduced to add a touch of boorishness and uncourtliness to Caxton's origins. One recent proposal has suggested that his birthplace was at Strood (Blake 1966).

His parents were probably merchants for they sent their son to school and then apprenticed him to Robert Large, an influential merchant who became Lord Mayor of London in 1439. It may not have been easy to place a boy with Large, and this argues that Caxton's parents had some influence in the merchant community. Caxton was already an apprentice by 1438, though it is probable he was enrolled with Large before then. The guilds in London traditionally dealt in one item of merchandise, and the mercers' guild in which Caxton was enrolled handled "mercery" or what today includes haberdashery, silk, and other cloth. Each company had a monopoly over its merchandise in the retail market in England, but no such restriction applied to the overseas trade in which the largest fortunes were made. At the end of the fifteenth century there was a flourishing trade between England and the Low Countries, involving the export of wool and the import of finished products like cloth and manuscripts. Important international fairs were held in the towns of the Low Countries like Bruges where merchants from different countries had established permanent settlements.

One of Caxton's most important acts was to enroll as an apprentice with Large in the Mercers' Company since this provided him with a well-marked career. He immediately became a member of the richest and most powerful guild in London. He met many other merchants who would remain friends and business colleagues in later life. He learned how to handle money, finance transactions, float loans, and market goods. Equally important was the link between the mercers and the Merchant Adventurers' Company, that loose organisation whose role was the regulation and protection of English merchants engaged in the overseas trade. The Merchant Adventurers' Company had no guild house in London, for it used the Mercers' Hall as its base, and it was there that its records were kept. It might not be altogether inaccurate to say that the history of the merchant adventurers at this time is the history of the mercers. Hence any apprentice joining the mercers would inevitably be drawn into the overseas trade with the Continent organised through the merchant adventurers. As it happens, the Low Countries were at this time part of the Duchy of Burgundy, a vast conglomerate of lands that stretched from Switzerland through the east and north of France to the North Sea. The dukes were princes of the French royal blood, and in the fifteenth century their duchy was usually richer and politically more powerful than the monarchy. The politics of the time involved manoeuvres among the three powers, England, France, and Burgundy. For their part the dukes became more closely linked with their Low Countries possessions during the fifteenth century because these lands provided the greatest revenue and affected their relations with England and France. Thus English merchants who traded with the Low Countries were necessarily involved in political negotiations which were partly economic and partly national. The merchants were also involved in arranging loans for the kings of England to support political and military developments. Consequently merchants like Caxton would have been familiar with members of different European courts, and they moved on the fringes of court life, although they rarely became courtiers as such.

Caxton's career followed what was probably a set pattern, and if he differs from some of his colleagues it may be simply because he rose higher up the ladder than they. Large died in 1441, but Caxton would have remained in the business until he issued from his apprenticeship. Then as a mercer he became involved in the trade with the Low Countries. It is not likely that he lived abroad at first even though in his prologue to the *History of Troy* he claimed that he had "contynued by the space of xxx yere for the most parte in the contres of Braband, Flandres, Holand and Zeland" (Blake 1973, p. 98). This statement is introduced as part of the humility formula and should not be taken literally. His home was probably in England, though he doubtless spent much of his time going back and forth across the Channel. At first he dealt in the traditional items of mercery, but later there is evidence to suggest that he became involved in the import of manuscripts. Flanders was at that time the most important centre for manuscript production in Northern Europe, and the manuscripts produced there were in great demand for their craftsmanship and the quality of their miniatures. The merchants provided the English gentry with these manuscripts, and there is every reason to suppose that it was at this period in his life that Caxton learned the value of literature as merchandise.

He continued to prosper, and in the 1450s he must have spent an increasing amount of time in Bruges and other towns in Flanders. In the early 1460s, possibly in 1462, he was elected to the governorship of the English Nation there. The nationals of each country were organised into nations under a governor whose job it was to discipline the members and to act as liaison with the local and national authorities in the Low Countries. It was an important job involving diplomacy and travel, and Caxton's election indicates his wealth and his reputation. Through it he met people of high rank. For example, in 1468 at Damme outside Bruges, Edward IV's sister Margaret married Charles the Bold who had succeeded to the Duchy of Burgundy the previous year. The marriage was designed to cement the Burgundian alliance, and it was celebrated with pomp and pageantry. Caxton may have had a hand in the negotiations for the marriage, and he would certainly have attended the celebrations.

A new phase in Caxton's life began when he decided to acquire a printing press to embark on a career as a publisher. I use this word advisedly because he is usually described as England's first printer. He was not indeed a printer in the modern sense of that word, for he did not operate the presses or even supervise the workmen on a day-to-day basis; he was not an artisan. He was in charge of a business which had a printing press as part of its equipment, though the physical production of books was only a limited aspect of that business. The most important part fell into the domain of what we today consider the role of a publisher: the choice of material to print and the marketing of the finished product. At that time the production and sale of goods were not as separated as they are today; a man who had a stake in the sale of manuscripts and books might naturally seek to acquire the means of their production.

It is first necessary to enquire why and how Caxton became involved in printing. The discovery of printing with movable type is attributed to Johannes Gutenberg in Mainz in the early 1450s. From Mainz the invention spread up and down the Rhine quickly, and the first printing press to be established in Cologne was operative by 1464. Its owner, Ulrich Zell, was probably an associate or pupil of Gutenberg. Cologne was then one of the leading towns of the Hanseatic League which had particular associations with England and which dominated the Low Countries. Trade flowed along the Rhine from the Low Countries to Cologne, which was also the seat of the local archbishopric. Many people from Holland and Belgium went to the university there. Developments in Cologne would quickly be known in Bruges, and it is not unlikely that Caxton soon became aware of the establishment of its first printing press.

The way in which Caxton acquired a press at Cologne has to be pieced together from several disparate sources. The first of these is the Register of Aliens at Cologne in which he was given permission to reside in Cologne for four continuous periods starting on July 17, 1471. The final renewal of this permission which was for a six-month period is dated June 19, 1472. Presumably Caxton stayed in Cologne until the end of 1472 since his permission was not extended again. It is accepted generally that he was in Cologne to acquire a press, since this was the nearest place to Bruges with one at that time. The second source is the material included in his prologues and epilogues to the *History of Troy*, his first printed book. There we learn that he began translating the *History of Troy* from Raoul Lefèvre's French version on March 1, 1469. After he had completed a few quires of the translation, he gave the work up in disgust at his incompetence. Two years later he showed this unfinished translation to Margaret of Burgundy, the wife of Charles the Bold, who ordered him to complete it and gave him a "fee." Caxton describes himself in a prologue as Margaret's "servant." Although he had started the book in Bruges, he continued it in Ghent and finished it in Cologne on September 19, 1471. A third source is the edition of the English translation of *De Proprietatibus Rerum* published by Wynkyn de Worde, Caxton's assistant and successor, in 1495. In that edition Wynkyn included some verses about the book, which include the lines:

> And also of your charyte call to remembrance
> The soule of William Caxton, first prynter of this boke,
> In Laten tonge at Coleyn [i.e., Cologne], himself to avaunce,
> That every well disposyd man may theron loke.

This verse implies that Caxton was associated with a Latin edition of the *De Proprietatibus* printed in Cologne. As it happens there is an edition from Cologne dated to the early 1470s, and we must assume that Caxton had some link with that text. This itself introduces the fourth source, the development of typography in Cologne and the Low Countries. Caxton is linked with an edition of *De Proprietatibus* printed in Cologne which was almost certainly produced in the workshop of Johannes Veldener, although there is no name or date given in the edition. Veldener is known to have been in Cologne at the right time though he later moved to Louvain.

These sources raise several questions. Why did Caxton stop his translation? What was his relationship with Margaret of Burgundy? Did he go to Cologne of his own volition? What was his business arrangement with Veldener, and what role did he play in the publication of books in Cologne? These questions are interrelated. The break in the translation of the *History of Troy* as described by Caxton was introduced as part of the humility formula. By this means he was able to suggest that, although his own abilities were limited because of his birth in Kent and long residence abroad, the book's style was courtly and fashionable because it had been corrected in accordance with the wishes of Margaret of Burgundy, who was a member of one of the most sophisticated courts. Even so, there may be some truth in the break in translation although the reasons Caxton gives for it are not likely to be the whole truth. If he was making an English translation of a Burgundian book, it can have been destined only for the English market. In 1469 Edward IV had been on the throne for eight years and might have seemed so well established that England would no longer be wracked with civil strife. However, in July 1469 Warwick the Kingmaker captured Edward and tried to restore Henry VI to the throne. It may be this return to civil disorder that caused Caxton to put aside his translation. Edward was freed by Warwick, but was forced to flee to the Low Countries. Eventually in 1471 his brother-in-law, Charles of Burgundy, helped him to regain the country, which he accomplished by defeating Warwick at Barnet on April 14, and the Henrician forces at Tewkesbury on May 4. Henry VI and his son were killed. Edward became undisputed ruler, and Caxton was in a position to resume his translation.

In the *History of Troy* Caxton said he was Margaret's servant and received a fee from her. Many scholars have taken this to mean that he was in her employ in some capacity, perhaps as secretary or librarian. This view cannot be accepted, for there is no evidence that mercers were employed in such positions for which they were not well fitted. Caxton's words here are part of the conventional language of the fifteenth century used to express deference to members of the aristocracy. Caxton was governor of the English Nation; he was not a courtier. He is not likely to have been in Margaret's service, and he probably remained governor until he went to Cologne. If he was not in Margaret's service, there is no likelihood that he went on her behalf to Cologne. Some scholars have suggested, on the other hand, that he was in Cologne purely fortuitously because he had been exiled from Bruges for political misdemeanours (cf. Painter 1976). There is equally no evidence for this assumption, which is in any event unlikely. Edward could not exile Caxton from Bruges, and if Charles of Burgundy exiled him he would more likely have returned to England. The most reasonable explanation of the available evidence is that Caxton went to Cologne on his own initiative and at his own expense with the express purpose of acquiring a printing press. After all he started his first translation in 1469, and it is likely that his intention to acquire a press dates from then. Otherwise there seems no adequate explanation of why he should have embarked on a translation at all.

When he arrived in Cologne he teamed up with Johannes Veldener, a type cutter and printer. Before the publication of the *De Proprietatibus* Veldener had produced relatively small quarto books, as was customary with the Cologne printers. *De Proprietatibus* is a large folio volume, and it can have been produced only with a massive influx of capital into the business. That capital was presumably provided by Caxton, possibly as part of the bargain by which he acquired a press and the necessary helpers. In that case Caxton would have been the financier and part-publisher of the volume; he was not the printer. A second volume, *Gesta Romanorum*, was probably also produced jointly by Veldener and Caxton, before the former left Cologne to set up in Louvain and the latter returned to Bruges. They remained in contact, and Veldener continued to supply Caxton with type.

Caxton returned to Bruges at the end of 1472 or the beginning of 1473 and embarked on his publishing career. His first edition, *History of Troy*, was issued in late 1473 or early 1474, and his second translation, *Game of Chess*, appeared on March 31, 1474. These books which were in English were meant for sale in England. However, Caxton stopped producing English books for the rest of his stay in Bruges, until 1476, and produced four books in French. These were probably produced in association with Colard Mansion, a Bruges scrivener, with whom Caxton apparently had some business link. Possibly Mansion had earlier produced manuscripts for Caxton to sell in England. When Caxton returned to England, Mansion carried on publishing in Bruges. Mansion could provide Caxton with access to retail outlets in Bruges and its environs. Caxton's switch to French texts may signal the difficulties he came up against in trying to dispose of copies of his editions in England when he himself was not there. He would be forced to use agents or other intermediaries. The difficulty of distribution may have prompted him to return to England so that the printing and distribution could be done together. The acquisition and translation of suitable texts were perhaps the least of his problems and did not demand his presence on the Continent, for through his contacts with people like Mansion he could get hold of the books being read there which he could then translate and print. It was the sale of books that demanded a personal touch.

At the same time we should not forget that although he became a publisher Caxton did not cease to be a merchant with all that entails. He was still employed on diplomatic missions by the crown, and he still continued to trade in a variety of goods, though as time progressed he probably limited his merchandise increasingly to manuscripts and books. These latter included many that were printed on other presses and which he had imported. Caxton's life did not change suddenly because of the printing press; the main difference was that he controlled the production of the goods he was selling.

When Caxton returned to England in 1476 he did not establish his business in London as one might have expected; he set up his press in the precincts of Westminster Abbey. Churches then were much more involved in the life of the surrounding town, as is still true of churches in some continental cities. It used to be thought that Caxton had avoided London because of the hostility of the scriveners, but this view is incorrect for there seems to have been cooperation between scriveners and printers; indeed many early printers were scriveners by profession. His choice of Westminster was positive rather than negative, for it was the seat of the court, the civil service, and the judiciary. It was not the financial centre of England, but it was the courtly and fashionable centre. In publishing books the most difficult problem is disposing of multiple copies of an identical text. The acquisition of a press and the physical process of printing require capital; but the disposal of possibly hundreds of copies of a book requires a distribution system which cannot be established so easily. Caxton had sold manuscripts earlier in his career, but they were individual works which could be sold on a personal basis. The advantage of Westminster was that because it was near the court, many rich, idle people were in the vicinity. Many shops besides Caxton's were established there to tempt courtiers and other hangers-on with their wares. In addition Westminster Abbey had a large scriptorium which may have been able to provide Caxton or his clients with other appurtenances to the book trade like rubricating and binding.

The average printer was an artisan who responded to the whims of his patron in his publishing work, and that meant considerable numbers of them went bankrupt. They did not have the necessary financial expertise to run a business as complicated as publishing. Caxton had that expertise, and he also developed a list as a modern publisher does. This sense of purpose can be understood from his very first printed book, *History of Troy*. Almost all books that had been printed by 1473 in Europe were in Latin and were either religious or scholarly. One might have expected Caxton's first book to follow this pattern, particularly if he had drifted into printing as some scholars have suggested. Instead, he produced an English translation of a French work, and this indicates that he had thought carefully about his publishing programme.

What were the alternatives available to Caxton in deciding his publishing policy, and how did he set about deciding which book to pick? First there was the question of language: should his texts be in English, French, or Latin? The number of people in England who could read French easily at the end of the fifteenth century was probably small, and so French was not a realistic choice. Latin was much better known, particularly in academic and religious circles where it remained the lingua franca. The problems with Latin were that the choice of texts would be restricted, the audience would be small, and the risk of competition from books printed abroad would be considerable. The same book was often printed at about the same time by different printers. Nevertheless, service books in Latin were a potential publication monopoly because the Sarum rite was based on English usage. Caxton decided that his principal effort would be devoted to producing books in English. Although this restricted his market to English-speaking people, a relatively small market at that time, it did mean that he did not have to concern himself about competition from continental printers, who only started to print books in English in the sixteenth century.

Works available in English can be divided into those that already existed and those that could be created. The former group included poetry in the courtly style, poetry in the alliterative tradition, historical prose, and religious and moral material, though these groups are not mutually exclusive. Of these four categories Caxton printed a wide selection of material from the first: he printed works by Chaucer, Lydgate, and Gower as well as those by lesser-known poets. On the other hand, he printed no alliterative poems; *Piers Plowman* and *Sir Gawain and the Green Knight* were ignored. This choice reflects a stylistic prejudice which I examine in greater detail shortly. He printed some historical prose, such as the *Chronicles of England*, and it is possible to consider Malory's *Morte Darthur* under this head. There was not, however, a great deal of material available in this category, for much of it overlapped. Finally, he did produce some religious and moral material, though he only published that which was of general rather than of special appeal. He did not print the fourteenth-century English mystics, though he did publish the English translation of the *Speculum Vitae Christi* and texts like the English version of *Ars Moriendi*. The texts in this last group are usually translations rather than original compositions in English. It is also true of the works in all these groups that there would not be sufficient texts available to keep the presses working continually. Hence Caxton had to face the problem of providing new material.

New material could be provided either by working with practising writers or through translation. The former has its difficulties in that one could not guarantee a continuous supply of work. Hence Caxton decided to rely on translation; and this was surely a sensible decision. It enabled him to provide new works, in the sense that they were translated for the first time into English, and to cash in on the prestige of those works in the parent language. Some of the texts he chose had already been printed in France, and others had links with well-known people such as the dukes of Burgundy. As we saw of *History of Troy* itself, it was written in French by one of the duke's secretaries. Nevertheless, translation posed one problem for him, namely who was to do it. If he was translating courtly literature he could not let any ordinary hack writer loose on the translation. The content was fashionable reading matter, and it could not be spoilt by the translation. Caxton never employed professional translators or members of his staff to do this work; Wynkyn de Worde was not allowed to try his hand at it. He employed people who were fashionable or who could be made to seem acceptable to his courtly clientele. Many of the translations he made himself. As the former governor of the English Nation at Bruges he had moved on the fringes of court life, and his name carried a certain cachet. Even so, he took care to present himself as the "servant" of Margaret of Burgundy in his *History of Troy* to show that he was a translator whose style had been improved by a member of the aristocracy and thus also to imply that he knew the taste of the higher reaches of society. It is partly for this reason that he refers to so many noblemen in his prologues and epilogues. These are often thought of as his patrons, though that is not the appropriate word to describe them. Many had no part in the choice of book to be translated. Margaret did not choose the *History of Troy*, and her brother George, duke of Clarence, did not choose the *Game of Chess*. Indeed, in the latter instance Caxton describes himself as Clarence's "unknown servant," a sure indication that Clarence knew nothing about the book or his patronage of it until after it was published. Caxton used the names of such noblemen to give his books prestige and a fashionable gloss. Some of them may have had a hand in choosing the book, but for the most part they were content to lend their names.

Two noblemen did make translations used by Caxton. One was Anthony Earl Rivers, who was responsible for at least three translations and possibly a fourth published by Caxton. Although Caxton is fulsome in his praise of the earl, his precise relations with him are not easily discovered since some of the negotiations concerning the publication of his translations were apparently conducted on the earl's behalf by his secretary. Whether Caxton knew Rivers as well as some scholars have suggested must remain doubtful. Caxton also published the translations by John Tiptoft, earl of Worcester, of Cicero's *Of Friendship* and Buonaccorsso's *Declamation of Noblesse*. Since Tiptoft had been executed before Caxton returned to England, it is possible that he acquired copies of these books through the Rivers family, though he may simply have wished to produce volumes made by noble translators. If the translators were not themselves noble, Caxton was quick to give them noble connections and to underline their abilities as translators. *Of Old Age* was translated by William Worcestre for Sir John Fastolf. In order to make the translation acceptable, Caxton in his prologue concentrates on the knight rather than on the translator. The impression given is that the book owes its existence more to Fastolf than to Worcestre. Another example of a similar process is provided by Caxton's edition of Trevisa's translation of Higden's *Polychronicon*. In this case he did two things. He stressed the connection with Lord Berkeley, but since he knew little about the particular Lord Berkeley, he was unable to expand upon the noble associations of the book. He therefore made Trevisa into an apparently well known translator by mentioning other translations he had supposedly made. These include the Bible, though Trevisa's link with a Bible translation is far from certain. In this way Caxton is able to suggest that Trevisa's credentials as a translator were impeccable. The most interesting case in this connection is Malory's *Morte Darthur*. The Winchester manuscript of Malory, which found its way into Caxton's workshop though it is not thought to be the manuscript he used to set up his own edition, contains quite a lot of information about Malory, including the description of him as a knight prisoner. Most of this information is omitted by Caxton so that the translation is simply said to be by Sir Thomas Malory knight. By these omissions Caxton is able to avoid any unpleasant associations with Malory who is presented as a knight pure and simple. He remains a noble translator untainted by any suggestion of prison or other wrongdoings.

The books that Caxton published were mostly translated from French. Even those that were ostensibly translated from Latin like the works by Cicero were normally based on a French version of the Latin original. Caxton himself knew Dutch and Latin, for his translation of *Reynard the Fox* was made from the former language and that of the *Saint Winifred* from the latter. There were not many works in Dutch available for translation, and as a language it was not as fashionable as French. Latin, on the other hand, was too much associated with the Church and liturgical and scholastic practices to yield many texts that he might have wanted to translate. His reliance upon French was also dictated by his audience and their expectations. French was a fashionable language used by the dukes of Burgundy whose life-style and ideas had considerable influence on English people at the end of the fifteenth century. Burgundy initiated what might be termed a North European renaissance in the fifteenth century which had particular meaning for England (Kipling 1977). Caxton was influenced by the kind of books being produced in Flanders, and he may have attempted to reproduce these varieties in English for the English market, for the categories of books found in the catalogues of the ducal library that survive from the fifteenth century are reflected in the type of work Caxton chose (Blake 1965). However, this analogy should not be pressed too far since many of the books were found in other libraries in the Low Countries (Hellinga 1981).

Caxton's publishing and translating policy has been considered by scholars as an aspect of his relations to his patrons. It has been debated whether he led or followed the taste of his time. The debate should not be framed in these terms, for there is little doubt that he shared the tastes of his contemporaries. However, only he had ready access to what was being published abroad, and so he naturally would have chosen the particular texts to translate and print. Yet he did not usually look for specific texts, he looked for texts that fell into particular categories. The actual text translated may have been fortuitously chosen because it happened to be in his stock when he wanted to start a new project or because it had recently arrived with the latest consignment of volumes from the Continent. Caxton sold the books he printed from a shop he had at Westminster, and in this shop he also had manuscripts. It is possible that members of the public did sometimes discuss with him what he should publish when they were in the shop, but his stories of conversations that are supposed to have taken place there are almost certainly fictitious. Yet the books he chose clearly reflected the interests of the public at the time, for if they did not he would have gone out of business.

As I have already noted, the problem of publishing printed books is how to sell multiple copies of the same work. To give his texts appeal to his audience Caxton included prologues and epilogues. These are not found in all his printed books, because not all of them needed to be promoted in the same way. As a general rule he did not include promotional material in editions of English poets because their works were usually well enough known to be sold without this support. The poets he printed were in the courtly tradition and most had been dead for some time; he did not produce the works of living poets. One work that was provided with a prologue is the second edition of the *Canterbury Tales*. This example is significant because it reveals that the market for works of this kind was limited and that Caxton had to persuade people who already had one edition to buy another. It does not follow that what he wrote in this prologue reflects the truth, though it has often been taken at face value by modern scholars. The prologue is worth looking at in depth (see Blake 1973, pp. 61ff.).

He opens with a rhetorical flourish, "Grete thankes, lawde and honour ought to be gyven unto the clerkes, poetes and historiographs," which is modelled upon the opening of his own prologue to the *Polychronicon* which he had borrowed earlier from the prologue to the *Historical Library* by Diodorus Siculus. The opening is not as suitable as it might be because it is more concerned with the writing of history than of poetry, though Chaucer is described as a philosopher. Among the noble writers Chaucer is especially to be praised, Caxton continues, because he embellished English "eschewyng prolyxyte, castyng away the chaf of super-fluyte, and shewyng the pyked grayn of sentence utteryd by crafty and sugred eloquence." These sentiments are borrowed from Lydgate's praises of Chaucer—and Lydgate was a poet Caxton knew well and whose output he may have imitated. In other words the opening sentences of the prologue are modelled by Caxton on other works so that he can praise Chaucer in a suitably rhetorical way. The potential purchasers needed to be impressed by the style to understand that the work itself was of some literary excellence. Caxton continues by turning to the *Canterbury Tales*, which contains accounts of the pilgrims and tales "whyche ben of noblesse, wysedom, gentylesse, myrthe, and also of veray holynesse and vertue, wherin he fynysshyth thys sayd booke." Unfortunately people had tampered with the text so that it contained parts that were not genuine. Six years previously Caxton had himself been brought a poor text of the poem which he had printed, supposing it to be satisfactory. These were then sold to gentlemen. However, one of them visited him to complain about the text and said that his father had a good manuscript which he would try to get his father to let the publisher have, if he agreed to print a sound text. Caxton accepted this proposal and the new text was produced.

The important thing to notice is that Caxton stresses the superiority of the second edition as compared with the first; it is said to have an authentic text. In actual fact the text of the second edition is if anything worse than that of the first, because it represents an amalgam of the first edition with the second manuscript. It was clearly important for Caxton to persuade his clientele that they were reading a better text, even though they were not. This behaviour is common enough in sales promotions. It is also significant that he does not mention who the gentleman in question was; he remains conveniently anonymous. Similarly the gentleman's father is not identified. Both are probably fictitious. Caxton invented the gentleman and his father to underline the request by the gentleman and the unwillingness of the father to part with the volume. In this way he is able to suggest that there is a demand for a new edition, while at the same time he can show that the text he is using is so valued by someone it was not easily relinquished to allow the printer to publish the second edition. By this story he is able to show how attractive his edition is so that all those with a first edition can be encouraged to get the second as well.

Reprints, however, represent a special case. For the most part Caxton included prologues and epilogues to the translated works, for they were new to the English audience and therefore needed introducing to them. Often, these works had prologues and epilogues in their French versions, and on many occasions he adapted what he found there. The result is an amalgam between a translation of the French prologue and pieces added by Caxton, though he did sometimes include two prologues, one by the original author and his own. In the *History of Troy* he included a preface before the prologue, because there was one in Lefèvre's version. In it he refers to Lefèvre's work and to his dedication of that work to Duke Philip of Burgundy before he introduces details about his own translation and its dedication to Margaret. The preface is followed by the translator's prologue. In this he refers to the French version which contained "many strange and mervayllous historyes wherein I had grete pleasyr and delyte as well for the novelte of the same as for the fayr langage of Frenshe" (Blake 1973, p. 97). The book contains excellent stories and is written in an approved style. He therefore decided to make a translation which he gave up in despair because of his faulty style. It was then that Margaret encouraged him to continue, provided he made some improvements in his style. After his own prologue he included a translation of Lefèvre's prologue. In the epilogues he refers to Lydgate's poem about the Troy story, which may have prompted him initially to make a prose translation, and to the fact that he had been asked for copies of his translation by so many gentlemen that he was forced to print it. All these details are included to attract attention and hence custom. The book was originally made for a duke of Burgundy; the translation was approved by and dedicated to Margaret, duchess of Burgundy. The story was exciting and written in a good French style. The account of Troy as found in Lefèvre's version is mostly new in England, though parts of it had been covered by Lydgate who was one of England's great poets. The translation has both novelty and tradition in its favour. Finally it was in demand among gentlemen and so it is implied it ought to be acquired by all gentlemen.

We can see from this work that Caxton needed to emphasise patronage, novelty, style, and demand among the characteristics of his books. These features reappear constantly in the prologues and epilogues, though they are supplemented by others such as the good quality of the second edition of the *Canterbury Tales*. However, although he had a formal dedication in *History of Troy* which was expressed in the preface, this was dropped in later works. It was important simply that the book be associated with someone fashionable, not that it should be formally dedicated to him or her. For the most part he liked to have a story about the translation's genesis, as here, for that helped to underline the book's attractiveness, but he was quite prepared to invent the details when necessary. To start with, the prefatory matter was rather long partly because he had not learned to amalgamate his own comments with those of the original author, but this changed as he gained in experience. Much of what we today know about Caxton and the contemporary taste for literature was introduced into the prologues and epilogues which were part of the promotional side of his business; it therefore needs to be interpreted with care.

As a final example of the way he set out his prologues and epilogues we may consider the prologue to his edition of Malory's *Morte Darthur*, a work peculiarly associated with Caxton. The prologue was probably written after the rest of the work had been set up in type, and so it may be later than the epilogue in which Caxton says briefly that the book is about Arthur and his knights, that it was translated by Sir Thomas Malory knight, and that it was divided by Caxton into twenty-one books. The prologue, however, is lengthy and was designed to make this version of King Arthur better known to potential purchasers by relating it to the general history of Arthur. The prologue opens with an impressive sentence which refers first to other books published by Caxton of a historical or didactic nature and then to a visit which "many noble and dyvers gentylmen of thys royame of Englond" (Blake 1973, p. 106) paid to him to complain that he had never printed anything about King Arthur who was the most famous of all English kings. In this way Caxton is able to begin his prologue with a rhetorical sentence, to refer to other works he had published, and to imply that he produced his version of King Arthur's deeds because there was a great demand for the book from unnamed gentlemen. He then goes on to refer to the theme of the Nine Worthies, consisting of three pagans, three Jews, and three Christians. The three Christians were Arthur, Charles the Great, and Godfrey of Bouillon. Caxton had published the deeds of Godfrey and was to publish those of Charles. The gentlemen demanded to know why he had not published anything about Arthur who was an

Englishman seeing that he had printed the deeds of Godfrey. Caxton's reply to this question was that many people considered Arthur to be fictitious and not historical.

The gentlemen replied that it was absolute madness not to believe in Arthur's historicity—and at this stage in the discussion one of the gentlemen present was most vociferous in the debate about Arthur's genuineness. This gentleman is not named. The historical proofs of Arthur's existence are listed. Caxton then goes on to say that he has read many accounts of Arthur in French, and that other accounts exist in Welsh and English though these are not complete. He has therefore decided to print a version translated by Malory from French from "a copye unto me delyverd" (Blake 1973, pp. 108–109). Finally he gives a very generalised account of the contents and says that he presents the book "unto alle noble prynces, lordes and ladyes, gentylmen or gentylwommen, that desyre to rede or here redde of the noble and joyous hystorye of the grete conquerour and excellent kyng" (Blake 1973, p. 109). Thus although he claims he had been asked to publish the work by certain gentlemen, he dedicates it to all gentlemen and gentlewomen rather than to those who had asked for it or to the one who was most vociferous in proving Arthur's historicity. He does not even say how he acquired the manuscript, although the implication is that he was lent it by a gentleman. It seems likely that most of what is found in this prologue is fictitious and that it was included to arouse interest in Arthur. Doubts about his historicity are raised and stilled; accounts of Arthur in other languages are mentioned; Arthur's place as a king of England and as one of the Nine Worthies is brought up; the demand for a work about Arthur by members of the aristocracy is specified; and the general moral and historical nature of the work is stressed. It all adds up to clever propaganda to promote the book.

Several points emerge from this discussion of Caxton's prologues and epilogues. He imitated the models found in his sources and was able to develop them to answer his particular needs. They formed a vehicle for his sales propaganda. As part of this promotion he needed to refer to the demand for each book by members of the gentry and to its wider appeal because of its links with French culture. At the same time he did not shrink from inventing stories that created an interest in his books and that introduced some apparent controversy. The whole approach is sophisticated, and this needs to be borne in mind when assessing Caxton's overall contribution to literature and publishing. It might be claimed that Caxton is the first English critic because he is forced to evaluate a book critically in contemporary terms in order to try and sell it. From his comments we can gauge how people responded to literary works and what qualities they expected to find in them.

It remains to consider Caxton's attitude towards translating and towards language in general. The fifteenth century witnessed a great flood of translation, the majority of which was made from French or Latin. Secular material was more likely to be translated from French, and religious and mystical work from Latin. This wealth of translation was motivated in part by Chaucer and in part by the prevailing attitude to Franco-Burgundian cultural superiority. Chaucer had translated Boethius's *De Consolatione Philosophiæ* as well as modelling many of his poems on French or Italian sources. His work was thought to have given English literature a new start, and it is not unnatural that many thought prose should be revivified in the same way. The dukes of Burgundy were the arbiters of fashion in the fifteenth century, and English people imitated the cultural developments initiated there. This applies to many aspects of culture other than literature. In his prologue to *Jason* Caxton refers to the duke's castle at Hesdin and all its magnificent properties. The Burgundian court was French speaking, and the dukes had acquired a library that, unlike many of the humanist libraries being assembled at the time, contained mostly works in French. It included romances, histories, and religious material in French, and this material reflects the type of book that Caxton himself was publishing in England, even if he did not imitate its contents deliberately.

The acceptance of French, and particularly Burgundian, superiority in cultural affairs also affected Englishmen's attitudes towards language. Many felt that English was an unsophisticated language that needed improving to make it as elegant as French or Latin. The ways of doing this were to introduce as much classical vocabulary as possible, to elevate the language through the use of rhetoric, and to follow French sentence patterns. In practice this meant that translators followed their originals slavishly as though the assumed excellence of the original's language would brush off on to the English translation. Caxton is no different in this matter from the bulk of fifteenth-century translators (cf. Workman 1940). As an example of his abilities as a translator we may consider the following passage from *Charles the Great* and its corresponding paragraph in the French *Fierabras* which Caxton used as his source.

J'ay parlé devant ou premier livre superficiallement du premier roy de France baptisé en descendant selon mon propos jusques au roy Charles, duquel on ne scauroit pas bonnement racompter la vaillance de luy et ses barons que se dient pers de France, desquelz a leur endroit je feray mencion selon que j'en pourray concepvoir en verité. Mais ce que j'ay dessus escript, je l'ay prins en ung auctentique livre nommé *Mirouer Historial* et es croniques anciennes, et l'ay tant seullement transporté de latin en francoys. Et la matiere suyvant que sera le second livre est d'ung

rommant fait a l'ancienne facon sans grant ordonance, dont j'ay esté insité a la re-
duire en prose par chapitres ordonnez. Et se dit celluy livre selon les aulcuns et le
plus communement *Fierabras* a cause que celluy Fierabras estoit si merveilleulx,
comme j'en feray mencion, que fut vaincu par Olivier et a la fin se baptisa et fut
apres saint en paradis.

    I have spoken tofore in the fyrst book superfycyally of the first kyng of Fraunce
baptysed in descendyng after my purpoos unto Kynge Charles, of whome may not
wel be recounted the valyaunce of hym and of hys barons, whych were named and
called pyeres of Fraunce. Of whome and of their behavyng I shal make mencion
after that I shal mowe conceyve by trouthe. But thys that I have tofore wryton I
have taken it oute of an autentyke book named *Myrour Hystoryal* and in auncyent
croncyles, and have onelye translated them oute of Latyn in to Frensshe. And the
mater folowyng whyche shal be the second book is of a romaunce maad of th'auncyent facyon wythoute grete ordynaunce in Frensshe, wherof I have been encyted
for to reduce in prose by chapytres ordeyned. Which book after somme and moost
comunely is called *Fyerabras* by cause that thys Fyerabras was so mervayllous a
geaunte, as I shal make mencyon, whyche was vanquysshed by Olyver and at the
laste baptysed and was after a saynt in heven. (Ed. S. J. Herrtage [1880] *The Lyf
of the Noble and Crysten Prynce, Charles the Grete*, pp. 36–37, EETS, es 36)

The first thing to be noticed is that the English translation reads well even though
it sticks fairly closely to the French original. No attempt has been made to recast
the sentences, though minor matters of syntax are rearranged in an English way.
Adjectives that come after the nouns in the French are placed before them in the
English, and some inversions of subject and verb in the French are replaced by
the ordinary subject verb order in the English. Thus "*Et se dit celluy livre*" becomes *Which book . . . is called*. It must be admitted that the easy stylistic flow of
the English reflects the syntax of the French, and it may be suggested as a general
principle that Caxton's own texts reflect the stylistic attainments of their originals.
At times Caxton preserves the word order of the French, and this can cause some
difficulty of interpretation. Thus the first sentence, which reads "I have spoken
tofore in the fyrst book superfycyally of the first kyng of Fraunce baptysed in descendyng after my purpoos unto Kynge Charles," is clumsy partly because he has
kept the *baptysed* after *Fraunce* and partly because he has kept some of the French
words like *descendyng*.
    Such sentences have led to a controversy about Caxton's methods and ideals as a
translator. It is thought by some scholars that he produced his translations quickly
and that he overlooked many of the resulting infelicities. This view can be supported by the sporadic mistranslations and misreadings that occur in his translations. It is clear that he took each phrase by turn and did not consider the wider
syntax and organisation of the sentence as a whole. In this he represents the translators of his time. Other scholars have, however, suggested that he was a more

perceptive translator, that he was trying to heighten the style of his translations, and that he deliberately produced sentences of this type. It is certainly true that he preserves the vocabulary of the French fairly closely and that he can on occasions introduce wordier phrases. Thus *se dient* becomes *named and called*, and *si merveilleulx* becomes *so mervayllous a geaunte*. Such attempts at improving the style do not invalidate the general assumption that he worked speedily at his translations, for the sheer bulk of material that he got through was enormous. For the most part, though, his translations read well and fluently; Caxton was certainly one of the better translators of his time.

When he had to deal with English material he was influenced by his prejudices regarding style. For him a book which had "no gaye termes ne subtyl ne newe eloquence" (Blake 1973, p. 68) was not likely to be a good one, and he constantly apologised for the absence of such features. He followed Lydgate and other writers in the fifteenth century in accepting that Chaucer had introduced such eloquence into English and consequently that this feature had been lacking in earlier English works. This meant in effect that alliterative writing was not stylistically sophisticated; it was old-fashioned and provincial. In his prologue to *Eneydos* he mentions that the abbot of Westminster had asked him to look over some old documents. The language was so old he had difficulty in understanding it. He goes on to imply that there were two types of style at the time, that which was rhetorical and was sometimes criticised for having "over curyous termes" and a second that was old and homely. The latter was linked with the older type of writing in English, namely alliteration. The old style lacked a proper vocabulary and the refinement of rhetoric.

This general attitude influenced the way Caxton responded to English texts. Some older texts were modernised because they used an antiquated vocabulary. In his epilogue to book seven of the *Polychronicon* translated by Trevisa in the fourteenth century he wrote that he had "chaunged the rude and old Englyssh, that is to wete certayn wordes which in these dayes be neither usyd ne understanden" (Blake 1973, p. 132). However, the *Canterbury Tales* which was composed almost at the same time as Trevisa's translation was praised for its ornate language. Yet Chaucer's prose contains as many old words as Trevisa's translation, but naturally Trevisa did not have the same stylistic reputation. This stylistic prejudice affected the way Caxton reacted to Malory's *Morte Darthur*, which was written only a few years before he printed it. Malory, of course, had used alliterative poems like the *Morte Arthure* as source material and had taken over much of their alliterative vocabulary. This applies particularly to certain parts of Malory's work, such as book five, which were based on earlier English material. Hence when Caxton printed Malory, he completely rewrote book five in order to exclude some of the alliterative vocabulary. This can be seen in the following comparative passages:

> *Malory:* Than the kynge yode up to the creste of the cragge, and than he com-
> forted hymself with the colde wynde; and than he yode forth by two
> welle-stremys, and there he fyndys two fyres flamand full hygh. And
> at that one fyre he founde a carefull wydow wryngande hir handys
> syttande on a grave that was new marked.
>
> *Caxton:* And soo he ascended up in to that hylle tyl he came to a grete fyre, and
> there he fonde a careful wydowe wryngynge her handes and makyng
> grete sorowe, syttynge by a grave new made.

Caxton eliminates the alliterative phrases like *creste of the cragge* and *fyres flamand*.
He replaces older words by French ones such as *ascended* for *yode up*. He also
introduces many vague adjectives such as *grete*, and he sometimes adds new
phrases to balance ones already there such as *makyng grete sorowe*. The drift of
Caxton's changes is to make his version more courtly and less specific. The language loses some of that individuality which makes Malory such an admired
writer today, for it becomes practically identical with the language in which most
other romances were written at the time. Nevertheless, one should recognise that
it was not alliteration as such to which Caxton objected, for alliteration was a
rhetorical embellishment; it was only the vocabulary of the alliterative tradition
that he was trying to eradicate.

What then of the future? Although several Caxton texts have appeared recently
in facsimiles, there is still a need for modern editions of his works. Until they
have been compared with the sources he used, it will not be easy to come to a
proper assessment of his linguistic and literary accomplishments. New work is
being done on the printing side of Caxton's career, and this may lead us to new
understanding of how he printed his works. It is likely that this approach will
lead to further insights into his edition of Malory in particular, for it is clear that
the Winchester manuscript (now in the British Library) was also in Caxton's
workshop when his edition was being set up. The typographical and com-
positorial constraints must be understood in any evaluation of the editorial procedures followed. Although we know more of Caxton's life now, we still lack a complete collection of the life records. A bibliography of all that has been written on
Caxton is also a desideratum. Finally studies on other authors and people who
moved in the court and merchant circles in the second half of the fifteenth century
will throw light on Caxton's career. His associations with Anthony Earl Rivers
remain obscure, and if they could be elucidated through a biography of Rivers,
we might come to a more complete understanding of Caxton's relations with other
members of the aristocracy whose names he sprinkled so liberally in his prologues and epilogues.

BIBLIOGRAPHY

CAXTON'S TEXTS

As many of Caxton's texts cannot be dated accurately, his editions are listed below alphabetically by short title. They are arranged in two groups, as is customary, according to their place of publication. Dates in brackets indicate that no date is given in the edition. Further bibliographical details of each edition may be found in de Ricci (1909), which in the following list is given simply as de Ricci, and in STC. Many of his editions have been published through the Early English Text Society, and some have been reissued as facsimiles. Details of these may be found in Blake (1969, pp. 224–249), Hartung (1972, pp. 771–807 and 924–951), and Watson (1974, pp. 667–674).

Not included in the list are Caxton's translations of the *Lives of the Fathers*, printed by De Worde in 1495 (STC 14507), and Ovid's *Metamorphoses*, of which no printed copy is extant. He claimed to have translated the *Life of Robert Earl of Oxford*.

BRUGES

Les Fais et Proesses du Noble et Vaillant Chevalier Jason [1474–1475?] De Ricci 3c. (For English version see *Jason*)

Game of Chess, 1st ed. March 31, 1474. De Ricci 1; STC 4920.

History of Troy [1473–1474] De Ricci 3; STC 15375. (For French version see *Le Recueil*)

Les Quatres Choses Derrenieres [1474–1475?] De Ricci 2. (For English version see *Cordial*)

Le Recueil des Histoires de Troyes [1474–1475?] De Ricci 3b. (For English version see *History of Troy*

Septenuaire des Pseaulmes de Penitence [1474–1475?] De Ricci 3d.

WESTMINSTER

Advertisement [1477?] De Ricci 17; STC 4890. (Advertising the *Ordinale*)

Æsop's Fables. March 26, 1484. De Ricci 4; STC 175.

Anelida and Arcite [1477?] De Ricci 24; STC 5090.

Ars Moriendi [1491?] De Ricci 5; STC 786.

Art of Dieing [1490?] De Ricci 6; STC 789.

Blanchardin and Eglantine [1489?] De Ricci 7; STC 3124.

Boethius's Consolation of Philosophy [1477?] De Ricci 8; STC 3199.

Book of Courtesy [1477–1478] De Ricci 11; STC 3033.

Book of Good Manners. May 11, 1487. De Ricci 65; STC 15394.

Canterbury Tales, 1st ed. [1476?] De Ricci 22; STC 5082.

    2d ed. [1482–1483?] De Ricci 23; STC 5083.

Caton [1483–1484] De Ricci 16; STC 4853.

Charles the Great. December 1, 1485. De Ricci 19; STC 5013.

Chronicles of England, 1st ed. June 10, 1480 De Ricci 29; STC 9991.

    2d ed. October 8, 1482. De Ricci 30; STC 9992.

Churl and Bird, 1st ed. [1477?] De Ricci 67; STC 17009.

    2d ed. [1477?] De Ricci 66; STC 17008.

Commemoratio Lamentationis sive Compassionis Beate Marie [1487?] De Ricci 32; STC 15847.3.

Confessio Amantis. September 2, 1483. De Ricci 48; STC 12142.

Cordial. March 24, 1479. De Ricci 33; STC 5758.

Court of Sapience [1480?] De Ricci 68; STC 17015.

Curial [1484] De Ricci 20; STC 5057.

Deathbed Prayers [1484?] De Ricci 34; STC 6442, 14554.

Description of Britain. August 18, 1480. De Ricci 35; STC 13440a. (A shortened version of *Polychronicon*)

Dicts or Sayings of the Philosophers, 1st ed. 1477. De Ricci 36, 37; STC 6826, 6827.

    2d ed. [1480?] De Ricci 38; STC 6828.

    3d ed. [1489?] De Ricci 39; STC 6829.

Directorium Sacerdotum, 1st ed. [1487?] De Ricci 77; STC 17720.

    2d ed. [1489?] De Ricci 78; STC 17722.

Doctrinal of Sapience. 1489. De Ricci 40; STC 21431.

Donatus Melior [1487?] De Ricci 41; STC 7013.

Eneydos. 1490. De Ricci 96; STC 24796.

Epitome sive Isagogicum Margarite Castigate Eloquentie. 1480. STC 24190.3. (An abridgment of *Nova Rhetorica*)

Feats of Arms. July 14, 1489 (or 1490). De Ricci 28; STC 7269.

Festial, 1st ed. June 30, 1483. De Ricci 79; STC 17957, pt. 1.

    2d ed. [1491?] De Ricci 80; STC 17959. (Not a reprint of the previous ed.)

Festum Transfigurationis [1491?] De Ricci 42; STC 15854.

Festum Visitationis [1480?] De Ricci 43; STC 15848.

Fifteen Oes [1491] De Ricci 44; STC 20195.

Four Sons of Aymon [1489?] De Ricci 45; STC 1007.

Game of Chess, 2d ed. [1482–1483] De Ricci 18; STC 4921.

Golden Legend, 1st ed. 1483. De Ricci 98; STC 24873.

    2d ed. [1487?] De Ricci 99; STC 24874.

Governal of Health [1489?] De Ricci 47; STC 12138.

Horae, 1st ed. [1477?] De Ricci 50; STC 15867.

    2d ed. [1480?] De Ricci 51; STC 15868.

    3d ed. [1490?] De Ricci 52; STC 15871.

    4th ed. [1490?] De Ricci 53; STC 15871.

Horologium Sapientiae, etc. [1491?] De Ricci 12; STC 3305.

Horse, Sheep and Goose, 1st ed. [1477?] De Ricci 70; STC 17019.

    2d ed. [1477?] De Ricci 69; STC 17018.

House of Fame [1483?] De Ricci 21; STC 5087.

Image of Pity, 1st ed. [1487?] De Ricci 54; STC 14077 c. 6.

   2d ed. [1490?] De Ricci 55; STC 14077 c.8.

Indulgence plural issue before December 13, 1476. STC 14077 c. 106.

   singular issue before March 31, 1480. De Ricci 56; STC 14077 c.107.

   plural issue [1480] De Ricci 57; STC 14077 c.110.

   singular issue [1481] De Ricci 58; STC 14077 c.112.

   plural issue [1481] De Ricci 59; STC 14077 c.113.

   singular or plural issue before April 24, 1489. De Ricci 60; STC 14077 c.114.

Infantia Salvatoris [1477?] De Ricci 62; STC 14551.

Jason [1476–1477] De Ricci 64; STC 15383. (For French version see *Les Fais*)

Knight of the Tower. January 31, 1484. De Ricci 63; STC 15296.

Life of Our Lady, 1st ed. [1484?] De Ricci 71; STC 17023.

   2d ed. [1484?] De Ricci 72; STC 17024.

Mirror of the World, 1st ed. 1481. De Ricci 94; STC 24762.

   2d ed. [1490?] De Ricci 95; STC 24763.

Moral Proverbs. February 20, 1478. De Ricci 27; STC 7273.

Le Morte Darthur. July 31, 1485. De Ricci 76; STC 801.

Nova Rhetorica [1479] De Ricci 91; STC 24188.5, 24189. (For abridgment see *Epitome*)

Of Old Age, Of Friendship, and *Declamation of Noblesse.* August 12, 1481. De Ricci 31; STC 5293.

Order of Chivalry [1484?] De Ricci 81; STC 3326.

Ordinale [1477?] De Ricci 81; STC 16228. (*Advertisement* refers to this ed.)

Paris and Vienne. December 19, 1485. De Ricci 83; STC 19206.

Parliament of Fowls [1477?] De Ricci 25; STC 5091.

Parvus Cato, Magnus Cato, 1st ed. [1477?] De Ricci 14; STC 4851.

   2d ed. [1477?] De Ricci 13; STC 4850.

   3d ed. [1481?] De Ricci 15; STC 4852.

Pilgrimage of the Soul. June 6, 1483. De Ricci 73; STC 6473.

Polychronicon. 1482. De Ricci 49; STC 13438. (*Description of Britain* is abridged version of this text)

Propositio Clarissimi Oratoris Magistri Johannis Russell [1476?] De Ricci 90; STC 21458.

Psalter [1480?] De Ricci 86; STC 16253.

Quattuor Sermones, 1st ed. [1483?] De Ricci 85; STC 17957, pt. 2.

   2d ed. [1483?] De Ricci 85; STC 17957, pt. 3.

   3d ed. [1491?] De Ricci 86; STC 17959.

Reynard the Fox, 1st ed. June 6, 1481. De Ricci 87; STC 20919.

   2d ed. [1489?] De Ricci 88; STC 20920.

Royal Book. 1484. De Ricci 89; STC 21429.

Saint Winifred [1485?] De Ricci 100; STC 25853.

Sex Epistolae. 1483. De Ricci 92; STC 22588.

Siege of Jerusalem. November 20, 1481. De Ricci 46; STC 13175.

Speculum Vitae Christi, 1st ed. [1486?] De Ricci 9; STC 3259.

   2d ed. [1490?] De Ricci 10; STC 3260.

Stans Puer ad Mensam [1477?] De Ricci 74; STC 17030.

Statutes of Henry VII [1489] De Ricci 93; STC 9348.
Temple of Glass [1477?] De Ricci 75; STC 17032.
Troilus and Criseyde [1483?] De Ricci 26; STC 5094.
Vocabulary in French and English [1480?] De Ricci 97; STC 24865.

SECONDARY MATERIALS

Details of earlier scholarship can be found in Bennett (1947), Blake (1969), Hartung (1972), Heilbronner (1967), Painter (1976), and Watson (1974).

Barker, Nicholas (1976) "Caxton's Typography." *Journal of the Printing Historical Society*, 11, 114–143.
Bennett, H. S. (1947) *Chaucer and the Fifteenth Century*. Oxford: Clarendon Press.
Blake, N. F. (1965) "William Caxton: His Choice of Texts." *Anglia*, 83, 289–307.
———— (1966) "William Caxton's Birthplace: A Suggestion." *N&Q*, 211, 52–54.
———— (1969) *Caxton and His World*. London: André Deutsch.
———— (1973) *Caxton's Own Prose*. London: André Deutsch.
———— (1975) "Caxton's Reprints." *Humanities Association Review*, 26, 169–179.
———— (1976a) *Caxton: England's First Publisher*. London: Osprey.
———— (1976b) "Caxton Prepares His Edition of the Morte Darthur." *Journal of Librarianship*, 8, 272–285.
———— (1976c) "William Caxton: The Man and His Work." *Journal of the Printing Historical Society*, 11, 64–80.
———— (1977) "A New Approach to William Caxton." *Book Collector*, 26, 380–385.
———— (1978) "Dating the First Books Published in English." *GJ*, 43–50.
———— (1979) "Continuity and Change in Caxton's Prologues and Epilogues: The Bruges Period." *GJ*, 72–77.
———— (1980a) "Continuity and Change in Caxton's Prologues and Epilogues: Westminster." *GJ*, 38–43.
———— (1980b) *William Caxton after Five Hundred Years*. Davis, Calif.: Library Associates.
Bornstein, Diane (1976) "William Caxton's Chivalric Romances and the Burgundian Renaissance in England." *ES*, 57, 1–10.
Corsten, Severin (1976) "Caxton in Cologne." *Journal of the Printing Historical Society*, 11, 1–18.
de Ricci, S. (1909) *A Census of Caxtons*. London: Bibliographical Society.
Duff, E. Gordon (1917) *Fifteenth Century English Books*. London: Bibliographical Society.
Hartung, A. E., ed. (1972) *A Manual of the Writings in Middle English 1050–1500*, vol. 3. New Haven: Connecticut Academy of Arts and Sciences.
Heilbronner, W. L. (1967) *Printing and the Book in Fifteenth-Century England*. Charlottesville: University Press of Virginia.

Hellinga, Lotte (1981) "Caxton and the Bibliophiles." *Actes du XIe Congrès international de bibliographie bruxelles 1979*, pp. 11–38.

———— (1982) *Caxton in Focus*. London: British Library.

Hellinga, Lotte, and Hellinga, Wytze G. (1976) "Caxton in the Low Countries." *Journal of the Printing Historical Society*, 11, 19–32.

Kipling, Gordon (1977) *The Triumph of Honour: Burgundian Origins of the Elizabethan Renaissance*. Leiden: Leiden University Press.

Lindström, B. (1977) "Some Remarks on Two English Translations of Jacques Legrand's 'Livre des Bonnes Meurs.'" *ES*, 58, 304–311.

Moran, J. (1976) "Caxton and the City of London." *Journal of the Printing Historical Society*, 11, 81–91.

Nixon, Howard M. (1976a) "Caxton, His Contemporaries and Successors in the Booktrade from Westminster Documents." *Library*, 5th ser. 31, 305–326.

———— (1976b) "William Caxton and Bookbinding." *Journal of the Printing Historical Society*, 11, 92–113.

Noguchi, S. (1976) "Caxton's Malory." *Poetica* (Tokyo), 8, 72–84.

Painter, George D. (1976) *William Caxton: A Quincentenary Biography of England's First Printer*. London: Chatto and Windus.

Penninger, Frieda E. (1979) *William Caxton*. Boston: Twayne.

Takamiya, T., and Brewer, Derek, eds. (1981) *Aspects of Malory*. Cambridge: D. S. Brewer. (Contains several articles dealing with Caxton and Malory and an up-to-date bibliography)

Thompson, Susan O., ed. (1976) *Caxton: An American Contribution to the Quincentenary Celebrations*. New York: Typophiles.

Watson, George, ed. (1974) *The New Cambridge Bibliography of English Literature*. Vol. 1:600–1600. Cambridge: Cambridge University Press.

Workman, Samuel K. (1940) *Fifteenth Century Translation as an Influence on English Prose*. Princeton: Princeton University Press.

CHAPTER 18

Works of Religious Instruction

Alexandra Barratt

Many of the prose works already considered in this volume count, in one sense or other of the phrase, as works of religious instruction. This chapter, however, is confined to works in which the didactic purpose is paramount and, more specifically, to treatises that in their various ways, cover—fully or partly—the official teaching curriculum for the laity of the medieval Church. They are precious evidence of the first programme of mass education ever carried out in the West, maybe in the whole world.

The importance of the Fourth Lateran Council of 1215 in the formation of the consciousness of Western Europe cannot be overrated. At that council the duty of yearly confession to their parish priest was laid on all Christians of both sexes, and, as confession is impossible unless the penitent has some notion of what constitutes a sin, and as the medieval priest was expected to use the sacrament of penance as an opportunity for checking on his parishioners' knowledge of the Church's basic doctrines, this decree (whether or not the bishops realised it at the time) committed the Church to educating its own clergy and, through them, the laity—both men and women. While Judaism had always demanded that males should be literate and informed in the law, it was the Christian Church of the West that first demanded from women too some minimum of basic knowledge in their faith. No Christian over the age of discretion was exempt from the council's decree. Lay or religious, literate or illiterate, all had to have a basic grasp of their belief, its key texts, and their moral obligations. We tend to forget what an incredibly ambitious programme the bishops undertook; for the clergy itself had to be accurately instructed in fundamental theology and pastoral care before the task of lay instruction could be delegated to it. But perhaps even more far-reaching was the resultant training in self-analysis which was propaedeutic to confession and must have left an indelible imprint on Western consciousness, influencing the writings of many a novelist, biographer, and autobiographer in the last two hundred years, little though they may recognise their debt to the Lateran

Council. A more immediate result, I suggest, was the development of a capacity for irony, currently regarded as the most interesting characteristic of late fourteenth-century English poetry and a major preoccupation of modern literary critics. Irony can only exist among those who have acquired a measure of detachment from self, a detachment that cannot but be nourished and fostered by systematic and regular self-examination, which Lateran IV demanded and the numerous treatises of religious instruction promoted.

The role of Lateran IV and the subsequent episcopal decrees issued in England which led up to Archbishop Pecham's famous 1281 Constitutions in stimulating Middle English works of religious instruction has been rehearsed by many scholars; see especially Gibbs and Lang (1934, pp. 94–170), Milosh (1968, pp. 140–168), Moorman (1955, pp. 90–109), Pantin (1955, pp. 220–245), Pfander's seminal article (1936, pp. 243–245), and Robertson (1947). The relevant episcopal documents can now be consulted in modern editions (Powicke and Cheney 1964), from which it is clear that even before 1215 there were moves to instruct the laity. The 1213–1214 Statutes of Canterbury laid down that all adult Christians should know the Lord's Prayer and Creed, and that every priest should urge his parishioners to learn them. Bishop Poore's statutes, first issued for Salisbury between 1228 and 1236, urged priests to instruct their people *in articulis fidei* in the vernacular, and to exhort them to learn the Creed, Lord's Prayer, and Ave Maria. Peter des Roches (?1224) who explicitly puts this instruction in the context of the sacrament of penance, mentions that the texts should be known *saltem in lingua materna*; William of Blois's 1229 statutes for the diocese of Worcester vary this, laying down that the priests should instruct a penitent before confession in the Apostle's Creed, *sub lingua ei nota*, and after confession, more fully, in the Seven Deadly Sins and their branches. Alexander of Stavensby, bishop of Coventry, sometime between 1224 and 1237 actually composed a systematic and thorough *tractatus de vii criminalibus* to be read on Sundays or feast days, and also a *tractatus de confessionibus*. Particularly influential were the statutes Grosseteste issued for Lincoln in ?1239, much repeated in other diocesan statutes, which seem to be the first to add the Decalogue and the Seven Sacraments to the expanding syllabus: "ut unusquisque pastor animarum et quilibet sacerdos parochialis sciat decalogum . . . eademque populo sibi subiecto frequenter predicet et exponat. Sciat quoque que sunt septem criminalia eademque similiter populo predicet fugienda. Sciat insuper saltem simpliciter ecclesiastica sacramenta."

In 1240 Walter de Cantilupe urged his priests frequently to preach and expound the Decalogue, the Seven Deadly Sins, the Seven Sacraments, and all three Creeds. William of Bitton II, bishop of Wells, made the same requirements (in different words) in ?1258, repeated for Winchester between 1262 and 1265. This gradual evolution of a set programme of instruction culminates in the famous paragraph *Ignorancia Sacerdotum* in the statutes issued by the 1281 Council of Lambeth under Archbishop Pecham; this requires sermons covering the fourteen Articles of Faith, the Decalogue, the two Evangelical Commandments, the Seven Works of Mercy, Deadly Sins, Principle Virtues, and Sacraments. Boyle (1955, p. 82) rightly points out that this is "simply a Syllabus which lists or defines what responsible parish priests should preach to their parishioners" rather than an exposition of these topics, though Peter Quinel or Quivel, bishop of Exeter, in his 1287 statutes, includes a *summula* which is "primarily a manual for the examination and instruction of penitents in the confessional" (ibid.) and does expound the Decalogue, the Seven Deadly Sins by *radices* and *species*, their aggravating circumstances, and the articles of faith. Robertson makes some acute comments on these various episcopal decrees and provides a useful analysis of the *Ignorancia Sacerdotum* which points out that Pecham's syllabus was not commonplace but elaborate and unusually sophisticated. He remarks, "The decrees merely reflect an effort to incorporate in sermons what has been aptly described as 'the large body of popular pastoral theology which was growing rapidly in this age'" (1949, p. 388).

Works instructing the clergy, at least in the thirteenth century, were written in Latin, but in the area of lay education the vernaculars, including of course Middle English from the fourteenth century on, came into their own. As Ackerman puts it, "The standard instructional programme . . . so intimately associated with confession also formed to a great extent the basis of a very large and diverse body of didactic writings in the Vernacular. . . . These seem mainly to have been written for Englishmen [and one should add women] who knew no Latin" (1962, p. 547). But works written in Latin to instruct the clergy are as important to the Middle English scholar as their vernacular derivatives. Pantin's pioneering summary of such works produced in England to assist parish priests in their considerable educational labours (1955, p. 219) and Boyle's seminal article on William of Pagula (1955) were for some time about the only aids available in this area. But we now have an indispensable tool: *Incipits of Latin Works on the Virtues and Vices* (henceforth ILWVV), which covers far more than its title might suggest. It is not confined to systematic treatments of the vices and virtues but includes summae and manuals of pastoral theology, incorporates an originally separate collection of incipits of works on the Ten Commandments and the Pater Noster, and another of Latin works *de contemptu mundi*—in short, "many works dealing in many ways with ethical and moral matters" (Bloomfield, Guyot, Howard, and Kabealo 1979, p. 3). Researchers may well find it more useful to know what is *not* included (ibid., p. 5)! The large number of *incipits*—6,553 of "Works on the Virtues and Vices" in the sense peculiar to this book, and 1,261 of "Works on the Pater Noster"—even though it overestimates the number of discrete treatises, indicates to a degree the vastness of the field and is a salutary reminder that the

surviving works of religious instruction in Middle English prose are no more
than minor figures in a vast European drama with a cast of thousands.

When it comes specifically to these Middle English works, there is as yet
nothing comparable to ILWVV, though the Index of Middle English Prose project will eventually fill the need. We are already fortunate to have Jolliffe's *Check-
List of Middle English Writings of Spiritual Guidance* (1974). His definition of
spiritual guidance does not entirely overlap with mine of religious instruction,
for he specifically excludes "very simple descriptions or explanations of the Decalogue, the seven deadly sins, the five wits, both corporal and spiritual, the seven
works of mercy, both corporal and spiritual, the seven sacraments, the seven gifts
of the Holy Ghost, and the articles of the faith," "somewhat longer didactic
tracts" unless clearly addressed to the Christian as an individual (a confusing distinction), and "the expositions of the Decalogue, the Pater Noster and the Creed,
so common in Middle English religious manuscripts" (1974, pp. 27–28),
partly because the former "are moralised writings on the commandments, intended to expound them rather than to apply them to the needs of the individual"
(pp. 28–29). Even so, without Jolliffe's book it would have been almost impossible to write this chapter.

Though much has been done on Middle English works of religious instruction, much remains. It has been well said in a recent review that "although plenty
of lip service has been given to the importance of the so-called 'Pecham programme' and of the 'literature of religious instruction' in late medieval England,
little substantive scholarly effort has been expended in showing the various ways
in which the programme might be communicated" (Hanna 1981, p. 151). In
contrast to this we may set the provocative remark of Blake (1974, p. 355): "We
have for too long been satisfied simply to edit the texts and trace their sources; it
is time we moved on"—apparently to an examination of the audience for which
they were composed and to "the purposes of the writers of Middle English prose
and how this purpose influenced the way they set about their works." However,
the basic tools for such research—adequately edited texts—are still few and far
between, mute evidence of the pusillanimity of modern editors. The heroic days
of editing, when men like Furnivall edited texts the way their contemporaries
built transcontinental railways, are over. Of the long compendia that effectively
and comprehensively cover the teaching ideal set out by Pecham, many derive
from the French *Somme le Roi*; we have available at present only two of the nine
complete or partial translations into English of this work: *The Book of Vices and
Virtues* (Francis 1942) and the *Aȝenbite of Inwit* (Morris 1866, rev. Gradon
1965, 1979)—rarely, one suspects, read for its contents. (For further information on the importance of *Somme le Roi* derivatives in Middle English, see
Gallagher 1965 who shows that two of Caxton's publications derive from the
French text and also has much of interest on the *Somme* and the *Manipulus*

Curatorum.) But there is probably no point in editing the remaining Middle English versions of the *Somme* until more work has been done on the French original. However, an edition of a prose version of the *Speculum Vitae* (itself derived from the *Somme*)—*A Myrour to Lewde Men and Wymmen*—has recently appeared (Nelson 1981), and one of the version of the *Manuel des péchés* in Cambridge MS Saint John's College G. 30 (197) is in preparation for Middle English Texts. Of other compendia, recently an edition of the *Memoriale Credencium* has appeared (Kengen n.d.), an encouraging sign. But we still have no edition of the *Ignorancia Sacerdotum*, though we have Hodgson's pioneering article (1948), nor of the *Pore Caitiff*, or the *Disce Mori* (related, apparently, to the *Ignorancia Sacerdotum*); these have been edited from one or more manuscripts for dissertations but have not appeared in print. It is unfortunate that others can only take advantage of the efforts that must have been expended on these texts with difficulty. The *Pore Caitiff* in particular seems to have been closely modelled on Pecham's syllabus; Brady outlines the instructional programme, points out that "all these points are covered in the first three tracts" (1954, p. 536), and raises the question "whether our compiler found at his disposal ready-made tracts on the Creed, Commandments and Pater Noster . . . or whether he himself actually put the material of the tracts together from various sources. The problem requires further investigation" (ibid., p. 538). The problem is not of course unique to the *Pore Caitiff*. We are fortunate to have Brady's article on this confusing subject, but we still await the promised critical edition. Such works are indeed daunting in their sheer bulk and sometimes also in the number of extant MSS.

Another available compendium well illustrates the subsidiary place of Middle English treatises. The *Speculum Christiani* (ed. Holmstedt 1933) covers the Pecham syllabus almost exactly, with some additional matter, but while there are sixty-six Latin MSS, there is only one version written completely in English. Other similar texts that are available include John Gaytryge's translation of Archbishop Thoresby's Latin Catechism (both texts were included in that bishop's register) in Blake (1972), printed from the Thornton MS. It gives instruction in the syllabus and was originally a treatise for the clergy to use to instruct the laity. It is one of the very few texts of this type available in a form suitable for use by students. The (misnamed) *Quattuor Sermones Printed by William Caxton* (ed. Blake 1975) are very similar in content, though the editor remarks: "In view of our limited knowledge of Middle English texts it is not possible as yet to determine the various affiliations . . . in any depth" (p. 14).

Although it was not originally a compendium of this fundamental and elementary type, we should mention here the various Middle English translations of Saint Edmund's *Speculum Ecclesie*. Although for a long time it was thought that the Anglo-Norman version of this text (Robbins 1925) was the original, Forshaw has recently demonstrated that the original version was written in Latin (1971, 1972, ed. 1973) and that it was early translated into Anglo-Norman and then retranslated into Latin. She shows that the treatise was not originally a composite treatise but in effect a summa of Victorine spirituality, a mystical work specifically composed for religious. However, much of the contents coincides with the Pecham syllabus—Part Two covers the Seven Deadly Sins, Virtues and Gifts of the Holy Spirit, the Ten Commandments, Twelve Articles of Faith, the Seven Sacraments and the Six Works of Mercy, the Seven Gifts of the body and the soul in Heaven and in Hell—to such an extent that it prompts the question whether Edmund's treatise (written ca. 1240) influenced the final form of Pecham's syllabus. In any case, some of the Middle English versions (MSS listed by Robbins 1925) do appear to function as works of religious instruction, whatever Saint Edmund's original purpose, and now that the vexed question of the original version has been settled and we have good editions of the two Latin versions, it should be possible to determine from which version the various Middle English translations were made and edit them appropriately, using the original in each case to help establish the text where necessary.

The foregoing survey of available texts suggests that Hanna's assessment of the present state of play is juster than Blake's. As to the tracing of sources, which Blake seems to regard as an inadequate scholarly goal, it is on the contrary of the utmost importance if we want to see how the Pecham programme was communicated. But it is a difficult, frustrating, and time-consuming task. One can proceed on the assumption that most works of religious instruction are translations or adaptations, and therefore require editorial treatment and critical attention very different from those appropriate to original work; the sources must be located, sometimes themselves edited, to present the Middle English text adequately. This makes very clear the symbiotic relationship that should exist between Middle English, French, and Latin studies, and it is perhaps unfair to criticise Middle English scholarship for failing to edit major basic texts (let alone the hoard of minor pieces Jolliffe's *Check-List* reveals) while the immensely influential French *Somme le Roi* itself remains unedited, though Brayer has published two substantial but tantalizing articles on this seminal compilation and the less well known *Mirroir du Monde* (1958). And Peraldus's *Summa Vicium ac Virtutum*, one of the *Somme*'s sources as it is, directly or indirectly, of many a Middle English treatise, is not only unavailable in a modern critical edition but we do not even have a modern reprint of any of the seventeenth- or eighteenth-century editions. The only source of information on Peraldus has for long been Dondaine's article (1947), and nothing seems to have been done on the sources Peraldus himself may have used. However two recent articles by Wenzel have increased our knowledge of certain derivatives of Peraldus (1971, 1974); they bring to our notice the *Quoniam* and *Primo* (ILWVV 5059, 4166), texts that are "part of an extensive process of adapting Peraldus's *Summa de Vitiis*," in their capacity as "the closest models we have so far discovered" for the Parson's Tale (1974, pp. 377, 378), probably the most neglected of Chaucer's texts, the source of which is generally agreed to be an unidentified French treatise that drew on Peraldus, and itself of course an excellent example of a work of religious instruction.

The lack of reliable texts, whether French or Latin, from which Middle English translations and adaptations were made, is a considerable deterrent to editing the Middle English texts. Often the original must be edited, or at least a version transcribed, and its own textual affiliations disentangled, before real work can begin on the Middle English. It is noticeable that two cases in which this has been done (Hackett, Colledge and Chadwick's work on William Flete's *De Remediis*, 1964, and my own on *The Book of Tribulation*, 1983), both concern short, relatively manageable texts. Longer texts could well demand a lifetime's work, or a concerted, carefully coordinated effort by a group of scholars.

A further reason for careful treatment of sources is that the current view often turns out to be misleading when work begins on the individual text. For example, the editor of the *Memoriale Credencium* has found that its sources were William of Pagula's *Oculus Sacerdotis*, the Peraldus derivative "Postquam," and a version of Saint Edmund's *Speculum Ecclesie*. In Jolliffe (1974), however, it is listed (item A 3) with *A myrour to lewde men and wymmen* as a version of the *Manuel des péchés*, while *A myrour*, in its turn, is an adaptation of the *Speculum Vitae*. Similarly, the various related texts on tribulation listed by Jolliffe as item J 3 are all there given as translations of the pseudo-Peter of Blois text, *De XII Vtilitatibus Tribulationis*. In fact three are translated, not from this short Latin text, but from the French *Livre de tribulacion*, itself a translation of the original long version of the text, the unpublished Latin *Tractatus de Tribulacione*, from which *De XII Vtilitatibus Tribulationis* derives. It is only when texts are thoroughly edited that their true sources gradually emerge; the task is the more daunting and confusing because such texts tend to bear a strong family resemblance to other texts of the same type, which can easily mislead on a cursory acquaintance.

Of the topics listed by Pecham, some receive separate treatment in shorter prose treatises outside the large compendia. There are a number of tracts on the Pater Noster, Creed, and the Ten Commandments; there are many treatises that deal in various ways with the Seven Deadly Sins in themselves and give model forms of confession or remedies for temptation; there are tracts on the virtues and allied subjects such as tribulation. Finally some treatises touch on these topics, though not systematically, but are clearly didactic rather than devotional, and we should include treatises on death and preparation for death, a subject included in the *Somme le Roi* though not explicitly listed in the episcopal decrees.

In the area of tracts on the Pater Noster and the Ten Commandments, some valuable work has long been available because of the Wycliffite associations (real

or illusory) of some of these tracts. In the future, work will be immensely helped
by the availability in *Incipits of Latin Works on the Virtues and Vices* of a list of
1,261 incipits of expositions of the Pater Noster. The diligent reader will also
find in the subject index, under various headings such as "*Decalogue*" and "*Decem
Dei preceptorum*," and "*Decem mandatis*," many incipits of Latin works on the
Ten Commandments. One hopes that this tool will stimulate, rather than over-
whelm, potential researchers; what is very clear is that practically nothing as yet
is known about the Latin tradition. The ultimate sources of many of the Latin
works on the Pater Noster are probably pseudo-Hugh of Saint Victor, *Allegoriae
in Novum Testamentum* II, ii–xiv, and *De Quinque Septennis* (PL 175: cols.
405ff.), which introduces the very popular interlinking of various Sevens, relating the seven petitions of the Pater Noster to the Beatitudes and Gifts of the
Spirit, together with patristic commentaries such as Augustine, *De Sermone in
Monte* (PL 34: cols. 1276–1308); but these were no doubt mediated through
later popularisations. On some of these Latin treatments, see Baron (1963).

On Middle English works on the subject, see particularly Kellogg and Talbert
(1959–1960), an article of great importance with far wider relevance to the topic
than its title suggests. Hussey shows how the Pater Noster "became a portmanteau
of doctrine" (1958, p. 9). The longest Middle English treatise on the Pater
Noster, which the editor points out is quite different from other treatments of the
subject, has been edited (Aarts 1967), and the introduction contains a useful section on the Pater Noster in Middle English literature; see also the same author's
article (1969). A number of shorter tracts on the Pater Noster are also available
in print, the one from the Vernon MS (ed. Horstman 1896, pp. 261–264)
which the editor notes owes something to Hugh of Saint Victor (PL 175: cols.
767–774) though it is a much abbreviated and simplified paraphrase of the Latin
rather than a translation. For other tracts, for example, from the Simeon MS,
printed by Francis (1942, pp. 334–336), Matthew (1880, pp. 198–202), and
Arnold (1871, p. 93), no Latin sources have been suggested, but it would be
surprising if these turned out to be original compositions. For some other texts,
see Jolliffe (1974, items M 9, O 9 and introduction, p. 29).

On the Ten Commandments, Kellogg and Talbert (1959–1960) print a text of
"the common orthodox treatise" from Rylands English MS 85, also printed from
the Simeon MS by Francis (1942, p. 317). "A notabill Tretys off the ten Com-
mandementys, Drawen by Richerde, the hermyte off Hampull" is in Perry
(1867, pp. 10–12). A very simple, catechetical treatment of the subject in Morgan MS 861 was printed by Bühler (1954); this whole manuscript is a representative compilation of religious instruction, containing as it does tracts on the
Seven Deadly Sins, Works of Mercy, Inner and Outer Senses, and the Four Cardinal Virtues. As in so many texts of this type, our main interest at present
is likely to be whether or not the vernacular treatments introduce any new ele-

ment not found in the Latin sources and analogues; Robertson in his article on Mannyng's verse treatment of the Commandments (1946a) gives valuable patristic and later sources (such as Bernard, Peter Lombard) for the conventional exposition of the Commandments which are equally applicable to prose treatments of the subject.

While the purely didactic treatments of the Pater Noster may have had some influence on other types of vernacular literature (such as the mysterious "Pater Noster play"), in contrast expositions of the Ten Commandments remained at a purely practical level. With none of the dynamic potential of the Seven Deadly Sins, their only more literary manifestation is the *Dives and Pauper*, "the only elaborate didactic treatise written originally in English prose and built on a framework of the Ten Commandments that has been presented to us from the Middle Ages" (Pfander 1933, p. 299). Volumes One and Two of a modern edition (Barnum 1976, 1980) have now appeared, and the third volume of introduction and notes, which will deal with sources and analogues, should prove of great value in adding to our knowledge of this area. In the meantime, we have Pfander's (1933) article on this treatise of unknown authorship written in the first decade of the fifteenth century.

A large body of writings in Middle English tries to prepare the layperson, in various ways, for the sacrament of penance, by analysing the sins, enumerating remedies, or providing model (comprehensive, all-purpose) confessions. The idea of the Seven Deadly Sins is probably the most widely known aspect of this type of writing, as it was productive in literature other than the purely didactic in a way that the Ten Commandments, for instance, (which were also used as a basis for the penitent's self-examinations) were not. The development of the concept of the sins and of the various standard schemes of presentation is of course covered in Bloomfield (1952); as Wenzel remarks, since this book "virtually no major study on the seven chief vices and closely related subjects has appeared" (1968, p. 1). He goes on to remark that the pastoral literature of the Middle Ages is "a type of literature which is as yet hardly even canvassed yet promises to yield a rich harvest of background material for medieval literature in general" (p. 18). Although Wenzel has in mind primarily Latin *pastoralia*, a wider knowledge of vernacular writings on the subject can also serve this purpose.

At the same time there is a need to relate what we know of vernacular writings on sin and confession to the wider context of the development of the Latin tradition. The whole history of confession is itself illuminating and delineates the context within which the very large body of Middle English writings on the subject (Jolliffe's classes C, D, E, F, and G all in their various ways bear on the topics of sin and confession) must be studied. McNeill (1952) gives a useful introduction to the subject, which is not confined to the Middle Ages, and includes just though inevitably now somewhat out-of-date comments on the various books of guidance for confessors, most though not all of which appeared after 1215. Tentler (1977) gives a more detailed and complex account, of Latin *pastoralia* in the main; he covers a few vernacular treatises but specifically excludes English ones; however his work shows the vast potential of this area of research. His theory that "sacramental confession provided a comprehensive and organised system of social control" (p. 345) has caused dismay in some circles, but he rightly stresses that he is concerned with the function actually fulfilled by these writings rather than with the author's conscious intentions. The Latin texts are in fact rather different from vernacular manifestations of the same movement, but there is a great need to begin to relate the Middle English texts to the Latin material of which they are often not so much translations as derivatives. We need to know just how the Middle English writers transmuted and modified their raw material, and this must surely have some bearing on the very different audiences concerned. Works in Latin are naturally for clerics, although even here there is great variety, depending on the level of education envisaged for the various potential audiences (the medieval clergy was of course a far from homogeneous body); on the other hand works in Middle English are not necessarily only for the laity but also for religious (specifically women) without Latin.

In the area of the Latin texts, there is some controversy over terminology; Tentler (1977) distinguishes between summae for confessors which are very large, comprehensive, and legalistic, much concerned with individual awkward cases; manuals of confession and pastoral care written for confessors; and purely devotional literature; while Boyle (1974) uses *summae confessorum* and manuals as synonyms, saying that the first work actually called a *summa confessorum* was that of John of Freiburg which did not appear until 1298, but regarding such works as those of Thomas of Choabham and Robert of Flamborough as summae. Fortunately the controversy is of only marginal interest to Middle English studies as the vast and legalistic summae are very distant relatives indeed of the vernacular texts. The manuals on the other hand, though not in any way reproduced in Middle English writings, are recognisably of the same type.

A great deal of work is now appearing on Latin *pastoralia*; in 1955 when Pantin listed eight manuals of pastoral theology written in England during the thirteenth century, none was available in print, but today a number of works of this type have been edited, and information is available in print about others—and of course all works of this type are listed in ILWVV. In 1945 Kennedy described Robert Courson's summa (written between 1204 and 1208) and printed the first fifteen chapters; two years later he listed the rest of the contents which show that Courson, though providing no sin-by-sin discussion as do some later writers, did cover the sacraments in general and in particular. This treatise also seems to be one of the earliest to list the distinguishing features of a good confession (Courson gives fifteen points) a *topos* familiar to readers of *Ancrene Wisse* and Chaucer's *Parson's Tale*, and it also enumerates eight "circumstances"; Goering's more recent articles on Magister Serlo (1976, 1978) are illuminating on the "new penitential literature" (1978, p. 290) of the thirteenth century, and for the Middle English scholar the fact that Serlo is himself second-rate and derivative hardly matters. His treatise, we are told, does consider the individual sins by species and *filiae* and also their remedies. There is a useful article on the late twelfth- or early thirteenth-century poem, probably composed in England, the *Poeniteas Cito*, to which many later treatments of confession can be traced, in MacKinnon (1969). More texts are also available: Thomas of Chobham, Robert of Flamborough, Petrus Pictaviensis, and Alan of Lille have all been edited within the last twenty years, but as yet do not seem to have attracted the attention of Middle English scholars. Such works are in the long run of great relevance to Middle English studies; but more immediately rewarding results might come from paying some attention to the kind of Latin formularies for confession, which contain little more than the list of faults on which a priest should interrogate the penitent, two of which are printed in Michaud-Quentin (1964).

As most Middle English works on sin and confession were written by clerics, we can also assume that it was exactly this sort of literature with which they were familiar and on which they drew. To ignore the all-pervasive Latin substratum can only result in absurdities. Robertson's article (1946b) on the traditional Latin background of the "circumstances" that aggravate sin for instance, is indispensable to a true assessment of such a text as *Ancrene Wisse*, though this is not immediately obvious; but as so often the benefit of such work on ultimate sources and influences is largely negative: it may save us from attributing originality to a vernacular work where it does not exist, or from assuming the direct debt of one text to another, where the true explanation is that both are written in a common tradition.

A few systematic Middle English treatments of the Seven Deadly Sins are available in print: Richard Lavynham's *Lityl Treatise* (ed. van Zutphen 1956), which considers each sin in turn, in the same way that the Latin manuals do, though the subdivisions of the sins are simplified, and the order of the sins themselves rather unusual, and also the so-called *Tretyse of Love* (ed. Fisher 1951), generally but perhaps wrongly believed to be a distant derivative of *Ancrene Wisse*, "a treatyse moche prouffitable for the reformacion of soules defoyled wyth ony of the vij dedely synnes." But another interesting, though even less studied, way of approaching and classifying the sins is found in the many Middle English forms of confession. These texts seem to be largely unexplored; of the forty-five listed by Jolliffe in his class C, only two are available in print—one published twice, by Horstman (1896, pp. 340–345) and by Baugh (1956), and the other

(Meech 1934) possibly unrepresentative because we know that it was written specifically for schoolboys. However they are all apparently highly formulaic: Jolliffe describes them as follows: "Almost without exception in the extant forms, the seven deadly sins form at least one basis for self-accusation. Usually, the forms not only list sinful thoughts, words and deeds under these seven headings, but go on to treat the Decalogue, the five wits, and the seven works of mercy in the same way," some adding confession "according to the five spiritual wits, the due observance of the seven sacraments, and belief in the articles of the Faith" (1974, p. 40). Again, this serves to emphasise the close connection between confession and the Church's teaching syllabus, and gives the forms of confession an interesting position as epitomes, so to speak, of the material covered at greater length in the compendia. Tentler (1977) has shown how much information can be derived from the numerous corresponding Latin *formae confitendi*, and it would be interesting to use the Middle English texts in a similar way, as well as to elucidate their connections with the Latin forms: are they simply translations and reworkings, or are there distinctive preoccupations in the Middle English versions? It has also been suggested that the scraps of specimen confession provided in *Ancrene Wisse* may represent a colloquial form of the language, and it may well be that these later Middle English pieces would reward the attentions of a researcher interested in language registers.

The sins inevitably call to mind works on the virtues. Jolliffe points out that "unlike the numerous tracts which discuss the deadly sins, very few deal with groups or collections of specific virtues," but, paradoxically, "if the forms of confession are excluded, extant tracts concerning virtue are almost twice as numerous as those concerning sin" (1974, p. 47). No doubt the relative absence of systematic treatments of the virtues has to do with the lack of as fixed a schema for them as was provided for the vices by the Seven Deadly Sins formula. Perhaps medieval writers found the subject of the virtues, their relationship with the Gifts of the Holy Spirit on the one hand and the Three Theological plus Four Cardinal Virtues on the other, as thorny as we do. A good starting point for those who wish to approach the subject is Tuve (1964, 1966), but in the area of vernacular texts, our knowledge is inevitably very imperfect: of the thirty texts listed in Jolliffe's section G (Specific Virtues) only one (item G 26) has been printed.

Writings on temptations and tribulations are closely related to works on the virtues, as in both the virtues of fortitude and patience are in question. The intrinsic link between temptation and tribulation is made clear by *Ancrene Wisse*, which refers to both in its section on *innre* and *uttre fondunges*. It is curious that, in contrast to many of the topics mentioned so far, literature on Tribulation is well represented in print. All the Middle English versions bar one of the *Livre de tribulacion* are now accessible (Barratt 1983; Horstman 1896). These are straightforward works of instruction with no mystical overtones and very little affective writing, solidly didactic in tone. The most important of the texts on Temptation (Version M.E. III of William Flete's *De Remediis contra Temptaciones*) has been edited not once but twice (Colledge and Chadwick 1968; Horstman 1896), though this text is not perhaps strictly a work of religious instruction; originally "a simple work of instruction, as practical as it is learned, to be read by anyone suffering the afflictions for which it offers alleviation, whether he aspire or not to a contemplative life" (Hackett, Colledge and Chadwick 1964, p. 211), it evolved into something more complex. In fact the article of Hackett and his collaborators raises interesting questions about genre and the way in which medieval texts can pass through a number of authorial hands, changing their nature and evolving into something quite different from their original form.

Both these texts were enormously popular in their original and Middle English forms, and it is important to study such works as a gauge of the taste of the audiences for whom Chaucer, Langland, and the Gawain-poet wrote. Such works were the nearest the Middle Ages had to the best-selling works on self-help of today; maybe later generations will find their popularity with us as perplexing, and as intriguing, as we find the popularity of such medieval treatises.

There are also a number of treatises that are hard to classify but seem to count as works of religious instruction in that they are certainly not mystical, and are didactic rather than devotional or affective in tone, such as *The Mirror of Sinners* (Horstman 1896), much concerned with death and judgment, and translated from a Latin text (ILWVV 4918); *The Abbey of the Holy Ghost* (in Blake 1972; see also Consacro 1976), an allegorical treatise translated from the French; *A Treatise of Ghostly Battle* (Horstman 1896), also allegorical, demonstrating how the didactic mode can be variously conveyed. Finally, although the *Ars Moriendi* (of which *The Book of the Craft of Dying*, Horstman 1896, is a translation) as such goes back only to the early fifteenth century (see O'Connor 1942), there are a number of other texts on preparation for death; the subject also had a place in the compendia. Beaty (1970, p. 34) comments on the Latin original that its "enormous popularity and influence . . . in western Europe remain as yet incomprehensible"—a remark that is applicable to so many of these texts. The *ars moriendi* in particular is an area in which students might study the Renaissance transformations of originally Middle English prose types (see El-Gabalawy 1978 who comments on "the sparse studies of this genre," p. 115, and of its florescence in the sixteenth and seventeenth centuries). But it is those Middle English prose works of pastoral intention concerned with "confession and spiritual guidance," "revealing a pastoral intention, employed to guide the Christian soul in his rejection of sin and his progress in a life of service to God" (Jolliffe 1974, p. 17) that make up the bulk of the texts listed in Jolliffe's *Check-List*. Is it self-evident that more need to be available in print? Perhaps not, given the dissatisfaction earlier expressed by Blake with "mere" editing. In an age of microfilm and microfiche, of good interloan services and fairly easy international travel, can we still regard the editing of unpublished matter as a good in itself? The question is particularly acute in the area of works of religious instruction, because the sheer bulk of unedited material is so great on the one hand, and the aesthetic value of much of it, on the other, so dubious. It may well be that it is the sociological and anthropological aspects of these texts that are really valuable, illuminating as they do subjects such as the history of deviance and the way in which earlier societies grappled with the problem of classifying types of behaviour in moral terms which later times would regard as partly criminal, partly psychopathological, and providing evidence, for instance, of the transition that took place in the Middle Ages from a society in which pressures on behaviour were collective to one in which the individual was stressed, and showing how a society could function in which legal justice was largely private. But in this case there is all the more need for specialists in Middle English to make available for those in other disciplines well-edited texts; as a minimum one would hope to set as a target editions of all the major compendia and representative selections—as long as the choice of texts had been carefully made by someone conversant with the range of manuscript material—of the shorter pieces. But as so often one suspects that in this area it is putting the cart before the horse to concentrate on the Middle English texts while the immensely more complex and sophisticated Latin material remains virtually unknown except to a few specialists in medieval canon law and *pastoralia*.

Perhaps my estimate of the aesthetic value of these texts is too pessimistic. Hodgson in 1948 was urging that works of religious instruction could be scrutinised by those in search of "the beauties of Middle English and for the sources of more modern prose" (p. 1), but as she went on to point out, such works were written "solely with a practical purpose," and it may well be that they are most profitably approached in a similar purely practical fashion. On the other hand, so much medieval literature, including for instance many medieval lyrics, seems to have been composed in a utilitarian spirit that instead of dismissing aesthetic criteria as irrelevant, it may be better to develop an aesthetic suitable for a period when the nineteenth-century concept of "literature" as opposed to other types of writing, had not yet appeared. It seems to me that the potentially most useful theoretical framework for an approach to works of religious instruction on lines other than that of content alone, are the ideas on "inorganic structure" developed by Jordan (1967) in the context of Chaucer's work. If anything, they are more applicable to such works, and it is significant that his ideas on quantitative structure, on sufficient enumeration, sufficient articulation, sufficient interrelation, for which he turns to architectural analogies, with the poet as a Gothic builder, are particularly well exemplified by his interpretation of the *Parson's Tale*. When he says of that prose work that "as a treatise on penitence the Parson's Tale offers little that will please or instruct the modern reader" (p. 228), or remarks that "in the prosaic nakedness of its rhetorical structure it displays with the utmost explicitness the principles of inorganic structure," he might be talking of so many other works of religious instruction. The ease with which such works are excerpted, abridged, expanded, and rearranged shows that they are intrinsically "modular" in construction. Furthermore we should bear in mind that the often asymmetrical numerical frameworks which articulate so many of these treatises may well be the distinguishing marks of works written in a predominantly oral culture, where mnemonic devices are deliberately cultivated.

A further question is that of the relationship between prose and verse works of religious instruction. Earlier works (e.g., *Handling Sin*) in Middle English are usually in verse, but by the fifteenth century prose is the favourite medium, though there are still a large number of very simple, mnemonic didactic poems. Are the prose works more complex, more theologically correct, than the verse? Are they perhaps directed at a different audience? McSparran and Robinson (1978, p. viii) make the interesting suggestion that some fifteenth-century didactic verses are specifically for the basic instruction of children. Or is the shift from verse to prose (which is not of course confined to works of this type alone) to be connected with increasing literacy (on which see Parkes 1973), itself bound up with the transition from an oral to a written culture? And how far are prose works still conceived primarily as oral literature, using oral formulae such as enumeration and subenumeration? Much of the Church's teaching, if the episcopal decrees were obeyed at all, must have continued to be oral, in the shape of sermons, in spite of the simultaneous existence of written works. It would be interesting to know if the original audience made any significant distinction between sermons and prose treatises; sermons were often simply written homilies read aloud, and conversely many works of instruction use the convention of the direct address to the individual. Was this an empty convention, or a reflection of the real situation? Such works would of course be read aloud rather than silently, whether in an individual or communal setting.

These are intriguing possibilities in the longer term. In the meantime we still need to concentrate on identifying and classifying the numerous unedited, maybe even unnoticed, works of instruction, which are surely of all types of Middle English prose the most neglected; editing at least the longer and more important texts with due regard to the Latin and French sources; producing editions that will be of use to scholars other than Middle English specialists; possibly developing a literary critique that bears in mind the peculiar constricting factors of this type of writing, especially its status as translations or adaptations, and that sets out to describe and appreciate positive aspects of its predominantly utilitarian structures. Further research into the audiences for which the various treatises were designed will be stimulated by the increasing tendency to study manuscripts as wholes (as advocated by Martin 1981), so that there is a concentration not so much on the individual treatise in the case of the shorter instructional pieces, as on the constellations they make up within particular manuscripts, and the other kinds of texts with which medieval audiences regarded them as making up appropriate collections. For instance, study of the recent facsimile edition of Cambridge University Library MS Ff. 2. 38 reveals a deliberate and systematic arrangement of material "proceeding from religious material which is meditative or didactic to exemplary items which combine a moral with a story and finally to secular works of entertainment" (McSparran and Robinson 1978, p. vii). We must not regard the audience for these works as homogeneous; readers' needs varied with education, age, class, and status, so that in some ways it can be misleading to classify works of religious instruction by subject matter alone; certainly one is struck by the range of levels of approach in texts ostensibly dealing with the same basic subject. Finally, we can see these works as playing a humble but essential role in our knowledge of medieval culture, for we can be confident that of all the types of prose considered in this book, it would be works of religious instruction with which any medieval reader would be most likely to come in contact, maybe at a very early age.

BIBLIOGRAPHY

The bibliography is divided into bibliographical aids, primary sources (Middle English and Latin), and secondary material. Items are listed within each section alphabetically by author or editor.

BIBLIOGRAPHICAL AIDS

Bloomfield, Morton W.; Guyot, B-G.; Howard, D. R.; and Kabealo, T. B., eds. (1979) *Incipits of Latin Works on the Virtues and Vices.* Cambridge, Mass.: Medieval Academy of America.

Jolliffe, P., ed. (1974) *A Check-List of Middle English Prose Writings of Spiritual Guidance.* Toronto: Pontifical Institute of Mediaeval Studies.

PRINTED TEXTS

MIDDLE ENGLISH

Aarts, F. G. A. M. (1967) *Þe Pater Noster of Richard Ermyte: A Late Middle English Exposition of the Lord's Prayer Edited from Westminster School Library MS 3.* The Hague: Nijhoff.

Arnold, T., ed. (1869–1871) *Select English Works of John Wyclif*. 3 vols. Oxford: Clarendon Press.

Barnum, P. H., ed. (1976, 1980) *Dives and Pauper*, vol. 1, pts. 1 and 2. EETS, os 275, 280.

Barratt, A. A. T., ed. (1983) *The Book of Tribulation*. MET 15. Heidelberg: Carl Winter.

Baugh, N. S., ed. (1956) *A Worcestershire Miscellany Compiled by John Northwood c. 1400*. Philadelphia: no publisher.

Blake, N. F., ed. (1972) *Middle English Religious Prose*. York Medieval Texts. London: Arnold.

———, ed. (1975) *Quattuor Sermones Printed by William Caxton*. MET 2. Heidelberg: Carl Winter.

Bowers, R. H. (1939) "The Middle English *St. Brendan's Confession.*" *Archiv*, 175, 40–49.

Bühler, C. F. (1954) "The Middle English Texts of Morgan MS 861." *PMLA*, 69, 686–692.

Colledge, E., and Chadwick, N. (1968) *"Remedies Against Temptations:* The Third English Version of William Flete." *Archivo italiano per la storia della pietà*, 5, 203–240.

Fisher, J. H., ed. (1951) *The Tretyse of Loue*. EETS, os 223.

Francis, W. N., ed. (1942) *The Book of Vices and Virtues*. EETS, os 217.

Holmstedt, G., ed. (1933) *Speculum Christiani*. EETS, os 182.

Horstman, C., ed. (1895, 1896) *Yorkshire Writers: Richard Rolle of Hampole . . . and His Followers*. London: Swan Sonnenschein and Co.

Kellogg, A. L., and Talbert, E. W. (1959–1960) "The Wyclifite *Pater Noster* and *Ten Commandments*, with Special Reference to English MSS. 85 and 90 in the John Rylands Library." *BJRL*, 42, 345–377.

Kengen, J. H. L., ed. (no date) *Memoriale Credencium: A Late Middle English Manual of Theology for Lay People Edited from Bodley MS Tanner 201*. Nijmegen: no publisher.

Matthew, F. D., ed. (1880) *The English Works of Wyclif*. EETS, os 74.

Meech, S. B. (1934) "John Drury and His English Writings." *Speculum*, 9, 70–83.

Morris, R., ed. (1866) *Dan Michel's Ayenbite of Inwyt*. EETS, os 23. Rev. ed. (1979) by P. Gradon. EETS, os 278.

Nelson, V., ed. (1981) *A Myrour to Lewde Men and Wymmen*. MET 14. Heidelberg: Carl Winter.

Perry, G. I. C., ed. (1866) *English Prose Treatises of Richard Rolle de Hampole*. EETS, os 20.

———, ed. (1889) *Religious Pieces in Prose and Verse from R. Thornton's MS*. EETS, os 26.

van Zutphen, J. P. W. M., ed. (1956) *Richard Lavynham, O. Carm: A Lityl Tretys*. Rome: Institutum Carmelitanum.

LATIN

Baron, R. (1963) "Note sur l'Indiculum du ms. Oxford Merton College 49 et les expositions sur l'Oraison dominicale qui s'y trouvent mentionées." *RTAM*, 30, 333–336.

Broomfield, F., ed. (1968) *Thomas of Chobham: Summa Confessorum*. Analecta Mediaevalia Namurcensia 25. Louvain: Editions Nauwelaerts.

Firth, J. J. F., ed. (1971) *Robert of Flamborough: Liber Poenitentialis. A Critical Edition
with Introduction and Notes*. Toronto: Pontifical Institute of Mediaeval Studies.

Forshaw, H. P., ed. (1973) *Edmund of Abingdon, Speculum Religiosorum and Speculum Ecclesie*. Auctores Britannici Medii Aevi 3. London: Oxford University Press.

Michaud-Quantin, P. (1964) "Deux formulaires pour la confession du milieu du XIIIe
siècle." *RTAM*, 31, 430–462.

Powicke, F. M., and Cheney, G. R., eds. (1964) *Councils and Synods*, vol. 2, pts. 1 and
2. London: Oxford University Press.

SECONDARY MATERIAL

Aarts, F. G. A. M. (1969) "The Pater Noster in Medieval English Literature." *Papers
on Language and Literature*, 5, 3–16.

Ackerman, R. W. (1962) "The Debate of the Body and the Soul and Parochial Christian-
ity." *Speculum*, 37, 541–565.

Beaty, N. L. (1970) *The Craft of Dying: The Literary Tradition of the "Ars Moriendi" in
England*. New Haven: Yale University Press.

Blake, N. F. (1974) "Varieties of Middle English Religious Prose." In *Chaucer and Middle English Studies in Honour of Rossell Hope Robbins*, edited by B. Rowland. London:
Allen and Unwin.

Bloomfield, M. W. (1952) *The Seven Deadly Sins*. East Lansing: Michigan State College
Press.

Boyle, L. E. (1955) "*The Oculus Sacerdotis* and Some Other Works of William of Pagula." *TRHS*, 5th ser. 5, 81–110.

——— (1974) "The Summa for Confessors as a Genre, and Its Religious Intent." In *The
Pursuit of Holiness in Late Medieval and Renaissance Religion*, edited by C. Trinkaus and
H. A. Oberman. Leiden: Brill.

Brady, M. T. (1954) "The Pore Caitif: An Introductory Study." *Traditio*, 10, 529–548.

Brayer, E. (1958) "Contenu, structure et combinaisons du *Miroir du Monde* et de la
Somme le Roi." *Romania*, 79, 1–38, 433–470.

Consacro, P. (1976) "The Author of the Abbey of the Holy Ghost: A Popularizer of the
Mixed Life." *FCEMN*, 2, 15–20.

Cumming, W. P. (1927) "A Middle English MS in the Bibliothèque Ste. Geneviève,
Paris." *PMLA*, 42, 862–864.

Dondaine, A. (1947) "Guillaume Peyraut: Vie et oeuvres." *AFP*, 17, 163–236.

El-Gabalawy, S. (1978) "The *Ars Moriendi* in More's Utopia." *Mosaic*, 11, 115–126.

Forshaw, H. P. (1971) "New Light on the *Speculum Ecclesie* of St. Edmund of Abingdon." *AHDLMA*, 38, 7–33.

——— (1972) "St. Edmund's *Speculum*: A Classic of Victorine Spirituality." *AHDLMA*, 39, 7–40.

Gallagher, J. E. (1965) "The Sources of Caxton's *Ryal Book* and *Doctrinal of Sapience*." *SP*, 62, 40–62.

Gibbs, M., and Lang, J. (1934) *Bishops and Reform 1215–1272*. London: Oxford University Press.

Goering, J. (1976) "The *Summa de Penitentia* of Magister Serlo." *MS*, 38, 1–53.

——— (1978) "The *Summa* of Magister Serlo and Thirteenth-Century Penitential Literature." *MS*, 40, 290–311.

Hackett, B.; Colledge, E.; and Chadwick, N. (1964) "William Flete's *De Remediis contra Temptaciones* in Its Latin and English Recensions: The Growth of a Text." *MS*, 26, 210–230.

Hanna, R., III (1981) Review of Kengen, *Memoriale Credencium*. *Speculum*, 56, 151–154.

Hodgson, P. (1948) "*Ignorancia Sacerdotum*: A Fifteenth-Century Discourse on the Lambeth Constitutions." *RES*, 24, 1–11.

Hussey, M. (1958) "The Petitions of the Paternoster in Mediaeval English Literature." *MAE*, 27, 8–16.

Jordan, R. M. (1967) *Chaucer and the Shape of Creation*. Cambridge, Mass.: Harvard University Press.

Kennedy, V. L. (1945) "Robert Courson on Penance." *MS*, 7, 291–336.

——— (1947) "The Content of Courson's *Summa*." *MS*, 9, 81–107.

MacKinnon, M. (1969) "William de Montibus: A Medieval Teacher." In *Essays in Medieval History Presented to Bertie Wilkinson*, edited by T. A. Sandquist and M. R. Powicke. Toronto: University of Toronto Press.

McNeill, J. T. (1952) *A History of the Cure of Souls*. London: SCM Press.

McSparran, F., and Robinson, P. R., eds. (1978) *Cambridge University Library MS Ff. 2. 38 (facsimile edition)*. London: Scolar Press.

Martin, C. A. (1981) "Middle English Manuals of Religious Instruction." In *So Meny People Longuages and Tonges: Philological Essays in Scots and Mediaeval English Presented to Angus McIntosh*, edited by M. Benskin and H. L. Samuels. Edinburgh: privately printed.

Michaud-Quantin, P. (1962) *Sommes de casuistiques et manuels de confession au moyen âge (XIIe–XVIe siècles)*. Analecta Mediaevalia Namurcensia 13. Louvain: Editions Nauwelaerts.

Milosh, J. E. (1966) *The Scale of Perfection and the English Mystical Tradition*. Madison and London: University of Wisconsin Press.

Moorman, J. R. H. (1955) *Church Life in England in the Thirteenth Century*. Cambridge: Cambridge University Press.

O'Connor, M. C. (1942) *The Art of Dying Well*. New York: Columbia University Press.

Pantin, W. A. (1955) *The English Church in the Fourteenth Century*. Cambridge: Cambridge University Press.

Parkes, M. B. (1973) "The Literacy of the Laity." In *Literature and Western Civilization: The Medieval World*, edited by D. Daiches and A. K. Thorlby. London: Aldus.

Pfander, H. G. (1933) "Dives et Pauper." *Library*, 4th ser. 14, 299–312.

———— (1936) "Some Medieval Manuals of Religious Instruction in England and Observations on Chaucer's *Parson's Tale*." *JEGP*, 35, 243–258.

Robbins, H. W. (1925) "An English Version of St. Edmund's *Speculum* Ascribed to Richard Rolle." *PMLA*, 40, 240–251.

Robertson, D. W., Jr. (1945) "The Manuel des Péchés and an English Episcopal Decree." *MLN*, 60, 439–447.

———— (1946a) "Certain Theological Conventions in Mannyng's Treatment of the Commandments." *MLN*, 61, 505–514.

———— (1946b) "A Note on the Classical Origin of 'Circumstances.'" *SP*, 43, 6–14.

———— (1947) "The Cultural Tradition of *Handlyng Synne*." *Speculum*, 22, 162–185.

———— (1949) "Frequency of Preaching in Thirteenth Century England." *Speculum*, 24, 376–388.

Russell, G. H. (1962) "Vernacular Instruction of the Laity in the Later Middle Ages in England: Some Texts and Notes." *Journal of Religious History*, 2, 98–119.

Tentler, T. N. (1977) *Sin and Confession on the Eve of the Reformation*. Princeton: Princeton University Press.

Tuve, R. (1964) "Notes on the Virtues and Vices, Part II." *JWCI*, 27, 42–72.

———— (1966) *Allegorical Imagery: Some Medieval Books and Their Posterity*. Princeton: Princeton University Press.

Wenzel, S. (1968) "The Seven Deadly Sins: Some Problems of Research." *Speculum*, 43, 1–22.

———— (1971) "The Source of the 'Remedia' of the Parson's Tale." *Traditio*, 27, 433–453.

———— (1974) "The Sources of Chaucer's Seven Deadly Sins." *Traditio*, 30, 351–378.

Index